ENCYCLOPEDIA OF INDIAN PHILOSOPHIES

ENCYCLOPEDIA OF INDIAN PHILOSOPHIES
General Editor, Karl H. Potter

The following volumes are published:

I. Bibliography, 2nd ed. (1984)
II. Indian Metaphysics and Epistemology: The Tradition of Nyāya-Vaiśeṣika up to Gaṅgeśa (1978)
III. Advaita Vedānta up to Śaṃkara and His Pupils (1982)
IV. Sāṃkhya: A Dualist Tradition in Indian Philosophy (1987)
V. The Philosophy of the Grammarians (1990)

ENCYCLOPEDIA OF INDIAN PHILOSOPHIES

VOLUME VI

Indian Philosophical Analysis
Nyāya-Vaiśeṣika from Gaṅgeśa to
Raghunātha Śiromaṇi

EDITED BY
KARL H. POTTER
AND
SIBAJIBAN BHATTACHARYYA

PRINCETON UNIVERSITY PRESS
Princeton, New Jersey

Published by Princeton University Press, 41 William Street,
Princeton, New Jersey 08540
In the United Kingdom: Princeton University Press, Oxford

Library of Congress Cataloging-in-Publication Data

Indian philosophical Analysis: Nyāya-Vaiśeṣika from Gaṅgeśa to Raghunātha Śiromaṇi / edited by Karl H. Potter and Sibajiban Bhattacharyya.
p. cm.—(Encyclopedia of Indian Philosophies; v. 6)
Includes Index.

ISBN : 0-691-07384-8

I. Pooter, Karl H. II. Bhattacharyya, Sibajiban.
III. Series: Encyclopedia of Indian Philosophies (Princeton, N.J.) vol. 6.

B131.E5 1977 vol. 6   181'.4' 03 s—dc20   [181'.43'03]   90-22379

This book has been composed in India by Jainendra Prakash Jain
at Shri Jainendra Press, New Delhi

Printed in India.

10 9 8 7 6 5 4 3 2 1

Contributors:

Nandita Bandyopadhyaya
Kali Krishna Banerjee
Gopika Mohan Bhattacharya
Janakivallabha Bhattacharya
Tara Samkara Bhattacarya
Kishor Kumar Chakrabarti
V. N. Jha
Bimal Krishna Matilal
Umesh Mishra
Yusho Miyasaka
Jitendra Nath Mohanty
P. K. Mukhopadhyaya
Madhusudana Nyayacarya
Sukha Ranjan Saha
Nani Lal Sen
Prabal Kumar Sen
Esther A. Solomon
V. Varadachari
Satis Chandra Vidyabhusana

CONTENTS

PREFACE xi

PART ONE:

INTRODUCTION TO THE PHILOSOPHY OF NAVYA-NYĀYA
(*Karl H. Potter* and *Sibajiban Bhattacharyya*)

1. Historical Résumé 3
2. Relations and Analysis of Awareness 15
3. Metaphysics 19
4. Epistemology 53
5. Logical Theory 69

PART TWO:

SUMMARIES OF WORKS

1. Gaṅgeśa 85
   Tattvacintāmaṇi (*Nandita Bandyopadhyaya, Sibajiban Bhattacharyya, Kishor Kumar Chakrabarti, V.N. Jha, Bimal Krishna Matilal, Jitendranath Mohanty, P.K. Mukhopadhyaya, Madhusudana Nyayacharya, Sukha Ranjan Saha*)
2. Vaṭeśvara 312
3. Vardhamāna 313
   Prakāśa on Udayana's Kiraṇāvalī, Dravya (*V. Varadachari*)
   Prakāśa on Udayana's Kirṇāvalī, Guṇa (*Nani Lal Sen* and *V. Varadachari*)
   Prakāśa on Vallabha's Nyāyalīlāvatī (*V. Varadachari*)
   Pariśuddhinyāyanibandhaprakāśa (*Umesh Mishra*)
   Prakāśa on Udayana's Nyāyakusumāñjali (*V. Varadachari*)
   (Supplement) Udayana, Nyāyapariśiṣṭa (*Esther A. Solomon*)
4. Rājaśekhara Sūri 363
5. Jayasiṃhasūri 363
   Tātparyadīpikā on Bhāsarvajña's Nyāyasāra (*V. Varadachari*)
6. Cinnam Bhaṭṭa or Cennu Bhaṭṭa 368
   Prakāśikā on Keśava Miśra's Tarkabhāṣā (*V. Varadachari*)
   Vyākhyā on Varadarāja's Tārkikarakṣā (*V. Varadachari*)

7. Tvantopādhyāya 374

8. Ghaṭeśa Upādhyāya 374

9. Nyāyalocanakāra 375

10. Gaṅgāditya 375

11. Jīvanātha Miśra or Jayanātha Miśra 375

12. Bhavanātha Miśra or Duve or Ayāci Miśra 375

13. Jinavardhana Sūri or Ādinātha Jain 376
Jivavardhanī on Śivaditya's Saptapadārthī (*V. Varadachari*)

14. Śivapati 380

15. Viṣṇubhaṭṭa 380

16. Rāmeśvara 380
Tārkikarakṣāsaṃgrahavivaraṇa (completion) (*V. Varadachari*)

17. Nārāyaṇa Ācārya 380
Dīpikā on Udayana's Ātmatattvaviveka (*V. Varadachari*)

18. Śeṣa Śāraṅgadhara 382
Nyāyamuktāvalī on Udayana's Lakṣaṇāvali *(Nani Lal Sen)*

19. Vāsudeva Sūri 389
Padapañcikā on Bhāsarvajña's Nyāyasāra (*V. Varadachari*)

20. Guṇaratna Sūri 394

21. Śaṃkara Miśra 395
Āmoda on Udayana's Nyāyakusumāñjali (*V. Varadachari*)
Bhedaratna (*V. Varadachari*)
Vādivinoda (*V. Varadachari*)
Kaṇādarahasya (*V. Varadachari*)
Upaskāra on Kanāda's Vaiśeṣikasūtras *(Karl H. Potter)*
Kalpalatā on Udayana's Ātmatattvaviveka (*V. Varadachari*)
Kaṇṭhābharaṇa on (Śri) Vallabha's Nyāyalīlāvatī (*V. Varadachari*)

22. Hari Miśra 453

23. Vācaspati Miśra (II) 454
Khaṇḍanoddhāra (*V. Varadachari*)

24. Mallinātha 465
Niṣkāntikā on Varadarāja's Tārkikarakṣā (*V. Varadachari*)

25. Pakṣadhara (the Vivekakāra) 470

26. Bhuvanasundarasūri 471

27. Śeṣānanta 472
Padārthacandrikā on Śivāditya's Saptapadārthī (*V. Varadachari*)

28. Narahari 473

29. Yajñapati Upādhyāya 473

Tattvacintāmaṇiprabhā (*Gopikamohan Bhattacharya*)
30. Pragalbha Miśra or Śubhaṅkara 486
31. Jayadeva or Pakṣadhara Miśra 486
32. Śrīnātha Bhaṭṭācārya Cakravartin 489
33. Vāsudeva Sārvabhauma 489
34. Kṛṣṇānanda Vidyāvinoda or Vidyaviriñci 490
35. Janārdana of Mithilā 490
36. Timmabhūpāla 491
37. Misaru Miśra 491
38. Virūpākṣa Miśra 491
39. Narahari Upādhyāya or Maheśvara Viśārada 491
40. Mādhava Miśra 491
41. Śrīkāra Kubjaśaktivāda 492
42. Śūlapāṇi Miśra 492
43. Vāsudeva Miśra 492
44. Rucidatta Miśra 492
Prakāśa on Gaṅgeśa's Tattvacintāmaṇi (*V. Varadachari*)
Makaranda on Varadhamāna's Nyāyakusumāñjaliprakāśa (*V. Varadachari*)
Vṛtti on Vardhamāna's Dravyakiraṇāvalīprakāśa (*V. Varadachari*)
45. Ratnākara or Viṣṇudāsa Vidyāvācaspati 520
46. Puruṣottama Bhaṭṭācārya 520
47. Janeśvara (or Jaleśvara) Vāhinīpati 520
48. Bhairavendra 521
49. Gadādhara Miśra 521
50. Raghunātha Śiromaṇi 521
Dīdhiti on Udayana's Ātmatattvaviveka (*V. Varadachari*)
Dīdhiti on Vardhamāna's Guṇakiraṇāvalīprakāśa (*Nani Lal Sen* and *V. Varadachari*)
Padārthatattvanirūpaṇa (*Karl H. Potter*)
Ākhyātavāda (*Prabal Kumar Sen*)
Nañvāda (*Janakivallabha Bhattacarya*)
Dīdhiti on Gaṅgeśa's Tattvacintāmaṇi (*Nandita Bandyopadhyaya, Kali Krishna Banerjee, Kishor Kumar Chakrabarti, Jitendranath Mohanty, Madhusudana Nyayacarya*)

NOTES 591

INDEX 633

PREFACE

Volume Six of the *Encyclopedia of Indian Philosophies* picks up the history of the Nyāya-Vaiśeṣika system where Volume Two left off. The time covered in this volume is much smaller than in any of the previous volumes of the *Encyclopedia*, a scant two hundred years between approximately 1310 and 1510. There are good reasons for this intensive attention to such a brief period. For one thing, two of Indian's most remarkable philosophers, Gaṅgeśa and Raghunātha Śiromaṇi, are covered in these pages—in fact, they initiate and terminate the period surveyed. More generally, we here begin to treat the literature of Navyanyāya, a movement comparable in its implication to the burgeoning of symbolic logic and its concomitant philosophical speculations found in the writings of Frege, Russell and Wittgenstein in the West at the end of the 19th and beginning of the 20th centuries. The excitement of newly pioneered techniques of philosophical analysis developed by Gaṅgésa spawned a bevy of philosophical talents. Indeed, this period is even richer than we are able to summarize here, since a good part of it is still unavailable in print.

The history of Indian philosophy, and specifically of Navyanyāya, has been treated in a quite extensive literature. The *Bibliography of Indian Philosophies* (New Delhi : Motilal Banarsidass, 1970, referred to below as "B"; Revised Edition, New Delhi: Banarsidass and Princeton, Princeton University Press 1983, referred to as "RB") provides assistance in suggesting a chronology of Indian thought in general within which Navyanyāya philosophers find their appropriate places.

The form of this book features an extended introductory section followed by summaries of works belonging to the system's literature. These summaries are arranged in relative chronological order to assist the reader in tracing the development of the school's thought. Summaries have been provided by scholars from India, England and the United States. Remarks in the Introductions to previous volumes of the *Encyclopedia* explaining the intended reading public to whom these volumes are addressed apply here as well.

Thanks are due to the American Institute of Indian Studies, the Indo-U.S. Subcomission for Education and Culture, the Bureau of Educational and Cultural Affairs of the U.S. Department of State, the Joint Committee on South Asia of the American Council of Learned Societies and the Social Science Research Council, and the National Endowment for the Humanities; all of these bodies provided needed assistance in the development of this volume through financial assistance of various sorts. Finally, special thanks are due to Laura Townsend for assistance in preparation of the manuscript.

June 1989 KARL H. POTTER

PART ONE

INTRODUCTION TO THE PHILOSOPHY OF NAVYA-NYĀYA

1

HISTORICAL RÉSUMÉ

This, the second volume on the Nyāya-Vaiśeṣika system, takes up where Volume II of the Encyclopedia of Indian Philosophies left off, in the early fourteenth century with the pivotal figure of Gaṅgeśa, author of *Tattvacintāmaṇi.* It covers what we know of the history of the school up to and including Raghunātha Śiromaṇi, who flourished (we estimate) about 1510. In the two centuries covered there are some 50 authors whose names have come down to us as identifiable as having lived in this period, who are held to be responsible for some 98 works expounding or defending the principles of Nyāya-Vaiśeṣika. Of these 98 works, 15 have been lost and are known to us only by name, sometimes not even that. Of the remaining 83 works, 45 have been published, at least in part, and the remainder are known to exist (again, at least in part) in one or more manuscripts. Only six of the works from this period have been translated, even in part. A complete list of authors and works treated in the following material is provided in Table I, below on pages 10–13.

1. Major Figures

Gaṅgeśa is viewed, and rightly, as the founder of Navyanyāya, the "new" Nyāya system. The term "Navyanyāya" is used in two senses. On the one hand, it is frequently employed to identify Nyāya-Vaiśeṣika literature that appeared from Gaṅgeśa's time onwards, but a more precise sense of the term applies to that literature which, as Gaṅgeśa's work does, utilizes a certain technical vocabulary to explicate Nyāya concepts. In this latter sense, not all of the 50 authors treated here are Navyanaiyāyikas, since some of their works are commentaries on old Nyāya-Vaiśeṣika works in traditional style and with little or no use of the technical terminology and methods in question. However, the bulk of the literature here surveyed is Navyanyāya in both senses of that term.

Navyanyāya flourished in the main in these first few centuries of its development in Mithila, that is, the northern part of what is now the Indian state of Bihar. The roster of authors in Table I (pp.10–13) represents in some measure a genealogy of scholarly families of Mithila. Gaṅgeśa was a Maithila. Many of these authors are in various relationships to the family whose earliest member listed here was Vaṭeśvara (1340). And practically all of them were related to each other either by family or by the relationship which binds teacher and pupil and pupil's pupil. While there have been suggestions that Navyanyāya also found its way into Bengal during this period, this has not been altogether substantiated. It was largely a Maithila monopoly until the time of Raghunātha, where this Volume ends. Subsequent Volumes will trace the process in which Navyanyāya gradually spread outwards from Mithila until exponents of it are found throughout the subcontinent.

Gaṅgeśa and Raghunātha are clearly the best known of these philosophers now, but a few others were equally important during the period treated. In particular, as soon as the *Tattvacintāmaṇi* had appeared commentaries on it began to be composed, and a lively controversy developed among the commentarial traditions. Notable is the debate between Narahari Viśārada and Jayadeva Miśra, both students and relatives of Yajñapati Upādhyāya (1460).

Jayadeva, otherwise known as Pakṣadhara Miśra (fl. 1470), is in many ways the central figure of the period. Navyanyāya was a family specialty inherited from Vaṭeśvara's time over a century before him. Jayadeva wrote a seminal commentary on the *Tattvacintāmaṇi* called *Āloka* and taught just about all the great figures of the next generation of the school, including Vāsudeva Sārvabhauma, Rucidatta Miśra, Raghunātha Śiromaṇi and others.

Vāsudeva Sārvabhauma was himself a great teacher, with many illustrious pupils, the most famous of whom was Caitanya, the great Vaiṣṇava saint and the leader of the Acintyabhedābheda school of Bengali Vaiṣṇavism. It was Vāsudeva who was (though this is disputed) mainly responsible for the development of Navyanyāya into a Bengali tradition. Vāsudeva founded a *ṭol*, a traditional place for study, at Navadvīpa (in the present-day Nadia district). In his later years he is said to have become first an Advaitin and then, eventually, a follower of Caitanya's. In addition to Caitanya and Raghunātha Śiromaṇi, Vāsudeva also is held to have taught Raghunandana, the jurist, whose commentary on Jīmūtavāhana's *Dāyabhāga* "is now held to be the best current authority on the Bengal school of Hindu law", [1] as well as Kṛṣṇānanda, the Tantrist, a well-known writer "on charms and other kindred subjects".[2]

Raghunātha Śiromaṇi is one of the most original thinkers in all of Indian philosophy, and is referred to regularly as the leader of the "Navyas", i.e., the "new" wing of Navyanyāya. Since Navyanyāya is "new" already the reference indicates the radical nature of Raghunātha's contributions, at least in the eyes of his fellow Naiyāyikas. His originality is matched by his reputation for irreverence and hubris, as recorded in various stories which have come down to us concerning him as a disrespectful pupil and brilliant but proud master.[3]

The line from Gaṅgeśa through Jayadeva and Vāsudeva to Raghunātha may be viewed as the major stream of development of the technical side of Navyanyāya, meaning by this the extensive use of methods which will be explained below together with a penchant for treating certain problems—notably the definitions of key notions in the theory of inference such as pervasion (*vyāpti*)—to a far more generous extent than many of the more traditional Nyāya concepts. These more traditional notions were also treated extensively in the literature of our period, notably by Vardhamāna (1350), Śaṃkara Miśra (1430) and Vācaspati Miśra II (1450) in their commentaries on some of the old Nyāya works. These writers, along with a number of others, are willing to accept the concepts of old Nyāya pretty much as they were taught by Udayana, say. Raghunātha is possibly the first and foremost commentator who undertakes to drastically revise Nyāya tradition, though some of his most extreme apparent innovations develop suggestions now known to have been pioneered by Bhāsarvajña the Bhūṣaṇakāra.[4]

It should be noted that critical historical scholarship on the philosophy of this period is still in its infancy. Picking out the half dozen or so figures named in the foregoing paragraphs may merely reflect accidental circumstances combining traditions of uncertain origin with the rather chance nature of which texts and names happen to have been preserved and which not. It may well be that others among the 50 authors here treated should be held to be as important as these are. For example, Gopikamohan Bhattacharya has studied some of the material found in manuscripts of lesser known figures such as the commentaries on the *Tattvacintāmaṇi* by Yajñapati and his son Narahari Viśārada, as well as by Rucidatta Miśra, another pupil of Jayadeva's. The contribution of Pragalbha (1460) is little known at this point, for his commentary is not studied.

2. The Literature of Early Navyanyāya

It will be seen that Table I below on pages 10ff. features numerous commentaries on such standard old Nyāya works as those of

Udayana, Keśava Miśra's *Tarkabhāṣā*, Śivāditya's *Saptapadārthī*, and Vallabha's *Nyāyalīlāvatī*. Only occasionally do writers of this period essay commentaries on the *Nyāya* or *Vaiśeṣika-sūtras* themselves, though Śaṃkara Miśra's *Upaskāra* on the *Vaiśeṣika-sūtras* is a highly authoritative reading within the school, if only by default, there being no extant commentary of any consequence prior to it. Several writers reply to the Advaita critique of Śrīharṣa's *Khaṇḍanakhaṇḍakhādya*. However, throughout this period, the work most commented on is the *Tattvacintāmaṇi*. It is, at least until Raghunātha, practically the only entirely independent Nyāya work composed in these centuries, at least among those that are extant and have been studied to any extent. It is arguable that Raghunātha's *Padārthatattvanirūpaṇa* should be viewed as an independent work on the Vaiśeṣika categories, though as mentioned it owes some of its inspiration to the Bhūṣaṇakāra.

It is, then, the *Tattvacintāmaṇi* that is the centerpiece of the period, and indeed of Navyanyāya through the centuries, although later on, to the present day, the commentators—Raghunātha, Jagadīśa, and Gadādhara especially—come to be studied more carefully than Gaṅgeśa's original. Two features of the *Tattvacintāmaṇi* are immediately noteworthy, before we turn to the innovations in the thought itself. These are Gaṅgeśa's style of exposition and the organization of his treatise.

Gaṅgeśa's method of exposition features the provision of a series of definitions of a topic. These definitions are in many cases clearly identified as the product of some rival theory, though in most cases the school responsible, much less the name of any particular author, is not mentioned, and in many of those cases it is definitions composed by rival Naiyāyikas that are criticized. Characteristically, a section of Gaṅgeśa's work will open with the quotation—or at least, a summary presentation—of one or more alternative definitions of the topic of that section, each definition being carefully expounded first and then as carefully criticized and emended, then criticized again until either one runs out of possible versions or the result of the emendations coincides with the correct account. The opponent's section is then followed by a section in which Gaṅgeśa proposes his own definition (or sometimes, several), which is once again considered with respect to possible criticisms and carefully defended.

This task of considering countless definitions calls for a technical terminology and methodological apparatus, and that is what Gaṅgeśa pioneers, although elements of his contributions can doubtless be discovered in his predecessors, especially Udayana. In the main, the technical terminology involves the manipulation of what may be called "relational abstracts" in order to indicate clearly what aspect of a topic one is speaking about. To take a simple instance, if one is speaking of the fire on the mountain in the context of the stock inference (about there being fire on the mountain because smoke is known to be there) and one wants to clarify that it is the general features of fire that one is speaking of and not the features of this particular fire, one may say that it is this fire as characterized (*nirūpita*) by fireness that he has in mind. Again, if one is calling attention to the role of this fire in the inference in question he may speak of the *sādhya*-ness resident in this fire, thereby indicating that it is this fire as the topic of this inference and not as, say, a locus of fireness or any other role this fire might be playing in the world that he has in mind. For example, this fire is the counterpositive of an absence of this fire; Navyanyāya will speak of that role of this fire by referring to it as the locus of the counterpositiveness to absence of this fire. This same fire is also the qualificand in the expression "(this) fire is on the mountain", and so has qualificandness resident in it. And so on through the myriad roles—i.e., types of relations to other things—which it might on reasonably frequent occasions become relevant to speak of.

Navyanyāya manages to achieve the results of quantification through its manipulation of relational abstracts. Ingalls provides a graphic account of how Navyanyāya renders such an intricately quantified expression as "no body of smoke occurs in any locus in which no body of fire is present". The result he translates from Sanskrit as "in smoke there is a generic absence of occurrentness described by locus of absence of fire, which absence describes a counterpositiveness limited by fireness and contact". He provides simpler illustrations of the same point. We have quoted this example to point up one practical outcome of Navyanyāya techniques for English readers, which is to make understanding a literal translation of Navyanyāya into English well-nigh impossible. Such translations can, to be sure, be produced, but one has to practice reading them systematically so that they may be in turn translated again into some more familiar mode—whether ordinary colloquial English or, say, a mathematical-logic-oriented reconstruction. The point is of direct relevance to the task essayed in this volume on Navyanyāya, for this feature of Navyanyāya forces us to choose between intelligibility and faithfulness to the style of the original. The practice that has been followed in our summaries is to provide some of each, but that is itself somewhat misleading viewed in a certain perspective, for the reader must still consult the original Sanskrit to discover whether a passage summarized in colloquial English is or is not written in the technical idiom.

The second point of innovation concerns the organization of the *Tattvacintāmaṇi.* Overall, it is divided into four Books, one for each of the four instruments of knowledge recognized by Nyāya. This method of division is not unusual; as early as Jayanta Bhaṭṭa's *Nyāyamañjarī* we find portions of works thus organized, and the *Nyāyasāra* is divided into three parts corresponding to the three instruments that its author admitted. However, these works in at least a general way follow the order of the *Nyāyasūtras* in introducing the topics treated, and the general assumption is that the reader is understanding the work in the light of the *sūtra* literature. On the other hand, a work such as Vallabha's *Nyāyalīlāvatī* demonstrates more independence in organization, but its orientation is toward the categories of Vaiśeṣika as the basis for the plan of the work, and anyway there is little rationale for the order of topics. Gaṅgeśa's method is independent like Vallabha's but follows a plan which is traditional and understandable, and that plan stems from the epistemological categories rather than metaphysical ones.

The sections within this plan are especially interesting. Gaṅgeśa makes no attempt to justify his choice of topics treated. They are apparently those topics which have occasioned controversy, whether within or without the system. He is not primarily concerned to react to critiques stemming from quite foreign standpoints, such as Buddhism or Advaita Vedānta. He largely deals with *pūrvapakṣas* which appear to represent either other Naiyāyikas or else one or another of the three main schools of Pūrvamīmāṃsā—the Prabhākaras, the Bhaṭṭas and the Miśras. The result resembles nothing so much as a series of philosophical journal articles on knotty puzzles of analysis. Combined with Nyāya technical apparatus and terminology the upshot is a formidably difficult work which is unquestionably deep and worthy of careful study. It is no wonder that it occasions a new beginning in the ever-continuing work of Nyāya commentators. It is likewise not surprising that the commentaries on the *Tattvacintāmaṇi* outdo the text in difficulty, some would say obscurity. One has the strong impression that these commentaries spring from earnest and searching discussions among a small group of initiates into a cult whose common bond is a special terminology. References by these commentators are largely to each other, but again without identification, suggesting that they were written for each other in a context where everyone knew—or ought to have known—whose view is alluded to and what is going on at each point in the exercise. The commentaries do not slavishly comment on quoted passages from Gaṅgeśa either. Especially in the *Dīdhiti* of Raghunātha Siromaṇi we find whole contexts laconically identified in a single word or phrase, and not always favorably:

Raghunātha was quite willing to reject Gaṅgeśa's opinions in favor of others, whether his own or those already proposed. The vast subcommentaries of Jagadīśa, Mathurānātha and Gadādhara are critical to the very life of this tradition, because it is dubious that these obscure references by Raghunātha could have been made intelligible outside of such authoritative renderings.

Raghunātha, furthermore, submits whole new sections of his own which break new ground. Notable among these is the section on the notion of the "limitor" (*avacchedaka*), frequently cited in modern times as at once the most crucial and the most difficult of the Navyanyāya technical notions. It is not that the term "limitor" had not occurred previously in Nyāya writings, indeed even before Gaṅgeśa. However, Gaṅgeśa does not devote a separate section to it. Raghunātha does. On the other hand, Raghunātha does not comment on every one of Gaṅgeśa's sections. The two concluding sections of Book Two of the *Tattvacintāmaṇi*, those on causal efficacy (*śakti*) and on liberation (*mukti*), are ignored by Raghunātha, and the section before those, on the inference justifying God's existence, is only summarily treated in the *Dīdhiti* in a few sentences. It seems unlikely that these comments have been lost, although that is of course possible, as it is also likely that his comments on the third and fourth Books—on comparison (*upamāna*) and verbal testimony (*śabda*) respectively—once existed but have been lost for the time being at least.

TABLE 1

Nyāya-Vaiśeṣika from Gaṅgeśa to Raghunātha Śiromaṇi: Checklist of Authors and Works

T—Translated
E—Not translated, but has been published
M—Not published, but manuscript(s) available
C—Commentary

	Name	*Date*	*Place*	*Works*
1.	Gaṅgeśa	1320	Darbhanga	*Tattvacintāmaṇi* (E; Part T)
2.	Vaṭeśvara	1340	Mithila	*Nyāyanibandhadarpaṇa* *Nyāyalīlāvatīdarpaṇa*
3.	Vardhamāna	1345	Mithila	*Dravyakiraṇāvalīprakāśa* (E) *Guṇakiraṇāvalīprakāśa* (E) *Nyāyalīlāvatīprakāśa* (E) *(Pariśuddhi) Nyāyanibandha-prakāśa* (Part E) *Nyāyakusumāñjaliprakāśa* (E) *Nyāyapariśiṣṭaprakāśa* (E) *Khaṇḍanakhaṇḍakhādyaprakāśa* (M) *Nyāyasūtrānvīkṣānayatattva-bodhinī* (M) Commentary on *Ātmatattvaviveka* (M) Commentary on *Tarkabhāṣā* (M)
4.	Rājaśekhara	1350	?	*Nyāyakandalīprakāśa*
5.	Jayasiṃhasūri	1366	?	*Nyāyasāratātparyadīpikā* (E)
6.	Cinnam Bhaṭṭa	1390	Andhra	*Tarkabhāṣāprakāśikā* (E) *Tārkikarakṣāsaṃgrahavivaraṇa* (M)
7.	Tvanto-pādhyāya	1400	Mithila	Commentary on *Tattvacintāmaṇi* *Nyāyakusumāñjalimakaranda*
8.	Ghaṭeśa Upādhyāya	1400	?	C on *Tattvacintāmaṇi*?
9.	Nyāyaloca-nakāra	1400		*Nyāyalocana*
10.	Gaṅgāditya	1400	?	C on *Tattvacintāmaṇi*
11.	Jīvanātha Miśra	1400	Mithila	
12.	Bhavanātha Miśra	1400	Mithila	C on *Nyāyakusumāñjali*
13.	Jinavardhana	1412	?	*Saptapadārthījinavardhanī* (E)

	Sūri			
14.	Śivapati	1420	?	
15.	Viṣṇubhaṭṭa	1420	?	*Tarkabhāṣāprakāśikāniruktivivṛti*
16.	Rāmeśvara	1420	?	Completion of Cinnambhaṭṭa's *Tārkikarakṣāsaṃgrahavivaraṇa* (E)
17.	Nārāyaṇācārya	1420	South?	*Ātmatattvavivekadīpikā* (E)
18.	Śeṣa Śārṅgadhara	1420		*Lakṣaṇāvalīnyāyamuktāvalī* (E) C on *Kiraṇāvalīprakāśa* (M?) *Tarkacandrikā* (M)
19.	Vāsudeva Sūri	1420	Kashmir	*Nyāyasārapadapañcikā* (E)
20.	Guṇaratna Sūri	1420	?	*Nyāyasiddhāntadīpaṭippaṇī* (E)
21.	Śaṃkara Miśra	1430	Darbhanga	*Nyāyakusumāñjalyāmoda* (E) *Bhedaratna* (E) *Vādivinoda* (E) *Kaṇādarahasya* (E) *Vaiśeṣikasūtropaskāra* (ET) *Ātmatattvavivekakalpalatā* (E) *Nyāyalīlāvatīkaṇṭhābharaṇa* (E) *Tattvacintāmaṇimayūkha* (E)
22.	Hari Miśra	1430	Mithila	
23.	Vācaspati Miśra II	1440	Mithila	*Khaṇḍanoddhāra* (E) *Nyāyatattvāloka* (M?) *Nyāyasūtroddhāra* (E?) *Nyāyaratnaprakāśa* (M) *Pratyakṣanirṇaya* *Anumānanirṇaya* (Part M) *Śabdanirṇaya* *(Tattva) Cintāmaṇiprakāśa* (Part M)
24.	Mallinātha	1445	?	*Tārkikarakṣāsārasaṃgrahaniṣkāntikā* (Part E)
25.	Pakṣadhara	1450	?	*Tattvacintāmaṇiviveka* *Dravyakiraṇāvalīprakāśaviveka* (M) *Kiraṇāvalīprakāśadravyaviveka* (M) *Nyāyalīlāvatīviveka* (M) *Nyāyalīlāvatīprakāśaviveka* (M)
26.	Bhuvanasundarasūri	1450	?	*Mahāvidyāviḍambanāvyākhyānadīpikā* (E) *Laghumahāvidyāviḍambanā* (E) *Mahāvidyāślokavivaraṇaṭippaṇa* (E)
27.	Śeṣānanta	1450	?	*Saptapadārthīpadārthacandrikā*

				(E) *Nyāyasiddhāntadīpaprabhā* (E)
28.	Narahari	1455	Navadvipa	
29.	Yajñapati Upādhyāya	1460	Mithila	*Tattvacintāmaṇiprabhā* (E)
30.	Pragalbha Miśra	1470	Mithila?	*Tattvacintāmaṇiprāgalbhī* (Part E) *Nyāyalīlāvatīviveka* (M) *Khaṇḍanadarpaṇa* (Part E) C on *Kiraṇāvalīprakāśa* (M)
31.	Jayadeva or Pakṣadhara Miśra	1470	Mithila	*Tattvacintāmaṇyāloka* (Part E) *Pramāṇapallava* (M) *Nyāyapadārthamālā* (M) *Saśadharavyākhyā* on *Nyāyasiddhāntadīpa* (M)
32.	Śrīnātha Bhaṭṭācārya Cakravartin	1470	Varanasi	Commentary on *Tattvacintāmaṇi*
33.	Vāsudeva Sārvabhauma	1480	Navadvipa	*Tattvacintāmaṇisārāvalī* (M)
34.	Kṛṣṇānanda Vidyāvinoda	1485	Navadvīpa	*Tattvacintāmaṇi(pratyakṣa) kṛṣṇa*
35.	Janārdana	1490	Mithila	*Tattvacintāmaṇiprakāśa* (M)
36.	Timmabhūpāla	1490	?	
37.	Misaru Miśra	1490	?	*Padārthacandra* (M)
38.	Virūpākṣa Miśra	1490	?	Commentary on *Tarkabhāṣā* (Part M)
39.	Narahari Upādhyāya	1495	Mithila	*Tattvacintāmaṇidūṣaṇoddhāra* (M) Commentary on *Ātmatattvaviveka* (M)
40.	Mādhava Miśra	1500	Mithila	Commentary on *Tattvacintāmaṇi*
41.	Śrīkāra Kubjaśaktivāda	1500	?	
42.	Śūlapāṇi	1500	?	
43.	Vāsudeva Miśra	1505	Mithila	*Nyāyasiddhāntasāra* (M)
44.	Rucidatta Miśra	1505	Mithila	*Tattvacintāmaṇiprakāśa* (Part E) *Nyāyakusumāñjalimakaranda* (E) C on *Tarkabhāṣāprakāśa* (M) *Nyāyalīlāvatīvibhāṣā* (M) *Kiraṇāvalīprakaśavivṛti* (E)
45.	Ratnākara Vidyāvācaspati	1505	Navadvipa	Commentary on *Tattvacintāmaṇi* and *Āloka* (M)

46.	Puruṣottama	1510		
47.	Janeśvara Vāhinīpati	1510	Navadvipa	*Tattvacintāmaṇyālokoddyota* (M)
48.	Bhairavendra	1510	?	*Saptapadārthīśiśubodhinī* (Part E)
49.	Gadādhara Miśra	1510	?	*Nyāyabhūṣaṇaprakāśa* (M)
50.	Raghunātha Śiromaṇi	1510	?	*Ātmatattvavivekadīdhiti* (E) *Nyāyakusumāñjalidīdhiti* (M) *Nyāyalīlāvatīprakāśadīdhiti* (M) *Kiraṇāvalīprakāśadīdhiti* (E) *Padārthatattvanirūpaṇa* (ET) *Nyāyalīlāvatīvibhūti* (M) *Ākhyātavāda* (ET) *Nañvāda* (ET) *Tattvacintāmaṇidīdhiti* (E, Part T)

2

RELATIONS AND ANALYSIS OF AWARENESS

Perhaps the most dramatic development from the time of elder Nyāya-Vaiśeṣika to our period of Navyanyāya concerns the treatment of relations. The tendency in old Nyāya was to conceive of relations as entities belonging to one or another of the Vaiśeṣika categories. Thus inherence (*samavāya*) is counted as one of the seven fundamental categories (*padārtha*) of classical Vaiśeṣika, while contact (*saṃyoga*) and disjunction (*vibhāga*) are viewed as types of the second category, of qualities (*guṇa*). As time goes by there is a growing realization that each and every individual falling into one of the categories sustains relations with other individuals, and the conception arises that any individual may relate *itself* to another thing. These self-linking connectors are known as *svarūpasambandhas*, and in Navyanyāya their varieties become virtually innumerable.

All relations are regarded in Navyanyāya as dyadic relations between two terms, the first called *anuyogin* or referend, the second the *pratiyogin* or referent. The Navyanyāya theory is that a relation is always a property resident in the referend, so that a natural way to analyze any relation is as follows: where *a* is the referend, *b* the referent, and R the relation, we can say "a- (R-b)". Thus, e.g., where Daśaratha is Rāma's father, we shall have "Daśaratha- (father of-Rāma)". This situation can be expressed most accurately and technically in Navyanyāya by saying that the father-of-ness resident in Daśaratha is determined by the son-of-ness resident in Rāma. This accurate but awkward expression becomes standard later on in Navyanyāya; an earlier and less awkward but more inaccurate manner of speaking was to say that the father-of-ness resident in Daśaratha is determined by Rāma.

Where R is inherence, contact or disjunction, "a-(R-b)" is to be read as indicating a triadic situation involving three distinct entities. Where R is a self-linking connector, there are only two entities involved, although the situation is still triadic in form. For example, take a self-linking connector recognized in old Nyāya, viz., the relation between the place where something is absent and the absence. This relation is called "absential qualification" (*abhāvīya-viśeṣaṇatā*), and can be symbolized as "ground-(R-absence of pot)". Here R does not designate a third thing beyond its relata; the ground is functioning as its own relation.

An absential qualification relation can only relate a positive entity with an absence. Inherence only relates certain sorts of entities to certain other sorts; likewise, contact. Thus relations can be classified according to the kinds of relata they connect. This is true of self-linking connectors. The relation *being the father of*, which we saw connecting Daśaratha with Rāma, is a self-linking connector, ontologically identical with Daśaratha. Clearly, there are indefinitely many such relations which could be appealed to in analyzing a complex situation.

Some self-linking connectors are especially useful because of their abstract nature. For example, being a *qualifier* (*viśeṣaṇa*) is something by which a great many entities are capable of being in relation to appropriate qualificands (*viśeṣya*). Thus the self-linking connector being the qualifier of, or qualifierness (*viśeṣaṇatā*), is a type of relation tokens of which are rife in the world. Likewise for qualificandness (*viśeṣyatā*). For example, whenever a universal property—say, cowness—is present in a cow, the cow is related by qualificandness to the cowness, and the cowness is related by qualifierness to the cow. Qualifierness and qualificandness have varieties, of course: we can distinguish temporal qualification (*kālikaviśeṣaṇatā*, spatial qualification (*daiśikaviśeṣaṇatā*), absential qualification (as we saw), etc. Other abstract relations of this type include the following: the relation called *anuyogitā* (in *x*) of being the referend (to *y*) and the relation of *pratiyogitā* (in *y*) of being the referent (to *x*); the relation of *pratiyogitā* (in *x*) of being the counterpositive (to some absence *y*); the relation of *viṣayitā* (in some awareness *x*) of having some *y* as its content, and the relation called *viṣayatā* in *y* to its locus, the awareness *x*; the relation called *pratibandhakatā* in *x* of obstructing the occurrence of something *y*, and its converse, the *pratibandhitatva* to *x* resident in *y*; the relation (called *ādheyatva*) of being resident in *y* which is found in *x*, and its converse *ādhāratva* or *adhikaraṇatā* which belongs to *y* relative to *x*; the relation called *kāraṇatā* which resides in *x* which is the cause of *y*, and its converse *kāryatā* which resides in *y* with respect to *x* in the same circumstance.

Some relations are direct, such as those just listed. Others are indirect, such as the ones identified by Uddyotakara[5] called "being inherent in what inheres", "being inherent in what is in contact", etc. Another indirect relation is that of *sāmānādhikaraṇya*, *having the same locus as*: *x* has the same locus as *y* if both are resident in some *z*.

An especially difficult and important relation is that of limitorness (*avacchedakatva*) and its converse limitedness (*avacchedyatva*). Though the term *avacchedaka* appears in early Nyāya literature, it is Raghunātha Śiromaṇi who makes of it an especially important tool of analysis.

Some relations are such that one of their relata occurs in or on the other. E.g., all cases of inherence are such—qualities and motions occur in the substances they qualify, wholes occur in their parts, etc. On the other hand, sometimes contact involves such occurrence, sometimes not. A classification used in Navyanyāya is that between "occurrence-exacting" (*vṛttiniyamaka*) relations and those which are not occurrence-exacting (*vṛttyaniyamaka*). Inherence, self-linking connectors and temporal relations are always occurrence-exacting. Among nonoccurrence-exacting relations we may class pervasion, identity, and most indirect relations.

Another classification among relations concerns whether the referend occurs in all of the referent or not. The most important application of this distinction is to the relation of contact and its absence. If a monkey is in contact with a tree, it is not in contact with all the places occupied by the tree, since it is sitting, say, on one of its branches. Thus contact is said to be a relation of incomplete occurrence or non-locus-pervasion (*avyāpyavṛtti*). Analogously, the absence of monkey in the tree through contact is a non-locus-pervading relation as well.

A special relation, discussed by Raghunātha Śiromaṇi, is that between a number (say, duality) and the pairs that it qualifies. The number two, i.e., duality, inheres in the two substances making up a pair which is, as we say, twofold. But what shall we say about a pair of qualities, or a pair of motions? Since number is itself a quality, a member of the second Vaiśeṣika category, and since qualities can only inhere in substances, we cannot say that the number two inheres in the two qualities which make up the pair. The Navyanaiyāyikas solve this problem by saying that there is a special relation which connects the number two, not to the members of the pair, but to the pair itself. This relation, called *paryāpti*, is a self-linking connector, and so it can perfectly well link a quality to a pair of qualities. Properties that occur in pairs, triples, etc., are known as *vyāsajyavṛtti* properties.

Identity (*tādātmya*) and difference (*bheda*) are two non-occurrence-exacting relations, the converse of each other. X and Y are related by identity just if X is the same individual as Y, i.e., they have the same nature or essence. It should be noted that "identity" as used to designate this relation cannot be equated with identity as it is normally understood in Western logic. Specifically, the Navyanyāya identity is between individuals: to say X and Y are identical is to say they are the very same individual. This will be interesting when X, that is, Y is known under different descriptions. Thus I may know the entity in question as a blue pot, and you may know it as a pot. Or, I may know it at one time as a pot, and later as an umbrella-stand. The identity relation obtains between any individual and itself regardless of what description or descriptions that individual is known under. Absence of identity is what is called "mutual absence" or difference, again, the difference being between two distinct individuals regardless of the descriptions under which they may be known.

Viewed in historical perspective, there is a great deal of development between Gaṅgeśa and Raghunātha in their use of relations of these exotic sorts to say accurately things that could only be phrased ambiguously in ordinary Sanskrit. Just how much of Raghunātha's apparatus was his invention, and how much he got from his teachers and the tradition they inherit, is impossible to say until closer study has been made of the figures which intervened between the two great Naiyāyikas.

The most intricate use of these relations occurs in connection with the analysis of awareness, to which we shall now turn. It is this side of Navyanyāya which is developed to an astounding degree in the further commentarial literature on *Dīdhiti* contributed by Jagadīśa and Gadādhara. That literature will be surveyed in another volume of this series.

3

METAPHYSICS

Navyanyāya developed a language to describe knowledge and other allied cognitive states and attitudes. This language, which is different from ordinary Sanskrit, is technical in the sense that it contains terms for concepts which were developed to deal specifically with cognitive mental states. This is why, even though the metaphysics of Navyanyāya is realistic, it could be taken out of the metaphysical system and made to apply *mutatis mutandis* not merely to other philosophical systems but to all serious discourse as well. A mastery of the techniques of this language came to be considered necessary not merely for students of philosophy but also for students of grammar, poetics, law and even medicine. All of these involve rigorous discussion of the nature of cognition. Navyanyāya is really a logic of cognition.

The Sanskrit term *jñāna* is used to denote not merely propositional acts like judging, believing, disbelieving, doubting, assuming, inferring, remembering, perceiving, but also nonpropositional states like sensing, feeling, etc. *Jñāna* is therefore identical with awareness (of facts, objects, sensory qualities, mental states, etc.). It will be translated as "awareness" henceforward.

Jñāna is always used in the episodic sense to denote an occurrence of an act, but never in the dispositional sense. The term *saṃskāra* is used for 'disposition' in general, physical as well as mental; in the context of cognition, *saṃskāra* is used to denote unconscious traces which when stirred up or activated produce conscious memory. We shall use "cognitive act" as an abbreviation for "actual conscious state of awareness", but not in the sense of any activity or action. Even sensing will be a cognitive act in this sense.

This concept of an awareness or cognitive act plays an important role in Navyanyāya logic. In this logic Navyanyāya makes use of a certain concept of a relation between two such cognitive acts which is novel and difficult to explain, viz., the preventer–prevented relation between two such acts. One awareness, under certain conditions, prevents the occurrence of another awareness, although it does not prevent or cancel the existence of a mental disposition. So the relation holds only between acts of awareness, not between an act and a disposition, or between two dispositions.

An awareness has generally (except for enumerative cognition) three moments or phases: (a) a moment of origination, (b) a moment of duration in which an act produces its own trace, and (c) a moment of cessation. Navyanyāya holds that two awarenesses cannot originate at the same moment. An awareness originating at *t* will prevent every other act from originating at *t*. It is a psychological law that we cannot attend to more than one thing at a time.

Although two awarenesses cannot originate at the same time, still one awareness can, and if introspection is to be possible, must originate, i.e., be in its first phase, when a prior awareness endures, i.e., is in its second phase. The introspective act is just one jump behind the act which is its content. In the waking state there is no felt gap between two awarenesses. When the preceding awareness is in its second phase the succeeding awareness originates and replaces the former; and so on. In Navyanyāya terminology the succeeding awareness "destroys", "kills" the preceding awareness.

An act of awareness may produce a disposition; indeed, no dispositions can arise except as caused by some act. The disposition which is caused by an awareness is a memory trace which will produce a memory when it is stirred up or activated. This dispositional memory–trace will not be the direct cause of any other type of awareness except memory, and will not be the direct cause of any behavior, even of speech behavior.

There is a controversy among philosophers of the Navyanyāya school on the nature of the relation between a disposition and an act of awareness. The question is whether, after an activated disposition causes a memory, the diposition continues to exist. According to one section of Navyanyāya a disposition after producing the memory act will itself be destroyed. It will no longer remain that disposition, although the memory act it produces will leave behind it a new disposition which will be stronger than the old disposition and so not require much excitation to bring about another memory. The difficulty in this theory would seem to be that it has to postulate innumerable dispositions of almost the same cognitive form. This is what has led other philosophers of the school to hold that a disposition is not destroyed even after the production.

The preventer–prevented relation, mentioned above, is not only this feature of the psychological impossibility of more than one awareness' originating at one time. The preventer–prevented relation holds between two awarenesses, not in virtue of their merely being awarenesses, but in virtue of their contents. Elucidation of the point helps to explain how there can be a *logic* of cognition given the episodic nature of cognitive awarenesses in Nyāya.

An interesting puzzle broached in Western philosophical analysis concerns whether it makes any sense to say 'A believes *p* and does not believe *p*'. According to Navyanyāya this puzzle can be solved easily by a distinction between an actual awareness belief and a disposition to believe. We have already seen that a second act can originate while a prior act endures. So, if we symbolize by *t* the time when the first act (of believing *p*) originates, and if we symbolize by *t*′ the time when that act endures, then we can say that it is logically possible that X believes at *t* that *p* and X believes at *t*′ that *q*. However, it is not logically possible, on Navyanyāya assumptions, that X believes at *t*′ that *p* and X believes at *t*′ that not–*p*, since, as long as X continues to consciously believe (i.e., be aware of believing) *p* X cannot even *start* believing that not–*p*. As long as the belief that *p* endures as a conscious state, the other act of believing that not–*p* cannot even originate. This impossibility has nothing to do with the psychological mechanism of the origination of acts, but is completely determined by the logical relation between *p* and not–*p*.

According to Navyanyāya the relation between a preceding and a succeeding act is that of the killed and the killer; the two acts have to meet, if only for one moment, so that the succeeding act can kill the preceding act. But in the case of awarenesses of two contradictory propositions, the presence of the one act prevents the origination of the other act, so that they can never be copresent, not even for one moment. This is because, under conditions specified below, the awareness of one proposition is a negative condition of the awareness of its contradictory; that is, the absence of one awareness is necessary for the occurrence of the other act. So the preventer act and the prevented act can never meet. If, however, the belief that *p* has lapsed into a mere disposition and is no longer a conscious state, if it is forgotten and not remembered at the moment, then the mere disposition will not prevent the same person from believing that not–*p*.

Thus we have come to a fundamental difference between disposition and act. So long as a conscious act of believing that *p* remains a conscious act, it will prevent a person from consciously believing that not–*p*; but if the belief is a mere disposition and is not recalled, then the same person can believe that *p* and also that not–*p*, and one of the beliefs can become also actualized at one time. A person can believe that not–*p* consciously only so long as she does not realize that she also believes that *p*; that is, a person cannot consciously, knowingly hold self-contradictory beliefs; but unknowingly, without realizing that she does so, a person can hold beliefs (as unconscious dispositions) which may not be consistent.

Note that the preventer awareness must be attended with belief—it must not be a supposition or a doubt; it may be either true or false, but if false, it must not be cognized, truly or falsely, as false; it must be about the proposition which is contradictory to the proposition cognized by the prevented awareness. The prevented awareness can be either true or false; it may or may not be attended with belief; it must not be a supposition; it must not be an ordinary perception, or an illusory perception due to any psychophysical defect; and it must be propositional.

To explain. If we suppose that S is P, then this supposition when it endures as an actual conscious state cannot prevent us from cognizing or even knowing that S is not P. So even if we know that S is P, this knowledge will not be able to prevent us from supposing that S is not P. However, in this case the supposition will be contrary to fact. Then an illusory perception cannot be prevented from occurring by any awareness of the contradictory proposition. Thus, if we are suffering from jaundice, then even though we know actively that the wall is not yellow, yet we shall see that the wall is yellow; but in this case the illusory perception will not be attended with belief. Thirdly, the preventer awareness can be either true or false; it is not always the case that only a true awareness can prevent the occurrence of a false awareness, for even a false awareness held with firm conviction can prevent one from cognizing the truth. But if our awareness is false, we must not know or even suspect it to be false if it is to prevent the awareness of the truth. For if we know or doubt that our awareness is false, then we shall withhold our belief from it, and this awareness without belief will not be able to act as the preventer awareness. The awareness which is prevented may, however, be a doubt, this is, an awareness not attended with belief; it we cognize with belief that S is P, then we cannot even doubt that S in not P.

There are certain propositions such that the conditions which produce the awareness of the one proposition are exactly the same as those which produce the awareness of the other. In such a case the two propositions are the contents of one and the same awareness. For example, the logical converse of a proposition is cognized by the same awareness that has that proposition as its content. Thus not merely the awarenesses of p and of not-p have the relation of preventer to prevented, but any awareness which is produced by exactly the same conditions as the awareness of p will prevent or be prevented by the awareness of not-p.

According to Navyanyāya the conditions of different kinds of awareness have different strengths. In every moment of waking awareness sufficient conditions for the perception of something or the other are present. A problem, then, is this: how is it ever possible for us not to be constantly perceiving objects but to have inference, or to understand what others say to us? Suppose I am now sitting in a chair; sufficient conditions for perceiving all objects in front of me are present. How then can I infer, as I do now, that it is going to rain very soon? According to Navyanyāya this is possible only if the conditions of making this inference predominate over the conditions of perception. Now in determining the relative strength of the conditions of perception, inference, or of understanding the meanings of heard sentences, Navyanyāya refers to the contents of awareness. If the contents of the awarenesses are the same, then the conditions of perception prevail over conditions of inference, verbal testimony, etc. Thus verification is possible; what is perceived may be the same as what is inferred or known from others, so what we perceive can be justified by inference or corroborated by what others say. If, however, the contents are not the same, then the conditions of inference prevail over the conditions of perception. Thus if conditions for perceiving that it is raining are present, then even if conditions for inferring the same are present, we shall have perceptual awareness and not inference. But if conditions for perceiving a table (say, for becoming perceptually aware that the table is brown) and conditions for inferring that it is raining are present, then because the contents of perception and inference are different, we shall draw the inference. In every case the desire to cognize in a certain way rather then in any other way will produce the desired type of awareness; desire to cognize in a certain way has overriding influence on the mode of awareness.

We said that Navyanyāya philosophers developed a logic of cognition. In developing this logic Navyanyāya starts with a certain presupposition, viz., that there must be a definite way of understanding the nature of cognitive awarenesses. If we do not understand or are uncertain about the nature of awarenesses themselves, we cannot develop a logic of cognition at all. The logic of cognition is not developed in order to clarify confused awareness of cognition but to describe in a rigorous manner what we already understand. The method of understanding the nature of awarenesses is introspection. According to Navyanyāya, introspection gives us an infallible understanding of our mental states, of our awarenesses. The technique of referring constantly to awarenesses in order to decide between two alternative hypotheses is due to Raghunātha Śiromaṇi and has been used very widely ever since.

This explains why Navyanyāya does not give any criterion of what it is to be one awareness or cognitive act. If there is any controversy whether the alleged awareness is one or many, the method by which this controversy is resolved is by reference to introspection. Likewise, there is no criterion for deciding whether a supposed fact is a single fact or a complex of many facts. In Western philosophy, the problem of identity of propositions or of facts has posed a very difficult problem. Navyanyāya does not distinguish between a proposition and a fact, i.e., does not believe in the existence of any proposition distinct from fact.

Whether a fact is one or a complex of many atomic facts can be discussed from various points of view. For example, it may be held that there is one fact corresponding to a certain type of atomic proposition and also of all propositions formed from it truth-functionally by adding an even number of negatives. It is sometimes said that two propositions, if they are logically equivalent, are then identical, and that corresponding to them there is only one fact and not two. This is, according to Navyanyāya, to approach the problem from a point of view different from that of a logic of cognition, for even if two propositions are logically equivalent, the awareness of one need not be identical with the awareness of the other. For example, to cognize that *p* is not the same as to cognize that not-not-*p*, even though *p* and not-not-*p* are truth-functionally equivalent. The point here is that unless we make an assumption of rationality which amounts to limited omniscience we cannot say that a person who is aware of a certain proposition is bound to cognize or even ought to cognize all the propositions which are either logically equivalent to it or follow logically from it.

So far as our actual awarenesses are concerned one person may cognize what is logically equivalent to it or what is entailed by it. Navyanyāya distinguishes between contents of awareness from this standpoint of the logic of cognition, so that contents will be distinguished from each other even if they are expressed by propositions which are logically equivalent or by some propositions logically implying others. A content is what becomes evident to a person through his awareness of it; that is, a content is what a person actually cognizes it to be and not what he ought to cognize it to be.

According to Navyanyāya, awarenesses are of two types, nonpropositional (*nirvikalpaka*) and propositional (*savikalpaka*). Propositional awarenesses are awarenesses of a complex whole containing a relation and its two terms (according to Navyanyāya all relations are dyadic).

This may suggest that what is cognized in this type of awareness can be schematically represented as "aRb"; but this representation is not sufficiently perspicuous. For, according to Navyanyāya, what is cognized in a propositional awareness becomes a term of another relation cognized in a more complex awareness. "aRb" represents a fact, but what is cognized in a propositional awareness cannot be said to be a fact; it is really a complex content. As has been said, we shall represent it by "a–(R–b)", which will stand for a complex term denoting *a*–as–related–to–*b*–by–R. The three elements of this complex term are designated by the technical expressions "qualificand" (*viśeṣya*), "qualifier" (*viśeṣaṇa*), and "qualification" (*vaiśiṣṭya*). In the content of the awareness represented by "a–(R–b)"

a (not "*a*") is the qualificand of the awareness,
b (not "*b*") is the qualifier of the awareness,
R (the cognized relation) is the qualification of the awareness,
a–(R–b) is *a*–as–qualified–by–*b* as the successor of the relation R, or *a*–as–related–to–*b*–by–R.

Propositional awareness is also called "qualified awareness" (*viśiṣṭajñāna*).

This representation of the content of an awareness, a–(R–b), is regarded as a complex term. But Navyanyāya makes no distinction between a sentence (which contains a finite verb) and a complex term. So, in speaking of propositions in the foregoing, the reader should understand these as structured as a–(R–b). So far as the nature of awareness is concerned, both a sentence and a complex term produce the same type of propositional or qualified awareness. Thus "(the) brown table" (in Sanskrit there are no articles, definite or indefinite), and "(the) table is brown" express the content of the same awareness; the "is" is redundant according to Navyanyāya, and in ordinary Sanskrit it is often omitted. (The grammarians, of course, insist that a sentence must contain a finite verb which, if not expressed, has to be understood. But Navyanyāya philosophers hold that a complex term is a sentence, or rather, in the context of cognition, that the content of an awareness expressed by a sentence is to be understood as a complex term with the structure a–(R–b).)

The relation R in this representation of the content of an awareness may be any relation. The qualificand is said to be cognized through the qualifier, which must have, therefore, already been cognized. To stop the infinite regress of qualifiers, Navyanyāya postulates nonrelational awareness, in which universals and other unanalyzable properties are directly cognized, that is, not cognized through any qualifier. Thus universals are self-evident in the sense that they are cognized in and through themselves and not through any qualifier.

By contrast with the nonpropositional kind of awareness, in a qualified or propositional awareness the awareness manifests something (the qualificand) *as* something else (the qualifier, also known as the "chief qualifier" (*prakāra*)). Both the qualificand and the qualifier are factors in the content of the qualified awareness.

Now according to Navyanyāya, a qualificand as qualified is ontologically the same thing as the qualificand without the qualification. For example, a blue pot is ontologically the same as the pot, and by cognizing the pot as blue we are not cognizing anything different from the pot. But, although this particular pot which happens to be blue is identical with this particular pot ontologically, still the awarenesses of this as a blue pot and of this as a pot are different awarenesses. To explain this difference between the awarenesses Navyanyāya introduces the important concept of a limitor (*avacchedaka*). The limitor is the mode under which an ontological entity becomes evident in an awareness. Thus, if we cognize an entity simply as (a) pot, then the mode under which it is presented to the awareness is *potness*, for the entity is cognized as an instance of (that is, as related in a specific manner to) the universal *potness*. Although the content cognized is expressed by a single word, "pot", still the awareness is of a complex of the form a–(R–b), where *a* is the pot, R is inherence, and *b* is the universal *potness* which is cognized directly. Here *b* (the universal) is the limitor of the property of being the qualificand and resident in *a* (the pot). A limitor is thus a qualifier, but all qualifiers are not limitors; the difference is that qualifiers may be expressed in language by words denoting them, or else they have to be understood by themselves, even though what they are understood *as* is not expressed. Limitors are qualifiers of the latter type, i.e., when the content of an awareness is expressed in words the limitors have to remain unexpressed, yet in the awareness of the object they have to be cognized as qualifiers.

The result is that on the Navyanyāya view no linguistic expression can adequately represent all the factors in the content of a propositional awareness. This is because whenever a content is expressed by a word, that word fails to express the manner of presentation (the limitor). This manner of presentation therefore has to be understood. That is, in the awareness the mode of presentation will be manifest but there is no way of expressing it in language.

It is widely held in Western philosophy now that thinking is impossible without using language. Navyanyāya shows the inadequacy of such a theory. It points out that using language is not possible without understanding the meaning of words, expressions and sentences. But understanding the meaning of expressions is an altogether different type of activity from the activity of perceiving, inferring, etc. Even if thinking be regarded as sub-vocal speech it nevertheless requires understanding the meaning of expressions used. The difference between understanding the meaning of expressions and other forms of awareness like perceiving, inferring, however complex those may be, is fundamental. The act of understanding the meaning of expressions is typically exemplified in reading or hearing what others write or say, and this act is unlike inferring, etc. So acts of awareness like inferring, etc., cannot be identified with understanding the meaning of expressions.

But, although inferring is not speaking, still isn't inference impossible without using language in some form or other? The reply to this question is not difficult to find. If inferring, for example, is not identical with speaking or soliloquizing, then if such activity is necessary it must be so only as a subsidiary process. This will lead to the theory that an act of cognizing like perceiving, inferring, etc., is really not one act, but is to be analysed into different sorts of acts—one of inferring and another of speaking, going on simultaneously in the mind. But this is an implausible theory and involves insuperable difficulties of all sorts. We can ask, for example, how can two altogether different types of cognitive acts be performed simultaneously? The theory also runs counter to introspective evidence. So Navyanyāya holds that an act of perceiving, inferring, etc., is not the same as speaking or whispering, that different acts cannot be simultaneous, that language is necessary only for expressing an act of awareness, and that the act of expressing is a subsequent and different type of act.

Next, let us consider a false awareness. If an awareness is false then the content cognized, namely a–(R–b), is not a reality. Thus, *a* as related to *b* by the relation R is not an actual existent. For example, if we cognize a certain thing as piece of silver when it is not, then according to Navyanyāya the content of this false awareness is of the form this-inherence–silverness. Yet although the relation cognized here is the relation of inherence, that relation does not actually obtain between the thing presented as *this* and the property of *silverness*. So even though the relation is a dyadic relation, yet because the awareness is false its two terms are not *this and silverness*, though the content of the awareness is of the form this–(inherence–silverness). The problem then is: This false awarness, being a propositional awareness, must have a qualificand and a qualifier, yet the qualificand and the qualifier cannot be identified with the first and the second terms of the relation of inherence which is manifested as the relation of the awareness.

But how are we to define what is cognized and the elements constituting what is cognized except in terms of the awareness itself? According to Navyanyāya in introspection when we become aware of our awareness we also become aware of all the special relations into which the three elements of its content enter with the awareness.

The awareness is related to its qualifier in one characteristic manner, to its qualificand in another characteristic manner, and to the qualification in a third characteristic manner.

We may represent this schematically as follows:

Awareness

1 3 2

a R b

The one awareness is related to *a* in the first characteristic manner, to *b* in the second characteristic manner, and to R in the third characteristic manner. These special relations in which the awareness is related to the three elements constituting its content become evident, and unmistakably identified, in introspective awareness. Thus we can define the "qualificand of an awareness" only in terms of the specific relation in which the awareness is related to it. So also in defining "the qualifier of the awareness" we have to make use of the introspective awareness of the special relation in which the awareness is related to it. And likewise with the relation which is the qualification we have to make use of a very special relation in which the act of awareness is related to it. These very special relations of one and the same act of awareness to the three elements of its content are introspectively differentiated and identified unerringly.

Now how do we fix the relation R in the content a-(R-b)? Not by resorting to the ontological situation, but rather by introspection. This appeal to introspective awareness in order to fix the relation R is necessary for Navyanyāya philosophers because there is nothing in the nature of entities which makes relations distinct from other entities. Relations do not form a separate ontological category, but are entirely relative to situations. Thus R, which is a relation between *a* and *b*, will itself be a term if we ask: What is the relation between R and *a*? According to Navyanyāya what is a relation in one context or situation will be a term in another context. So if we want to fix on something as the R in a-(R-b) we have to refer to the awareness of a-(R-b).

That what functions as a relation in a particular content of awareness is cognized in a special and very determinate way is shown in Navyanyāya by its theory that in the linguistic expression of what is cognized the relation can never be represented by a word. We have already seen that according to Navyanyāya qualifiers of awarenesses, i.e., modes of presentation of the things cognized, cannot be expressed in language except through predicative expressions whose modes of presentation have then to be understood. Now

Navyanyāya holds that no relation can ever be expressed by words, for if a relation is expressed by a word, then it is no longer meant as a relation, but rather it is meant as a term. A relation is always understood from the word order of the expression representing the content of an awareness. The mode of presentation of an object in an awareness *can* be expressed in language, but if it is, then a higher mode has to be understood. But a relation can never be expressed by any word.

How then can Navyanyāya explain the possibility of a false awareness? For in a false awareness the relation R does not really unify the two elements *a* and *b* together. So the question arises: what is the content of a false awareness? According to Navyanyāya, even in the case of false awareness the three elements *a*, R and *b* are all real. Only the a-(R-b) unity is not real. But that does not mean that the unity is made by the cognitive act which goes wrong and produces a false awareness. Even in false awareness we can find by introspection three characteristic relations, different from each other, in which the one awareness is related to each of the three elements in its content. According to Navyanyāya in all cases of illusory perception, and false awareness generally, the content has to be analysed into its parts or elements, and since a false awareness is necessarily a propositional awareness, the elements will always be three, a relation and its two terms. All these three elements are actually existent, but it is not necessary that the three must form an actual existent "fact" in order to be cognized.

It was said earlier that Navyanyāya has developed a technical language adequate for serious discussion. In order to understand the need for and nature of this technical language it is necessary to realize the inadequacy of ordinary language, i.e., ordinary Sanskrit.

The problem is: How can we talk about awarenesses, which are inner states? It is necessary somehow to communicate these inner states of awareness through language. So we shall have to examine how cognitive states can be communicated. One natural answer will be that to talk about cognitive states one has to *express* them in language. But according to Navyanyāya to express an awareness in language is to say what is cognized in the cognition, is to represent its content. Thus if I perceive that the chair is brown, what I shall say in expressing this awareness is simply "the chair is brown." This expression describes a content, not an awareness.

In contemporary Western philosophical analysis it is regularly assumed that a proposition is something which remains constant even though the so-called propositional attitudes change. Thus the proposition that the chair is brown remains the same proposition whether I assert it, doubt it, entertain it, or reject it. But according to Navyanyāya the so-called proposition is not something which remains constant through these different propositional attitudes. Rather, they say that since a judgment and a doubt differ in that the former is a state of belief or certainty while the latter is a state of uncertainty, i.e., since these attitudes differ psychologically, what is believed and what is doubted cannot be identical. The content of belief, for example, will be "the chair is brown"; the content of doubt will be "the chair is either brown or green." There must be a difference between the contents of belief and of doubt.

Furthermore, since Sanskrit has no articles and finite verbs are not mandatory in expressing contents of awarenesses, the content of the awareness of the brown chair may well be expressed by the Sanskrit phrase equivalent to English "brown chair". Semantically, what this expression conveys is that some one thing is both a chair and brown, that an identity relation obtains between the chair and the brown chair. Yet so far as the content of the awareness is concerned, it is the relation of inherence which obtains between the brown color and the chair. Thus the relation cognized is inherence, while in the language one has to use to express the awareness the relation semantically made necessary is the relation of identity. And generally, the relation which has to be understood in order to construe grammatically the words constituting a description of the content will not be identical with the relation which is cognized as the qualification obtaining between the qualificand and the qualifier. So, even though it is necessary to express our awareness through language, the linguistic units will require some relations to be understood in order to form a unified expression, and this relation will not normally be the same as the relation between the qualificand and the qualifier, i.e., will not be the relation which is cognized.

That is why it becomes necessary to *describe* our awarenesses in a technical language. If we want to describe the awareness expressed by the expression "brown chair" it will be as follows: it is an awareness which has the brown color as its qualifier, the chair as its qualificand, and inherence as its qualification. Of course, this technical language again has to be understood grammatically, but then here we have expressed the qualifying relation by a relation word, so this language is really a second order language where what has to be understood in the first order language is made explicit. Indeed, in such a second order technical language the qualifiers, i.e., the modes of presentation of the elements involved in the content, which have necessarily to be understood when we want to express our awareness in language, can be explicitly named. Thus the awareness expressed as "brown chair" is to be described even more perspicuously as follows: it is that awareness the qualifier of which is brown color cognized under the mode of the property of brownness, the qualificand of which is the chair cognized under the mode of chairness, and the qualification of which is the relation of inherence. The special feature of this higher order language is that what was understood as a manner or mode of presentation when an awareness is expressed in ordinary language has become explicitly named in this higher-order-language description, and the higher-order-language therefore is not the ordinary expression of an awareness.

In Navyanyāya parlance the phrase "under the mode of" in higher-order descriptions of the above sort is rendered through use of the technical notion of a "limitor" (*avacchedaka*). Specifically, the part of the description offered in the preceding paragraph which speaks of "the qualificand of which (awareness) is the chair cognized under the mode of chairness" will be rendered by "the property of the qualificand, resident in the chair, is limited by the property of being a chair." But the qualifier (here, the brown color) also has got to be cognized under its own mode; so according to Navyanyāya this entire awareness can be perspicuously represented in the technical language as "the cognition which has its qualifierness limited by brown(color)ness and by inherence, and whose qualificandness is limited by chairness."

If we understand that the concept of the limitor is the concept making explicit the modes of presentation of the qualifier and the qualificand, we can then indicate certain rules concerning limitors. First of all, if one object is cognized under more than one mode then all the modes become, separately, limitors of the qualificandness or the qualifierness in this cognition. According to the older school of Navyanyāya, when a thing is cognized under a mode which is a heavier property, then the limitor should be a lighter property, wherever possible, if it is coextensive with the heavier property. For example, when something is cognized as *possessing a certain shape, etc*. rather than as a *jar*, according to this older school it is *jarness* that should be regarded as the limitor of the qualificandness, and not the property of possessing a certain shape, etc., since this latter property is analyzable and so heavier, while *jarness* is a simple property and lighter. But according to Raghunātha Śiromaṇi and the "new" wing of Navyanyāya this is a wrong application of the principle of parsimony, which they say should only be applied in ontology, not in epistemology. According to Raghunātha, if a jar is cognized under the mode of having a certain shape, etc., then that property should be the limitor of the qualificandness, not *jarness* which is not the mode under which the qualificand is cognized. According to Raghunātha, which property is the limitor of the qualifierness or the qualificandness is to be determined by introspecting to see under which modes the qualifier and the qualificand have been cognized.

The concept of limitor is used in Navyanyāya for various other purposes as well. It is sometimes wondered how Navyanyāya can dispense with words indicating quantity while discussing universal judgments, for example. The answer is that in Navyanyāya the quantity of an awareness is always understood, not expressed in the first-order representation of it; its representation comes in the higher technical language in terms of the limitors of the qualifier and qualificand. By the "quantity" of an awareness we mean whether the awareness concerns a single item falling under a description, some of them, or all of them. E.g., when the qualificand of an awareness is expressed by the word "cow", there is nothing in the word to indicate whether the reference is to Bossie here, a group of cows, or all cows there ever were, are or will be. By contrast, the "quality" of an awareness—by which we mean the positive or negative force of the awareness—is indicated directly in the expression of it through the use of the negative particle.

To illustrate through an example. Suppose one expresses his awareness by saying "here there is absence of cow." There is no indication from what has been said as to whether the absence of all cows is intended or the absence of a particular cow is meant, for the Sanskrit expression whose English literal translation we have just provided is ambiguous as regards the quantity. In Navyanyāya this ambiguity is always resolved by appeal to the manner in which the cow is cognized. If I cognized the cow under the mode of *cowness* then "absence of cow" will mean the absence of all cows (i.e., there are not any cows here). If the cow is cognized under the mode of its particularity as that cow, then "absence of cow" will mean absence of that cow (i.e., the awareness is that Bossie is not here). In the higher order language we shall say that the cow whose absence is cognized, i.e., the cow which is the counterpositive of the absence in question, has counterpositiveness limited by *cowness*. Thus the sign of quantity which is absent in the expression of an awareness is always to be understood and can be expressed only in the higher order technical language by means of the concept of limitor.

This use of the concept of a limitor is only one use of that concept. It is technically called the limitor as self-linking connector (*svarūpa-sambandha*), and has to do with the mode under which an object is cognized. The concept of limitor explicated in the previous chapter has to do with objective features without reference to awareness. Actually, these two concepts, though designated by the same term "limitor", do not have anything essential in common, and therefore do not admit of one definition.[6]

An objection might be raised at this point to the effect that the Navyanyāya analysis of an awareness saddles it with an infinite regress. The analysis requires that in every propositional awareness a qualificand is cognized through a qualifier, and the qualifier, in turn, has to be cognized through a second-order qualifier, i.e., a limitor, and so on. This threat of a regress does not bother the Navyanaiyāyikas. For there is no regress of entities involved here. The distinction between qualificand and qualifier is not an ontological distinction. One and the same entity can, and in various cases does, function in a cognition in two capacities of qualificand and qualifier. For example, when we cognize that a jar is identical with itself, the relation cognized is identity, and its two terms, the qualificand and the qualifier, are the same entity, viz., the jar.

I. Substance

Characteristically, Navyanyāya discussions of substance tend to collect around the defining characteristic of substance, that is, substanceness. Udayana offered several definitions of substance, one of which was that a substance is a thing which is not the locus of an absolute absence of qualities.[7] But, objects the Advaitin Citsukha, your doctrine requires that a substance exist for a moment before it acquires any qualities; so the definition just offered fails to cover such a substance. Śeṣa Śārṅgadhara's answer is that the substance at that moment is qualified by being at that moment, so it isn't the locus of an absolute absence of qualities. Śaṃkara Miśra utilizes this definition of Udayana's, and Raghunātha Śiromaṇi also defends it.

A. *Atomic Theory and the Theory of Cooking.* For the most part the Navyanaiyāyikas of this period appear to have accepted Praśastapāda's account of atomic theory and cooking. The exception is Raghunātha Śiromaṇi. Raghunātha dispenses entirely with atoms and dyads. For him the smallest substance, indivisible, is the minimal perceptibilium (*truṭi*). The arguments of Praśastapāda and the tradition that follows him are dismissed on the ground that they produce infinite regress.[8] Raghunātha is aware that his theory is not original with him—he associates it with the Bhaṭṭa Mīmāṃsakas, and Bhaduri points out that it was criticized many centuries earlier by Uddyotakara.

B. *Earth, Water, Fire, Air.* Both Vardhamāna and Śaṃkara Miśra support the view of Vyomaśiva[9] and Udayana (against, e.g., Śrīdhara) that trees are alive and constitute organic bodies. Otherwise nothing startlingly new is suggested about earth by these writers. The same is true of water.

Śaṃkara Miśra classifies fire into four kinds according to whether its color and/or touch are manifested or unmanifested. Thus the sun's rays are fire where both color and touch are manifested, while in the fiery sense-organ, i.e., the visual organ, both color and touch are unmanifested (otherwise it would be seen and it would burn things up that are seen by it). In hot oil the touch but not the bright color is manifested, and in gold the color but not the hot touch is manifested.

Gaṅgeśa gives an entire, though small, section to the topic of gold. The occasion is the position taken by Mīmāṃsakas that gold is an earthy object. Gaṅgeśa refutes a number of arguments purporting to establish the Mīmāṃsā thesis. For one thing, gold is not bright, as it ought to be according to the analysis in the previous paragraph. Gaṅgeśa's answer is that, though gold has manifested color, being a fiery object, its brightness is overcome by the color of the earth that surrounds it, which is why we don't see gold in the dark. Gold can't be the surrounding earthy stuff itself, since it would be immediately burnt up by the fire inside; the reason the surrounding earth doesn't get burnt up or change color is because it is in contact with something which has accidental liquidity, viz., fire.

Cennu Bhaṭṭa and Jinavardhana also have extensive discussion of gold. Śaṃkara Miśra implies that the moon is also a fiery object.

A classical problem concerns the proof of the existence of air or wind. In the older literature it had been proved by inference,[10] on the assumption that it is not perceptible and thus cannot be proved through perception. The reasoning is as follows: since air is (doctrinally) supposed to be without any color, and since possession of manifested color is a prerequisite of perceptibility (again doctrinally), it must follow that air is not perceptible. This, however, does not seem to be a happy outcome. The responses of Navyanaiyāyikas range from attempts to justify the tradition (Gaṅgeśa) to complete rejection of possession of manifested color as prerequisite of perceptibility (Vyomaśiva and later, Raghunātha Śiromaṇi).

Gaṅgeśa again devotes an entire section to the topic. Although we cannot be clear that Gaṅgeśa is actually reporting Vyomaśiva's views consciously, he summarizes the sorts of arguments presented by Vyomaśiva[11] and unlike his predecessors, answers them.[12] Vyomaśiva's position was that when Kaṇāda says that possession of middlesizedness, composition and color is the prerequisite of the perceptibility of a substance[13] he doesn't mean that all three have to be present in every case of perceptibility. Rather, they are disjunctive requirements, so that, e.g., the self can be perceived because it has middlesizedness, composite perceptible substances satisfy all three requirements, and air satisfies two out of the three—viz., middlesizedness and compositeness. Furthermore, it would seem that air (wind) is tactually perceived, and Kaṇāda's requirements seem to be addressed to visual perceptibility rather than perceptibility by other organs. Therefore, concludes Vyomaśiva's position, or at any rate the position opposed to Gaṅgeśa's tradition, possession of compositeness and middlesizedness together with manifested color is the condition for visual perceptibility, while the first two coupled with manifested tangibility constitute the conditions for tactual perceptibility, conditions that air satisfies. Therefore air is perceptible.

Gaṅgeśa, however, insists that both manifested visibility and tangibility are required for perception. Otherwise, he says, we should be able to perceive things such as the warmth of summer, hot wind, and such things, and so we should also be able to perceive their size, contact, disjunction and motions, which is absurd. He says that is the view of the "new school", but adds that there is also an opinion supporting the original view of, e.g., Praśastapāda, that possession of manifested color alone (together with middlesizedness and compositeness) are the requisite conditions.

C. *Time and Space.* Śaṃkara Miśra, presumably recognizing that some members of his school were proposing the reduction of time, spatial direction and *ākāśa* to a single substance, is moved to inquire what the intrinsic distinction between time and space in fact is. In *Kaṇādarahasya* he proposes that the difference is that temporal divisions are the same for everyone, while distinctions among spatial directions are relative to the location of the person appealing to them. In the *Upaskāra* on the *Vaiśeṣikasūtras* he explicitly notes and rejects the reduction of spatial direction (*dik*) and time (*kāla*) to a single substance, giving essentially the same reason in more picturesque fashion. He adds other reasons, some not very convincing.

Raghunātha Śiromaṇi not only accepts the reduction of spatial direction and time to a single entity, he goes farther and treats these two as identical with the self we call "God". In this he follows at least one earlier author, Aparārkadeva the commentator on Bhāsarvajña.[14] Raghunātha announces this reduction in his *Padārthatattvanirūpaṇa;* in other places, such as the *Kiraṇāvalīprakāśadīdhiti*, he seems to accept the older distinctions among these ubiquitous substances at least for the sake of argument.

D. *The Internal Organ.* The traditional view of the size of the internal organ in Nyāya is that it is imperceptibly small (*aṇu*). Gaṅgeśa devotes an entire, though short, section to the defense of this thesis, in the course of which some fresh opposing views about the nature of the internal organ are developed by the opponent, only to be carefully considered and rejected by Gaṅgeśa. Some of these views are referred to in subsequent discussions of the same topic by Vardhamāna, Śaṃkara Miśra, and others.[15]

E. *Selves*. Jinavardhana appears to have proposed an Advaitin interpretation of "*ātman*" and attempted to combine it with the Nyāya theory. However, the general thrust of the Nyāya authors covered in this volume is toward criticism and rejection of Advaita tenets, though many authors will cite Upaniṣadic passages where they believe such can be squared with Nyāya theory.

F. *God*. It will be seen by consulting the section on God in the Introduction to Volume II that the major questions about God raised by older Naiyāyikas relate to His nature, whether He has a body, and the arguments for His existence. These very topics occupy the limelight in Navyanyāya discussions of God as well, along with a growing concern that God's awareness, with its peculiarities, not be excluded from general definitions of "awareness" and other epistemological notions.

After Udayana's refutations of Buddhist arguments, with the possible exception of Vallabha, the most important contributor to discussions of theism in Nyāya is Śaśadhara. Indeed, Gaṅgeśa can be seen to have had Śaśadhara's treatment very much in mind, as John Vattanky has shown in his detailed discussion.[16] In particular, the way in which Gaṅgeśa goes about his task in the section of *Tattvacintāmaṇi* devoted to God is precisely that of Śaśadhara. Both consider various ways of expressing the main terms of the cosmoteleological argument that Nyāya offers for God's existence. The procedure begins with an opponent's section in which possible formulations of the *pakṣa, sādhya* and *hetu* of such an argument are reviewed. In the *siddhānta* section in which the correct view is propounded Śaśadhara gives and defends correct formulations of each of the terms. Gaṅgeśa follows a somewhat different plan: he provides the entire argument, or rather, several versions of the entire argument. Still, the formulations of the terms in those full statements can be seen to depend to a large extent on Śaśadhara.

If Gaṅgeśa depends so fully on Śaśadhara what, if anything, is original in his own treatment? Well, he does not change anything in the Nyāya position, although we saw that Udayana displays some ambivalence on certain points—such as God's having a body—on which Gaṅgeśa adopts a consistently clear position with a generous defence. Gaṅgeśa's contribution is to develop Śaśadhara's definitions, add some technicalities of his own, and in general to answer explicitly or by implication the objections of (mainly) Buddhist authors against theism. This is all done in a somewhat formal and technical fashion.

The form of this technical method is straightforward enough. In the opponent's section each of the three main terms in the classical inference are criticized by the opponent, who attempts to demonstrate that all relevant formulations involve commission of fallacies of one sort or another. The *pakṣa*, *sādhya* and *hetu* are taken up in turn in this way. In the "correct view" or "*siddhānta*" section Gaṅgeśa sets forth three carefully qualified and clarified forms of the cosmoteleological argument for the existence of God. They are all considered to be valid. Then the *p*, *s* and *h* terms of each are defended from various objections both of the sort produced in the *pūrvapakṣa* section earlier and others that arise for the first time. These objections cover the various criticisms that were urged by Buddhists of former times and especially by Mīmāṃsakas of Gaṅgeśa's time. For example, the problems relating to the question whether God must have a body in order to create are taken up in the course of these discussions, and Gaṅgeśa is able to defend the interpretation that God is completely bodiless (an interpretation which, as we saw, Udayana is less clearly committed to). Likewise, God's eternality, His existence despite not being perceptible, His desire, awareness and effort and how they differ from those of ordinary selves, are all topics which come under consideration.

Gaṅgeśa depends entirely on the cosmoteleological argument, and does not offer the argument from language and thought nor the negative ontological argument, which were proposed by some of the old Naiyāyikas. However, Gaṅgeśa does agree that God is the author of tradition; indeed, it is God who promulgates the original conventions governing the meanings of words, for example. However, only a brief section relates to this function of God's.

Among the authors that follow Gaṅgeśa over the next century or two, Vardhamāna shows clear awareness of his father's contribution, as do those who comment on the *Tattvacintāmaṇi*. Others, however, key their discussion of God's nature and existence to Udayana's work, sometimes because they are commenting on it, sometimes not, but with surprisingly little reference to either Śaśadhara or Gaṅgeśa.

As for the commentators on *Tattvacintāmaṇi*, to the extent that we can tell, few show much originality in their discussions, with the exception, as usual, of Raghunātha Śiromaṇi. Raghunātha has some interesting remarks to make about God in various places among his works. We have already noted that Raghunātha collapses time, spatial direction and *ākāśa* with God to highly simplify the Vaiśeṣika list of substances. In another place[17] Raghunātha shows more than any other up to his time a growing awareness of the threat that devotionalism poses for Nyāya theory. He has in mind a view according to which knowledge of God is the cause of liberation. Raghunātha insists that it is self-knowledge, not knowledge of God, which is the required condition, and engages in some interesting Upaniṣadic exegesis to demonstrate the difference. He is careful to distinguish his aversion to devotionalism from his position towards Advaita Vedānta, which has led some (for example, Professor Varadachari in his summary below) to attribute "Advaitic leanings" to Raghunātha. (This is not the only point at which such leanings have been supposed to be displayed.)

II. Qualities and Motions

The second Vaiśeṣika category is that of *guṇa,* the particular qualities of particular substances. The student of classical Vaiśeṣika will recall that seventeen of them were mentioned in the *sūtras,* and that Praśastapāda added seven more to make the canonical list of twenty-four.

There is apparently some discomfort felt about the principle by which we classify these twenty-four together under the rubric "quality". Such discomfort is fairly apparent in Vardhamāna's discussion at the beginning of the *Guṇa* section of *Kiraṇāvalīprakāśa.* The occasion for discomfort is the Bhūṣaṇakāra's proposal to make motions, the third major category in Praśastapāda's system, into a twenty-fifth quality. Since both qualities and motions are related to their loci by the same relation, inherence, it is a puzzle how one is to characterize the principle which will distinguish the twenty-four classical qualities from motions. One can, of course, say that qualities are those specific properties of particular things which are not motions, but this is rather obviously *ad hoc.* At best it will leave us without a proper universal which characterizes the twenty-four classical qualities, since a "proper" universal must satisfy a number of tests (authoritatively laid down in the *Kiraṇāvalī* by Udayana) of which crossconnection (*jātisaṃkara*) is one. If both qualities and motions behave in relevant respects in the same way, then the properties of qualityness and motionness will apply to all and only the same things, which constitutes crossconnection if we suppose qualities and motions to be different kinds of things. Vardhamāna's solution is to admit that qualityness is not a proper universal. Presumably then it must be an *upādhi* or imposed property.

Subsequent writers prior to Raghunātha Śiromaṇi, such as Śaṃkara Miśra, do not address this issue directly but content themselves with providing definitions of qualityness and motionness which differ. They are also ultimately *ad hoc,* however. It is Raghunātha who takes the bull by the horns, characteristically, and declares flatly that qualityness is not a proper universal, on pain of having to postulate an infinite number of universals of that sort, as well as for the reason of crossconnection. It is, for him as for Vardhamāna, a "partless" (*akhaṇḍa*), "distributive" (*vibhājaka*) imposed property (*upādhi*).

On Raghunātha's view, then, there is no single cognizable property shared by the twenty-four items in the classical list; each has its distinctive property by which items described by each of the twenty-four quality-kind-terms (viz., "color", "smell", "contact", etc.) are distinguished and identified. This presumably undercuts the question whether motion is a twenty-fifth quality, since there is now no general principle upon which items are classed as qualities and which not.

Classically, qualities were classified in several ways. One distinction sometimes cited is that between specific and generic qualities, used by Vātsyāyana and others in distinguishing an individual material (*mūrta*) substance. Generic qualities are identified by Praśastapāda as number, size, separateness, contact, disjunction, farness, nearness, weight, instrumental fluidity, and impetus.[18] The rest are specific qualities. Udayana in his commentary on that section (not summarized in Vol. II) attempts to define specific qualities as those qualities that have "lower" or "specifying" (*avāntara*) universals differentiating the substances which are their loci,[19] i.e., qualities which have varieties that are limited to qualifying specific kinds of substances. Various authors studied in the present volume complain that Udayana's definition overextends to include unwanted qualities within the scope of "specific" ones. Notably, Vardhamāna and Śesa Śārṅgadhara propose various alternative definitions, some acceptable and others to be avoided. Raghunātha in turn analyzes and criticizes Vardhamāna's definitions.

Praśastapāda distinguishes between those kinds of qualities that are locuspervading and those that may or may not not be. The latter group includes contact, disjunction, sound, and the specific qualities of the self. The rest are always locuspervading. Vardhamāna defines "x is not-locuspervading" as "x's having the same locus as its absolute absence". To understand this one has to understand that, remarkably, the later Nyāya notion of an absolute absence is that it is compatible with the concurrent occurrence of its counterpositive, analogously to the existence of a universal at the time and place where it does not occur in any individuals.

Raghunātha points out that, although classically each kind of property must be either locuspervading or non-locuspervading, the assumption need not be binding. Some colors may be locuspervading, others not, and thus the problem occasioned by a thing's being mottled or "variegated" (*citra*) resolves itself: there is no need to postulate an additional kind of color called variegated-color. The same analysis allows some touches, tastes, smells and motions to be non-locus-pervading.

Still another distinction among the qualities is that between those that have arisen or are "manifest" (*udbhūta*) and those which, though present, are unanifest (*anudbhūta*). The distinction is necessary since Vaiśeṣika doctrine has it that atoms have colors (otherwise how to explain the colors of the wholes produced from them) and yet we cannot see atoms. Thus a condition for visual perceptibility of a substance is said to be its possessing manifest color. The color of an atom is unmanifest.

Gaṅgeśa points out that manifestedness may be understood as the property of those qualities which possess a universal pervaded by colorness (in the case of manifested color; likewise for the other sense-qualities). In that case, however, manifestedness cannot be considered a proper universal, since instances of the same kind of quality—a color—may be either manifested or unmanifested. This deviates from tradition, which viewed the two properties as proper universals.

Raghunātha notes that not everyone accepts unmanifested qualities. Air, for example, which appears colorless, *is* colorless, even though it is perceptible. Again, if the visual organ is a middle-sized colored substance with tangible qualities it should be perceptible. To account for the differences among substances in their ability to be visually or tactually experienced by postulating different manifested or unmanifested qualities in each case is highly complex. One feels that Raghunātha sympathizes with the intentions of the "independent" thinkers who take this line, although he has doubts about the viability of the positive proposal they make. In the *Padārthatattvanirūpaṇa* he accepts their view, denying the existence of unmanifested colors, and citing the various streamlining aspects of the rejection of unmanifested qualities.

1. *Color, Taste, Smell, Touch.* How to define that which colors have in common and differentiates them from tastes, smells, etc.? Śaṃkara Miśra proposes that colorness is the universal property *being perceptible by the visual organ only.* He insists that it is a proper universal, since if it were only an imposed property we should not immediately experience color when our eye falls on a red quality; we should have to momentarily consider and construct the red. For the same reason, redness, blueness, etc., are also proper universals. An objector who wishes to treat shades of color, such as blue, as each a single, eternal entity is refuted.

Raghunātha Śiromaṇi, however, states that colorness, as well as blueness, etc., are imposed properties (*akhaṇḍopādhi*), without giving any reason. Presumably *his* reason is that, as we saw, he treats *all* universals as imposed properties, and thus feels no need to answer Śaṃkara Miśra's argument.

We saw above that opinions vary in the tradition about whether there is a color called "variegated" or not, with Raghunātha characteristically in the negative, most everyone else in the positive. A parallel discussion arises about the existence of a variegated kind of taste, smell, etc. The question is raised in the following terms: The myrobalan (*haritakī*) tree produces a fruit which presents different tastes under different circumstances. Shall we then say that the myrobalan has variegated taste, on analogy with the variegated color admitted by most Naiyāyikas?

Vardhamāna answers no. Rather, he suggests, the myrobalan should be held to possess six different unmanifested tastes, each of which is manifested under appropriate circumstances. He takes the matter up in at last three different places, so one infers the issue is of some importance for the theory in his opinion. Tradition does speak of a taste called "*kṣara*" which has sometimes been interpreted as referring to a variegated taste. Vardhamāna suggests it means "salty", and that it is one of the several kinds of taste possessed by the myrobalan. What happens is that when we taste a piece of myrobalan fruit one of the several kinds of taste-quality is manifested in the portion we taste but not the others. In the case of color we see an entire mottled surface, a whole possessing variegated color; in the case of tasting the fruit we do not taste the entire fruit. The rule which causes the difficulty, a rule Vardhamāna feels it is important to observe strictly, is that a whole has the quality of its parts. Since we never taste a whole at once, but only the several bites of it, we need not suppose that the whole manifests all the several tastes at once, and thus in turn we do not need to postulate a variegated taste in order to protect the rule.

Despite Vardhamāna's efforts a few later Naiyāyikas continue to speak of variegated taste. E.g., Jinavardhana and Mādhava Sarasvatī are cases in point. For the most part, however, Naiyāyikas following Vardhamāna reject variegated taste whether or not they accept variegated color.

2. *Number*. Bhāsarvajña, author of the *Nyāyabhūṣaṇa*, denied that number was a quality at all. Among the writers surveyed here only Raghunātha Śiromaṇi agrees with the Bhūṣaṇakāra in this regard. However, Raghunātha's view is, as usual, unique. Raghunātha proposes that number be accepted as a separate category in addition to the classical Vaiśeṣika seven (or what remain of them after his critique). His reason is that we cognize numbers not only of substances but of qualities and other things—since if number were a quality it could only reside in substances, we need a category which is not restricted in that way. The classical way out of this problem—for the old school was aware that we can count qualities and attempted

to explain that fact by appealing to a relation called inherence of two-qualifiers-in-one-locus (*samānādhikaraṇatā*)—is considered and refuted by Raghunātha.

Bhāsarvajña's proposal was to treat numbers larger than one in terms of difference. Another quality in the classical list is separateness; the separateness of two things (*dvipṛthaktva*) may be considered to perform all the necessary functions that duality (*dvitva*) is classically supposed to perform. Vardhamāna objects to this argument: our awareness of duality and separateness-of-two have different causal conditions, he responds, since to cognize the number we may not be aware that there are *only* two things while we must cognize that in becoming aware of the separateness of two things. Raghunātha rejects Vardhamāna's rebuttal; he asserts that the two have precisely the same causal nexus and thus are not different. Given Raghunātha's belief that number is a new additional category we may understand that he denies separateness of two things though not the quality separateness itself.

Bhāsarvajña also proposed to treat unity—the number one—as a universal propety (*ekatva*), and his follower Aparārkadeva tends to treat all numbers as universals. Vardhamāna, following Udayana, argues that unity is not a universal, since if it were we should speak of the unity of duality. Raghunātha remarks that we do indeed say just that, though Raghunātha doesn't treat unity as a universal. As for the numbers from two on up, Vardhamāna does not think they are proper universals, following Udayana and Vallabha in his arguments. Raghunātha reviews a host of opinions on this topic without clearly indicating his affiliation with any one of them.

Running through this discussion of the categorial status of number is the important question of how numbers come into being at all. Praśastapāda traced the production of numbers to what he called an "enumerative cognition" (*apekṣābuddhi*), suggesting that duality, e.g., comes to be in two things—each one itself a unit—when we consider the two as a group. However, we must not confuse this enumerative cognition which produces duality with the subsequent cognition in which we cognize that duality. The enumerative cognition actually produces first a nonpropositional awareness, which then in turn produces the propositional awareness of duality, and finally we come to have a qualified awareness of two things in front of us. Sadananda Bhaduri reports this account, and also reconstucts the Vaiśeṣika argument against Mīmāṃsakas who think numbers are in existence before the enumerative cognition.[20] He points out, too, that the problem of how a thing can be one (by nature) and two (as member of a group) is resolved in Navyanyāya by the postulation of a relation called *paryāpti*; this is the relation by which duality (the number 2) resides in the two items collectively. This relation seems to have been first introduced by Raghunātha Śiromaṇi in his *Avacchedakatva* section of the *Tattvacintāmaṇidīdhiti*.

Śrīdhara and Udayana differed on whether "manyness" (*nānātva*) is to be included as a very large number. Śrīdhara thought manyness is a number, since one can be aware of plurality without being able to count, while Udayana denied this since it is always the case that a group, however large, is of some definite number or other. Śaṃkara Miśra adds a new suggestion to this debate: he argues that any group above two has two numbers, the actual number of members plus the number *many*. This explains how we can cognize that there are many things in the distance without cognizing any particular number of them.[21]

3. *Contact and Disjunction*. Vardhamāna and Raghunātha appear to differ slightly on the question whether the self comes into contact with other substances, e.g., atoms. Raghunātha says it does. Vardhamāna says this is not literally contact.

Śaṃkara Miśra considers the view espoused by Bhāsarvajña, that there is no such quality as disjunction since disjunction is just the absence of contact. He argues that none of the possible kinds of absence fit. In the main, these discussions reflect older treatments and arguments.

4. *Size and Shape*. The classical qualities farness and nearness are rejected by Raghunātha on the ground that everything that needs to be said about these relations can be said in terms of spatial and temporal relations among entities without invoking such qualities. In this he once again follows the Bhūṣaṇakāra. Raghunātha remarks that on his view all substances need not have size, and thus God can be a substance even though he has no size. He adds that size terms are comparative: "small" (*aṇu*) is used to mark something judged relatively smaller than something else.

5. *Psychological Qualities: Awareness, Pleasure, Frustration, Desire, Aversion, and Effort.* As Nyāya becomes Navyanyāya one of the results is a vast increase in attention to theories about awareness (*jñāna*). We have consequently devoted a whole preceding section (Chapter 2) of this Introduction to that topic.

6. *Dispositional Qualities: Weight, Fluidity, Viscidity, Inertia, Elasticity, Mental Traces.* An object's weight was cognized only by inference, according to the old Vaiśeṣika theorists. However, Vardhamāna suggests that weight is sometimes perceptible through touch assisted by *adṛṣṭa*. Śaṃkara Miśra says that this view goes back to Vallabha.

Śaṃkara Miśra specifies liquidity as well as viscidity as conditions for the agglutination of bodies, agreeing with Vātsyāyana in contrast to Praśastapāda and Śrīdhara.[22]

Vardhamāna tries to clarify the role of mental traces in experience. When we remember something traces provide the relation between the present cognition and what is remembered; however, a trace cannot serve as the causal condition *par excellence* (*karaṇa*) since that condition must "have an operation", i.e., must be what triggers the experience at that moment rather than some other time. In recognition (*pratyabhijñā*) traces only function indirectly through the memories involved. They also function in determining the content of perceptual awareness, etc.

7. *Merit and Demerit, and Adṛṣṭa*. Śaṃkara Miśra drops the fascinating comment that what the Advaitins call *māyā* and the Sāṃkhyas call *prakṛti* is actually just *adṛṣṭa*. It is not clear in precisely what connection he is proposing this equation.

A new development in Nyāya literature, ushered in by Gaṅgeśa's extensive treatment in the *Śabdakhaṇḍa* of *Tattvacintāmaṇi*, is its interest in and attention to Mīmāṃsā topics such as the aim of life called *dharma* and its relation to the sentences (*vidhi*) in which *dharma* is enjoined. This is a part of the general orientation of Navyanyāya led by Gaṅgeśa toward Pūrvamīmāṃsā opponents and arguments. The Mīmāṃsakas were specialists in ritual, in exegesis and thus in language. Navyanyāya is characterized by its own version of the "linguistic turn", and it is not surprising it picked on the Mīmāṃsakas as foils for its own increasingly sophisticated linguistic analyses.

8. *Sound*. Rucidatta provides an extensive discussion of how sound travels depending on the air currents. Classical arguments as to why sound is a quality and not a substance, arguments directed against the Mīmāṃsakas, are reviewed by several of our authors.[23]

Cennu Bhaṭṭa and Raghunātha Śiromaṇi discuss how the last sound in a series gets destroyed. Praśastapāda is said to hold that each sound is destroyed by a sound produced subsequently to it, which would seem to mean that the last sound in a series goes on indefinitely. Therefore Cennu Bhaṭṭa provides a new account according to which the last sound is destroyed by the destruction of the previous, penultimate one.

Vardhamāna has a different problem with the traditional account, pointing out that to hear a sound it must last for more than a moment, and on the classical view the last sound will only last one moment at most. Raghunātha mentions another old view according to which the effect of the first sound destroys the cause of the last sound, which in turn destroys the last sound, thus preserving the account which traces the cause of destruction of any sound to its predecessor.

Raghunātha comes out with a positive theory which has a sound lasting for four moments, viz., the moment of its origin, a second moment when the air stops moving, a third of disjunction through the air movement, a fourth moment when the specific contact between that portion of *ākāśa* and air is destroyed. After those comes the moment when the sound is destroyed.

9. *Motion*. We have seen already that Bhāsarvajña proposed to count motion as a quality. As with other proposals of the *Bhūṣaṇakāra*, Raghunātha Siromaṇi is the only one of our authors to accept this proposal. It is noticed, and argued against, by others, for example, by Vardhamāna.

III. Remaining Categories

A. *Universals*. The classical treatment of universals is, by and large, maintained throughout our period in the same fashion as in the older school. However, by Raghunātha's time the number of proper universals has, perhaps without its being recognized, dwindled away. The implications of Udayana's six requirements have gradually become recognized as precluding the status of a proper universal to just about any candidate. By Raghunātha's time there are virtually no universals. Instead, generic properties are treated as "composite" (*sakhaṇḍa*) imposed properties (*upādhi*), and the status of a separate category is sometimes granted to them. This allows Navyanyāya to bypass certain problems that had haunted earlier discussions, such as those about the supposed status of substanceness, qualityness and so on as universals. Since essentially nothing passes Udayana's requirements these generic properties are no different from supposedly "proper" universals such as potness. Umesh Mishra notes two prime reasons for classifying a property as "imposed" rather than universal: (1) if it's "always necessarily apprehended through something else", as are all the myriad properties such as locusness, qualifierness, and so on; (2) if it is a "composite" applying to individuals of more than one category.[24]

By reclassifying this legion of properties it is arguable that Navyanyāya makes a serious concession to idealism. Imposed properties have a questionable metaphysical role. While Raghunātha sturdily invents a new categorial status for them, it is not surprising that idealist critics, such as Advaitins, find in this reclassification evidence of the unstable character of Nyāya leanings. However, to pass judgment at this point goes far beyond our present function; we merely point out that one may well question on what gound all conceptual distinctions are accorded the status of ontological distinctions as well. Indeed, since, as we have seen, not *every* conceptually distinct item can be given a distinct ontological status, the problem is to provide a satisfactory criterion for demarcating ontological distinctions from merely conceptually convenient ones. It is to be expected that as Navyanyāya proceeded to develop after Raghunātha one finds attempts to reinforce this distinction, or else to ignore it altogether following classical Vaiśeṣika tenets.

B. *Individuators*. It is well known that Raghunātha rejected the individuator (*viśeṣa*) entirely as a category. As Ingalls notes, "He says quite properly that it is as reasonable to suppose that the atoms are by nature distinct, as to suppose further entities, whose nature it is to distinguish, residing in them. He deals with the blind belief in tradition in a manner not only scientific but not without humor. 'Yogis (are said to) see ultimate difference. Well, then, let them be asked on their oath whether they (really) see ultimate difference or not.'"[25]

C. *Inherence*. Gaṅgeśa devotes a chapter of his *Tattvacintāmaṇi* to inherence. In it, he tries to show that inherence is a separate category, that it is ineliminable, that it is perceptible, and it is single. Of special interest is the concluding defence of the theory against an opponent who argues that nondifference (*abheda*) can do the jobs inherence does. The argument is shown to founder on the inconsistency of holding that two different things can be nondifferent, but it is carried out in a highly technical fashion which already presages the convoluted character of later treatments.

Classical Vaiśeṣika held that there is only one inherence, that the appearance of different inherence-related pairs was unnecessarily "heavy". Thereafter throughout the "old" period of Nyāya-Vaiśeṣika that was the canonical view, not questioned but not much defended either. By Gaṅgeśa's time it had begun to be questioned. Śaṃkara Miśra mentions that some were of the opinion that there are many inherences and indeed seems to favor that view himself, though he does not clearly attack tradition. Raghunātha Śiromaṇi in predictable fashion does so, delcaring flatly that there are as many inherences as there are pairs to be related.

The ineliminability of inherence is defended vehemently by Gaṅgeśa as well as its perceptibility. The latter is equally vehemently denied by Śaṃkara Miśra.

D. *Absence*. One of the most arresting features of the development of Navyanyāya from Gaṅgeśa to Raghunātha is the remarkable increase in the use of absences as a means of quantification. This has been partly shown in preceding sections. However, there are a few points about the position of absence as a category that should be noted here.

One problem much on the mind of, e.g., Raghunātha Śiromaṇi concerns an absence whose counterpositive is itself an absence (i.e., the absence of an absence). Is *it* an absence or not? Since there is more than one kind of absence (e.g., prior, posterior, mutual, absolute) the problem is even more complex. Traditionally it is tacitly assumed that the absence of an absence of *x* is just *x* itself, but this doctrine is evidently open to question. E.g. how can something be both an absence and a presence, given that absence (*abhāva*) is differentiated categorically from the six positive categories (*bhāva*) of classical Vaiśeṣika? On the other hand, if an absence of *x* is always a different additional category from *x*, then infinite regress ensues, since absence of absence of *x* is another category, absence of absence of absence of *x* another, and so on *ad infinitum*. Raghunātha is the most notable, though not the first, to tackle this problem. He is preceded at least by Śeṣa Śārṅgadhara, who denies that the absolute absence of an absolute absence is a presence. However, Gaṅgeśa's section on absences does not raise the question.[26]

In at least three different places Raghunātha Śiromaṇi tells us that an absolute absence of an absolute absence of *x* is the same thing as *x*, agreeing with Śeṣa Śārṅgadhara.[27] Otherwise, he argues sensibly enough, there will be infinite regress. However, just prior to the relevent passage of the *Padārthatattvanirūpaṇa* he seems to argue the reverse, that an absence of an absence is *not* a presence but a new category. The way to avoid the infinite regress, he explains, is to equate a triple absence (absence of absence of absence of *x*) with a single one (absence of *x*). Raghunātha does not really explain why he treats mutual absence differently from the other kinds in this way.[28]

What about the absence of *x*'s absence prior to its destruction, or the absence of *x*'s absence when *x* comes into being? Raghunātha says these have to be added to the list of kinds of absences. As for prior and posterior absences, he disposes of these in favor of functions of the other remaining kinds of absences. He concludes this tantalizing section by denying that prior absence is not even an absence. What it is according to those with this opinion he doesn't tell us.[29]

Another hotly debated issue, discussed in a separate section of *Tattvacintāmaṇi*, is whether a generic absence is or is not the product of the collection of a number of specific absences, e.g., whether *absence of cow* is a product of *absence of Bossie* and all the other absences of specific cows.[29]

Gaṅgeśa's own view is that generic absence cannot be the product of specific absences. His problem centers around the fact that air is colorless, but that though this is well known to everyone, in Vaiśeṣika metaphysics it is nevertheless argued whether air has color or not. If this doubt can occur it must be about something. Gaṅgeśa's position is that, while we can know for sure that air lacks each specific kind of color on the color-wheel, that still leaves it possible to doubt that it lacks *any* color at all—otherwise the doubt that arises about air's lacking color can't be explained.

Frauwallner's study proceeds to examine the pre-Raghunātha commentators. Yajñapati expands Gaṅgeśa's argument, considering various ramifications. Jayadeva, however, proposes a completely new definition of "absence of color" as "the absence of any locus of colorness". The application to the present case is that even though one knows that A is not blue, not red, not yellow, etc., since we do not know how many colors there are we don't know that A is colorless. Using this definition he argues further that generic absence is not a single absence, but many absences. He derives this conclusion from the consideration that there are several different *kinds* of absences the counterpositives of which are the same entity (e.g., mutual absence of *x* in *y*; absolute absence of *x* in *y*, etc.). Since different absences may have the same counterpositive the difference between them has to be derived from somewhere else. Thus a prior absence of *x* is the absence of *x* at a time before *x* occurs, the absolute absence of *x* its absence from a given locus at any time, etc. A generic absence, then, is not a single absence but a whole family of these kinds, as illustrated.

Rucidatta's explanation, which Frauwallner argues is frought with difficulty, seems to come eventually to the same conclusion as Jayadeva. But Vāsudeva Sārvabhauma's discussion, the longest of them all, takes exception to all his predecessors.

Raghunātha, characteristically, criticizes everyone's view. For example, he rejects Jayadeva's differentiation of generic absence from single absences. He points out that differences between specific absences is due to their loci being different, not to their counterpositives being different. Since the locus of a specific absence of pot *a* is a different locus from the specific absence of pot *b*, the generic absence of all pots is not just located in all the loci of a collection of component specific absences. Just as a universal inheres in many things and is not identical with any of them, so generic absence characterizes the loci of each of the several specific absences and yet is not identical with any of them.[31]

E. *New Categories*. Raghunātha, besides eliminating motions and individuators from the canonical list of seven categories (along with his sizable revision of the types of entiries compressed within each category) adds at least eight new categories to the list in his *Padārthatattvanirūpaṇa* alone, as well as others elsewhere (e.g., certain absences of absence, as we just saw). These specific eight are as follows:

(1) Moment (*kṣaṇa*). On the old view time was classified as a substance, and a moment then comprised a limited portion of this substance. The limitor was taken to be, e.g., the motion of a ray of sunlight measured by its contact with a certain mountain. And a motion constituted the third category of things postulated by the old school.

Raghunātha, we know now, rejected motion as a category. Furthermore, he argues here that the moments supposedly comprising the limited portion of a substance cannot be the limitors of motions. According to him there is no momentariness in motions; motions are *sui generis* and have no proper universal inhering in them. So they are not members even of the category of quality (*guṇa*). Indeed, we are forced to admit, says Raghunātha, that motion must constitute a hitherto unrecognized category of entities.

(2) Possessedness (*svatva*). Raghunātha's keen originality is nowhere more in evidence than in his argument for the second new category. When we say that something belongs to someone, a statement that is sometimes true, how does this get "mapped" onto the Nyāya-Vaiśesika scheme of things? In terms of what can it be analyzed? Raghunātha cleverly argues that any attempt to analyze ownership or possessedness in terms of other notions involves appealing to the notion of ownership (or possessedness) in the analysans. That being the case, there is no alternative but to admit, say, possessedness as a fundamental category itself.

(3) Causal efficacy (*śakti*). Students of Pūrvamīmāṃsā will be aware that causal efficacy or power is postulated as a separate category by the Prābhākaras, and the postulation is even found in an occasional old Vaiśeṣika.[32] Gaṅgeśa, who has Prābhākara opponents very much on his mind, takes on the task of refuting the theory of causal efficacy. Gaṅgeśa's contention is interesting: it is that if the arguments for causal efficacy are allowed to stand they will generate infinite regress. The argument goes as follows: some things burn and some don't; the kind that does must possess something else that explains why *it* burns but the other kind doesn't; this something else is an entity called causal efficacy. But this postulation of an additional entity must be repeated when we ask what is the cause of this causal efficacy, since every distinct occurrent entity must have a distinct inherence cause. And so on and so forth *ad infinitum*. Causality should instead be treated as a universal property. (Arguments with Mīmāṃsakas about causality reverberate as a recurrent theme throughout our literature.)

Raghunātha Śiromaṇi reverses the Nyāya view, and subscribes to the previously rejected view that causal efficacy needs to be admitted as an additional entity. His reason is simplicity. If we do not admit causal efficacy, he argues, we will have to postulate legions of things that are clearly individuals of the same generic kind. For example, we can make a fire in several ways. Does that mean there are several different kinds of fire? Raghunātha, the defender of simplicity at all costs (despite the complexity of some of his arguments!) finds the argument telling, and postulates a new category of things. The application here is that a single causal-efficacy-to-produce-fire attaches to the several distinct sets of kinds of connecting relations between cause and effect.

(4) Causality (*kāraṇatva*). Consider several causes—the substance that catches fire, the disjunction that produces an absence of contact, and so on. Do they share a common property of causality? No, says Raghunātha, since the supposed universal causality will inhere in different categorial kinds, the first in a substance, the second in disjunctions (a kind of quality), etc. On pain of crossconnection, therefore, we shall have to explain otherwise what the fiery substance and the disjunction have in common, and we can do that only by postulating another new category of things, namely, a distinct category of causality.

(5) Effectness (*kāryatva*). Analogously we shall have to postulate a new, distinct category common to all effects. Since there is no valid reason to reduce either causality to effect-producing or effectness to being-causally-produced, both need to be admitted.

(6) Number (*saṃkhyā*). Classically number is treated in Vaiśeṣika as one of the qualities. Raghunātha notes, however, that we rightly say "this cloth is three-colored". We thus predicate triplicity of the colors in the cloth, and color is itself a quality. Now a quality can only inhere in a substance in Vaiśeṣika. It follows that triplicity, i.e., the number three, cannot itself be a quality. It can't be any of the other traditional categories either, or for that matter any of Raghunātha's new additions up to now. Therefore it must be added to the list of new categories.

(7) Being qualified (*vaiśiṣṭya*). One of the earliest canonical Nyāya-Vaiśeṣika list divides sense-object connection into six kinds: (1) contact, (2) inherence in what is conjoined, (3) inherence in what inheres in what is conjoined, (4) inherence, (5) inherence in what inheres, and (6) the qualifier-qualified relation. These are themselves entities (as relations are in this system), and it is easy to see that (1) is a quality and (2)–(5) belong to the category of inherence. What about (6)? Classically this was treated as a self-linking connector relating an absence or (an) inherence to its loci.[33]

However, Raghunātha questions this classification. Inherence is a category, he notes; presumably the reason something is classed as a category is that its postulation is found to be necessary to explain what certain kinds of judgments—e.g., that a certain substance has a certain quality—are about. Likewise, since the qualifier-qualificand relation is postulated to explain what a certain kind of judgment is about, it too should be a category. That relation is postulated to explain what "the pot is not on the table" is about. So it must be a separate category just as inherence is.

(8) Contentness (*viṣayatā*). In the same manner contentness, which connects the contents of judgments with the judgments themselves, should be counted as still another separate category.

4

EPISTEMOLOGY

Concern with theory of knowledge is high during the period we are surveying in this volume. We have already seen, in Chapter Two of this Introduction, how Navyanaiyāyikas develop a highly technical method of limitors and self-linking connectors to accomplish quantification and other procedures for precise reference. In a broad sense of "epistemology" all these concerns fall within its purview, but we forbear to repeat them here. In the present section we survey developments in Navyanyāya ways of treating only a section of epistemology, specifically that of the instruments of knowledge.

Before considering the several instruments, however, we should first review the account of truth and error developed in the system. The main part of what is new here involves critique of other systems, notably of the Pūrvamīmāṃsakas, who bulk large in Gaṅgeśa's view of his opposition, and also of the supercritical stance of Śrīharṣa in his *Khaṇḍanakhaṇḍakhādya*, which wins extended attention from several Naiyāyikas in our period.

1. *Truth and Error*. An awareness (*jñāna*) is, in the sense we understand it here, an act.[34] It is something which happens at a time, an occurrent. If it involves belief, it does so only in the sense of a believing as a fleeting act of awareness. It is not a belief in the dispositional sense. And not all *jñānas* are beliefs even in the occurrent sense—believing is only one sort of *jñāna*. Any act of awareness which has intentionality constitutes a *jñāna*. Entertaining a doubt, vaguely sensing the presence of something or other, drawing a *reductio ad absurdum* inference, and understanding someone's meaning are all *jñānas*. None of them are believings. And since they are not beliefs (in any sense) none of them are true beliefs, and none of them are justified beliefs. Rather a *jñāna* is, as indicated, *an* awareness. It is not knowledge, or even *a* knowledge, *per se*, though it remains open to further scrutiny whether all, some or no acts of

awareness constitute instances of knowledge in some sense other than justified true belief.

Now here is Gaṅgeśa's analysis of truth (*prāmāṇya*) as formulated in the *Prāmāṇyavāda* section of the first Book of *Tattvacintāmaṇi*. He says, truth is:

> "Either (a) being an awareness whose chief qualifier, *x*, is in what possesses *x*, or (b) being an awareness of a relatedness of *x* to what possesses *x*."[35]

This says that a piece of knowledge (*pramā*) is an awareness (a) whose predicate term (as we might put it) belongs to its subject term, or (b) which attributes some property *x* to a content which actually has *x*. Gaṅgeśa argues, in favor of his analysis, that only when (a) or (b) is satisfied does one undertake action predicated on the awareness in question. In addition, he argues, this is the most economical account of what truth is.

It is important to emphasize that Gaṅgeśa puts forth this analysis as a conception which is common to all theories about truth. Gaṅgeśa's idea is that, however each different believer in intrinsic validity thinks the truth of an awareness A is made known to us, in any case *what* is made known is a combination of two things, (1) that the qualificandum (i.e., the subject term) of A possesses a certain property, and (2) that that property is the chief qualifier (predicate term) of A. The claim is that the joint satisfaction of (1) and (2) is a requirement common to all those who hold to the intrinsic validity position, and it is a necessary condition (though possibly not a sufficient one) even according to an extrinsic validity theorist that (1) and (2) be satisfied whenever truth is present.

Among those philosophers who have become caught up in the intrinsic/extrinsic validity debate we may count some Buddhists, several kinds of Mīmāṃsakas, the Naiyāyikas and not a few Advaita Vedāntins. Let me start with Buddhism. In Dharmottara's *Nyāyabinduṭīkā* we find the following passage explicating the notion of "right awareness" (*samyagjñāna*), which I take to be his term for knowledge.

> "Right awareness is awareness that is not contrary to what it is right to attribute (to something). In ordinary usage it is said that what is right to attribute (to something) is that which causes us to attain a purpose which has been previously identified.... 'Attaining the purpose' here means just causing our activity to have to do with the purpose identified, and nothing else. Now, awareness does not produce the purpose, but it does cause us to attain it. In causing a person to initiate activity toward a

purpose, it causes him to attain it. This initiating of activity is merely the identification of a content of activity..."[36]

As I read this passage, Dharmottara's idea is that the function of a right awareness is to direct the attention of the person having it toward the content of that awareness as being relevant to a previously identified purpose or purposive object. That sort of awareness which does this regularly deserves to be called an instrument of knowledge. What sort of awareness does this regularly? According to Buddhism of Dharmottara's school it is perceptual awareness, defined as direct awareness, i.e., awareness which does not involve conceptual construction (*kalpanāpoḍha*).[37] What we might call sensation constitutes such perception, since it is a moment of sensory awareness prior to association with language or memory. Sensation is right awareness *par excellence* for the Buddhist, since its entire function consists in calling its content to our attention as something which is a possible object of successful purposive activity.

For Dharmottara, then, the relation between right awareness and its content requires that the awareness apprehends the content as an objective suitable for successful purposive activity. And if (as Gaṅgeśa himself will not admit) sensation can be supposed to ascribe a property to something, then a right awareness ascribes to its content the property of being an object of successful activity, which property that content (which Buddhism calls the *svalakṣaṇa*) indeed possesses.

Next let us consider those schools which are treated by Gaṅgeśa himself. First we may consider the Prābhākara Mīmāṃsaka. According to the Prābhākara there is no cognitive error at all;

> "When we say an awareness is false we really mean that it leads to unsuccessful behavior."[38]

A rather late Prābhākara, Rāmānujācārya, distinguishes between three relations called *yāthārthya, prāmāṇya* and *samyaktva*:

> "*Yāthārthya* belongs to all awareness (including memory and what ordinarily passes for erroneous apprehension), *prāmāṇya* to all awareness excepting memory (but including even the so-called erroneous apprehension) and *samyaktva* only to such knowledge other than memory which leads to successful practice."[39]

As in Buddhism, the function of knowledge is to present to us a content which is an object of successful activity—the Prābhākara adds that it must do so for the first time, and that it not be a memory, but that does not materially affect the point being made, which is that the analysis is the same as before.

Turning next to the Bhāṭṭa Mīmāṃsakas, followers of Kumārila,[40] we find a divergence of explanations but essential agreement that either truth involves the relation that we have seen Buddhists and Prābhākaras to emphasize, viz., the picking out of a content as an object of successful activity, or else (for some Bhāṭṭas) it involves a relation they term *viṣayatathātva*, which might be rendered as "an awareness' being as its content is". I submit that this relation can well be taken as truth, and it nicely satisfies Gaṅgeśa's analysis of truth.

A third type of Mīmāṃsā is that known as the Miśra school, a system whose literature is largely lost to us but which appears in an important role in Gaṅgeśa's discussions. The Miśra account of truth is rather more complex than those of the other Mīmāṃsakas. The Miśra analysis is that truth is *tadvadviśeṣyakatve sati tatprakārakatva*,[41] that is to say, a *pramā* must satisfy two tests, (1) that the awareness in question must present a qualificand, C, which has a chief qualifier, Q, and (2) that it must present C as qualified by Q. When we compare this with Gaṅgeśa's analysis we find that tests (1) and (2) are precisely Gaṅgeśa's (1) and (2).

Next, consider the Vivaraṇa Advaita Vedānta school's analysis of truth as the property of being an awareness which is capable of picking out that content which accords with its purposes.[42] It should be clear that this conception again satisfies Gaṇgeśa's general requirement.

Finally we must consider the Nyāya analysis itself, which is just what Gaṅgeśa himself proposes, viz., the simultaneous satisfaction of Gaṅgeśa's (1) and (2).[43] *A fortiori* this satisfies (since it is identical with) Gaṅgeśa's analysis of truth.

Now what is the extrinsic/intrinsic validity debate about? The intrinsic validity theorist holds that whatever causes us to be aware of A causes us to be aware that A can satisfy its purpose, i.e., can lead to successful activity of the relevant sort. The extrinsic validity theorist denies this, holding that to become aware that A can satisfy its purpose we need a further awareness, presumably inferential, which is over and beyond the awareness which causes us to be aware of A itself. The point comes out most dramatically when we contrast the Miśra theory with the Naiyāyika's. On both theories we first have an awareness A, which is not self-aware but for the awareness of which we require an "aftercognition" B. The Miśra theory holds that B not only makes us aware of A but also of A's truth, i.e., A's capacity to evoke successful activity. The Nyāya theory denies that B makes us aware of A's truth. Nyāya holds that only an inference, e.g., one based on successful action or on reasons to think that such activity would be successful, can attest to A's truth.[44]

Notice that it doesn't matter to the debate so posed whether A is true or false, or thought to be true or false. Whether a theorist holds that all awarenesses are true, or all are false, or that some are one and some the other, the issue about truth remains a real one. Nor does it matter whether a theorist thinks that only true awarenesses can lead to successful activity or, alternatively, thinks that some awarenesses capable of leading to successful activity can be false. The issue concerns whether, when one becomes aware that A is a potential purpose-satisfier, he does so through the same awareness by which he became aware of A's occurrence, or through some *other* awareness.

Gaṅgeśa's main argument against the intrinsic validity theorist is that if the intrinsic validity theory were correct it would make it impossible for one to doubt A's truth immediately after A's occurrence. That is, since the intrinsic validity theory says that the awareness by which we first become aware that A occurred always involves an awareness that A can satisfy its purpose, has *prāmāṇya*, this precludes our doubting at that moment that it is true. But we *do* in fact sometimes doubt the truth of an awareness as soon as we become aware that it has occurred. So the intrinsic validity theory has to be wrong, concludes Gaṅgeśa.

What are the conditions that are sufficient for true awareness, that is, for knowledge to occur? Gaṅgeśa spends some time formulating his answer in a later section of the *Prāmāṇyavāda* section. The upshot is this. Those factors which are sufficient to impede the production of any awareness opposed to the awareness in question are sufficient to produce true awareness. Gaṅgeśa concludes this remarkable chapter by considering a host of wrong definitions of truth and rejecting them all for cogent reasons. The very number of such formulations, in this and other sections of *Tattvacintāmaṇi*, indicate that Gaṅgeśa must have been engaged in spirited discussion with a host of other scholars.

The literature following Gaṅgeśa's time, to the extent that it is uncovered, is largely engaged in clarifying and expounding the old and the new Nyāya. The discussion turns into highly technical clarifications of terms, a development which will reach its climax after our period in the vast subcommentaries of Jagadīśa and Gadādhara. Beyond this clarifying there are extended critiques of all the various opposing theories known at the time. One newcomer to the scene is Śrīharṣa, whose expostulations against Nyāya earned extended attention by various of our writers. The new onslaughts of Śrīharṣa occasioned renewed efforts at rebuttal, as in Vācaspati

Miśra II's *Khaṇḍanoddhāra*, which develops a new line of refutation of skepticism. Vācaspati's way of dealing with the skeptic who questions the use of instruments of knowledge is just to point out that for Śrīharṣa to prove that *pramāṇas* are not workable he must convince us, and to convince us he needs to use *pramāṇas* or something, otherwise we should be justified in dismissing what he says as cavil.

A different topic is raised in the *Anyathākhyātivāda* of Gaṅgeśa's *Tattvacintāmaṇi*. The question here is how to prove the existence of error, given that at least one school, that of the Prābhākaras, seems to hold (in a sense) that all awarenesses are true. Gaṅgeśa's discussion of this is again highly technical. But the nub of the answer appears just to be that an awareness is true precisely when the awareness has a content whose appropriate relatedness to its object really exists. The length of this section is almost entirely due to the remarkable complexity of the Prābhākara's opponents' arguments. That remark can in fact be generalized to the whole of the *Tattvacintāmaṇi*, whose length and complexity can largely be ascribed to the large number of arguments of Prābhākara opponents it refutes. Who these Prābhākara opponents actually were we do not know.

2. *Perception.* Several sections of the first Book of Gaṅgeśa's *Tattvacintāmaṇi* provide important changes and improvements in Nyāya theory. Section Four concerns the question of characterizing perception. Gaṅgeśa is aware of several problems in earlier treatments of the topic.

The problems partly concern the scope of the term "perception". For one thing, Nyāya treats both "ordinary" and "extraordinary" perception under the same rubric, "perception". In order to clarify which kind of perception one is talking about Nyāya developed by our period terminology distinguishing "occurrent" (*janya*) perception, the "ordinary" sort, from "eternal" (*nitya*) perception, the "extraordinary" sort. (The latter is itself of three kinds: (1) yogic perception, (2) perception of a universal characterizing all members of a class one of whose members is presented, and (3) perception of the features of a thing which was known previously or elsewhere.) Gaṅgeśa's procedure in Part Four on the definition of perception is first to define ordinary perception, and then to propose a definition which will cover both ordinary and extraordinary perception. The definition is this: a perceptual awareness is an awareness that has no other awareness as its causal condition *par excellence.*

There are several problems that call forth this definition, and these are thrashed out in various sections of Book One of the *Tattvacintāmaṇi*. The problem that most occupies Gaṅgeśa has to do with the kind of awareness we call recognition (*pratyabhijñā*). When we have seen Bossie before, see her now and judge, correctly, that this is Bossie again, we must have some type of knowledge, since our judgment is correct. But how can recognition be perceptual knowledge if it involves the memory of an earlier perception of Bossie? Furthermore, isn't recognition essentially linguistic, since in recognizing Bossie we cognize that what we now see has the same description as what we saw before? So mustn't recognition be a kind of awareness that is either inferential or verbal but at any rate not perceptual? Yet Nyāya theory regularly classes recognition as perception, so Nyāya theory must be wrong.

Gaṅgeśa's definition seems on the face of it to exclude recognition from the scope of perception. Yet Gaṅgeśa clearly views recognition as a type of propositional (*savikalpaka*) awareness. So he needs to explain how the proposed definition can be understood so as to include recognition, and to do that without violating the distinction between perceptual and linguistic awareness.

Now what is a "causal condition *par excellence*"? According to Gaṅgeśa it is a causal factor which has no mediating condition (called in Nyāya the "operation", *vyāpāra*) through which it is connected to the result—it is *immediate*. So Gaṅgeśa must explain how recognition can be perceptual if that involves immediacy of its causality.

Nyāya theory maintained there are two kinds of perception, propositional and nonpropositional. (Since Jayanta's time this distinction is equated with the distinction between an awareness that has a structure—involves a "qualifier" (*viśeṣaṇa*) and an awareness that has no structure, involving no qualifier.) Recognition is viewed by Gaṅgeśa as a variety of propositional awareness; it has a structure involving a qualifier. It is not the only kind of propositional awareness, however; there is also at least one other kind, viz., a straightforward judgment of classification such as "this is a cow".

Gaṅgésa's answer to the problems about recognition is as follows. Recognition *is* perception, not inference, because memory does not come in essentially. "This is Bossie", a recognition of Bossie, though it is of course assisted by memory of one's earlier acquaintance with Bossie, does not involve memory as a part. In this it differs from the "straightforward" kind of propositional judgment, e.g., "this is a cow", which *does* involve a memory, of *cowness.* Neither "this is Bossie" nor "this is a cow" involve memory as a "constituent" part of the awareness; where memory comes in as a *constituent* part of an awareness that awareness is not perceptual at all, but an inference, verbal testimony or some other sort of awareness.

The second problem was this: isn't recognition essentially linguistic? No, answers Gaṅgeśa,

> "... perceptual cognition is a unique type of cognition and is completely independent of all sorts of lingusitic elements. In a perceptual cognitive state we are directly aware of individuals, universals and unanalysable common properties. Our consciousness directly refers to objects lying outside the cognitive state itself. Even our erroneous consciousness refers to objects which are not mental. According to them the facts of the world are neither subjective construction nor as such stamped as true or false. Whenever our senses come in contact with an object, the senses being conjoined with the mind and the mind with the self, a perceptual cognition instantly arises referring to the object as something. Gradually the objective constituents are presented to us as combined into a concrete object. In this way the intitial nonrelational consciousness is replaced by a relational consciousness. Whatever memory-elements might be involved in this process, they are in no way subjectively determined; they are determined objectively."[45]

So thc perceptual awareness of a cow or recognition of Bossie are not about memories, even though memory may come in along the way as a causal element in shaping our awareness. The demarcation between perception and verbal testimony is thus maintained.

In later sections of Book One Gaṅgeśa reverts to this discussion to clear away objections and confusions. In Section Eleven he considers an objection to his definition: the objector claims the definition will not cover our perception of our own pleasures and pains unless the internal organ is held, contrary to Nyāya tenets, to be a ubiquitous entity. Gaṅgeśa is not moved by this argument.

In Section Thirteen Gaṅgeśa refutes an opponent—perhaps a Grammarian—who holds that there is no nonpropositional awareness at all, that *all* awareness is propositional. Gaṅgeśa makes the obvious retort that this breeds an infinite regress, and cleverly meets the "and you're one too" response, showing that his own position is not guilty of infinite regress.

As a codicil to this last Gaṅgeśa offers a thought-provoking point. It is natural to suppose that any judgment is either propositional or nonpropositional. We have, indeed, been further classifying these two varieties. But in fact, says Gaṅgeśa, a judgment may be both—that is, the distinction consists of viewing one and the same judgment from different aspects.

Aftercognition (*anuvyavasāya*) (which is to be carefully distinguished from recognition) is seen by Gaṅgeśa as critical in refuting an important element in the various epistemological theories ranging from Prābhākara Mīmāṃsā to Yoga and Advaita Vedānta. These theories view an awareness as having by its very nature a multiple content. E.g., the awareness of a certain pot has that pot as part of its content, they say, but in addition it has itself—the awareness—as its content too. Every awareness thus is, for these theories, self-aware. Taken to its extreme conclusions this thesis allows the Advaitin to defend his characteristic doctrine that objects other than consciousness are illusory, that consciousness is the only real thing there is.

Gaṅgeśa devotes a section of Book One of the *Tattvacintāmaṇi* to refuting this doctrine of the self-awareness of every awareness. The Nyāya view is rather that when one has a simple awareness, say of a certain pot, one is not aware of oneself as having this awareness. One may become aware that one is having the awareness; this subsequent awareness is then an aftercognition that I am (was) aware of the pot. But it is an entirely different awareness. Gaṅgeśa devotes a generous section to clarification of the notion of an aftercognition.

3. *Unusual Forms of Perception.* It was said in the Introduction to Volume II of this Encyclopedia that Navyanyāya accepted as a "well-defined tradition" three kinds of extraordinary perception: (1) yogic perception (*yogipratyakṣa*), (2) perception of a universal characterizing all members of a class (*sāmānyalakṣaṇasannikarṣa*), and (3) perception here and now of the features of a thing which was known previously at another place and time (*jñānalakṣaṇasannikarṣa*). On closer inspection our general statement about Navyanyāya must be modified. Although Gaṅgeśa does accept, and indeed defends, all three of the kinds of extraordinary perception just listed, Bimal Matilal tells us that Maṇikaṇṭha Miśra rejected (2) and that Raghunātha Śiromaṇi did so too.[46] Umesh Mishra also reports that Śaṃkara Miśra counted (2) and (3) as kinds of qualifier–qualificand-relation (*viśeṣaṇatā*), the sixth of the classical kinds of relations that make up perceptual connections of objects to our awarenesses of them.[47]

Vācaspati Miśra also rejects the standard view. For him, the only extraordinary perceptions are those experienced by God and by yogīs.

Of the three kinds (1)–(3) it is the theory of (2) *sāmānyalakṣaṇasannikarṣa* that is questioned most often. Yajñapati accepts it, but criticizes several of Gaṅgeśa's arguments in favor of it. And Raghunātha rejects it completely.

Raghunātha divides the arguments for (2) into two sorts. On the first argument, (2) is needed to account for our perceptual awareness of generic absence, e.g., an awareness that there is no pot on the table. On the second argument, (2) explains how we can be aware perceptually of the prior absence of something we haven't seen yet. Raghunātha is unconvinced by either argument.

The first argument is refuted by dividing it in turn into two sorts. On the first version of the first argument, call it (2a), the universal *potness* itself is the connecting link between all pots and the eye that perceives its absence on the table. On the second version, (2b), one's *awareness* of potness' absence is the connecting link. But, Raghunātha contends, if (2a) is the preferred version then no extraordinary perception at all is needed, since the universal *potness* inheres in each pot, and generally any kind of thing's absence can be known by appealing to whichever of the six classical kinds of relations is appropriate. On the other hand, if (2b) is the view favored, Raghunātha patiently explains all supposed problems away. E.g., the opponent might ask how we can know *all* the counterpositives in "there are no pots here". Raghunātha's answer is, well, even if we can't we can know some of them, and anyway, one doesn't one himself first have to know *x* in order to know absence of *x.* And this last point also is sufficient to meet the second argument, though Raghunātha provides additional refutation.

4. *Verbal Testimony (śabda).* One of the most remarkable features of Gaṅgeśa's *Tattvacintāmaṇi* is the distinctive and extensive attention he gives to the fourth Nyāya instrument of knowledge, verbal testimony. In part, this indicates the growth in importance of theory of language in Indian philosophy over the centuries. In particular, it reflects a recognition within Nyāya of the importance attaching to a correct exposition of the Nyāya theory of meaning in the light of Grammarian encroachment into issues hitherto treated within philosophy alone. Gaṅgeśa's extensive Fourth Book occupies itself with problems lying on the border between linguistics and philosophy. Perhaps as a result, scholarship on the material in this Book has dwindled to almost nothing in recent years. The dearth of scholarship is furthered as well by the difficulty in obtaining printed editions of Book Four. Only one full edition has ever been published, and it is long out of date and extremely difficult to find.[48]

It is reflective of this situation that we have been unable to find summarizers for large sections of Book Four. Where summarizers were lacking we have made do with the relevant sections from Satischandra Vidyabhusana's years-old summary, though it is in many cases far short of the detail readers of our Volumes are receiving in most of the summaries provided.

The most philosophical portion of Book Four is its first section. What Gaṅgeśa attempts to do here is to establish verbal testimony as an instrument of knowledge, *pace* e.g. Buddhists, but also as an entirely separate instrument of knowledge, *pace* Prābhākara

Mīmāṃsakas and Vaiśeṣikas. The Prābhākara holds that the meanings of "ordinary", i.e., nonVedic, utterances are grasped by inference from their speakers' intentions. For them, however, the awareness conveyed by the utterances of the Vedas are of nonhuman origin and must be known by a different instrument of knowledge, verbal testimony. As for the Vaiśeṣikas, they hold that the meanings of all utterances, Vedic or not, are grasped by inference, so that a separate instrument of knowledge called verbal testimony is not needed.

Against the Buddhists and Vaiśeṣikas Gaṅgeśa presents, in his characteristic fashion, a series of arguments. In this instance he considers four arguments (V1–V4 in our summary) attributed to the Vaiśeṣika which purport to prove that knowledge derived from language can be classified as inferential. Discussion of these arguments leads Gaṅgeśa to make moves of intrinsic interest for modern philosophers of language.

The Vaiśeṣika proposes, for example, V2 to show how we gain knowledge when we hear somebody utter words we remember the meaning of; what we do is to infer, e.g., from hearing "this is a cow", that the animal in front of us has the property *cowness* that we have confronted in the past. Gaṅgeśa rejects this argument. For one thing, the argument begs the question, or if not, it depends on another instrument of knowledge eventually, not inference. To know that the utterance "this is a cow" should call forth the thought of (the "expectancy" of) cows one must know that the word "cow" means cows, but how do we know that? Not by perception, evidently. If by inference, infinite regress ensues. So another instrument is needed after all, and that is verbal testimony.

To bolster this rebuttal Gaṅgeśa offers a couple of counterexamples to V2—the liar and the parrot. Suppose a liar says "this is a cow", pointing to a cleverly dressed horse. His hearer believes him, basing his belief on the expectancy the liar intends him to base his belief on. According to V2 the liar's remark should be true and the hearer's judgment knowledge. But his remark is false; the judgment is not knowledge.

The Vaiśeṣika's initial response to this is that "this is a cow", though false, is still *meaningful* for the reason given, namely that there is expectancy between the words. Gaṅgeśa's retort to this is to invoke a parrot, who produces the noises "this is a cow". It cannot be supposed that, just because the noises uttered happen to be English words, the parrot has uttered a sentence. The parrot doesn't know what the noises mean. So it is not enough for the hearer just to *judge* expectancy; for it to *be* there more is required.

Nevertheless the argument moves the Vaiśeṣika to admit that it is not enough for the speaker's words to convey fitness; the speaker must be aware that they do. (The parrot lacks this awareness.) This is the key for Gaṅgeśa's case. The point is that what the hearer believes about the speaker's beliefs is irrelevant; what *is* relevant is what the hearer believes about the world. Truth or falsity relate to *that*. The proper analysis of lying is that the liar's false utterance, known by the liar to be false, is intended to make the hearer believe it is true and to act in a certain way. The hearer, if he is taken in by the liar, himself frames a false belief that the animal in question is a cow. This false belief is not the same false belief as the false belief that the speaker (in this case, the liar) spoke truly.

The Vaiśeṣika has misconstrued the role of inference. Inference can certainly provide us with knowledge of a speaker's intention, what he means to say. What it can't do is provide knowledge that what he says is true, that things are related as they are said to be. Something more is needed for that. Indeed *none* of the three conditions of meaning as normally constituted—expectancy, fitness or contiguity—nor even all three together are sufficient. Fitness, if construed in a certain way, might be held to be sufficient, but construed in that way, as absence of the truth of any contrary belief, it can't be *known* to be present, since an indefinite number of contrary beliefs would have to be tested. So one cannot *infer* that knowledge is present. One can only know this in some *other* fashion.

But then how does one know, if not by inference, that a judgment is true? The Nyāya view is that it can only be by the instrument of knowledge called verbal testimony.

This conclusion is followed by a long section that considers an alternative suggestion of the Prābhākaras. What the Prābhākaras propose is that verbal testimony, properly understood, pertains only to the words of the Vedas. The Vedas, unlike ordinary words, have no speakers. We need, so the Prābhākara contends, to postulate a separate instrument to explain how ordinary words can convey knowledge. But, leaving Vedic knowledge aside, ordinary nonVedic knowledge can be understood as derived by inference.

The Prābhākara argument is this. There must be something that is shared by those utterances that are both true and understood to be true. Provided that something is itself a thing that can be perceived when it occurs, then the proper view must be that we infer the truth of an utterance by perceiving that something. The Prābhākara thinks he knows what that something is. He carefully explains what it cannot be, and concludes that it is just the speaker's intention to produce the belief intended in his hearer.

Gaṅgeśa's criticism of the Prābhākara's contention is essentially the same as his final criticism of the Vaiśeṣika position. We cannot perceive upon hearing it that an utterance involves the speaker's intention to produce the belief intended. Yet we do understand what the speaker says, and it has to be admitted that some things speakers say are true and that we correctly judge them to be so. Therefore we must postulate an added instrument by which the correct judgment is justified, and that is what we are calling verbal testimony.

The remainder of Book Four takes up a variety of more specifically linguistic problems. The *Vidhivāda* raises the question: what exactly is it that induces a person who hears a Vedic injunction to act? The main foil here is, once again, the Prābhākara, who holds that the hearer's desire to act arises from his knowledge of what he wants to accomplish. His action arises from his desire together with his awareness that he has the means to accomplish his desires and is not stopped in some way from acting. It is not, according to the Prābhākara, due *merely* to his knowing that something is a means to his desired end, since if that were the case one would spend one's time trying to catch the moon! Gaṅgeśa's response to all this is that knowing something to be a means to a desired end *is* in fact what induces one to act to get the means to one's desired end. The defence of his contention runs in a wide variety of directions.

In the next section, *Apūrvavāda*, the basic question seems simple enough. Does an injunction—e.g., (A) "one desirous of heaven should perform the *darśapūrṇamāsa* sacrifice"—essentially involve merit and demerit (*apūrva*) or not? Both Prābhākaras and Naiyāyikas agree that karmic results of actions do occur, and that knowing the karmic outcomes of actions is required if one wants to know what will transpire. They disagree, though, on whether the injunction itself expresses that merit and demerit or whether it is rather known by inference. The Prābhākaras adopt the former position, Gaṅgeśa the latter.

The general rule Gaṅgeśa relies on is that one should not invoke something in explanation if explanation can be achieved without it. Gaṅgeśa holds that we can know by inference what the merit and demerit occasioned by the sacrifice is; one need not postulate it as any part of the meaning of the injunction. Where the Prābhākara will analyze (A) as "one desiring heaven should earn merit by sacrificing", the Naiyāyika prefers on grounds of simplicity the following analysis: "one desiring heaven should sacrifice."[49]

The (*Kāryānvita*) *Śaktivāda* section that follows reports a discussion between two arms of the Prābhākara Mīmāṃsā camp. One arm—called "imperativist" by our summarizer Sukharanjan Saha—supports the classical Mīmāṃsā contention that injunctions are primary in conveying the knowledge we gain from scripture. Their view is that *all* meaning primarily consists of specification of what ought to be done. The other arm, of "nonimperativists", thinks knowledge of what is enjoined presupposes knowledge of a more basic sort, viz., knowledge of what words mean. These two contingents carry on an extended argument, during which considerable attention is paid to how children learn language. A basic question is raised, as well, as to whether awareness of the mere relationship between the things meant by the words of a sentence is sufficient for understanding the sentence's meaning, or whether there is always reference as well to what ought to be done, or at least to something else, this last view being referred to in our summary as "context theory". Gaṅgeśa finds both views—imperativist and nonimperativist—at fault. What is *meant* by an utterance is just the object or objects spoken of, not those objects in relation to each other. We saw the nub of this analysis earlier in this introduction, when it was made clear that the basic form of a simple judgment is a–(R–b), and that its meaning involves *a* and *b* but not R. (If we want to speak of R we shall need to relate *a*, R and *b* by further relation or relations so as to differentiate, e.g., a–(R–b) from b–(R–a), etc.) The "limitor" of R in *any* judgment of the form a–(R–b) is, to use contemporary jargon, only used but not mentioned.

Following this *Śaktivāda* there is another, *Jātiśaktivāda*, also having to do with meaning. A topic of discussion for centuries among the schools is whether a word means a universal or a particular or both. Prābhākaras say the meaning is the universal, since if it were the individual there would have to be a different meaning invoked for each expression uttered—an infinite number of meanings. Gaṅgeśa disagrees. It is the individual that is meant and not the universal, he submits, but a general term means each of the individuals possessing the universal. Thus flagrant infinite regress is avoided.[50]

5. *Nonapprehension a Pseudo-Instrument.* The Bhāṭṭa Mīmāṃsakas consider nonapprehension (*anupalabdhi*) to be an additional instrument of knowledge, since they do not allow that we grasp absences by perception. Gaṅgeśa devotes a section of Book One of *Tattvacintāmaṇi* to criticism and rejection of this view.

We know that at least since Uddyotakara's time Nyāya has counted at least six kinds of perception of which the last one is the qualifier–qualified relation or qualifierness (*viśeṣaṇatā*). The Naiyāyika classifies the awareness, say, of the absence of a pot on this floor as a case of perception of the qualifierness sort. The Bhāṭṭa does not agree with this theory, believing it unnecessarily complex, but must find a defensible alternative. He postulates an added instrument, nonapprehension, as his alternative. But just how is this nonapprehension to be understood? For example, if we *see* that no pot is there, but it isn't visual perception, what's to stop a blind person from knowing that there's no pot there? The Bhāṭṭa attempts to meet this by requiring that the absence that is "nonapprehended" must have as its locus something graspable by a sense organ, so that the blind person, who cannot see the pot, cannot apprehend its absence either. Gaṅgeśa points out that this isn't sufficient. The blind person can still know, e.g., that air is colorless, or that a stone has no smell. He is not deprived of knowing such truths by even the revised theory. In fact, the knowledge that air is colorless, i.e., of the absence of color in air, *must* be perceptual, since it is not inferential and does involve a sense organ.

5

LOGICAL THEORY[51]

It is to inference (*anumāna*) that Navyanyāya devotes its most innovative efforts. The innovations are not so much in theory as in method. Notable among methodological innovations is the remarkable increase in complexity of analysis, using abstract relations of the kind described in Chapter 2 of this introduction. The methods developed using these abstract relations have a general application that stretches far beyond the theory of inference. They were commandeered by the leading practitioners of many scientifically studied subjects. To understand medieval discussions of topics as disparate as jurisprudence, medicine and linguistics it is essential to master the technical terminology of Navyanyāya analyses.

We do not have space here to provide a full scale introduction to Navyanyāya procedures. Such an introduction does not fully exist in a Western language.[52] What such an introduction will require is a manageable notation rendering the complex Navyanyāya analyses of judgments in the way that symbolic logic renders propositions. Suggestions for such a notation were made initially by Ingalls, and alternatives have been devised by Staal[53], Sibajiban Bhattacharya[54], and B.K. Matilal[55] and perhaps others. None of these methods is particularly useful for our present purpose, though development of a usable procedure for representing Navyanyāya analyses is undoubtedly a *sine qua non* for understanding later Navyanyāya formulations.

1. *Pervasion Defined*. Navyanyāya analysis of inference centers on the key relation of pervasion (*vyāpti*). A valid inference is distinquished from invalid ones in that its *sādhya* pervades its *hetu*, assuming that its *pakṣa* is a member of the *hetu* class. E.g..

(1) "this mountain has fire, because it has smoke"

is a valid inference, as is shown by the fact that all cases of smoking things are cases of fiery things together with the fact that this mountain indeed is a smoking thing.

To provide an instance of pervasion is not the same thing, however, as saying what pervasion is. For that the optimal need is for a definition that specifies the necessary and sufficient conditions for validity together with foolproof directions for applying those conditions in the form of a test. Naiyāyikas since the beginning have proposed such definitions.[56] That none of them prior to our period is deemed fully satisfactory by Gaṅgeśa and his followers is not surprising. For the problem is arguably the same as the one known in Western thought as "the justification of induction".

If this is not entirely evident, notice that to justify truth of (1) we would have to *know* that "all smoky things are fiery things" is true. To know it is to have conclusive reason to accept it, to be in a position where no conceivable example of a non-fiery smoky thing can be provided since no such counterexample exists. It is now rather generally accepted in Western contemporary philosophy of science that no such justification is possible. One may well question, therefore, whether the Naiyāyika's problem is at all solvable.

Gaṅgeśa cites a goodly number of definitions of pervasion without naming those who proposed them. It is likely they *were* actually proposed; at least there are traditions about the proposers that are recorded in commentaries on *Tattvacintāmaṇi.* Gaṅgeśa himself, though he doesn't name names, does refer to two of the definitions as those of "lion" and "tiger", suggesting that he knew of persons who were so called. He criticizes some twenty-one such definitions before offering eight that he finds acceptable. One can cull additional definitions from those discussed by, among others, Śaṃkara Miśra in his *Kaṇādarahasya* and *Vaiśeṣikasūtropaskāra*, and Raghunātha Śiromaṇi in his *Tattvacintāmaṇidīdhiti* discusses fourteen definitions other than those in Gaṅgeśa's list.

Gaṅgeśa's first considers five definitions based on the most generally accepted definition of pervasion in later classical Nyāya, one that requires nonwandering (*avyabhicāratva*) of *h* from *s*. Let's call this definition "NW". Consider first a favorable case for NW, namely (1) above. Here the *h* is smoke, the loci of *h* are mountains, kitchens, etc., the loci of absence of *h* are lakes, red-hot iron balls, and so on. The *s* of NW is fire, loci of *s* are mountains, kitchens, red-hot iron balls, etc., and loci of absence of *s* include bodies of water such as lakes, etc. Suppose we construe the meaning of NW in the fashion proposed in the definition designated as Dl in the summary of *Tattvacintāmaṇi* below:

(Dl) the *hetu* must not occur in loci of absence of the sādhya.

It can easily be seen that smoke does not occur in a lake or in any place where there's no fire. So NW appears to work for this example, at least when understood as Dl.

However, now let's consider

(2) "everything is nameable because it is knowable".

Here *h* is knowableness, *h* is located everywhere and there is no locus of absence of *h*; *s* is nameableness, *s* is located everywhere and there is no locus of absence of *s*. For Dl to apply to this case its *h*, knowableness, should not occur in the loci of absence of nameableness. But since there are no loci of absence of nameableness the test can't be used. And a "test" that can't be used to test is no test at all!

In a similar way D2–D7 are not tests at all, since they cannot be applied to inferences of the sort exemplified in (2), namely inferences about universal classes. After considering and rejecting (in Section Four) a clever way of trying to *provide* a locus of absence of *h* in such cases involving universal classes, Gaṅgeśa goes on to consider other definitions, all of which commit an even more general fault, a fault committed, he claims, by all the definitions from D1 to D21. This fault consists in using of the terms "*hetu*" and "*sādhya*" in the definition of pervasion. The reason this is a fault is that the understanding of those terms presupposes that pervasion is already understood, so that D1–D21 beg the question.

Having set aside all these unsatisfactory definitions Gaṅgeśa is ready to propose his own. Obviously, given the criticism just levelled, the preferred definition must not have the terms "*hetu*" and "*sādhya*" occurring in it. D21–29 satisfy this requirement. An innovation in some of them is the introduction of a new technical term, "limitor" (*avacchedaka*). A further characteristic, though not altogether a uniquely new feature, of these definitions is their fundamental appeal to the notion of "having a common locus" (*sāmānādhikaraṇya*).

The new definitions provided are of two sorts: generic and specific. Gaṅgeśa's "conclusive" definition (D22) is generic in that it invokes the idea of all instances of a kind. Since that idea includes future as well as past and present instances, (D22) raises problems about whether we can know facts about future entities. For those who prefer to avoid these problems Gaṅgeśa proceeds to give us several versions that he considers satisfactory which only refer to absences of specific things. It will be seen that in this way Gaṅgeśa admits the problem we alluded to about justifying induction.

All in all Gaṅgeśa discusses 29 definitions of pervasion (D1–D29 of our summary). Goekoop has summarized the gist of these: what we provide now is his summary revised to fit our terminology.

"Pervasion is having a common locus."

This property, when not explicitly mentioned in a definition of pervasion, must be assumed as implied by the fact that the terms of pervasion are supposed to be terms of inference. For inference is not conceivable without some common locus connecting the terms... There are two ways two terms can have a common locus: pervasion or deviation. It follows that pervasion is definable either as a form of having a common locus or as nondeviation. Since deviation involves an obstruction (*upādhi*) and vice-versa, nondeviation can be identified as having a common locus without an obstruction. So we have three manners of defining pervasion:

(I) as nondeviation;

(II) as the absence of obstruction;

(III) as a special kind of having a common locus.

(I) Nondeviation is the absence of deviation. Deviation of A from B is the fact that some locus of A is a locus of B and some is not... Deviation of A from B can therefore be said to be the fact that some locus of A is not a locus of B, i.e., (1) there is something which is a locus of A but not a locus of B. The same is conveyed by saying (2) there is something which is not a locus of B but is a locus of A.

(1) may be expressed as (a) "A (= *hetu*) occurs in a locus of (absolute) absence of B (= *sādhya*)", or (using the corresponding mutual absence) as (b) "A occurs in a locus other than a locus B" or as (c) "a locus of A is a nonlocus of B". The negation of (a) is D1, that of (b) is D5, and that of (c) is found in D6 and D7. D2 is a refinement of D1, D3 a verbal variant of D5, and D4 a logical variant of D1. D8 is a refinement of D6, and D19 a verbal variant of D1.

(2) may be expressed as (a) "B is absent from a locus of A", i.e., "B is the counterpositive of an absolute absence having a common locus with A", or (using the corresponding mutual absence) as (b) "any locus of B is the counterpositive of a mutual absence having a common locus with A (residing in a locus of A)." The negation of (a) is D9 and, with a refinement, D23. The negation of (b) is D10, D24 and D25. The conclusive definition D22 is a variety of D23. All these definitions mention explicitly A and B having a common locus, and evidently do so because otherwise A would not be stated as the subject of pervasion, B or the loci of B being the subject of the absence of deviation.

(II) The negation of any obstruction is the absence of the property of being an obstruction. There are several properties of an obstruction; the property which is used here is the common property which (incompletely) describes an obstruction as a property pervading the *sādhya* without pervading the *hetu.* If a property which pervades a *sādhya*, call it B, does not pervade the corresponding *hetu* A, then B itself does not pervade A, i.e. A deviates from B.

And if A deviates from B, we can imagine a property (whose locus may be coextensive with the locus of B) from which A deviates, i.e. which does not pervade A and which pervades B. This deviation is equivalent to the definition of obstruction, and pervasion is the failure of that definition to apply. This failure can be formulated in two ways: (a) no property that pervades B fails to pervade A, or (b) no property that does not pervade A pervades B. Both (a) and (b) are found in D12. Formulation (a) is adopted by definitions D13 and D28, formulation (b) by D26 and D27.

(III) The special kind of having a common locus is a relation involving the *hetu* class. This characteristic of the relation of pervasion is correctly expressed by definitions D14 and D29. D18 may be interpreted in the same way. D15 and D16 add a wrong qualification to the connection which is the having of a common locus, and D20 makes no qualification at all.

There remain D11, D17 and D21. D21 is a combination of D20 and D5. D17 deals with the having of a common locus which connects the *sādhya* indirectly with the whole of the *hetu* by connecting it with all the properties that have a common locus with the *hetu*. Its parallel in the nondeviating type (type I) is D11."[57]

Has Gaṅgeśa then solved the problem of induction? No. He has, or so he would argue, said in a variety of ways what one would have to know in order to know that *s* pervades *h*. However, this is not to say that he has given foolproof directions as to how to achieve that knowledge. The fact that one hasn't found deviation or an obstruction doesn't, of course, prove there isn't any. But Gaṅgeśa doesn't attempt to solve the problem of induction. What he proposes are various ways of thinking up test cases, of finding counter-examples. There is an alternative way of doing that, less general but probably more helpful for one having in mind a general statement whose truth he wants to assess: that way is to hunt for fallacies.

2. *How is Pervasion Known?* We may distinguish between three distinct kinds of inference.

(A) There is a type of inference in which we infer the presence of an individual present in a particular thing on the basis of the presence of another individual present in the same thing. For example, when we infer that this piece of fruit has this color because it has this particular taste, both the *hetu* (this taste) and the *sādhya* (this color) are particulars which can be present in only one thing, this piece of fruit. *This* color quality which is present in this piece of fruit is not the same as the color quality that is present in another object, though both these color qualities may be of the same kind. So also with the taste which is a particular and can belong only to this piece of fruit. The relation of pervasion underlying this inference can be stated thus: whatever has this taste has this color. But although the pervasion is stated in the form of a universal proposition, there is no generalisation here from observed cases to unobserved cases, for there is only one thing to which this taste and this color belong. Only one object has to be observed in order to cognize the pervasion between its two qualities.

(B) A second type of inference, too, has a single object as its *hetu*, and another single object as its *sādhya*. For example, we may infer the presence of the universal *substancehood* from the presence of the universal *pothood.* This will be the case, generally, when the *h* and *s* are both universals. The pervasion underlying this type of inference will be a relation between two objects, between one universal and another. The difference between cases (A) and (B) is that although in both cases the *h* and *s* are single objects, yet in (B) because they are universals they are necessarily present in many, namely, all particicular instances of them, whereas in (A) these single objects are nonrepeatable qualities and can be present in only one object.

(C) The third variety of inference is the most common one, for example where we infer the presence of fire on the basis of the presence of smoke there. Here both "smoke" and "fire" are general terms, they denote many particulars present in different places. The pervasion "wherever there is smoke there is fire" involves a passage from observed cases to unobserved ones, and it is this type of case which has been the source of many problems.

The Mīmāṃsakas assert that we need repeated observations (*bhūyodarśana*) to ascertain pervasion. It is not enough that we perceive that both smoke and fire are present in one instance. We have to perceive many instances. This is because even though we perceive smoke and fire together in one place, we may still have doubts about their being together in other places. But when we find that smoke and fire are co-present uniformly in all instances which we have observed, we become convinced of the invariable concomitance of smoke and fire.

Naiyāyikas, however, find this theory unsatisfactory for the following reasons. (a) The term "many observations" is ambiguous. It may mean (i) observation of many loci of the *hetu* and the *sādhya*, or (ii) observation of many loci of many individual *hetus* and *sādhyas*, or (iii) (simply) many observations. But in none of these senses of "many observations" can the term explain how pervasion is ascertained in all types of cases. For example, if we accept sense (i), then we cannot explain how pervasion canbe known in cases (A) where a relation between two individual qualities is to be known—qualities which cannot have many loci, which cannot belong to more than one object. If we accept sense (ii), then we cannot explain how pervasion can be ascertained in cases (A) and also in cases (B) where the *h* and *s* being universals are single objects and there cannot be many individual *hetus* and *sādhyas* as in cases (A). Sense (iii) is very vague; it does not say how many observations are necessary for knowing pervasion or how long one should continue observation. If we accept sense (iii) then we cannot explain why, in spite of repeated observations of concomitance of two objects in (C)-type inferences, we do not always cognise that they are invariably related. This leads us to the main objection of the Nyāya philosophers to the Pūrvamīmāṃsā theory.

(b) The problem to be solved here, as has been emphasized by Western philosophers as well, is to explain why in many cases only one observation of a concomitance produces cognition of pervasion where in many other cases repeated and careful observation of innumerable instances fails to convince us that the observed concomitance is invariable. Mīmāṃsā philosophers are concerned with the cognition of pervasion in cases (C), ignoring cases (A) and (B). But even in cases (C) sometimes one perception suffices to produce conviction, but in other cases a number of observations, even varying the instances does not convince us. The Pūrvamīmāṃsā philosophers are not aware of the real issues here.

The Nyāya theory is based on a theory of blocking of cognitive acts by other cognitive acts. To explain how pervasion is cognised in cases (C) we have to take into consideration the presence or absence of doubt in the mind of the knower. Sceptical philosophers like the Cārvākas argue that we can never be sure that the unobserved cases will be like the observed cases. If one has a doubt of this sort, then the presence of this doubt will prevent one from knowing pervasion even after repeated observations of uniform concomitance. If, however, one does not have this sceptical doubt one can acquire knowledge of pervasion even by observing only one favorable instance. For acquiring knowledge of pervasion, therefore, two conditions are to be fulfilled: (1) the knowing subject must be free from doubt that the *h* may be a deviating *h*, i.e., may be present where the *s* is not present, and (2) the subject must have observed the concomitance of the *h* and the *s* in at least some cases.

The Nyāya solution to the problem of induction—that in some cases only one observation suffices, while in other cases innumerable observations do not suffice, to produce knowledge of pervasion—may appear to be a psychological one. The Nyāya theory is that the deciding factor here is the presence or absence of doubt in the thinker. But whether one has doubts or not seems to be a purely subjective affair. To reply to this charge of psychologism Nyāya philosophers make a very important distinction. Although whether one has doubts or not is a purely subjective affair, still the Nyāya theory is not psychological. Nyāya states a universal law: whoever has a doubt that the *h* may be a deviating one will not be able to know pervasion between *h* and *s* as long as he has that doubt. The question here is: is this law a psychological law?

Nyāya distinguishes between two types of blocking or obstruction of inner states by other inner states of an individual subject. In one type of blocking, the inner states by their intrinsic nature prevent the subject from knowing. For example, the excessive love of a mother for her son will prevent her from making a correct assessment of his shortcomings. This type of prevention is psychological, and Nyāya philosophers are not concerned very much with this sort of blocking. They are interested in a different type of blocking of one cognitive state by another by virtue of their objects. Thus if a man is habitually sceptical, then he will not be able to acquire knowledge about anything at all. But what prevents one from knowing a particular pervasion is not one's mental makeup, but the fact that one has a particular doubt, e.g., the doubt that the *h* in this case might be a deviating one. Pervasion and deviation are logically contradictory. Pervasion has been defined, though not flawlessly, as nondeviation, and a cognition of deviation, even though it be of the nature of a doubt, prevents the cognition of pervasion. This law is a law of epistemic logic and not of psychology. A psychological law states a causal law among mental states as mental states; a law of epistemic logic states a relation among cognitive acts as determined by their objects. Only when we become clear how cognition of pervasion is blocked can we set about solving the problem of induction. When we are clear about the factors involved in the cognition of pervasion, we can know that if someone does not know a particular pervasion although he has relevant observational data he must have doubt about the *h* not being of the right type. At this stage Nyāya gives us a method of deciding whether the doubt is justified or not.

For deciding whether one is justified in one's doubt that a particular *h* may be a deviating one the Nyāya philosophers have offered an elaborate argument called *tarka* (rendered in our summaries as *reductio ad absurdum*). Let us explain the essential features of this type of argument with the stock example of pervasion of smoke by fire.

The pervasion in this example can be stated thus: smoke is pervaded by fire; or, wherever there is smoke there is fire; or, in every locus of smoke fire is present. If we have a doubt which prevents us from knowing this pervasion, then this doubt will be that fire may be absent in a locus of smoke, i.e., that smoke may deviate from fire. The doubt in this case is resolved by appealing to a more fundamental relation between smoke and fire, namely, the causal relation. This may be compared with Mill's theory that induction is based on the law of uniformity of nature and the law of causation. But the argument which proves the pervasion of smoke by fire from the causal relation between them is, according to Nyāya, of a peculiar nature, not ordinary deduction or inference. That is, the Nyāya theory is different from the theory of some Western logicians that induction is nothing but deduction with the law of uniformity of nature or the law of causation as the major premise. The nature of the Nyāya form of argument involving *tarka* may be explained by contrasting it with ordinary inference.

(N) Nyāya inference:

(1) Smoke is pervaded by fire.
(2) The mountain possesses smoke.
(3) The mountain possesses smoke pervaded by fire.
(4) Hence, the mountain possesses fire.

(T) Argument based on *tarka* (tentative form):

(5) Deviation of fire (from smoke) is pervaded by absence of being caused by fire.
(6) Smoke possesses the property of deviating from fire.
(7) Smoke possesses deviation of fire (from smoke) pervaded by absence of being caused by fire.
(8) Hence, smoke possesses the absence of being caused by fire.

But (8) is unacceptable to both the parties in the argument, for both accept that smoke is caused by fire. The difference between (N) and (T) consists essentially in this, that if we know that the hill does not possess fire then inference (N) is not possible, whereas unless the contradictory of the conclusion (8) is accepted by both parties to the argument, argument (T) will not be possible. Knowledge of the contradictory of the conclusion is an impediment for inference but is *necessary* for *tarka.* The reason for this fundamental difference between (N) and (T) is obvious. In (N) the conclusion has to be asserted, i.e., has to be firmly believed. But if the contradictory of the conclusion is known to be true, then anyone who has this knowledge will be prevented from asserting conclusion (4). But it is essential for *tarka* to know that the contradictory of (8) is true. Now when one knows that the contradictory of a certain proposition is true, then he can, at best, merely entertain the proposition but without believing in it for a moment. Such an awareness with full realisation that what is cognised is false is called *āhāryajñāna*, contrary-to-fact supposition. Thus *tarka* will have to be put in the form of a counterfactual hypothesis. This form is

(T') (5) Deviation of fire (from smoke) is pervaded by absence of being caused by fire.
(9) If smoke deviated from fire then it would not have been caused by fire.
(10) But smoke is caused by fire.
(11) Hence, smoke cannot deviate from fire.

That is, the doubt is resolved.

Every *tarka* is based on a pervasion, for example, (5) of (T'). Can that pervasion, in its turn, be doubted? The answer is yes, for we can surely doubt whether deviation of fire from smoke is really pervaded by absence of being caused by fire. But this doubt will not arise, for it is admitted by everyone that if one thing deviates from another then the first thing is not caused by that. The causal principle guarantees uniformity of agreement in presence and absence—that which being present a thing is produced, and which being absent it is not produced, is that thing's cause. Thus anyone who admits that this notion of cause is adequate and also accepts that fire is the cause of smoke does not have the option of doubting that smoke may deviate from fire, i.e., of doubting whether fire is present while believing that smoke is.

Now what happens if one doubts whether smoke is really caused by fire? One immediate consequence of this doubt will be that the *tarka* (T') will not be possible against him, for it is necessary for *that* argument that both the parties to the argument accept that smoke is caused by fire. If an opponent does not accept this, then this argument will not be possible against him, for step (10) will not be available. So what procedure can be followed against such an opponent? The procedure of Nyāya in such a case is to show that such a doubt cannot be seriously held at all. Doubts that smoke may not be caused by fire may have one of the following three forms: (i) smoke is perhaps produced only when fire is absent, (ii) perhaps in some cases smoke is produced without fire, or (iii) perhaps smoke is produced by no cause. But none of these doubts can really arise at all. The Nyāya theory is that one cannot even start doubting that smoke may not be caused by fire. This doubt is blocked, i.e., prevented from arising in the mind, by the person's knowledge of agreement in presence and absence of smoke and fire (viz., that in all cases where smoke is produced fire is present, and all cases where fire is absent smoke is not produced). If one persists in maintaining that even though one knows that there is uniform agreement in presence and absence of smoke and fire one may still doubt that smoke may be caused by fire, then the Nyāya reply will be that such a doubt is insincere, for one's action will give the lie to such a statement of doubt. It is important here to distinguish between doubt which is really there and a mere statement that one has a doubt.

Doubt, being an inner state, cannot be directly inspected by anyone except the doubter himself. But one's own statement of the presence of doubt in his mind becomes suspect when his actions come into conflict with his avowal. Suppose someone says that he has doubts whether smoke is caused by fire, but regularly lights a fire to produce smoke. Then it is clear that his action does not conform to his statement, for his action follows from his undoubting belief that fire causes smoke. In a novel situation one may launch on a doubtful course of action to test the result, but if one regularly follows a particular procedure to obtain a particular result, then one must be acting from conviction and not from doubt.

Thus the Nyāya philosophers have shown that in this particular case, i.e., the case of smoke and fire, one cannot doubt that if smoke deviates from fire then smoke is not caused by fire as long as he believes that smoke is caused by fire. One cannot doubt that smoke is not caused by fire so long as one invariably lights a fire to get smoke. Thus the pervasion that wherever there is smoke there is fire is established.

We must note here carefully exactly what this type of argument based on *tarka* can achieve. The function of *tarka* is to resolve doubt about pervasion, so it will not be the case that one person may fail to know pervasion because he has doubts about deviation while another person who does not have any doubt about deviation has no difficulty in being convinced of the pervasion. These individual differences among different thinkers are resolved by *tarka.* But *tarka* by itself does not guarantee that the awareness of pervasion which *tarka* helps to produce is, *ipso facto,* true. The truth of the awareness of pervasion is not guaranteed by *tarka,* but by the *truth* of *tarka*. If the counterfactual conditional is true, and not merely not doubted, then the awareness of pervasion, too, is true. To solve the logical problem of induction is not to give necessary and sufficient conditions of the truth of induction.

This brings us to a fundamental difference between the Nyāya theory of the awareness of pervasion and the Western theory of induction. Induction is supposed by many to give us only a probable conclusion, whereas according to Nyāya the awareness of pervasion can be as certain as any other type of knowledge. In their attempt to justify inductive inference many Western philosophers have reduced induction to a deduction having the principle of the uniformity of nature or the law of causation as its major premiss. We have seen that according to Nyāya even when *tarka* is needed it is not deductive inference. But now we note that according to Nyāya we cannot appeal to the law of causation to resolve doubts about deviation in every case. For, according to Nyaya, inferences are of three types: *pūrvavat, śeṣavat,* and *sāmānyatodṛṣṭa.*[58] Only in *pūrvavat* and *śeṣavat* inferences is the causal law involved, not in *sāmānyatodṛṣṭa* inferences. So the pervasion underlying this type of inference cannot be justified by any appeal to causal connections.

On this point the Nyāya theory of pervasion is radically different from the Buddhist theory of pervasion. According to the Buddhists there must be some reason why something is invariably co-present with another, and this reason, according to them is that either the two things are causally connected or that they are essentially identical. That is, the Buddhists use the causal principle to justify invariable concomitance between two things. According to Nyāya it is enough to know that two things are invariably co-present; we need not try to give any cause for this fact. Moreover, according to Nyāya the causal principle cannot justify pervasion, for the causal connection between two things is itself a case of pervasion. In Mill's theory there is a paradox of induction, because Mill holds that the principles of the uniformity of nature and of causation are the grounds of induction, that they justify inductive inferences, yet he holds that they are themselves results of induction. The Nyāya theory does not involve this paradox, for although Nyāya uses, in two types of inference, the causal connection to remove doubts about deviation and therefore to establish pervasion, yet Nyāya never tries to justify pervasion by the causal principle, and any causal connection can be an object of doubt unless contradicted by action. So there is no difficulty for the Nyāya philosophers holding that the causal connection is itself a special case of pervasion.

The Cārvāka philosophers have argued that doubt about a general awareness cannot be resolved because we have to pass from observed cases to unobserved cases and this passage is never logically justified. As pervasion cannot be known there can be no inference. This position of the Cārvākas has been refuted by Udayana in a famous verse. He points out that to doubt that smoke may not be pervaded by fire is to have already made an inference. For cases of smoke which have been observed to be attended with fire cannot admit of any doubt. We can have a doubt only about unobserved cases of smoke, cases which are in different places and times. If we do not know that there are such cases of smoke at a different place we cannot have a doubt about *them,* or *their* being pervaded by fire. How can we be certain that there are unobserved cases of smoke? The Cārvāka philosophers admit perception as the only source of knowledge, so they cannot talk of unobserved cases of smoke as being known. To talk of unobserved cases of smoke inference is necessary; if to pass from observed cases of concomitance of smoke and fire to unobserved concomitance is unjustified, then to pass from observed cases of smoke to the *existence* of unobserved cases of smoke is equally unjustified. The Nyāya philosophers offer their theory of *sāmānyalakṣaṇa* perception to explain how we can talk of unobserved cases of smoke.

The Nyāya theory of blocking of one awareness by another, if the things cognized are contradictory, has been misunderstood by Śrīharṣa, the author of the *Khaṇḍanakhaṇḍakhādya*. He has argued that contradiction is a relation between two awarenesses such that if one awareness is the contradictory of another both awarenesses must occur. So if doubt is to be contradicted by *tarka,* then both doubt and *tarka* must exist: but the existence of *tarka* as the contradictory of doubt must imply the existence of doubt, and so *tarka* cannot resolve doubt. Now this is a misunderstanding of the Nyāya theory of blocking, as has been pointed out by Gaṅgeśa. The Nyāya theory is that if two awarenesses are contradictory only one can occur. For the blocking of doubt it is not necessary that the doubt should exist; on the contrary, the blocking insures that the doubt cannot arise at all.

In this connection we should note another point. Existence of doubt about deviation is an impediment only to the perception of pervasion (by *sāmānyalakṣaṇa*), but not to inferential or verbal awareness of pervasion. For even when one has doubt about the presence of fire in a room, one can still infer its presence by seeing smoke there. So also when one has doubt about the existence of a snake in a hole, one can still come to know it on hearing that it is so from a reliable person. The point here is that the presence of doubt is an impediment only to perceptual knowledge of pervasion, but not to being aware of it altogether.

PART TWO

SUMMARIES OF WORKS
(Arranged Chronologically)

1

GAṄGEŚA

While one might argue about the origins of "Navyanyāya" (the claim that Udayana is the "real" origin of that tradition is commonly maintained) there is no doubt that Gaṅgeśa's *Tattvacintāmaṇi* is the premiere work on which the crux of Navyanyāya turns. Whatever may be the estimate of Gaṅgeśa's dependence on others, something that still lies ahead of scholarship on Navyanyāya, it is hardly likely that his place in the movement can ever be usurped. As the summaries to follow will amply demonstrate, Gaṅgeśa's was a unique talent, one which places him securely among the premiere philosophical minds the world has produced.

Gaṅgeśa was a native of Mithila. He seems to have been born and brought up in a village named Chadana, which is no longer identifiable, but he lived in later life at Karion, which was Udayana's village, about twelve miles southeast of Darbhanga.

He belonged to the Kāśyapa *gotra.* Tradition has it that he had several wives, three sons and a daughter. One of the sons was Vardhamāna (see below). Contradictory traditions say that Gaṅgeśa was either (a) a great prodigy or (b) an illiterate child. That is about all we know about his life.

Estimates of Gaṅgeśa's date vary widely. Bodas (whose view of Gaṅgeśa's contribution is uncharitable) places him at the close of the eleventh century.[1] Various writers find him in the twelfth century.[2] The most common estimate is a mid- to late-thirteenth-century date.[3] But the most recent opinions place him in the early fourteenth century.[4] As Ingalls points out,[5] he must be later than Śrīharṣa, whose *Khaṇḍanakhaṇḍakhādya* he quotes, and Śrīharṣa is clearly prior to 1233, for a manuscript exists from that date. On the other hand, Gaṅgeśa must be earlier than his son Vardhamāna, and a manuscript of Vardhamāna's *Kusumāñjaliprakāśa* exists which has been identified on epigraphic evidence as stemming from the period 1300-1360. Since Gaṅgeśa knows the work of other scholars of this period—e.g., of Śaśadhara and Maṇikaṇṭha, covered in Volume II of this series—he appears to have flourished toward the end of the period in question. Our estimate for the present is fl. 1320 A.D., which is closely supported by Matilal, G.M. Bhattacharya, and Umesh Mishra.

Ingalls points out that the appellation *navya* or "new" Nyāya is in fact Gaṅgeśa's own. He also argues that Gaṅgeśa's "newness" is more a matter of style and organization than any startling revolutionary theory. "He is far more precise, more careful to define his terms, than were his predecessors."[6] Furthermore, where Udayana and other "old" Naiyāyikas had argued most vociferously against Buddhist opponents, Gaṅgeśa's major opposition is Pūrvamīmāṃsā.

The following summary of the *Tattvacintāmaṇi* is the work of many hands. Responsibility is indicated for each section. Large portions of the work are untranslated; where translations exist, and other helpful studies, we shall try to indicate them. For the entire work S.C. Vidyabhusana (B and RB: HIL) provides a helpful summary, from which some of our summaries below are drawn. Surendranath Dasgupta (RB5327) offers an extended analysis. Through the first book, on Perception, unless otherwise indicated the edition referred to by "E" references is that by N.S. Ramanuja Tatachariar (RB5346).

TATTVACINTĀMAṆI

BOOK ONE: PERCEPTION (*pratyakṣa*)

Section One: Invocation (*maṅgala*)[7]

Summary by Kishor Kumar Chakrabarti

(E1-5) Gaṅgeśa's work begins with an invocation to the three-faced (*trimūrti*) Lord. This leads to a discussion of the function of an invocation.

(E6-80) It is held that an invocation is performed at the begining of a project for the sake of its completion.

Objection (O_1): That an invocation is the cause of the completion of a work cannot be established through positive or negative concomitance, for there are cases of a work's being completed even without the performance of an invocation.

Objector to O_1: That is because the invocation was offered in a previous birth.

O_1: No, that is circular, and anyway, offering of an invocation is rendered superfluous by the empirically known causes of the completion of a work.

Objector to O_1: The proof that the invocation is a cause of completion involves a two-stage inference. First, it may be inferred that the invocation is fruitful on the ground that invocation is an activity which is not denounced and is practised by cultured (*śiṣṭa*) men.[8] Then it may be inferred that the completion of the work is the fruit since it is completion which is regularly sought after, and since no other fruit is available.

O_1: This will not work. Since it is already known that there may be completion without an invocation, the causal connection cannot be established by any amount of reasoning.

Objector to 0_1: We invoke a Vedic injunction to support the contention that invocation is the cause of completion. Though no such Vedic statement is actually found, it can be inferred from the fact that an invocation is performed by cultured people.

At this point Gaṅgeśa enters into a long discussion of whether the invocation could be regarded as a subsidiary cause. By a "subsidiary cause" is meant that which does not produce the chief result, but produces the operation (*vyāpāra*) which leads to the chief result. He discusses in particular whether the invocation could be regarded as the cause of completion by way of being the cause of the removal of obstacles. He also discusses whether one could suppose that in those cases where there is no completion in spite of the performance of an invocation, completion will take place in a future life. He finally concludes that the invocation cannot be regarded as either the principal or the subsidiary cause of completion.

Answer: The appeal to a Vedic injunction is of no help. Since the invocation is not invariably present before the completion of work, it cannot be made out to be the cause of completion even with the help of scripture.

(E81-113) Gaṅgeśa: Though the invocation cannot be regarded as the cause of completion, then, it may still be regarded as the principal cause of the removal of obstacles. The causes of completion may be said to be the absence of obstacles together with the known empirical causes. Noncompletion may be due to there occurring an obstacle after the performance of the invocation, or due to the absence of some known empirical cause. An existing obstacle cannot be removed except through the performance of an invocation. The absence of obstacles, which is a cause of completion, may be either eternal or due to the performance of invocation. Since the absence of obstacles may be eternal, it can be explained how in some cases there can be completion even without the performance of an invocation. The invocation is offered out of the apprehension that there may be obstacles, hence it should be performed as long as there is such an apprehension.

This is followed by a long discussion of what precisely is meant by "invocation." Gaṅgeśa concludes that a number of different activities such as saluting (*namaskāra*), eulogizing (*stuti*), uttering specific words like "*atha*", etc., are signified by "invocation" and that there is no characteristic common to all of them. There is also a discussion of what is meant by saluting, by being "cultured", etc.

Section Two: Truth (*prāmāṇya*)
Summary by Jitendranath Mohanty
Part One: *How Truth is Grasped* (*jñapti*)

For Part One only, "ET" references are to the edition and translation by J.N. Mohanty is his *Gaṅgeśa's Theory of Truth* (RB 5338). Numbering of paragraphs corresponds to numbering in Mohanty's work.

1-5. (ET81-89) The work begins with an invocation in which Gautama's first *Nyāyasūtra* is quoted to show that all the other fifteen of Gautama's categories depend on the first, viz., instrument of knowledge (*pramāṇa*).

Objection (O_1): Since it is not possible to ascertain the nature of the instruments of knowledge it is not right to hold that gaining the highest good depends on apprehension of the instruments of knowledge. For it is impossible to apprehend truth either intrinsically or extrinsically, and apprehension of the nature of truth is necessary in order to ascertain the nature of the instruments of knowledge.

Another objector (O_2): Why should we have to apprehend truth? There is no general connection between it and activity in general. Even in cases where something is difficult or expensive to achieve what is needed is belief (*niścaya*) in an object only (and not in the truth of any awareness).

Objection (O_3) to O_2: Belief in truth is necessary. For there is the rule that wherever it is the case that either doubt about x's presence or conviction about x's absence or both obstruct the arisal of some awareness J, then conviction about the presence of x must be the cause of the arisal of J. For example, this rule is instantiated in the case of inference, where knowledge of pervasion is the cause of inference, since doubt about it or conviction of its absence blocks inference.

O_2: This rule is irrelevant here, since what obstructs activity is not conviction about truth but rather belief in the object.

Gaṅgeśa (answering O_2): No, once doubt has arisen about the truth of an awareness belief in an object—which belief is a requirement for unwavering activity (*niṣkampapravṛtti*)—can only arise from conviction as to the truth of that awareness.

6-13. (ET90-106) Suppose the ascertainment of truth is intrinsic (*svatas*). Then there are the following alternatives (*vipratipatti*):

(A_1) The truth of an awareness J is grasped by any awareness K which is produced by the same conditions as give rise to the awareness of J without producing awareness of J's falsity.

(A_2) The truth of J is grasped by an awareness K which is not produced by any awareness that has J as its content.

(A_3) The truth of J is grasped by any awareness which grasps the locus of J's truth, i.e., by J.

(A_4) The truth of J is grasped by its own locus.

(A_5) The truth of J is apprehended by J itself or by that awareness K which grasps J.

Contrasting with each of A_1-A_5 are five further options which fit the position that truth is grasped extrinsically. Generally, the distinction is that on the extrinsic view truth is apprehended only after the awareness J has itself been grasped, whereas on the intrinsic view the awareness is grasped *as* true.

Pūrvapakṣa (the opponent's position)

14. (ET107) Gaṅgeśa now reviews arguments in favor of the intrinsic-truth view. First, he clarifies the sense in which "truth" is to be understood under the intrinsic-truth view. He shows that certain definitions of "truth" will not do for that view. Truth, for instance, cannot consist in (a) J's not having a qualifier which is absent in the qualificand, or (b) J's grasping what has not been grasped before, or (c) J's being an awareness other than memory. None of these can be the sense of truth which fits the intrinsic-truth view, since each of them would involve the absurd assumption that at the time of entertaining J we have already entertained the qualification *not having a qualifier which is absent in the qualificand*, etc. (since to know that J has these we must have known them earlier).

15. (ET111) Rather, the sense of "truth" appropriate for the intrinsic-truth view must be either (d) J's having the property of being an awareness whose qualifier is in its qualificand, or (e) J's having the property of being an awareness of the relatedness of its qualifier with its qualificand.

16-21. (ET113-126) Gaṅgeśa next argues in defence of the intrinsic-truth view that, since an awareness is determined by its content, an awareness of that awareness amounts to an awareness of that content. Let us call that second awareness an "aftercognition" (*anuvyavasāya*). On all versions of the intrinsic-truth view the aftercognition grasps a content comprising three things, viz., a qualificand (*dharmin*), a qualifier (*dharma*), and the relation between them (*vaiśiṣṭya*). So, even a false awareness is *cognized* as true; its invalidity must be held to be cognized extrinsically.

Objection: If the aftercognition K in apprehending intrinsically the truth of a false judgment J apprehends the total content of J, it would seem that any judgment that judges that J is false must itself also be false, which is absurd—we could never validly detect error!

Answer: As long as J is not sublated one who entertains K (that J is true) also entertains a false judgment, viz., although as yet he does not know that it is false. Once J has been sublated the absurdity will not occur either, since J will then be known to be false.

After dealing with some other objections to the intrinsic-truth view, Gaṅgeśa concludes his defence of the theory by summing up two main arguments. (1) Since an aftercognition K of awareness J is capable of apprehending the fact of its having a certain content, it should also be able to apprehend its truth. (2) If truth is not apprehended intrinsically, the question would arise as to how to ascertain the truth of any other judgment offered as establishing the truth of the initial one; one would be landed, as a consequence, in an infinite regress.

Siddhānta (the correct position)

22–25. (ET128–131) Gaṅgeśa rejects the intrinsic-validity view. The central point of his attack is the fact that often, soon after we have an awareness, we ask ourselves "Is this awareness true or not?". This is more often so in the case of unfamiliar awarenesses. Now, according to a well-known Nyāya theory, doubt presupposes (a) awareness of the qualificand, (b) memory of the mutually contradictory alternatives, and (c) absence of the perception of any of those specific qualities with which either of the two alternatives is universally concomitant. In the present case ("is J true or not?") the qualificand is J whose truth is doubted, and the alternatives are truth and falsity. Since such doubt does occur, there must be awareness of its qualificand J, that is to say, aftercognition of J must occur. But aftercognition of J is also, on the intrinsic-truth view, apprehension of its truth, and if J's truth is apprehended at the time in question a doubt about J's truth or falsity cannot occur at the same time. Hence the intrinsic-truth theory cannot account for the possibility of doubt about the truth of an awareness soon after its occurrence. Here "soon after" means "in the third moment after the origin of the awareness (J)."

25. (ET137) Objection: Awareness of the qualificand is not a prerequisite of doubt.

Gaṅgeśa: Yes it is. Otherwise (1) there would not be the rule that every doubt is apprehended as a doubt about something (the qualificand), and (2) it could not be explained why it is that in many cases of doubt one of the two alternatives has more *prima facie* strength than the other.

26-29. (ET139–146) Objection: A person may believe that a conch shell is white and nevertheless, due to defects in the senses, perceive it to be yellow. Likewise, even after one has the initial belief in the truth of an awareness, due to defects doubts may subsequently arise.

Answer: No, the cases are not analogous. In the conch shell case though we see yellow we behave on the basis of our earlier belief that it is white. But in the supposedly analogous case in question, we cease behaving on the basis of our initial belief and act instead on the basis of the doubt. Secondly, whereas in the case of perceptual error (the conch shell case) it is belief based on perception which produced it that removes it, in the case of doubt belief based on anything may remove it—perception, inference, whatever.

Furthermore, there is no universal property of defectness (*doṣatva*) present whenever there is doubt.

Objection: Just as doubt about the object of J arises from doubt about the truth of J, so doubt about the truth of J arises from doubt about the truth of the aftercognition K.

Answer: No, for on your intrinsic-truth view the doubt about the truth of K cannot arise at all, since that truth is known intrinsically.

Objection: Mere awareness does not preclude awareness of its opposite, for even after a false judgment there arises the sublating one. The awareness that precludes sublation or doubt is an awareness which cannot occur without its object being as it says it is (*ananyathāsiddha*). So any awareness suspected of being *anyathāsiddha*, that is, of being about an object that is not as it says it is, is thereby weakened. And such an awareness, though initially believed, may come to be doubted. So doubt about the truth of K may arise after all.

Prima facie answer: Just as there never arises a doubt whether J is an awareness or about what its content is, since these things are the objects of aftercognitions, so also there should not be any doubt about the truth of J, since it is a rule that aftercognitions are true.

Objector: No, for aftercognitions never grasp the awarenessness or the content of a J except when those properties are necessarily present in J, while truth may be the content of an aftercognition even though it is actually absent.

Gaṅgeśa (answering the original objection): No, for the opposite of *ananyathāsiddhi* is just falsity (*bhramatva*). So, when there is doubt about the falsity of K there also arises doubt about the truth of J. But doubt about the falsity of an awareness is not possible, whether its truth is apprehended or not.

30. (ET148) Objection: Very well. Doubt does not arise from doubt about the truth of an awareness. Rather, doubt may arise with respect to the content of any awareness which has the generic property of having a content. Both the content of true judgments and of false ones share the common characteristic of being contents of awareness. Now the truth of J is the content of K, and since J possesses the property of being a content of an awareness the doubt can arise with respect to K "is it true or isn't it?".

Gaṅgeśa: But doubt does not always occur whenever a content is entertained, so it needn't arise in the case in question. And indeed it won't arise, since *ex hypothesi* there is belief in its truth!

31–32. (ET150–154) Objection: Truth is the property of having a chief qualifier (*prakāra*) which is present in the qualificand (*tadvati tatprakārakatva*). It is *this* truth which is apprehended by K, which also apprehends J—so there can be no doubt about *this* kind of truth. Nevertheless truth in some sense is doubted subsequently.

Gaṅgeśa: But it is truth in the original sense (the one you have just explained) which is doubted subsequently—not some other kind of truth.

Objector: It can't be. Consider "this is silver" as our J. The aftercognition K ("I know this (to be) silver") must apprehend the content of J with all its appropriate qualifiers. So there is no way that doubt about this can occur.

Gaṅgeśa: You don't properly understand what an aftercognition apprehends. An aftercognition is a mental awareness, not a perception of external objects. Thus K, the aftercognition, cannot grasp the external objects *this* and *silverness,* etc., as J, a perceptual awareness, does. Rather, it grasps J with its qualifiers. So K is not "I know this (to be) silver", but rather "I have an awareness of J, whose qualifiers are *thisness* and *silverness.*"

Objector: Nevertheless, if K does not apprehend that *this* is really (i.e., externally) related to *silverness* it will be nonpropositional.

Gaṅgeśa: No, since K is a judgment which has a qualificand and qualifiers and so is propositional. The qualificand and qualifiers are not entities but epistemic entities appearing in J.

34–38. (ET159–175) Gaṅgeśa next proceeds to formulate his objection in standard-form arguments. We shall not here try to summarize these. The important philosophical question he raises is: How does our first notion of truth arise? According to Nyāya we infer that an awareness is true from the fact of its verification in practice. But how is such an inference ("this awareness is true, because it leads to successful behavior") possible? According to the rules of inference, the *sādhya* (in this case not only truth in general but the specific truth of this particular awareness) must be already known. Hence the relevance of the question: How do we get our first notion of truth?

Gaṅgeśa examines several answers. Universal skepticism, which denies that there is truth, is dismissed on the ground that a total denial of truth is absurd. If truth exists, its denial is false; if it does not exist, its denial is pointless. Though the concept of truth may be established in this manner, still it presupposes someone else who denies the possibility of truth. In the absence of such an opponent, and in the case of the first inference for oneself, the question remains as to how to arrive at the first notion of it. One answer is suggested, and possibly upheld by some Naiyāyikas: according to it, the concept of truth is recollected from experiences in past lives. Gaṅgeśa does not favor this view, and instead offers his own suggestion along the following lines. At first, we establish the absence of falsity with the help of an inference in the negative (*vyatirekin*) mode: the positive notion of truth will then follow from the negative by implication. Gaṅgeśa offers a series of such negative inferences, which establish the absence of falsity in an awareness of the form "this is fire". E.g., here is such a negative inference: "J (viz., "this is fire") is not an awareness whose qualifier is absent in its qualificand; because it is a belief which has fireness as its qualifier and something capable of burning as its qualificand; whatever is not a belief having fireness as its qualifier and something capable of burning as its qualificand *is* an awareness whose qualifier is absent in the qualificand; like a false awareness of fire."

39. (ET182) The question nevertheless remains, how do we get our first notion of falsity? Gaṅgeśa answers in the following manner. As soon as a false awareness is corrected, we say "my awareness was about fire, but its object lacks fireness." This amounts to saying that my awareness is false in the strict sense of having a qualifier that is absent in its qualificand. Granted that this is how we get our notion of falsity, still it may be asked, where do we get the notion of "absence of falsity" from which we are going to infer the presence of truth? Here we have to depend upon a negative pervasion (*vyatirekivyāpti*), i.e., one in which the absence of the *s* is apprehended as pervaded by the absence of the *h.* In this connection, Gaṅgeśa lays down that a prior acquaintance with the *s* is only necessary where the absence of the *s* is apprehended as a negative entity. In the present case, the absence of the *s*, i.e., the absence of the absence of falsity, is apprehended as the positive entity called falsity, so that a prior acquaintance with the *s* (i.e., absence of falsity) is not presupposed. Once the said negative inference has taken place, it may be followed by a positive (*anvayin*) inference for establishing the positive truth of the awareness.

Among the other points Gaṅgeśa makes out in this connection the following is important. An awareness may establish the truth of another awareness even if its own truth is not yet ascertained. An awareness involves belief in the existence of its own content, though its truth is not thereby ascertained. It is only when there has taken place a doubt about the truth of the awareness, and consequently a doubt about the existence of its content, that the truth of the awareness must be ascertained in order that unwavering activity with regard to that object may be established. Unwavering activity does not ordinarily require ascertainment of the truth of the awareness. Nonapprehension of its falsity suffices. In this respect the Naiyāyika effects an economy in explanation as compared to the Mīmāṃsaka who demands that apprehension of truth is necessary for unwavering activity.

40. (ET186) Objection: How can we infer the truth of something before we are acquainted with the concept of truth? In order to judge that *x* has *phi* we must already be acquainted with *phi*—so, in order to judge that J is true we must already be acquainted with truth.

Gaṅgeśa: The initial inferential conclusion is rather "there is truth in J", and there is no rule that we must already be acquainted with the qualificand *truth* here. Then, once we have that judgment, we can easily move to "J is true", i.e., "J possesses truth". It is analogous to awareness of absence—first we are aware that there is absence of pot on the floor, and subsequently that the floor possesses the absence of pot.

41. (ET188) Gaṅgeśa now reformulates the argument so far in terms which will suit Naiyāyikas who hold a certain special view about the relational abstracts involved in the knowledge situation.

42. (ET191) Objection: Successful activity doesn't necessarily prove the truth of an awareness. Suppose I see, a long way off, the light cast by a jewel. Judging "that is a jewel" I set out to find it and do find it, but the awareness is false since "that" is the light of the jewel, not the jewel itself.

Gaṅgeśa: The activity was directed toward the light, which was the actual qualificand in the awareness in question.

Objector: The inference "J possesses absence of falsity, because it leads to successful activity" involves the fallacy of being too specific (*asādhāraṇa).* Its *h* ("leading to successful activity") is absent from both *vp* (erroneous awarenesses) and from *sp* (e.g., nonpropositional awarenesses).

Gaṅgeśa: The rule is that the *h* must not be absent from what is apprehended as possessing the *s.* Now we are discussing the very first inference to truth, and *ex hypothesi,* although nonpropositional awarenesses do have absence of falsity they are not yet apprehended as having absence of falsity.

43. (ET194–200) Again, arguments are rephrased to fit those Naiyāyikas with special epistemological theories.

48. (ET202–204) Objection: The inference "J has absence of falsity, because it leads to successful activity" requires for its validity that the *h* be known to reside in the *p*. But how could we know that in this case? I may judge "this is capable of burning" but only later, after the judgment has lapsed, do I test whether it does indeed burn, and the testing does not relate to J at all.

Reply: It is known by the aftercognition K "I know that this is capable of burning."

Objector: No, since K, being a mental awareness, does not ascertain that the qualifier *really* belongs to the qualificand; all it tells us is that I know that I had a judgment to this effect. And if the aftercognition can somehow apprehend the *real* fireness through the experience of being burned, then our intrinsic-truth theory is shown to be justified.

Gaṅgeśa: It's like this. First we apprehend J_1 ("this is fire") and have an aftercognition K_1 of it ("I know that this is fire"). Then we (may) test J_1 by getting ourselves burned, so judging J_2 ("this is capable of burning"). Now, recalling J_1 and J_2 I can have the mental perceptual awareness "J_1 has as its content an object capable of burning," just as one may have the visual awareness that a piece of sandalwood is fragrant (through *jñānalakṣaṇasannikarṣa*).

49. (ET205–206) Objection: Precisely. So, since truth is cognized by mental perception—one thus perceives that the awareness J_1 possesses the absence of a qualifier that is nonresident in the qualificand—your view amounts to the intrinsic-truth view.

Gaṅgeśa: No, it is extrinsic, since J_1's truth is only made known through a different awareness, viz., the mental perception.

What *is* intrinsic truth? It can be formulated in three ways: (1) The property of being apprehended by an awareness J that is caused by the same conditions as also give rise to all those awarenesses which apprehend J. (2) The property of J's being apprehended by any awareness which apprehends the locus of J's truth. (3) The property of J's being apprehended by an awareness K that is caused, but not caused by an awareness—itself caused—about J. Any account other than these three entails the extrinsic-truth view. Now in the case of the mental perception mentioned, since truth is apprehended by an awareness (the mental perception) that is caused by an awareness (the memory of J_1—itself caused—about J_1) the account is clearly different from (3) above, and so constitutes an extrinsic-truth account.

50. (ET208–210) Once one has gotten the first awareness of truth through a negative inference to absence of falsity leading to a positive inference from absence of falsity to truth, we can subsequently reason positively and directly, since now we *have* the notion of truth and can recognize cases of it.

51. (ET216) Objection: An awareness whose truth is not believed cannot ascertain the truth of another awareness—if it could, we would have an infinite regress. Or else, if it can, then let the original awareness J ascertain its object without itself being believed to be true.

Counterobjection: But an awareness such as J is often found to be false! So we cannot be sure of the existence of its content until we are convinced of its truth.

Objector: Yes, but the same applies to Gaṅgeśa's inference to truth, which often turns out to be false; since it does so we shall have to ascertain its (the inference's) truth, etc., etc.—infinite regress.

52. (ET217–218) Gaṅgeśa: I do not maintain that in order to believe in the existence of J's content I must believe in J's truth; in fact I deny it. As long as there is absence of doubt about the existence of J's content unwavering activity may arise. But sometimes doubts do arise, for example, when we have not entertained that kind of awareness (and object) before. Now in such a case we need to resort to inference to remove such doubts, i.e., to prove J's truth. But the inference we use to prove it does not, again, have to be one we are sure of—it is enough if we are not in doubt about it. The infinite regress, therefore, does not arise unless *you* assume, contrary to what I assume, that in order to believe in the existence of J's content I must be convinced of J's truth.

53. (ET222) One should not confuse my view with a different answer to the infinite regress charge, according to which one might doubt the truth of an awareness without having doubts about the existence of its content.

54. (ET224–226) Objection: Inferential awareness in any case involves an infinite regress, since in order to infer I must cognize the *p*, the *h* and the pervasion, but in order to cognize *them*—being in doubt and thus perforce having recourse to other inferences, on Gaṅgeśa's account—I shall be forced from inference to inference without end.

Gaṅgeśa: No. Again, as long as there is absence of doubt no regress occurs.

Objection: On your view, then, belief in the truth of an awareness has no relation to unwavering activity regarding its object. It should follow that we would seldom if ever find it worthwhile to go to the trouble of inferentially justifying the truth of awarenesses, especially since by the time we did so the awareness would be past and cannot inspire activity any more.

Gaṅgeśa: Even though that awareness is past another awareness may arise concerning the same object, and because of the truth of the previous awareness the new one may be free from doubt and thus will inspire unwavering activity.

55. (ET227–229) Objection: Since we sometimes act quickly and immediately on the basis of an awareness we should assume that at least for *those* awarenesses their truth is cognized intrinsically.

Gaṅgeśa: No. Truth in the sense we are discussing (viz., the property of not being limited by a qualifier that is the counterpositive of an absence residing in the qualificand) cannot be cognized intrinsically. As for the quick action, this must occur because the conditions for the inferential justification are directly at hand, or more likely, that because the case is similar to previous ones, no doubt about the truth of the awareness arises at all—e.g., when a thirsty man sees water and reaches out to drink it.

Part Two: *How Truth Arises (utpatti)*

1. (E306–320) J's truth arises extrinsically, not intrinsically, i.e., not merely from the collection of conditions sufficient for the production of J itself. For if the doctrine of the intrinsic origination of truth so understood were correct then a false awareness would be true. Since a true awareness is different from a false awareness, they must be due to different causes. A true awareness is produced through some excellence (*guṇa*) in its cause, while a false awareness is produced through some fault (*doṣa*) in its cause. There is no general cause in the absence of specific causal factors. The generic cause operates only together with specific conditions. Therefore, in the absence of both excellences or faults, the merely generic causes of awareness *qua* awareness cannot bear any consequence at all.

Pūrvapakṣa

The difference between truth and falsity is analogous to the case of two pots, or two twins, arising from the same causal conditions. Secondly, truth is a common (*anugata*) property and should have a single common causal condition, but excellence (*guṇatva*) is not such a common property. Thirdly, excellence cannot be said to be the cause of truth, for even a fault may produce truth regarding one part of an awareness. The awareness "the conch shell is yellow", which is due to a fault in the sense-organs, is nevertheless true in one part, i.e., inasmuch as it actually does grasp a conch shell.

Siddhānta

2. (E321–386) For these same reasons falsity ought also, according to the (Mīmāṃsaka) opponent, to arise from the generic causes of awareness *qua* awareness. In fact, however, the two effects, true awareness and false awareness, are heterogeneous, and so their causes must also be heterogeneous. There is, Gaṅgeśa points out, a common cause of truth: it is produced by those factors which possess the property of impeding the production of awarenesses opposed to it. The joint methods of agreement and difference also bear out the same conclusion. There is truth, when there is (in the case of perception, for example) sense contact with a large number of parts of an object there is absence of truth when such contact is absent. So also in the case of other types of awareness such as inference. Furthermore, defects no more possess a generic property than do excellences; there is no reason why the Mīmāṃsaka should choose to operate with the former concept but discard the latter. In fact, the excellence need not be exactly the same in all cases of truth: it will indeed differ from case to case, and there is nothing objectionable about this.

3. (E386–407) Against the Prābhākaras, who do not admit any falsity at all and would at best define truth as the property of being other than memory, Gaṅgeśa insists that truth must be opposed to falsity. If a philosopher does not recognize this ordinary usage and make his analysis conform to it, his talk about "truth" would be rendered arbitrary, and the word "truth" ("*pramā*") would become a mere technical term (*paribhāṣika*), which it isn't. As opposed to falsity, "truth" means the property of being an awareness of relatedness (*viśiṣṭajñānatva*). Truth in this sense, it is easy to show, is not apprehended intrinsically. Indeed, Gaṅgeśa has already shown it.

Prābhākara: Truth is the nonapprehension of a nonexistent difference (*avidyamānabhedāgraha*), for falsity is the nonapprehension of an existent difference.

Gaṅgeśa: Even in that sense truth cannot arise intrinsically, for the counterpositive of this nonapprehension is a nonexistent difference which, being nonexistent, cannot be apprehended.

Part Three: Truth's Definition

1. (E408–415) Gaṅgeśa examines a series of definition of truth. Truth is *not* a proper universal property (*jāti*) for three reasons: (1) it is inferred even though it inheres in particulars that are capable of being perceived; (2) it overlaps with such properties as immediacy (*sākṣāttva*); and (3) it may belong to an awareness in virtue of pervading only one part of it, whereas a proper universal should be locus-pervading, i.e., should belong to its substratum in all of its parts.

2. (E416–433) Here are some mistaken definitions, and the reasons why they are mistaken:

(D1) The truth of J is J's not having as its chief qualifier what does not occur in its qualificand. Reason why mistaken: This is not what "truth" means in ordinary usage.

(D2) Truth of J is J's grasping what has not previously been grasped in conformity with its object. Reason why mistaken: This definition fails to apply to consecutive awarenesses of one and the same object.

(D3) The truth of J is J's being the direct awareness of the object as it actually is. Reason why mistaken: "As it actually is" (*yathā*) means resemblance, and there is no resemblance of a pot to the awareness of it. Fruthermore, whatever resemblance there is is also there in the case of error.

(D4) The truth of J is J's being a direct awareness produced by an excellence. Reason why mistaken: This is not a generic (*anugata*) property, which a definiens should be.

(D5) The truth of J is J's being a direct awareness of what is unsublated. Reason why mistaken: The sublating awareness is itself an opposite truth.

(D6) The truth of J is J's being a direct awareness of what is consistent. Reason why mistaken: Consistency or coherence with other awarenesses is common to both true and false awarenesses.

(D7) The truth of J is J's being a direct awareness which produces successful activity. Reason why mistaken: This does not apply to awarenesses which are neglected and do not produce any activity at all.

(D8) The truth of J is J's being a direct awareness of reality. Reason why mistaken: The definition is pointless, for there is nothing other than reality (*tattva*).

(D9) The truth of J is J's being a direct awareness which has as its chief qualifier a property which is the counterpositive of an absolute absence resident in its qualificand. Reason why mistaken: This definition does not apply to a true awareness about contact, the absence of contact belonging to the same qualificand as contact itself does (since contact is nonlocus-pervading).

(D10) The truth of J is J's being a direct awareness the absence of whose chief qualifier does not occur in the qualificand. Reason why mistaken: This definition fails to apply to cases of true collective (*samūhālambana*) awarenesses if we take the chief qualifiers collectively and the qualificands distributively.

(D11) The truth of J is J's being a direct awareness whose chief qualifier has the same locus as J's contentness. Reason why mistaken: The chief qualifier *thisness* in the false awareness "this is a snake" also has the same locus as the awareness's contentness.

3. (E434–461) *Siddhānta*: Gaṅgeśa now shows that truth can be defined, and in a simple manner, i.e., as either (D12) or (D13):

(D12) the truth of J is J's being a direct awareness of something where that object actually is, or

(D13) The truth of J is J's having a chief qualifier that belongs to J's object.

In the same way, a false awareness may be defined either as an awareness of a thing where it is not, or as a direct awareness whose chief qualifier is absent from its object. The clause "whose chief qualifier" should be understood either as meaning "having its relatedness for content" or as "produced by awareness of it as qualifier". The first interpretation will comprehend both finite and divine awarenesses; the second applies only to finite ones, for divine awarenesses do not have any origin. Furthermore, God's awareness is of a thing as a related object, but it does not have that as its chief qualifier. Nonpropositional awareness is neither true nor false.

Gaṅgeśa emphasizes in this connection that a true awareness need not be true always and everywhere, but only sometimes and somewhere. The definition of truth in each case should therefore best be formulated by considering the particular object.

Section Three: Error (*anyathākhyāti*)
Summary by K.K. Chakrabarti
Pūrvapakṣa

1. (E463–472) Prābhākara: Mīmāṃsaka: All awarenesses are true. So there is no point in giving definitions of truth as was just done. There is no proof that things are ever cognized as other than what they actually are.

Objector to the Prābhākara: Here is an inference to prove that things are sometimes cognized as other than what they are:

(Inf1) Being the intentional object of someone looking for silver is pervaded by the property of being the content of a direct awareness having silverness as its chief qualifier; because it is a property that belongs only to the intentional object of someone looking for silver; like a property belonging only to silver.[9]

Prābhākara: Inf1 is mistimed (*aprāptakāla*). *Belonging to silver alone* is an obstruction vitiating it.

Objector to the Prābhākara: Then consider Inf2:

(Inf2) (Where J is an awareness of shell): The contentness of J belonging to shell has silverness as its qualifier; because it is a contentness which belongs to the intentional object of an activity arising from the desire for silver; like the contentness (in an awareness of silver) belonging to silver.[10]

Prābhākara: Inf2 is vitiated by an obstruction, viz., belonging to silver (since belonging to silver pervades the *sādhya* but does not pervade the *hetu*).

Objector to the Prābhākara: Then

(Inf3) Silverness is the chief qualifier of the content of an awareness of something other than silver because it is the content of an awareness which causes activity directed toward what is not silver; like *shellness.*

Prābhākara: Inf3 has not belonging to silver as its obstruction.

Objector to the Prābhākara: Then consider Inf4:

(Inf4) The awareness of silver has the shell as its content; because it is an awareness which causes volition toward the shell; like the awareness of the shell itself.

Prābhākara: Inf4 involves the *asiddhi* fallacy, since the awareness of silver cannot be the cause of the said volition.

Objector: Then

(Inf5) The shell is the locus of the contentness of the awareness of silver; because it is the intentional object of the volition of someone looking for silver; like silver.

Prābhākara: In Inf5 silverness is the obstruction.

Objector to the Prābhākara: Then

(Inf6) The volitional activity toward the shell on the part of someone looking for silver is caused by an awareness having silverness as its qualifier and the shell as qualificand: because it is a volitional activity of someone looking for silver; like the volitional activity toward silver.

Prābhākara: Now having silver as content is the obstruction.

2. (E473–484) Gaṅgeśa: (But there are some nondefective inferences to show the existence of error):

(Inf7) The volitional activity toward the shell that arises from the desire for silver is caused by the awareness of the desired intentional object of the volition; because it is volitional activity, like the activity towards the shell on the part of a person looking for a shell.

Objection to Inf7: Here being a volitional activity toward the desired object is the obstruction.

Gaṅgeśa: No, since that is precisely the *sādhya* further qualified.[11] Again,

(Inf8) The awareness having silverness as its chief qualifier, which causes the volitional activity towards the shell arising from desire for silver, has the shell as its qualificand; because it is an awareness which is conducive (*prayojaka*) to the activity towards the shell; like the awareness which causes the activity towards the shell on the part of a person looking for the shell.

Objection to Inf8: This involves the *asiddha* fallacy.

Gaṅgeśa: Hardly, since we both accept that there is volitional activity toward the shell!

Objection to Inf8: This is not a case of cognizing something other than it actually is, but rather merely the cognizing of two things, shell and silver.

Gaṅgeśa: No, since apprehending something other than it actually is (*anyathākhyāti*) is precisely to have an awareness whose chief qualifier exists in a different locus (*vyadhikaraṇa*).

Objection to Inf7 and Inf8: In both arguments *being deviant (visaṃvādinī)* is an obstruction.

Answer: No, for that property does not pervade the *s.*

Objection: Then not being caused by a defect is the obstruction.

Gaṅgeśa: That doesn't pervade the *s* either.

Objection to Inf8: There is lack of adequate support (*aprayojaka*) for the *h.*

Gaṅgeśa: No, since the awareness that the desired object is in front of one causes the volitional activity toward it.

3. (E484–496) Prābhākara: The "lack of support" we mean is that we can account for the volition through postulating two independent presentations together with the failure to grasp the difference (of the silver) from the desired object. Since the matter can be thus explained there is no need to invoke the awareness of something erroneously qualified.[12]

Objection to the Prābhākara: Since the awareness of this as silver is the cause of volitional activity towards silver when there is silver, the same should be the cause here (where the *this* is the shell).

Prābhākara: It is economical (*lāghava*) to regard the awareness that the desired object is in front and lack of awareness of difference as the cause of all volitional activities. Even though the relational awareness is present (in the case of true awareness) it would therefore be unnecessarily complex to regard it as the cause.

Objection to the Prābhākara: When there is silver there can be no awareness of the difference between what is desired and what is in front of one. How can the absence of that awareness of difference then be the cause?[13]

Prābhākara: What we mean is that the absence of the difference from what is in front of one is the cause as it is the counterpositive of the awareness of silver. Alternatively, the cause is the absence of the object in front being the content of the awareness of difference from what is desired as the qualifier.[14]

Objection to the Prābhākara: Talk of identity (with silver) must be caused by the awareness of silver, not merely by the lack of awareness of the absence of that identity; otherwise it should be that whenever there is lack of awareness of identity we shall for that reason alone talk of difference.[15]

Prābhākara: No, for desire, etc., have as their contents only what one is aware of in front of one. Furthermore, talk of identity is due to the lack of awareness of the absence of connection of the identity (with the object in front), hence there is no such usage with reference to what one is unaware of altogether.[16]

Objection to the Prābhākara: When the (erroneous) awareness that the conch shell is yellow and not white is followed by the (corrective) inference that it is identical with what is white, there is volitional activity towards it by one looking for a white thing; the awareness of identity is then the cause of that activity.

Prābhākara: This isn't so. You too would have to admit that from awareness of identity of the conch shell with what is yellow no activity takes place if there is also inference of the difference between them. Thus the absence of awareness of difference must be the cause of the activity.

Objector to the Prābhākara: The awareness of identity which is known to be false is merely inoperative towards the production of activity.

Prābhākara: Then the awareness of difference which is known to be false should be so too. Alernatively, the awareness not having difference from what is desired as the content is conducive to the activity (i.e., exclusion of the awareness of irrelevant things is implied). It is not that in the inference to identity (with what is desired) difference from what is desired becomes the content.

Objector to the Prābhākara: If that is true, a unitary qualified awareness need not be accepted even when silver *is* there; the activity may be accounted for through the absence of awareness of difference. The awareness "this is experienced as silver" or "I am aware of this as silver" is equally available in the case of shell also.[17]

Prābhākara: This is not so. In the case in question, in which something just produced is perceived, there can be no memory of silver, for it has not been experienced before. The awareness of silver is a unitary one comprising both the qualificand and the qualifier; this is so because of the nature of things, that is, because the awareness arises from that of silverness together with its connection to the proper qualificand. Silverness of course cannot be the cause of the awareness of the shell.

Objector to the Prābhākara: The causes are the sense organs and the traces, as also in the case of recognition.

Prābhākara: No, for their contents are different.[18]

4. (E496–502) Doubt occurs when there is absence of the awareness of the difference among many incompatible independent presentations attributed to the same thing at the same time. The alternative would be to suppose that it arises from absence of awareness of the difference of many incompatible presentations which are successive,

not simultaneous, so that there take place two successive errors (e.g., the erroneous awareness "this is a tree" followed by the erroneous awareness "this is a man"), and that alternative would lead you to the absurd position that doubt is impossible.

Objector to the Prābhākara: Suppose the doubt (e.g., is this a tree or a man?) is followed by an erroneous awareness (e.g., this is a man). If there is absence of the awareness of difference from both there would be doubt; but if there is absence of the awareness of difference from only one (since the thing has been erroneously identified with the other) this would be a case of error, of cognizing something differently from what it is.

Prābhākara: It is because of some defect that the one thing is not presented independently but rather as being qualified by an absence (i.e., as "this is a man and not a tree"); therefore absence of the awareness of difference from that is immaterial.

Objector to the Prābhākara: Suppose the doubt (e.g., whether there is fire in the lake) is followed by an erroneous apprehension of smoke (in the lake); this may lead to the activity of someone looking for fire.

Prābhākara: The activity is caused by the absence of the awareness of lack of connection with fire.

Objector to the Prābhākara: No, since that absence is already there as the cause of the doubt. So the inference that there is fire in the lake must be the cause of the activity.[19]

Prābhākara: No. Since the erroneous apprehension of smoke obstructs the awareness of absence of fire, the independent memory of fire on the basis of the regularity (that smoke is pervaded by fire) is the cause. Thus there is in this case neither doubt nor error.[20] Likewise, absence of the awareness of difference between what is not desired and what is independently presented is the precluder (*nivartaka*, i.e., the cause of not undertaking activity). If awareness of being identical with what is not desired were the precluder, the awareness that this is not silver when silver is present would not become a precluder (which of course it may). Although there is the awareness that this is not silver when silver is there, there results neither activity toward it nor the awareness of something being different from what it really is, for what there is is absence of the awareness of lack of connection of difference from silver.[21]

Objector to the Prābhākara: Suppose both a piece of silver and a piece of silvery-painted foil are in front of one, and the silver is taken to be foil and the foil to be silver. Since there is absence of awareness of difference from both with respect to each, there should take place both attraction to and repulsion from both simultaneously.[22]

Prābhākara: Not so. There is no evidence for that. The things which are posited on the basis of their effects have to be posited in accordance with the nature of the effects (i.e., there is no veridical awareness of any such effect as simultaneous activity and preclusion of activity). Furthermore, the seeming unity is due to the lack of awareness of differences among cognitions occurring successively. Otherwise (if the cognitions of silver and foil took place simultaneously), since there is absence of awareness of difference from both, there should have taken place the doubt as to whether this is silver or foil with reference to each of them. Or else, that which is the cause of the confusion should at least be the regulator of attraction and repulsion.[23]

5. (E502–509) Objector to the Prābhākara: Sublation (*bādha*), which consists in the rejection of what has been erroneously cognized, does not fit with your view but it does fit with ours.[24]

Prābhākara: The opposite is the case. If *anyathākhyāti* were the right view, since both J and its denial are mutually opposed, there can be no regularity about which is sublator and which sublated.[25]

Objector to the Prābhākara: It is the later cognition that sublates the earlier one.

Prābhākara: Not always. So the right thing to say is that it is the usage (*vyavahāra*) (that occasions the activity) that is sublated by the awareness of difference. And in the case of so-called "error" that results in indifference (i.e., in no activity) what is sublated is that usage.[26]

Since an awareness with a content is restricted by nature to what pertains to that content alone, how can what is only an awareness of silver also be an awareness of what does not pertain to silver? That would be opposed to a thing's nature. And it cannot be an awareness of both (what pertains to silver and what doesn't) because that involves the difficulty of why every awareness having silverness as qualifier doesn't have something nonsilver as its qualificand as well.

Objection to the Prābhākara: But an awareness of X can perfectly well take place without any X being presented.

Prābhākara: That leads to *Sākāravāda* (i.e., the idealist position that objects are merely mental contents). If awarenesses could be false then every awareness would be subject to doubt on that score, and then unwavering activity could not ever take place.

Objector to the Prābhākara: Confidence can be placed in an awareness (so that unwavering activity becomes based on it) when it is known that the causal conditions of the awareness are free from defect.

Prābhākara: No, since the awareness of being free from defect is itself an awareness and thus subject to distrust.

If error has only actual entities as its contents then how can it be false? On the other hand, if its contents are nonactual one will have to accept the *asatkhyāti* position (of the Buddhists).[27]

There is no ground for accepting *anyathākhyāti.* Cognitions arising from authoritative statements and flawless inferences do not provide any ground. Nor do cognitions which are held by Gaṅgeśa to be false support that view; they consist in two cognitions the lack of connection between which is not apprehended. Nor does perception provide any case for *anyathākhyāti,* since the senses apprehend only that with which they are in contact.

Objector to the Prābhākara: A different kind of effect (viz., a false awareness) may be produced even when the senses are in contact because of some defect.

Prābhākara: No, for defects are not productive. No awareness has a chief qualifier which does not belong to the qualificand, because it is an awareness, like a true awareness. A desire having silverness as its qualifier and which is directed towards the shell provides a case which shows that the *hetu* (in the inference stated in the previous sentence) is known.[28]

The property of being an awareness does not belong to the relatum of a contentness (*viṣayatā*) which is limited by a qualifier which does not belong to the qualificand, because it is a property that belongs to awarenesses alone, like the property of truth (*pramātva*).[29]

Objector to the Prābhākara: This inference is obstructed by the following inference: The visual organ is the cause of an awareness which is other than a true visual awareness, because it is a sense organ, like the gustatory organ.

Prābhākara: No. This inference is devoid of supportive reason (*aprayojaka*). Furthermore, *being the cause of an awareness which is other than visual awareness* is a vitiating obstruction here.[30]

So it is clear that two distinct awarenesses (and not one (false) relational awareness), which are not discriminated as to their nature and contents, become the cause of deviant activity. Although only usage is the result of the lack of awareness of difference (and usage alone may be sublated) awarenesses are designated as true or false on the basis of the congruence or deviance of the usage itself. This is why people do not regard the cognition that water is hot as false. So far as an awareness that results in indifference (i.e., no activity at all) is concerned, it is designated as true or false because it has the potentiality for those usages.[31]

Siddhānta

6. (E510–521) Gaṅgeśa: Since it is accepted by both of us that the awareness that the desired object is in front of one is the cause of all activity in the cases we call "true", it is hypothesized (*kalpyate*)

on grounds of economy that relatedness (*vaiśiṣṭya*) itself and alone insofar as it is a content (*viṣaya*) is the limitor of causality (*kāraṇatāvacchedaka*), so that unwanted consequences (such as that the activity may take place even when one is aware that the object in front is not desired) may be avoided.[32] Having relatedness as a content should be regarded as the limitor of causality also for the reasons that it becomes the object of the aftercognition, that it becomes presented to thought quickly (i.e., inevitably), and that there are no overriding considerations to the contrary.

Objection: Lack of the awareness of difference of what is before one from what is desired is the cause of the activity, and the fact of there being the lack of awareness of such difference is the limitor of the causality.

Gaṅgeśa: But this is uneconomical. It also involves assuming the presence of the alleged lack of awareness of which we are not aware.

Objection: Lack of awareness of difference is the cause of relational awareness (*viśiṣṭajñāna*) as well (in all cases, "true" or "false").

Gaṅgeśa: Not so. That could only be if one admits the relational awareness exists, which is contrary to your own view. Furthermore the lack of awareness does not occur at the time of becoming aware of the cause of the activity. Furthermore, there is this argument: Deviant activity also is caused by a relational awareness, because it is activity, as in activities occasioned by truth. Since explanation is impossible without assuming some cause the defective sense organ, etc., are assumed as the causes of (false) relational awarenesses. It is inexplicable otherwise.[33]

Moreover, activity cannot be accounted for by lack of awareness of difference, since that would involve there being simultaneous activity (*pravṛtti*) and withdrawal (*nivṛtti*).

Objection: There is no evidence for that.

Gaṅgeśa: Yes, there is. Just as in the case of true awareness that two things are respectively foil and silver, so in all cases the causal conditions for mistaking the foil as silver and the silver as foil are found to be present at the same time. And that is a matter of experience. Otherwise collective awareness (*samūhālambana*, i.e., an awareness with multiple contents) would turn out to be impossible and that would involve as a consequence that the perception of duality, etc., would not be possible. Likewise, the error that occurs when the true identity of each of the two objects is reversed can be explained. From my point of view it is because of the defects in the organs that the silver is taken to be different from silver and the foil is taken to be different from foil and thus doubt does not take place. However, from your point of view doubt as to whether each is foil or silver should take place, since there is lack of awareness of difference between two independent presentations with respect to the same thing in both cases.[34]

Objection: Attraction and repulsion will take place in accordance with what has been presented through the awareness of a property belonging to it and where there is lack of awareness of difference from it.[35]

Gaṅgeśa: No. Where the desired thing and its opposite are presented through language or through perception it is because of the absence of the thing. Though according to my account also both the opposed properties (of being foil and being silver) are presented through awareness of the same property (being colored silver), neither the silver nor the foil are cognized respectively as silver and foil because of some defect, and it is also because of a defect that they are cognized in reverse (silver as foil and foil as silver).

Objection: Then let attraction and repulsion be regulated by the defect.

Gaṅgeśa: No, for defects are not there in the case of true awarenesses, though there is attraction or repulsion. It is also not the case that perceptual or inferential defects, etc., share an identical nature. So far as awarenesses caused by defects are concerned there are differences in kind among them.[36]

6. (E522–533) *Navyas* (i.e., neo-Prābhākaras): There is a property, a particular kind of sheen, which is known to belong to foil but produces a strong inclination for silver because it has often been known to go with silver. But it does not produce a strong inclination for foil because it is only seldom found to go with foil. The same goes for another property sometimes found in silver but which produces a strong inclination for foil. Now since the strong inclination for one obstructs the weak inclination for the other there is neither repulsion from foil nor attraction to silver.

Gaṅgeśa: This is not satisfactory. It still involves the consequence that there will be simultaneous attraction and repulsion when the cognition is produced by words, for in cases of things presented through words the inclination is equal. Furthermore it is dubious what can be meant by "being strong".[37]

Prābhākara: Congruent activity is different from deviant activity. Let relational awareness be regarded as the cause of the congruent act and lack of awareness of difference be regarded as the cause of the deviant act, rather than making both the result of relational awareness, which is both uneconomical and unsubstantiated.[38] After all, the awareness that the desired object is in front of one is the cause of his attraction, and the presentation of an undesired object is the cause of his repulsion. The cause is not possession of a relational awareness, which would be uneconomical. Now in the case of the foil and silver above deviant activity takes place because there is failure to be aware of their difference, and congruent activity doesn't take place, since there is no relational awareness.[39]

Objection to the foregoing: But since there is lack of awareness of difference of silver from the silver and of foil from the foil (since both are present), attraction toward silver with activity toward silver and repulsion from foil with withdrawal from foil should take place, since all the causal conditions required on your account are present. But it doesn't happen.

Prābhākara: No. Activity is said to be deviant if it is directed toward what is not desired and withdrawal is deviant if directed towards what is desired. Lack of awareness of difference is the cause of activity toward what is not desired and of withdrawal from what is desired. How can it then be the cause of activity toward what is desired? It lacks the capacity for that.

Gaṅgeśa: Everyone agrees that an awareness produces an activity toward just whatever is its content; we learn this when we see babies seek their mother's milk. Therefore that awareness that causes activity toward, say, the shell must have the shell as its content.

Objection: No, it is better to assume that an awareness may be the cause of activity toward what is not its object, since the factors of lack of awareness of difference, perception of the thing presented and the memory of silverness are necessarily present and since to postulate a false relational awareness in every case of deviant activity is uneconomical.

Gaṅgeśa: No. On the strength of the already established evidence a relational awareness has to be posited in cases of deviant activity also. Without some reasons to reject that evidence no assumption contrary to it can be entertained. And under these circumstances appeal to economy is not relevant.[40]

Objection: It may be true that an awareness produces activity towards its content alone. Still in the case of deviant activity the awareness of *this* alone is the cause, and not the awareness of what is desired. The latter is a limitor of causality with reference to the lack of awareness of difference between what is apprehended and what is desired (which lack is itself the cause of the activity), because that leads to economy. So the awareness of *this* is irrelevant as cause, like stickness (is irrelevant as cause in the production of a pot).[41]

So the awareness of silver is neither conducive to activity toward the shell nor has the shell as its content. Otherwise there is the consequence that the true awareness of silver also should have the shell as a content. In cases of congruent activity, however, the awareness of what is desired is the cause; there it cannot be the limitor of causality, because it is the same as the cause.

Gaṅgeśa: Since the awareness of what is desired is independently related to the effect by way of positive and negative concomitance, it must be the cause and not the limitor of something else that is the cause. It is not the case that lack of awareness of difference from what is desired is related by way of positive and negative concomitance to the effect so that that lack can be viewed as a limitor of causality like stickness. It is also not the case that the awareness of what is desired is related by positive and negative concomitance to the activity insofar as it involves lack of awareness of difference and thereby it (awareness of what is desired) can be regarded as irrelevant like the color of the stick. Otherwise, why should it not be that awareness of what is desired should be regarded as the cause and lack of awareness of difference as the limitor of causality? Therefore, because of being independently related by postive/negative concomitance, both awareness of *this* and of the desired silver are causes.[42]

Since awareness of the desired is the cause of activity, deviant activity is also caused by such awareness, since without its cause no activity will take place.

Objection: The cause must be awareness of the desired limited by being an activity having the desired thing as its object.

Gaṅgeśa: No, since such a limitation is cumbrous. Unless there is a difficulty the generally concomitant entities themselves should be regarded as related as cause and effect.

Objection: In the case of congruent activity also awareness of *this* is the cause; that awareness only happens by chance to have the desired thing as its content.

Gaṅgeśa: But then the activity toward what is desired could only be caused by awareness of *this*.

Objector: The awareness of silver does not have the shell as its content, because it is not the cause of activity towards the shell.

Gaṅgeśa: This inference suffers the fault of *asiddhi* (since its *hetu* does not belong to its *pakṣa*).

Objection: Every awareness is true. This pervasion obstructs the possibility of a false relational awareness.

Gaṅgeśa: No; that alleged pervasion is undermined by the fact that false relational awareness has been shown to be the cause of unsuccessful activity on the basis of positive and negative concomitance.

Objection: The sense organ and the trace cannot produce a single awareness of two mutually unrelated things (viz., the perceived *this* and remembered silverness).

Gaṅgeśa: No. The effect must take place if the collection of causal conditions occurs.

7. (E533–539) A few (Prābhākaras) say the following: Since there is no awareness of difference of silver and foil from silver and foil

simultaneous attraction and repulsion do not take place. But it does not follow that this is a case of *anyathāsiddhi*, for because of some defect the two things in front are not taken to be different from themselves but rather from remembered silver and foil.

Gaṅgeśa: No. The difficulty involving the opposed four things will only ensue where one foil and silver have been cognized (so that there is no question of remembering any others). Alternatively, it will be a case of *anyathākhyāti* for silver and foil, will be cognized to be different from themselves.

Others say: The awareness with respect to silver that "this is not silver" involves lack of awareness of the lack of connection of *this* with silver as well as lack of awareness of lack of connection of difference of *this* from silver, and thus becomes the obstruction to activity.

Gaṅgeśa: That is not satisfactory. If there is in the foil lack of awareness of lack of connection of difference from silver and of lack of connection of silverness which are presented as belonging to others, there would be repulsion from foil. On the other hand, if there is awareness of lack of connection of those in the foil, it will be a case of *anyathākhyāti.*

Objection: The refusal to act is due to lack of awareness of lack of connection of lack of connection of lack of connection of difference from silver in silver.

Gaṅgeśa: This is not so. Since lack of connection of lack of connection with difference is of the same nature as connection with difference, there will be repulsion from the foil due to lack of awareness of lack of connection of lack of connection with difference from silver. On the other hand, if there is awareness of lack of connection of connection with difference from silver, it will be a case of *anyathākhyāti.*

Another opinion: Lack of awareness of difference between difference from silver and some difference known to belong to silver is the obstruction to activity; similarly lack of awareness of difference between difference from foil and some difference known to belong to foil is the obstruction there.[43]

Gaṅgeśa: No, for even then an erroneous statement would produce simultaneous attraction and repulsion.

Still another: The awareness that what is desired is not the counterpositive of the difference that is known to belong to what is in front leads to attraction; likewise the awareness that what is not desired is not the counterpositive of the difference that is known to belong to what is in front leads to repulsion. Although difference from silver belongs to foil (i.e., foil is different from silver and silver is the counterpositive of a difference belonging to foil), it is not apprehended due to some defect; but difference from something else (say, a pot) is apprehended. In this way from the correct awareness that silver is not the counterpositive of any difference that is known to belong to foil there takes place attraction to silver leading to activity towards foil. Although foil (which is not desired) is not the counterpositive (of any difference that belongs to foil) it is not apprehended due to some defect; hence there is no repulsion from it. Similarly, since there is awareness that foil (i.e., what is not desired) is not the counterpositive of any difference that is known to belong to silver, there is repulsion from foil leading to withdrawal from silver. Although silver is not the counterpositive of any difference that belongs to silver, it is not apprehended due to some defect. Hence there is no room for simultaneous attraction and repulsion.

Gaṅgeśa: But that is not acceptable. It is well-known on the basis of positive and negative concomitance that the awareness that this is silver is the cause of attraction.[44] In the case where this awareness ("this is silver") is true it is a relational awareness. What is controversial is whether in false cases "this is silver" is one (relational) awareness or two awarenesses. To hold that in the false cases the awareness "this is silver" is not the cause of activity conflicts with what is known to everyone through experience.

Objection: That awareness too (i.e., together with the nonapprehension of difference, etc.) is the cause of the activity.

Gaṅgeśa: No, for (1) the nonapprehension of difference is not invariably found in the cases of true awareness, and (2) it is a more complex explanation than the mere appeal to the relational awareness alone. Likewise for the explanation of repulsion.[45]

8. (E540–550) Other: Apprehension of a property which is believed to belong to what is desired and also believed not to belong to what is not desired is the cause of attraction toward its locus. Such a property is silverness in the case of activity for silver taking it as silver, and similarity to silver in the case of activity for foil taking it as silver. Similarly also for repulsion, i.e., apprehension of a property believed to belong to what is not desired and not to belong to what is desired is the cause of repulsion, such a property being foilness in the case of repulsion from foil taking it as foil and similarity with foil in the case of repulsion from silver taking it as foil. Hence there is no room for simultaneous attraction and repulsion.

Gaṅgeśa: That is not right. If the above were true, attraction to foil taking it as silver and repulsion from silver taking it as foil would not have taken place from the erroneous statement "these are foil and silver" accompanied by the perception of foil and silver as *these.* This is because in the case of foil the property belonging to silver (viz., similarity with silver) and in the case of silver the property belonging to foil (viz., similarity with foil) are not presented by the statement.

Still others say: Silverness is not apprehended in silver due to a defect. So, since there is awareness of the difference between silverness and all the properties believed to belong to silver, the attraction to silver does not take place. However, since there is lack of awareness of difference between silverness and some property believed to belong to foil, there is attraction to foil. Similarly also for repulsion (i.e., since there is lack of awareness of the difference between foilness and some property believed to belong to silver, there is repulsion from silver).

Gaṅgeṣa: This is not acceptable. The relational awareness "this is silver" is both simpler as well as related by way of positive and negative concomitance with the activity, and so should be regarded as its cause.

Objection: But the causes of relational awareness are absent.

Gaṅgeśa: No, they aren't: just as recognition, this relational awareness may be produced by the trace together with the sense organ.

Objetion: Say that recognition is not a single awareness but a composite of two awarenesses.

Gaṅgeśa: Then a thing cannot be the same for two moments, since it is recognition which is the sole proof of such continuance.

Objection: But suppose the trace and sense organ work together in recognition because they have the same content?[46]

Gaṅgeśa: Not so, since in recognizing a thing by name (e.g., "that is Devadatta again") there is no trace of the *that*.

Objection: Even if recognitive perception is regarded as a single awareness, its "that" part is not a case of immediate awareness, for there is no sense-object contact there and furthermore it is produced by the previous awareness of *that*, so the "that" part is memory. The "this" part (i.e., what is presented in experience now) and the awareness which identifies *this* and *that* are cases of immediate awareness, however.

Gaṅgeśa: Then you would have to admit that a thing with which there is no sense-object contact may still be presented through a trace. In a similar manner the unitary awareness that "this is silver", of which the "this" part is perceptual and the silverness part is recollective, should also be produced, because the causal conditions for it are present. From my own point of view, however, since the recognitve awareness is produced by a sense organ and since universals do not overlap, both the parts (*this* and *that*) are cases of immediate awareness.[47]

Objection: Immediate awareness through any sense organ can take place only through connection with that sense organ. But there is no sensory connection with silver where the remembered silver has been cognized.

Gaṅgeśa: An exception to the above rule is to be found in the immediate awareness of thatness and its name, since recognitive perception, which is produced by a sense organ, is an immediate awareness. Furthermore, the trace or the memory provides the sensory connection.[48]

Objection: According to your view perception of silverness requires the sensory connection called inherence in what is in contact (*saṃyuktasamavāya*). How can perception of the shell having silverness as qualifier take place without that relation (of *saṃyuktasamavāya*)?

Gaṅgeśa: *Saṃyuktasamavāya* is not a causal condition for the perception of what is qualified by that silverness. Although contact with silver is a cause of the direct awareness of silver, it is not a cause because it happens to be contact as such, but only insofar as it is in connection with the qualificand.[49] It is also the case that to regard connection with the qualificand as the cause of the immediate awareness of silver is simpler than regarding the lack of awareness of difference between what is desired and what is presented independently to be the cause of activity.

As a matter of fact it is accepted by both of us that error is caused by a defect. But it cannot be that error is nothing but the lack of awareness of some relation. For on the one hand, if the lack of connection were the same as the locus (which is the Prābhākara's own position regarding the ontic status of negative entities) it could not be produced; on the other hand if the lack of connection were the same as the awareness of the locus it would be a true awareness and not caused by any defect.

Objection: A true awareness pertaining to what has been labelled as an error can be produced by a defect.

Gaṅgeśa: No, for a true awareness is produced by a different set of conditions, one that excludes defects. So perceptual error is nothing but false relational awareness taking place because of some defect although the appropriate sensory connection is missing.

(Objection: Although error is caused by a defect error should be construed as nondeviant usage, so the above theory is out of place.)

Gaṅgeśa: It is just the relational awareness itself which is the effect of the defect, for it is the relational awareness which has to be admitted as the cause of activity,and not the lack of awareness of difference, for that is only an assumption.

9.(E550-564) It has been said that defects do not produce any effect (i.e., a defective seed does not produce a sprout). But "defect" in the case of a sense organ is not the same as "defect" in the case of a seed.

It is also the case that my knowing this as silver is reported by aftercognition. Thus aftercognition testifies to the fact that things are cognized otherwise (*anyathākhyāti*). Aftercognition alone can provide evidence for what has become the content of an awareness. An awareness J not having something X as content is never cognized by aftercognition K as having X as its content, for aftercognitions are always veridical. The aftercognition is not in the form "I know this" but rather of the form "I know silver".

Since a relational awareness always has a qualificand and a qualifier, a false awareness does likewise. Further, since it is not accepted that silverness belongs to the awareness of silver (as the *sākāravādin* thinks), and since it is held that the qualifier and the qualificand are the contents of the awareness, there is no commitment to the view that awareness is *sākāra*.

Objection: If an awareness can be false, it cannot be settled which awareness is to be sublated by which.

Gaṅgeśa: This is not so, for an awareness which is such as to be *ananyathāsiddha*—not possible to cognize otherwise—cannot be sublated.

Objection: What is it in an error that is sublated? Not the thing's nature, for that exists. Nor the fact of having silverness as the qualifier and the shell as the qualificand, for these cannot be set aside. Not practical usage (*vyavahāra*), for such usage does take place. Not the production of future activity, for that will not be produced at any rate because of lack of causes for it.

Gaṅgeśa: Sublation is just the awareness on the part of the sublater that the error is an error.

Objection: How can one place confidence in awareness if an awareness may be false?

Gaṅgeśa: But the method of discerning truth (*prāmāṇya*) has been explained.

Objection: A defect cannot be a cause of an awareness.

Gaṅgeśa: Certainly it can, as shown on the basis of what happens.

Objection: How can the awareness that this is silver be false, for both *this* and *silver* are existents? On the other hand, if the contents are nonexistents, one will have to accept *asatkhyāti* (the Buddhist view).

Gaṅgeśa: Although an erroneous awareness has only what exists as content, its erroneousness consists in the fact of its having that as its qualifier which does not belong to its qualificand. The old theorists, however, hold that the only nonexistents that can be contents of awareness are nonexistent relations of identity. This does not amount to acceptance of *asatkhyāti*, since what is accepted in old Nyāya is that there is awareness of something absolutely unreal which is imposed on what is real. On the other hand, *asatkhyāti* is the view that there is awareness of something absoutely unreal which is simple and not imposed on what is real. But there is no evidence for this *asatkhyāti* view.

Section Four: The Definition of Perception (*pratyakṣalakṣaṇa*)

Summary by Pradyot Kumar Mukhopadhyaya

1. (E567-571) Correct awareness (*pramā*) has four varieties: perceptual awareness(*pratyakṣa*), inferential awareness(*anumiti*), comparative awareness (*upamiti*), and linguistic awareness (*śābdabodha*). There are four instruments, the causal conditions *par excellence* (*karaṇa*) of these four types of *pramā* respectively: viz., perception (*pratyakṣa*), inference (*anumāna*), comparison (*upamāna*) and verbal testimony (*śabda*). We hold that all other instruments of knowledge are included in these. Gaṅgeśa now considers a number of definitions of perceptual awareness and rejects them.

(D1) Perception is the undeviating (*avyabhicārin*) awareness that results from the connection (*sannikarṣa*) of the sense organs with their respective objects.

Gaṅgeśa's reasons for rejecting D1 are: (1) D1 overextends, since it applies to inferential awareness of oneself, memory of oneself, and for that matter to awareness in general (none of which are counted by Nyāya as perceptual). For every awareness results (partly) from the contact between the internal organ and the self, and since the internal organ is a sense organ and the self is an object the definition is satisfied in the unwanted cases mentioned. (2) D1 underextends, since it fails to apply to God's perception (which is not caused by sense-object contact). (3) The term "connection" in D1 refers to a variety of relations such as contact, inherence, etc. No one of these relations is present in all instances of perceptual awareness. Therefore any attempt to distinguish the class of perceptual awarenesses in general from cases that are not perceptual awareness on the basis of D1 will fail, since we cannot distinguish a class of things in terms of a property which is not present in every member of the class. (4) Besides, D1 as a ground for distinguishing perceptual awareness is unduly complex, since it seeks to distinguish perceptual awareness in terms of the connection between sense and object, whereas that purpose can equally well be served by defining it simply as what is produced by a sense organ or as what is produced by an object. But for all that being produced by either of the two (organ or object) cannot by itself be an adequate definition of perceptual awareness. For every kind of awareness comes either from the self or from the internal organ. Finally, the notion of a sense organ itself involves the notion of perception for its explanation.

(D2) Perceptual awareness is a direct awareness (*anubhava*) which is not produced by any known causal condition *par excellence.*

This will not do, as it applies to inferential awareness. Inferential awareness results from awareness of the *hetu* (here, *liṅga*), but this *liṅga* is not the causal condition *par excellence* of the inferential awareness. That causal condition *par excellence* is an awareness which is not itself known (e.g., *parāmarśa* or *vyāpti*, etc.).

(D3) Perceptual awareness is a direct awareness that is not caused by another awareness.

This will not do either, since it would exclude qualified awareness from the scope of perception, since such awareness is produced by awareness of its qualifier.

(D4) Perceptual awareness is an immediate veridical awareness.

This also fails because immediacy cannot be apprehended as a universal property. (1) There is no common feature of perceptual awarenesses which could suggest that all of them share a single universal. (2) If there were any such feature then it itself would suffice to accomplish whatever might be accomplished by such a universal as immediacy.

Gaṅgeśa: Immediacy is a defining feature of perceptual awareness. In reply to (1) above it needs to be pointed out that in the absence of any sublating reason it must be admitted that the form of our awareness, viz., "I know (this) immediately" is common to visual and other instances of perceptual awareness. And the content of this awareness is a universal.

Objection: The relevant universal property is (rather) *being produced by a sense organ.*

Gaṅgeśa: No, for (a) to define perceptual awareness in terms of "sense" or "organ" is circular, and (b) the sense organs being imperceptible, the property of *being caused by a sense organ* cannot be the content of the sort of awareness that counts as evidence for a universal property.

In any case, contrary to what the Prābhākaras believe, awareness of a single common feature of all instances of a kind is not necessary for our being aware of a universal property present in all those instances. For just as we apprehend the universal *cowness* through awareness of a feature like the dewlap which is not the only feature uniformly suggestive of cowness, so also we can apprehend immediacy through our awareness of such a feature as *being a nonrecollective experience produced by the visual organ as cause par excellence* even though it is not the only feature that forms the basis of our apprehension of the universal *immediacy.* Indeed, in the case of such a universal property as may be apprehended in qualities like awareness, satisfaction, frustration, etc., there is no necessity for the presence of any common feature whatsoever.

However, objection (2) to D4 is accepted by Gaṅgeśa who says that in case such common features are present they would suffice as an explanation of why we have the same form of awareness with respect to diverse instances, and so to admit a universal would not be necessary.

2. (E571-589) In nonpropositional, God's or yogic perceptual awareness the perceptuality is established through the fact that the property-possessor (*dharmin*) has been grasped. The perceptuality of ordinary perception (*janyapratyakṣa*, i.e., *laukikapratyakṣa*, perceptual awarenesses other than the above three kinds) is defined by some as follows:

(D5) An ordinary perception is an awareness which is produced by a sense organ,

i.e., by some sense organ or other, for no single sense organ produces all ordinary perceptions. Furthermore, the internal organ is to be understood in this context as the cause of memory, inference, etc., but not as internal sense organ, for otherwise memory, etc., would have to be regarded as perceptual.

Lest there be any suspicion of circularity *being a sense organ* means being the seat of that contact with the internal organ which is the cause of some awareness but not the cause of memory. Breath (*prāṇa*), body (*śarīra*) and self (*ātman*) are the loci of such contacts with the internal organ which causes memory. Alternatively, "sense organ" may be understood to mean that which, while it is not the locus of manifested qualities other than sound, is the locus of contact with the internal organ which produces awareness.

3.(E590-602) (D5 is a definition of ordinary perception only. As a definition of ordinary and extraordinary perceptual awareness *in toto* Gaṅgeśa says) We define perceptual awareness as:

(D6) (Perceptual awareness is) an awareness which has no other awareness as its causal conditon *par encellence*.

One need not fear that this definition fails to cover propositional awareness, for awareness of the qualifier is not the causal condition of propositional awareness, for it has no mediating causal condition or "operation" (*vyāpāra*) which it should have if it is to be regarded as the causal condition *par excellence*. Furthermore, awareness of the qualifier is (also) the cause of the qualified awareness since it is itself qualified and there is no evidence to prove that in such cases the awareness of the qualifier is also the casual condition *par excellence* so that infinite regress doesn't arise.

Objection: Recognition, which is perceptual awareness, has awareness of the qualifier as its causal condition *par excellence* together with a memory trace.

Answer: No, memory is the causal condition *par excellence.* If (on the other hand) the recognition were caused by a trace alone then it would be a case of memory, since it is simpler to regard the property *being caused by a trace* as determining memory, since a trace has in any case to be inferred as a cause of memory.

4. (E607-610) The Prābhākaras offer the following:

(D7) Perceptual awareness is just immediate awareness. However, according to them immediacy is not a proper universal. For nothing is there in every case of perceptual awareness the awareness of which may reveal the presence of immediacy.

Objection: Immediacy is the property of being an awareness that is not dependent on any other propositional awareness (and so is a proper universal after all).

Prābhākara: No, for then D7 would be too narrow, since it would exclude recognition as well as the perceptual awareness of similarity, duality and so on. What is intended by D7 as immediacy is that an awareness is immediate relative only to such among its contents in respect of which the awareness is not causally dependent on any other propositional awareness. Every awareness is perceptual *qua* awareness of itself and the perceiver insofar as with respect to those items the awareness is not caused by another qualified awareness. Though a recurring awareness of the same thing has the same form (through its different occurrences in the presence of individually different contents) as we have when a proper universal is present, and is caused by another awareness, still it is perceptual in that the other awareness is nonpropositional, having for its content the universal and its individual instances taken independently.

Objection: A perceptual awareness "this is similar to that", having relation to something qualified (the thing said to be similar) as its content, is caused by the awareness of the corresponding qualifier.

Prābhākara: No, for even without the previous awareness of the qualifier the awareness under discussion results from contact of the sense organs with their objects and has contact simultaneously with both the qualificand and its qualifier. Perception of things as "long" has no causal dependence on the awareness of things as "short", although there is such dependence on our ability to correctly use expressions such as "long" and "short".

Inferential and recognitive awarenesses are each indirect (*parokṣa*) if we consider the *sādhya* (in inference) and pastness (in recognition) parts of their contents. For insofar as those awarenesses are awarenesses of those contents they are caused by other awarenesses.

However, with respect to themselves, their cognizer and the *this* portions of their contents they are perceptual awarenesses.

Objection: Indirectness of an awareness of the *that* which causes recognition is not necessary for the awareness of the past to function as cause; all that is necessary is that there be such an awareness.

Prābhākara: No, for by the same reasoning inferential awareness can be classified as perceptual with respect to the *sādhya* part of its content on the ground that that which functions as cause in its production functions as cause qua awareness.

Gaṅgeśa: If recognitive awareness must be indirect in respect of its *that* part (i.e., if in "this is that same Devadatta", the *that* cannot itself be immediately cognized but must be inferential), then recognition can never take place, since the relevant awarenesses of *hetu*, etc., do not occur.

Prābhākara: The sense organ together with the awareness of the *that* portion constitutes the cause of recognition.

Gaṅgeśa: Then recognition becomes immediate awareness with respect to the *that* portion.

Prābhākara: What characterizes an immediate awareness is that it is produced by a sense organ independently of any other awareness.

Gaṅgeśa: That is unparsimonious, for the sense organ alone is sufficient as the characterizer. Anyway, recognitive awareness would become nonperceptual even with respect to the *this* portion, since it is caused by a sense organ jointly with awareness of *that*. But in the same awareness there can't be both dependence and nondependence on the same (other) awareness.

Prābhākara: But one part of the same awareness can be dependent and another part nondependent.

Gaṅgeśa: No, for the parts of an awareness, being contents (of that awareness) are not themselves produced by other awarenesses. So (pace the Prābhākaras) every awareness cannot be perceptual with respect to itself and its cognizer. For awarenesses (in these respects) are not produced by a sense organ, and to be an immediate awareness is to be produced by a sense organ.

Objection: Suppose we say that these respects are produced by a sense organ, viz., the internal organ.

Gaṅgeśa: Then inferential awareness would become perceptual with respect to the *sādhya* part of its content.

Objection: What determines the perceptual character of an awareness is just the property of being produced by the conditions of awareness as such.

Gaṅgeśa: That would be uneconomical. Furthermore, not every awareness is an ordinary one—thus not every awareness has causal conditions at all. And not even every ordinary awareness is perceptual. Moreover, no single kind of awareness is conditioned by awarenesses in general, nor is there such a thing as the collection of causal conditions of awarenesses in general.

5. (E610-612) Furthermore, what is called a "part" (*avayava*) of an awareness is really nothing other than its content. For awareness is without parts. Now an awareness is not (as the Prābhākara assumes) the cause of its content. What therefore follows is this: Inferential awareness and recognitive awareness are perceptual so far as their respective contents of *sādhya* and *thatness* are concerned. For, as we just remarked, a content is not caused by a propositional awareness (or any awareness at all, for that matter.)

Prābhākara: Since a recognitive awareness has *thatness* as its content, it must be caused by (previous) awareness of *thatness*. Likewise inferential awareness of the *sādhya* must be caused by previous awareness of the *sādhya*. These awarenesses, however, are not caused by any other awareness in respect to the cognizer, the *thisness* and the awarenessness they exhibit.

Gaṅgeśa: This cannot be accepted. For (a) an awareness being about some content does not consist in its being caused by an awareness of that content. Rather, it consists in the presence of that content in that awareness which is its possessor. Being present in that awareness, the content determines the character of that awareness as effect relative to whatever is its cause. (b) Besides, the Prābhākara account of perceptual awareness as an awareness not caused by any other awareness is too narrow, for it excludes, e.g., a perceptual awareness of the form "This is a man holding a stick." For such an awareness, being propositional, is as much caused by previous awareness of a qualifier as an inferential awareness.

Objection: Mediacy (*parokṣatva*) is an obstruction here (i.e., only mediate propositional awarenesses are caused by a previous awareness of the qualifier).

Gaṅgeśa: No, since mediacy does not pervade the *sādhya* (as it must to be a real obstruction). Here the *sādhya*, the property *being caused by a previous awareness of the qualifier*, is there in the recognitive awareness as well as in, say, the awareness of the recurrence of something which has a universal for its content. In neither of these awarenesses is the alleged obstruction *mediacy* present.

Objection: But this latter awareness, of recurrence, is not caused by previous awareness of a qualifier.

Gaṅgeśa: Yes it is, for being a recurrent feature means being present in a previously experienced individual as well as in the individual confronted now. Thus the previously experienced individual functions as the qualifier, and awareness of this previously experienced individual causes the perceptual awareness of recurrence. If this is not admitted the very first experience of the previous individual will have to be accepted as a perceptual awareness of recurrence. (But when we perceive an individual for the first time we do not perceive it as of this or that kind, i.e., we do not perceive it as sharing a recurrent feature with other individuals of the same kind.)

Prābhākara: These cases can be accommodated if D7 is understood as follows:

(D7a) Perceptual awareness is awareness not directly caused by a propositional awareness.

Recognitive awareness (even if it is caused by previous awareness of *thatness*) is directly caused by memory traces. Similarly the awareness of recurrence of a universal is directly caused by memory traces. Even the awareness of similarity is directly produced by the memory trace of the referent (*pratiyogin*, i.e., the thing to which it is similar). Thus the charge of underextension against D7 is answered.

Gaṅgeśa: Even so, D7a is too narrow to cover the perception of a man with a stick, which is caused by a previous direct awareness (not a memory trace) of the stick. It also fails to cover continuous perception (*dhārāvāhika pratyakṣa*). Generally, a previous awareness of a qualified object, being awareness of a qualifier, is the cause of the subsequent qualified perceptual awareness of that object. And memory traces do not cause any awarenesses other than memories. Otherwise recognition will become, as was said earlier, a case of memory.

Section Five: Sensory Connection (*sannikarṣavāda*)
Summary by K.K. Chakrabarti

(E613-615) A specific kind of sensory connection (*sannikarṣa*) is a causal condition of a specific kind of perception. Not all sensory connections are of the same kind. To enumerate: a substance is perceived through the sensory connection of contact, qualities and motions are perceived through inherence in what is in contact with the senses, etc., and absences are perceived through qualifierness.[50]

Objection: A substance may not be perceived even if the sense organ comes into contact with a small part; hence not contact, but contact with a big part, should be regarded as the causal condition.

Answer: Contact with a big part cannot be accepted as a causal condition of perception of substances in general, for this clearly does not hold in such cases as perception of the self, perception of the minimal perceptibilium etc.[51]

(E616-628) Objection: Since inherence in what inheres in what is in contact with the senses has to be accepted as a sensory connection for perception of color, etc., why not regard it as the sensory connection for perception of substances as well (and dispose of contact as a kind of sensory connection)?[52]

Answer: Since contact has to be accepted as the causal connection for perception of the self, it is regarded as the causal condition for the perception of other substances as well. Furthermore, even for the perception of substances which are wholes, or for the perception of external substances, it is more economical to regard contact as the causal condition.[53]

Objection: Why not regard inherence in (its) locus as the sensory connection, instead of inherence in what is in contact?

Answer: Unless contact with (its) locus is further specified as contact with that in which smell is inherent, it will be obviously unacceptable; with this specification, however, you've got what we say (i.e., contact of sense organ with smell's locus, i.e., that in which smell inheres).

Objection: Instead of "inherence in that which is in contact", why not take "contact with that in which the thing is inherent" as the connection?

Answer: This is the same thing turned around.

Objector: "Inherence in that which is in contact" is neither contact, nor inherence, nor both.

Answer: It is an indirect relation, viz., inherence in the locus of contact with the sense organ.

Objector: It has been held that colorness, etc., are perceived through inherence in what is inherent in what is in contact. But colorness, etc., don't exist.

Answer: Even if colorness, etc., were nonexistent this sensory connection would still have to be admitted for the perception of similarity among colors, etc. Similarity of color cannot be simply due to similarity of substance, for colors may be apprehended to be similar even when their loci are dissimilar.

On the strength of the awareness of sameness, tasteness, sweetness, smellness, etc., can be admitted to be universals. In the case of colorness, however, we do not have cognitions like "this is a color", "that is a color", etc.; instead we have cognitions like "blue is a color", "yellow is a color", etc. On the strength of such cognitions colorness can therefore also be admitted as a universal.

Objection: Why not say that the property of being a color is nothing but the property of being perceptible by the visual organ, the property of being a smell is nothing but the property of being perceptible by the olfactory organ, etc.?

Answer: No. Unless there are overriding considerations to the contrary the awareness of sameness should be the basis for the admission of universals. Further, if your suggestion were accepted, it would not be possible to infer the existence of unmanifested colors, smells, etc. Similar considerations go to show that blueness, etc., also are universals.

(E628-639) Objection: Why not suppose that there is only one blue, one red, etc. (instead of supposing that there are many blue colors, etc.)? The fact that the same blue belongs to many individuals does not prove that it is a universal: universals are revealed only by the configuration of parts and belong only to wholes made of parts.[54]

Answer: No. For we do have such an awareness as "the blue color has been destroyed by the application of heat and red color has arisen." Such an awareness cannot be dismissed as false, for there is no contrary evidence. Nor can it be said that it is inherence which is the object of this awareness of origin and decay, for inherence does not figure as the content of the awareness. Further, if one opts for one blue, one red, etc., one should also opt for one sweet taste, one fragrance, etc. It may be said that one could do so; but that would not be acceptable, for their origin and decay are also factors of experience. Finally, if there were only one sweet taste, how could one explain that some tastes are sweeter than others?

Objection: It has been said that sound is perceived by the auditory organ through the sensory connection called inherence. But then one should hear all sounds (all the time, for inherence is one and the same everywhere). It cannot be said in reply that only that sound which is originated within the periphery of the auditory organ is heard; for the locus of sound is *ākāśa*, which is one and the same everywhere.

Answer: Not so. Since sound is perceived, a sensory connection has got to be admitted. We hold that inherence as specified by contact with the ear is that sensory connection. Only that sound with which such a sensory connection is established is heard. Since we have such an awareness as "the sound is here and not there", it is established that sound is nonpervasive (even though the locus of sound is one and the same everywhere).[55]

Objection: It has been held that *ākāśa* as specified by the ear is the auditory organ. But why not say that *ākāśa* as specified by the source of sound, e.g., a musical instrument, is the auditory organ?

Answer: Since sound is heard only within the limit of the ear, *ākāśa* as specified by the ear is held to be the auditory organ; such a supposition is both necessary and economical. Further, only that which is in contact with the body and is also a necessary condition of direct awareness may be regarded as a sense organ.

E (639-644) Question: How can we account for the fact that the noise of the thunder in the sky is heard by many on the ground?

Answer: It may be supposed that due to the contact of a big volume of wind with the clouds, etc., another sound spreading in all directions and covering a wide region of space is produced from the initial sound; thus the same sound may be heard by everyone. Since the wind moves very fast, the subsequent sound may be heard without delay after the lapse of the initial sound.

Alternatively, it may be supposed that ten different sounds giving rise to sound streams in ten different directions are produced from the initial sound. Many sounds may be produced from the same sound either due to contacts with many gusts or due to many prior absences.

Prior absence has to be accepted as a causal condition for every effect, for otherwise we cannot explain why in spite of the availability of all causal conditions something originated is not produced once again. It cannot be objected that a totality of causal conditions can by virtue of its very nature produce only one effect (and that hence it is unnecessary to suppose that prior absence is a causal condition), for nonorigination of the effect should be explained on the basis of the nonavailability of the sum-total of causal conditions.[56]

Question: Do the causal conditions have to endure until the time of the origin of the effect?

Answer: No, except in the case of the inherence cause.

Objection: Inherence in what inheres has been admitted as a kind of sensory connection to account for the perception of soundness, etc. But there is no such thing as soundness.

Answer: The existence of soundness can be proved in the same manner as the existence of colorness, etc., above.

Section Six: Inherence (*samavāya*)
Summary by K.K. Chakrabarti

1. (645-655) Objection: The alleged inherence relation between the qualificand and the qualifier in an awareness such as "the cloth is white" is a content of that awareness. The universal property, quality or motion are experienced as mutually related to their possessors.

Gaṅgeśa: But in a relational awareness the relation is not apprehended as a qualifier, for it is not what one is initially aware of, nor is one aware (initially) that the relata (property and possessor, e.g.) are related by inherence to each other. The relation is not the qualificand either, for there is no such inherence that relates itself as qualificand to a qualifier. It cannot be either that inherence is apprehended as neither qualificand nor qualifier but just as itself, for there is no such perceptual awareness as "I am aware of inherence."[57]

Objection: An awareness such as "the pot is blue" has as content an inherence relation between qualifier and qualificand, because it is a relational awareness, like the awareness of one holding a stick.[58]

Gaṅgeśa: This argument is not sound. It is vitiated by the defect called "*arthāntara*" (having a different object) because the argument is applicable to self-linking connectors, inasmuch as there are negative relational awarenesses in which the relation is a negative self-linking connector. Furthermore the *hetu* (being a relational awareness) suffers from the fault of *aprayojaka* (it is supportless) because it is clear from cases of awarenesses of absences, etc., that a relational awareness may take place without a relation which is different from the relata.[59]

Objection: The awareness "this is here", involving a whole apprehended in its parts, etc., is caused by a relation between the substratum (*ādhāra*) and superstratum (*ādheya*), because it is a true (*yathārtha*) awareness of some thing being the substratum of some other thing, like the awareness "fruits are in the pot."

Gaṅgeśa: No. The *hetu* (being a true awareness of some thing being the substratum of some other thing) is deviant (*vyabhicāra*) as is clear from such cases of awareness as "absence of pot is here on the ground." For by a substratum is meant anything which is requisite for origination or maintenance in existence or making known.[60]

Objection: Sounds, universals, colors, etc., become connected with the sense organ, because they are perceived, like a pot. The connection is not contact. So it must be inherence. Now only what is in contact with a sense organ can be perceived, and this is why inherence is not perceived: there is no means of connection between inherence and any sense organ.

Gaṅgeśa: No. Self-linking connectors will have to be admitted in spite of the admission of inherence. Sound should be held to be perceived through a sense-object-connection called *indriyaviśeṣaṇatā* (a kind of self-linking connector), the universal through *indriyasambaddhaviśeṣaṇatā,* and so on.

Objector (a Prābhākara): A black pot turns into a red pot when baked. This change cannot be due to the two colors, for color is eternal and so both colors should have been perceived at the same time. Since colors are eternal, they are neither originated nor destroyed. Hence it must be the relation between them which is destroyed. That relation is inherence.[61]

Gaṅgeśa: This cannot be accepted. There is uncontradicted awareness that the black color is destroyed and the red one produced. Furthermore, we do not become aware that inherence is produced or destroyed. For you hold that inherence is imperceptible. Moreover, if you accept the above argument, why do you not accept also that wholes and smells, etc., are also eternal and that it is their inherence (in their loci) which is noneternal? The awareness of origin and decay cannot be set aside as false without sufficient reason.

Inference: An awareness of being qualified by a quality, a motion or a universal has a relation with the qualifier as its content, because it is a relational awareness, like the awareness of one holding a stick. In this inference the *hetu* is not deviant, because the awareness of a thing qualified by absence also has a self-linking connector as a content. The defect of *arthāntara* mentioned above does not arise, since the relation which is being proved to be the content of awarenesses of being qualified by qualities, motions or universals is also proved by virtue of the nature of the *pakṣa* (being such an awareness) to be the same relation, on the grounds of economy. And that relation is inherence, not self-linking connection, for the respective natures (of relata) are infinitely various, and moreover other relations are not admissible in the present case.[62]

Alternatively, it might be argued thus: The (perceptual) awarenesses of being qualified by a quality, or by a motion, or by a universal property, are caused (partly) by the relation with the qualifier, because they are true relational awarenesses, like the awareness of one holding a stick. A relation with a qualifier, insofar as it is a cause, is admitted to be a single thing: on the grounds of economy a certain kind of effect has to be causally explained by an identical kind of cause. The said relation thus is not a self-linking connector, for self-linking connections are unique to each situation. The charge of being "supportless" (*aprayojaka*) is not valid: if perception of relatedness did not have the relation as a content or were not caused by a relation, even such things as a cow or a horse could also be known to be so related.[63]

2. (E660–665) The Navyas argue: An awareness of being qualified by a quality, motion or universal has as content a relation with a qualifier different from the relata of that relation, because it is an awareness of being qualified by a qualifier whose content is not dependent on the content of the other relation, or (alternatively) because it is an awareness qualified by a qualifier not determined (*nirūpya*) by a determination (*nirūpaka*) of the other (relation). Thus an awareness qualified by an absence, etc., is not a counterexample. A relation is a regulator (*niyamaka*) of that awareness that is characterized by the qualifier in contrast to that which is not characterized by the qualifier.[64]

Alternatively, inherence may be proved as the sensory connection required for the perception of quality, motion or universal. For perception cannot take place without sensory connection and other sensory connections (like contact) are eliminated. Inherence is proved to be one only on the strength of its own nature and of economy; therefore, it cannot be a case of self-linking connector, for those are many.

Inherence is perceptible whenever its two relata are perceptible.[65]

3. (E666–674) Objection: Then, on the basis that there are qualified awarenesses involving absences and since contact and inherence have to be eliminated as the connector there, it should also be admitted that absence is related to its locus by a numerically single relation which is both a content and a cause of such an awareness.[66]

Answer: No. If the relation called qualifiedness (*vaiśiṣṭya*) were regarded as numerically single in the way inherence is, it would follow that even in a locus where there is a piece of cloth, but no pot, there would be the awareness of absence of cloth; for the relation with absence of pot and with absence of cloth would have to be one and the same![67] To avoid this difficulty those relations may be regarded as as numerous as absences are. But in that case the loci and the absences may be regarded as self-connected.

Objection: If inherence is numerically single, how can it be explained that some things are colored and some not?[68]

Answer: Although inherence of color resides in air (which is colorless) there is absolute absence of color in air, but not in a pot. That this is so is due to the respective natures of the loci.[69]

4. (E675–698) Objection: Color and pot are not related by inherence but by nondifference. Like the awareness "the man holds a stick" (where the man and the stickholder are nondifferent) the awareness "the pot is blue" is an awareness of nondifference between blue and pot. If "the pot is blue" and "the man holds a stick" are supposed to be awarenesses of relationships, then like the awareness "the pot is blue" there should be the awareness "the man is a stick", and like "the man has a stick" there should be "the pot has blue."

Alternatively, what one is aware of in "the pot is blue" is that blueness and potness, which are respectively the limitors of the fact that blue is the qualifier and pot is the qualificand, belong to the same thing, just as it is known through "the man holds a stick" that the property of being a stickholder and the property of being a man belong to the same thing. The thesis of nondifference is not being advanced merely on the basis of linguistic usage, but on the basis of the awareness of nondifference between blue and pot.

Gaṅgeśa: If the words "white" and "cloth" meant the same thing, just as there is no such usage as "the pot is pitcher" (which should be distinguished from "the pot is a pitcher"), there should not also have been the usage "the cloth is white". Again, just as a blind person perceives a piece of cloth, he should also have perceived color, or just as he does not perceive color, he should not have perceived cloth also. Furthermore, just as "pot is not pot" is contradictory, so also "the pot is not white" should have been contradictory, for white and pot are allegedly identical. Moreover, when the black color of the pot is destroyed due to the application of heat and the red color is produced in the pot, the pot too should have been destroyed and produced.

On the other hand, if whiteness is different from the substance, then such a usage as "the cloth is white" becomes in order. It also explains why a blind man perceives the (white) thing but does not perceive the white color.

Objection: When we say that whiteness and the substance are nondifferent we mean that the relation is not inherence but a self-linking connector, i.e., the nature of the substance itself constitutes the relationship.

Answer: But then whiteness should have been perceived by the tactual organ, by which the substance is perceived. And then it would not be the case that each should be regularly cognized through one organ and not another. The fact that there is this regularity between apprehending organ and the kind of thing apprehended is itself evidence for the difference between the quality and the substance. If they were nondifferent, how could there be such an awareness of the differences as "the white color of the cloth"?

Objection: The substance and the quality are both nondifferent and different (*bhedābheda*), as proved by the reasonings just reviewed.

Question: How can such mutually exclusive categories as nondifference and difference be combined together?

Objector: There is no contradiction, any more than there is when we speak of the presence and absence of contact in a single thing. Anyway, you too have to admit with reference to a pot which was previously black and has become red that the black thing is not a black thing. This commits you to identity and difference. It may also be argued thus: Difference is nonlocuspervading, because it is a property pervaded by an absenceness which belongs to an eternal absence, like absolute absence.

Gaṅgeśa: The absence of the counterpositive may belong to the same thing in which the counterpositive is present insofar as different limitors are involved. Similarly, the pot insofar as it is black is different from the pot insofar as it is red. Thus it is clear that in such an awareness as "the pot is blue" the relation with blue becomes the content (which implies that blue and the pot are different). It is intended that the awareness amounts to "the pot has blue (color)." The word "blue" in "the pot is blue" singnifies "possessor of blue color."

Objection: But why shouldn't the sensory connection in question be qualifierness or being a qualifier of what is related to a sense organ etc.? Why inherence?

Gaṅgeśa: Sounds, etc., are experienced as qualifying their loci through inherence. Hence necessarily inherence is cognized first and then the fact of their being qualifiers. (Hence it is preferable to regard inherence as the sensory connection.)

Objection: In the awareness of an absence, being a qualifier of what is related to a sense organ must not be the sensory connection, for then one could perceive with one's eyes even absence of waterness, etc., belonging to atoms, etc., with which the visual organ is connected. Instead, *svagrahasambandhaviśeṣaṇatā* should be taken as the sensory connection (i.e., it should be held that absence is perceived insofar as it qualifies that with which the sense organ is connected provided that thing is perceptible by that sense organ). And qualifierness should not be regarded as a sense-object connection, for then absence of waterness, which qualifies the visual organ, could be perceived by that visual organ.

Gaṅgeśa: Because of economy, being a qualifier of what is related to a sense organ should be regarded as the sensory connection in cases of absence. The difficulty you allege does not arise: where the presence of something is opposed to its nonperception, only there is its absence perceived through the senses. The presence of waterness, etc., in the eyes is however not opposed to nonperception. Similarly, there is no difficulty in regarding qualifierness as the sensory connection for the perception of absence of sound: presence of sound is opposed to its nonperception; the presence of waterness, etc., in the eyes is however not opposed to nonperception.

Objection: Let us suppose that an absence is related to its locus not through qualifierness (a kind of self-connector) but through inherence, for absence is also apprehended to qualify its locus.

Answer: If that were so posterior absence would have ceased with the destruction of its inherence cause. (When the inherence cause is destroyed, so is also the effect which is related to it by way of inherence.) It cannot be said that only positive entities may cease to exist, for prior absence too ceases (when its counterpositive is produced).

Section Seven: Nonapprehension (*anupalabdhi*)
Summarized by K.K. Chakrabarti

1. (E699–709) (According to Gaṅgeśa, an absence is perceived through a sense organ by way of the sensory connection called qualifierness, i.e., absence is perceived insofar as it qualifies its locus with which the sense organ is connected. This was explained in the previous section.)

Pūrvapakṣa

Bhāṭṭa Mīmāṃsaka Objection: An absence is not grasped through any sense organ, but rather through nonapprehension of what is perceptible (*yogyānupalabdhi*), since the absence of something is cognized only when there is nonapprehension of that thing. And nonapprehension (or nonperception) is a separate instrument of knowledge.

Objection to the Bhāṭṭa: Then why not say that awareness of the presence of something also does not take place through a sense organ but through nonapprehension of its absence?

Bhāṭṭa: No. A sense organ is invariably required for grasping the presence of a thing; otherwise visual perception of a pot could take place even with the eyes closed through nonapprehension of absence of the pot. That is why, although nonapprehension of absence may be invariably involved as a converse process in awareness of a presence, it cannot be regarded as its cause, for it is rendered dispensable by the sense organ.

Objector to the Bhāṭṭa: So, since a sense organ is invariably required for (direct) awareness of an absence, it should be regarded as the cause of (direct) awareness of absence (just as it is regarded as a cause of direct awareness of presence).

Bhāṭṭa: No. The visual organ, etc., cannot be connected to an absence. Its role is limited to apprehension of a locus.[70]

Objector to the Bhāṭṭa: Awareness of the locus is the operation of the sense organ; the sense organ cannot be rendered dispensable through its own operation![71]

Bhāṭṭa: Not so. First the sense organ has to be established as a cause of the direct awareness of an absence; then one can speak of its operation. But the sense organ cannot be established to be the cause, for there is no conceivable connection between it and an absence. A sense organ cannot apprehend something which qualifies that with which the sense organ is connected if there is no connection between that qualifier and the sense organ. If that were not so, there would have been no need to admit sensory connections such as inherence in what is in contact, etc., and a sense organ would be able to apprehend, say, a stick belonging to the man with whom the sense organ was connected even though there was no connection between the stick and the sense organ.

Objector to the Bhāṭṭa: Precisely. Qualifierness is the needed relation, just because the other connections like contact, etc., are not suitable, in the same way as it is inferred that inherence in what is in contact is the proper connection for the perception of color.

Bhāṭṭa: In those cases the connection (such as inherence in what is in contact, etc.) is admitted because sense organs are in any case required and their function is not exhausted otherwise. In the present case, however, it is simpler to suppose that the function of the sense organ is exhausted in apprehending the locus. So an additional kind of sensory connection need not be hypothesized, since it would be superfluous. Otherwise why not hold that air is perceived because the skin is invariably required for its cognition and the function of the skin is not exhausted in apprehending touch qualities.[72]

Again: On the one hand if qualifierness is admitted as a sensory connection absence may be said to be cognized through a sense organ; on the other hand, if absence is said to be cognized through the sense organ, qualifierness has to be admitted as a sensory connection. Thus there is circularity.

Furthermore, qualifierness is the very nature of what is apprehended. In the other cases the nature of what is apprehended is not posited as the sensory connection; instead contact and inherence are posited as (distinct) sensory connections, etc. Indeed, in every such case the connection is different from the things connected. If the nature of the thing apprehended could be the connection, let that be the case also for apprehension of color, etc.; where is the need for distinct relations such as contact or inherence?

Objector to the Bhāṭṭa: Light is sometimes required for the awareness of absence. This shows that the visual organ is also required, for light is an aid to the visual organ alone. (And if it is accepted that a sense organ, such as the visual organ, is the cause of the awareness of absence the postulation of nonapprehension as a separate instrument of knowledge is ruled out.)

Bhāṭṭa: No. The visual organ cannot be the cause since there is no way it can be connected to an absence. On the other hand, that light is required for the awareness of an absence is due to the fact that light is required for the awareness of its counterpositive.

Objector to the Bhāṭṭa: Since the counterpositive is apprehended through the visual organ it should be admitted that the absence of that counterpositive is also apprehended by the visual organ.

Bhāṭṭa: The visual organ cannot be accepted as the cause, for lack of connection and because its function is exhausted in apprehending the locus.

Objector to the Bhāṭṭa: If that were true, even a person who has become blind could directly apprehend absence of a remembered yellow color in something blue which he has apprehended through touch. This difficulty would not arise if it is admitted that absence is apprehended through that sense organ through which the counterpositive is apprended, for the blind person lacks the visual organ.

Bhāṭṭa: Not so. Absence may be cognized through nonapprehension only when its locus is apprehended through the sense organ through which the counterpositive is apprehended. Otherwise the absence of waterness too could be apprehended in an atom with which the visual organ is in contact.

Objector to the Bhāṭṭa: If the above were true, how can it be apprehended that there is absence of color in air, or absence of the bitter taste in water or absence of fragrance in a stone? For air, which is the locus of absence of color, cannot be apprehended through the visual organ through which the counterpositive, viz., color, is apprehended, and similarly *mutatis mutandis* in the other cases.

Bhāṭṭa: No. Inferential cognitions of the absence of color in air possess nonapprehension as their mark.

Objection to the Bhāṭṭa: I can prove my thesis by inference as follows: The given awareness of an absence is through a sense organ (and not through nonapprehension); because it is a direct awareness. The sensory connection called "qualfierness" can also be postulated on this basis. It cannot be said that the awareness in question is not a direct awareness, for if it were a mediate awareness it should have had another awareness as its causal condition *par excellence.* In some cases of course the awareness of absence may be mediate, as when that awareness is produced through verbal testimony or through inference. In those cases the awareness of an absence is produced through some awareness as causal condition *par excellence.* But in the present case (e.g., when it is known just by looking that there is no pot on the floor) the awareness has been produced without any awareness as the causal condition *par excellence.* Hence it must be direct.

2. (E711–716) Bhāṭṭa: This cannot be accepted. First of all, mediateness (*parokṣatva*) is not a proper universal, because it overlaps with being a direct awareness (*anubhavatva*).[73] On the other hand, by "mediate awareness" should be meant any awareness other than an immediate (*aparokṣa*) one. If construed in this way, an awareness of an absence has to be regarded as mediate, like memory (which is also mediate but not produced by an awareness functioning as its causal condition *par excellence*). still they are different from one

another. Similarly, neither nonapprehension nor direct awareness is produced by an awareness playing the role of causal condition *par excellence,* still they are different, because the latter is produced by a sense organ and the former is not. Thus "direct" awareness may be construed as any awareness which is produced by a sense organ, "indirect" awareness as any awareness not produced by a sense organ. The difference between these two kinds of awareness is that the latter is produced by an awareness functioning as the causal condition *par excellence,* while the former is not so produced. But such an explanation is unnecessarily complex and also fails to apply to memory.

Objector to the Bhāṭṭa: Nonapprehension cannot be an instrument of knowledge of absence, for an external object may be apprehended through the internal organ only when it is aided by a positive instrument of knowledge (viz., the sense organ).

Bhāṭṭa: If the above were true inference too could not give us knowledge about external objects.

Objector to the Bhāṭṭa: In every other case, such as inference, etc., absence is apprehended by the same instrument by which the counterpositive is apprehended. In the present case too the counterpositive is apprehended by the sense organ, so its absence likewise should be apprehended by the sense organ.

Bhāṭṭa: No. Only positive existents may be apprehended through inference, etc. Absence(s), being (a) negative (thing, a nonexistent) cannot be apprehended through any of them.

Objector to the Bhāṭṭa: Nonapprehension cannot be an instrument of knowledge, for it is devoid of any operation. Only that which is characterized by an operation can be a causal condition *par excellence.*

Bhāṭṭa: By a "causal condition *par excellence*" we mean that condition which is invariably followed by origination of the effect. On that understanding there is no difficulty in regarding nonapprehension as a causal condition *par excellence* of knowledge.

Siddhānta

3. (E716-724) Gaṅgeśa: Apprehending the locus of absence by the same sense organ through which the counterpositive is apprehended cannot be a causal condition for apprehending absence, for no such condition is required for knowing that something was absent somewhere. (So the objection to the Bhāṭṭa view that even a blind person could apprehend absence of color under certain conditions remains unanswered.)

Furthermore, it has to be admitted that the absence of color in air, e.g., is apprehended through the sense organ and not through nonapprehension as its mark; for in these cases nonapprehension cannot become known. Indeed, no authoritative statement conveying such a nonapprehension is available either.

Objection: The nonapprehension of color in air could still take place, like the absence of pot on the ground.

Answer: But remember that on your (Bhāṭṭa) view awareness is imperceptible. Therefore, absence of awareness cannot be apprehended through *yogyānupalabdhi*—nonapprehension of what is perceptible (since awareness is not perceptible). Mere nonapprehension which remains unknown cannot produce an awareness of absence.

Objection: Then let us say that awareness *is* perceptible!

Answer: Then in the case of absence of pot on the floor also the known nonapprehension of the pot could be the mark for apprehending the absence; there would then be no need to admit nonapprehension as a separate instrument of knowledge.

Objection: The awareness of the absence of a pot on the floor is not produced by an awareness functioning as its instrumental cause (i.e., it is not inferential) , because it arises without any involvement of such a mark.

Answer: So also is the case of absence of color in air, etc.

Objection: Absence of being known as possessed of color, etc., or alternatively nonapprehension of possession of color, etc., inferred on that basis could be the mark for awareness of absence of color in air.

Answer: Not so. Absence of being known as possessed of color likewise cannot be apprehended. Nonapprehension cannot be inferred merely from the lack of physical and linguistic activity, for an awareness which produces indfference (*upekṣā*) also does not lead to any physical or linguistic activity. Furthermore, if the above were true, absence of being known as possessed of a pot or such nonapprehension inferred from that basis could be the mark for inferring that there is absence of pot on the floor. Why admit an additional instrument of knowledge called nonapprehension?

Again, since the awareness of an absence is produced by an absence which (we both agree) is an objective entity, and since it is of the nature of a direct awareness, it should be held that such awareness is caused by the sense organ.

Objection: Suppose that Caitra, who has come out of a room, is asked by another whether Maitra was in that room. Suppose further that Caitra thinks for a moment and realizes that Maitra was not in that room since he did not apprehend Maitra there and says accordingly that Maitra was not there. Such an awareness to the effect that something is absent somewhere cannot be a case of memory, since there was no original experience of absence of Maitra in that room. Further, awareness of the said absence takes place through nonapprehension alone, without any operation of the sense organ. Thus it is clear that awareness of absence arises through nonapprehension in some cases. The thesis may then be extended to other cases as well.

Answer: The nonapprehension through which the said absence is supposedly known in the above case cannot itself remain unknown. If, however, nonapprehension were to be itself known there would be an infinite regress; since nonapprehension is itself a case of absence, it would have to be apprehended by another nonapprehension, and so on. On the other hand, the said absence may be apprehended through the mark; then the admission of nonapprehension as a separate instrument of knowledge is not necessary.

Since the awareness of the absence of color in air cannot be inferential, and since the sense organ is invariably required for such an awareness to take place, it becomes established that such awareness is produced by the sense organ. Then it also becomes necessary to hypothesize qualifierness as the requisite sensory connection. Thus the awareness of absence (in the given case) may be regarded as perceptual.

Section Eight : Absence (*abhāva*)
Summary by K.K. Chakrabarti

"T" references are to the translation in Bimal Krishna Matilal, *The Navya-Nyāya Doctrine of Negation* (RB 5341)

Pūrvapakṣa

1. (E730-731; T109-111) Opponent: An absence is a positive entity (*bhāva*), and is grasped through contact, etc., and not through qualifierness (as supposed by Gaṅgeśa).

Old Nyāya: There is no such unsublated awareness as "there is no pot in this place." This awareness of absence does not have the place as its content, for then such an awareness might occur also when there is a pot on the floor.

Objection: The content of the awareness is the bare place.

Old Nyāya: No, since the bare place is nothing but the floor. If the said awareness had only the bare ground as its content it could not be explained why an absence is known to be located on the ground, though it is clear that the place is the locus.

Objection: An absence must be located somewhere. So there must be, according to you, some special feature in the place where the absence is located, a property other than being that place, since that place might have a pot on it.

Old Nyāya: No, since this special feature is just the presence of each absence.

Objection: Where in particular does an absence occur, then?

Old Nayāya: Where it is apprehended to do so, i.e., where it does in fact occur. If it were otherwise,one would reject universals too, since we could substitute an appeal to some special feature in cows.

2. (E731-732; T111-113) Opponent: Still, in what kind of place does an absence occur?

Answer: If the question is what kind of place it was before the absence occurred on it, the answer is that it was a place with a pot in it. And at the time of the absence, it is a place with an absence of pot in it. And there is no time in between.

Opponent: What is cognized in a negative awareness is the ground's property of being a content of an awareness of a mere *that* i.e., of the place alone.

Answer: Oh what an explanation! Awareness of a place on the ground that has a pot on it is also an awareness of "a mere *that*."

Opponent: No, in that case we cognize both the place and the pot.

Answer: If we did we wouldn't cognize the ground alone, but just *place-and-pot*!

Opponent: We do cognize the place alone, since immediately after cognizing the pot in that place we cognize the place as distinct from the pot.

Answer: Then it is that second cognition that is the awareness of a mere place.

3. (E733-735; T113-115) Opponent: We define "absence (of pot)" as an awareness of the place which arises only from causal factors other than the counterpositive (viz., pot) and anything pervaded by that counterpositive.

Answer: "Only" indicates negation and so begs the question—which is, after all, how to analyze negation.

Opponent: All right: the absence of pot is simply an awareness which has the place and not pot as its content.

Answer: Same problem: negation has yet to be analyzed. Anyhow, you cannot reduce an absence to an awareness. An absence depends for its identification on being aware of what its counterpositive is, while an awareness can be cognized without knowing a counterpositive.

Opponent: Though in order to speak of an absence we must be aware of its counterpositive, we can nevertheless have a simple awareness of absence *per se* (without being aware of its counterpositive).

Answer: There is no evidence of that.

Opponent: The awareness of an absence takes place when the sense organ is connected with the locus, but not with both the locus and the counterpositive, and there is memory of the counterpositive. The absence is nothing other than such an awareness of only locus preceded by memory of the counterpositive.

Answer: Absurd! One couldn't know a mere locus in the dark, then, and since one doesn't remember—say—thorns, one would be pricked by the thorns. Again, if a dam breaks where no one is watching the water would not flow out, since no one would be there to cognize the bare place (which cognition, *ex hypothesi*, is the absence of water!). Finally, as soon as one stops being aware of a bare place, a pot that was smashed should reappear, since the absence of absence of pot is just pot. If absence is not an independent entity, as you claim, we can never first have an awareness of pot in a place and then be aware of the absence of that pot at that place when the pot is smashed, since on your view nothing has been changed by the fall of the hammer.

5.(E736-739; T115-119) Prābhākara: The cause of our speaking of absence of pot in a place is just that awareness of the place which is different from the awareness of the place having the pot. Actually there are two kinds of absences—(1) locative (*vyadhikaraṇa*) absences, in which the locus and the counterpositive are named by nouns with different case-endings, and (2) nominative (*samānādhikaraṇa*) absences, where the nouns have the same, e.g., the nominative case-endings. The cause of our speaking of a locative absence is our awareness of the locus (the place, say), an awareness which is *not* an awareness of the locus as lacking the counterpositive. The cause of our speaking of nominative absence, on the other hand, is just the denial of identity, i.e., the declaration that two things are different in nature from each other. So no mutual dependence arises, since what the Nyāya takes to be the cause of the awareness of an absence we take as the cause of our speaking of absences.

The Naiyāyika, on the other hand, is forced to recognize as we do direct awarenesses of absences, since he analyzes qualified awarenesses into their simple constituents. So, just as an awareness of a blue pot requires awarenesses of blue and of pot, so awareness of the absence of pot on the ground presupposes conception-free awarenesses of pot, ground and absence.

Objector to the Prābhākara: The cause of speaking of an absence is the nonapprehension (*anupalabdhi*) of a locus as possessing a counterpositive.

Prābhākara: No, since even when we apprehend a locus as possessing a counterpositive we may still speak of its absence, as e.g. in "this pot was not here before." Furthermore, we do not accept an entity such as "mutual absence" (*anyonyābhāva*). The difference between "there is a pot on the ground" and "there is no pot on the ground" is an essential (*svarūpa*) difference and not a case of mutual absence; otherwise there will be infinite regress or self-dependence. Even if for argument's sake we accept that absences are independent entities, still there is no proof for mutual absences or, for that matter, absolute absences, held in Nyāya to be eternal. The reason is that in these cases no actual entity is involved other than the mere locus. The counterpositive is thought about but is not there in actuality. Indeed, it cannot be either identical with or possessed by the locus. (E.g., in "the pot is not a cloth" or "air has no color" the counterpositive is never present in the locus.) After all, it is for precisely the same reason that you yourself do not allow an absence to be the locus of another absence.

6. (E740-747; T119-124) Objector to the Prābhākara: What differentiates one awareness from another is difference between their contents. But between awareness of a place and awareness of the-place-with-pot-on-it there is, on the Prābhākara view, no difference.

Prābhākara: No, for the whole complex of causal factors help to differentiate them. We only disagree in that you invoke mutual absences instead of essential natures in differentiating them.

Objector to the Prābhākara: How can the place which is that place that has the pot be different from it?

Prābhākara: You have the same difficulty in establishing your mutual absence through awareness that the two things do not have a common locus. After all, you allow that the same place is limited by pot at one time and absence of pot at another—yet it's the same place!

Objector to the Prābhākara: How can there be a doubt whether there is a pot on the ground or not on your view? In both cases the counterpositive will be something merely thought of, and so there should be (not doubt but) awareness of absence, which you take to be either the same as the mere locus or as the awareness of that locus.

Prābhākara: Doubt can happen because of some defect in the sense organs that precludes our properly ascertaining whether the locus is or is not different from (say) the-place-with-a pot-on-it.

Objector to the Prābhākara: Since each case of a place and or awareness of a place is different from the next, they have no common property—so how is it that we speak of them all as cases of absence?

Prābhākara: The same problem arises for you who take absence as a separate entity: there is no proper universal absenceness, since mutual absences cannot have absenceness in them (since absenceness is the property of having mutual absence with presence).

Objector to the Prābhākara: Then we explain absenceness as being contradictory to a presence (*bhāvavirodhitva*).[74]

Prābhākara: No, since being contradictory can be explained only by reference to an absence.

Objector: O.K., absenceness is to be that which has a presence as its counterpositive.

Prābhākara: No, for absence of absence is the positive thing itself and that does not have something positive as its counterpositive.

Objector: Absenceness is being devoid of existence (*sattāśūnyatva*).

Prābhākara: But existence itself lacks existence, yet it isn't an absence! And "being devoid of" involves the notion of absence.

Objector to the Prābhākara: Absenceness is that property of a thing *x* such that *x* has the constant absence of existence; that constant absence can be cognized even when absenceness is not cognized.

Prābhākara: No, for *x* must be an absence, and we do not accept (nor do you!) that an absence can have another absence.

Objector to the Prābhākara: Absenceness is that property of *x* such that there is no cognition of existence in *x*. There is no existence in universal properties but it is erroneously cognized there; our reason for rejecting it is because of the contradiction that results. Since we are quite aware that existence is incompatible with absenceness there is no problem with this analysis.

Prābhākara : But "incompatibility" is nothing other than the very nature of a thing (here, the nature of absence).

Objector: No, incompatibility is the nonconcurrence (*sahānavasthāna*) of two things in the same locus.

Prābhākara: That involves self-residence, since nonconcurrence is the absence of concurrence.

Objector: Absenceness is difference from presence (*bhāvabhinnatva*).

Prābhākara: Well, either this difference is the same as the thing's nature or as a mutual absence, and we have shown the problems with those answers above.

7. (E747-750; T125-128) Objector to the Prābhākara: Let us say that absence is a single entity though instanced in various places.[75]

Prābhākara: Then this single absence must be eternal. But prior and posterior absences are not eternal. Besides, what happens to absence of pot when a pot is produced? So it is better to adopt our view, and to accept that it is a specific awareness of the ground which occasions a specific awareness of an absence. And this specific awareness is both the content and the instrument of our knowledge, since cognitions are according to us self-illuminating (*svaprakāśa*).

Objector to the Prābhākara: If awareness of mere locus is the same as the absence, and awareness is self-illuminating, one need not cognize the counterpositive at all.

Prābhākara: Yes, there is need, not in order to become aware of the absence, but in order to speak about it.

Objector: The rule is: where one desires to speak about *x* and is aware of *x*, one needs nothing further in order to speak of it.

Prābhākara: Surely not. One can know that *x* is long by contrast with *y*, and yet not be able to speak of it, since he needs to know that length is a matter of a greater number of units lying between in comparison with what is "short" in order to be able to express the difference accurately.

(As for objections raised above:) The smashed pot does not reappear, for absence of absence of pot is not a pot, but rather an awareness—just as absence of pot is an awareness, so absence of that awareness is another awareness. And it doesn't follow that water will not flow from a broken dam just because no humans are around to cognize it, because there will after all be birds and insects around, etc.

Objector to the Prābhākara: On your view everyone should be liberated merely by being aware of themselves. Since liberation is absence of bondage (*saṃsāra*), and on your view that absence is nothing but an awareness of the bare locus—here, the self—anyone aware of himself will be liberated![76]

Prābhākara: But we postulate a cause only if some specific effect—here, liberation for everyone alike—is found to occur. But it isn't.

Siddhānta

8. (E751-759; T128-134) Gaṅgeśa: (Here is) the correct view: An absence is always apprehended along with a counterpositive, since we only cognize an absence as absence of *x* or *y*, etc. Awareness of the counterpositive contributes to the awareness of the absence itself, not merely to our ability to speak about it; the speech act could not occur without the prior awareness of the counterpositive. Absence cannot be explained away either as the bare locus or its awareness, for the bare locus may be apprehended without the awareness of the counterpositive, and the counterpositive likewise does not become the content of the awareness of bare locus.

Objection: It is only talk of negation that can be shown to require awareness of the counterpositive.

Gaṅgeśa: No. In an awareness that the pot is not here it is the pot that is experienced to be the counterpositive of the absence, and talk of negation presupposes awareness of absence.

(You argued above that talk of "long" and "short" required more than awareness of size. But) long and short are themselves different sizes, not properties of sizes. At the time of becoming aware of a substance we may not become aware of these sizes and so we shall not be able to speak of them. (The rule cited by the objector in Section 7 holds. Usage presupposes acquaintance.)

Objector: All right, we'll grant that prior to our awareness of an absence we must have been aware of its counterpositive. Still, assuming such awareness, it is our awareness of the bare locus—the ground—which is grasped as the absence of which you speak.

Gaṅgeśa: No. We don't say "the place is an absence of pot," but instead "absence of pot is at that place," and that is because in the latter something besides the place is manifested, viz., the counterpositive. Besides, on your view it is a sufficient condition for *x* to be an absence that someone speak of it thus, but this creates circularity, since to speak of it thus one must first be aware that it is an absence.

Or if you mean that the place necessarily possesses a counterpositive, then it will never appear without that counterpositive, which is absurd. Or if you say that it has a counterpositive only when we speak of it as having one, this will again bring in circularity.

Section Nine: Connection of Content and Illumination (*viṣayālokasannikarṣa*)

Summary by K.K. Chakrabarti

1. (E770-787) The six kinds of sensory connections are causal conditions of specific different kinds of perceptual awareness. A particular contact between light and the content is also a causal condition of (visual) perceptual awarenesses. Contact between light and the visual organ is not such a causal condition, however, for an object which is in the dark cannot be perceived by the visual organ even when that organ is in contact with the light, while perception does take place if the object is in contact with light while the visual organ isn't.

The manifested color of light is also a causal condition, for it is related by way of both positive and negative concomitance.

Furthermore, the manifested color in the content is also a causal conditon, for otherwise the visual organ, warmth, and so forth would also be visible.[77] It should be noted that manifestedness is a characteristic which belongs to color and not to the substance possessing color. Manifestedness cannot be large-sized-ness (*mahattva*) belonging to the substance. One way of explaining the nature of manifestedness is as follows: manifestedness is the possession of a universal pervaded by colorness; absence of that is nonmanifestedness; similarly of touch, etc. Upon such a construction neither manifestedness nor unmanifestedness is regarded as a universal.

Only those substances which have manifested color are visually perceived. All substances which are visually perceived also have the twin characteristics of possessing large-sized-ness and of being made of many substances or parts. Of these two latter features, however, only large-sized-ness and not the property of being made of many parts is regarded as a causal condition of the visual perception of substances, since the resulting view is more economical. Both manifested color and large-sized-ness should be accepted as causal conditions, because additional excellence of the object in these two respects results in the improvement of one's perception.

Section Ten: Perceptibility of Air (*vāyupratyakṣa*)
Summary by K.K. Chakrabarti
Pūrvapakṣa

1. (E788-797) Opponent:
(Inf1) Air (*vāyu*) is perceptible, because it is the locus of perceptible touch, like a pot.

Inf1 is not without support. Largesizedness and possession of manifested touch are conducive to tactual perception. Possession of manifested color is not a conducive factor because it is superfluous. Furthermore, we have the awareness "the wind is blowing" as a result of contact with the skin, as well as the awareness "the wind is cold."

Objector to the opponent: A substance that is not visually perceived cannot be tactually perceived; air is not visually perceptible, and so it isn't tactually perceptible either.

Opponent: Then it would follow that only the visual organ can grasp substances, and that the only thing the organ of touch (the skin) apprehends is the touch quality. But it is difficult to set aside our awarenesses that these things happen (that we see colors and feel substances). So, we should admit that both the tactile substance and its quality are perceived through the organ of touch. And thus air should be held perceptible.

Objector to the opponent: When a substance is perceived its number, etc., are also perceived, unless that is made impossible by some defect. But in the case of air these characteristics are never perceived. Hence air is not perceived.

Opponent's answer: There is no such regularity. A cloth hanging down the shoulder may be perceived although its number and size, etc., are not perceived.

Objector to the opponent: A substance is perceptible through an external sense organ only if it possesses a specific quality (*viśeṣa-guṇa*) that is perceptible through a noneternal sense organ, or alternatively if it possesses both a nonatomic size that is noneternal together with a specific quality.

Opponent: If either were the case, even the bilious substance belonging to the tongue and the wind-blown fragrant substance should be perceptible.

Objector to the opponent: Then having both nonatomic size and manifested color are the factors conducive for the perception of a substance through an external sense organ. Thus air is imperceptible.

Opponent: But having manifested color cannot be a conducive factor, for then the bilious substance in the eyes would have been perceived.

Objector to the opponent: Then having manifested touch is alone the conducive factor for perception of a substance through an external sense organ. (This supposition is possible because all visually perceived substances, with the exception of the disputed case of radiance (*prabhā*), possess manifested touch.) And radiance is not thus rendered imperceptible, for radiance is really a quality, the color of a fiery substance and not the substance itself. So air is perceptible, since it has manifested touch.

Siddhānta

2. (E797-806) Gaṅgeśa: Inf1 is not acceptable. If possession of manifested touch alone were the conducive factor for tactual perception of a substance, summer warmth and wind-blown hot and cold things would be perceived, not to speak of their number, size, contact, disjunction and motion. But we don't perceive such things. Similarly, possession of manifested color cannot by itself be the conducive factor. Hence the two together must be held to jointly be the conducive factors for external perception of substances. It then follows that air cannot be perceived. This is the view of the "new ones" (*navīnāḥ*).

The "knowers of the tradition" (*sampradāyavid*), however, prefer to regard possession of manifested color alone as the conducive factor and hold air to be imperceptible for that reason.

Objection: But it can be inferred that the air is cold.

Gaṅgeśa: No, this is an erroneous assumption.

Objection: Like air, the self also should not be perceived, since the self lacks manifested color and only substances possessing manifested color can be perceived.

Gaṅgeśa: The self is perceived, for there is recognitive perception (*pratyabhijñā*) that "I who saw the pot am now touching it." No such recognitive perception takes place in the case of air, for air is constantly moving.

The following inference provides proof of our view:

(Inf2) Air is not perceptible by an external sense organ, because it is a colorless substance, like *ākāśa*.

Objection: Inf2 is vitiated by the obstruction *not being the locus of manifested touch*.

Gaṅgeśa: No, for that property does not pervade the *sādhya*.

Section Eleven : The Fierriness of Gold (*suvarṇataijasatva*)

Summary by K.K. Chakrabarti

1. (E808-812) Gold belongs to the class of fiery substances in spite of the fact that it is not felt to be hot. It possesses unmanifested touch; it possesses manifested color, but its color is subdued by the yellow color of the adjoining earthy substance.

Objection: Fire can be seen in darkness. If gold is a fiery substance it too should be seen in darkness without the aid of light.

Answer: A substance can be visually perceived only if its color is visualized. The color of gold is not perceived because it is subdued by the color of the adjoining substance but, due to the lack of light, that color itself may not be perceived in the dark.

Objection: What proof is there to think that gold consists of a fiery substance in addition to the "adjoining" earthen substance that has weight and yellow color?

Answer: The yellow color of gold is not changed despite the application of high heat. This fact cannot be explained without assuming contact with a liquid substance. For whenever high heat is applied to an earthen substance, its color is changed; however, an earthen substance is not burnt up as long as it is in contact with a liquid substance such as water. Unless the yellow substance within gold were in contact with a liquid substance, its color would change when heated. Since its color doesn't change under that condition it must be in contact with a liquid substance, a substance of the nature of fire, for its liquidity is not natural but accidental.

Objection: Since the liquidity of gold is accidental it may as well be regarded as entirely made of earth.

Answer: No, for if a liquid earthen substance were responsible for the preservation of color in spite of being heated to a high temperature, that should hold good in the case of ghee (clarified butter) as well. But it is not so (since the color of heated ghee changes when burned). Just as the yellow color of the earthen neighbor of the gold is preserved in spite of the application of heat, so too the liquidity of that neighbor. This latter phenomenon is also due to contact with the liquid fiery substance that is gold, just as the liquidity of clarified butter is not destroyed when heated as long as the butter remains in water.

2. (E812-822) The new school argues thus:

Inf1: The locus of perceived liquidity which is not destroyed in spite of being heated to a high temperature is fire, because it is different from both water and earth and it has color. It is not water because its liquidity is accidental and not natural, or due to the fact that it has viscidity. It is not earth because its liquidity is not destroyed even when it is heated.

Others argue this way:

Inf2: Fireness belongs to this liquid object (viz., gold), because fireness is a universal which belongs to something colored and has substanceness as its immediately pervading universal, like waterness.

Objection: *Belonging to what has taste* is a vitiating adjunct that defeats Inf2.

Answer: No, for *belonging to what has taste* doesn't pervade the *sādhya.*

Objection: The liquidity of gold is destroyed when gold itself is destroyed because it is heated to a high temperature. This shows that Inf2 suffers from the fault of *asiddhi* (i.e., the presence of its *hetu* in its *pakṣa* is unproved).

Answer: The liquidity of gold is destroyed due to the destruction of its locus, viz., gold, but not due to the application of heat.

A final argument:

Inf3: The atoms producing gold are not earth atoms, because they possess a liquidity which is not destroyed in spite of the application of high heat, like water atoms.

Section Twelve: Atomicity of the Internal Organ (*mano'ṇutva*)

Summary by K.K. Chakrabarti

Pūrvapakṣa

1. (E823-828)[78] Objection: The definition of perception as that which arises through the sense organs is too narrow, for it fails to apply to the perception of satisfaction, etc., which perception does not arise through any external sense organs.

Opponent: Although the awareness of satisfaction, etc., does not arise from an external sense organ, it must arise from a sense organ, since such awarenesses are perceptual. So it is proved that there is an internal sense organ. This organ must be partless on grounds of economy. It is devoid of touch—its presence cannot be felt. Unlike the external senses, it is not restricted to the perception of only one kind of quality as the external organs are.[79]

This internal organ is ubiquitous, for any of the following reasons: (1) it is the locus of contact with a noninherence cause of an awareness;[80] (2) it is an eternal sense organ like *ākāśa*; (3) it is an eternal substance which does not produce any substance; (4) it is a substance which is devoid of specific qualities like selves, etc. (only ubiquitous substances lack specific qualities according to Nyāya-Vaiśeṣika).

Objector to the opponent: The specific locus of the effect of something ubiquitous is determined by a noninherence cause. But if the internal organ is also ubiquitous, there can be no fixed locus for the origin of satisfaction, etc.

Opponent: The alternative supposition—that the internal organ is atomic—also involves difficulty. For if it is held that the noninherence cause produces the effect only in that part which is limited by itself it would follow that satisfaction, etc., would only occupy an atomic-sized space.

Objector to the opponent: The size of the locus of satisfaction, etc., is determined, not by the noninherence cause, but by such conditions as sandalwood paste, etc. (which is applied to a part of the body, say). Although the internal organ is ubiquitous, satisfaction is produced in just that part of the body where the paste has been applied.

Opponent: But this solution is equally available to us who take the internal organ to be ubiquitous.

Again, both satisfaction and frustration may be experienced at the same time, say, if sandalwood paste and fire are applied to different parts of the body at the same time. Such simultaneous origination of satisfaction and frustration may be explained if the internal organ is regarded as ubiquitous, but not if it is construed as atomic (for something atomic cannot come into contact with two different bodily parts at the same time).

Objection: But in other cases (e.g., the circle of fire), some apparently simultaneous events have been found on closer examination to be successive, and so it is here.

Opponent: No, for elsewhere the successiveness of experiences is due to the succession of the occasions for those experiences, but here we have no successive occasions.

Although the internal organ is ubiquitous, it helps cognize satisfactions, etc., only within the limits of the body, just as although the auditory organ is ubiquitous, it produces auditory perception only within the limits of the ear-cavity.

Objection to the opponent: In that case a pain in the foot should pervade the whole body!

Opponent: No, the specific location of the pain is determined by the contact of that location with the occasion. Those who view the internal organ as atomic have to say the same thing. Otherwise it could not be explained how the pleasure from a cool dip on a hot day could pervade the whole body although the internal organ is atomic!

There are other opinions: Some say that the internal organ is ubiquitous but that the contact between self and internal organ *per se* is not the noninherence cause of experience, but is so only within the limits of contact with the occasion. Others prefer to hold that satisfactions, etc., are produced only in those parts where there are prior absences of them.

Siddhānta

2. (E828-836) Gaṅgeśa: It is well-known that although several sense organs may be at the same time connected with their respective proper objects, perception may take place through only one of them, and not through the others, when one pays special attention to only the one of them. That simultaneous perceptions do not take place in such a situation may be explained by supposing that the internal organ is connected with only one of the sense organs and not with the others. Thus it has to be supposed that the internal organ is such that it may be connected with the different external organs only successively, not simultaneously. Then it may be held that satisfaction, etc., are perceived by the same internal organ. So it becomes clear that the very reasoning which shows that there is an internal organ militates against the thesis that it is ubiquitous. If it were ubiquitous, it could simultaneously be connected to several sense organs.

Objection: Although the internal organ is ubiquitous, the successiveness of perceptions taking place may be explained on the basis of the interest the perceiver has in cognizing through them.

Gaṅgeśa: Not so, for perception may take place even of something in which one has no interest. Moreover, perception of a cloth may take place in spite of one's being interested in perceiving a pot. Interest is immaterial when the internal organ is applied and attention directed to something else.

Objection: Suppose that the succession of cognitive acts in the above-mentioned situation is due to the characteristic nature of the causal conditions *par excellence* that cause each. One such condition suffices to produce only one action in the same thing. Although the internal organ is ubiquitous, it still is only sufficient to produce, say, the visual perception in the self at a given moment.

Gaṅgeśa: In that case that which is responsible for the production of one out of the five possible perceptions should be so conceived that the production of more than one is ruled out (i.e., the internal organ should be regarded as atomic rather than ubiquitous). Otherwise, how would the tussle among the five possibles over being produced be resolved? It has to be noticed that all the other causal conditions for the origin of each of the five possible cognitions are fulfilled at the same time. Hence it must be left to the nature of the internal organ that it leads to the production of only one of them.

It may so happen that although numerous sounds have been received by the auditory organ at the same time only one of them gets perceived and not the others. For an explanation of this phenomenon we must appeal to the factors of selective interest and attention. These factors have to be regarded as auxiliary causes in those cases where one out of many sounds gets perceived. This does not, however, mean that these factors are auxiliary causes for the perception of sound in every case.

3. (E837–840) Objection: If the internal organ is atomic, how can on certain occasions several perceptions be produced simultaneously, as e.g., when one eats a piece of fruit?

Another: Since on some occasions only one of several possible perceptions is produced and on other occasions all of them are produced simultaneously, the internal organ is made of parts and is capable of expansion and contraction. (When it contracts to a very small size only one perception is produced; when it expands, several may be produced.)

Objector: No. There is no reasonable explanation of this supposed expansion and contraction of the internal organ. If the explanation involves appeal to *adṛṣṭa*, it would be better to regard *adṛṣṭa* itself as the cause of the origin of one perception sometimes and several simultaneous perceptions at other times, and do away with the internal organ altogether.

Another objection: Suppose that there are five atomic internal organs and that, depending on such factors as selective interest, etc., from one to all five of them get connected with the external sense organs at the same time, and that that is why there is simultaneity of perceptions on some occasions and nonsimultaneity on other occasions in spite of the fact that all the five external organs are simultaneously connected with their objects.

Objector: Although there may be interest in all the five objects, still only one perception takes place. This phenomenon can be (best) explained by there being only one internal organ and not five. So the internal organ should be regarded as ubiquitous rather than multiple or made of parts, since ubiquity is the more economical view.

Gaṅgeśa: Simultaneous perceptions do not take place on any one occasion. When at the time of eating a piece of fruit there is an aftercognition of all the five kinds of perception having occurred, five different aftercognitions of five different acts of perception actually take place at very short intervals, but their difference is not noticed due to the brevity of the temporal gap. Alternatively, it may be the case that from the disposition of the five aftercognitions arises the memory of the objects of the five perceptions; when this memory is mistaken for a direct experience of them there results the aftercognition of simultaneous perceptions.

Since it is thus established that there is an internal organ that is atomic in size, it may now be held that satisfaction, etc., are perceived through the internal organ. So it follows that the definition of perception is not too narrow.

Section Thirteen: Aftercognition (*anuvyavasāya*)
Summary by K.K. Chakrabarti
Pūrvapakṣa

1. (E841–847)[81] Opponent: An awareness (J_1) is not apprehended through the internal organ. Rather, it is apprehended through itself and does not require another awareness to be apprehended. There is neither positive nor negative concomitance between a J_1 and any other awareness J_2 of it. Since an occurring awareness is apprehended through itself, it is superfluous to have recourse to another awareness for this purpose. A past or a future awareness of course cannot be apprehended through itself, but only through another awareness.

Objection to the opponent: Then should we hold that desire, etc., are also self-revealing like awareness?

Opponent: No. Talk about and awareness of desire, etc., can take place only through awarenesses that are distinct from desire, etc., themselves.

Objector to the opponent: An awareness must be different from its content. How then can an awareness be cognized through itself?

Opponent: It is the special nature of awareness that it also has itself as its object and reveals itself. An awareness of the pot, for example, is not only capable of producing usage regarding the pot, but is also capable of producing usage regarding itself. This capability of producing usage regarding itself is due to the inherent nature of awareness. Such a special nature of awareness cannot be articulated through language but is nevertheless an experienced fact.

Prābhākara: All awarenesses have the form "I am aware of this." Thus not only the thing known, but also the self, insofar as it is the knower, as well as the awareness insofar as it is the (mental) act, become the contents of every awareness. Such is the position of those who hold that the contents of every perception are threefold (*tripuṭī-pratyakṣavādinaḥ*, i.e., the Prābhākaras).

Objection to the Prābhākara: An awareness (J_1) has only *this* as its content. It is the subsequent aftercognition (J_2) that has the form "I know this", and that aftercognition J_2 takes place through the instrumentality of the internal organ.

Prābhākara: Since an awareness is self-revealing, appeal to another awareness is redundant. Furthermore, the possibility that an awareness is revealed by another awareness has to be rejected on the ground that it makes such an awareness impossible. First of all, it cannot be held that awareness of awareness is inferential and takes place through knowness (*jñātatā*) as the mark, for knownness does not belong to the past or the future. Secondly, it cannot be held that an aftercognition is perceptual and takes place through the internal organ, for either such an aftercognition will be preceded by a desire, or it won't. If aftercognition is preceded by desire the awareness would be destroyed by the desire and could not be apprehended by the aftercognition. On the other hand, if the aftercognition could take place without any desire, the series of aftercognitions would go on *ad infinitum*. These considerations serve to set aside the following argument and others similar to it: An awareness is an object of the internal organ, for it is a perceptible quality of the self, like satisfaction; a visual awareness cannot be a content of a visual awareness, for it is not connected with the relevant sense organ.[82] Since an infinite regress is inevitable if it is held that an awareness must be revealed through another awareness, such a view has to be rejected and it has to be accepted that awareness is self-revealing. As a matter of fact, by a "perceptual awareness" is meant an awareness which arises without the intervention of any awareness through the instrumentality of a sense organ. Thus it should follow that every awareness is perceived by the self through the contact between the self and the internal organ, without the intervention of any other awareness.[83]

Siddhānta

2. (E847–849) This cannot be accepted. Perception does not furnish evidence for saying that awarenesses are self-revealing. For it is not established that initial awarenesses (*vyavasāya*, i.e., awarenesses that

are not aftercognitions) have the form "I am aware of this." To question this does not involve any conflict with our experience, for our activities ensuing upon an awareness may be fully accounted for in terms of the awareness of the object alone without supposing that the self and the awareness itself are contents of that same awareness. Further, so far as our experience is concerned, it is felt that the object alone becomes the content of our awareness. To suppose that the awareness is a content of itself is superfluous, for such a supposition is not required to give an account of our activities. In fact our experience is of the form "this is silver", which shows that neither the self nor the awareness are contents of the awareness.

This does not imply that an awareness of the form "I am aware of this" never takes place. Such an awareness indeed may take place after an intitial awareness, at the time of aftercognition.

Objection: If aftercognition J_2 is different from the initial awareness J_1 there will be an infinite regress. Therefore, they should not be regarded as different.

Gaṅgeśa: If awarenesses were thus proved to be self-revealing it must follow that all awarenesses have the form "I am aware of this." Since awarenesses have not been proved to be self-revealing it does not follow that all awarenesses have that form. Furthermore, in the supposed initial cognition J_1 with the form "I am aware of this" the self is supposed to be known as the agent, and the awareness as the (mental) act, etc. However, by an agent is meant a person characterized by the will to act, and by (mental) action is meant the meaning of a verb, etc. How can the property of being an agent and the property of being an action be contents of J_1 without the sense organ being connected with these things? So, what is reasonable is to hold that it is cognized by the self (after J_1 occurs), that it, the self, is qualified by the awareness of *this*. Such an awareness J_2 can take place after the initial cognition, but not at the same time as it. Thus the initial awareness J_1 cannot have the form "I am aware of this"; rather it is the aftercognition J_2 which has such a form.

Objection: Let it be conceded that it is not apprehended at the time of the initial awareness J_1 that the self is qualified by agency. Still, it may be supposed that J_1 has itself (the mental act) as a content and is thus self-revealing.

Gaṅgeśa: No. Since the sensory connection through which J_1 has been originated is not connected with J_1, J_1 cannot be its own content.

3. (E850–856) Despite this it should not be thought that no awareness is ever self-revealing. Specifically, the following awareness of pervasion, viz., all cognitions are cognizable, does have itself as a content, since cognitionness (*jñānatva*) functions as a sensory connection (in *sāmānyalakṣaṇa* perception). Further, since God's

perception is uncaused and has everything as its content, it too is self-revealing.

Objection: Won't there be an infinite regress if every awareness has to be revealed by another?

Gaṅgeśa: No, since not every awareness has necessarily to be cognized itself.

Objection: Since an awareness may be perceived by the internal organ through inherence-in-what-is-in-contact (*saṃyuktasamavāya*), and nothing else is required, why shouldn't every awareness be invariably cognized as soon as it arises?

Gaṅgeśa: Not so. The awareness of an awareness may be obstructed by the causal conditions of the awareness of satisfaction, etc. (or any other alternative state). It is common experience to find that the internal organ has moved on to something else, from which it may be inferred that the causal conditions of that thing are stronger. Some even say that the awareness of an awareness may not take place because the initial awareness remains unmanifested.

Objection: All awarenesses are perceived, since they are special qualities of the self fit for perception. Thus an awareness is invariably cognized and so it must follow that it is self-revealing.

Gaṅgeśa: It is not the case that all cognitions are perceived. If it were true and cognitions were not self-revealing there would be infinite regress. On the other hand, cognitions cannot be self-revealing, for the required conditions for being so are not present. Only that with which there is sensory connection can be perceived, but there is no sensory connection with the initial awareness itself.

Objection: We know through eliminative inference (*pariśeṣa*) that awarenesses are self-revealing, for the alternative is refuted through its leading to infinite regress.

Gaṅgeśa: But this eliminative inference—is it self-revealing? That it is will have to be proved by yet another inference, and so on ad infinitum. So infinite regress arises from your position as well.

Opponent: Ah, but the regress is stopped, both because the internal organ moves on to something else and because the regress goes only up to the point that there is desire to cognize.

Gaṅgeśa: These ways out are easily open to us.

Opponent: That the above eliminative inference is self-revealing is known through *sāmānyalakṣaṇa* perception.

Gaṅgeśa: We who hold that awareness is revealed by another awareness can appeal to the same reasoning to prove our thesis. Remember too that those who advocate the view that awarenesses are self-revealing do not accept *sāmānyalakṣaṇa* perception.

Objection: When something other than awareness is to be perceived sensory connection is required. But here it is only awareness itself that is perceived; where is the need for a sensory connection? There is no fault in holding that such awareness is self-revealing and perceptual without a sensory connection.

Gaṅgeśa: No exception can be made for the awareness of an awareness, even through itself, for sensory connection is a causal condition for all perceptual awarenesses; otherwise there would be lapse of uniformity.

Objection: An awareness that is not cognized cannot be proved to exist at all, due to lack of evidence. Since something can become the content of an awareness only if there is an awareness of it, even the existence of the content of awareness would be questioned.

Gaṅgeśa: We do not admit an eternally uninterrupted series of awarenesses. However, the existence of an awareness is sometimes inferred through such marks as memory, usage, etc. Thus evidence for the existence of both an awareness and the content of awareness is available.

Objection: If the awareness that this is a pot is different from the awareness that I am aware of a pot, we should be aware of some awareness the content of which is burdened by hundreds of thousands of contents of the preceding serial awarenesses of awarenesses... of pot![84]

Gaṅgeśa: Not so. An aftercognition is specified by the content of the initial awareness alone, and not by the successors of that content. Thus all such awarenesses are apprehended by us as simply awarenesses of an awareness.

Objection: Having something as a content is just having the capacity for using (i.e., speaking or practical behavior about) that something.

Gaṅgeśa: No. The awareness of having the capacity for using *x* can be gained only through the awareness of having *x* as a content. If the reverse were true as well there would be mutual dependence.

Objection: An awareness produces both usage (*vyavahāra*) and a trace (*saṃskāra*) without having itself as content.

Gaṅgeśa: No, for it has to be admitted on the evidence of awarenesses elsewhere that an awareness may produce usage or traces only of that which is its content.

Objection: An awareness cannot be cognized through the internal organ. For the awareness of being qualified by an awareness must be preceded by a nonpropositional perception of awarenessness. But such a perception cannot take place, for the initial awareness would have ceased to exist by that time.

Gaṅgeśa: Not so. It is possible for an awareness J_2 that J_1 is qualified by awarenessness to take place at the moment that J_1 ceases to exist, for J_1 is existent in the previous moment. It is not required that J_1

be existent at the time of perception; its existence at the immediately preceding moment will suffice.

As a matter of fact it may be held that both J_1 and awarenessness become the contents of aftercognition. An aftercognition may be construed as a hybrid awareness part of which is nonpropositional (viz., the part of which awarenessness is the content) and part of which is propositional (viz., J_1). In other words, the aftercognition may have the following form: I possess an awareness which is characterized by awareness and in which (say) potness is the qualifier.

Section Fourteen : Nonpropositional Awareness (*nirvikalpaka*)

Summary by Sukha Ranjan Saha

1. (E857–860) Perception is of two kinds: nonpropositional (*nirvikalpaka*) and propositional (*savikalpaka*). A nonpropositional awareness, one without a chief qualifier (*prakāra*), is an awareness without connection to a name or a universal property, etc., and which does not have as its content a qualification-relation.

Pūrvapakṣa

Opponent (one who thinks all awarenesses are propositional, a *savikalpakavādin*, hereafter called SV): How do you know that there are any awarenesses other than propositional ones? Not by perception, for that begs the question. And not by appealing to common usage, since usage is always propositional.

The believer in nonpropositional awarenesses (hereafter called NV): But we commonly say "I didn't reflect on it earlier but am doing so now", which indicates a difference between nonpropositional awareness and reflective or propositional awareness.

SV: No. We hold that in both kinds of awareness one is aware of a qualifier.

NV: Here is an inference to prove the existence of nonpropositional awareness:

NVInf1: The perceptual awareness "(it is a) cow" is produced by an awareness of a qualifier; because it is a qualified awareness; like inferential awareness.

SV: There is a general rule that

SVR: We only know the qualifier (for the first time) when we have a qualified awareness (involving it).

Awareness of qualifier and qualificand, being related by mutual expectancy, is a sufficient condition for having a qualified awareness. Since SVR can be shown to be satisfied in the case of inference, comparison and knowledge gained through language, there is no special reason for perception to be different.

NV: According to your SVR, since recognition is a qualified awareness we should have had no awareness of the qualifier before the qualified awareness that is recognition. But clearly we must have been aware of the qualifier before (how else could we recognize anything?). So likewise in perceptual awareness we must have awareness of the qualifier before we have a qualified awareness.

SV: What is recognition? Is it memory? No. So it must be one of the four instruments of knowledge. But it isn't inference, comparison, or knowledge gained from language. So it must itself be a kind of perception. Thus you cannot use it as an example to prove your case about perception.

NV: But from what does the remembered aspect in the recognition arise?

SV: Traces, even though not risen to consciousness, can produce a memory. Furthermore, a false awareness (*bhrama*) is yet another case of an awareness which is not preceded by awareness of a qualifier (or at any rate, of a qualifier which actually belongs to the qualificand).

NV: No. *Our* general rule is the following:

NVR_1: Whatever awareness we consider, if we consider it to be a case of qualified awareness, we must consider it also as preceded by an awareness of the qualifier.

SV: Take the awareness (A) "(this) possesses fire." Awareness of fire is not a cause of (A), since it may not be recognized that the fire *is* fire (i.e., has fireness). It is only the awareness of the quality as having the relevant property that is the cause of the qualified awareness.

NV: Even so, it *is* an awareness of the qualifier (so the point has been granted).

SV: No. NVR_1 overextends to include causation by a qualifier not known to be such, and therefore NVR_1 should be rejected.

NV: This is wrong. You yourself accept that a cause of an awareness of a qualified qualifier (*viśiṣṭavaiśiṣṭyajñāna*) is an awareness whose chief qualifier is the limitor of the qualifierness (i.e., in "this is a blue pot" you accept that a cause is the previous awareness of blueness). So by parity of reasoning you should accept the same thing in the case of the simple qualified awareness ("this is a pot") viz., that a cause is the previous awareness of potness. Thus awareness of the qualifier *simpliciter* (i.e., whether recognized as such or not) is sufficient to cause a qualified awareness. Otherwise the causal principle that general causal relationships match particular cases of causes and effects will be abrogated.

SV: Mediacy (*parokṣatva*) is an obstruction here. (I.e., we will grant that NVR_1 applies to mediate awarenesses, but not immediate awarenesses.)

NV: No, for you yourself admit that recognition, which is immediate awareness, satisfies NVR_1. Anyway, SVR is mistaken, since it will mean that some awarenesses (e.g., "this is a cow") cannot fall under it, since being aware that this is a cow requires awareness that one is aware of cowness, and awareness of cowness requires that one is aware of cownessness, and so on; thus one can never be aware that this is a cow.

SV: Not so. According to both of us memory is produced by traces born of prior experiences. (And those experiences also involve traces of experiences prior to them—indeed, all awarenesses involve traces.)

NV: And those prior experiences are just awarenesses of qualifiers.

SV: Then in the case of recognition there should also be a preceding awareness of a qualifier—otherwise recognition will be only memory (which after all involves traces). So it is not the case that NVR_1 holds, e.g., for recognition, as you claimed.

NV: In the case of immediate perception of a color at a time, since it is not a memory, traces do not operate. Thus the awareness of the qualifier is itself nonpropositional. By parity of reasoning we prove our point for other cases (like recognition).

SV: Suppose we are aware of a qualifier for a second time. Now either it is a case of an awareness of something qualified by a qualifier (*vaiśiṣṭyaviśiṣṭajñāna*) (e.g., "(this is a) thing with white-color qualified by white-color-ness") or it is merely a qualified awareness (e.g., "(this is a) thing with white-color"). The second case is impossible, since no one can be aware of something as white without being aware of white-color-ness. So this awareness of a qualifier for the second time must be an awareness of the first type (i.e., *vaiśiṣṭyaviśiṣṭajñāna*). But you admit that in such a case white-colorness is remembered and the white color perceived. So why do you object to my view? Or else you may invoke your doctrine of *sāmānyalakṣaṇasannikarṣa* (which we don't accept). In any case, parity of reasoning works in favor of my view, not yours.

2. (E860–862) NV: We propose the following inference:

$NVInf_2$: A nonrecollective awareness other than that which occurs at the first moment of waking is produced by an awareness of a qualifier; because it is a case of qualified awareness.

SV: Either (a) a previous nonrecollective awareness of the qualifier is the cause even with respect to the awareness at the first moment of waking, the former related to the latter by traces, or (b) memory produced by the previous awareness is the cause.

NV: No. Without an exciter (*udbodhaka*) traces can't produce memory or any other qualified awareness. Now, since it is a generally accepted rule that

NVR_2: An exciter is some awareness or other,

this must be the case here also. Now this exciter can't itself be a qualified awareness, for that leads to infinite regress. So we must admit a nonqualified (i.e., nonpropositional) awareness as the exciter.

SV: Awareness is not always followed by the excitement of traces. So awareness *qua* awareness can't be the exciter.

NV: The specific awareness produced by specific traces is the exciter which revives those traces.

SV: No, there is no general rule to that effect.

NV: Yes there is, viz.,

NVR_3: The exciter is what arises from the revival of traces.

SV: You admit that in the case of the awareness that occurs at the first waking moment there is some exciter operative as the cause, and evidently in that instance there are traces excited. But your NV Inf2 implies that the awareness that occurs at the first waking moment is an exception. So we conclude that there cannot be any such general rule as NVR_3.

Furthermore, as to your reason (in either NVInf1 or NVInf2) "because it is a case of qualfied awareness", why is the adjective "qualified" required? If it means something, you must assume the existence of an awareness that is not qualified, but that's just what you have to prove. And even if that assumption be admitted, the argument is of no avail (as we have shown). And if you then revise the reason to read "because it is a case of awareness", then the invariable concomitance between this *hetu* and the *sādhya being produced by the awareness of the qualifier* will fail in respect of nonpropositional awareness, or else there will be infinite regress.

3. (E862–863) Furthermore, what is the content of a qualified awareness? If you define a qualfied awareness in terms of its content, and hold that

QAD_1: The content of a qualified awareness comprises the two entities (*vastu*) which are in fact the qualifier and the qualificand,

your definition will overextend to include nonpropositional awareness, for according to you nonpropositional awareness has a qualifier and a qualificand. If you hold instead

QAD_2: That a qualified awareness has as content a qualifier that is not only in fact such but is also known to be such,

this cannot be accepted, because only if we can distinguish the bearer of such a qualifier from other things which don't have it does the definition make sense, but what you take to be qualified awarenesses do not always involve this discrimination.

NV: So, we shall define qualified awareness as

QAD_3: An awareness whose content is the relation between qualifier and qualified (technically known as *vaiśiṣṭya* or "qualification-relation").

SV: Let us take a case of an awareness where one is merely considering (*vikalpa*) a content—as, e.g., when one thinks to himself "this thing might be a cow." According to you one who merely considers in this way does not ascribe cowness to the thing, but rather the qualification-relation is itself the qualifier of the awareness. However, since this is a qualified awareness it should be preceded by a nonpropositional awareness according to NVR, and that nonpropositional awareness must have as *its* content the qualifier of the considering, viz., the qualification-relation. But then QAD3 fails, for since the nonpropositional awareness has the qualification-relation as its content it is after all a qualified awareness! Either this constitutes overextension of QAD3 or else (if you insist that nonpropositional awareness *is* a qualified awareness) infinite regress will result.

NV: Then we define a qualified awareness as

QAD_4: An awareness with a chief qualifier

A "chief qualifier" is a specific kind of content which is not definable in terms of any other concept.

SV: No, for we do not admit any unique status for the notion of chief qualifier. A chief qualifier is just that which figures as the content of an awareness.

NV: An awareness with a chief qualifier is due to (previous) awareness of that qualifier. If an awareness is due to the awareness of a qualifier, then it is "with a chief qualifier" and that qualifier (viz., the qualification-relation) is the chief qualifier of that awareness.

SV: Since you hold that merely considering something is an awareness with a chief qualifier and that its chief qualifier is the qualification-relation, unless you can prove that this considering is due to the awareness of the qualification-relation. Your position is inconsistent. Furthermore, God's awareness is with qualifier, but it is admitted by all to be eternal, so it cannot be due to a previous awareness of a qualifier.

NV: Then a qualified awareness is

QAD_5: An awareness where the content is known as something distinct from things other than itself (*atadvyāvṛtti*).

SV: That is tantamount to (the Buddhist's) *apohavāda* (and thus reprehensible to both of us). Also, QAD_5 won't apply to mere considering, as you yourself have shown.

NV: Your remarks on mere considering cannot be accepted. Such an awareness as merely considering leads to an awareness of its content as something distinct from things other than itself.

SV: No. What is this awareness of a content distinct from things other than itself? The only common feature of such awareness must be difference from nonpropositional awareness. (But this begs the question.)

NV: Consider awareness(B):

(B) "(This is a) cow."

Now either (1) (B) is other than some awareness (X) which is distinct from a qualified awareness (Y) from which (B) is different, because (B) is a content of knowledge (*prameya*), in which case (X) must be a nonpropositional awareness and (B) is different from it; or (2) the visual organ is the cause of some awareness other than a visual qualified awareness because it is a sense organ (and that other awareness is nonpropositional).

SV: Neither (1) nor (2) will do. In both cases, unless you have the theory of nonpropositional awareness already in mind one may easily come up with some other awareness that is to be considered "other than a qualified awareness."

Siddhānta

4. (E863-865) Gaṅgeśa : *My* inference is

GInf: The initial perceptual awareness of (say) (B) "(this is a) cow" is produced by a previous awareness of a qualifier; because it is a case of qualified awareness that occurs at a particular moment; like an inferential awareness.

It is presumed that this awareness of qualifier is not a case of memory, since we have specified this to be the *initial* experience of cowness, i.e., the first experience of a cow in this life.

Objection: The child's instinctive volition for its mother's breast can't be explained without the presumption of memory produced by traces from a former birth. So it is here.

Gaṅgeśa: No. In the case of the child what excites the traces is the human instinct for preservation(*jīvanādṛṣṭa*). But in the present case there is no exciter of any trace (*ex hypothesi*). If memory of cowness can arise without an exciter there will be the undesirable outcome that even without sense-object connection one could perceive cowness!

Objector: So, the connection of a sense organ with cowness is the cause of your nonpropositional awareness, and that in turn excites the traces leading to memory.

Gaṅgeśa: No, because you admit that this sense-object connection is sufficient by itself for sensory awareness. Even if we admit that it is also sufficient for the excitement of traces, still the resultant awareness will be perceptual (not memory) for it is a universally accepted rule that

NVR_3: Conditions sufficient for nonmnemic awareness will be operative even if they are also sufficient for mnemic awareness.

So, the previous awareness of a qualifier is not itself a case of qualified awareness, because there is no previous awareness of the qualifier. And this proves the thesis of nonpropositional awareness.

Objection: A qualified awareness is present just when there is awareness of a qualifier.

Gaṅgeśa: Then you presume that the awareness of a qualifier is an awareness, and that it is a qualified one, and so in your philosophy awareness and qualified awareness are the same thing. But that isn't right, since if so, and if NVR_3 is correct, it will be preceded by some other awareness, or else infinite regress will ensue.

Objector: Still, there may be memory due to the operation of conditions sufficient for nonmnemic awareness.

Gaṅgeśa: No, for then we should have mnemic awareness about Vedic matters (which conflicts with the accepted view that the Vedas are linguistic (*śābdika*, understood by the instrument of knowledge called verbal testimony and thus nonmnemic in nature).

Objection: Awareness of cowness may be due to (1) awareness of cowness, (2) previous awareness, (3) previous awareness of (the qualifier) cownessness. Any of these descriptions are true, as is evident from known cases of qualified awarenesses. This proves that awareness of cowness is never initial in the manner of your (B), i.e., never nonmnemic.

Gaṅgeśa: You are taking cause and effect as identical, which is fallacious. Moreover, it will lead to infinite regress.

Objector: In (B) the relation of the qualification-relation to cowness appears in the cow. It should be preceded, according to your principles, by a previous appearance of this relation, and that previous appearance should be nonpropositional. But you define "nonpropositional" as being free from a qualification-relation.

Gaṅgeśa: No. Cowness is the qualifier, on my position, and not the qualification-relation. So your criticism is off the mark.

Objector: I presume the qualifier (cowness) in (B) appears qualified by cownessness. If it does, you will say it only does in qualified awarenesses, for if it does so in nonpropositional awarenesses you will have conflated qualified with nonpropositional awareness. But then we shall get an infinite regress.

Gaṅgeśa: In a qualified awareness cowness doesn't appear as qualified by any further property.

Objector: But every thing (on your account) has *some* qualifier in it! So cowness must itself have some qualifier. Since you say it is not cownessness, we shall say that, just as cow is qualified by cowness, so cowness is qualified by cow! (And if that be so, cowness cannot appear unqualified by any further property.)

Gaṅgeśa: Let it be so as far as ontology is concerned (i.e., let it be that every qualifier is qualified by some property). But it isn't necessarily the case that every qualifier is *known as* qualified by a further qualifier.

5. (E865-868) Objection: In GInf the *hetu* "because it is a qualified awareness" is redundant: the adjective "qualified" is of no use. If every awareness is preceded by awareness of a qualifier, then it is unnecessary to add "every qualified awareness is preceded by awareness of a qualifier."

Gaṅgeśa: An adjective (such as "qualified" in "qualified awareness") is significant if it is required for us to be aware of pervasion. Now in my system "every awareness is preceded by a previous awareness of qualifier" does not state pervasion, for it would lead to infinite regress or else would necessitate (in order to block the regress) the admission of an awareness not preceded by any previous awareness.

As for your "mere considering" (*vikalpa*): The qualification relation is a relation by reference to which we become aware of the distinction between its relata and things not related by it. E.g., in "this man is a stick-bearer" the relation of the stick to the person is cognized and serves to distinguish the person who is a stick-bearer from others who are not stick-bearers. This is true also in the case of merely considering. The definition of a qualified awareness is

QAD_6: Awareness of the qualificand as qualifier by a qualifier. This must involve the distinguishing of something from something else.

Objection: In the case of the relation of stick to person it is the *relation* that is cognized as residing in the person, and we can thereby distinguish that person from any other person who does not possess a stick.

Gaṅgeśa: I accept your point, but must add that there can't be any awareness of the relation of stick to person without previous awareness of the stick itself. (Not just awareness of the relation, but awareness of the stick itself is required.)

If the awareness of the qualifier can be taken to be generated by conditions sufficient for a qualified awareness, it is not a nonpropositional awareness. Among awarenesses which have another awareness as their causal condition *par excellence*, awareness of a qualifier can never be nonpropositional. Thus it is only in *some* cases of perceptual awareness that the preceding awareness of a qualifier is nonpropositional. For example, an awareness of an absence is not preceded by a nonpropositional awareness, for there cannot be any awareness of an absence without previous awareness of its counterpositive as well as of the locus of the absence.

Objector: Awareness of absence seems to be an exception to NVR_1, for admittedly it is not preceded by awareness of a qualifier, and even if you say it *is* preceded by an awareness of a qualifier, that awareness cannot be said to be nonpropositional. (That is, the qualifier in the case of absence is the absence itself, and according to your theory the counterpositive, say, the pot, cannot be cognized by a nonpropositional awareness.)

Gaṅgeśa: In the case of an awareness of absence, say the one expressed in "there is no pot on the ground", the ground is the qualifier and the absence is the qualificand. Here mere awareness of the qualificand (viz., the absence) is not a cause of the awareness of the absence in relation to the ground. First we have an awareness of the form "there is no pot on the ground", and then subsequently we may turn this into "the ground has absence of pot", where the order of qualifier and qualificand are reversed. (But the former order is primary, and so NVR_1 doesn't fail in the case of awareness of absence.)

Objection: In your theory of sense-object connection (Section 5 above) you said that in an awareness of absence the sense-object connection is qualifierness, which is the relation in which the absence stands to its locus, the locus in turn being in contact with the sense organ. Now you say the reverse, that the ground is the qualifier and the absence the qualificand!

Gaṅgeśa: In that section I was using the word "qualifierness" in its ontological sense (*svabhāvapratyāsatti*), in relation to the order of the natures of things. I did not mean thereby that what is a qualifier in the ontological sense will also be so epistemically (*bhāṇam*). And what I'm saying here is corroborated by the Ācārya (Udayana) when he says, "We may have visual awareness of an absence in the form, there is absence of color in air" (which amounts to saying that absence of color is, in the context of awareness, the qualificand and air is the qualifier, but ontologically air is the qualificand and absence of color the qualifier). The Ācārya said so because air cannot be an object of straightforward visual connection.

One and the same awareness may be regarded as both propositional and nonpropositional, the former because something is known as qualified by something else, the latter because there is no qualified awareness of the qualifier and the qualificand in J_1, though such a content belongs to the aftercognition J_2 which cognizes J_1.

In my system neither being propositional nor being nonpropositional are proper universals, for there is cross-connection in such lower properties as visual-perceptibility, etc.

Finally, then, awareness of cowness involved in the qualified awareness (B) "(this is a) cow" is a nonpropositional awareness, for cowness has been cognized as such. To deny this will produce infinite regress.

Section Fifteen: Qualifier and Indicator (*viśeṣaṇopalakṣaṇa*)[85]

Summary by Sukha Ranjan Saha

Pūrvapakṣa

1. (E869-871) A chief qualifier (*prakāra*)must be either a qualifier (*viśeṣaṇa*) or an indicator (*upalakṣaṇa*). But if both qualifiers and indicators are differentiators (*vyāvarttaka*), what is the difference between them? A series of definitions are considered and criticized:

(D1) A qualifier is a resident differentiator, while an indicator is a nonresident differentiator.

Criticism: No. Consider (A) "Devadatta's house is the one with the crows (on it)" or (B) "the saint is the one with matted hair." It may be the case that the house of Devadatta actually does have crows on it at the time (A) occurs, or that the saint has matted hair at the time of (B); still, both are indicators, not qualifiers.[86]

(D2) A qualifier is what is resident in the qualificand and is its differentiator.

Criticism: No, since a qualificand is whatever has a qualifier, so that the definition is circular.

(D3) A qualifier is what is resident in the locus of differentiation ensuing upon a qualified awareness, and is itself its differentiator.

Criticism: This definition doesn't apply to the redness which is admittedly a qualifier in the (false) awareness reported by "the crystal is red" even though the crystal is not in fact red (so that redness is qualifier in that case even though it doesn't satisfy D3).

(D4) When a qualificand (i.e., a locus of differentiation) is differentiated by the property which generically delimits it (e.g., as crystalness generically delimits crystal, or potness a pot), some other property appears as co-resident with that property in a qualified awareness, and this other property is the qualifier. (Since redness appears in the crystal in "the crystal is red" it qualifies as a qualifier under D4.)

Criticism: No, for in (B) "this saint is the one with matted hair" the saint actually has matted hair, so matted hair satisfies D4, but *ex hypothesi* matted hair is an indicator, not a qualifier there.

(D5) A qualifier is that which is represented by a word with the same case-ending as the word representing the qualificand.

Criticism: No, There are instances where an indicator is represented with the same case-ending as the qualificand. In (A), which in Sanskrit is "*kākavad devadattagṛham,*" the two words have the same case-ending. Furthermore, D5 will not cover the instances of qualifiers involved in qualified awarenesses had by people who cannot express them in language (e.g., children, dumb persons).

(D6) A qualifier is that differentiator which figures as the content of a qualified awareness.

Criticism: Since we support the doctrine of self-illumination (*svaprakāśatva*) of awareness, every qualifier will statisfy D6.

Defender of D6: A qualifier figures as the content of a qualified awareness only *qua* differentiator of the qualificand, not as endowed with its character of being a qualifier; otherwise, it would not be possible to account for our being able to question whether a chief qualifier is to be regarded as a qualifier or an indicator. In Nyāya philosophy an initial qualified awareness is held to be a case of perception by an external sense organ; since qualifierness is not manifest in that qualified awareness there cannot be any question of cognizing the qualifier there as endowed with its character of qualifierness. D6 implies that an indicator is that differentiator which does not figure as the content of a qualified awareness. I.e., even if there are no crows on Devadatta's house a person can still have a qualified awareness of the house as qualified by its structural features. It would be wrong to suppose that a man may have a qualified awareness of the house as qualified by crows when there are no crows there. If he does so, it would have to be a case of false awareness.

Critic: Then your interpretation doesn't explain the significance of the use of the word "crows" in (A), for the resulting qualified awareness isn't about crows at all!

Defender of D6: But that's how the meaning of the sentence is in fact understood. It is in this respect like (C) "the Ghosh family lives in the Ganges" (*gaṅgāyām ghoṣa ity*). One doesn't take the word "*gaṅgāyāṃ*" in (C) to refer to a volume of water flowing—it rather has the secondary meaning of a *bank* of the river.[87] For if "Ganges" were interpreted literally the sentence would make no sense, for a family can't live in water.

Critic: Then do you treat an indicator as a secondary meaning?

Defender of D6: No, because the word "crow", if treated as a word with a secondary meaning, would stand for the structural features of the house. But in fact the word "crow" produces in the hearer awareness of crows, and this awareness then by association presents further awareness of that region of the house over which the crows are hovering. Therefore it is not a case of understanding that region as the direct denotation of the word "crows".

Critic: No, that is not right. The sentence in question doesn't contain any word which stands for the structural configuration of the house. The word "crow" does stand for the object crow, which is here the indicator, and also for the structural configuration, which is the thing indicated by that indicator. And if you deny that this is a case of secondary meaning I do not see why you would accept *anything* to be a case of secondary meaning, for your sort of explanation can always be offered.

2. (E872-874)

(D7) (The qualifier is that differentiator which is related to the verb (*kriyā*) of the sentence. The indicator is that differentiator which is not so related.

Criticism: No. In Sanskrit not all sentences have verbs, although they contain words for the qualifier and the indicator. For example, "this staff-bearer, lucky (because of his) long arms" (*subhāgo ayaṃ daṇḍī mahābāhur*)—here "this" refers to the qualificand, and the rest to the qualifier. Moreover, a word for an indicator can always be found one way or another.

(D8) A qualifier is a content of an awareness which is a cause of qualified awareness, and is also co-resident with revealed distinctness (*pratyayavyāvṛtti*) (of the qualificand from things lacking that qualifier). This definition implies that neither the qualifier nor the indicator is a content of qualified awareness; therefore, what seems to characterize the qualificand in a qualified awareness is its distinctness from things that do not have the qualifier.

Criticism: No. In the qualified awareness (E) "The lotus is blue" no mention has been made of *nonblue* and thus of *distinctness from nonblue*. Furthermore, the view is inconsistent with the aftercognition (F) "I know a blue thing", which clearly indicates that blueness is the character that has been taken in the original awareness (about which (F) reports) to characterize the thing. The definition has the further defect of embracing the Buddhist doctrine of *apoha*.

(D9) (The differentiator *blueness* in (E) is directly related to the thing differentiated while crows in (A) are not so related to the thing differentiated. Therefore the directly related differentiator is the qualifier and a differentiator not so related is an indicator.)

In the qualified awareness (G) "the person is a stickbearer" the qualifier happens to be the stick according to this definition and not stickhood, which is directly related to sticks and not to stickbearers. Thus a relation that does not involve any further relation for relating its relata is to be treated as a *direct* relation. Such a relation might be contact, inherence, or self-linking connection. Thus we may say that the content, negation and inherence stand directly related by way of self-linking connection to awareness, the locus and the terms of inherence respectively, and hence all of them may be regarded as qualifiers in the relevant contexts. This view is held by Śivāditya Miśra.

Criticism: No. In (H) "the cow is noneternal", (I) "a colored object is passing" and (J) "there is taste in colored things" the universals cowhood (in H) and colorness (in I and J) are directly related by way of inherence to the thing differentiated. Thus they should be regarded as qualifiers. But as they are obviously indicators in such contexts, the definition suffers from overextension. Moreover, if redness is understood to be related in an indirect manner to the crystal in "The crystal is red" redness, though not directly related to the thing differentiated (since the judgment is false), is treated as qualifier and the definition fails to cover it.

(D10) If something is understood as related to the differentiated through its being capable of representing something else (which alone is understood as directly related to the differentiated), that is an indicator; that which is understood as directly related to the differentiated is a qualifier.

Thus crows in (A) are relevant by being able to represent structural features by reference to which Devadatta's house is identified. If, however, in a situation where crows do not function in this way, that is, if they are understood as directly related, they are to be treated as qualifier like *stick* in (F).

Criticism: No. This implies that the word for the indicator is to be understood in its secondary meaning. Furthermore (in a negative judgment "there is no cow" when the utterer was asked to bring cows that are pulling carts but definitely saw other cows there) the hearer understands the statement (as he himself was sure of the presence of some cows there) as expressing an absence whose counterpositive is *cow in general.* In this example *cow* (i.e., the counterpositive) is the indicator though it doesn't represent any other thing by reference to which negation is understood. Hence the definition of indicator suffers from underextension and that of qualifier from overextension.

(D11) The differentiator which happens to be related to the

qualificand at the time of awareness of differentiation is a qualifier; otherwise it is an indicator.

Thus matted hair in (B), if present in the saint at the time of awareness of differentiation, is to be treated as a qualifier and, if absent at that time, is to be treated as an indicator.

Criticism: Color, though an indicator in (K) "there is some taste in a colored pot", would have to be treated as a qualifier. Furthermore, *stick*, which is admitted to be a qualifier in (L) "he was a stick-bearer", cannot be treated as a qualifier according to this definition, since the sentence implies that the person is not *now* a stick-bearer.

Gaṅgeśa makes here a further remark that a color, which is an indicator in (K), would have to be treated as a qualifier if it is defined in (D11) as something co-resident with the limitor of the qualificandness (which in (K) is *potness*).

Siddhānta

3. (E874-879) After rejecting these Dl-D11 Gaṅgeśa makes the following observations. After the qualified awareness "the person is a stick-bearer" there arises an awareness of difference from non-stick-bearer in the stick-bearer. The person is so differentiated by reference to the stick and not by reference to any other property, say manhood, for in that case the stick-bearer could not have been differentiated from other men. So far as the indicator in (A), (B) and the other cases is concerned, the locus of differentiation is not limited by crow in (A) or by matted hair in (B), since in their absence also Devadatta's house or the saint are differentiated by reference to the structural features in (A) or ascetic appearance in (B).

Gaṅgeśa now offers his own definition:

(D12) That differentiator which is also the limitor of the locushood of differentiation (i.e., by reference to which the thing is differentiated from other things) is a qualifier; if it is not so, it is an indicator.

Something which is in fact a qualifier will not be understood in its character of being a qualifier if there is no mention of such a differentiation.

Gaṅgeśa here quotes the following sentence from Udayana in support of his position: "A differentiator, whether it is existent now or not, is a qualifier if it is co-resident (in a locus which is known as distinguished from other things by reference to it); a differentiator which is not so co-resident is an indicator." Gaṅgeśa thinks that this statement may be interpreted in any of the following senses:

Something is a qualifier if

(i) with reference to all its loci and with reference to these only differentiation is made;
or if (ii) the locushood of differentiation is limited by it,
or if (iii) no differentiation every locus of which is different from any of its loci is made with reference to it, and some differentiation is made with reference to it.

So understood, this account will not cover an indicator which admittedly serves to distinguish a thing which is not its locus from other things.

At this point Gaṅgeśa discusses approvingly five more definitions which, though different from D12, come close to it.

(D13) The limitor of the referentness (*pratiyogitā*) of the relation which is intended by the utterer is the qualifier; and what is not such a limitor is the indicator.

(D14) After the qualificand is presented as related to something, it is intended to be understood as related to some other differentiator, which latter is to be regarded as qualifier; otherwise, as indicator.

(D15) The qualifier is the referentness of a relation with the thing to be differentiated and a differentiator not so related is an indicator.

(D16) That differentiator which has to be understood to be related to another referent of the qualificand is a qualifier; otherwise, it is an indicator.

(D17) A property which is the referentness of a relation which has the designated (*uddeśya*) for its relatum (*anuyogin*), or which is the referent of the relation that has been intended to be understood by the utterer, is a qualifier; otherwise, it is an individuator.[88]

Section Sixteen: Propositional Awareness (*savikalpaka*)

Summary by Bimal Krishna Matilal

Pūrvapakṣa

Objection : In the judgment "this is a cow" the "this" part represents the presentation of something now, while the "cow" part refers to something remembered. So this judgment must be false.

Answer: No, though the "cow" part derives from memory, it is applied to the "this" as present now, and it is present now. Thus the judgment is true.

Prābhākara: Then the judgment is actually a case of recognition, since the "cow" part derives from memory.

Pūrvapakṣa answer : Yes, and if the memory is accurate the identification of the object as cow will be accurate and the judgment will be true.

Siddhānta

Gaṅgeśa: No. Recognition through memory is different from propositional perception. When we remember something we cognize it as "that", but when we perceive something we cognize it as "this". Propositional perception is a kind of perception, so it can't involve cognizing something as "that". Thus the Prābhākara answer is incorrect.

In fact, when we cognize this as pot, recognition doesn't come into it. The moment you see the object (cow) you immediately cognize it as a cow without any memory trace playing a role; your cognition is not based on memory. Recognition involves the awareness that you have seen this object before, but when you say "this is a cow" you are not recognizing this as the cow you saw before.

BOOK TWO: INFERENCE (*anumāna*)
Section One: Inferential Awareness (*anumiti*)

("ET" references in the following Sections 1-8 are to the edition and translation by C. Goekoop, RB5338. The summary of these sections is by K. H. Potter.)

(ET55) Since inference depends on perception, and is more generally recognized by all the systems, it is considered before comparison.

D1: An inferential awareness is an awareness produced by awareness that the qualification of the *pakṣa* by the *hetu* (*pakṣadharmatā*) is qualified by pervasion.

Its causal condition *par excellence* is inference (*anumāna*), which is the consideration (*parāmarśa*) of the *h* (*liṅga*), not the *h* considered—this will be explained later.

(ET57-58) Objection: Inference is not an instrument of knowledge. For even when we believe that there are no visible obstructions (*yogyopādhi*) there may still be doubt about possible deviation (i.e., the failure of the inference), since there may be an invisible obstruction. Furthermore, even when things have occurred together a hundred times we find there still may be deviation. In the world, a man speaks of fire just after seeing smoke because he supposes it to be present and because it fits experience; so he thinks his inference may be valid. But in fact nothing other than perception is an instrument of knowledge.

Answer: No. (1) In trying to prove the invalidity of inference you offer a positive example, but to do so amounts to offering an inference!

(2) "Inference is not an instrument of knowledge" means either that "inference is an instrument of knowledge" is doubtful or else that it is false—but neither of these statements can be known by perception. (3) The statement "inference is not an instrument of knowledge", whether true or not, involves contradiction. (4) If inference were invalid, perception would be too, since it is by inference that the validity of perception is proved. If perception's validity were grasped intrinsically we wouldn't have doubt about it.

Section Two: Five Definitions of Pervasion (*vyāptipañcaka*)

(ET 60) In the foregoing definition of inferential awareness what is meant by "pervasion"? It is not nondeviation (*avyabhicāritatva*) of *h* from *s*. For the following five ways of understanding "nondeviation" won't do.

D1: Nondeviation is the nonoccurrence of *h* in a locus of absence of *s*.

D2: Nondeviation is the nonoccurrence of *h* in a locus of absence of *s* which is different from a locus of *s*.

D3: Nondeviation is *h*'s not having the same locus as a mutual absence whose counterpositive is a locus of *s*.

D4: Nondeviation is *h*'s being the counterpositive of an absence which resides in all loci of absence of *s*.

D5: Nondeviation is *h*'s nonoccurrence in what is other than the locus of *s*.

All five of these definitions fail to apply in the case of only-positive (*kevalānvayin*) inferences.

Section Three: Lion and Tiger Definitions (*siṃhavyāghra*)

(ET64) The following two definitions of pervasion are also unsatisfactory:

D6: Pervasion is *h*'s not being a locus of the property *not-having-a-common-locus-with-s*.

D7: Pervasion is *h*'s not being a locus of the property *having-a-different-locus-from-s*.

Both D6 and D7 mean that the *h* does not have as its locus what is not a locus of *s*. But this will apply neither to (a) only-positive inferences, as above, nor to (b) smoke in the valid inference to fire, since whatever *s* you have in mind, smoke has as its locus what is not a locus of it.

Section Four: Absence Limited by a Property whose Loci are Different from its Counterpositive (*vyadhikaraṇāvacchinnābhāva*)

(ET66-67) Objection: In only-positive inferences such as "it is nameable because it is knowable" a negative example *is* available. Every entity is a locus of an absence the counterpositiveness of which is limited by a property whose loci are different from the counterpositive. So a pot, which is an entity, *can* serve as the *vp* for the only-positive inference quoted.

Counterobjection: Then there will be deviation (i.e., the inference will be invalid), since the *h* (knowableness) resides in the locus of the absence of *s* (viz., the pot).

Objector's reply: Not so, since deviation only occurs when the *h* occurs in the locus of an absence whose counterpositiveness is limited by the limitor of *s*-ness, which is not the case here.

Gaṅgeśa: If what you (the objector) say is true, you must offer as your *vp* an absence of something which has the same locus as absence-of-*s*, and this you haven't done. So the difficulty about only-positive inference is unresolved. Furthermore, a property which does not occur in the counterpositive cannot be a limitor of the counterpositiveness, for it is only an awareness qualified by this limitor that produces an idea of an absence. Otherwise the idea of an absence would arise from a nonpropositional awareness as well. This is why the statement "On the cow there is no hare's horn:" makes no sense: "there is no hare's horn" means "there is absence of horn in a hare."

Section Five: Fourteen More Faulty Definitions of Pervasion (*caturdáśalakṣaṇa*)

(ET70-109)

D8: Pervasion is *h*'s not being the locus of the property of not having a common locus with *s*. (This includes only-positive inferences, since the property of not having a common locus with *s* is present in *ākāśa* and other eternal things, thus *ākāśa*, etc., are the required *vipakṣas*.

Gaṅgeśa: No, since whichever way you quantify "not being the locus of the property of not having a common locus with *s*" it either fails to cover only-positive inferences or else it fails to cover the typical case of smoke and fire, for example.

D9: Pervasion is *h*'s having a common locus with *s*, where *s* is not the counterpositive of an absolute absence which has a common locus with *h*.

Gaṅgeśa: No. (a) Mountain-fire is the counterpositive of an absolute absence which has a common locus with kitchen-smoke, so the definition will not apply to the valid inference to fire from smoke. (b) Substanceness, etc., will not be pervaded by what is only non-locuspervading (since a substance *will* be the counterpositive of an absolute absence which has a common locus with *h*).

D10: Pervasion is *h*'s having as locus something which is the locus of *s* but is not the counterpositive of a mutual absence residing in a locus of *h*.

Gaṅgeśa: No. (a) Pervasion is being defined, yet the phrase "locus of *s* which is not the counterpositive of a mutual absence residing in a locus of *h*" presupposes pervasion, and for that matter we can't understand the terms *h* and *s* without presupposing pervasion. (b) The definition underextends; it fails to impart validity to valid inferences such as "X has contact with monkey because it is this tree" (since part of the tree—the roots—has no contact with the monkey), or 'X has fire because it has smoke" (because the mountain, which is a locus of fire, is the counterpositive of a mutual absence residing in kitchen, which is a locus of smoke).

D11: Pervasion is *h*'s having a common locus with an *s* which is not a locus of the property of differing in locus from some *x*, if this property is described by all the properties which have a common locus with *h*.

Gaṅgeśa : No. (a) Some properties, e.g., knowability, do not differ in locus from any *x*, so there are no such *hetus*. (b) Among properties which have a common locus with *h* (smoke) is fire, since they both reside by contact in kitchen. But fire also inheres in the particular of fire by inherence. So in the valid inference "this has fire because it has smoke" *h* nevertheless has a common locus (viz., a kitchen) with *s*, a kitchen being a locus of the property of differing-in-locus-from-fiery-particles...

D12: Pervasion is a relation free from obstructions. An obstruction is something *x* which pervades *s* without pervading *h*. And pervading something *y* is not being the counterpositive of an absolute absence residing in a locus of *y*. And counterpositiveness does not presuppose pervasion, since it is a self-linking connector.[89]

Objection to D12: Either the obstructor is to be chosen as relevant to the inference in question or not. Suppose the inference in question is (A) "It has fire because it has smoke." If we can choose as obstruction something vitiating any old inference different from (A) then (A) cannot ever be valid, since we can easily find some other inference (B) in which some property P pervades the *s* of (B) without pervading the *h* of (B), which property happens to accompany smoke.

On the other hand, if the above procedure is disallowed the definition becomes unworkable. In a valid inference like (A) no obstruction is possible, and so the term "absence of obstruction" (in D12) is meaningless, having no counterpositive.

Supporter of D12: Then I will expand my definition:

D12a: Pervasion holds when the following two conditions are satisfied: (1) for all *x*, if *x* pervades *s* then it pervades *h*; (2) for all *x*, if *x* does not pervade *s* then it does not pervade *h*.

Gaṅgeśa: This won't do, since pervasion is not a property of the *h* (which it ought to be).

Supporter of D12: All right, then:

D12b: Pervasion holds when the following two conditions are satisfied: (1) *h* is a thing for whose *s* it is the case that for all *x*, if *x* pervadas *s* then it pervades *h;* (2) *h* is a thing for whose *s* it is the case that for all *x*, if *x* does not pervade *s* then it does not pervade *h*.

Gaṅgeśa: No. Let fire be *h* and smoke be *s* (so that the inference is the invalid "it has smoke because it has fire"). The idea of D12 is that an obstruction, say wet fuel, is forthcoming, and that is why the inference is invalid. But wet fuel is not the requisite obstruction, because *all* wet fuel doesn't pervade fire, and no single particular instance of wet fuel satisfies the formula. (It is not the case that for wet kitchen-fuel which pervades the fire in question that it pervades smoke, since it does not pervade mountain-smoke.)

D13: Pervasion is a relation free from obstructions, i.e., it is nondeviation from all things from which *h* does not deviate.

Gaṅgeśa: We have already refuted equivalent definitions involving the notion of nondeviation (cf. Section Two of this Book, above).

D14: Pervasion is a relation involving *all* of *h*.[89A]

Gaṅgeśa: No. If there is only one instance of *h* there is no "all" And even where there are several instances of h, no single instance of *s* has for its locus the loci of all instances of *h*.

D15: Pervasion is a relation involving *all* of *s*.

Gaṅgeśa: No, for the same reasons. Furthermore, the number of instances *s* and *h* may not be the same.

D16: Pervasion is a relation involving instances of *h* which corres- pond to instances of *s*.

Gaṅgeśa: The difficulties adduced against (14) still apply.

D17: Pervasion is *h*'s having a common locus with an *s* which has a common locus with all those properties which have a common locus with *h*.

Gaṅgeśa: This fails in the same way that D11 did, or else it is just ambiguous.

D18: Pervasion is a natural (or "essential") (*svābhāvika*) relation.[90]

Gaṅgeśa : A "natural" relation may mean (1) that it is self-caused (*svabhāvajanya*) or (2) that it resides in what is natural (*svabhāvāśrita*). But in sense (1) the definition underextends, and in sense (2) it overextends.

D19: Pervasion is inseparability (*avinābhāvatva*).[91]

Gaṅgeśa: No, for then it would not apply to only-positive inferences.

D20: Pervasion is just a relation (between *h* and *s*), since even a relation involving deviation becomes nondeviant when something is supplied.

Gaṅgeśa: No. Our problem is to define the pervasion which involves the consideration of the *h* (i.e., *liṅgaparāmarśa*), the fourth member of the inference-for-others formula that is the specific occasion for inferential awareness. Since successful inferential awareness does not arise from consideration of any old relation, D20 fails.

D21: Pervasion (a) in only-positive inferences is the relation of *h* with the only-positive property of *s*, (b) in only-negative inferences it is nonoccurrence of *h* in what is other than locus of *s*. On this view the occasion for successful inferential awareness is the awareness that *p* has *s* (*pakṣadharmatā*), but this is not a fault, since we hold that the complete set of causal conditions leading to a successful inferential awareness includes not only the occasion (that *p* has *s*) but also the specific conditions involved for each kind of inference (only-positive, only-negative, and positive-negative).

Gaṅgeśa: No. As for (b), there is no nonoccurrence of smoke in what is other than locus of fire, since there is smoke in what is other than mountain, which is a locus of fire.

In all these definitions there is circularity, since the very notions of *h* and *s* presuppose understanding of pervasion.

Objection: An *s* is that which is, or needs to be, proved.

Gaṅgeśa: No. Kitchen fire (which is fire) is not what is, or needs to be, proved in the inference "the mountain has fire because it has smoke."

Objection: We must already know in a general way the meaning of pervasion; otherwise how can we find the fault in someone else's reasoning? So we need not define pervasion.

Gaṅgeśa: But we need to know when our own inferences are valid, and for this, we need to have a complete understanding of the nature of pervasion.

Section Six: The Conclusive Definition (*siddhāntalakṣaṇa*)

(ET109-110) Gaṅgeśa:

D22: Pervasion is the having of a common locus of something with something else that differs from what is limited by the limitor of the counterpositiveness to the absolute absence that has a common locus with *h* and has no common locus with its counterpositive.

Section Seven: General Absence (*sāmānyābhāva*)

(ET116-117) Gaṅgeśa: There must be, in addition to the absence of kitchen-fire, absence of mountain-fire, etc., a distinct item called "absence of fire in general", not reducible to the product of the specific absences. Otherwise, once we are aware that air has none of the colors known to us, we should not continue to wonder whether air has color—but we do!

Section Eight: Particular Absence (*viśeṣavyāpti*)

(ET119-138) Gaṅgeśa: Here are some more definitions of pervasion (that are acceptable):

D23: There is pervasion of A by B if, and only if, A shares a locus with B in such a way that B is not the counterpositive of a constant absence which shares some locus with A and differs in locus from its counterpositive.

D24: There is pervasion of A by B if, and only if, A shares a locus with B in such a way that locus of B is not the counterpositive of a mutual absence which shares some locus with A.

D25: There is pervasion of A by B if, and only if, A has a locus of B such that the locus of B is not the counterpositive of a mutual absence which shares some locus with A.

These definitions differ from D22 in that they operate with absences of particular instances of fire and smoke rather than with the general absence discussed in the preceding section. The virtue is that on these definitions pervasion is a relation between a particular set of fires and a particular set of instances of smoke.

Gaṅgeśa next discusses a way of speaking which overcomes the difficulties posed (for certain inferences) by the fact that absence of contact incompletely occurs in (e.g.) substances. On the other hand, mutual absences cannot occur incompletely, so no such difficulty arises there.

Objection: We see that the pair fire-and-lake are absent from any locus of smoke. So we can say that in a locus of smoke there is constant absence of fire and mutual absence of locus of fire, which in turn means that D22-D25 fail to capture the necessary relation.

Gaṅgeśa: We do not admit absences of pairs of the sort you mention (i.e., absence of fire-and-lake from locus of smoke). Or if you insist on our admitting them, it is still clear that their counterpositives are *pairs,* not the members of those pairs taken distributively.

Pervasion may also be defined as being free from obstruction, in one of the following senses:

D26: There is pervasion of A by B if, and only if, A shares a locus with B in such a way that B shares a locus with absolute absence whose counterpositive is that which is determined by all limitors of counterpositiveness to absolute absence sharing a locus with A;

or D27: Pervasion is *h*'s sharing a locus with that *s* from which deviate all things that deviate from *h*;

or D28: There is pervasion of A by B if, and only if, A does not share a locus with an absolute absence whose counterpositive is all that is no counterpositive of an absolute absence sharing a locus with B.

An *h* with an obstruction *x* will not satisfy these definitions, since *s* (say, smoke) does not share a locus with the constant absence of *s* (say, wet fuel), where *x* is the counterpositive of an absolute absence sharing a locus with *h* (say, fire). (Similarly for D28.)

D29: Pervasion is A's being connected with B, where the connectedness has for its limitor the proper universal belonging to A. Thus, where A is smoke and B is fire, since smokeness *is* the limitor of the connectedness (the whole of smoke being connected with fire), the definition is satisfied; while where A is fire and B smoke, since fireness is not the limitor of the connectedness (not all fires being smoky) the definition is not satisfied.

However, if A is fire-with-wet-fuel and B is smoke, the definition is satisfied, since all fire-with-wet-fuel is connected with smoke. Thus, in general, for B to be pervaded by A is for A to have a nature determined by the limitor of (the property of) sharing the locus with B. Now, since pervasion is thus understood, and with it the terms "pervader" and "pervaded", the circularity mentioned earlier is not a problem. E.g., we can define an obstruction as "that which does not pervade *h* but does pervade *s* limited by *h.*"

Section 8A : *ata eva catuṣṭayam*
Three Definitions of an Obstruction[92]

(ET142-143) Since the above definition of an obstruction holds, people say (1) An obstruction is a qualifier of the *h* which is different from the limitor of the *h*-ness and which limits the relation with the *s* in what is considered to be the *h.* But equally legitimate is (2) an obstruction is what is not a pervader of the *h* but is a pervader of *s* as limited by *h.* Likewise, (3) the obstruction is that pervasion which is marked by a nature which limits the connectorness to the *s* and shines in what is considered to be the *h* as a flower shines in a crystal (nearby). All these points follow from the definition of obstruction given in the previous paragraph.

Section Nine: The Means of Grasping Pervasion
(*vyāptigrahopāya*)
Summary by K.H. Potter and K.K. Chakrabarti

The edition and translation referred to here by "ET" is that of Mrinalkanti Gangopadhyaya, *Journal of Indian Philosophy* 3, 1975. The sections numbered here correspond to the numbering of ET.

(ET167-172) Prābhākara objection: Pervasion is not grasped through repeated observation (*bhūyodarśana*) because no observation by itself can cause such ascertainment, and because, since observations are momentary and nonsimultaneous, a collective experience of them is impossible.

Counterobjection: The traces of the observations, together with the sense organs as accessories, are the cause of ascertainment of pervasion, because in the case of recognition the sense organs are likewise accessories.[93]

Prābhākara: No. A trace laid down by an observation of *x* can cause memory or recognition only of *x.* So how can traces produce awareness of pervasion?

Furthermore, what does "repeated observation" of the relation (of *h* and *s*) actually mean? Does it mean (1) observation of that relation in many loci? Or (2) the observation of the relation between many *sādhyas* and *hetus*? Or (3) many observations of the relation?

None of the alternatives is acceptable. (1) By observing only one locus of the relation between taste and color, or (2) between (the single *h*) potness and (the single *s*) substanceness, one may grasp pervasion. Again, (3) will lead to ascertainment of pervasion merely by the continuing stream of awareness (*dhārāvāhikajñāna*) of a single locus. And (3) also fails because manyness (*bhūyastva*) is not a consecutive property (*anugatadharma*).[94]

Moreover, even though we can repeatedly observe the concurrence of earthness and being scratchable by iron, there is no pervasion between them.

Counterobjection: Then we say that repeated observation together with *tarka* as accessory causes the grasping of pervasion.

Prābhākara: If so, then let *tarka* itself be the cause, with observation of concurrence and nonperception of deviance being the accessories?

Counterobjection: There can be no *tarka* without repeated observation.

Prābhākara: No, for a person who has understood (through words) can use *tarka* in respect to the very first observation.

(ET174-175) Counterobjector: Then let us accept your suggestion that *tarka* with the accessories you mentioned above causes grasping of pervasion.

Prābhākara: No, for *tarka* presupposes grasping of pervasion; thus infinite regress.

Counterobjector: The newborn child must have the awareness of pervasion producing the inference leading him to activity or inactivity, and this must be without *tarka*. So there is no infinite regress.

Prābhākara: In that case, *tarka* is obviously not the cause of grasping pervasion!

(ET177) Counterobjector: Grasping pervasion is caused when all (the *sādhyas* and *hetus*) are known through their connection with universals; but since repeated observation is required to have this knowledge of connection with universals, it is a necessary condition.

Prābhākara: No, because it is simpler to think that the universal is the connection, not the knowledge of connection. In any case, we don't accept such a connection.

Counterobjector: Repeated observation is required to remove the doubt as to whether the concurrence is merely accidental, like that of the crow and the fruit.

Prābhākara: But even after further observations that doubt may persist.

(ET179-185) Counterobjector: The cause of awareness of pervasion is the awareness of the absence of any obstruction. A doubt whether the presence of a particular thing (e.g., a pot) at a certain place or time is due to an obstruction can be sometimes removed by discovering that the thing is a pervader of the *h*, sometimes by discovering that the thing is not a pervader of the *s*, but in any case it requires repeated observations.

Prābhākara: No, since the awareness of the absence of an imperceptible obstruction will require inference, and so infinite regress will result.

(ET181) Counterobjector: But if there is doubt about whether obstructions are present pervasion cannot be ascertained. The awareness that there are not obstructions arises from awareness that there are not pervaders of *s* (or that there are pervaders of *h*), and that awareness in turn is derived from repeated observation. The number of observations required is determined by the nature of each case, and no problems about consecutiveness need arise.

Even though a doubt whether an object does or does not pervade the *s* or the *h* does not obstruct ascertainment of pervasion, still, since from such a doubt there arises another doubt about the regularity of the connection (between *s* and *h*) which *does* block ascertainment, it is necessary to remove the first doubt.

Prābhākara: No, since as we pointed out before to remove such a doubt requires awareness of imperceptible obstructions. Furthermore, the traces produced by repeated observation cannot serve as accessories to the external sense organs (as was contended they could by the counterobjector), since even without such mediation a person may be aware of pervasion (on only a single observation). And the traces cannot be accessory to the internal organ as well, since then any ascertainment of pervasion will require the traces and as a result the traces—or the memory the traces produce—will have to be counted as an additional instrument of knowledge!

So pervasion is ascertained by a single observation; pervasion is just the absence of obstructions. And an absence is either the mere locus or the relation to a point in time or the self-illuminating awareness of these. Again, awareness of the counterpositive is not required for awareness of the mere locus, etc., and therefore awareness of an obstruction is not required for ascertainment of pervasion. Thus once one is aware of the absence of obstruction nothing further needs to be observed. However, awareness of the obstruction *is* required in order that one speak about pervasion (=the absence of obstructions), just as in order to speak about the length of something one must know what is the standard of comparison.

(ET188) Counterobjector: Then any old awareness of a relation between two things will produce ascertainment of a pervasion!

Prābhākara: No. When there is a memory of the obstruction together with the collection of all the conditions required for perceiving the obstruction—excluding the obstruction itself and what is pervaded by it—then there is produced awareness of the mere locus accompanied by the nonperception of any obstruction.

(ET190) Counterobjector: But if pervasion is ascertained by a single observation, and then there is perception of a specific thing, no question about pervasion arises any more than one who has seen a donkey and a fire together would suspect pervasion between them.

Prābhākara: No. Even after ascertaining pervasion one may experience a doubt as to whether an unsuspected obstruction is actually present, a doubt which may indeed be removed by repeated observation. Alternatively, doubt as to the presence of pervasion can arise from doubt about the validity of the awareness derived from a single observation, e.g., even when the collection of causal conditions requisite for producing awareness of pot is present, still one may doubt that collection is in fact present and thus doubt the validity of one's awareness.

(ET192-193) Counterobjector: All right, then there may as well be ascertainment of pervasion between the donkey and fire (where of course there isn't any pervasion).

Prābhākara: No. An erroneous awareness—that there is pervasion between donkey and fire—results from two distinct awarenesses which are actually unrelated—here (1) perception of the donkey and (2) memory of pervasion based on perception of pervasion elsewhere. Because of a failure, based on a defect, to realize that there is no relation between the two awarenesses speech-behavior (*vyavahāra*) arises. But such an error (=superimposition, *āropa*) doesn't occur in the present case, for there is no such memory.

(ET194-197) A section of the Mīmāṃsakas say: Pervasion is either (1) the *h*'s sharing a locus with an *s* which is not the counterpositive of any constant absence occurring in a locus of *h*; or (2) the locus of *s* not being the counterpositive of a mutual absence occurring in a locus of *h*. (I.e., they accept one or another of Gaṅgeśa's definitions of pervasion.) In either case pervasion is perceptible and is ascertained by a single observation, since when one perceives either the constant absence or the mutual absence of *h* in, say, the kitchen, one is not aware of either fire or the locus of fire as being the counterpositive of such absences. As for the donkey-fire case, pervasion may be cognized even there until it is sublated.

Prābhākara: This won't do. For according to the above view pervasion occurs only between particular things—this fire or that smoke—and it is pervasion between smoke and fire in general that is required for inference. Furthermore, if only one observation is made it cannot be determined that neither fireness nor being a locus of fire is the limitor of the counterpositiveness in question.

(ET198-199) Gaṅgeśa: This position (of the Prābhākara) is wrong. An obstruction can be defined either as (1) that which pervades the *s* under discussion and does not pervade the *h*, or as (2) a qualifier which limits the relatedness of the *s* with what is thought to be the *h*. Whichever definition is accepted, pervasion cannot be the absence of obstuction, since (in inferential awareness depending on awareness of pervasion) one is aware neither of the presence or absence of obstructions.

The property of *not having an obstruction* should be defined as the *h*'s sharing a locus with an *s* which deviates from objects which themselves deviate from the *h*. But such a property cannot be ascertained by a single observation.

Furthermore, the cause of inference is not awareness of pervasion alone, but awareness of pervasion as qualified by *pervasionness*. And this *pervasionness* is identified by the Prābhākara as *being an absence of obstruction*. But awareness of pervasion as qualified by *that* property is not possible without being aware of the obstruction itself, since a qualificative awareness presupposes awareness of the qualifier. We are not aware of the obstruction prior to ascertaining pervasion.

(ET200-201) Let it be, as the Prābhākara said, that awareness of the counterpositive is only required for speech about absences and not for awareness of an absence. Still, the result will be that no inference can involve speech about absence of obstructions, and thus an inferential awareness grounded on awareness of absence of obstruction will result even without any awareness of obstruction, which is not the case.

Pervasion cannot be ascertained by a single observation, for there may be doubt as to whether the *h* deviates, and such a doubt requires awareness of general properties such as coexistence, as well as nonapprehension of specific characteristics.

(ET202) Prābhākara: But such a doubt—as to whether *h* deviates—does not obstruct the ascertainment of invariable concomitance, since a doubt about the object to be grasped does not obstruct the grasping of that object—otherwise we could never ascertain an object at the moment following a doubt.

Gaṅgeśa: Agreed. What we mean is this: if the factors (awareness of common properties, nonawareness of specific characteristics) conducing to doubt are present, only doubt can follow, not ascertainment (and this can well be the case at the first moment of observation). Moreover, if the collection of causal conditions required for awareness of *x* obstructs some other awareness (say, *y*) then *x* itself would obstruct *y*, provided no specific characteristic is grasped.

(ET203-204) So, repeated observation cannot remove doubt, and *tarka* is of no help because of infinite regress. How can pervasion be ascertained, then? We say: the cause of the ascertainment of pervasion is the perception of the co-occurrence (of *h* and *s*) together with absence of awareness of any deviation (of *h*).[95]

An awareness may be either an ascertainment or a doubt. Doubt sometimes arises from questions about an obstruction being present, sometimes from perception of common properties together with absence of awareness of specific characteristics. And absence of such doubt arises sometimes from *tarka*, which negates the opposite alternative (viz., that deviation is present), sometimes absence of doubt merely stands by itself.

Objection: Then infinite regress results, since *tarka* involves awareness of pervasion.

Gaṅgeśa: No, since *tarka* is only invoked when there is a possibility of doubt. When one alternative involves "practical contradiction" (*vyāghāta*) and no doubt can arise, ascertainment of pervasion follows without any use of *tarka*.

Section Ten: Reductio Ad Absurdum (*tarka*)
Summary by Kishor Kumar Chakrabarti

"E" references are to N.S. Ramanuja Tatachariar's edition of *Anumānakhaṇḍa* with the commentaries of Rucidatta and Dharmarājādhvarīndra (Tirupati 1982).

(E192-208). If it were the case that smoke is not caused by either what is concomitant with fire or by what is not concomitant with fire, smoke would have been uncaused.[96]

When it is doubted whether smoke is caused by fire, there may be three different kinds of doubt: (1) Is smoke always caused by something different from fire? (2) Is smoke in some cases caused by something different from fire? (3) Is the occurrence of smoke uncaused? All three these kinds of doubt are incompatible with one's own action.[97]

In every known case smoke is found to be accompanied by fire; further, in every known case absence of fire is accompanied by absence of smoke. The skeptic knows this. Moreover, he invariably lights up a fire if he wants to produce smoke. If he is doubtful about fire being the cause of smoke he should not do so invariably, and if he does so invariably he should not be doubtful. Since he does so invariably, and since this is incompatible with sustaining the doubt, the doubt cannot be sustained. Thus the skeptic's own action stultifies the doubt. Hence there is no infinite regress.[98]

Repeated observation of the co-presence and co-absence of the pervaded and the pervader is conducive to *tarka*. Though the impression of such repeated observation is a cause of *tarka*, such impression should not be regarded as an additional source of knowledge, for *tarka* is not a kind of knowledge.[99]

Tarka is required for perceptual knowledge of pervasion; but knowledge of pervasion through inference and testimony may take place without *tarka*.[100]

The *tarka* offered in support of a generalization should not itself be faulty; otherwise the generalization based on it may be faulty too. This is similar to the relationship between awareness of the "differentiating factor" (*viśeṣa*) and the resolution of doubt.[101]

Others have held that although *tarka* is required as the support of the original awareness of pervasion, it is not required as the support in some cases of remembrance of pervasion, so that there is no occasion of an infinite regress. One case where the knowledge of pervasion can only be a remembrance is when a just born infant engages in such activities as sucking the breast after having inferred that it is beneficial. A beginningless regress of previous cognitions of pervasion is involved here.[102]

Section Eleven: Comprehensiveness of Pervasion (*vyāptyanugama*)

(The summary is based on S.C. Vidyabhusana (B and RB: HIL). "E" references are to N.S. Ramanuja Tatachariar's edition (Tirupati 1982).

Comprehensiveness (*anugama*) is the property of a pervasion which exhibits in one form all the various kinds of pervasion previously defined. The pervasion involving mutual absence is a comprehensive one and should be accepted as a cause of inference for simplicity's sake. Of the definitions of pervasion given in *Tattvacintāmaṇi,* definitions D3, D5, D9 and D10 (in the summary of *Tattvacintāmaṇi* above) involve mutual absences. The conclusive definition of pervasion may also be modified so as to involve mutual absence. Of these D10 is by far the simplest.

Section Twelve: Perception through Connection with the Universal (*sāmānyalakaṣaṇa*)

Summary by K.K. Chakrabarti

("E" references are to the edition by N.S. Ramanuja Tatachariar, Tirupati 1982.)

1. (E230-233) The awareness of pervasion of all cases of smoke (by cases of fire) takes place by means of *sāmānyalakaṣaṇa* (connection between sense organ and object through a universal). Otherwise, how can the smoke on the mountain, which is not known to be pervaded, be the basis of an inferential awareness? The said connection is either what qualifies that with which the sense organ is related or it is something else. Since the sense organ must be

connected with what is perceived and since there can be no contact with what is past or future, it must be the latter.

Pūrvapakṣa

Others (commentators say Mīmāṃsakas) think not. For the pervasion of what is limited by smokeness (i.e., all smokes) is perceived in an instance of smoke with which a sense organ is connected through the perception of smokeness; then that pervasion is remembered; and then it is cognized as the property of the case of smoke which is the *pakṣa*; after all of these take place the inferential awareness arises. Alternatively: in a case of smoke with which the sense organ is connected it becomes known that that instance inasmuch as it has smokeness is pervaded by fire; then the pervasion is remembered in the same manner; then there is the awareness that this instance involves smoke which insofar as it has smokeness is pervaded by fire; and then results the inferential awareness.

2.(E234-235) In order to be the basis of inference the awareness of pervasion, the memory of it and the awareness that it (the pervasion) belongs to the *pakṣa* must all share the same chief qualifier. In the case of a word like "cow", etc., also the awareness of designative capacity (*śakti*), the memory of that and the understanding of the meaning of the sentence are related as cause and effect insofar as they share the same chief qualifier. After all this there is the awareness that smoke is pervaded by fire, but not the awareness that all cases of smoke are pervaded by fire. So it cannot be maintained that *sāmānyalakṣaṇa* connection accounts for the awareness of all smokes (as fiery).

Objection to the Mīmāṃsaka: The inference that this mountain has fire must be preceded by the awareness of fire as the qualifier, because the said inference is a qualified awareness. The *sāmānyalakṣaṇa* connection has to be admitted to account for the awareness of fire on the mountain.[103]

Mīmāṃsaka: The above argument is not acceptable. With respect to qualified awareness it is both necessary and more economical to regard the awareness having as its qualifier the limitor of the property of being a qualifier to be the causal condition. Such awareness is already there (and so there is no need for *sāmānyalakṣaṇa* connection). For the qualified awareness "(this is a) cow" the simultaneous connection of the sense organ with the qualificandum and the qualifier is the cause (not just the awareness of the qualifier). The nonpropositional perception (of cowness) is not (a prerequisite). Sufficient evidence (for postulating nonpropositional perception) is lacking. The fact that the awareness is qualified cannot of itself provide the requisite evidence, for no *sapakṣa* is available.

Objection to the Mīmāṃsaka: The awareness "the man is a stick-holder" is the *sapakṣa.*

Mīmāṃsaka: No, no awareness of qualifier is a causal condition there, and anyway it is an awareness of a qualified qualifier (*viśiṣṭavaiśiṣṭyajñāna*). Furthermore, a person who happens to have a *sāmānyalakṣaṇa* awareness where the qualifier is knowability should be omniscient. If so such a person should not even question whether something cognized by another is potness or not. Such a person should be able to ascertain that it is or it isn't by his awareness of knowability.

Objection to the Mīmāṃsaka: Such a person does come to know all pots through knowability, but not potness.

Mīmaṃsaka: Why? Isn't potness a knowable? Then why should it be different? Since the property which belongs to all pots is a knowable, it is impossible that it should remain unknown.[104]

Siddhānta

3. (E235–249) Gaṅgeśa: If there were no *sāmānyalakṣaṇa* awareness one could not have a doubt as to whether smoke, etc., are deviant (from fire) except through recourse to *reductio ad absurdum* (*tarka*). For the known cases of smoke are cognized as being together with fire, but the instances of smoke occurring at other times and places are uncognized, since there would be no way of coming to be aware of them. If, however, all instances of smoke are presented through the universal (i.e., the property smokeness), there can be no doubt as to whether some other particular item is (or is not) smoke where the particular features of the thing are not seen (otherwise).

Objection: (No, the argument is this:) (Without *sāmānyalakṣaṇa* awareness) there would have been no interest in cooking, etc., and no desire for satisfaction, etc., since one does not desire what already exists, and what does not exist (now) is not cognized (unless we admit *sāmānyalakṣaṇa* awareness). So it should be admitted that of all the things that are known through the common property of satisfactionness, etc., desire is felt for those which do not exist (yet), though not for those that do exist (now).

Gaṅgeśa: This is not right. Although what doesn't yet exist may be uncognized, out of the awareness of what does exist there originate by their very nature desire and volition for what doesn't yet exist. And this does not overextend, for the causal connection of cognitions with desires and volitions is not based on them having the same contents but on their having the same qualifier. Not on them having the same content, for even when the contents are the same desire and volition do not come into being if there is no awareness having the same qualifier.

As for the argument that since there is omniscience doubt (about potness) would be impossible, it is the awareness "that is a pot", having potness as qualifier, which is opposed to the doubt (on the objector's view). But that awareness doesn't occur, since the causal conditions for it are not present. Therefore, although there is the awareness of everything, including potness, etc., still there may be the doubt as to whether a thing is a pot or not.

Section Thirteen: On Obstruction (*upādhi*)
Summary by K. K. Chakrabarti

("E" references are to the edition of *Tattvacintāmaṇi* by Vindhyesvara Prasada Dvivedin and Vamacarana Bhattacarya (B3400; RB5308), Chowkhamba Sanskrit Series 42, 1913–1927)

Pūrvapakṣa

(E877) An obstruction may be defined as:

D1: That which pervades the (putative) *sādhya* and does not pervade the (putative) *hetu.*

This is not circular: although there can be no ascertainment of pervasion once an obstruction is detected, the awareness of being free from obstructions is not a causal condition of the awareness of pervasion. Alternatively, "being the pervader of *x*" may be defined as "not being the counterpositive of any absolute absence belonging to the locus of *x*." Then also the charge of circularity cannot be raised.

Nevertheless, D1 is not satisfactory. It fails to apply to an obstruction which (does not pervade the *s* as such, but) pervades the *s* as limited by a property of the *p* or as limited by the *h*.[105]

(E893–908) In this connection it may be asked whether "being other than the *pakṣa*" (*pakṣetaratva*) is acceptable as an obstruction. Some have held that it should not be regarded as an obstruction, for then even good inferences would be vitiated by it.[106]

In this regard a distinction should be drawn between inferences possessing the fault of sublation and other inferences. For the former kind "being other than the *pakṣa*" may be accepted as an obstruction. In such cases the *p* is devoid of the *s* and hence the said property ("being other than the *pakṣa*") may with certainty be said to pervade the *s*.[107] But insofar as inferences which do not possess the fault of sublation are concerned, "being other than the *pakṣa*" may not be accepted as an obstruction.[108]

(E910–912) Another definition of an obstruction is:

D2: An obstruction is that which is coextensive with the *sādhya* but does not pervade the *hetu.*

This too is not a good definition. To say that an obstruction is coextensive with the *s* implies that the obstruction is pervaded by the *s* (and also that the obstruction pervades the *s*). But that the obstruction is pervaded by the *s* does not contribute towards the reason which determines an obstruction as a fault. An obstruction is a fault primarily for the reason that it proves that the putative *h* is deviant. That the obstruction pervades the *s* but does not pervade the *h* proves that the *h* is not pervaded by the *s*: there is indeed the law that what is not pervaded by the pervader is not pervaded by the pervaded. Thus it is clear that the obstruction pervaded by the *s* cannot be the ground for proving that *h* is deviant. It is also clear from the above that the *h*'s deviance would follow from the condition that the obstruction is coextensive with the *s* (and does not pervade the *h*) as also from the condition that the obstruction is not coextensive with the *s*, but pervades it without being pervaded by it (and does not pervade the *h*). Hence that the obstruction is coextensive with the *s* should not be included in the definition of an obstruction, for it includes the superfluous condition that the obstruction is pervaded by the *s*, besides the required condition that the obstruction pervades the *s*.

(E913–914) So far as ordinary usage is concerned, by "obstruction" is meant that the property of which is transferred to something else. But so far as scientific discourse (*śāstra*) is concerned, by "obstruction" is meant that which pervades the *s* and does not pervade the *h*.

(E915–924) Others have defined an obstruction as:

D3: That the absence of which is opposed to deviation.

(Since an obstruction proves deviation, the absence of an obstruction may be thought to prove the opposite of deviation.) The absence of what pervades without being pervaded, however, is not opposed to deviation, for there may be deviation in spite of its absence. For example, knowability pervades noneternality and qualityness (*guṇatva*) as well, but there is no pervasion between noneternality and qualityness.

But that is not correct. While it is true that what is pervaded by what is pervaded by the *s* does not deviate from the *s*, it is not true that what is pervaded by what pervades the *s* does not deviate from the *s*. It has also to be borne in mind that by a fault is meant that the presence of which would obstruct an inference, but not that the absence of which would always lead to an inference.

(E924–929) Again, an obstruction may be defined as:

D4: That which does not pervade the *hetu* but pervades the *sādhya* as limited by a property of the *pakṣa*.

But this is not acceptable, for it fails to apply to an obstruction which pervades the *s* as limited by the *h*. It also fails to apply to those obstructions, such as wet fuel, where the *s* is not limited by such a property of the *p*.

(E930–935) Again, an obstruction may be defined as:

D5: That which does not pervade the *hetu* but pervades the *sādhya* as limited by the *hetu*.

But this fails to apply to an obstruction which pervades the *s* as limited by a property of the *p*. It cannot also be that deviation from the *s* as limited would lead to deviation from the actual *s*, for that is vitiated by the fault called *arthāntara*.

(E936–944) Next, an obstruction may be defined as:

D6: That which does not pervade the *hetu* but pervades what amounts to the *sādhya* (*paryavasitasādhya*).

(This definition is suggested by the author of *Ratnakośa*.) For example, consider the inference "sound is possessed of that property which is different from those properties of sound which are different from noneternality, because sound is cognizable." In this inference the *s* resolves into noneternality; the property of being a product which pervades noneternality may therefore be regarded as the obstruction.[109]

This definition too may be open to objection. Take the following inference: the dyad is not inherent in noneternal substances, because it is a substance which is devoid of noneternal size. (Since it is already known that the dyad inheres in substances,) here the *s* resolves into *being inherent in eternal substances*. Then *being inherent in substances which are devoid of touch* turns out (wrongly) to be an obstruction, because it pervades what amounts to the *s* and does not pervade the *h*.

Siddhānta

(E952–989) A correct definition is:

D7: An obstruction is that because of deviation from which the *hetu* becomes deviant from the *sādhya*.

But D6 is acceptable also, if we interpret "what amounts to the *sādhya*" as the *s* limited by those properties through which the *s* is determined.[110] The character through which the *s* is determined could be the *h*, etc. It is obvious that the *h* would deviate from the *s* if it deviates from what is coextensive with the *s* or from what pervades the *s* without being pervaded by it. It is also clear that if the *h* deviates from what pervades the *s* as limited by the *h* or some character of the *p*, it deviates from the *s* itself. This will hold if the *h* does not deviate from the qualifier (of the *s*, such as the *h* or some character of the *p*). In that case, if the *h* deviates from the qualified (i.e., the *s* as limited) it must deviate from the qualificand (the *s*) as well. It thus follows that the fault called *arthāntara* does not arise. Accordingly, being positive (*bhāvatva*) would be an obstruction in the inference "destruction (*dhvaṃsa*) is noneternal, because it is produced."[111]

(E991–998) Alternatively, the following is the case. The property of being the locus of perceived touch deviates from the property of being perceived, for it does not deviate from the property of being a substance and still deviates from what pervades the property of the perceptibility of a substance, like largeness (*mahātva*). Again, the property of being a child of Mitra (a woman) deviates from the property of being dark in color, for it does not deviate from the property of being Mitra's child and still deviates from what pervades the property of being a dark child of Mitra.

(E999–1007) Alternatively, an obstruction may be defined as that which does not pervade the *hetu* and establishes the fact of deviation from the *sādhya* directly or indirectly. It does not follow then that *not being audible* would be an obstruction in the inference "sound is nameable, because it is knowable"; nor would it be that earthness would be an obstruction in the inference "water is knowable, because it has taste." In these cases the *s* is an only-positive (i.e., omnilocated) property and must belong to the *p* to which the said properties do not belong; hence the said things cannot be obstructions because of failing to pervade the *s*.

(E1007–1009) It is also not the case that being other than the *pakṣa* would be an obstruction. Since there is lack of supportive (*anukūla*) *tarka*, it would be doubtful whether it pervades the *s*. This, however, would not hold where it is certain that the *s* does not belong to the *p*, for there supportive *tarka* is available (i.e., being other than the *pakṣa* may be accepted as an obstruction in cases of *bādha*).

(E1009–1016) Further, the following would be acceptable as obstructions: *being a case of fire produced from wet fuel* in the inference from smoke to fire, *being possessed of manifested color* in the inference to being a substance which is externally perceived, *consumption of vegetables* in the inference that Mitra's children are dark-complexioned, and *being positive* in the inference that something is noneternal. In each of these cases supportive *tarka* that the obstruction pervades the *s* is available.

(E1023–1024) Should it be said that pervasion holds only between the cause and the effect? No. It may hold also between other things if supportive *tarka*-based causation is available.

In some cases the evidence for the pervasion between the *s* and the obstruction on the one hand and the evidence for the pervasion between the *h* and the *s* may be equally strong; in such cases there will be doubt that an obstruction is involved. If in such a case a supportive *tarka* becomes available on the side of the *h*, it will be settled in favor of the latter evidence, while if supportive *tarka* is found for the obstruction it will be settled in favor of the former.

Being other than the pakṣa (except in cases of sublation) cannot be said even to lead to the doubt that an obstruction is involved, for that would be self-stultifying. (In cases of sublation, however,) the property *being other than the pakṣa,* assuming that it pervades the *s*, is acceptable as a fault, for it may lead to the doubt that the *h* may be deviant.

Objection: The admission of an obstruction as a fault is dispensable in favor of the admission of the absence of supportive *tarka* as the fault.

Answer: No, both have to be admitted as separate faults.

(E1031–1046) Others (commentators such as Maṇikaṇṭha Miśra hold that an obstruction is:

D8: That because of the absence of which the *hetu* becomes dissociated from the *sādhya.*

It is because of the absence of the obstructing property that the *h* fails to be connected with the *s* in the *p*. An example of such an obstruction is *being made from wet fuel.* It is because of its absence that smoke (the *s*, where fire is the *h*) is absent from a red-hot iron ball. Hence the co-presence of the *s* with the *h* in the *p* does not hold. This account, too, allows for the acceptance of *being positive* in the inference to noneternality and of *possessing manifested color* in the inference to perceptibility as obstructions and does not allow *being other than the pakṣa* to be an obstruction except in the case of *bādha.*

(E1046–1056) Obstructions are of two kinds: believed (*niścita*) and doubted (*saṃdigdha*). If it is believed that the obstruction pervades the *s* and does not pervade the *h* then, since the fact of deviation is believed, it is called a believed obstruction. On the other hand, if it is doubtful whether the obstruction does not pervade the *h* or whether the obstruction pervades the *s* or whether both are doubtful, it becomes doubted whether the *h* is deviant and hence it becomes a case of doubted obstruction, as, e.g., being the result of consumption of vegetables in the inference to Mitra's dark-complexioned children.

(E1056–1057) Objection: Under the circumstances, in the inference of fire from smoke, too, the totality of causal conditions will be an obstruction.

Answer: No, in such cases the pervasion of smoke by both fire and the totality of causal conditions of fire are believed, for the requisite conditions for generalization are available, while they are not available in the case of Mitra's children. Accordingly (as Udayana has said), where the requisite conditions for establishing the pervasion between the *h* and the *s* are available, the collection of causal conditions of the *s* will not be an obstruction, while where the requisite conditions for pervasion are not available, it will be an obstruction.

(E1058) It should not be thought that the doubted obstruction does not qualify to be an obstruction. Like the *saṃdigdhānaikāntika hetu* it can lead one to the doubt that the *h* is deviant and hence is a fault.

(E1059–1064) Objection: What precisely is the basis for regarding an obstruction as a fault? It cannot be said to counterbalance the *h*, for it fails to pervade the *h* which is (supposed to be) pervaded by the *s*. Indeed the absence of what is not the pervaded does not follow from the absence of pervasion: since it does not pervade what is pervaded by the *s*, it follows that it does not pervade the *s* as well.

(E1065–1091) Answer: As already said, where the obstruction is believed, deviation is believed; where the obstruction is doubted, deviation is doubted. Thus it is by means of the awareness of deviation that an obstruction is a fault. Alternatively, the fact of its being a fault is due to its proving the absence of pervasion by virtue of the *h*'s not being pervaded by what pervades the *s*.

(E1092–1093) The following are fallacious obstructions (*upādhyābhāsa*):

1. That which is absent in all *sapakṣas*, e.g., *being other than the pakṣa* except in cases of sublation, the *s* being related to the *h* by way of agreement in presence and absence (*anvayavyatireka*).[112]

2. Where absence of the *sādhya* is not a fact, e.g., *being other than the pakṣa,* etc., in cases where the *s* is omnilocated (*kevalānvayin*).[113]

3. Where absence of *sādhya* in the *pakṣa* is known not to be a fact, e.g., *not being a product* in the inference "fire is hot because it has fireness."

4. That the absence of which does not pervade the *pakṣa*, e.g., *being different from atoms* in the inference "earth, etc., have a causal agent, because they are produced."

5. Nullification of the previous *hetu* (where one inference is counterbalanced by another).

6. Nullification of what is pervaded by the previous *hetu.*

7. Being different from either the *pakṣa* or the *vipakṣa*; and

8. Absence of the *sādhya* which is qualified by being other than the pakṣa.[114]

Section Fourteen: Being the Pakṣa (*pakṣatā*)

Summary by Madhusudana Nyayacharya

"E" references are to Ramanuja Tatacarya's edition (Tirupati 1982).

1. (E337–340) In order that the qualification of the *p* by the *h* be understood the nature of the *p* needs to be explained. Gaṅgeśa is of the opinion that *being the p* is a cause of inference. He discusses and rejects three definitions of *being the p* before giving his own definition.

Pūrvapakṣa

(1) According to the first of these three definitions, the *pakṣa* is that about which there is doubt about the presence of the *s* in it. If we already know definitely that the *s* is present in the *p* then there can be no inference. Therefore we must be in doubt upon that point, and inference is appealed to settle the question.

Against this view, Gaṅgeśa points out that in many cases of inference we do not consciously doubt whether the *s* is or is not present in the *p*. To cover such cases of inference a different definition is required, such as:

(2) The *pakṣa* is something about which we can have doubt as to whether the *sādhya* is present in it.

Against this definition Gaṅgeśa points out that inference takes place even when we have certainty that the *s* is present in the *p*. Thus still a different definition is needed:

(3) The *pakṣa* is what possesses the property which is the *sādhya* that we desire to infer.

Against this Gaṅgeśa points out that in daily life most inferences are made without any conscious desire to infer.

Siddhānta

Gaṅgeśa states his own definition thus: The *pakṣa* is that with respect to which there is absence of an instrument of knowledge of the presence of the *sādhya*, or which, even if we have such knowledge, we may still desire to infer. That is, there is no *p* only in case both conditions are satisfied, viz., we have knowledge of the presence of the *s* in it and we have no desire to infer it.

Section Fifteen: Consideration (*parāmarśa*)

Summary by Sibajiban Bhattacharyya

"E" references are to Ramanuja Tatacarya's edition (Tirupati 1982).

1. (E352–416) A cause of inferential awareness is awareness of pervasion of *h* by *s* qualified by the *p*'s being an *h*.

Pūrvapakṣa

Mīmāṃsaka: But this qualification is unnecessary. It is sufficient (1) to remember pervasion *qua*: the limitor of the pervadedness as chief qualifier and (2) be aware of the presence of the *h* (property in the *p* (*pakṣadharamatā*)—(1) and (2) are first-order qualifications and their concurrence is sufficient to produce inferential awareness. Moreover, these two awarenesses are necessary for the production of the awareness of their combination which, according to you, is the immediate cause of the awareness of the inferential awareness.

(First) Objection to the Mīmāṃsaka: Then awareness of the pervadedness (i.e., (1) above) alone may be regarded as the cause of inferential awareness, because it is simpler as well as being a necessary factor.

Mīmāṃsaka: No, (1) cannot be the cause since it is not present immediately prior to the arising of the inferential awareness.

(Second) Objection to the Mīmāṃsaka: As in recognition of the form "This is that (same) Devadatta", so also in the case of inference, the smoke which is perceived is known to be identical with *smoke pervaded by fire*, and this knowledge of the identity between the particular (perceived) smoke and the remembered smoke-as-pervaded-by-fire produces the recognition "This is pervaded (by fire)", and this is the cause of the awareness of the conclusion "this (mountain) possesses fire."

Mīmāṃsaka: If the two awarenesses are present then they will produce inferential awareness and not the recognition of the perceived smoke as being identical with what is pervaded by fire, for conditions of inference prevail over conditions of perception (in the case of different objects). Otherwise, even according to your (second) objection above another consideration or aftercognition of consideration would follow upon this consideration, and no inferential conclusion will ever be drawn.

(Third) objection to the Mīmāṃsaka (made by an old Naiyāyika): The memory that smoke is pervaded by fire, together with the perception of smoke on the mountain, is sufficient to produce the awareness of the pervasion of smoke by fire and smokeness. Alternatively, anyone hearing the sentence "this has what is pervaded by fire" will also have awareness of the pervasion of smoke by fire and smokeness. In both cases it will be simpler to suppose that the awareness of the relation between the *p* and *being pervaded by fire* is the cause of the inferential awareness. And likewise in other cases as well.

Mīmāṃsaka: That is not possible in cases where the *p* is not perceived or not perceptible: there won't be any awareness of the relation between the *p* and smokeness when smoke isn't perceived.

(Fourth) Objection to the Mīmāṃsaka. In such cases the unpresented smoke may be recalled by association with the remembered pervasion.

Mīmāṃsaka: Then memory would become an instrument of knowledge.

Siddhānta

2. (E367-392) Gaṅgeśa: It is not necessary to know the specific character of the *h*.The inference "this is fiery" can take place in spite of the doubt whether the *h* is smoke or light, each of which is pervaded by fire.

Mīmāṃsaka objection: Here the *h* is either-smoke-or-light!

Gaṅgeśa: But in such cases it is not necessary to believe that the *h* is either smoke or light—even a doubt whether it is one-or-the-other will lead to the inferential conclusion.Even where the specific character of the *h* is known, this awareness is not relevant for drawing the conclusion. What is necessary and sufficient is just to know that *something* pervaded by the *s* is present in the *p*.

Section Sixteen: Only-Positive Inference (kevalānvayin)

Summary by Sibajiban Bhattacharyya

"E" references are to Ramanuja Tatacarya's edition (Tirupati 1982).

1. (E424-439) Inference is of three kinds: only-positive, only-negative and positive-negative. An only-positive inference is one in which there is no *vipakṣa*. More technically, it is an inference in which the *s* is not the counterpositive of an absolute absence which has no locus at all. Or again, it is an inference the *s* of which is not absent anywhere.

An absolute absence which has no locus at all may be said to have a counterpositive, but the *s* of an only-positive inference cannot be the counterpositive of such as absence. E.g., absolute absence of *ākāśa* has no locus; any *s* of an only-positive inference must not be the counterpositive of such an absence. An example of an only-positive inference is: "The jar is an object of knowledge, because it is knowable".

Objection : *Being an object of knowledge* is not the *s* in an only-positive inference, for it is not a single property—it differs with different objects of knowledge.

Answer: There may be a second-order property common to all objects of knowledge, and indirectly common to all the instances of the first-order property *being an object of knowledge.* Or, we can consider the inference as this: "the jar is the content of a valid awareness, because it is knowable": *being an object of knowledge* is a proper universal common to all such contents.

Objection: If the *s* is present everywhere it cannot be doubted (and so no inference about it will occur). It can, of course, be doubted whether some particular thing is an object of knowledge (rather than some other). However, that doubt will not lead to *this* inferential conclusion!

Answer: Doubt about the *s* is not a necessary antecedent of inference. But even supposing (for the sake of argument) that it were, the doubt might be about whether (a) (A) *being an object of knowledge* is in (B) the jar, or about whether (b) (B) the jar has (A) *being an object of knowledge* . Are these two doubts? Which is the doubt about the absence of the *s* which, according to you, leads to the inference in question?

Objector: Both doubts (whether A is in B and whether B possesses A) have the same contents,with the elements differently arranged. So they're really the same.

Another opponent: No, the order of arrangement is essential, because depending on which of the two doubts occurs, the conclusion drawn will be in that form (the former having A as *p* and B as *s*, the latter having B as *p* and A as *s*)

Gaṅgeśa: Both doubts are relevant, not because they have the same contents (as the first objector claimed) but because both of them block ascertainment of the *s* in the *p.*

Section Seventeen: Only-Negative Inference (*Kevalavyatirekin*)

Summary based on S.C. Vidyabhusana.

"E" references are to Ramanuja Tatacharya's edition (Tirupati 1982).

(E441-515) An only-negative inference is an inference in which there is no *sapakṣa.* It may also be defined as the inference in which the *s* does not abide in anything else but the *p.* An example is "The earth is different from other things, because it possesses smell".

By contrast a positive-negative inference (*anvayavyatireka anumāna*) is an inference in which the major term has both *sapakṣas* and *vipakṣas*. An example is "the hill has fire, because it has smoke, as kitchen and unlike lake."

Section Eighteen: Presumption
(*arthāpatti*)
Summary based on S.C. Vidyabhusana.

"E" references are to Ramanuja Tatacharya's edition (Tirupati 1982).

(E517-538) Mīmāṃsaka: Presumption is a separate instrument of knowledge. On hearing that Devadatta who is fat does not eat in the day we at once conclude that he eats at night. Since a person cannot become fat unless he eats either in the day or at night, it follows by presumption that he eats at night.

Gaṅgeśa: No, presumption is not a separate instrument of knowledge. Rather it is a variety of negative inference which establishes the absence of the *h* through the absence of the *s*.

Section Nineteen: Members of an Inference
(*avayava*)
Summary based on S.C.Vidyabhusana.

"E" references are to Ramanuja Tatacharya's edition (Tirupati 1982).

1. (540-606) A member (*avayava*) of an inference is a sentence that gives rise to an awareness which contributes to the production of an entire awareness that produces consideration.

When one hears the five members one first gets an awareness from each of them separately. Then there arises collective awareness from the five members combined together. This collective awareness which produces consideration is based on each of the five awarenesses which are parts or members.

Section Twenty: Fallacies
(*hetvābhāsa*)
Summary by Nandita Bandyopadhyaya

"E" references throughout this section are to the edition of *Tattvacintāmaṇi-Anumānakhaṇḍa* by Vamacharan Bhattacharya and Dhundiraja Sastri (B3400; RB 5308).

Part One: General Definition
(*sāmānyanirukti*)

1. (E1579-1634) Gaṅgeśa gives three general definitions of a fallacious *hetu* (*hetvābhāsa*):

D1: A fallacious *h* is the content of a veridical awareness which (content) is the counterpositive of some absence which is the causal condition of an inferential awareness.

D2: A fallacious *h* is something which has the nature of being the content of an awareness of the *h* and contradicts the inferential awareness of the *h* and contradicts the inferential awareness.

D3: A fallacious *h* is something which has the nature of being a content of an awareness and which prevents the occurrence of an inferential awareness.

Objection: (Two rubrics listed below as types of fallacies, viz.) sublation (*bādha*) and counterbalancing (*satpratipakṣa*) prevent perceptual and verbal awarenesses (not inferential ones), so they are not fallacious *hetus* (according to these definitions).

Answer: Since they have the characteristics of what is only fallaciously cognized, and since when perception is sublated no awareness is prevented but rather the invalidity of some already-arisen awareness is made known, the arising of an inferential awareness *is* prevented.

Part Two: Deviation (*savyabhicāra* or *anaikāntika*)

(E1637-1682) There are three varieties of deviation: (1) too-general (*sādhāraṇa*), (2) too-specific (*asādhāraṇa*), and (3) inconclusive (*anupasaṃhārin*).

First Section: Definition of Deviation
Pūrvapakṣa

Opponent: A deviating *h* may be defined as follow:

D4: A deviating *h* is that which leads reasoning (*prasañjaka*) to both the *s* and its absence.

Gaṅgeśa's criticism: D4 fails, since one thing cannot lead reasoning to both such opposing items.

D5: A deviating *h* is something thought of as the *h*, which becomes the content of an awareness of its being property of the *p*, which content causes the presentation of two opposing alternatives, which presentation leads to doubt about the *s*.

Criticism: D5 is not to the point, since even in the absence of the awareness specified by it each of the three kinds (1-3 above) of deviating *h* may prevent either one's own awareness of concomitance (of *h* with *s*) or lead to another's showing the lack of concomitance—thus satisfaction of the condition specified in D5 is irrelevant.

D6: A deviating *h* is something which, though occurring in the *p*, is not excluded from standing in a contradictory relation to the inferential conclusion.

Criticism: But whether we are aware, or are not aware, of this general character of our *h*, its fallaciousness is determined by the specific conditions respectively occasioning (1-3) above. So D6 is irrelevant too. Besides, the condition "occurring in the *p*" (which is intended to exclude the unproved (*asiddha*) fallacy from being included in the general definition of deviation) actually is a useless specification, since far from showing that the proposed *h* blocks an inferential conclusion it instead states a condition necessary for any successful inference.

D7: A deviating *h* is something which is different from a term that occurs only in a locus of the *s* other than the *p*, and is also different from what occurs only in a locus of the absence of *s* other than the *pakṣa*.

Criticism: But D7 will not apply to (3) the inconclusive deviation, since there the *p* is "everthing"—so "occurring in a locus of the *s* other than the *p*" is an empty term. Furthermore, D7 will overextend to the valid inference "the mountain has fire, because it has smoke", since *smoke-possessing* is a term that satisfies the conditions specified.

Siddhānta

(E1685-1701) Gaṅgeśa:

D8: A deviating *h* is one which possesses a nature limiting the establishment of both (of two opposing) alternatives. That is the too-general, etc.

D9: A deviating *h* is one which, while occurring in that *p* which is different from what is contradicted, is not excluded from standing in a contradictory relation to the inferential conclusion.

D10: A deviating *h* is one which, being other than what occurs only in what possesses the *s*, is other than what occurs only in what possesses absence of the *s*.

These are defended. Nevertheless, none of these definitions provides a general characterization of a fallacy which all and only (1), (2) and (3) involve. At best they may indicate a property which is present whenever any of (1-3) are, in order that the other four kinds of fallacy (which also have such a property) do not fall within the definition too, for they are excluded *ad hoc* by specific conditions added for that purpose only. So perhaps fallacies of the *h* should be classified into two varieties, those which directly prevent an inferential awareness, and those which indirectly do so through blocking consideration. But one cannot dictate to or question the freely expressed desire of Gautama.

Second Section : Too-General
(*Sādhāraṇa*)

(E1702-1705) A putative *h* is said to be "too-general" if it occurs in the *vp*.

Objection : Unless one adds "and also occurs in the *sp*" this definition will overextend to include the fallacy called "contradiction" (*viruddha*).

Answer: No, for the definition given amounts to "a too-general *h occurs in* what possesses absence of *s*" while a contradictory *h* is *pervaded by* absence of *s*. No doubt the second always involves the first, but the decision as to which fallacy is being identified depends on whether one is merely aware that this particular *h* occurs in the *vp*, or whether one is aware that the whole class of *h*s is pervaded by absence of the *s*.

It is not unusual for two fallacies to overlap each other and yet be distinct. Consider "everything is noneternal, because everything is knowable". This is inconclusive (*anupasaṃhārin*) as well as too-general. Or "sound is eternal, because it is sound." This is both too-specific and too-general. Or "the earth is eternal, because it smells," which is too-specific and too-general both. Thus which fallacy is identified depends on how the matter is considered.

Third Section: Too-Specific (*asādhāraṇatva*)
Pūrvapakṣa

(E1721-1726) Gaṅgeśa begins with a detailed examination of the old concept of "too-specific" which is defined as:

D11 : Being too-specific is the *h*'s absence both from all *sp* and all *vp*.

But, says Gaṅgeśa, absence from *vp* cannot be a part of the fault, for it is conducive to pervasion through contraposition(*vyatireka*). A debater not moving beyond the inference-for-others such as "sound is noneternal, for it has soundness" can be easily faulted by showing the definition's incompleteness due to the omission of a supporting example, without that counting as the *h*'s absence from all *sp*. But the contrapositive statement "whatever has absence of noneternalness has absence of soundness, e.g., big-time" is too strong to be countered by the absence of the *h* from *sp*, which is thus not a fault in debate. At best it is a fault in inference-for-oneself.

Siddhānta

(E1728) Gaṅgeśa: In both inference-for-oneself and in debate the *h*'s absence from *sp* as well as from *vp* both taken together can be treated as the fallacy of too-specific, through blocking inference through the indecisive clash between equal possibilities of presence and absence of the *s* in the *p*. The difference between counterbalanced (*satpratipakṣa*) and too-specific fallacies is that in the former there are two *h*s countering each other while in the latter there is one *h*. But the definition of too-specific-ness is constituted by the *h*'s absence from all *sp* alone. Its absence from *vp* is redundant for the purpose of the definition. According to Gaṅgeśa both "sound is noneternal, for is possesses soundness" and "sound is eternal, for it possesses soundness" may be treated as too-specific fallacies. But the former can be an instance of the fallacy only when one does not notice the valid contrapositive pervasion. In the latter inference there is also contradictoriness (*viruddhatva*) which however passes into too-specific according to this way of thinking. Too-specific-ness is thus only a relative fallacy.

Fourth Section: Inconclusive (*anupasaṃhārin*)
Pūrvapakṣa

(E1740-1742) A traditional example of inconclusiveness is "everthing is nameable because it is knowable". Things unknowable to men are known to God who, being ominiscient, knows everything in the universe by name. So nothing is unknowable and nothing unnameable. The implied pervasion is "all that is knowable is nameable." Outside the *p* there is no possible *sp* or *vp*. We have seen that being-the-*p* (*pakṣatā*) is determined by doubt about the existence of the *s* in the *p*. Now if the doubt about the existence of nameability (the *s*) invades everything (*p*), the very state of pervasion "whatever is knowable is nameable" is vitiated by doubt. Beyond the *pakṣa* there is no instance to facilitate the knowledge of the collocation between the *h* and the *s*.

Siddhānta

(E1747-1748) Gaṅgeśa first defines the inconclusive *h* as follows:

D12: The inconclusive *h* is that which is thought to be the *h* but where there is absence of conclusiveness (*upasaṃhāra*) in that *sp* which secures pervasion.

Or D13: The inconclusive *h* is that *h* which involves a p limited by the only-positive property, i.e., where everthing is the *p*.

But (says Gaṅgeśa) in the inference "everything is nameable because it is knowable" we have a nonfallacious *h*, for the limitor of the *p*-ness is not only-positive, since it is believed to occur in what possesses the *s*; when there is no belief in the *s* because of doubt about all cases then alone do we have inconclusiveness.

(Better,) The fault (of inconclusiveness) occurs with respect to the contrapositive (*vyatirekī*) *s* (as in "everything is impermanent, because it is knowable"), where there is no *vp* in which both absence of knowability and absence of impermanence are found together, so that the contrapositive pervasion (viz., "whatever is not impermanent is not knowable") is precluded from our awareness. Gaṅgeśa points out that this general account overlaps the account of too-general, since where the *h* coexists with the absence of the *s* (e.g., as in "noneternality is found in time or space," etc.) one may have either too-general (if one is aware of this) or inconclusive (if one is not). The fallacy some call *vyāpyatvāsiddhi* depends on this fault of inconclusiveness.

Part Three: Contradictoriness (*viruddhatva*)
Pūrvapakṣa

(E1769-1775)

D13: The contradictory *h* is what is pervaded by the absence of the *s*.

Criticism: D13 is defective, for it overextends to a correct *h* as in the case "it possesses contact, for it is a substance", which is correct even where the substance lacks contact, being nonlocus-pervading.

D14: The contradictory *h* is that which is pervaded by the counter-positive of an absolute absence located in the locus of the *s*, so that "sound is eternal, because it is an effect" is contradictory because the absolute absence of the *h* *effectness* is located in the locus of the *s* *eternalness*, viz., time, space, etc.

Criticism: But D14 overextends to another example of a correct inference, viz., "it is a substance because it has a quality", since the locus of substanceness is also the locus of the absolute absence of contact, as shown above.

D15: The contradictory *h* is that which is pervaded by absence of the *s* that is not collocative with the presence of the *s*. This avoids the difficulties with D13 and D14, for contact, being a quality, cannot be pervaded by the absence of substanceness, and absence of contact is collocative, not noncollocative, with the presence of the *s*.

Gaṅgeśa goes on to explain that the term "absence of the *s*" in D15 simply means being contradictory to the *s*, not necessarily a negation of it, so that when something's absence is itself the *s*, absence of *s* will mean absence of absence of that something and this double-absence is the same as the original presence. Or, says Gaṅgeśa, you may take not-not-A as an absence different from (the presence) A and it is still directly contradictory to not-A.

D16. : The contradictory *h* is that which is pervaded by difference from that which possesses the *s*.

Criticism of D15 and D16: These definitions are not finally satisfactory. They overlap the scope of the too-general, having the same root, viz., the *h*'s presence in *vp*s.

Siddhānta

(E1776–1781) Gaṅgeśa offers the following preferable definitions:

D17: The contradictory *h* is the counterpositive of that absence which pervades the *s*.

But this is equivalent to Gaṅgeśa's definition of too-specific. So better are:

D18: The contradictory *h* is that which (existing in the *p*) has no existence in the locus of the *s*.

or D19: The contradictory *h* is that which (existing in the *p*) is not the locus of *existence in the s*'s locus.

or D20: The contradictory *h* is that property of the *p* which is not the locus of *existence in the s*'s locus.

D17–20 do not overextend to a correct only-negative *h*, since in only-negative inference, there being no *s* in any locus (except the disputed *p*), it is not at all possible to have an awareness of the *h*'s absence in a locus of the *s*. According to the present concept of contradictoriness an only-negative *h* is also a contradictory *h*.

Objection: In order to contradict the awareness of pervasion awareness of the *h*'s absence in *sp*s should be reduced to awareness of the presence of the *h* in *vp*s. But in that case the "contradictory" *h* turns out to be the "too-general" *h*.

Answer: No. The awareness of a too-general *h* is dependent upon the awareness of contradictoriness, and since there is this relation the contradictory should be counted as different from the too-general type. Pervasion has two parts—collocation (*sāhacarya*) and nondeviance (*avyabhicāra*). Awareness of contradiction *qua* noncollocativeness contradicts the one, while awareness of deviance contradicts the other.

There are six kinds of contradictory *h*, three each of a positive and a negative variety:

1. Where the *s* is a positive variety:
   (a) Where the *h* is directly pervaded by the absence of the *s*, e.g., "this has smoke, for it is not cognized as something for having smoke";
   (b) Where the *h* is pervaded by the negation of the pervader of the *s*, e.g., "this has smoke, because it has absence of fire";
   (c) Where the *h* is cognized as contradictory to that which is the pervader of the *s*, e.g., "this has smoke, for it has the character of being a body of water."
2. Where the *s* is a negative entity:
   (a) Where the *h* is cognized as the counterpositive of (the absence which is) the *s*, e.g., "this has absence of fire, for it is fire";
   (b) Where the *h* is cognized as the negation of the pervader of (the negative) *s*, e.g., "this has no fire, for it has absence of smoke";
   (c) Where the *h* is cognized as contradictory to the pervader of (the negative) *s*, e.g., "this has absence of fire, because it has smoke."

Part Four: Counterbalanced Hetu (*satpratipakṣa*)
Pūrvapakṣa

(E1784) A counterbalanced *h* is one in respect of which there is another *h* of equal strength by which the negation of the proposed *s* is made to be understood.

Criticism: Mutual blocking makes any such understanding impossible. The law of contradiction requires that two *h*s pervaded by contradictory *sādhya*s cannot belong to the same *pakṣa* and that either pervasion or the qualification of the *p* by the *h* must be false in one case. Even as in illusion it is not possible to entertain two contradictory propositions at once.

Opponent: Then we will amend the definition by adding that the negation of the proposed *s* is made to be understood by failure to determine which of the rival pervasions is true and which false.

Answer: No. Two such rival pervasions in respect to the same *p* cannot lead to any such understanding. When two contradictories are presented for consideration there is always at least this much determination—that one is negated in fact. But without knowing which one it is not possible to come to the understanding that the proposed *s* is negated.

Siddhānta

(E1787–1802) Gaṅgeśa's definitions are these:

D1: The counterbalanced *h* is an *h* the operation of which is blocked by a contrary *h* having equal strength and having the capacity to introduce the contradictory of the *s*.

D2: A counterbalanced *h* is one whose effect (viz., whose inferential conclusion) is blocked by a counter-*h* which is being cognized as having the characteristics producing a counterconclusion which is, however, different from what causes a counterconclusion (for it is likewise blocked by the proponent's *h*)

Objection: In actuality a thing cannot possess two contradictory characters. Hence when two counterinferences present two contradictory conclusions such as "*p* has *s*" and "*p* has no *s*," one must be false. In that case, even if the disputants fail to identify which one of the two syllogisms is wrong, they cannot escape the feeling that either of the two must suffer from either breach of pervasion (i.e. deviation) or breach of the qualification of the *p* by *h* (i.e., from unestablishedness). Therefore counterbalance is not a separate fallacy.

Gaṅgeśa: In counterbalance consideration of these (just-mentioned) difficulties arises only after the awareness of one *h* being blocked by the other, and so deviation is the basic fault.

Objection: Just as an *s* and its absence are not contradictories, so two *h*s, one pervaded by the *s* and the other pervaded by the absence of the *s*, are not contradictories either. In counterbalance when two such *h*s are presented as belonging to the same *p*, the confused disputants are in doubt about the existence of either of the two *h*s in the *p* and it is then a case of unestablishedness of *h*'s belonging to *p*. If one objects that the contradiction between *s* and its absence is not the same as the contradiction between a *h* pervaded by *s* and a *h* pervaded by absence of *s*, and that there is no problem with cognizing two such *h*s in the same *p*, then both the pervasions are subject to doubt and the case becomes one of the unestablishedness of *h*'s pervadability by *s*.

Gaṅgeśa: The root of the fault in counterbalance is the nonproduction of any decision due to a clash between two contradictory considerations (appearing to be of equal strength), and not the lack of pervasion or the qualification of the *p* by the *h*, the reckoning of which comes only after the sense of blockage. That is why in a debate even a correct inference can be blocked by an opponent.

This does not, however, mean that the value of inference as an instrument of knowledge is totally lost there by, for any inference, correct or incorrect, may be blocked. The strength of an inference is pervasion and *pakṣadharmatā.* If either of the disputants can convincingly demonstrate this strength, there is no question of blockage.

(E1804–1825) The *Ratnakośakāra* (viz., Taraṇi Miśra): In counterbalance want of decision does not mean nonemergence of any conclusion. Because two counterinferences are evenly balanced since appearing to have equal strength, nothing can stop the emergence of two respective counterconclusions. The point is, however, that since there is no feeling of decision each conclusion is attended by a feeling of doubt. Each conclusion rises separately from its relevant premisses, but doubt is not separately produced by each inference. The doubtful nature of both the conclusions is an implication (of the apprehension) of equal strength.

Gaṅgeśa: Just as since *s* and not-*s* are contradictories and the awareness of one blocks awareness of the other, so likewise an *h* pervaded by not-*s* being opposed to *s,* awareness of having an *h* pervaded by not-*s* blocks awareness of *s.*

According to Gaṅgeśa the result of counterbalance is not doubt but an inquiry into the nature of things. Hence from the standpoint of its result a counterbalanced *hetu* may be defined as follows:

D23: A counterbalanced *h* involves the presence of two pervasions and *pakṣadharmatā*s which produce the desire to know which of the two *hetu*s in relation to the two *sādhya*s concerned is actually correct.

Objection: The desire to know can arise either from the awareness that the desired knowledge leads to the desired result, or from doubt. Without either of these two how can the desire to know arise simply from the awareness of contradictory instruments?

Gaṅgeśa: There is no desire to know unless a contrary possibility is considered. Where there is such a consideration there is such a desire. So the causal relation between awareness of contradiction and desire to know is established by positive and negative concomitance.

The *p* in two counterbalanced inferences does not have to be the same. The fallacy consists of unresolved contradiction only. Anything more is irrelevant. E.g., here are two counterbalanced *h*s with different *p*s:

Arg. 1 : The jar is nameable, because it is knowable, like a piece of cloth.

Arg. 2 : Nameability is the counterpositive of an absence of it in a jar, because along with its being different from a universal property, it is a property different from an exclusive property of jar, like mutual absence resident in jar.

Part Five: The Unestablished Hetu (*asiddha*)
Pūrvapakṣa

(E1836) D24: The unestablished *h* is the absence of pervasion and *pakṣadharmatā.*

Criticism: If D24 involves two distinct absences it cannot include all the three types of unestablished *h* within its scope, for both absences cannot belong to the one and the same type of unestablishedness. On the other hand, if it is meant to be read "the unestablished *h* is the single absence of the *h*'s existence in *p* as qualified by the pervasion of *h* by the *s*," this understanding is also defective, because the awareness of the whole complex is not necessary for identifying a case of unestablishedness. For *vyāpyatvāsiddhi* (unestablishedness of the *h*'s pervadability by *s*) we require only awareness of the absence of the qualifier, while for *āśrayāsiddhi* (unestablishedness of *h* due to the unestablishedness of *p*) and *svarūpāsiddhi* (unestablishedness of *h*'s belonging to *p*) we require only awareness of the absence of the qualificand. Thus the separate awareness of each separate absence being indispensable, neither the construal of D24 as two negations nor as one can constitute the fallacy of unestablishedness.

(E1838–1850) For the same reason:

D25: The unestablished *h* is the absence of either pervasion or *pakṣadharmatā.*

or D26: The unestablished *h* is the absence of the knowledge (*pramiti*) of pervasion and *pakṣadharmatā (or, pakṣadharmatā* in conjunction with pervasion),

since each separate absence creates a fallacy.

Siddhānta

(E1852–1867) Gaṅgeśa: Actually there is no general definition of unestablishedness. Each of the three sorts (*āśrayāsiddhi, svarūpāsiddhi* and *vyāpyatvāsiddhi*) are fallacies in themselves, with no common property shared by them all. Gaṅgeśa, however, acknowledges that Gautama has brought the three types under a single class on the strength of a comprehensive common property, viz., that they all involve absence of the content of consideration.

Objection: How can *āśrayāsiddhi* arise from an unestablished locus? (The previous establishment of the counterpositive is a necessary condition for there being an absence of it.) Consider the inference-schema "the sky-lotus is fragrant, because it has lotusness." If we consider the sky-lotus as the *p*, since it doesn't exist at all there can be no absence of it, and so the definition (of Gautama) doesn't apply to it. Rather, it is a case of the way of losing an argument called "*apārthaka*" (see Vol. II of this Encyclopedia, p. 680).

Answer: Take *lotus* as the *p* and *belonging to the sky* as the qualifier which is absent in it; then the unestablishedness of the qualifier in the *p* constitutes the fallacy of unmixed *āśrayāsiddhi*.

Part Six: Sublated (*bādha*)

Pūrvapakṣa

(E1869) Before stating his own view Gaṅgeśa examines and rejects some definitions of the elders:

D27: Sublation is the *h*'s being attributed to a *p* which possesses absence of the *s*.

D28: Sublation is the *h*'s being assigned to such an *s* as is the counterpositive of an absence located in the *p*.

D29: Sublation is the *h*'s existence in the *p* which possesses absence of *s*.

Criticism: Gaṅgeśa argues that mere awareness of the absence of the *s* in the *p* is not enough for the direct cancellation of a conclusion. It is the awareness of the *truth* of that awareness which gives superior strength to the contradictory of the conclusion that the inference draws and thus blocks our drawing it.

As regards D29 there is a further objection: the *h*'s existence in the *p* precludes *svarūpāsiddhi* and *āśrayāsiddhi*, but there may be sublation along with such unestablishedness. The definition obviously falls short of a generally satisfactory account of sublation.

So Gaṅgeśa suggests three more definitions:

D30: Sublation is the *h*'s being attributed to such a *p* which is known to possess absence of *s*.

D31: Sublation is the *h*'s being attributed to such a *p* as possesses absence of *s* which is known to be such.

D32: Sublation is the *h*'s being assigned to such a *s* as is the counterpositive of that absence located in the *p* and which is an object of knowledge.

Criticism: In this second set of definitions the differentiating element is the insertion of "knowledge" in the definition of the fallacy itself. According to the generalization of these definitions, a fallacy is a fault only insofar as it figures as an object of knowledge, i.e., of true awareness. Hence Gaṅgeśa argues that the mere *existence* of the awareness of absence of the *s* is not the fault of sublation, but rather it is that awareness' being *cognized* as true. That is how the contrary proposition "p has no *s*" gathers superior strength, and why an inference is arrested even when an invalid awareness is taken to be true.

(E1871–1881) Dharmakīrti: When the *p* is already cognized as possessing the absence of *s* (thus constituting a counterpositive) any possible knowledge of the *h* being located in such a locus would constitute the fault of deviation. The absence of such an awareness would constitute a case of unestablishedness. If the awareness of the *s*'s absence in *p* involves belief—subjective certainty—the supposed *p* loses the character of *p*-ness since there can be no doubt (which is part of the definition of *pakṣatā*). Thus the fault of *āśrayāsiddhi* is also there.

Counterobjection: But awareness of deviation depends upon the awareness of the absence of the *s* in the *p*, and that sublation, being dependable, is different from what depends on it (viz., awareness of sublation).

Gaṅgeśa: No, for the same awareness comprehends the absence of the *s* in the *p* as well as the presence of *pakṣadharmatā.* So one awareness does not depend on the other.

In answer to the original objection (of Dharmakīrti): The feeling of cognitive certainty about the existence of an object follows from belief in the truth of the awareness of it. That is why one has to proceed to a subsequent (inferential) awareness for ascertaining the validity of a previous awareness. Otherwise objective certainty could have been derived even from a falsely cognized object. So, it is this knowledge of validity which confers superior strength on the awareness of the absence of the *s* from the *p* and so becomes the basis of the fault of deviation.

Siddhānta

(E1882–end) Hence, Gaṅgeśa concludes, the fault of sublation is the precognized validity of the awareness of the absence of the *s* in the *p*.

Objection: But the listing of sublation as a separate fallacy is unnecessary. That very knowledge of the absence of the *s*, since it entails the awareness of the *h* going along with the absence of the *s*, signals the fault of deviation, and one does not need the precognized *validity* of the awareness.

Gaṅgeśa: If that were so, one could not entertain a false inference by taking a piece of knowledge to be invalid, nor could one have got one's inference blocked by taking a false awareness of the absence of the *s* in the *p* as true (both of which happen).

Thus the inference "the mountain possesses kitchen-fire, because it possesses smoke", which is invalid even though the *h* property does reside in the *p*, is a case of sublation and not of deviation. Smoke entails fire in general, which means any fire, i.e., anything limited by fireness. Kitchen-fire is not different from fire. So kitchen-fire cannot be debarred from the mountain by deviation, but only by sublation. Otherwise "the mountain has kitchen-fire" would be a sound statement. So sublation is an independent fallacy.

Furthermore, deviation does not simply mean the *h*'s collocation with any absence of the *s*. Otherwise such inferences as "the pitcher possesses smell, because it is earthy" or "the pitcher has a quality, for it is a substance" would have been deviant, because a substance has no quality at the moment of its production or after its destruction, so that substanceness becomes collocative with the prior absence and posterior absence of the *s* (in either case). But this collocation of the *h* with this sort of absence of *s* does not in reality constitute deviation. What is required in a fault of deviation is the *h*'s collocation with the absolute absence of the *s*. That is why, when a quality is sought to be established in a substance as qualified by the prior or posterior absence of that quality, such an inference can be refuted only by sublation, not by deviance.

In conclusion, Gaṅgeśa offers ten types of sublation divided into four classes:

I. Sublation by the same awareness as grasps the *p*.
 1. by perception, e.g., "the pitcher is ubiquitous, because it possesses existence" (it is clearly not ubiquitous);
 2. by inference, e.g., "the atoms have parts, for they are material" (atoms are known not to have parts);
 3. by verbal (here, scriptural) testimony, e.g., "Mount Meru is rocky, because it is a mountain" (since Mt. Meru is said in scripture to be a golden mountain).

II. Sublation by the same awareness that grasps the counterpositive of a negative *s*:
 4. by perception, e.g., "fire is not hot, for it is produced" (where fire is perceived as hot);
 5. by inference, e.g., "sound is not heard by an auditory organ, for it is a quality" (whereas sounds are known to be heard);
 6. by comparison, e.g., "*gavaya*-ness is not the occasion for the usage of the word "*gavaya*", because it is a universal" (where it is already known that "*gavaya*" connotes *gavaya*-ness).

III. Sublation by the same awareness that grasps the *sādhya*:
 7. by verbal testimony, e.g., "a human skull is sacred, because it is an animal organ" (the skull is polluted).

IV. Sublation by the same awareness that grasps the *hetu:*
 8. by perception, e.g., "water and air are hot because their tactual quality is the opposite of that of earth" (for water and air are felt to be cool);
 9. by inference, e.g., "the internal organ is ubiquitous, because it has awareness inhering in it (where one already knows by inference that the internal organ is of small size);

10. by verbal testimony, e.g., "the *Rājasūya* sacrifice is the duty of a Brahmin, for it is a means to heaven" (where it is at best the duty of others than Brahmins).

Part Seven: Fallacies are Serviceable as they Point out Inefficiency (*hetvābhāsānāmasādhakatāsādhakatvanirūpaṇam)*

The "E" reference is to the edition of Anumānakhaṇḍa by Somanathopadhyaya (B3391; RB 5299), pp. 1235–1241. The summary is by Satischandra Vidyabhusana (B and RB: HIL)

A fallacy when exposed is a good reply to an opponent, whose argument is thus pointed out to be inefficient. Quibbles and far-fetched analogies are not good replies as they are of no use in this respect. Far-fetched analogies are moreover self-destructive.

Section Twenty-one: The Inference to God's Existence (*īśvarānumāna*)

Edition and translation by John Vattanky, *Gaṅgeśa's Philosophy of God* (Madras 1984). Section numbers refer to this work. The summary is by Sibajiban Bhattacharyya and K.H. Potter.

Introduction (ET169): Since inference has now been explained, the existence of a person (*puruṣa*) who creates (*nirmātṛ*) the universe (*jagat*) is proved through Inf1:

Inf1: Earth, etc., has a maker, because it is an effect, like a jar.

(I.1) (ET169–173) Objection: Earth, etc., cannot be the *p* of a sound inference, for the various things such as earth, water, fire, and so on, all of which are created, cannot be cognized under one form, since they are so different from one another.

(I.2) Counterobjection: Then let the *p* be whatever is in doubt and occasions the doubt whether it is created or not, or is argued about in discussion.

Objector's answer: No, since all sorts of different things might be that.

(I.3) Counterobjection: Then the *p* should be (a) that which is made with dependence on a body, or (b) that which is made but is not made by a body.

Objector's answer: No, for then a lot of things alleged to be made by God at the beginning of creation, such as the specific qualities of the self, sound, the Vedic tradition, etc., will be left out of the *p*, and the *p* itself will be unestablished, since according to Nyāya tradition the creation of the world requires not only God but also the collective *adṛṣṭa* (i.e., karmic merit and demerit of men).

(I.4) Counterobjector: Then let the *p* of the inference be something made but not made through effort which is itself produced. Or else let it be something produced but different from something produced by an effort and accepted by both (of us disputers) as such.

Objector's answer: No, since earth, etc., are produced through *adṛṣṭa* by an effort which is itself produced.

(I.5) Counterobjector: Then make the *p* (a) something produced but not produced by an effort which produces *adṛṣṭa*, or else (b) something produced but not directly produced by an effort which is itself produced.

Objector: No, for God's effort is the cause of *adṛṣṭa* and so earth, etc., will not fall within the *p* so described.

(I.6) Counterobjector: Then let's just understand the *p* as earth alone.

Objector's answer: No, for then there will be doubt about the possible deviation of the *h* and *s*. God is the creator of all things, not only earth: for example, he creates plants. We know that plants are created objects, so if we infer the presence of the property *being made* only in earth there will arise a doubt about the presence of this the *s*-property in plants where we already know the *h*-property is present. And this is an instance of doubtful or inconclusive deviation (*sandigdhānaikāntika*).

Counterobjector: Even though plants are not included in our (revised) *p*, still they are similar to the *p* and so, once we have inferred the *s* to be in earth we can also infer it to be present in plants as well.

Objector's answer: This will not do. You have proposed confining the *p* to earth, but now you propose to include plants as well, which amounts to changing the thesis of the inference.

Counterobjector: There are two distinct inferences, one about earth, the other about plants.

Objector: Then a doubt will arise as to which depends on which, and neither will be sound. Besides, even if one can prove both earth and plants to have a creator, this doesn't prove God as the creator of all effects.

Counterobjector: All right, then let us propose a completely different *p* but one which picks out a proper single kind. Our proposed new *p* is *dyads at the beginning of creation.*

Objector's answer: But the opponent doesn't accept that there *is* a beginning of creation!

(II.1) (ET173–176) (So much for difficulties about the *p*. Now we show problems with the proposed *s* of Infl, viz., *having a maker.*) What is this *s* property? Is it (a) coexisting with one possessing effort or (b) being produced by one possessing effort? Neither, since the creator proved under either of these meanings is, e.g., the potter who makes an earthy object, and since that is already accepted the inference will prove what is already proved.

(II. 2a) Counterobjection: Then let the *s* be as follows: *being produced by one having immediate awareness about the materials* (*to be used*) *together with desire and effort* (*to create*).

Objector: But the potter satisfies this also. Furthermore, the *adṛṣṭa* of humans is produced by immediate awareness, desire and effort to perform the sacrifice, and so human beings become creators of the world by the argument so understood.

(II. 2b) Counterobjector: Then understand the proposed *s* (just given) as *being produced mediately by one having immediate awareness,* etc.

Objector: That won't do, since the jar (the *sp* in Inf1) is not produced immediately by one satisfying these conditions, for, e.g., a pot is produced immediately by the potter, as it is the result of actions of his body.

Counterobjector: Then change the *sp* to *human action.*

Objector: Then there will be inconclusiveness (*anaikāntika*) in the case of a jar (since it will not be made by the potter!). And having bodily motion (*ceṣṭātva*) becomes an obstruction (which is unallowable since as a result only those things have makers which are the effects of bodily motions, contrary to the intention of the proposer of Inf_1.

(II. 2c) Counterobjector: Let us change the *s* to *being produced by someone having immediate awareness of the material cause of earth, etc.*

Objector: But then there will be no *sp* (since no one has such immediate awareness of the material cause of all things).

Counterobjector: What we mean is immediate awareness of the respectively relevant material cause for each such thing.

Objector: This would depend on the intentions of the speaker, which is out of place when considering inference where words must be understood in their generic meaning, since it is in their generic form that the *h* must be pervaded by the *s* in a sound inference. The proposed *s* is not invariably concomitant with the *h* of Inf1. And since we (ourselves, though not our bodies) exist at the beginning moment of creation and since it is accepted that we possess effort, desire to create and immediate awareness of the materials for creating earthy things, etc., the argument so construed will prove what is already accepted.

(II.3) (ET176–179) Counterobjector: In order to avoid these objections we need another, a revised, inference. Here are two versions of such a new inference.

Inf2a: (*Pakṣa*:) What is produced but not produced by one possessing effort, desire to make and immediate awareness of the material cause, where (the effort, desire and awareness) are produced but not produced by *sāmānyalakṣaṇasannikarṣa* nor produced by a propositional awareness nor produced by yogic merit, is (*sādhya*:) produced by one possessing effort, desire to make and immediate awareness of the material cause, where they (effort, desire and awareness) are not produced by *sāmānyalakṣaṇasannikarṣa* nor by a propositional awareness nor by yogic merit, because (*hetu*:) it is an effect, like a (*sapakṣa*:) jar.

Inf2b: Same *pakṣa* as in Inf_2. *Sādhya*: produced but not produced by a produced awareness which is not produced by connection (*sannikarṣa*) which produces the immediate awareness of future events. Rest as in Inf2a.

Inf2c: Same *pakṣa* as in Inf2a. *Sādhya*: produced by one having effort, desire and immediate awareness of the material cause, where these are not produced by a connection which produces an immediate awareness of future events.

Objector's answer: Firstly, the opponent does not admit the existence of some of the things mentioned in these inferences—for example, *sāmānyalakṣaṇasannikarṣa* or immediate awareness of future events. Secondly, Inf2 still proves what is already accepted, viz., that individual selves are creators of their *adṛṣṭa* and the results accruing therefrom.

(III. 1) (ET180–183) (So much for difficulties about the *p* and the *s*. Now as to the *h*:) What does "being an effect" mean? Does it mean "being suitable to be brought about directly by effort"? No, since the opponent (e.g., the Mīmāṃsaka) does not accept that the earth is brought about directly by anyone's effort. Does it mean "occurring at a later time without occurring at an earlier time (to the *p* and *sp*)"? But then, since time prior to the *p* is a different span from time prior to the *sp* such a "prior time" will be unestablished. Does "being an effect" mean "occurring at some time or other"? But then prior absence will be an effect, since it occurs at some time or other. Does it mean "being the counterpositive of a prior absence"? But the counterpositives of posterior absences will then not be effects. Does it mean "existing at a time and at that time being the counterpositive of a prior absence"? No, for the opponent (e.g., the Mīmāṃsaka) does not accept existence as a proper universal.

(III.2) Friendly objection: But the following inference works: This pot is produced by awareness, etc., difference from the noneternal awareness, desire and effort that produces this pot, because this pot is an effect, like a cloth.

Answer: No, because since the proposed *h* is unsupported it is not absent in any contrary example or *vp*. Furthermore, in a similar fashion one would be able to prove a locus of eternal merit and demerit, eternal satisfaction and frustration from the noneternal varieties of these qualities, which (you and I agree) is objectionable. Anyway, there are counterinferences such as: this jar is not produced by awareness, etc., different from the noneternal awareness, etc., which produce it, because it is a jar.

(III. 3) Another friendly objection: Then let's prove God's existence as follows: The mental activity that produces the first awareness of a human being after creation has as its cause an effort which is not the effort of a human being, because it is a mental activity that occurs after an effort taking place before any human being is capable of awareness.

Answer: No, for the mental activity might be the final one in the previous period just prior to dissolution.

Siddhānta

(I) (ET183–184) Gaṅgeśa: Here are three versions of a sound argument which proves that the world has a creator, viz., God.

Inf3a: (*Pakṣa*:) All things which are produced, which are not due to the merit or demerit of individual selves, which are not produced by bodily movements which are themselves effects of volition, and which inhere in something[115] are (*sādhya*:) created by a self which has effort, desire to infer, and immediate awareness (all three) concerning the appropriate material, (these three) not being counterpositives to any prior absence pervaded by a prior absence of merit and demerit,[116] because (*hetu*:) all such things are the counterpositives of prior absences and inhere in something.

Inf3b: The *pakṣa* is as in Inf3a. The *sādhya* is: are created by a self which has effort, desire to infer, and immediate awareness concerning the appropriate material, which awareness ranges over future objects;[117] the *hetu* is the same as in Inf3a.

Inf3c: Same *pakṣa* and *hetu*. The *sādhya* is: are the objects of immediate awareness, desire to infer, and effort.[118]

(II.1) (ET184–188) Objection: The *p* in Inf3 is present in a variety of objects which do not have any common property shared by all of them. So, they cannot be cognized under one description. Therefore Inf3a is impossible.

Answer: There is such a common property, viz., "not being produced by bodily movements which are themselves effects (of volition)." All such things can be cognized under the description "being different" by the perception born of *sāmānyalakṣaṇasannikarṣa.*

Objection: Since everything is created (according to us) there is nothing that is not produced and the qualification is redundant.

Answer: Not every proper qualifier has to differentiate—in "this jar is knowable" knowableness is a qualifier even though it applies to everything.

Gaṅgeśa points out that the *pūrvapakṣin*'s argument (under Section A.I above) excluding specific qualities of the self, sound, etc. from the scope of *p* is now answered in the present specification, which does not render the *p* unestablished. We cannot create the qualities of our own selves except through our karmic merit and demerit, so such qualities are included in the *p* of Inf3. Sound cannot be produced by us since we do not directly perceive its material cause, *ākāśa*.

Objection: But then destruction or posterior absence, which does not have any material cause, must be excluded from the *p*, and so God won't be able to destroy anything!

Answer: In that case, read the *p* and *h* without the qualification "which inheres in something." Or alternatively, replace that qualification with another, viz., being not produced by a desire to do and by produced effort. Then destruction will be included, since it is not produced by desire.

(As the counterobjector claimed in Section A.1,) One may alternatively take the *p* to be simply *earth*. The *pūrvapakṣin*'s response to that (in Section A.1 above), alleging doubt about whether the *s* property then will occur in plants as well, is confused, for such a doubt is inevitable in any dispute, and not a fault. When one knows for sure that the *h* as pervaded by the *s* occurs then the *s* will be inferred both in the *p* and in objects similar to the *p*. There is no circularity in such inference, since inference of the *s* in *p* and in objects similar to *p* is not mutually dependent. That is, we do not infer the presence of the *s* in the *p* by first inferring it in objects similar to the *p* and vice versa.

Objection: If plants, etc., are not included in the *p* the presence of the *h* property in them will not be ascertained, and so there will not be inference of the *s* in objects similar to the *p*.

Answer: Any object concerning which there is absence of conviction of the presence of *s* together with the absence of desire to infer will be an object where the *s* is inferred on the basis of conviction as to the presence of *h* as pervaded by *s* there. Even though the consideration involving earth (the *p*) is established by the five-membered argument form, and the consideration involving plants is not, still there is no difference in the result. However it is established, consideration leads to inference.

Objection: If the things similar to the *p*, being cognized as having the *h* property, are still doubted to have the *s* property, then no awareness of pervasion will arise.

Answer: If that were right no inference at all would be possible! Even the inference of fire from smoke will be impossible, since there will be no way of becoming aware of the pervasion of smoke by fire. For objects like the mountain (*p*), together with those objects other than the mountain where smoke is ascertained but the presence of fire is doubtful, do not share any common property among them. So we must conclude that all objects where the *s* is doubtful but the *h* is ascertained are objects where the *s* can be inferred, and a doubt about such an *s*, where the *h* is known to be in the *p* or in objects similar to the *p*, is not a defect but is in fact a necessary condition of inference.

Objection: If one thing, such as earth, is taken as the *p*, then the inference cannot prove the existence of an ominscient self (i.e., God).

Answer: Then add still another qualification to the *p*, viz., that it not be produced through an awareness which has a content that is limited. This inference will then prove the existence of an omniscient person.

Answer: Effort, desire and awareness are qualifiers (*viśeṣaṇa*) of the *s*. Now since yogis do not have these qualities just before the beginning of creation, their existence is not established by Inf3, even without the added qualification mentioned at the end of section II.1.

Objection: In the *s* of Inf3a and Inf3b let productivity belong to the collection of effort, desire and immediate awareness of the material cause of the jar; then there will be the proving of what is not intended to be proved (viz., the existence of yogis).

Counterobjection: Hardly, since the *s* so understood (viz., being produced by effort, desire and immediate awareness of the material cause of the world) does not exist prior to the creation of the world.

Objector's answer: No, for time is beginningless and there might perfectly well be such a person.

Counterobjection: So there is no possibility of proving what is not intended, since the *p* is qualified by "at the beginning of creation".

Objector's answer: It can't be so qualified since some of the opponents (e.g., the Mīmāṃsakas) don't admit any beginning to creation.

Gaṅgeśa's answer to the objector: The objection is unsound, because God's awareness causes destruction which is related to its locus (what is destroyed) by a self-linking connector, while the yogis' desire, etc. do not do so.

Objection: This inference alleges that only God produces things such as breaking the earth, increase in the oceans, or the production of dyads from atoms. But indeed humans sometimes do such things; they break the earth when tilling, increase the ocean by pouring water into it, create a dyad by moving their hand into contact with something. So there is the fault of proving what is already established (viz., that humans—at least yogis—are the creative agents).

Answer: No, humans do not do the first and third things, for they do not have the requisite awareness. E.g., they break whole pieces of earth into parts, but not the parts ultimately, since they don't have any awareness of the ultimate parts—atoms. Similarly for the creation of a dyad in the manner alleged. But they do know the material cause of the increase in the ocean, so *that* result could be counted as part of the *p* of the inference.

Objection: It is the awareness, and not its owner, that produces (say) a jar, and the *s* as formulated is defective.

Answer: No, for it takes bodily effort and action by someone for a jar to be produced.

Objector: Not really. The self is always there prior to an event (here, the production of a jar), but the bodily action does not take place unless effort inheres in the self just prior—so it is that, effort, and not the self, which is the cause of the production of the jar.

Answer: Every causal situation requires a noninherence cause. The bodily action is an effect produced by an effort (as we say), but effort cannot be the noninherence cause (for it is its instrumental cause), rather the noninherence cause is the contact of the self with its body, and so the self is involved in the causal factors after all.

(II. 2d–e) (ET192–194) The specification of immediate awareness in the *s* of Inf3 is defective, since the object of the desire can only be inferred, not perceived, being still in the future at the time of the effort and desire.

Answer: It is what is present—the material cause—which has to be perceived, and what is future, the resultant object (e.g., the pot) that has to be inferred.

Objection: We move our internal organ to effect contact with a sense organ; but though this is a causal situation there is no perception of the material cause of the movement, viz., the internal organ. Therefore the *s* is deviant.

Answer: But we do perceive the *nāḍī* or channel in which the internal organ moves. Or if you don't believe we do perceive these channels, we suggest a proof that we do: when we drink water we feel tactually the water coursing along *nāḍīs*.

Objection: In the case of production of the jar we find that among the causal factors there is inference. Now just as God's perception is eternal while ordinary selves' perceptions are not, so God's inference should be eternal; otherwise He could not produce the beginningless dyad, etc.

Answer: God has no such inferences as are relevant in the case of our productive activities. For our inferences have to do with the production of satisfaction or the avoidance of frustration, but these states are never found in God.

(II. 2f–g) (ET195–196) An action done out of hatred toward something is not done from desire. So it is not true that every action is performed from a desire to perform it. And if you admit that hatred is also a cause of the producing of something by an act, then hatred becomes attributable to God.

Answer: No, for it is not true that hatred is the only cause of an action. The desire to kill a snake, for example, is not prompted solely because of our aversion to snakes. The reason is rather this: no wise man ever performs anything solely to produce frustration. The desire to kill snakes is due to our desire to avoid frustration. To avoid frustration by destroying its source is a desirable goal, is good for me. It is this awareness that killing snakes is good for me which prompts the desire to kill snakes. So hatred is not the immediate cause of the effort to kill a snake, but only a mediate condition. This doesn't mean that there is no hatred, for everybody has experienced through introspection hatred, e.g., of their enemies. But hatred cannot be the only or the immediate cause of effort to perform an action.

Objection: God is not an object of perception. This nonperception of God produces awareness of his absence, and this awareness contradicts the inference intended to prove his existence.

Answer: If nonperception were a sufficient reason for awareness of the absence of a thing, then no imperceptible objects could ever be inferred. It is not nonperception alone, but nonperception of perceptible objects, that is the cause of the perception of absences. Since God is not a perceptible object, nonperception of Him cannot be a sufficient reason for awareness of His nonexistence.

Objection: If so, one could infer the existence of invisible horns on a horse on the ground that it is an animal!

Answer: Horns aren't invisible: they are very clearly visible! Moreover, everyone knows through perception the nonexistence of horns on a horse, and this sublates the alleged inference.

(II. 2h) (ET197–199) Objection: To establish a causal relation between two things we have to see not only their agreement in positive instances, but also in negative instances. According to Nyāya God's effort is eternal, it is not absent at any time anywhere. So there can be no negative instances of God's effort. Furthermore, there can be no agreement in positive instances between God's effort, which is eternal, and created things which are not eternal.

Answer: You have to understand the nature of positive and negative instances. Take for example the causal relation between fire and smoke. To establish this causal relation, it is necessary and sufficient to observe some instances where smoke of a certain sort is present with fire of a certain sort. And in the negative instances we have to observe the absence of smoke of that sort accompanied by the absence of fire of that same sort.

Objection: If it is admitted that by observing the positive and negative concomitance of kitchen fire and kitchen smoke we can know the pervasion of something else, say of hill fire and hill smoke, then it will be possible to know the pervasion between any two things by observing positive and negative concomitance between two other things.

Answer: No, since by observing positive and negative concomitance between instances of two universals we know the pervasion between any two instances of these universals. So by observing concomitance of particular smokes and fires we know the pervasion between smoke and fire in general. Now in the concomitance between particular efforts (like those of a weaver) and particular effects (like production of a cloth) we know the pervasion of effects by efforts in general. It is not that the specific *s* which is present in this *p* has to be known in positive and negative instances with the *h* in order to know the pervasion between this *s* and this *h*.

Objection: If one can infer an imperceptible cause from pervasion between observable effects and observable causes, then we should be able to infer the invisible fire which digests food in the stomach.

Answe.. No, for there is no visible smoke coming out of a person's mouth on the basis of which we can infer that fire in his stomach.

(II.2i–j) (ET199–201) Objection: The absence of effects is not due to the absence of all (three) of awareness, desire and effort, but to the absence of any one of these. So Inf2 commits the fallacy of redundant qualifiers.

Answer: No, since by the presence of effects each of the three qualifiers is established.

Objection: Inf2 is meant to establish the existence of a bodiless agent with eternal awareness, etc. But the example given is a pot, where we find pervasion between having an effect and being an embodied agent with no eternal awareness, etc. So Inf2 is guilty of the fallacy of having a contradictory *sp.*

Answer: There is no fault in the *h*'s having omnipresence with the *s* in an *sp* with properties contrary to those of the *p*. If it were a fault no inference would be possible at all. E.g., supposing one wishes to infer fire from seeing smoke in a field of hay, and offers as his example the kitchen, where not hay fire but (say) coal fire is found to be concomitant with smoke. And there is no pervasion of having an effect by being an embodied agent with no eternal awareness, etc., since then Inf2 would be invalid, having one *s* in its pervasion and another in its *pakṣadharmatā.*

(II.2k) (ET202-203) Objection: Awarenessness and eternality, on the one hand, and bodilynessness, on the other, are mutually opposed and so cannot be compresent in one locus. So how can God, an agent with eternal awareness, be proved?

Answer: Each of these properties must be present in their own loci. Inf2 proves a locus, God, for all four of these properties. It doesn't first prove a locus of some of them, and then another locus of the others.

(II.21) (ET203-207) Objection: Efforts are the causes of effects (such as a pot) other than bodily movements only through the mediacy of bodily movements (of the hands, etc.). Since God doesn't have a body, He has no bodily movements, so God cannot produce any effects.

Answer: The causes of effects other than bodily movements cannot in general be bodily movements, for then plants, the earth, etc., cannot be caused at all. So the causal relation between pots and their creators—embodied agents—is a special case, and it cannot be generalized to all causal relations. So a paralyzed potter cannot create a pot because he lacks specific features required for producing pots, not because he lacks the generic feature for producing anything at all.

Objection: Effort does not coexist with the effect it is said to produce, since when bodily movement intervenes the effort has vanished before the effect is produced. So it has to be admitted that effort is the cause of effects in general only through bodily movements and not by itself. Since God has no body He cannot therefore create anything.

Answer: Though inherence cause and noninherence cause must coexist with their effect, we cannot also require the same of the instrumental cause. And there is no general argument against causes first ceasing to be and then producing their effects. A cause is something capable of producing an effect, yet it may not produce its effect if auxiliaries are lacking. To hold that these auxiliaries must be compresent with the effect would be to require far too much. E.g., a prior absence could not then produce its counterpositive. For no absence can coexist with its counterpositive. So God can be an instrumental cause of the world even though the world and God are not coexistent..

15. (ET208-213) Objection: We first see that individuals like Rāma, Shyāma, etc., are embodied, have noneternal awareness, will, effort, etc. We are aware of the pervasion of such properties by (the property) *having-effect-ness.* This awareness of pervasion, previously acquired, will operate as an obstruction, so that doubt about the pervasion on which Inf2 is based must result.

Answer: There is no pervasion found between awarenessness and noneternality. So even if we first become aware that all effects of a certain sort are produced by agents having noneternal awareness, etc., this does not prevent us from coming to learn later on that effects of other sorts may be produced by agents having eternal awareness, for we have not learned any rule that awareness cannot be eternal.

(II.2m-n) (ET211-214) Objection: The limitor of *being produced by an agent* is not *being produced* but rather *jarness, etc.*, since jars are found to have agents always but not everthing that is an effect has an agent (e.g., the earth).

Answer: An alleged pervasion must be accepted when there is concomitance (*sahacāra*) of *s* and *h* together with supporting arguments (*tarka*). This is the case here. The supporting argument is just this, that when there is causal relation between particulars of certain kinds and no contrary instances one should accept the general concomitance between the universals associated with those kinds, since if we were to reject such a principle we could never accept any inference at all. As long as this *tarka* is available for us (the *siddhāntin*) and no counter *tarka* is available for the opponent (the *pūrvapakṣin*), the general relation between the *s* and *h* in Inf2 should be accepted.

Here the "new" thinkers say: We have only experienced cases of noneternal awareness. But that in itself does not contradict the awareness that there is eternal awareness, unless we already have such an awareness to be contradicted.

(II.3a.i-ii) (ET214-217) Objection: An agent is an agent only as having a body. Since God doesn't have a body, he cannot be an agent. Even if his existence is proved, he can only be an onlooker, not a creator.

Answer: The sentence "an agent is an agent only as having a body" can be interpreted in three ways: (1) "an agent is an agent of pots, etc., only as having a body"; (2) "an agent is an agent of any effect only as having a body"; (3) "an agent is an agent of his own actions only as having a body". From (1) it does not follow that an agent cannot do anything without a body. If (2) is intended, even then the objector will not achieve his purpose. For he does not intend that effects in general are produced by agents. Or if he does, still *being produced by a body* will not be an obstruction of the *s* (which is) *being produced*, for the property of being produced is present in effects not produced by a body. And if (3) is intended, then the property of *being produced by an agent* becomes the limitor of the property of *being produced by an agent*, which is absurd, involving circularity. Furthermore, an agent is not an agent only as having a body, for when a person wants to infer a certain conclusion, and performs the act of inferring, his action as an agent of inference is not produced by his body.

(II.3.iii) (ET217-220) Objection: There is pervasion of *being produced* by *being produced by a body*.

Answer: But just as jar may be considered as limited by jarness, so being produced by an agent can be taken as the limitor of being produced. So, everything produced is produced by an agent, and production by a body doesn't come into it.

Objector: But being produced by a body is known to pervade being produced by an agent.

Answer: No, for being produced is the limitor of being produced by an agent, and so being produced by a body can't be so known.

(II.3 remainder) (ET220-223) Objection: There is a counter-inference:

CInf1: The earth, etc., are not produced by an agent, since they are not produced by a body.

Answer: This inference is only meaningful if we questionbeggingly assume that an agent of earth (viz., God) exists, since to cognize the absence of an agent for earth's production one must have cognized its counterpositive (God). Furthermore, there are various faults in CInf1, e.g., (a) its *h* not being produced by a body is absent from its *p*, earth, since earth, etc., do have *adṛṣṭa* as causal condition and *adṛṣṭa* belongs to embodied things. This and other faults in CInf1 are discussed at some length and substantiated.

(II.3.4a-c) (ET233-238) Objection: Even if it be admitted that earth, etc., has an agent, still it is not established that it has only one agent. For the *h* is not pervaded by *having only one creator*.

Counterobjection: It can be shown by appeal to parsimony.

Objector: No. Parsimony is not an instrument of knowledge.

Counterobjector: Then the instrument of knowledge which proves *having* (*at least one*) *creator*, together with parsimony, proves that there is only one creator.

Objector: No, for parsimony is not a regular concomitant of instruments of knowledge. There is no example of an inference failing to take place when the consideration has been recognized simply because parsimony is not present.

Counterobjector: Then parsimony is a cause of a simple inferential conclusion.

Objector: No, that is circular.

Gaṅgeśa's answer: In cases where the contents of an instrument of knowledge may be either simple or complex, simplicity is an auxiliary cause of an inferential conclusion. E.g., if one knows that if the cause of a piece of cloth may be conceived either as simply thread or as soft thread, and he knows that the property of being a thread is simpler than the property of being a soft thread, then he will realize that the cause of a piece of cloth is simply thread, not soft thread.

Objection: If this way of arguing is admitted, one can infer that a huge quantity of cloth has all been produced by one weaver!

Answer: Yes, one can infer that from parsimony; but then one comes to doubt whether one single individual can possibly produce so much cloth. Then subsequent thought convinces one that so much cloth was not produced by one weaver. But the case of the creator of the earth is not like that, for any doubt that may arise whether God is the only creator of the earth can be set at rest very easily. It may be impossible for one weaver to produce a million pieces of cloth, but there is no impossibility of the omnipotent creator creating the whole universe.

(II. 3d) (ET238-240) Objection: Even if God's existence is established by Inf2, it is not yet proved that His awareness is eternal and ranges over all objects. All that the inference establishes is that there is an agent of the universe who has immediate awareness of the material. But it is not established that this immediate awareness of the material is eternal awareness of all objects.

Answer by an old Naiyāyika: An inference establishes those objects which have necessarily to be known as implied by the relation between the *p* and the *s*. Here, the *p* is the beginningless cycle of creation of dyads, etc., and immediate awareness of this requires the immediate awareness of the material involved in such creation, and since any beginningless positive entity is also necessarily endless, this immediate awareness of the material is eternal.

The new Naiyāyika's answer: The *p* of Inf2 has a qualifier *not being produced by noneternal awareness.* So when Inf2 is established it cannot establish an agent with noneternal awareness, on pain of contradiction.

Vācaspati Miśra's answer: The inference (i.e., Inf2 or some equivalent) first proves the existence of one awareness through simplicity. Now we know (through *tarka*) that that awareness, which is the cause of beginningless cycles of creation, cannot itself have a beginning, and that proves the beginninglessness and hence eternity of divine awareness. In the same way God's will and God's effort are to be proved eternal. Then, it is proved that God's awareness is of all objects, since only awareness that has a beginning is determined by objects which are their contents. But if an awareness is eternal, then that awareness is tied to any object, and is therefore about all objects.

Still another answer: God has created the Vedas which contain knowledge about the six (positive) categories (of the Vaiśeṣika system), so God must be omniscient.

(ET240-241) Objection: How can God be the cause of every effect, e.g., of the production of a jar, which is after all produced by a potter? Doesn't this imply double agency for the pot—God's and the potter's? So we shall have to say that every effect has an agent, but this will not prove the existence of God as the creator of everything that is created!

Answer: God's omnipotence—his being the cause of everything created—is established in the same manner as his omniscience is. So, just as the weaver's awareness of the threads is a cause of the cloth, God's awareness of them is also a cause. Udayana has said: "God's existence is proved as the creator of the dyads, etc.; and his existence and agency being proved, it is proved that God is the creator of the pot that the potter is making. But God's existence is not proved in order to explain the creation of the pot by the potter."

Objection: If God is omniscient then he must know the errors of men, so he will also have erroneous awarenesses. For if God knows every object as it is then men's erroneous awarenesses have to be known by God as erroneous awarenesses. So God has erroneous awarenesses.

Answer: No, since God is omniscient, he knows everything, and thus he knows the erroneous awarenesses of human beings. If Devadatta takes a piece of shell for silver, he has a false awareness, for the qualificand of his awareness is the piece of shell but the qualifier is silverness. His perception is illusory, because he perceives something as silver which does not actually have the property of silverness. But when God knows, he does not know a piece of shell as silver (as Devadatta does) but he knows that Devadatta knows a piece of shell as silver, and this is a true awareness. So God knows about human errors, but he does not himself have erroneous awarenesses.

(II.3e) (ET241-243) Objection: God is without satisfaction or frustration, and so does not act from any purpose. If he acted to produce satisfaction and remove frustration he would have created heaven only. If God is dependent on human merit and demerit in allotting them the fruits of their actions then he is dependent. But if God acts without such dependence creation and destruction should be always happening simultaneously. Finally, if God acts from compassion, he must have a body and be a transmigrating self.

Answer: No. God's desire to create or destroy is the presence of that collection of causal conditions such as *adṛṣṭa*, etc., and which come in order. When the presence of this collection of conditions is accompanied by God's awareness and effort creation takes place.

(II.3f) (ET243-246) Objection: If God has no body how can he originate usages of language such as either the Vedas or the (meaning of the word) "pot"?

Answer: At the beginning of creation a fish gets created, and then through relation with *adṛṣṭa*, etc., or through relation to God's effort assisted by *adṛṣṭa*, motions occur in the neck and palate of the fish and in this way the Vedas originate. Similarly through God's effort and the potter's *adṛṣṭa* activity arises in or near the potter's body and creation of a jar results. And similarly is the tradition passed on from teacher to pupil.

Objection: No, Manu and other sages who have gained knowledge and who exist at the beginning of a creation for the purpose of experience perceive the Vedas existing in omniscient God, and repeat them. Later Manu, having taken many other bodies, originates the usage of words like "jar", etc.

Answer: No, this explanation is too complex, assuming many omniscient beings who might themselves create the world, rather than the simpler explanation that a single God creates the world.

Objection: The pupil taught the meaning of a word thinks it is this teacher's words that produce his understanding, but his opinion is false since it is God that is responsible. Thus all verbal cognition is erroneous.

Answer: It is true that the pupil's opinion that his teacher is responsible for his understanding is false, but that does not mean his verbal cognition is false. For if he learns that "jar" means jars his cognition is unsublated by experience and so correct. The falsity of its origin does not vitiate this correctness, any more than it would if he had happened to learn the meaning of the word "jar" from a puppet he mistakes for a person.

Section Twenty-Two: Power or Causal Efficacy (*śaktivāda*)

Summary by Sibajiban Bhattacharyya

"E" references are to the edition of *Tattvacintāmaṇi* by Dvivedin and Bhattacarya (B3400; RB5308).

Pūrvapakṣa

(E2001-2002) A causally necessary condition may be either positive or negative. A positive necessary condition is an object the presence of which is necessary for the production of the effect. A negative necessary condition is an object the absence of which is necessary for the production of the effect. The presence of a negative condition is, therefore, enough to prevent the production of the effect. An obstructor (*pratibandhakāra*) is sufficient to preclude the arising of the effect. There is, however, a type of object which can neutralize the action of an obstructor: such an object is called an exciter (*udbodhaka*). So an effect may be produced even in the presence of an obstructor if there is an exciter neutralizing the operations of the obstructor. Fire, for example, is a necessary condition for burning. The presence of a moon stone, however, prevents a fire from burning anything; so the moon stone is an obstructor. But if a sun stone is present, then even the moon stone will not have its obstructing effect, and fire will produce burning. So there are three cases to consider:

(1) fire alone is present, and burning is produced.

(2) fire and moon stone are present; no burning is produced.

(3) fire and moon stone and sun stone are present; there is burning.

The Mīmāṃsakas seek to explain these cases by reference to the hypothesis of a power or causal efficacy (*śakti*) in the cause producing the effect. In the above example, fire has the power to produce burning; this power is restrained or made ineffective by the moon stone. The sun stone neutralizes the effect of the moon stone and so the power in the fire, becoming effective again, produces burning.

Objection: The *adṛṣṭa* (i.e., the merit and demerit) of human beings explains this difference in the effects of fire (viz., fire's sometimes burning and sometimes not).

Mīmāṃsaka: No, since unseen factors such as *adṛṣṭa* cannot interfere with observable conditions sufficient to produce an effect. *Adṛṣṭa* can only function as an obstructor by removing an observable cause. Otherwise the regularity of causality will be abrogated: causal relations would be intered with arbitrarily.

Objection: Sometimes *adṛṣṭa* directly causes or obstructs, as for example when food prepared for a king is also eaten by cats and dogs it can be inferred that that part of the food eaten by the cats and dogs cannot be eaten by the king.

Mīmāṃsaka: If that were so, someone with his hands in the fire who drops the moon stone he is holding might not be burned, but we know this never happends. The obstructive power of the moon stone is established through the positive and negative concomitance observed between cause (fire plus moon stone) and effect (absence of burning). Only in cases where there is no difference in observable causes but yet there is a difference in the effects they produce can one infer *adṛṣṭa* as a cause.

Objection: *Adṛṣṭa* is the instrumental cause of everything that is produced.

Mīmāṃsaka: Then a bad act (like eating prohibited food) which produces pleasure will be said to do so by instrumental causality of merit, but that is inconsistent, since merit cannot produce pleasure from morally bad actions.

(E2002-2003) Old Naiyāyika: There is no need for this hypothesis of a causal efficacy. A necessary causal condition is that which is just a necessary and immediate antecedent of an effect. Now take

"O" to stand for "an obstructor is present", and "E" to stand for "an exciter is present". Then the cause of fire's producing burning is the presence of the following condition: not (O and not E). This can be seen by considering the four cases possible, viz.,

(O and E)	(a) the obstructor is present and the exciter is present.
(O and not E)	(b) the obstructor is present and the exciter is absent.
(not O and E)	(c) the obstructor is absent and the exciter is present
(not O and not E)	(d) the obstructor is absent and the exciter is absent.

Only in case (b) does fire not burn, and it is the only case where the condition not-(O and not E) is absent.

Objection: This Nyāya theory involves a vicious circle. An obstructor is the counterpositive of an absence which is a cause, and the absence of a cause is an obstructor.

Answer: Though an obstructor is a counterpositive of an absence which is a cause, still it is not the absence of a cause *qua* cause which is an obstructor, but rather the absence of (in this case) the moon stone. i.e., the limitor of the causeness is not *absence-of-obstructor-ness,* but *absence-of-moon-stone-ness.* So the circularity is specious.

Objection: An absence cannot be a cause.

Answer: But the validity of the Vedas, for instance, is due to the absence of defects in (them or their author), and that absence is thus accepted as the cause of their validity by all except unbelievers.

(E2003-2004) Mīmāṃsaka: The (Nyāya) theory is not correct, for there is (for them) no such thing as a real, qualified object and so there is no possibility of being aware of the absence of such an entity *qua* this or that. According to Nyāya there is no additional qualified entity over and beyond the qualificand, the qualifier and their relation. If we take the absence of each of these as a cause, then in some cases absence of an obstructor, in some cases absence of an exciter, and in some cases both are necessary conditions. But neither the absence of the moon stone, nor the absence of sun stone, nor the presence of the moon stone and the sun stone together, are causes of burning, since neither of them (moon stone and sun stone) is sufficient, i.e., neither of these is always present when burning occurs.

Naiyāyika: This objection is worthless. For even if ontologically there is no qualified object over and beyond the qualifier, qualificand and the relation between them, still that does not mean that epistemically there is not any difference. In awareness *what* is known (the ontologically real) is as important as the mode under which the real is known. So an absence differs from another absence if their counterpositives are different, but this is not the only reason why one absence differs from another. Even when the counterpositives of two absences are ontologically the same object, they may yet differ if the limitors of the counterpositives differ. Thus even though both a qualified object and the pure object (without qualification) are identical ontologically, still their absences are not the same, for the limitor of the counterpositiveness of the absence of a qualified object is the property of being qualified, while the limitor of the counterpositiveness of the same object not qualified is just objectness. The absence of *a*-as-qualified-by-*b* is known uniformly in all three of the following distinct cases, viz., where *a* is absent, where *b* is absent, and where both *a* and *b* are absent. Furthermore, a power as postulated by the Mīmāṃsakas is an unobservable object, so it cannot be known uniformly in the different types of cases where fire burns.

(E2004) Mīmāṃsaka: What is the nature of the absence of the obstructor when the obstructor is present along with the exciter? It cannot be prior or posterior absence, for the counterpositive (the obstructor) is present. It cannot be absolute absence either, for absolute absence is eternal; it cannot be present sometimes and absent sometimes. And the assumption of a fourth type of (relational) absence is not justified.

Answer: Even though absolute absence is eternal, yet it is not always perceived in its locus, as the relation between the locus and the absence is not eternal. So when a thing is present in a locus, its absolute absence, though present there, is not present in that locus in the relevant relation, for the relation between the absolute absence and the locus gets broken when the counterpositive of the absence becomes present in the locus.

(E2019-2021) So far the Mīmāṃsakas have tried to prove power as an independent category by recourse to presumption. They have not been successful. So now they try inference.

The inference is of the following sort: Fire possesses a property which explains why the causally ineffective sort of fire (e.g., with a moon stone in one's hands) does not occur—i.e., why one gets burned; because fire is in the effective state (i.e., it does burn one); just as a sharp ax must have some property which explains why it has different effects in use from a dull ax. The inference is valid (claims the Mīmāṃsaka), and the property in question is the possession of causal efficacy.

Naiyāyika: The alleged causal efficacy is the effect of the causes which produce fire. The causes of the power to produce fire and the causes of fire are exactly the same. So even when the obstructor (the moon stone) is present, causal efficacy too must be present, since fire itself is present.

Mīmāṃsaka: Even though the causal efficacy is the effect of positive causes, still when the obstructor is present it remains unmanifested.

Siddhānta

(E2023-2024) Gaṅgeśa: the Mīmāṃsā argument is not valid. For the same argument will serve to prove an infinite number of positive properties besides the power in question. The argument goes as follows: "Fire possesses an imperceptible positive property other than the power (already proved) that explains why the causally ineffective sort of fire does not occur; because the fire is in the effective state; etc."

Mīmāṃsaka: Since the fact of burning is explained by the first power to be inferred, there is no need to infer any added imperceptible positive properties to explain the same fact.

Gaṅgeśa: But even if the power is not inferred, still all the facts about burning can be explained.

Mīmāṃsaka: Just as the Nyāya philosophers have proved the existence of one God by their argument, so also we infer one and only one imperceptible positive property, viz., causal efficacy, and not many such properties.

Gaṅgeśa: Our inference proves a maker (of the world) *qua* agent, not *qua* God or *qua* some second agent. Effects such as a piece of cloth do have two agents, since the weaver is the agent of the cloth *qua* cloth, while God is the agent of the cloth *qua* effect (God is the agent of every effect). But there is no such causality residing in both. Just so, in the case of the Mīmāṃsā thesis, there is a causality explaining why the fire burns (i.e., why the causally ineffective sort of fire does not burn), but not as some positive imperceptible property. Moreover, every positive effect must have an inherence cause, so another power has to be inferred in which the first power can inhere. So there must be an infinite regress of powers of more and more complexity. And finally, the example (in the Mīmāṃsaka's proposed inference) is not valid, for the sharpness of the ax is not imperceptible—it is due to the superior metal of which it is made, which is perceptible.

(The Mīmāṃsakas distinguish between two kinds of power. One, called here "simultaneous power" (*sahajaśakti*), comes into being at the same time as its locus does, since the causes of, say, fire are exactly the causes which produce the efficacy of fire to burn. The other kind of power is created in something already in existence by causal factors which are different from those which produce the thing.

This kind of power is called "located power" (*ādheyaśakti*), being located in the pre-existing power. An example of located power is that which is produced by the Vedic oblation ritual using *vrīhi* (a kind of barley). The barley is already there and the power is created in it by chanting Vedic *mantras*. There are different arguments for these two different kinds of power. The next section deals with arguments concerning simultaneous power, the succeeding section with located power.)

Simultaneous Power

(E2026-2027) Mīmāṃsaka: Fire can be produced by different causal conditions—grass, flint, crystal. All these produce fire because they have the same causal efficacy. Even though the fires produced by the different causal conditions are different kinds of fire, still all fires are of the same kind *qua* fire. And the causal rule is that effects of the same kind are produced by causes of the same kind. This rule is justified by noting that if the different types of fire were held to be produced by different types of causes, then there will be no cause of fire as such. Moreover, there is no reason for specifying the effects ignoring the common cause. We do not detect through observation any differences among the so-called fifferent types of fire (produced by grass, flint or crystal). (There are other cases— log fires, lamp fires, etc., where different powers need to be postulated for observably different kinds of fire.)

Objection: If plurality of causes is not admitted, then there would be no inference of a specific type of cause from a specific type of effect, or from the absence of a specific type of effect to the absence of a specific type of cause. If effects are to be regarded as of one kind, then in the absence of a specific type of cause the effect could be produced by the presence of another type of specific cause.

Answer: If different types of fires are to be regarded as being caused by different types of causes, then different types of smokes should be regarded as being produced by different types of fires. But then it will be impossible to come to know that smoke in general is pervaded by fire in general, for there will be neither smoke in general nor fire in general.

(E2028-2032) Gaṅgeśa: If power is produced by exactly the same causal conditions that produce the thing which has it, then every piece of grass, every piece of flint, every crystal will have a different power, for the conditions that produce one piece of grass don't produce the next piece. So there still have to be an infinite number of powers belonging to an infinite number of pieces of grass alone. Instead of this, it will be simpler to hold that grass together with blowing, say, is the cause of one type of fire (the characteristic of which may be regarded as a proper universal), and so on. So instead of having a power belonging to each and every particular condition, there will be one type of causal condition as cause of one type of effect.

Objection: We observe fire produced by different types of causal conditions, but we do not perceive these different proper universals belonging to them.

Answer: We do perceive such differences. For example, for a sacrifice we need fire caused by flint. No other fire will have the required effect. But any fire caused by flint will do. Thus we have to admit specific types of effects produced by specific types of causes, and as limiting properties of causeness and effectness we shall have to admit specific proper universals.

Objection: If this is so, won't there have to be a general causality to account for general effects, over and beyond the specific causality for specific effects?

Answer: General causes of fire will include hot particles, contact among them, and nurturing (e.g., blowing on grass). But these general causes cannot produce any fire by themselves, for each fire produced is of some specific nature. So, over and beyond the general causes there must be specific causes such as grass or flint or crystal, etc. For the rule is: without the help of specific causes the general causes do not actually produce any effects.

Located Power

(E2032-2034) Mīmāṃsaka: In the Vedas it is stated that there should be ablution (*prokṣaṇa*) of barley grains and that the grains should be pounded. It is implied by this that in sacrifices like the *jyotiṣṭoma* the grains should first be purified with *mantras* and then pounded. So pounding without first purifying the grains is prohibited. Thus it has to be admitted that an imperceptible something is produced in the grains by ablution prior to their pounding at a subsequent time. As there is no perceptible change in the grains produced by the *mantras*, and since without ablution the pounding of the grains is not effective, this imperceptible something in the grains brought about by the *mantras* is a power.

Objection: The Vedic injunctions do not necessarily mean that the ablution had to be done first. The context, of course, requires that only those grains which have been purified by *mantras* are to be pounded. So the grains are objects to which *both* the actions of ablution *and* pounding are to be directed. But this does not mean that ablution causes the proper pounding at a later time.

Mīmāṃsaka: Even though ablution is not cognized as the cause of proper pounding simply by the rules of interpretation of language, still inference justified this conclusion. The inference is this: ablution is the cause of proper pounding, because it is prescribed only for pounding, as in the case of the grains. Since grains pounded without prior ablution are not productive of the result, it has to be admitted that it is ablution which produces a power in the grains. Still, it is not necessary that the pounding should immediately follow the ablution, for the power that has been produced in the grains by ablution is not a momentary entity. For example, by performing the *aśvamedha* sacrifice a power is created which sends the performer of the sacrifice to heaven. But the effect of the power is not immediate; the performer goes to heaven only after his death which is often long after the performance of the sacrifice. This power, then, must be admitted to exist in the grains. The ablution produces the power in the grains, not in the performer of the ablution. For if ablution is regarded as producing the power in the performer of the ablution, then there will be no direct relation between the grains and the power. It will be necessary to postulate a very indirect sort of relation to relate the grains with the power via the acts performed by the performer. This postulation will be heavy.

Objection: The power (here, *apūrva*) is produced in the performer, since Vedic injuctions are addressed to persons.

Mīmāṃsaka: It is not true that all injunctions, even though addressed to persons, produce a causal efficacy in the performers.

For example, in agriculture and medicine the injunctions, even though addressed to men, still produce fertility in the soil or health in the body.

Objection: If power is produced in the grains by ablution, then it must be assumed that each grain has this single power produced in it. So if some of the grains after ablution are somehow spoilt, then the sacrificial cakes produced from them will not be effective, for at least some of the grains will not have this power.

Mīmāṃsaka: The limitor of the causality resident in the grains is their potency (*saṃskāratva*), not the number of grains unspoiled. Just as even though all pens are causes of writing as pens (the limitor of the causality resident in pens is penness) writing can be done even if only one pen is present, so also the sacrificial cake will be effective even if produced by some grains having the potency of ablution. Alternatively, it may be supposed that there is one causal efficacy resident in all and only those grains, taken together, which have gone through the process of ablution.

(E2035-2043) Gaṅgeśa's response: In the case of agriculture or medicine the power does not reside in the performer of the acts, because the results are empirically observable, and perception determines where the power resides. But in the case of Vedic injunctions there is no perceptible result. In these cases it will be simpler to assume that what the performance of Vedic rites produces is a power in the performers. There is no reason other than a power residing in the performer that can explain why sacrifice, charity, oblation to fire, etc., are causes for being in heaven after the death of the performer. There is no rule of logic that actions performed by men with special material produce some special power in the material.

Objection: The rule is that a substance that has once produced *adṛṣṭa* cannot produce *adṛṣṭa* a second time. If ablution of grains produces *adṛṣṭa* in men, then those grains cannot be used again for pounding to produce another *adṛṣṭa*. If the act of ablution did not produce any specific change in the grains, then grains after ablution and grains without ablution cannot be different from each other. So even grains without ablution ought to be usable for pounding and making sacrificial cakes.

Gaṅgeśa: The injunction "pound the grains" means one should pound the grains after ablution. To explain *why* the grains to be pounded have to be pounded after ablution is not possible. There is no explanation why the Vedic injunctions say what they say. Whatever is said in the Vedas, for whatever reason, is obligatory. Furthermore, one act may produce effects in many things, but these effects will be of various sorts. The ablutions may produce *adṛṣṭa* in the performer and other changes in the grains. For example, a performer of the *kārīri* sacrifice has a good *adṛṣṭa* come to him, but also has his paddy crop saved from drought (since that rite brings immediate rain).

Objection: Vedic rites, even when performed according to prescribed rules, do not always yield results. For example, even when a person has properly performed the *putreṣṭi yāga* he (or she) does not always get a son.

Gaṅgeśa: How can Mīmāṃsakas raise this objection? If Vedic injunctions fail to produce observable results (where appropriate) what guarantee is there that they don't fail to produce imperceptible results, like a power?

Objection: If ablution of grains produces *adṛṣṭa* in the person, then the rule requiring that the results accrue to the agent will be violated.

Gaṅgeśa: It is just as in touching an untouchable, which destroys merit residing in the self. So in such cases we have to admit that the rule is violated.

(E2043-2054) What then is the meaning of the word "*śakti*"? It is causality (*kāraṇatva*). Power is nothing but causality.

Section Twenty-Three: Liberation (*muktivāda*)

Summary by Sibajiban Bhattacharyya

"E" references are to the edition of Gaṅgeśa by Dvivedin and Bhattacharya (B3400, RB5308)

(E2055-2057) One naturally learns about liberation, the self and things of the other world from the scriptures, especially from the Vedas. But after learning about these things from the scriptures one may confirm one's knowledge by inference. This presupposes the epistemological theory that one can know about the same object in different ways by different instruments of knowledge. In the case of the self, this presupposition is sought to be justified by the Vedic injunction "one ought to hear about the self, think (argue) about it, and meditate on it (in order to obtain liberation)". Thus there is scope for inference and argument about the nature of liberation, the means of attaining it, etc.

Liberation is defined as the permanent and total cessation of frustration. In our daily life many of our frustrations cease, but this cessation of frustration is neither total nor permanent. This is expressed in the technical language of Nyāya as follows: it is the cessation of frustration copresent with the prior absence of frustration.

Objection: If this be the real nature of liberation it is not a human goal. For past frustrations are over, and future frustrations cannot be prevented by anything that can be done now, and present frustrations will cease automatically without any human effort, for a present frustration will be destroyed by the origination of the succeeding internal state. The rule is that an internally or externally perceptible special quality of a ubiquitous substance is destroyed by its succeeding special quality. Present frustration, being a perceptible quality of the self, will necessarily be destroyed by a succeeding state of the self, say, the introspective awareness of frustration.

Objection to the objector: By destroying the cause of frustration (viz., ignorance) by correct awareness, frustration itself will be removed, in the same way that by destroying sin by expiation one is rid of frustration caused by sin.

Objector: Then destroying the cause of frustrations by itself becomes an end. But it is in fact not an end, since happiness and absence of frustration are ends in themselves, but not the destruction of the cause of frustration, which is just a means, not an end in itself.

Answer: Although destruction of temporary frustration is not attainable by human effort, total destruction of frustration is. By destroying false awarenesses one can achieve liberation.

Objection: To achieve liberation one has to destroy all frustrations, which means there will be a last frustration, the cessation of which will result in the cessation of all frustrations to come. But as this final frustration is a state of the self, it must be destroyed by its successor, say, the introspective awareness of the one who is frustrated. If, on the other hand, this awareness cannot destroy all frustrations permanently, the total destruction of all frustrations can be achieved only by ending the final frustration. Now if the emergence of this last frustration is necessary to attain liberation, and that can be destroyed by introspective awareness of it, then how can the attainment of correct knowledge of reality be regarded as the cause of liberation?

Answer: The cessation of all frustrations for all time to come cannot be achieved without knowledge of reality. Without this knowledge a cessation of frustration will be followed by emergence of new frustrations.

Objection: We do not have that last frustration, which is the necesssary condition of its cessation that is liberation.

Answer: Then why do a few individuals like Śukadeva have this last frustration which is destroyed automatically by their introspective awareness of it, after which they are liberated? What do these few persons have that we ordinary folk don't so that we are not liberated? It is the knowledge of reality which is peculiar to those who are liberated, as is established by positive and negative concomitance.

Objection: If the cessation of the last state of frustration is regarded as the highest good, then the last state of frustration too becomes the highest good. No state of frustration, not even the final one, can be the highest good; it is against human nature to desire frustration as an end in itself.

Answer: It is not necessary to hold that frustration be regarded as an end in itself to explain liberation as the highest good. The means for attaining the end is also desirable, and men do desire lesser frustration in order to avoid more terrible results, like taking bitter medicine to avoid death.

(E2057-2059) Objector 1: We hold that liberation is the destruction of frustration. Everyone experiences innumerable frustrations, so their destruction is not a single destruction, there must be innumerable destructions if there are innumerable frustrations. Yet these innumerable destructions may be regarded as a single destruction, just as darkness, which is really innumerable absences of innumerable sources of light, is regarded as single.

Answer: This theory is not tenable, for a collection of different objects cannot be the goal of single action, just as a collection of different objects—a pen, pencil, paper, ink, etc.—cannot be produced by any one cause.

(E2059-2060) Objector 2: We say that liberation is the destruction of the cause of a frustration which is not accompanied by the prior absence of any (further) frustration. Just as in ordinary life we find people striving to eradicate thorns which cause pain, so also the destruction of the cause of a frustration which will not be succeeded by any future frustrations is a desirable goal.

Counterobjection against Objector 2: Men act in order to avoid frustration, as the goal of human action is just the nonorigination of frustration, not the destruction of the causes of frustration.

Answer by Objector 2: The nonorigination of frustration is simply prior absence of frustration, a beginningless absence. So this cannot be the result of human action, and so not the goal of such action. So it is destruction of the cause that is the goal.

Gaṅgeśa's answer to Objector 2: Men act, pray, expiate, use medicine with the idea "May I not suffer". Hence nonorigination of frustration is the goal of human action. The objection that nonorigination, being beginningless, cannot be a goal of human action is not tenable, for by removing causes of frustration its nonorigination can be achieved. Thus nonorigination of frustration is the goal. Destruction of the causes of frustration is the means, not the end. This causal relation between the destruction of the causes of frustration and the nonorigination of frustration is established by positive and negative concomitance.

(E2060-2063) Objector 3: The prior absence of frustration is destroyed by acts of religious purification like fasting, ceremonial bathing, atonement, penance. When the prior absence is destroyed no frustration can originate, so in order to originate a thing must have prior absence.

Counterobjection to Objector 3: Even if a person performs sinful actions he will not suffer frustration, for by penance, atonement, etc., the prior absence of frustration has been destroyed, and without prior absence nothing can originate.

Answer to this by Objector 3: Expiation will not be useless, for it will destroy sins, and persons perform expiatory actions for destroying sins which lead to hell after death.

Gaṅgeśa's refutation of Objector 3: Destruction of the causes of frustration cannot be the goal of human action. Everyone acts with the idea of avoiding frustrations; therefore that is the goal, and destruction of the causes is the means.

(E2063-2065) Objector 4: Liberation is the absolute absence of frustration. Although another's frustration is obviously absent in one's own self, and there cannot be absence of one's own frustration in another's self, still the absolute absence of one's own frustration is causally related to the destruction of all the causes of one's own frustrations and so it is attainable by men.

Answer to Objector 4: This view is not tenable. Destruction of one's own demerit, though it causes frustration, is not conducive to liberation.

Objector 5: Liberation is the absolute absence of prior absence of all frustration.

Answer to Objector 5: An absolute absence of a prior absence cannot be an independent goal in itself.

(E2065-2066) Objector 6 (Prābhākara): Liberation is the final prior absence of frustration. When one has destroyed all demerits by attaining knowledge, the prior absence of one's frustration remains firmly established for all time to come and therefore cannot be destroyed by the emergence of new frustrations.

Counterobjection to Objector 6: To say that the prior absence of frustration remains firmly established through the destruction of all demerits is to say that all that one can do is to destroy all of one's demerits—for prior absence is beginningless and cannot be the result of any action. Hence liberation becomes the same as the destruction of all demerits.

BOOK THREE: COMPARISON (*upamāna*)
Summary by Satischandra Vidyabhusana[119]

A man who does not know the meaning of the word *gavaya*, hearing from an elder person that that word signifies an animal which is like a cow, goes into a forest where he sees an animal like a cow. Recollecting the instructive assertion of the elder person he institutes a comparison by which he arrives at the conclusion that the animal which he sees is the thing signified by the word *gavaya*. The means that this conclusion has been arrived at is thus called "comparison" (*upamāna*). It is the knowledge of likeness between a cow and a *gavaya*. The word "comparison" is ordinarily taken to signify the whole process.

The operation (*vyāpāra*) in the case of comparison consists in the recollection of the instructive assertion by the elder that the word *gavaya* signifies an animal which is like a cow. The result of comparision (*upamiti*) is the knowledge of the relation of a name to something so named.

The Mīmāṃsakas maintain that similarity (*sādṛśya*) is a distinct object which is not included in the seven categories of the Vaiśeṣikas. The meaning of the word "*gavaya*" is, according to them, an animal which possesses similarity to a cow. Gaṅgeśa opposes this view by saying that it is cumbersome. A thing is said to bear similarity to another thing if it, while possessing the special property of the latter thing, is different from that latter thing in its generic nature. Such being the definition of similarity, we have to admit an infinite number of similarities corresponding to the things that are similar. The real significance of the word *gavaya*, according to Gaṅgeśa, is not an animal which possesses similarity to a cow but an animal which possesses the generic nature of a *gavaya* (that is, which has *gavaya*-ness). Hence the result of comparison consists of knowledge of the relation between the word *gavaya* and the animal which possesses the generic nature of a *gavaya.*

Some say that the knowledge of the meaning of the word *gavaya* is derived through perception. This is absurd. Though the relation between the word *gavaya* and the animal in question may be perceived if our eyes are in the proper relation to it, it is impossible for us to perceive such a relation when the animal is beyond our vision. Therefore the knowledge of the meaning of the word *gavaya* is not derived through perception, but through a separate instrument of knowledge called comparison.

Neither can the knowledge of the meaning of the word *gavaya* be derived from inference, inasmuch as in the case of comparison knowledge is derived through the knowledge of likeness, independent of awareness of invariable concomitance which is indispensable to inference. Moreover, in the case of knowledge derived through comparision there is in us a self-awareness of the form "I compare" not of the form "I infer".

BOOK FOUR: VERBAL TESTIMONY (LANGUAGE)

"E" references for the summaries of this Book not otherwise identified refer to the Bibliotheca Indica edition of 1897 by Kamakhyanatha Tarkavagisa.

Section One: Language as Instrument of Knowledge (*śabdaprāmāṇyavāda*)

Summary by Pradyot Kumar Mukhopadhyay

(E1-22) Language (*śābda*) is that instrument of knowledge produced by awareness of the nature of actual entities (*bhūtārthajñāna*) which is the cause of usage (*prayoga*).

Objection (by a Buddhist, say commentators): Language cannot be an instrument of knowledge. An instrument of knowledge must be a particular instrument *par excellence* (*karaṇa*). Such an instrument *par excellence* is always followed by the effect. But knowledge does not always follow language—e.g., when we listen to liar. So language cannot be such an instrument of knowledge.

Counterobjector: This position of you (Buddhists) is self-contradictory since it turns out false no matter whether or not you are right in contending that language is not an instrument of knowledge. (If it is an instrument your rejection of it is false, and if it is not an instrument what you say is not knowledge-generating, for what you say is language!.)

Objector's answer: No, since even if language is not always veridical, still what we say may be correct about this specific matter.

Gaṅgeśa: No, you Buddhists are not right. Knowledge does result from hearing a linguistic utterance if the words constituting it have such properties as expectany (*ākāṅkṣā*), etc., and if the hearer remembers what the linguistic elements mean. Of course, utterances which do not have these properties fail to yield knowledge, but in this language is parallel to other admitted instruments of knowledge like perception or inference, which fail to produce knowledge when other necessary conditions are lacking.

(E22-33) Vaiśeṣika: Even so language is not an additional instrument of knowledge beyond inference. We can prove that this is so by the following inference:

V1: The words (*pada*) in such an utterance as "Drive the cow home with the help of the stick" or of any Vedic utterance are preceded by awareness of the intended relation between the things signified by the words and the memory of the things intended.

Because these words are related to each other through expectancy, etc.

Like the words in the utterance "Bring the pot".

Gaṅgeśa: How could we come to cognize the presence of the *h* property indicated in V1? That property is the relation of expectancy among the words. One might suggest that if we knew that the words had fitness (*yogyatā*) and proximity (*sannidhi*) and signified things related to each other we would then have reason to assume the presence of expectancy among the words. But we could never know that the things are related to each other prior to drawing the inference V1, since that knowledge is just what is supposed to be produced through the inference!

Vaiśeṣika: It is not knowledge of the relation among the things which justifies knowledge of the presence of the *h*-property, but merely awareness (i.e., belief) that the things are so related.

Gaṅgeśa: But mere awareness or belief is found not to always amount to knowledge—error occurs. So the mere awareness that the things signified by the words are related is not sufficient to yield the knowledge that the words are related by expectancy. And so the reason offered in V1 cannot be something known to be the case, and in turn that reason cannot be known; but since knowledge of the reason is a prerequisite for accepting the conclusion of an inference, it follows that V1 cannot succeed.

(E34-40) Thus in order to know the facts stated in V1 inference is not available, and we shall need language as the instrument of that knowledge. Indeed, the thesis of V1 is precisely what language as instrument is able to convince us of. Note the appearance of the qualifier "intended" in the formulation of the thesis—the "intended" relation between the things signified and the memory of the things "intended". Why is it necessary to qualify these clauses in that way? Because otherwise language would be an instrument of knowledge of any old relation between the words. In fact, this is another reason why the Vaiśeṣika inference cannot, but language can, give us conviction about the words. Some philosophers formulate the Vaiśeṣika inference in another way, viz.,

V2: These words have the relation that holds between the things remembered.

(Reason and example as in V1).

The words are said to "have the relation" in the sense that they inform us of this relation as much as the *hetu* of any inference informs us about *pakṣa*. Gaṅgeśa points out that this way of expressing the inference begs the question (*anyonyāśraya*), since in order to draw the inference about words having the relation among the things remembered one must have already remembered that relation among those words. Or if it is a different cognition about the words, there will be an infinite regress required of such cognitions.

Objection: This regress is not a fault; it is not a vicious regress.

Gaṅgeśa: V2 might enable us to infer the relation in question among the things, but to infer this is not to know that relation in the way such an awareness can be derived from hearing an utterance. True, we get understanding of the relation between the things recalled by the words in the utterance from hearing the utterance, but we do not cognize the relation merely as one that the words inform us of (the awareness constituting the *hetu* in the inference V2 is about words, not about an utterance). Again, to know by inference that the words were generated by belief about the relation between the things recalled is not to prove that those things have that relation. The words being related to each other through expectancy, etc., do produce in us a cognition concerning the connection between the things recalled, but cannot produce *knowledge* that that cognition is true.

Vaiśeṣika: Yes it can, since it is a rule that awareness J2 of an awareness J1 requires awareness of J1's content. And the inference in question, being an awareness J2 about a connection cognized J1 and now remembered, must involve awareness of J1's content, viz., the connection in question.

Objection to the Vaiśeṣika: Inference may prove somehow some connection between the things signified by the words in an utterance, but the instrument of knowledge that is language proves a specific connection between them, one on which people are disposed to act. (One is disposed to act on the basis of specific beliefs, but not of merely general ones about "some connection or other".)

Vaiśeṣika: But the conclusion of our inference is a specific connection, through the force of *pakṣadharmatā*, i.e., since the *s* property is claimed to characterize the *p* that is these specific words.

(E40-44) Objection to the Vaiśeṣika: As you understand the "rule" adduced three paragraphs back it has dangerous consequences. If J2 is the belief that J1 is false, then J2 must itself be false, since it is an awareness which has a content (J1's content) that is not the case. As a result, for example, God cannot be omniscient or infallible. If He were omniscient and infallible He could know that false beliefs are false, but the "rule" precludes that! Furthermore, one who cognizes by J2 that an awareness J1 is erroneous should nevertheless act on the basis of J1's truth according to the "rule", since the J2-knower believes in J1's content, which belief is taken by the Vaiśeṣikas themselves as the occasion for positive activity by the cognizer.

Response to these objections: These objections cannot stand, since a false awareness can't have content or for that matter fail to have one. If it has no content then there is no false awareness (since any awareness must have a content), while if it *has* a content and one is aware of it one's awareness must be true.

Objector to the Vaiśeṣika: Well, there are false awarenesses and they have contents, so this argument won't wash.

Vaiśeṣika response: The trouble is that you are assuming that the awareness J2 of an erroneous J1 has something unreal as its content. Rather, a false awareness is one whose chief qualifier is a property which does not reside in the qualificand of the cognition. J1 is a false awareness since its chief qualifier (say, silverness in "this is silver") does not reside in the qualificand *this.* But J2 ("J1 is false") has as its qualificand J1, and as its chief qualifier *falsehood.* The "rule" in question merely stated that the content (here, *silverness*) of J1 be involved in J2's content, which it is: the rule doesn't require that that content be the chief qualifier.

(E45-48) Gaṅgeśa: Now as to V1 and/or V2: these inferences are faulty because the *h* "wanders"—it is found sometimes in the absence of the *s.* For example, a liar makes an utterance intending to deceive his hearer: he knows that what he intends to convince his hearer of, which is what is expressed through the relation among the words he utters, is not the case, but yet the words are related to each other through expectancy, etc.

Vaiśeṣika: But of course the liar knows the relation that his utterance conveys, since no one can utter words that make a sentence without knowing the relation which the sentence expresses. So the case of the liar is not a case where the *h* of V1 (or V2) is not accompanied by its *s* property, it has not been proved that the *h* "wanders".

Answer: Well, a parrot utters sentences, but you must admit the parrot doesn't know the relation among the words. Perhaps we can say it knows the words, but no one supposes it knows the relations among the things the words mean. And so also it is not in general the case that knowledge of the relation among the things referred to by the words is required for an utterance to display expectancy, etc. And thus our example of the liar stands.

Vaiśeṣika: No. Every conscious and deliberate utterance of a sentence is preceded by an intention having the form "let this utterance convey to the hearer such and such a relation between the things which correspond to the words of the sentence uttered". Even an utterance by a liar is preceded by the knowledge of such a relation. So the charge of "wandering" has no force. Moreover, in the cases of both the liar and the parrot the *h* property isn't present, since in both cases there is absence of fitness. So not only is it the case that the *s* property is present in the case of the liar, but it is also the case that the *h* property is absent in both the two cases. Thus no charge of deviation can possibly be supported.

Question: Then how does the hearer manage to understand something about the things from the liar's or parrot's utterances, if fitness is lacking?

Vaiśeṣika: Because the hearer wrongly believes the fitness to be there, though it isn't.

(E48–50) Objection to the Vaiśeṣika: If an utterance is true, no matter who or what utters it, there cannot be absence of fitness. And if the liar is mistaken then what he utters (intending to deceive) turns out (unknown to him) to be true, and once again it must display fitness. So the *h* property *is* present in any true utterance, and so in particular it is present even in an utterance where the hearer fails to have the *s* property of gaining knowledge of fact from hearing it. In the cases in question (of a parrot who speaks truth, or the liar who mistakenly speaks truly) the hearer cannot correctly infer the awareness on the speaker's part of knowledge of the relations among the things he is understood to speak of. Yet according to the Vaiśeṣika it is only through inferring such a belief of the utterer that a hearer comes to have true belief about a fact.

Vaiśeṣika: If knowledge arises from such an utterance it will have to be considered in the way we consider the truth of Vedic utterances, viz., that either they have no speaker, or that their speaker is God, so that in any case we never find a case where the *h* property is present without the *s* property. That expectancy, fitness and contiguity assist the hearer (by providing the *h* for his inference as to what an utterance means) follows from the fact that hearers sometimes *misunderstand* a speaker—that wouldn't be possible unless they could form some cognition on the basis of what the speaker uttered.

(E50–53) Gaṅgeśa: Neither is the speaker's belief in the relation of things the cause of his uttering the sentence in question, nor does the volition of the hearer depend on the hearer's belief about the speaker's belief about that relation. Volition with regard to a piece of silver results from the belief on the part of the agent that it is a piece of silver; this volition does not presuppose as its cause a belief to the effect that the speaker has the appropriate belief about silver.

Objection: But the (hearer's) belief about the (speaker's) belief about silver is also a belief about silver. Why isn't it thus an occasion for volition?

Gaṅgeśa: Only the belief about silver has *silverness* as its chief qualifier, not the belief about the belief, and it is only with respect to the *chief* qualifier that volition is aroused. Otherwise, if the belief about the belief caused volition, then just as the mistaken person would have volition aroused in him by his awareness, so also would the person who detected the mistake, since their awarenesses both have *silverness* as a qualifier. The difference is that the mistaken person experiences an awareness in which *silverness* is the chief qualifier, while the one who discovers the mistake does not.

(E53–55) These considerations also disprove the theory according to which a hearer comes to know the relation among things expressed by the speaker's utterance through inferring the speaker's intention. This intention about the relation consists in the desire of the speaker to the effect that the hearer know the relation from his (the speaker's) utterance. Such an intention must indeed be admitted in order to explain what determines the hearer to disambiguate the meaning of the speaker's utterance, especially in cases where the speaker intends his utterance to be understood in some indirect or metaphorical fashion (in its secondary meaning, as Indian grammar has it). Furthermore, just as the inference from smoke to fire provides knowledge of the fire as being fire but not as being a substance, being knowable, etc., likewise V1 or V2 can provide knowledge that the utterance was preceded by the speaker's belief about the relation among the things as signified by those words but not insofar as they are silver, etc. Now what causes volition is not belief that there is a relation among things signified by the words and remembered, but rather the belief that this is silver. So V1 and V2 are not capable of giving rise to a judgment of the sort that induces volition. Instead, that judgment is provided by a distinct instrument of knowledge, language (*śabdapramāṇa*).

(E55–57) This disproves as well the view that language only gives us knowledge we must already have. Although inference can yield awareness of the truth of an utterance on the ground of the authoritativeness of the speaker or the expectancy, etc., present in the sentence uttered, the awareness derived is not the kind which brings about volition, as was just shown. The information derived from language and the information obtained from inference are different, since they have different chief qualifiers. The inference's chief qualifier is what is believed to be the relation holding among what is signified by some words, while the chief qualifier of the knowledge produced from hearing a speaker's utterance is a thing as having a certain property.

(E57–63) Vaiśeṣika: Well, then, we offer the following alternative inferences:

V3: These things are related to each other by the relation intended, because they are remembered through awareness that the words have expectancy, etc.

or V4 : These things are related by the intended relation, because they are recalled through awareness that the words indicate that relation, since those words possess fitness and contiguity.

(E63–64) Utterances of nonauthoritative persons (such as one who is mistaken, or a liar) do not constitute counterexamples to V3 or V4, because such utterances, being false, lack fitness. An utterance has or lacks fitness depending on whether or not the corresponding contradictory utterance is false or true.

(E64) Objection to the Vaiśeṣika: But what are expectancy, fitness and contiguity? Expectancy is what causes something to be inquired into by the knower (or hearer), so that there is expectancy for "B" given by "A" when it is the case that whenever "A" is heard there occurs a desire to come to know the thing(s) signified by "B." Specifically, it may be defined as the prior absence (on the hearer's part) of awareness of the relation capable of arising from those words. Fitness is the absence of contradictory knowledge. And contiguity is the immediate awareness of the other term of the relation intended. Now it is true that these three features are operative in generating understanding on the part of the hearer, but what causes that understanding is the presence of the features in the utterance, and not the hearer's awareness of them. The reasons for this are three: first, it is a simpler explanation to appeal to the features themselves than to the awareness of them. Second, understanding of the meaning of the utterance occurs immediately after hearing the words having these features, and there is no time for an intervening awareness of its having them. Third, awareness of the features presupposes prior awareness of the relation intended to be conveyed. For the hearer to be aware that word "A" leads to a desire to know the thing signified by "B", he has to become aware of the relation between the things signified by A and B—but that relation is precisely what he is supposed to become aware of by inferences V3 and V4 only after having heard the utterance.

(E64–66) Vaiśeṣika answer: No. If the features of expectancy, etc., are themselves capable of generating understanding, then either a hearer must not understand a given utterance (it lacking these features) or (if it possesses them) it must immediately produce true awareness. There would then be no possibility of false awareness arising from hearing someone speak. But this is absurd, since everyone knows false beliefs are regularly generated in hearers. They could only be so if the hearers had the false belief that expectancy, etc., are actually present in the utterance they heard. So, since false belief about things arises from false belief about the presence of the three features, true belief about the presence of an intended relation must arise from true belief that the features are present in the utterance heard.

Furthermore, it is not even the case that true belief about the presence of the three features is required for understanding. One hearing an ambiguous utterance, even though he does not know whether or not the features are all present, still does understand the utterance; he is *aware* of the features despite his doubt or rejection of the truth of the utterance, where the awareness in question may be doubt, rejection as well as belief.

(E66–67) Objection to the Vaiśeṣika: You say this because you think it difficult to know the presence of some of the features. For example, to know that fitness obtains one must (given the definition offered above) know that no one, oneself or any other, believes the opposite of what is uttered to be the case. But this is very difficult to know in practice. Realizing this, you have relaxed the requirement from knowledge to doubt or even false awareness.

Vaiśeṣika: No, we realize that fitness can be known. For example, the awareness that there is no pot here can be seen to be such that no one, neither oneself or anyone else, believes there is a pot here. So sometimes, at least, fitness may be ascertained. So that is not why we argued that belief in the presence of the features is not a prerequisite for understanding. Rather it is, as we said, because it is frequently found that the hearer understands an utterance even though he is in doubt as to whether the features are actually present in that utterance.

(E68–69) In any case, even you appear ready to admit that it is belief about fitness, etc., that is the proof of truth of the utterance, a belief which arises from the presence of that fitness in that utterance. Thus you seem to admit that an inference is required on the hearer's part to arrive at correct understanding. But what could be the *h* of such an inference for you? It must be either the authority of the speaker or the presence of the three features under discussion. But you cannot allow that the reason for the truth of the utterance is the authority of the speaker, since this would violate the principle of economy. This is because, in order to know that a speaker is authoritative one will have to know that the speaker is not a liar and that the speaker's utterance has expectancy, fitness and contiguity due to his knowledge of the things signified. This is unnecessarily complex: one can more simply hold (as we do) that the understanding derives directly from the awareness that the utterance displays the three features in question. Moreover, since a nonauthoritative person may accidentally happen to say something true, being spoken by an authoritative person cannot be a necessary condition of truth or correct understanding resulting. So even you must admit what we claim, that the hearer's understanding of an utterance derives from his inference to the truth of what is said on the basis of his awareness of the presence of the features of expectancy, fitness and contiguity in the utterance.

(E69–74) Objection: The presence of the three features is not enough. A fourth condition must be cognized as present, viz., awareness that he has heard just the words and all the words intended by the speaker. (An example is discussed the meaning of which is lost in English translation but which depends on the hearer hearing only some but not all of the words and drawing an incorrect inference about the speaker's meaning.)

Vaiśeṣika: No, since one understands or misunderstands even if he is in doubt.

Objector: But at any rate the hearer doesn't derive correct understanding when he doesn't get all the words; he comes to believe something that is false.

Vaiśesika: No. It is just the words that produce false belief, and so it is better to hold that it is the presence or absence of faults in those words that is responsible for the truth or falsity of what is understood, even if only some of the words are heard.

(E74–77) Objection: When false belief arises under those conditions (where all the words are not heard) the reason is the failure to grasp the lack of relation among the things signified by the words that are heard.

Vaiśeṣika: No, for such a situation does not constitute false belief but merely absence of awareness of anything contradicting the relation in question.

Objection: Being spoken by an authoritative person is the ground of inference or a qualifier of that ground. This will take care of the case under discussion, since this authoritativeness is absent from the utterance the hearer heard, which is why he draws an incorrect conclusion.

Vaiśeṣika: Who is an authoritative person? Everyone says something true sometime, and no one tells the truth always and in an unqualified way.

Objector: Authoritativeness belongs to a person not in general but in relation to a particular utterance. To say that a person is authoritative in relation to utterance U is just to say that he correctly knows the relation among things signified by U.

Vaiśeṣika: But on this construal how can we know that the speaker is authoritative prior to knowing what his utterance means? In order to know that a given S is authoritative in uttering U one must know that things are as U states them to be, and in order to do that one must know what U states them to be—so S's being authoritative can play no part in the hearer's inference leading to understanding or to knowledge. Again, prior to inferring what an utterance means a hearer, according to Vaiśeṣika theory, cannot ascertain whether or not one who acts on it acts successfully. So one cannot ascertain, through noting the success of the resulting volitional activity, the authoritative character of the speaker after having inferred the meaning of the utterance. Indeed, we sometimes act even on the basis of suspicion and not only on belief—as when one decides to carry an umbrella when he suspects it may rain. Finally, men do understand utterances of a type not heard before, and since that is sometimes the case, one cannot infer before one understands an utterance that the speaker is an authoritative person, since he does not necessarily know beforehand that the utterance is true.

(E77–79) Gaṅgeśa now offers his final view ("But *we* say ..."). According to the Naiyāyikas fitness consists in the absence of truth of any sublating awareness, i.e., of any contradictory belief. But this is not a reason or part of a reason which one might use to infer the meaning of an utterance, since one cannot ascertain beforehand absence of every contradictory belief. Besides, even if a hearer is in doubt as to whether or not there is a true utterance contradictory to a given U, he can still understand U. Now awareness of this fitness is a factor in the production of linguistic knowledge. But since the awareness of fitness can be a state of doubting, it is not by itself the cause of the resulting linguistic knowledge, which it would be if fitness itself were the inferential ground or part of it in which the understanding of the hearer consists. Since fitness is not the inferential ground, nor belief about it the cause of the resulting belief about the meaning of the utterance, the understanding of the hearer is derived from the utterance (i.e., language as a distinct instrument of knowledge.)

(E83–85) Older Mīmāṃsaka (*jaranmīmāṃsaka*): The information conveyed by an utterance must already be known by the hearer when he infers that the speaker is authoritative. This being the case, an utterance can convey only information known already to the hearer, ordinary language cannot be an instrument of knowledge but rather something that reiterates information the hearer already has. The point is that ordinary speakers sometimes utter false assertions. So the hearer must use some other means, like fitness, to ascertain the truth of what the speaker says. However, since Vedic utterances have no speaker, being eternal, the hearer does not require any knowledge of the authoritativeness of the speaker. The power of scriptural statements to convey truth is not therefore impaired by actual or possible defects of the speaker, and thus a hearer can derive the information they convey immediately on hearing it. This is how we learn information initially. And so, Vedic utterances cannot be said to merely repeat what is already known, and therefore qualify as an independent instrument of knowledge.

Answer: No. For Vedic utterances, just like ordinary ones, get understood on the basis of the collection of conditions such as expectancy, fitness and contiguity. Otherwise the hearer would have had to understand the information conveyed already (and would not need the utterance to understand it), in which case it can't be alleged (as the Mīmāṃsaka wishes to) that Vedic utterances don't repeat old information.

Objection: Then you should conclude that the hearer's understanding is inferential and does not derive from an independent instrument of knowledge called "language!"

Answer: The mere presence or even the awareness of the thing which may serve as *h* of an inference is not sufficient by itself to produce inferential awareness. One must also remember the pervasion of that thing by something else, the *s*, as well as the consideration of this pervasion together with the *pakṣadharmatā*. All of this takes time. However, the hearer immediately gets linguistic awareness from hearing the utterance, an awareness about the same thing cognized by the subsequent inferential awareness. So it is the inference which repeats information already gained (by the hearer), and thus inference is in this case not the instrument of knowledge. Rather, since ordinary utterances also exhibit the conditions of expectancy, fitness and contiguity as much as do scriptural sentences, language itself is an independent instrument of knowledge.

(E85–87) Objection: Those conditions are present in the case of the false utterances of untrustworthy persons as well. So the hearer needs to first infer trustworthiness of the speaker in order to know the utterance is true.

Answer: This cannot be accepted. We know that our visual organ has occasionally yielded false belief in the past, but we do not on that account deny that we can have visual knowledge. Likewise, even though expectancy, etc., hold, sometimes the utterances are false; however it does not follow that inference is needed to provide true awarenesses, any more than it follows that because the visual organ sometimes yields falsity one needs inference even when there may be doubt about the truth of a perceptual awareness.

Objection: There is a difference between the organ of vision on the one hand and conditions of fitness, expectancy, etc., on the other. The former produces knowledge while itself remaining unknown. If one has normal powers of vision one will perceive the color of the pot; one need not have to know for this purpose that he has the visual sense organ or power. But conditions like fitness yield knowledge only when one is aware of them. One will not be able to understand an utterance even when the conditions of fitness, etc., obtain if one does not believe that these conditions do obtain. In this respect these conditions are like the ground (*h*) of inference. Even when a thing like smoke is there, one may not arrive at the inferential belief that fire is there unless one also believes that the smoke is there. So conditions of knowledge are of two sorts. One kind functions to produce knowledge only when they are known: call them conditions operative through knowledge of them. The other sort is effective merely by being there, whether or not they are believed to be there. Sense organs are examples of the latter kind. Now normally conditions which obtain in the case of belief arrived at through language belong to the first kind. The characteristic feature of this first kind of condition is that once their ability to produce the effect comes to be doubted because of our awareness of their failure in the past, they cease to yield knowledge. If this is granted, conditions like fitness, etc., cannot be regarded as sufficient to yield knowledge in the case of ordinary utterances, since these conditions, like the inferential ground, fail to produce knowledge once their past failure has come to be known.

Answer: This argument does not hold. What is it that we may doubt about a speaker's utterance? We do not entertain doubt whether something was uttered or whether what was uttered is a sentence. Nor can we entertain doubt about the truth of the information that is to result from the utterance, for that information has yet to be conveyed. Nor do we doubt the trustworthiness of the speaker, since that trustworthiness is not a condition for linguistic knowledge.

(E87–90) Objection: But since there is always doubt about the trustworthiness of the speaker we do not derive any belief from his utterance; so belief in the speaker's authoritativeness *is* a condition for our understanding his utterance. So we must come to understand the utterance by ascertaining through inference that the utterance has been caused by knowledge on the part of the speaker about the information in question.

Answer: No, since in the case of Vedic sentences, which have no speakers, we still gain knowledge. So knowledge that a sentence has been uttered, etc., is not necessary for the sentence to produce knowledge. Furthermore, consider a foolish Mīmāṃsaka (literally, one who hails from Bengal ("Gauḍa"), who is not an expert in Vedic literature and hears someone utter something from the "Laws" of Manu employing Vedic intonation. Believing falsely that what is uttered is a Vedic sentence and so eternally true, he believes in what Manu says and his belief is correct on that score, for no contradicting awareness arises. What is more, even when he is told and comes to know that the sentence he heard has an author, this Mīmāṃsaka may continue to have the belief he had earlier and his belief continues to be true.

Objection: In a case like this the hearer actually misunderstands what Manu said!

Answer: He does not misunderstand. He fails to recognize the kind of sentence it is, and so wrongly assumes he needn't investigate the source of his belief. But if this were sufficient to support the misunderstanding of what is being conveyed by an utterance there would never be any understanding of what is attempted to be conveyed. If one can deny his understanding of an utterance for no reason at all then one can do so anytime.

Objection: In this case there is a reason for doing so, since the authoritativeness of the speaker is not accepted by the hearer. So, since understanding arises regardless, this belief in authoritativeness cannot be a condition at all.

Answer: No, since there is no evidence for such a contention. What an utterance signifies is (may be) something new. Thus, since the meaning of the utterance is not a recognized fact, it cannot function as a ground in an inference of the sort the objector appeals to.

(E90–92) Objection: What is a necessary condition for understanding an utterance is the belief that the utterance has not been uttered by a nonauthoritative person. This condition applies in the case of both ordinary utterances and Vedic sentences. In the case of the latter, if it is believed that the sentence has no author, it of course cannot be believed that it has been produced by a nonauthoritative person. In the case of the former, however, one must be convinced that the speaker is authoritative.

Answer: If this were so, then even Vedic sentences become noninstruments of knowledge because repetitive, since the only way one could become convinced that a sentence has no author is through some such inference as: the things mentioned in the Vedic sentence are related in the way stated, because they are recalled through hearing words spoken by nondeceptive, nondefective, etc., persons and such words are related by expectancy, etc. But this inference already presupposes understanding of the meaning of the sentence, and thus once again the sentence itself reiterates information already presupposed on the part of the hearer. And this undermines your position. Udayana is quoted here in approval.

(E92–99) Prābhākara: There must be a condition which is shared by all those sentences (or utterances) which are true and which are understood. We shall have to assume such a condition in order to explain how it is that some utterances fail to yield knowledge. The condition must furthermore be one which involves awareness of its presence. Just as inferential awareness is caused not by the *h* but by the awareness of the *h*, likewise understanding of an utterance or sentence is caused not by the words, etc., but by the awareness of the words, etc. So in the case of understanding an utterance or sentence, the special condition is the awareness of the words. But since this condition is present in cases of falsity as well as truth, some added condition is also called for, e.g., the presence of pervasion or of significative power (*śakti*). These (pervasion or power) are not the *cause* of belief in what the utterance says, but they assist in producing such belief.

If this is not admitted we could never have false awareness arising from hearing a sentence. But false beliefs do arise on the part of hearers. Thus the condition mentioned must be accepted.

Now what *is* this added condition? It cannot be merely that the words of the sentence are spoken by some authoritative person, for one sometimes finds true beliefs occasioned by utterances which are not spoken by authoritative persons. For example, if a parrot "utters" a sentence, or a liar who is himself mistaken, the hearer may be caused to develop a true belief. Furthermore, there is no *h* to enable us to infer that the words have been uttered by an authoritative person, since at least occasionally the correlation between that ground and the authoritativeness may fail. Or even if we grant there is some such feature which is always present when an authority speaks, the words themselves can with greater simplicity be supposed to display that feature. So we do not need to admit this feature as a ground for inference to authoritativeness.

(E100-102) Likewise, the production of false belief in the hearer cannot be ascribed to error, inadvertence, desire to deceive on the part of the speaker, deficiency in the appropriate organ or in its functioning, since any one of these is sufficient to make the hearer's belief false, and any of them may be accompanied by another.

Objector to the Prābhākara: Still, even though we cannot infer these conditions from the falsity of a hearer's belief, we can infer from that falsity that these words are not spoken by an authoritative person. And so we can proceed to infer that the condition of true belief is the feature of being spoken by an authoritative person.

Prābhākara: No, since, as pointed out above, we cannot draw such an inference prior to actually acquiring the relevant belief from the utterance in question.

Objector to the Prābhākara: Perhaps belief in the speaker's authority is not a condition of the hearer's belief in the information conveyed by the utterance; still, it does suffice to quiet doubt which the hearer may have about the veracity of the information. Likewise, in the case of Vedic sentences the fact of authorlessness (*apauruṣeyatva*) functions in the parallel fashion to quash doubt.

Prābhākara: This too is not correct, for the same reasons as before. Doubt is not terminated except by certainty, but for that an inference is required, which is just what has been refuted previously. And furthermore the Vedas come out repetitive again.

Objector to the Prābhākara: Then we propose that absence of defect is the condition which produces the hearer's correct belief.

Prābhākara: No, since the proposed condition is absent in the case of the correct belief produced in a hearer when hearing a deceiver who is himself mistaken.

(E102-104) Gaṅgeśa: This argument cannot be sustained, for it flies in the face of experience. The belief a hearer has when he hears a mistaken deceiver may later on be revealed as a case of verbal awareness. Furthermore, if one accepts that absence of defect is the condition of linguistic knowledge, this will reduce the Vedas to mere reiteration.

Moreover, if absence of defect is admitted as the condition of truth then the presence of defect must be likewise admitted as the condition of falsity. But the presence of all defects, or at least one? Now no single defect can be said to be both a necessary and sufficient condition for falsity. But the collection of all of them cannot be held to be so either, for one among them is sufficient to produce false belief.

(E104-108) Prābhākara: All right. It is more economical to hold that the condition that causes true belief is the intention of the speaker to convey exactly that information which is understood by the hearer on hearing the utterance, i.e., the condition is the "right sort" of intention. Absence of this right sort of intention is then the causal condition of false belief. No utterance as such is defective or non-defective, but an utterance causes true or false belief because of the presence or absence of the right sort of intention in its speaker. If this right intention is lacking it is, of course, due to one or another of those types of defect referred to previously.

Now in the case of the mistaken deceiver and the parrot this right sort of intention is present, and so, since the information conveyed is corroborated, what they say is true. But suppose the speaker utters "there is a certain jar in this room" having in mind a different jar from the one the hearer takes him to be referring to. Then the hearer's belief about this other jar cannot be said to have been caused by the utterance the speaker intended. How then did the hearer come to have the belief about the jar he identified? He must have gotten it from perception. Likewise when a speaker says "make the sticks enter" intending to mean that all the men with their sticks be taken to the dining-hall for dinner, and the hearer takes him to be referring to the sticks only, it cannot be said that correct understanding was produced by language, since that was not what the speaker intended, and the rule is that the meaning of an utterance is what the speaker intends it to mean.

(E108-110) The speaker's "right sort" of intention functions in the production of a hearer's belief (or other appropriate response) where the hearer understands that intention. In this way linguistic knowledge derived from utterances is like pervasion and the signifying power (*śakti*) of words—they are all conditions which contribute to the production of an effect only through their being *understood* as holding. If it were not so, it would not be possible to be mistaken about what an utterance means (since the presence of the "right sort" of intention would automatically insure the resulting understanding to be true or appropriate). But it is evident that hearers sometimes misunderstand speakers and arrive at false belief and inappropriate behaviour thereby. Likewise, it is recognition of the speaker's intention that enables us to disambiguate his expressions and to decide whether what he says should be understood in a secondary rather than primary meaning.

(E110-115) Objection to the Prābhākara: If there were such a rule that utterances or words mean only what is intended by the speaker it couldn't ever occur that we would misunderstand an utterance which the speaker had intended to be meaningful in terms of the primary meanings of the terms involved, and resort to secondary meanings wouldn't help either. Again, if words meant only what they were intended to mean then we could not be led to understand an utterance of, say, "cook" as meaning "cook the peas". But these things do happen. It must be recognized that the speaker's intention does not become effective in producing a hearer's correct response unless that intention is known, and this means that there must be some means of ascertaining the speaker's intention. This means is the context (*prakaraṇa*) of the utterance, etc. And therefore it is better to admit this context, etc., as the auxiliary condition which along with the words uttered produces the hearer's belief or appropriate response, rather than knowledge of the speaker's intention.

Prābhākara: No, for there is no general procedure for identifying conditions like context which may be operative. There are many such conditions, each of which is sufficient but none of them necessary. (Whereas apprehension of speaker's intention is a necessary and sufficient condition for hearer's understanding.)

Objector to the Prābhākara: It is not required that a condition should be a necessary condition to be operative and properly termed as a means. Neither smoke nor light is necessary to infer fire; nevertheless awareness of smoke is a means for inferring fire. So in the same way context, etc., being each sufficient to bring about hearer's understanding of speaker's intention, though not necessary, should each still be identified as operative means bringing about the hearer's understanding.

Prābhākara: We come to apprehend this intention in the case of Vedic sentences through reasoning (*nyāya*). But in the case of ordinary utterances we cannot apprehend the intention through reasoning, since the intention in these cases is determined by the desire of the speaker to get his hearer to apprehend a certain sentence-meaning. If that desire has been itself preceded by the speaker's correct cognition of the sentence-meaning, the hearer can apprehend that the speaker has the "right sort" of intention, but not otherwise. Therefore it has to be inferred first that the speaker understands the meaning of the sentence correctly: this inference is based on the speaker being an authoritative person. Then from that awareness that the speaker understands the sentence-meaning we in turn infer that the speaker has the "right sort" of intention and is describing what is actually the case.

(E115-122) The order of inferences needed is as follows. First, the hearer infers "This utterance has been produced by some (awareness) other than the qualified awareness characterized by error, etc.; because it is an utterance." The second inference is: "This speaker has correct awareness about the fact meant by his utterance; because he is the speaker of an utterance that has not been produced by error, etc., just as is the case with me." Notice that authoritativeness of the speaker is not made the ground of this inference, since that has not yet been proved. Thirdly, the hearer now infers: "These things are related properly (i.e., in the fashion the utterance declares them to be); because they are contents of correct awareness or are recalled by words uttered by authoritative persons; like the things I speak of."

Objector: Now, in this chain of inferences the thesis of the second one must be about some specific correct awareness that the speaker has. But to infer that particular bit of knowledge is impossible for the hearer, since it is not known prior to the hearer's understanding the utterance. There is no way we can become aware of pervasion relating that awareness to anything before knowing what the utterance means. And thus this second inference, and the third one that follows, are impossible. It follows that it is not inference but rather language (the utterance, the words) itself which brings about understanding on the part of the hearer.

(E122-129) Prābhākara: No. Even the opponent admits the need for ascertaining the intention of the speaker, at least in some cases, as requirement for understanding an utterance. He must therefore admit that there must be some way of ascertaining speaker's intention independent of language. And further he must admit that the speaker must have already come to believe in the facts about which he intends to speak, since otherwise the speaker's intention to assert those facts could not be correctly arrived at. So it is easy to see how it becomes known to the hearer that an utterance has been asserted by an authoritative person. Linguistic awareness of the facts does not occur first and so the cause of our understanding cannot be language operating as an independent instrument of knowledge. What an utterance tells us is already known to us by inference.

It should not be concluded that language is not an independent instrument of knowledge, since you would then have to admit that Vedic utterances are not instruments.

Objection: Even so, how can the particular thing meant by an utterance be known? The pervasion involving such a particular thing cannot be available to the hearer prior to his understanding the utterance.

Prābhākara: Yes, we can come to know that pervasion in a general way. One is aware of that toward which his activity is directed. For example, we can infer from the fact that someone is cooking that he was aware that he intended to cook. Likewise, having perceived a person holding up ten fingers we first infer that he means the number ten, and then, relating his gesture to, say, jars we come to know the specific meaning of his gesture, namely ten jars.

Alternatively, one may put the matter this way. The hearer first infers "This utterance has been caused by a single awareness about just these things meant that are related through expectancy, because this utterance has been uttered by an authoritative person and gives information about just this fact, just like my own utterance (of the same sort did, or would)". This inference is followed by another: "These things meant stand related to each other by expectancy and constituting a fact, because being related to each other they are also the content of a single awareness". This, then, leads the hearer to infer the speaker's knowledge of the fact expressed by his utterance. Then from context, etc., we infer that the speaker has the right sort of intention, and thus, coming to know through inference what the speaker's intention is we derive from his utterance the relevant belief, just as we do in the case of scriptural sentences, i.e., depending on our awareness of features such as expectancy, fitness, etc. And this shows that language reiterates what was already known at the time of inferring the speaker's knowledge, since the fact the words in the utterance signify is the content of that speaker's knowledge.

(E129-135) Objection: Error consists in absence of awareness of the relational fact. Thus the opposite of it, viz., knowledge, consists in cognizing that relational fact itself. So when a hearer infers absence of error on the part of the speaker, he must come to know the fact itself. Thus the inference that the speaker knows what he is talking about is included in the inference that the speaker is an authoritative person, and so the knowledge of authoritativeness cannot be the ground for inferring the speaker's knowledge.

Prābhākara: No. Error consists in failure to distinguish between two awarenesses. The absence of error, viz., truth, consists in recognizing the distinction between two awarenesses. Otherwise, if error were merely absence of awareness of the distinction then we should consider deep sleep to be a case of error. Therefore we do infer the knowledge of the speaker from the absence of error. Furthermore, if those inferences are one and the same, then it is evident that the same ground which serves in the one also serves in the other.

(E135-139) Gaṅgeśa: Now we shall answer the (entire Prābhākara) position. It cannot be that an awareness that the speaker intends to generate true belief about the fact in question is sufficient to cause true belief on the part of the hearer. For one thing, this account is overly complex. For another, it is impossible that the hearer should arrive at the knowledge about the speaker's specific intention prior to understanding what the speaker means. Again, in the case of worldly utterances, the explanation given will not stand. It was said that we can infer knowledge on the part of the speaker when, having removed the possibility of error, we come to know what the speaker intends the hearer to understand, and that this knowledge of the speaker's intention is gotten from context. But we cannot rule out the possibility of error before we know what fact it is that the speaker alleges to be the case, since we cannot test the claim until we know what the claim is. Or if we can we shouldn't need anything more than the mere uttering of the words to guarantee truth. Finally, even in the case of Vedic sentences one cannot infer the truth of what they say without knowing first what they say, as you yourself have admitted.

(E139-142) Objection: In both cases, then, we must learn what is meant by some other means.

Gaṅgeśa: The meaning of Vedic sentences cannot be the object of any other instrument of knowledge; those sentences do not tell us anything prior (to conveying the relations among the meanings of the constituent words).

Objector: Then let us say that the meaning of the Vedas is known through reasoning (*nyāya*) while worldly speaker's intention is known by some other instrument.

Gaṅgeśa: Then the Vedas will merely reiterate and not be an independent instrument, and this is as objectionable to you as to us.

Objection: If the meaning of Vedic sentences were apprehended through doubt or *tarka* the charge of reiteration is without force. Doubtful awareness or awareness of the *tarka* sort is sufficient to establish the intended relation.

Gaṅgeśa: No, for doubt or *tarka* concerning a specific fact (i.e., relation among things) is not possible unless this fact (relation) is already present to our awareness. Otherwise in the case of ordinary utterances, since we would already know the fact as soon as we experienced doubt or *tarka* about it, we would not need to infer the speaker's awareness of that fact to ascertain his intention.

(E142-147) Actually, if the right sort of intention produced belief in the hearer only after being cognized, then we could infer in both the cases of Vedic sentences and ordinary utterances the relation (fact) just from their being remembered, and then language would not be an independent instrument of knowledge. Furthermore, once a person's utterance is inferred to have been caused by some awareness other than a belief associated with faults, when it is eventually ascertained that the utterance is not caused by any defect at that time, the conditions that are available in the case of Vedic sentences are also available in the case of ordinary human utterances. Thus human speech becomes as much an instrument of knowledge as Vedic sentences. The inferential belief, being itself inferred, is delayed by the intervening memory of pervasion, etc., so that the inference does become a case of reiteration.

Objection: Whether a Vedic sentence or a human utterance, a linguistic item is said to be an instrument of knowledge if it produces uncontradicted belief about a fact. Now there are ordinary utterances which do not do so (i.e., are false). So in the case of ordinary utterances the hearer first needs to ascertain the absence of a sublating fact. He does so sometimes by perception and sometimes through inference from the authoritative character of the speaker.

Answer: In the case of Vedic sentences, however, the same ascertainment can only occur through inference, since such sentences are not amenable to the other instruments of knowledge. Thus it is not the case that Vedic sentences are in a different position from ordinary ones in terms of the conditions for the ascertainment of their truth.

(E147-149) No doubt if one needs to know first either the authority of the speaker or the absence of error inference will be required. But in that case the Vedas will turn out to be reiterative. So, if one is to avoid falling into the Vaiśeṣika position that inference is the instrument of knowledge in all cases, it must be held that features like "not being false", "being spoken by a trustworthy person", "having the right sort of intention", etc., features which distinguish true utterances (or sentences) from false ones, are conditions which operate in virtue of their existence and not only when they are cognized.

(E149-151) Vaiśeṣika: Suppose a child witnesses that a junior person, being addressed by a senior person in the linguistic community, performs a certain act. From this the witness infers that the junior had a certain kind of experience occasioned by the words addressed to him by the senior. So far the witness, the child, realizes that the words uttered are the cause of the act insofar as they signify relationships among things. He does not realize those words to be the ground of any inference, but they are.

Gaṅgeśa: If the understanding arises from utterances themselves then it would be heavy to insist that the words function as cause of understanding only insofar as they possess features like expectancy, etc. Furthermore, if an inferential process is involved, then as has been shown the Vedas become reiterations as much as ordinary utterances. Thus the Vaiśeṣika view is refuted.

(E151-154) Awareness of the right sort of intention is not a cause of the understanding of the meaning of an utterance.

Objector: Then we should add some qualifications to it.

Gaṅgeśa: No. Since it cannot be previously ascertained that the utterance has been uttered with the right sort of intention, the inference is not possible, the pervasion cannot be grasped. It is to be noted, however, that the pervasion or power of the words to signify (*śabdaśakti*) is itself not the cause of understanding an utterance's meaning, since for one thing even when the *h* of the inference is absent the inference may still take place, in the case where we get to know what an utterance means on the basis of a mistaken notion that some ill-formed expression (*apabhraṃśa*) it contains has meaning.

Objector: In order that an utterance have meaning some awareness has to be produced; so the first thing to be inferred is that the speaker uttered his expression intending to produce that awareness in his hearer.

Gaṅgeśa: No, that is not possible at the beginning. Therefore where the generating condition functions only when it is known to go with its result, that is, where a condition functions as cause only after it has been known to be a cause; only there the awareness of the absence of deviation is required (for there to be understanding of the meaning). Otherwise, if this is not admitted and this awareness of the absence of deviation is required everwhere, then words could be cognized as giving us meaning only after we had come to know that they stand in an invariable relation to such meaning, and that would turn the words themselves into the inferential ground.

(E154-156) Objection: Even granting this, we know that the thing meant by an untrustworthy speaker doesn't exist. Now since the words uttered by both trustworthy and untrustworthy persons alike can have features like expectancy, etc., hearing an utterance there must arise in the hearer a doubt to the effect "Does what these words signify exist or doesn't it?" Now if the words thus generate doubt how can they generate correct awareness? But if they can't generate correct awareness how can language be regarded as an independent instrument of knowledge? So there must be something more than mere expectancy, etc., some extra condition that causes the words to produce correct awareness.

Gaṅgeśa: No. Doubt regarding the existence or nonexistence of the thing meant by an utterance cannot prevent the occurrence of correct awareness. For example: Even when there is doubt regarding the existence of fire in a place, correct awareness of its existence there may be generated by perception or by inference. If this were not so we would have to conclude that there is no correct awareness and no instruments of knowledge.

(E156-170) The doubts you have in mind can arise only after the hearer has already derived an awareness from the utterance in question, and so those doubts cannot block his correct awareness about the meaning of the utterance.

(E170-173) Therefore the following features, even if they are apprehended as regularly present, are not conditions of the hearer's awareness: (a) having been uttered by some authoritative person, (b) not being produced by error, (c) being about something unsublated, (d) having been uttered with the intention to produce correct awareness about what the utterance signifies. These are not conditions because they cannot be known prior to one's having the linguistic awareness. Rather, one or the other of two features are well-known to be the means by which the hearer ascertains the speaker's intention—namely, (e) awareness produced by argument or (f) context. That is what is entailed, so to speak, by the utterances being pervaded by intentionality. These two along with awareness of expectancy and of contiguity are the causal conditions of understanding an utterance. That these last two are causal conditions is shown by the realization that if one does not have correct awareness of their presence one fails to have the relevant linguistic awareness. As for fitness, awareness of it is a general condition for any awareness, correct or not. Furthermore, it is also a necessary condition for every linguistic awareness that the words should be uttered with the proper inflections and that all of them should be uttered. Where the expressions are ambiguous reference is made to context, etc., to interpret the utterance.

(E173-176) We resort to the indirect rather than the direct meaning of an expression involved in an utterance not because otherwise the intention cannot be understood, but because otherwise the utterance makes no sense in the context, the context including the utterance itself. For example: from the context one is aware that there are men waiting to be shown in for dinner; someone says "show in the man with the stick", and we understand his utterance to mean that the guests including the one with the stick should be shown in. In another kind of case an expression may be such as to be understood in both its direct and indirect sense. So, if pointing to a procession of men which includes a man with an umbrella, one says "there goes the man with the umbrella", one means to say both that the man with the umbrella is going and so are the others.

(E176-177) Now suppose someone says "cook" and someone else says "rice": should we understand the first utterance to allude to cooking rice? No, we do not do so, and this shows that only words uttered by a single person and taken all together count in the context of linguistic awareness.

(E177-182) Some say that understanding the speaker's intention is only required when the utterance is equivocal. In fact, however, intention consists in uttering something with a desire to convey the information that a thing signified by one word is related to a thing signified by another word. And this intention is ascertained by reasoning in the case of Vedic sentences, and either by reasoning or from context in the case of ordinary utterances. So it cannot be said that there is no uniform condition of linguistic awareness resulting from ordinary utterances and Vedic sentences.

Objection: The awareness of the relation between a thing signified by one word and a thing signified by another, which you call the "intention", is in fact just the linguistic awareness itself.

Answer: When we know the intention we know the general relation between those kinds of things, but when we come to have the linguistic awareness we come to have the specific awareness about the particular things the speaker wants to refer to and the particular relation he wishes to assert to hold between them. Thus it is shown that language constitutes an independent instrument of knowledge. But since expressions which lack expectancy, etc., do not yield linguistic awareness we take them to be auxiliary conditions too.

Section Two: Expectancy (*ākāṅkṣā*)
Summary by S.C. Vidyabhusana

(B and RB: HIL) with stylistic emendations.

(E185-244) A word is said to bear the relation of expectancy to another word if it cannot without the latter produce awareness of its interconnection in speech. For instance, "*Devadattaḥ grāmaṃ gacchati*" ("Devadatta goes to the village") is an utterance in which the word *Devadattaḥ* (in the nominative case) bears expectancy to the word *gacchati ('goes'*, the verb), and this latter in its turn bears expectancy for *grāmam* ("village", in the accusative case). In the same way the stem *Devadatta* bears expectancy for *ḥ* (the same as *su*, the first case-ending), the stem *grāma* for *am* (the second case-ending) and *gam* (the root) for *ti* (the verbal suffix). A stem (*nāma*) and a case-ending (*vibhakti*), a root (*dhātu*) and a verbal suffix (*ākhyāta*), and a verb (*kriyā*) and a case (*kāraka*) bear expectancy for each other.

Section Three: Semantic Fitness (*yogyatā*)
Based on S.C. Vidyabhusana (B and RB: HIL)

(E245-285) Fitness characterizes a word's not bearing a meaning which is incompatible with the meanings of other words in an utterance. For instance, no verbal awareness is derived from such an utterance as *agninā siñcā* ("sprinkle with fire") because fire cannot be an instrument in the act of sprinkling. Fitness may be certain or doubtful, but in either case there will be verbal awareness.

Section Four: Contiguity (*āsatti*)
Summary based on S.C. Vidyabhusana (B and RB: HIL)

(E286-318) Contiguity consists in the enunciation of words, which are connected with each other, without a long pause between them. For example, the utterance "bring water" will convey no meaning if one utters the word "bring" now and the word "water" after an hour.

Section Five: Speaker's Intention (*tātparya*)
Summary based on S.C. Vidyabhusana (B and RB: HIL).

(E319-374) Intention, which indicates the wish of a speaker, consists in the utterance of a word with a special meaning. If at the time of eating a meal one says "bring *saindhava*" we are to understand by the word "*saindhava*" a quantity of salt and not a horse.

Section Six: Noneternality of Sounds (*śabdānityatā*)
Summary based on S.C. Vidyabhusana (B and RB: HIL).

(E375-464) Sounds such as "*ka*", etc., are multifarious, inasmuch as we find that a sound uttered by a man is different from the corresponding sound uttered by a parrot. On the ground that sounds are many, each of which is produced and destroyed, we must admit them to be noneternal. In fact, such an expression as "the uproar that arose in the market has now ceased" proves beyond a doubt that sound is liable to destruction.

Section Seven: Sounds Destroyed, Not Concealed
(*ucchannāpracchanna*)
Summary based on S.C. Vidyabhusana (B and RB: HIL)

(E465-525) If sounds are destructible, their aggregates, the utterances, must also be so. The Veda, a collection of utterances, is consequently noneternal. The Mīmāṃsakas say that though the Vedas as a collection of utterances are liable to destruction, having come down through a succession of teachers their continuity is uninterrupted. Gaṅgeśa opposes the above view by saying that from memories occurring in socio-religious institutions and from usages that have prevailed from older times we can infer that once there existed certain branches of the Vedas which have since disappeared. Therefore the Vedas are noneternal.

The Vedas are defined by Gaṅgeśa as a collection of valid utterances which are not the outcome of awareness of things signified by words, and the things singnified by which are not the objects of those kinds of awareness which are derived from means other than verbal testimony.

Section Eight: Injunction (*vidhi*)

Summary based on V. N. Jha's translation.[120]

Pūrvapakṣa

(E1-6) A Vedic injunction is the instigator of activity, since it generates the (linguistic) awareness which induces a person to act. Therefore, his inducing awareness is explained in this chapter.[121]

Here there are different views. Some say that the inducer is the awareness of the mood-suffix (*abhidhā*);[122] others that it is the awareness of desire (*saṃkalpa*);[123] others that it is the awareness of karmic traces (*apūrva*);[124] still others that it is the awareness of volition (*bhāvanā*).[125] But none of these views is tenable, since there are cases when even though these awarenesses are found no inducement is seen, and likewise inducement to activity is found in the absence of each any any of these.[126]

(E6-18) The Prābhākaras (*guravaḥ*) hold that the inducer to activity is the awareness that something is to be done (*kāryatva*).[127] That is, they say that if an awareness produces volition it must also produce the desire to do the act in question.[128] Sometimes even though there is presence of that desire a delay in volition occurs because other causal factors are absent.[129] A desire to do something is a desire which has *being the thing one wants to accomplish* (*kṛtisādhyatva*) as its chief qualifier and the action to be performed as its qualificand.[130] That desire to do is thus produced by awareness of it's being the thing one wants to accomplish.[131] This is why one goes on to perform the action—say, of cooking—which is the thing one wants to accomplish.[132]

This desire to do, however, is not produced merely by the awareness that the act is a means to a desired goal (*iṣṭasādhanatā*), because if it were we would desire to do things which are impossible for us to accomplish.[133]

(E18-24) Objector to the Prābhākara: The reason why we are not induced to try to do something impossible for us to do is that there is an obstructor (*pratibandhaka*), namely, the awareness that the act in question is not possible for us to perform.[134]

Prābhākara: No, that is too complicated.[135]

Objector: But we both accept that there is absence of awareness of capability to perform the action at that time, so there is no question of simplicity.[136]

Prābhākara: No. For example, it is simpler to explain the inducement to action from the hearing of an utterance through inference or even by chance. Also, a desire is always produced by that awareness the chief qualifier of which is the desire in question, and so it is necessary to postulate the awareness that such and such an act can be accomplished as one of the factors that produce inducement to act. Moreover, for an awareness to obstruct activity it must destroy the awareness that produces the effect.[137] Otherwise mere awareness of an act could be postulated as the inducing factor; and not only the state of not being possible to do, but also the states of being an instrument of an undesired result, of being fit to be ignored, and of having no result at all could be postulated as obstructors.[138]

(E24-27) Objection to the Prābhākara: The desire to do (*cikīrṣā*) is grammatically related to desire (*icchā*) and is caused by awareness of something's being a thing one wants to accomplish, e.g., as when one's desire to bring rain is caused by one's awareness that rain is a means by which a good harvest can be obtained.[139]

Prābhākara: No. You say that a thing's *being a means to a desired goal* is what the relevant grammatical suffix means while *we* say the relevant meaning is *being the thing one wants to accomplish* (*kṛti-sādhyatva*). Now the awareness of what one desires comes before the awareness of the action which one intends to take to accomplish that end; thus being produced by volition, not being desired, is the relevant causal antecedent to action. When one wants to cook something one doesn't desire cooking as such, he desires the rice to be cooked. Thus the action is connected directly to volition, not directly to desire; the desired thing is qualified by the wish to produce it.

(E27-40) Objection: But if the desire to do stands for the desire to accomplish by volition, then even when the cooking which was desired to be accomplished is already accomplished by other means the desire to accomplish it will still not be over. For the desire to accomplish something by one means is not ruled out by the accomplishment of that result by some other means. For instance, even if one obtains wealth as a gift out of love, one remains desirous of obtaining it as a right (*pratigraha*).

Prābhākara: No. The awareness that the desired object has already been gotten is an obstructor to the desire of the means for it, just as is the absence of any desire for the result. Now in the case in question both the cooking and the rice are already gotten. So it isn't the case that one will go on having desire to cook rice. As for the argument about wealth, it is a fact that the desire for greater wealth does not cease, so the fact that one has received a gift does not end one's desire for wealth. If he doesn't want any more than X one will not desire X after he has procured it.

Actually, the volition which causes activity is the means to the desired goal and therefore that the activity is to be accomplished by volition and that it is the means to the desired goal are understood only through activity. And so, on account of that understanding, as there will be desire for volition there will be desire for activity as well, since the activity is the thing one wants to accomplish. And thus the qualifier, namely the state of being the thing one wants to accomplish, is present invariably in each desire to do. So the desire to do is the cause of volition *qua* a desire the object of which is what one wants to accomplish, not *qua* the desire to want it, since it would result in overcomplexity if different objects were postulated for the desire and the volition.

(E40-44) It is an established fact that in whatever form something is known as the means of a desired goal, in that same form that something has to be desired. For instance, rain is known to be the means of one's desired goal *qua* rain falling on one's own field; so it is in just that form that rain is desired. Similarly, since cooking is the means to what one wants to accomplish *qua* activity to be accomplished by volition, there will naturally be a desire to do it in that same form (and so there is no desire to do something if the awareness arises that it is not possible for that something to be accomplished).

Objection: Just as one desires "let me accomplish it by fire" so one desires "let me accomplish it by volition". Both desires arise just from the awareness of a thing's being the means to a desired result.

Prābhākara: Then just the awareness that one wants to accomplish it by fire is required as the cause of cooking, likewise in the present case the awareness that one wants to accomplish it by doing is the cause of the desire to do. In the case of volition, however, there is an additional qualification, namely the state of being dependent upon a desire to do that is established by experience. That is why one who wishes to live does not have the desire to breathe. (He just breathes.)

(E44-49) Objection: Well, if the desire to do is treated as merely an indicator, since the notion of mere volition is very wide (e.g., it will include the will to live also), it becomes necessary to indicate particular volitions as each having its own particular sort of volition-ness, and since it is not possible to unite all those volitions, it is difficult to connect them to activities by causal relations. However, if desire to do is treated as a qualifier, then both desire to do and awareness will be causal conditions with respect to desire to do as well as activity; this is overly complex, and anyway there is no reason to think that desire to do produces desire to do. Finally, since it is contradictory to treat a volition, which is in the state of being accomplished by desire to do, as a means which is required to be already accomplished, the state of being accomplished cannot be cognized in the case of cooking.

Prābhākara: No. There is a particular volition, known by mental perception, different from the will to live, which is indicated by the desire to do; from it one gets the awareness of having desire to do as its cause. That particular volition is what you call "mere volition". According to us it is an imposed property that unites all relevant causal conditions. So, the particular volitions (other than the will to live) which are described as "desires to do" are brought into one class by this property.

(E49-50) Objection: The volition cannot be a qualifier of that which is what one wants to accomplish, since that doesn't exist yet! If it is held that it does exist then there will be interdependence (between volition and the thing desired). And it cannot be an indicator because that will lead to overextension (to cases where one knows it is not possible to perform the action).

Prābhākara: No. Volition is indeed a qualifier in an awareness as the content of that awareness, and to that which is desired to be accomplished it is an indicator since it causes awareness of that thing. If not, the same objections you raise can be raised against your doctrine also, e.g., the desired goal cannot be a qualifier of the means to what is desired, since it doesn't exist yet, and it can't be an indicator since that will produce overextension.

(E50-53) Objection: If awareness of being the thing one wants to accomplish dependent on a desire to do is treated as the cause of the desire to do, then, since it is possible to become tired by willing oneself to work dependent on one's desire to do, becoming tired should be something one desires to do! Thus some say that tiredness is accomplished through experiencing, etc., not by volition for that experiencing, since tiredness is not the object of a desire to do. A volition is a cause only with reference to an object of the desire to do in addition to the volition's own destruction and awareness of it. It is never the case that the act of going is accomplished by the volition to go dependent upon the desire to accomplish eating.

Prābhākara: That is not correct. When one tries to lift a very heavy weight which he can't possibly lift, or attempts to walk when he is tied up, although neither the lifting nor the walking is accomplished, the person concerned does not feel tired and so volition is the cause of it, not the action produced by that volition. Otherwise it will violate the causal relationship in the case of satisfaction. Satisfaction is not the object of a desire to do that is the cause of volition; indeed, a volition is caused by the desire to accomplish the means to satisfaction, not by the desire to be satisfied.

(E54-64) Objection: Some say that work succeeds merely *qua* volition and not as dependent on a desire to do. Otherwise, they say, since we desire to eat and not to go out to find food, we shall not succeed in going out but only in eating. Or else (if work is produced by volition despite its not being the object of desire to do, then) the going will have to be viewed as produced by the volition to accomplish the act of eating. In fact, the act of eating is produced by the particular volition dependent on the desire to eat. Or else one can say that work is not accomplished by the will to eat but is produced from the desire to stay alive. Now neither of these explanations is correct. Even though one wants to stay alive, that alone does not make one tired; work is required for that. It is the volition to eat itself which produces as well the work of finding food. A sleeping person's work cannot be inferred from the fact that he is sweating. Otherwise, by parity of reasoning we'll have to suppose that one is always working since one wishes to stay alive.

Prābhākara: No. Work is always produced by a volition dependent on a desire for something else (other than the work), for to desire just to work is to desire something unsatisfactory. If the volition to eat produces the activity of eating this will be cumbersome. (The nature of the cumbersomeness is spelled out in detail.)

(E64-72) Naiyāyika: Someone who knows that taking poison will bring bad results may still do it out of the illusion that it will bring about some desired goal. Thus a belief that something is a means to a desired goal may bring about action even with such dire results. On the other hand, one who is fed does not seek food, even though he knows it to be a desired goal; on your view he should do so, since you don't count that kind of knowledge as an obstructor.

A Prābhākara supporter: There is no knowledge that will bring about a desired goal in the former case (of poison-taking), since there is no bringing about of action.

Naiyāyika: But there may well be! Suppose a reliable person misinforms you (and you believe him) that taking this (that is in fact poison) will get you to your goal.

Prābhākara: No, in that case there is no awareness that taking poison will bring about the desired goal, since one is aware that poison is harmful. (It is only in the case of illusion that there is awareness of being the means to a desired goal.) As for the second case, though one knows it is a desired goal he does not desire it *now*, i.e., he has no awareness of its being a means to a desired goal at present.

(E77–81) Others (commentaries say the author of a *Mahārṇava*) say that since it is possible to have the knowledge of work's being the thing one wants to accomplish just by knowing that one is alive, one will have to exclude this knowledge specifically from requirements of the doer.

Prābhākara: No, knowledge of what one wants to accomplish is not caused merely by one's desire to work.

Another objection: The cause of inducement to action is one's knowledge that something is what one wants to accomplish obtained on the basis of its being a means to a desired goal.

Prābhākara: No, since in the case of required (*nitya*) acts (where there is no mention of desire) there can be no such knowledge that a thing is what one wants to accomplish.

Naiyāyika: A simpler account than yours is merely to specify that what one wants to accomplish be something gotten by a means other than the taking of poison. Furthermore

(InfA): The desire to perform X is produced by the awareness that X is the means to a desired goal, because X is desired as means, like the desire for rain.

Prābhākara: But there is nothing known here to be the thing one wants to accomplish that is known to be a means to the desired goal.

(E81-90) Prābhākara: Your line of reasoning here is wrong. It is not possible to know at the same time that one and the same thing is both what one wants to accomplish *and* a means to its accomplishment. The state of being what one wants to accomplish belongs to something that doesn't yet exist; when it does exist it will not be in that state of being what one wants to accomplish.

Naiyāyika: It can be known now that one thing is what one wants to accomplish and later that it is accomplished.

Prābhākara: No, for there is no one thing that is both "now" and "later". Therfore, the cause of desiring to do something is the knowledge that the object is what one wants to accomplish; the something will come into existence in the future by another volition. This type of being what one wants to accomplish is indeed contradictory to its being a means.

(E90-95) Others say there is another property, *being the thing to be named* (*uddeśyatva*), and that this property is what is meant by being a human aim. It is a common property which causes desire for satisfaction and the avoidance of frustration and the means to these. They say that it is this property that is the cause of desire for satisfaction.

Prābhākara: No. For even without the awareness of a thing's being the thing to be named there still may arise the desire to do something just because it is expected to cause satisfaction.

Objection: Then let the expected satisfaction be the cause of desire by itself.

Prābhākara: No. The desire can be produced directly in satisfaction, awareness, etc. just on the ground of being the cause. Being what one wants to accomplish arises after the arising of volition and only then.

(E95-109) Objection: Well, after the volition is destroyed the *apūrva* cannot be called "what one wants to accomplish". So how can a person desirous of a result be related to *apūrva* which is what one wants to accomplish, since a volition is momentary and gets destroyed?

Answer (by the "others" of E90-95): It is not so. The state of being the means to a desired goal prompts the knowledge that the goal object is desired, not the property of being a means to a desired object qualified by this being desired.

Objection: But awareness of being what one wants to accomplish, say cooking, is not possible directly by perception, since after the volition arises and the resulting action occurs this awareness of what one wants to accomplish will arise, and so there will be mutual dependency.

Prābhākara: No. One can have awareness by inference as follows: (The action of) cooking can be accomplished by me, because it is not possible without my volition and because it is the means to my goal, like my action of eating. That is, the general rule is that the means to a goal desired by X and which does not arise without X's effort comes into existence through the effort of X. (Objections are refuted.) So, though a person who is hot does not go for a dip in the river when it is raining since he expects to get cool without effort (i.e., since there is no *being a means to the goal* there is no *being what one wants to accomplish*), a person who realizes that without effort he will not find water will make an attempt.

(E109-113) Some Prābhākaras: One who merely wants to get cool does not know the *being a means to the goal* of having a dip in the river, since that comes about also from its starting to rain.

Prābhākara: No, since the cause of getting cool is contact with water, which occurs in both river-dipping and being rained on.

Some Prābhākaras: *Being the means to a desired goal* cannot be the *hetu* from which *being what one wants to accomplish* is inferred, since there is no ground, just as there is no ground to infer that eating rice is what one wants to accomplish before one is actually induced to eat it.

Naiyāyika: Then let awareness of *coming to be the object of desire* be the inducer, since it occurs before and is a prerequisite for *being the thing one wants to accomplish.*

Prābhākara: No, since if in that awareness *being the thing one wants to accomplish* does not appear it can't be the inducer. For that reason no awareness of any *hetu* can be the inducer.

(E113-115) Objection: Neither past nor present cooking can be the *pakṣa* of InfA since it is contradictory to being the thing one wants to accomplish. And future cooking cannot be either since there is no proof and there is no locus.

Prābhākara: Then consider this inference:

(InfB): The act of cooking is future (as well as past and present),
Because it is universal,
Like the universal *cowness.*

Naiyāyika: There is still no proof of the future existence of *cowness.*

Prābhākara: But the mere action of cooking (timeless) can be the *pakṣa.*

Naiyāika: No. If "mere" means *being* the act of cooking then there is again contradiction (since a universal cannot be the *s*); also, the *h* will be unestablished (*asiddha*). If what you mean is cooking *in general* then the future cooking will be both past and future, which is a contradiction. A *pakṣa* must be already established as existent; thus any (proper) *p* is bound to contradict *being the object of one's volition.*

Prābhākara: From the very awareness of *being the thing one wants to accomplish* in past and present cooking there can arise the desire to cook and the resulting volition to start cooking.

Naiyāyika: Then that type of *being the thing one wants to accomplish* which qualifies the desire is not present in the awareness, and the desire to cook will arise from an awareness whose qualifier is different from what it is desired to do. Therefore let *being a means to a desired goal* together with *being the thing one wants to accomplish* be (jointly) the cause of inducement, since both are understood at the first step.

(E115–123) Some Prābhākaras: The inducement arises from awareness of *being a means to the desired goal*; this causes the nonawareness of the lack of *being the thing one wants to accomplish* in the remembered cooking.

Naiyāyika: No. It is already established that the act of cooking is remembered, so it could hardly not be known to be related to *being the thing one wants to accomplish.* Or else a person who wants to eat rice will not cook it, or one who is satisfied having eaten, would want to eat it again.

(E123–132) Here is our view. Being the thing one wants to

accomplish can be established in cooking (in general). Because this (being the thing one wants to accomplish) contradicts the cooking's already being one (thus past) it is concluded that it is the future action of cooking that is established.

There are indeed three kinds of cases: (1) the future *being the thing one wants to accomplish* is inferred to be present in known (present or past) cooking, (2) known cooking (present or past) is inferred from known (present or past) *being the thing one wants to accomplish*, and (3) future (unknown) *being a thing one wants to accomplish* is inferred from future (unknown) cooking.

(E132–139) The desire for a thing one wants to accomplish in the future can be established by *sāmānyalakṣaṇapratyāsatti*, e.g., just as we infer that future rain will be accompanied by satisfaction. If you say you do not accept *sāmānyalakṣaṇapratyāsatti* then we say that however your *being a means to a desired goal* is known to you, in the same way one knows that the end is a desired one.

Prābhākara: In a parallel way for me whatever way *being a thing one wants to accomplish* is known, in that same way one knows it as evidence of future cooking. A child (who does not know the connection between acting and being an object of volition) tries to suck milk from its mother's breast, and this must be due to memory that sucking milk satisfies hunger, i.e., that satisfying one's hunger is a thing one accomplished. You, on the other hand, musı say that it is due to remembering that it is a means to a desired end. Actually, what happens here is that the child, feeling frustrated because of his thirst and hunger, remembers satisfaction (not *being the thing one wanted to accomplish*) as forthcoming from sucking the breast.

(E139–143) Later (*navīna*) Prābhākaras: Being aware that I can get this is not (as has just been claimed) a cause of inducement, since neither perception nor inference can generate awareness of a future object. But when one observes someone else doing an action one may judge himself similar to him and having remembered that goes about acting. Thus, seeing that X desires cooked rice and that X knows that cooking is the means to cooked rice remembers that he is like X and starts cooking. Likewise for other actions. Since one knows that worshipping Caitya or taking poison is not the means of a desired end one does not do those things.

Still later Prābhākaras: More than that, this person knows that taking poison or worshipping Caitya will bring bad results (not just that it won't bring good ones, and thus *not being a condemned object* (*avagītatva*) has to be added to *being a thing one wants to accomplish.* On the other hand the futureness of being the object doesn't come into it—a thing one wants to accomplish is not associated with time.

Siddhānta

(E144–149) Naiyāyika's final reply: After the knowledge of X's being a thing one wants to accomplish arises, X's being the means to a desired goal, excluded from the eating of poison and the like, is to be treated as the limitor of the contentness (i.e., of X's X-ness). This view is simpler than the alternative (Prābhākara) view that X is qualified by desire for the result.

Objection: Two contradictory properties, *being accomplished* (*as means to a desired goal*) and *being a thing one wants to accomplish*, cannot belong to the same X.

Answer: Yes they can, for the two properties are cognized at different times. First one judges that X is to be accomplished; subsequently he judges that it is accomplished as a means to some further end. Otherwise nothing can ever be judged to have been accomplished.

Furthermore, one cannot claim that when it is known that X is a thing one wants to accomplish the knowledge of X's being the means to a desired end is what incites activity. When the *Vājapeya* sacrifice is already established as what needs to be done to obtain a kingdom it does not still have to be shown that it should be done to obtain a kingdom!

(E150–153) Prābhākara: Two contradictory properties can be cognized to be in one thing if they are limited by different limitors. But *being the means to a desired goal* and *being the thing one wants to accomplish* are not like that (and so *are* contradictory properties).

Naiyāyika answer: No, these are not contradictory properties, since as we have just seen they refer to different times. Furthermore, if the two properties conflict (as you suggest) then one cannot infer the one from the other as we both assume one can here.

(E153–157) Prābhākara: When X is a thing one wants to accomplish which is the object of awareness of satisfaction—that in turn being the cause of desire—then one who desires to experience satisfaction does the act which is the means to X. (So there are three features operative.) Or, alternatively, the desire itself is the cause of the act, and the other two—*being the means to a desired goal* and *being a thing one wants to accomplish*—are the two causes of that.

Answer: When being a thing one wants to accomplish appears in the awareness that produces desire then there will be the desire to do the act—or else desire alone is the cause. This is simpler. Thus in the case of cooking when the thing to be cooked is both the means to a desired end and the thing one wants to accomplish then the desire to cook it arises. But, e.g., when one wants it to rain, being a thing one wants to accomplish is not there, merely desire.

Actually, the desire to accomplish the means to the desired object is produced by awareness that X is the object of volition, because it is a desire to accomplish a means, like the desire that it should rain (which is desired to accomplish a means to pleasure).

(E157–159) Objection: The desire to accomplish something can arise even without awareness that the thing is a means, e.g., when one desires to accomplish pleasure itself, so it cannot be a cause.

Answer: No, for the desire to accomplish something stands the test of positive and negative concomitance with being a means to a desired end. Anyway, rain is not by nature satisfying so the desire for it cannot arise.

Objection: Why not make the prompting factor to being the means to a desired goal just one's desire to get it?

Answer: No, this would be heavy, and anyway the property of being the means is absent in the case of desire for satisfaction itself. So, since it is evident that knowledge that X is the means to a desired end is the cause of X's being a thing one wants to accomplish, let the latter together with the former be both limitors of the causality.

(E159–163) Objection: But the property of being an instrument is counter to being a desire, which is a property of something already established. The desire for rain, etc. is due to the knowledge of the desired object (satisfaction) which will be gotten through that (rain).

Answer: No, there is no contradiction between something being an instrument as well as a desire.

(E163–164) This argument also refutes the neo-Prābhākara argument (of E139–143) according to which awareness of another's knowledge that X is an object of volition is the inducement. It is simpler to make awareness of one's own *being a thing one wants to accomplish* and of oneself having a means to a desired end the cause, rather than making the awareness of another's awareness the cause.

(E166–170) Neo-Prābhākara: We do hold that it is the awareness of one's own *being a thing one wants to accomplish* which induces one to act, and it is for this reason that no inducement of a farmer is seen with regard to making it rain, etc. Furthermore that the object is desired is an auxiliary cause.

Naiyāyika: Then why not admit what we say, that both *being a thing one wants to accomplish* and *being a means to a desired goal* are causal factors?

Neo-Prābhākara: Because though satisfaction is not a means to a desired end (being the end itself) there is desire to have it; so it is *being a thing one wants to accomplish* together with *being a means to a desired goal* that are the causal factors for action.

Naiyāyika: All this is not correct. Knowledge of X's being the means to a desired end is always the cause of the desire for the means to X; the same knowledge produces a desire to do the act, and we know that a desire does not produce another desire with the same object as the first one.

(E170–172) Prābhākara: Well, why is it that one who has already gotten cooked rice does not go to cook again?

Naiyāyika: Because he does not view rice as a means to a desired end anymore (having the cooked rice to hand). (Thus, in the absence of a desire for the result there is no desire to accomplish the means, and so a person does not initiate action.)

Objection: But (to take a different example) suppose someone is informed by a palmist that he might become King (which he views with pleasure) and suppose he believes it possible for him to climb the throne and that it is the means of his desire: why doesn't he make any attempt to accomplish it? It can only be because the time for the future King is not yet; any inducement to act requires an already established object—or else that he does not know the means to get the kingdom (and so doesn't try). When he knows the means he will try.

Answer: No, that's not right. Nobody desires to get something already gotten, such as the results of sacrifice or worship; the result would be that no one would sacrifice.

Objection: Even though one desires a kingdom and knows that it can be achieved, he still needs to know the means to it to be induced to act.

Answer: No, that is heavy, and anyway, the object of the getting the desired end and of the action are different.

(E173–197) Naiyāyika: This is all wrong. A reason why someone might not try to become a king might be that one is a child and thinks that it is not now possible for him to become king. Likewise one who has no rice does not try to cook rice. But if he knows that worship will get him the kingship and that he can perform it he will do so.

This is why, since it is not possible to get *apūrva* without sacrificing, since one can't sacrifice without the sacrificial cake and one can't have the cake without husking paddy, a person performs these acts in a sequence and not simultaneously. After the sacrifice is performed no one tries to get *apūrva*, because the *apūrva* is produced by the same effort required for the sacrifice itself.

There is a digression into some matters relating to the theory of sacrifice, to show that one will not take more trouble than necessary to produce the desired result.

(E197–209) Objection: Then "*na kalañjaṃ bhakṣayet*" cannot mean "one should not eat *kalañja*", since eating *kalañja* is a means of satisfying hunger (and thus would be appropriate in certain cases).

Answer: One should construe the sentence as meaning in effect that the eating of *kalañja* produces more unhappiness than necessary in producing the desired object..

Objection: But the injunction to a man who desires to kill his enemy does enjoin him to do something (the *śyena* sacrifice) which will produce more unhappiness!

Answer: In that case the properties of *being a thing one wants to accomplish* and *being means to a desired goal* only relate to the root sense (viz., perform the rite) and not to being the producer of more unhappiness, which is not fit in this case. This is why a wise man does not attempt that kind of sacrifice even though it is enjoined in the Veda. (Other opinions on this are discussed.)

(E211–219) Objection: Killing is violent (*hiṃsā*), since it is an action that has death as its result, and that produces hell.

Tentative answer: No. Violence cannot be understood merely as an action which (either directly or indirectly) causes death, since if that were so the maker of a well would be the killer of the cow that falls into it. For an act to be violent it must be produced with anger and be such that death invariably occurs as a result of it. The performance of the sacrifice for one who desires to kill his enemy is not like that.

Objection: Well, an action performed with a view to kill and which causes death is violent, and the sacrifice under discussion is indeed like that; by contrast, the making of a well is not intended to kill anyone.

Tentative answer: It has to be the immediate consequence of the act that determines whether a case is one of violence. Otherwise, e.g., when after being struck with a sword one later dies through food poisoning the person who gave the poison cannot be the killer and does not need to atone for a sin.

Answer: No. Designating such a person a "killer" in such cases is a secondary usage intended to bring those actions into the class of those that require atonement. But they are still killers.

(E219–224) Actually, "violence" applies to an action which is aimed at killing and which does not produce death through *adṛṣṭa*. Since the *śyena* sacrifice is an instrument of death through *adṛṣṭa* it cannot be violence. This is why the cow that dies in the well is not killed by the well's maker, but the one who gives poison (say) to one already wounded is a killer. Thus violence is not necessarily the action immediately preceding death, or else one who dies accidentally by food sticking in his throat will be a suicide.

Objection: Then one who throws his arrow at someone else and kills a Brahmin will not be called the killer of the Brahmin.

Answer: And rightly so. To call him "killer" is a secondary use of language.

(An alternative definition of "violence" is suggested and refuted. Thus the claim that being the means to a desired goal is the meaning of an optative suffix in injunctions to act has been defended.)

(E224–233) Being the means to a desired end cannot be what is meant by the optative suffix since in the case of obligatory rites (such as the *sandhyā* ritual) there is no result, no "goal".

Naiyāyika: Where there is no mention of any result that ritual is not obligatory.

Mīmāṃsaka: No. If so obligatory rites become noneternal like the optional (*kāmya*) sacrifices, to be done only occasionally when one wants something. As a matter of fact what the injunction "one should perform *sandhyā* everyday" means that anyone alive at that time should perform it. That is why eradication of sins cannot be the result of obligatory rites, since in that case their performance would be prompted by a desire to eradicate one's sins and, being only occasional, the obligatoriness of those rites will vanish.

It is only when one is aware of an obligation that he incurs sin by not complying. Prior to that if, as you Naiyāyikas say, there is no *being the means to a desired end*, there is no injunctiveness. But this results in interdependence, since to know sin the operation of injunction is required, but for the operation of injunction one has to postulate the sin of not performing what should be performed.

So what needs to be understood is that failing to perform *sandhyā* is the cause of frustration through producing sin. Performing *sandhyā* is desired, since it is not a means to frustration. It is meant by the optative suffix.

(E234–235) Prābhākara: No. If obligatory rites become optional they will no longer be obligatory. Furthermore, in supplementary texts what is understood as the cause of sin is the failure to perform only, not the absence of the object of performance (i.e., *upāsanā*). Otherwise how can you explain that a person who does not perform the obligatory rites gets sin, but not the person who performs them? The absence of the object of performance is common to both cases.

Really, the knowledge of *being the means to a desired end* together with *being a thing one wants to accomplish* induces a man to action. And since an action is not the result of an action the views advanced by others are not worth consideration.

(E235–237) Navyanaiyāyikas: The prior absence of *apūrva* produced by obligatory rites becomes the cause of frustration through producing sin. The absence of that prior absence—i.e., the *apūrva*—is desired, as it is the absence of the means of frustration. And the performance of *sandhyā* is enjoined as the means of that *apūrva* and as being the object of volition.

Prābhākara: No. What is meant by the *arthavāda* as the cause of sin is nonperformance of *sandhyā*, not the absence of *apūrva.*

(E238–242) Others say that the attainment of Brahma-world (*brahmaloka*) is the result of the performance of all those rites, obligatory and occasional, that are enjoined for the respective phases of life. Thus, even the obligatory rites have results.

Prābhākara: No. The meaning of the optative suffix is only that the thing is to be done (is the effect, *kāryatva*). The obligatory injunction does not mention any result.

Objection: But without any knowledge of purpose how can there be inducement to do the obligatory rites? Even a fool does not proceed to act without aiming at some result.

Prābhākara: No. The knowledge of purpose cannot be the prompting factor for inducement in general, since in the case of the obligatory rites the result is contradictory. Even in the case of the occasional rites knowledge of purpose is not the direct inducer, since the means is not known and one does not go to perform the end (but only the means to it). But that a thing is to be done can be known from the Vedas.

(E242–245) Naiyāyika: We reply. In every case of obligatory rites a result is mentioned either in the injunction or in the supplementary text. Thus a collection of factors makes the performer eligible to undertake the activity. So, since a result is mentioned, the performance of *sandhyā* is also an occasional rite, while since hell is mentioned on the consequence of not performing it, it is also understood as an obligatory rite.

You said (E224–233 above) that someone desirous of a result is not eligible to perform the *sandhyā.* But that is not correct, for what is understood is that a person who is alive and desires a result possesses the collection of factors which makes him eligible to undertake the performance. And if the result presented by the supplementary text is not construed with the injunction the sentence-unity will be broken.

(E245–250) Prābhākara: Well, if it is said that a living person who desires a result is eligible to perform an obligatory rite, then when he lacks desire he won't be eligible; then the rite will not be performed every day. Furthermore there will be no sin for nonperformance alone, since sin accrues only if someone is both eligible and does not perform.

There can be no general desire of the result, since knowledge of a result naturally produces the desire for its object. If one has only desire for liberation, even if he does not perform the occasional acts he does not incur sin; so there is no knowledge that occasional rites must be regularly performed. Furthermore it *is* sinful not to perform an obligatory act: there is a passage which says so (beginning "one who does not perform a prescribed act...") and there is an atonement prescribed (in the Vedas) for such nonperformance. Thus even if one does not desire the result he still performs the obligatory act to avoid sin.

Your argument that a person performs an obligatory rite, even when there is no mention of any result, because he is prompted by knowledge of what is to be done from the Vedas, is also not correct. For when it is known that the performance of an act will cause pain wise people regularly avoid doing it.

Your other argument that the nonoccurrence of results can by itself be the purpose that induces a person to act is likewise not correct, since the result will be that for you the obligatory rites will turn out to be optional. Since satisfaction and the absence of frustration is not functional here the *apūrva* which arises from performing obligatory rites cannot be such; it is an *apūrva* which does not produce any result.

(E250–253) Naiyāyika: The person who is to be induced to act does not know that the nonoccurrence of results is a purpose in the case of obligatory rites. Even though Prabhākara has said that eternal *apūrva* is the purpose of an obligatory rite, wise people have no faith in that.

So our conclusion is this. As for obligatory rites, it must be that the performance is prompted by some result, either the absence of the means to frustration or the nonoccurrence of undesired results. That is why every day one desires such results; otherwise it is not possible to explain it. Thus the result mentioned in the supplementary text is itself the inducer (not any *apūrva*). When there is no mention of any result it will be (as for you) heaven that is to be taken as the result.

Prābhākara: But since it is observed that inducement arises either from becoming aware that this is the means to the desired goal or from becoming aware that this which is to be accomplished is desired, what decides that the first and not the second is the inducer?

Nyāya answer: Because it is clear that with reference to desiring a result the awareness in which the object of the desire is the qualificand is the cause, and desire for the means (to a desired goal) plays the same role.

Actually, on your view two awarenesses contribute, one the awareness that the sacrifice is what one wants to accomplish, and then the awareness that the desired object is to be accomplished by that sacrifice. On my view, however, there is only one awareness that induces, namely that the sacrifice which is to be accomplished by the volition is the means to the desired object. A word cannot convey both its own relation to another word-meaning and the relation of that related meaning with another meaning.

(E253–260) Prābhākara: We propose that the meaning of the optative suffix is "whose *sādhya* is the desired object", (so we know the sacrifice simultaneously as both being the thing one wants to accomplish and being the means to a desired goal and there will be two awarenesses to induce).

Naiyāyika: But it is simpler, and it will keep *being the means to a desired goal* as the meaning of the optative suffix, if we construe the compound as a *tatpuruṣa*, not a *bahuvrīhi.* (Further grammatical clarifications.)

Prābhākara: Here is a suggestion. The awareness of being desired induces the person to eat again even after his hunger is satisfied, since he still knows that satisfaction of hunger is the desired object.

Naiyāyika: No. Even though being the means to a desired goal is there, still the cause of inducement is the desire for the result (the satisfaction of hunger) and since that desire is already satisfied there is no desire now for satisfaction of hunger.

(E260–263) Prābhākara: Then let desire for the result be the inducer and not awareness that something is the means to a desired end, since that will be overly complex. Moreover, if awareness of desire is treated as the cause of inducement desire cannot be the cause, since when we become aware of it it is destroyed. Again, the awareness "satisfaction is the object of desire" cannot be a mental awareness, because satisfaction is not established before taking up the activity. Even in the case of starting to cook there is no possibility of knowing that, e.g., cooked rice is desired, since the internal organ has no capacity to reach external objects.

(E263–267) Naiyāyika: Here is our answer. It is an established fact that awareness of being an instrument for that which is desired is the inducing factor for action. Although satisfaction, absence of frustration and their means, which are desired, cannot be united in one class by any common factor, still, being the object of desire can itself be treated as the uniting factor of these three. Similarly, when there is desire for satisfaction, and when one is aware that a thing is a means to obtaining what is desired and that it can be performed, then one begins to cook, etc.

Prābhākara: Then the optative suffix will be polysemous, since the objects of the awareness which induces a person are more than one.

Naiyāyika: No. The optative suffix expresses the instrumentality of sacrifice, etc., with reference to the desired result which although not united by the property of being satisfying is still united by the property of being the object of desire.

(E267–275) Prābhākara: On your position the optative suffix would not be the inducer, since being the means to a desired end is not really the inducer.

Naiyāyika: True, the optative suffix is not directly the inducer. But after it causes the awareness that the sacrifice is the means to a desired goal there arises the expectancy of what that goal is, and then the awareness that the sacrifice is the means to the desired goal (viz., heaven) is produced because of the juxtaposition with the word "one who desires heaven" (*svargakāma*). Thus the inducing awareness is that awareness which is produced by the awareness produced by the optative suffix.

Some other opinions on the same point are considered and refuted. A Grammarian objection is also rejected.

(E276–291) New logician: It is simpler to say that the desire to cook is the cause of volition, not the desire that something is the object of volition.

Prābhākara: How can one have the desire "I want to accomplish cooking by (my) volition"?

New logician: Just as one can have the desire "I want to accomplish cooking by fire". According to my doctrine, mere awareness of the state of being the means to a desired goal is the cause of the desire for those means. Thus when someone says "he wants to cook" cooking is understood as the object of the desire to do. Likewise the desire to accomplish satisfaction amounts to the desire of a volition which will produce satisfaction, since the volition is the instrument to that goal. So, the performance of *sandhyā* is desired as being the absence of nonperformance which will cause frustration, and the means to that performance is one's volition, and this is then what the optative indicates.

When something is known as the means to a desired goal and as a thing to be accomplished by volition there arises the desire to accomplish it. But such a desire does not arise from mere knowledge that something is a means to a desired goal.

Udayana holds that the knowledge that a thing is the means to a desired goal induces activity. However, the meaning of the optative suffix is the reliable speaker's desire, since it is logically simpler to suppose that.

This leads to the following generalization:

> Whatsoever performable activity or volition of a person or whatsoever volition the object of which is the activity of that person, is desired by a reliable speaker, that activity is the means to his desired goal and not the producer of any great harm,

and from knowledge of this generalization one infers that the sacrifice is the means to the desired goal, viz., heaven. Or, to put it another way:

> The sacrifice is the means to my desired goal,
> Because it is desired by a reliable speaker as the object of my volition,
> Just as the eating of food is desired by my father as the object of my volition and is the means to my desired goal.

Likewise, "one should not eat *kalañja*" means my volition to eat *kalañja* is not the object of the desire of the reliable speaker. From this follows the inference:

> The eating of *kalañja* is the means to my downfall,
> Because it is not desired by the reliable speaker as the object of my volition in spite of the fact that it is the means to my desired goal,
> Just as the eating of food mixed with honey and poison and not wanted by my father as the object of my volition is the means to my downfall.

The reliable speaker is Śiva.

(E291-295) Mīmāṃsaka: Then simplicity will have to be given up, since (if the speaker's desire is the meaning of the optative suffix, since desires are many, it will lead to) cumbersomeness with regard to the speaker's intention. Also one will have to postulate various reliable speakers (like Śiva, etc.)

Naiyāyika: No. It is simpler to accept what is well-known, that the optative suffix expresses desire. (That the optative suffix causes the awareness of desire is the result, and that is already established from the fact of verbal behaviour; even if it is not precise, there is no harm.)

Section Nine: Verbal Potency (I)
(*kāryānvitaśaktivāda*)

The following summary is by Sukharanjan Saha. We also offer as supplement the S.C. Vidyabhusana summary (B and RB: HIL) of the same section. "E" references are to the Kamakhyanatha Tarkavagisa edition (B3379; RB5287), Bibliotheca India 198, 1897.

THE IMPERATIVIST CLAIM[140]

(E460-466) The section begins by stating a thesis, which we may call the "imperativist" thesis. Sentences in the imperative mood or its equivalent can generate in a hearer an awareness of what ought to be done (*kāryatā*). But a sentence not containing such forms, e.g., a sentence in the indicative mood—whether a supplementary text of the Vedas or an ordinary indicative sentence—is about things in the world and not about what ought to be done. So, such a sentence cannot give us knowledge of what ought to be done.

Suppose a child who has not yet learned the language is present where A is giving instructions to B. The child finds that after listening to what A says B acts. The child reasons: before A spoke B did not act, but when he spoke B did act. Therefore, if the speech made by A is a case of normal behaviour it must have a purpose, and this purpose must be the activity of B. But since the speech did not directly cause the activity it perhaps generated in B an awareness to the effect that the activity ought to be performed. The child is aware that in his own case activity is preceded by an awareness that the activity ought to be performed.

It can't be supposed that the child could reason that A's speech produced B's activity by producing in B an understanding that the activity ought to be performed. For the child has no previous experience of such a complex causal relationship; these are his first ruminations about language. So he concludes that speech in general may act as a source of knowledge, but only of knowledge about what ought to be done. He does not yet know the meanings of specific words. So we shall have to suppose that he learns those meanings subsequently through assimilation and discrimination of certain sounds with and from certain kinds of activity. So, what he learned initially about the use of language regulates and determines his learning the meanings of specific words; meaning cannot be learned without involving reference to awareness of an activity to be performed.

(E466-470) Objection by a nonimperativist: Even if we agree that the activity of B is due to his awareness of what ought to be done, still it is not necessary to hold that his knowledge of what ought to be done is due to language in general. It is more reasonable to suppose that the understanding of language is due to language in general and that knowledge of what ought to be done is due to those words which convey the idea of obligation, provided there is mutual expectancy among the relevant words. Since this is at least as reasonable an explanation as the one the imperativist thesis provides, let us call this opposing explanation the "non-imperativist" thesis.

We nonimperativists rely on the indispensability of mutual expectancy. If the words in a sentence were not related by mutual expectancy no understanding would arise and no knowledge of what ought to be done would result. On the other hand, if other relevant conditions are present mutual expectancy is followed by understanding, though not necessarily by knowledge of what ought to be done. Thus the minimum conclusion is the indispensability of mutual expectancy.

Both the imperativist and nonimperativist here are Prābhākara philosophers. The Prābhākaras hold that the part played by a word in producing understanding of a sentence is just that it presents a universal property. Though the individual instantiating the universal is understood as a term of the relationship of knowledge which results from the hearing of a sentence, a word *qua* word, the Prābhākaras hold, does not present the individual since the presentation of the universal excites the psychic traces left over by previous awarenesses and produces memory of the individual. The nonimperativists argues that, though knowledge of what ought to be done can be explained by reference to the presence in a sentence of appropriate ought-indicative components, the sentence in general should not be taken as generating the knowledge of what ought to be done.

If, however, the imperativist still wants to maintain that speech in general generates knowledge of what ought to be done, he will be doing so on the basis of his hypothesis that the activity of H (the hearer) must be due to knowledge of what ought to be done. This knowledge is due to H's hearing of the sentence uttered by S (the speaker). Now if a child learns the use of language from the behaviour of elders, the imperativist should maintain that the child will eventually make a guess to the effect that the sentential understanding by H is an understanding of a relationship the terms of which were presented to him by the constituents of the sentence uttered by S. Therefore, consistently with this, the imperativist should further maintain that on hearing, e.g., "... the door" H arrives at the sentential understanding only after supplying in mind the missing word (here "close"). But this, the nonimperativist points out, amounts to embracing the Nyāya position and abandoning the general Prābhākara stance that what is to be supplied is not the word but only its meaning.

In order to escape this criticism the imperativist may put forward the bold hypothesis that even at the time of the child's initial learning of language he may have observed an H acting on hearing an S's single word sentence which is in fact an elliptical sentence. But as it must be the case that H has acted on the basis of understanding the relationship between the terms, and since not all of them have been presented to him through words actually uttered, the criticism of the imperativist (in the previous paragraph) by the nonimperativist is not well-founded.

But the nonimperativist hastens to point out that if the imperativist can be bold enough to imagine that such a sentential understanding in the context of an elliptical sentence may coincide with a child's initial learning of language, the imperativist need not feel shy of accepting the more natural hypothesis that a child's initial learning of a use of language may be in a situation where an addressee's sentential understanding is only about matters of fact and does not involve knowledge of what ought to be done. It is clear that in such a case the sentence uttered by the addresser does not contain any word enjoining the addressee to do something.

The imperativist may suggest that though such a sentence may not contain words indicating that an activity is to be performed we shall have to take at least one word of such a sentence not in its direct literal meaning (*śakti*) but in its indirect signification (*lakṣaṇā*) as suggesting the performance of an activity. Such a strategy, the nonimperativist points out in reply, can be adhered to only if there cannot result any sentential understanding when the word is understood in its direct meaning. But there cannot be any guarantee that such is actually the case. The nonimperativist takes this opportunity to remind his opponent that the principle followed in treating a use of a word as signifying indirectly is parsimony, since if what is taken to constitute the indirect meaning of a word were treated as its direct meaning the word would then have more than one direct meaning and this violates the law of parsimony.

If there is any lesson to be drawn from this, it is that we should accept that sentential understanding is about the relationship among terms and does not necessarily involved knowledge of what ought to be done. This is clearly in keeping with the law of parsimony. It will not be necessary to treat a word in a sentence seemingly clearly lacking an imperative as a word used indirectly to signify performance of an activity.

Furthermore, if the general strategy of the imperativist is to interpret every word in a sentence as standing for something relating to some activity to be performed, what interpretation will he offer of a word that directly means that an activity is to be performed? The meaning of such a word has to be understood as related to the meanings of other words not indicative of any activity to be performed. If, therefore, the imperativist has to abandon his general strategy in respect of such words, he cannot claim the general success of that strategy that every sentence constituent involved in sentential understanding embodies knowledge of relationship with what ought to be done.

(E470-480) The imperativist responds: When a child first learns language, the child, on the basis of observing an addressee trying to act, infers that the addressee's efforts must have been preceded by his understanding what ought to be performed; this is then how the child understands the speech of the addresser. The two ends of this chain are the speech of the addresser and the efforts of the addressee to perform the activity. There is an intermediate factor, viz., the addressee's understanding of what ought to be done. If this intermediate factor is not accepted, what will take its place? The nonimperativist holds that what takes its place is a chain comprising (1) a sentential understanding about relationship in general, (2) the grasping of the meanings of the constituent words, including those indicating injunction, and (3) knowledge of what ought to be done. The nonimperativist theorist,like the Naiyāyika, could perhaps dispense with (1). But the imperativist points out that if the addressee's efforts in performing his activity are what we are to account for then an explanation will have to attribute to him an understanding of what ought to be done, and that will have to figure in any alternative account proposed by the imperativist's opponents. Thus any explanation without (3) will be a bad explanation.

Nonimperativist: In attributing to a person an understanding of what ought to be done, knowledge of a relationship to what ought to be done gets admitted (being the awareness of the relation between qualificand and qualificandum). And thus it is simpler merely to postulate awareness of the qualificandum alone, viz., awareness of a relation, not necessarily of what ought to be done; that is all that comes to the hearer's mind when he hears the speaker.

Imperativist: It would be unreasonable to admit the more complicated relation if the simpler one will do. But it is not so in this case. Here is a parallel example.[141] Awareness of a bare floor accounts for our awareness of there being no pot on the floor, whereas awareness of the floor having a pot on it cannot account for it. So one cannot sensibly take the simpler awareness as basic in that case, and likewise with the case here. Thus we can conclude that in initially learning language the child can and does actually infer the addressee's awareness about the language's referring to what ought to be done from observing the adressee's behaviour,and that he can legitimately proceed to the conclusion that this awareness of the addressee results from hearing an utterance spoken by the addresser.

The imperativist does not accept the nonimperativist's argument that the imperativist theory fails to account for words indicating obligation. Such a meaning, says the imperativist, can be directly understood as involving relationship with what ought to be done, while also involving awareness of the meanings of the other terms in the sentence.

As for mutual expectancy, the nonimperativist is wrong to give the impression that the imperativist cannot admit mutual expectancy as a condition necessary for understanding sentences referring to what ought to be done. In fact expectancy is absolutely necessary.

Now how can it be the case that utterances which do not seem to involve obligation really do involve it? Well, if awareness of such a sense of obligatoriness is not produced on hearing the utterance, no understanding of the sentence can really result. At best what arises in such cases is a sequence of ideas unrelated to each other. Such a failure to understand sometimes occurs in children, but adults who understand utterances must relate the terms involved by appealing to a notion of obligation.

Nonimperativist: The initial learning of language by a child may not work as the imperativist assumes it does. A child may begin learning a language by attributing to an addressee understanding of utterances not involving reference to what ought to be done. E.g., a child who has not yet learned a language may hear someone say, on the occasion of his mother giving birth to a baby brother, "Caitra, a son has been born to you". Seeing a large smile on the face of the one addressed, the child infers that the birth of a baby is the cause of that smile through the sentence uttered on that occasion.

Imperativist: It might be so if the child had reason to exclude other reasons for smiling in the case in question. But he doesn't have any reason to preclude other causes for smiling. So the account given by the nonimperativist cannot be a good theory about language-learning. On the other hand, suppose the child later on sees Caitra performing the prescribed rites on the birth of a son: then he might learn the proper use of the sentence. But this favors our thesis, not yours.

Nonimperativist: All right, then consider this case. Suppose someone hears the sentence "the *pika* is singing in the mango tree", and assume he has learned the meanings of all the words except "*pika*". He looks at the mango tree and sees only one thing singing sweetly there, and thus concludes this must be what is referred to by the word "*pika*". In all this there is no involvement of any understanding of obligation. So there imperativist theory must be mistaken.

Imperativist: This is hardly a counterexample, as it is not a case of initial learning. Anyway, we have already outlined our procedure for explaining cases apparently lacking any reference to obligation. In this case he may well have run into the word "*pika*" previously in a sentence involving obligation.

Therefore words are used to lead men towards activity. Some do it directly, others in association with words indicating obligation. Since this is so, those sentences of the Vedas that don't contain words indicating obligation should be interpreted as auxiliary to those that do. This is how we are advised to understand historical and mythical stories, as auxiliaries to prescribed courses of action. The same approach should be taken toward poetry, drama and fiction, the expressions of which can at best convey sequences of undiscriminating discrete ideas but no awareness of their relationship.

The Nonimperativist Response[142]

(E484-488) Nonimperativist: Your analysis of children's language learning is incorrect. Instead, the correct account is rather like this. The child, hearing A say "Bring the pot" to B, sees that B brings a pot. Thus he begins by observing B's specific activity. The child next seeks the cause of B's activity, and concludes that the cause of that activity is B's understanding that a pot is to be brought (not knowledge in general, which is irrelevant). But he can't distinguish the different meanings of the specific words used by A. These he learns by a process of assimilation (*āvāpa*) and discrimination (*udvāpa*). First he observes bringing, and a pot, and assumes there are words for these in what was said. Then he may hear another speech "bring the book", and finds someone bringing a book. Likewise he hears "remove the book" and observes a different activity. In this way he learns to distinguish the different meanings of the constituent parts of the speech acts.

Imperativist: No. The child sees the bringing of the pot as due to B's will to do something or other, and this in turn is due to the hearer's knowledge in general of what ought to be done. Then the child subsequently arrives at the specific causal relationship between "bring the pot" and the hearer's awareness that the pot ought to be brought.

Nonimperativist: It is not necessary to assume that the awareness of the specific causal relation depends on awareness of the general causal relationship. On any account the child must learn the meanings of "pot", "bring" etc., and it would be unjustified to suppose the child must learn causality in general before coming to recognize a specific cause and effect. After all, knowledge of causal relationship is based on agreement in presence and in absence between what is taken to be effect and what is taken to be its cause.

Imperativist: But the knowledge of causal relationship of which you just spoke justifies one assuming the general relation of cause and effect as well as the specific one. If we learn that some particular smoke is the result of a specific fire, we also learn that fire causes smoke, and without any additional evidence. So our general theory need not be given up.

Nonimperativist: Nevertheless it would be unjustified to suppose that we should postulate general causal relationships just because we perceive a specific one. This requires an act of inference, and so our point is made, viz., that awareness of the specific causal relationship is prior to knowledge of general relation of cause to effect.

(E488-491) Furthermore, you argued that if one supposes speech to be generative of awareness of mere relationship and not of relationship involving reference to what ought to be done a double fault occurs, viz., (1) ignoring the role of the latter awareness which the child rightly infers to be the cause of the hearer's activity, and (2) accepting the role of speech in the former awareness (of mere relationship) even though the child is not justified in postulating it as the cause of the activity. Awareness of a relationship involving reference to what ought to be done is a case of qualified awareness; the relationship is the qualificand and what ought to be done is the qualifier. Awareness of the qualificand involves awareness of the qualifier, just as it was argued awareness of the floor as having a pot on it involves awareness of the floor.

Prābhākara philosophers consider the universal to be the meaning of a word on grounds of simplicity. It is perhaps tempting to suppose on that basis to argue that here the qualifier is knowledge of the relationship involving reference to what ought to be done, and the qualificand is the relationship itself. But by parity of reasoning, since we can account for the awareness of the qualifier as emanating from our awareness produced by the indicative, it is not necessary to hold that the understanding generated by the utterance is that of the qualificand qualified by this qualifier.

(E491-494)[143] One who has received satisfaction from an object will naturally desire to acquire another of that kind. So he will desire also to do what is required to get that kind of object. Thus his activity is due to his firm resolve to perform an activity sure to lead to the wanted result. This activity is also preceded by the agent's awareness that he can perform the action in question.

Now the nonimperativist criticism of the imperativist view is this: the child infers from the addressee's performance that he must have had an intention to perform it. And from that he further infers that the addressee believes he can perform the act in question. But if that is the imperativist view it is wrong, since, e.g., "bring a pot" does not involve any reference to any ability of the hearer's.

Imperativist: Yes it does. The hearer can infer from the fact that he is being addressed that the relevant intention took place.

Gaṅgeśa: Then you admit that the sentence has nothing to do with this particular hearer, in which case it can't place any obligation on any particular hearer.

Imperativist: The reference to the specific hearer is unnecessary in any case. All that is needed is that there be reference to hearer's ability, not of any particular hearer's ability. It will suffice for volition to take place that e.g., one knows that one is like someone who has been successful in performing this kind of action. It is sufficient for one's being moved to act that he believes the act is capable of being performed.

Gaṅgeśa: All right. But your imperativist account of the cause of the volition is not correct. You contend that the hearer's understanding that the act is capable of being performed is caused by his awareness that he is similar to someone else who has been successful in performing the activity. But it wasn't the same activity; that activity is past, the one we are contemplating is future. By removing the second part of the original analysis you have removed the connection between past and future. Our view, by contrast, can explain that connection; this was shown in the *Vidhivāda* section above.

(E494-501) Nonimperativist: Reverting to your argument at E470-480 above: The knowledge (3) of what ought to be done may figure in the initial learning procedure of the child, but that doesn't mean it will be involved in such a chain as you suppose. It needn't be. To be sure this constitutes a revision in the child's mature understanding of the situation, but this is to be expected: at the time of learning the language, the child couldn't understand the whole situation; now he does.

Imperativist: But the child began the process of learning with knowledge (3); it is basic to his reasoning.

Nonimperativist: That doesn't matter. Having corrected the mistaken classification of a shell as a piece of silver we do not have to impute the mistake to a subsequent experience of another shell.

Does the child grasp a connection between what the speaker says and what ought to be done? Or does he rather not involve that, but only sometimes, in which case the speech merely imparts the meanings of its interconnected words? In fact, a child once she has learned the language may remain in doubt whether the hearer's understanding is specific or general as regards what ought to be done. It is similar to the question whether one who hears a statement uttered also is aware that the speaker is claiming to know what he is stating to be true. Maybe so, maybe not.

The next point in the imperativist argument was that awareness of things on the basis of hearing a sentence does not necessarily involve reference to what ought to be done. The nonimperativist used the child's supposed recognition of a new brother as providing him joy as an example. But the imperativist points out that the child cannot be confident it is his brother's awareness of a new baby that is the reason for the smile—lots of things might make him smile. The nonimperativist refutes this line of thought by eliminating all other reasonable causes of Caitra's smile.

Anyway, continues the nonimperativist, even if a given argument for my conclusion happens to be faulty it doesn't follow the argument's conclusion is false. So the learning of language by the child may be correct even if an inference forming a part of it be faulty.

(E501-532) The next section deals with the initial imperativist point about indicatives, whether Vedic explanations or not, not giving knowledge unless appended to a context involving obligation. Gaṅgeśa points out that some explanatory sentences function to explain the meanings of terms referring to things or persons and not to actions alone. Thus such sentences can be used independently of injunctions to report regularities about the meanings of words, etc. This section explores the use of Vedic explanations in such a connection. The conclusion aimed at is to show that such explanations, contrary to the imperativist thesis, may well give us knowledge.

Siddhānta

(E533-534) Gaṅgeśa: The nonimperativist believes that the meaning of a word consists in its efficacy in producing understanding in general about things as related, though not as related to what ought to be done. Using the same kind of argument as the nonimperativist used against the imperativist, Gaṅgeśa argues that it is simpler to understand the thing meant as the qualificand alone, not as one object qualified by another.[144] It may be that when the child begins to learn language he may suppose that meaning consists in producing an understanding about a thing as related to some other thing. But as he learns he will give up this hypothesis. If the context theorist, no matter whether he is imperativist or nonimperativist, supposes that the child starts with the interpretation that speech produces understanding of a relationship between two or more things, he is only misleading his respectful and credulous disciples (*svaśiṣyavyāmohanam*!) and will be unable to win over his listeners.

(E534-541) In fact it is no part of the meaning of a word that it denotes any relationship between its referent and some other thing. The answer to the question how we come to know that things referred to by words are related is not that the relationship is part of the meaning of the words. If an utterance mentions only "a" and "b" and the meaning of the entire expression is that *a* is related by R to *b*, the meaning of "R" is not part of the meaning of either "a" or "b" but rather a result of mutual expectancy, well-formedness, appropriateness or intention. The mechanism transmitting these relations is memory. That this theory is the correct one is attested by its greater simplicity.

Moreover, if the context theorist were right then there would be no way to explain the difference in understanding "aRb" and "bRa". This consequence might have been averted by the nonimperativist if he could hold that the meaning of one constituent, say "y", consists in generating a memory of *y* only and that the other constituent, say "x", consists in generating the nonmnemic understanding of *x* as related to *y*. But that would involve giving up the context theory with respect to "y".

The nonimperativist might argue against Gaṅgeśa thus: If relationship figures as content of the hearer's understanding, then if it does not enter into the meaning of any constituent of the sentence, what is to guarantee that various other things not involved in the meanings of the sentence constituents will not figure as contents of the understanding of the sentence? Gaṅgeśa's reply will be that while we must understand the constituents in their relationships we do not have to take the same approach with regard to the relationship itself.

Nonimperativist: But according to you words too generate awareness of things only as related, not independently. So the words for the relation too must generate awareness only as related to the relata.

Gaṅgeśa: That is so. But to understand an utterance the hearer does not have prior awareness of the relation, though he must have an understanding of the meanings of the terms for the relata. And you (nonimperativist), who represent the Prābhākara camp, should agree, for you too hold that the meaning of a word is the universal property, though the awareness generated by hearing the word is an awareness of an individual as qualified by a universal.

Nonimperativist: If the meaning of "pot" (say) is its efficacy in generating awareness of a pot, then that awareness is involved in some relationship constituting the meaning of "pot".

Gaṅgeśa: No, for the awareness of a relationship can be viewed as a result of factors other than the meaning of words. Thus though the meaning of a word produces awareness of a thing denoted by the word as involved in some relation, the awareness of meaning operative here is only with respect to the term and not with respect to the relationship of which that is a term.

Nonimperativist: So our theories are not different. For according to us too there can be awareness of *x* without involving awareness of any relationship, e.g., when we remember something.

Gaṅgeśa: Memory has nothing to do with it. In memory a noise may recall a memory but it does not necessarily have any meaning-relation to the thing remembered. But when a sound creates an understanding involving relationship it is considered to be a word.

(E541-549) Nonimperativist: Even according to you the understanding of a sentence involves relationship. So words must be understood as having as their purport that a relationship be understood. But purport involves either direct meaning (as when a sentence is disambiguated—"bring *saindhava*" meaning to bring salt, not a horse), indirect meaning (as when "the Ghoṣas are Ganges-residents" means they live on the bank, not in the river), or secondary meaning (as in "the boy is a lion"). But the last two kinds aren't relevant here, so it must be the first kind, direct meaning, and that is what the nonimperativist theory holds.

Objection to this by another party (not a Bhāṭṭa): No, it is not direct meaning that operates; direct meaning can only provide a memory of the thing meant. Since the relationship in question is nonmnemic, but is not secondary meaning in the present case, it must be a case of indirect meaning here.

Nonimperativist: Just as awareness of the direct meaning of a word is necessary for the generation of the memory of the thing meant, so by parity of reasoning the understanding in a nonmnemic case must be generated by previous awareness of the relationship. But in the present case the relationship cannot be said to have been known before. So it can't be a case of indirect meaning. Anyway, our own view is simpler than this.

Gaṅgeśa: You assume that purport requires that the things meant must be either related through a direct or indirect relation. But that is not necessary. There are counter examples. For one thing, if I say "there's smoke over there" in hinting that there's a fire over there it would be irrational to suppose that the word "smoke" means fire either directly or indirectly. Rather we are drawn to make an inference ourselves to understand what is meant. A second example is called *ākṣepa* in rhetoric, e.g., when one says something intended to imply the reverse of what the sentences literally means.[145] These examples show that understanding the meaning is not necessary in fixing the purport behind the use of a word or sentence. Other factors are at work in arriving at the intention of the speaker. The words are operative by first producing memory images, which in turn produce understanding of the meaning of the sentence.

(E549-555) Bhāṭṭa: No. It is not the words that lead us to understand the relationship through producing memory images, but the things themselves produce the memories directly, and these generate understanding of the relationship (providing other conditions are present). E.g., a poet must know what he wants to express; this knowledge is an understanding of the things as connected with each other already.

Gaṅgeśa: Your (Bhāṭṭa) expalanation is less satisfactory than ours. You have the things produce the understanding of relationship by first producing the relevant memory images. Our theory is simpler, since understanding the complete context of the words is necessary. E.g., someone who hears "bring the cow" may understand bringing and cows but he will not have an understanding of the sentences without knowing the specific relationship intended here between bringing and cows. So the memory of bringing and cows isn't sufficient to explain how the sentence can be understood in the requisite way. Of course the poetry case you cite is not like this, but we don't claim that every case is as we describe it.

Section Ten: Verbal Potency (II)
(*jātiśaktivāda*)
Summary by Sukha Ranjan Saha

"E" references are to the Kamakhyanatha Tarkavagisa edition (B3379; RB5287).

(E556-559) Gaṅgeśa now undertakes an investigation as to what constitutes the meaning of a term. He first takes up the view of the Prābhākara Mīmāṃsā. The Prābhākara holds that what constitutes the meaning of a term is the universal and not the particulars exemplifying it.

Hearing a senior person say "bring the cow", and seeing a junior person bringing a particular cow, the child learns that the term "cow" stands for that particular cow. But hearing "bring the cow" at a later time and finding that the very same cow is not brought he learns that "cow" does not always refer to the same specific animal.

Suppose, however, he did not take a particular animal as the referent of the term but took it to refer to *any* cow. But when he hears "give away cow"[146] he must decide whether he should give away all cows or just a specific cow. He can't very well do the former. And *which* cow is the one he is being told to give away?

One might suppose that the difficulty only arises as long as one assumes that "cow" stands for something uniform in all contexts, and that if that assumption is given up there is no problem. But such an assumption amounts to admitting diversity of meanings of the same term as well as diversity of identifying properties any one of which will entitle its locus to be referred to by the term. This is unacceptably complex. Furthermore, on the hypothesis of such diversity of meanings one cannot explain how the hearer can understand the meaning of a term he has not heard before.

(E559-562) Against the Prābhākara view one may propose distinguishing between the qualifier and the indicator.[147] Suppose we treat *cowness* as an indicator rather than a qualifier.[148] Then, even though each individual has its own distinct marks as qualifiers, they are all "cow" as sharing the same indicator. In this way the difficulties raised in the previous paragraphs can be avoided.

Prābhākara: No. The indicator *crows* in "the house of Devadatta has crows on it" is a separable feature of the thing having it, the house; but *cowhood* is not separable from cows since nothing can be a cow which lacks *cowhood.* So *cowhood* must be a qualifier, not merely an indicator, of cows. And so "cow" does have diversity of meanings as alleged, referring as it does to various diverse things as referents.

Opponent: Just as a stick is a causal condition of a pot in virtue of *stickness* being the limitor of the causality in making a pot, even though *stickness* is not the cause of the pot, analogously a cow is denoted by the term "cow" in virtue of *cowness* being the denotative property (*śakyatā*) of "cow", even though *cowness* is not the meaning of the term "cow".

Prābhākara: This argument is self-defeating. The argument presupposes that the hearer understands cows by "cow", which implies that he knows that "cow" means thing having cowness.

Since it has been shown that particulars cannot be referents of terms *simpliciter* a universal is required. The view that the meaning is the particular as qualified by the universal involves the same difficulties. Therefore, by parsimony we conclude that it is the universal alone that is the meaning.

Opponent: You admit that particulars cannot constitute meaning if not qualified by the universal, thus admitting that nothing can constitute the meaning of a term if it is not taken as qualified by a qualifier. Now applying the same principle to your own thesis I can argue that the universal can constitute the meaning only if taken as qualified by some qualifier or other. So treat *cowness* as the universal and some distinctive mark—such as *having a dewlap*—as the qualifier. (*Having a dewlap* is generally agreed not to be a universal.)

Prābhākara: This involves a vicious circle, if particulars are differentiated by reference to a universal and it is also the case, as the opponent would like to have it, that the universal is differentiated by reference to those particulars.

How does the Prābhākara propose to explain the situation? He cites the Vaiśeṣika theory of individuators, which is held to be self-differentiating, and proposes that here we should make the same claim for universals, viz., that they are self-differentiating. If one demurs at this it is pointed out that otherwise there will be an infinite regress of higher-order properties needed, and that constitutes no viable alternative.

(E562-567) Naiyāyika: If a term has only the universal for its meaning it cannot very well generate awareness of a particular. The Prābhākara may hold that it is the very nature of a term that it can generate the awareness of a particular. But doesn't this imply that the particular is part of the meaning of a term?

Replies of the Prābhākara and others to the above objection: (a) If we accept the causal hypothesis that the hearer's knowledge that particulars constitute the meaning of the term is necessary for his having the awareness of the particular this will surely violate the law of parsimony.

(b) Though the particular does not constitute the meaning of a term, the knowledge that the universal constitutes its meaning generates the hearer's awareness of the particular, the determining condition being the fact that the particular is the locus of the universal. It is true that this involves postulation of an additional factor, namely the fact of the particular's being the locus of the universal.

(c) The question is how the hearer comes to have an awareness of the particular merely on the basis of the knowledge that the universal constitutes the meaning of the term. The answer relies on the principle of *ekavittivedyatā*. The principle is this: if A does not figure in any cognition without B also figuring in it, the conditions sufficient for the awareness of A are also sufficient for the awareness of B also. For example, everyone admits that an introspective awareness A about an awareness B has as its content the contents of B.

Nyāya objection: If awareness of a particular always involve awareness of a universal and vice versa, then the conditions for one should be conditions sufficient for the other too. But there are counterexamples. For instance, contact between sense-organ and a particular substance is the cause of awareness of the particular, but is not the cause of awareness of the universal (that cause is a relative product of the contact along with inherence). Again, the perception of a particular due to contact leaves behind impressions different from those left behind by perception due to contact plus inherence, so that memory of the particular generated by the activated traces of perception of the particular cannot be generated by the traces of perception of the universal.

Opponent's answer: It is indeed true, as the Naiyāyika points out, that the conditions for perceptual awareness of the universal cannot account for the perceptual awareness of the particular, and if recollection about the universal and the particular is based on the activated residual traces of previous perception about them the same is true of recollection also. But that does not justify extending the analysis to cases of testimonial awareness involving, where otherwise permissible, apprehension of the particular as having its universal in it. We shall have to treat this testimonial awareness as a class by itself.[149]

Objection to the opponent: The power (*śakti*) of terms is actualized by giving rise to the hearer's awareness, which is admittedly about both the particular and the universal.

Answer: It cannot be a rule that whatever figures in a hearer's awareness as a content of that awareness must be counted as the meaning of some term or other in the sentence expressing the awareness. We have seen earlier that there is always a relationship which is not a referent of a statement. Secondly, it is knowledge of the universal, and not of the particular, which is necessary for the hearer's final understanding.

(E567-572) The "humped-dwarf" (*kubjaśaktivāda*) theory of meaning is that words only mean universals and not other things like particular or relations.

Gaṅgeśa: People sometimes have wrong beliefs about the meaning of words, thinking that a certain word means A when in fact it means B. A and B are typically particulars. Since it makes sense to think that the meaning of a word should certainly include whatever figures as the content of a sentence using that word, and since particulars certainly do so figure, particulars must constitute at least part of the meaning of words.

Humped-dwarf answer: Surely if the awareness of a content of a sentence can be accounted for by reference to factors other than awareness of the meanings of words, those other conditions constitute the meaning of the sentence, not the word-meanings. E.g., though the bank of the Ganges is part of the meaning of "the Ghose family lives on the Ganges" it is not directly referred to and so is not part of the meaning of the sentence; rather it is a secondary meaning. Now since in general meaning can be explained without reference to any particular it is correct to conclude that the awareness of a particular plays a necessary part in the account of meaning.

Objection to the humped-dwarf: Many sentences either report the performance of an action or contain a command or request that an action be performed. Now the actions in question are particular, involving a specific place and time, agent and purpose. These cannot be accounted for if the meaning is merely the universal.

Possible answers to this: (1) What is related to action is indeed a particular, but a particular appearing only as an exemplification of some universal. (2) The agent in a sentence like "the cow is moving" is not simply a particular, but a particular identified as a cow, that is, as having cowness. (3) (Attributed to Śrīkara) The universal acts as a limitor with respect to the qualified particular related to an action; so the understanding of a sentence involves at least two instruments of knowledge, the universal together with language.

Prābhākara: Though meaning is constituted by the universal alone the antecedent mnemic representation of an object as well as the final sentential awareness do of course involve the particular. A universal cannot figure as content in an awareness without also making the particular co-content (*ekavittivedya*). But parsimony dictates that only the universal is needed as the meaning of a word. As for the secondary meaning (e.g., the bank in "the Ghose family lives on the Ganges"), it is not a part of the meaning either, but not for the same reason that the particular is not. While the principle in the case of secondary meaning is the above-cited one of co-content, the principle that excludes secondary meaning significance from the meaning of a sentence is different (say, it comes about through implication), which is why the particular is not thought of as a kind of secondary use. In fact, the use of a word to designate a particular is a primary use of language. Nevertheless Śrīkara is wrong to point to the universal as an instrument of knowledge, since it involves admitting an additional, unnecessary instrument. Since no sentential awareness can be only about the universal without a particular, the particular also may be assigned the status of limitor in respect to such an awareness, just the reverse of Śrīkara's suggestion.

(E572-578) Gaṅgeśa: What the meaning of a word is can be decided from what awareness the word produces. What is produced is an awareness not simply about a universal but also about a particular, as is implied by the Prābhākara's critique of Śrīkara and others as well as by the Prābhākara adherence to co-contentness of the universal and particular in memory and in the final awareness at the end of hearing a sentence.

Meaning is constituted by what figures as content in the sentential awareness produced by the knowledge of that meaning. Since by the Prābhākara's admission such an awareness is about the particular also, reference to the particular cannot be eliminated from the account of meaning. Again, it is evident that the particular figures as a content of linguistic awareness only along with a universal. But it was also admitted that the universal appears as indicative of some particulars. Thus the same principle that makes one constitutive of meaning makes the other also.

As for the charge that to suppose both universal and particular as meaning commits the fault of diversity of meaning (making two things "the" meaning): When the particular is taken to be constitutive of meaning it is not the particular *qua* particular that is so held. Thus, *this* cow falls within the meaning of the word "cow" insofar as *this* is a cow and not because that animal is a definite specific thing referred to as "this". Also, since there are words (such as "beast") which are not associated with any universal (since that would involve cross-connection of universals) strict adherence to the demand of unity of meaning by fixing the universal as the meaning will render such words meaningless.

As for the Prābhākara argument that if a particular were meant by a word then all the particulars the word applies to would be included—so that "bring a cow" would mean "bring all cows"!—since the universal is part of the meaning of a word one hearing a word thinks not just about the universal property but also about all the things to which the property applies. The specific reference to a particular cow must then be determined by other relevant factors. So both universal and particular are necessary parts of meaning.

(E578-591) Now Gaṅgeśa recounts the Bhāṭṭa Mīmāṃsā theory of meaning, that only the universal constitutes the meaning but that the particular figures in the content of an awareness by presumption (termed *ākṣepa* by the Mīmāṃsakas). Gaṅgeśa retorts that presumption can be valid only if the two things involved are related by pervasion, and since the universal is not pervaded by the particular one cannot cite presumption to justify a move from the universal to the particular.

Gaṅgeśa also records certain views held by Maṇḍana Miśra that are different from the Bhāṭṭa's. On Maṇḍana's view both particular and universal constitute meaning, but the universal is the direct meaning while the particular is indirect, since in a sentence predicating nonexistence of something that thing cannot be the eternal universal of existence but must be the particular, which is signified through indirect meaning. Gaṅgeśa denies that the initial meaning must always be the universal. In fact it is the particular as qualified by the universal that constitutes the direct meaning of a word.

Gaṅgeśa's view is closer to that of the Prābhākaras than to the Bhāṭṭas, since he holds that both the particular and the universal appear in the same awareness as bound together by a tie in which the former appears as qualified by the latter. In support of his view Gaṅgeśa quotes Gautama's *sūtra* (the last *sūtra* of 2.2) wherein his use of the word *padārtha* is in the singular though what constitutes this meaning is cited as consisting of the universal, the configuration and the individual—all three. The implication of the *sūtra*, according to Gaṅgeśa, is that the individual as qualified by the configuration and the universal constitutes the direct meaning of a word. There may be exceptions—e.g., saying "this is a cow" when speaking of a clay cow. Gaṅgeśa maintains that the word "cow" here refers to the configuration alone through secondary implication and envisages that there may be occasions when the universal only or the particular only may function similarly. But in such cases the mode of reference is through the process of secondary signification; generally we can retain the truth of the claim that what constitutes primary meaning is the qualified particular.

Section Eleven: *Apūrva*

This summary is based on the edition and translation by V.N. Jha, *The Logic of the Intermediate Causal Link* (Sri Garib Dass Oriental Series 46 (Delhi 1986). "ET" references are to this work. The numbering of passages referred to follows the above work as well.

(ET1-3)1-6. The question arises: is the meaning of the optative suffix corresponding to "should" in "one desiring heaven should sacrifice" related to the meaning of the root 'to sacrifice' or to something else?

Prābhākaras: The optative suffix cannot directly convey the root's meaning. The one who desires heaven cannot be *niyojya*, i.e., cannot be aware that he is enjoined to do this since he desires heaven. Having this awareness requires that one previously has had the awareness that the sacrifice is a means to heaven. But the optative suffix is not capable of conveying that the root meaning is the direct or indirect cause of heaven. That knowledge is going to occur at a time considerably later. The root's meaning is going to be destroyed soon, and its meaning will not be remembered (in the next life, etc.).

If the meaning of the optative suffix is *being the means to a desired goal* the problem just raised is clear enough. If the meaning is taken to be *being the thing one wants to accomplish* that presupposes as well that *being the means to a desired goal* has been understood, so there is no difference between the two doctrines. Therefore the meaning of the optative suffix is different from the "sacrifice!"; its meaning points to something which is the means to getting heaven and which causes the performance of the sacrifice.

(ET3-6) 7-17. Objection: But, e.g., drinking *ghee*, though it perishes quickly, nevertheless causes good health in the future.

Prābhākara: No. The reason why fire is not fit to cause sprinkling is because it is not a liquid substance. Likewise in the *ghee* case *ghee* is known to cause good health. In those cases we know whether the fire (or *ghee*) has the requisite similarity (*sājātya*) to the sprinkling or health. But in the case in question now (the sacrifice) the similarity cannot be known (since the result is far in the future).

Objection: Let's define "fitness" (*yogyatā*) as the absence of any proof against the awareness that one is enjoined to sacrifice. Then one can say that sacrifice is fit to get heaven.

Prābhākara: No. What is actually meant by "fitness"? Does it mean the absence of a valid awareness contradicting it? Or does it mean the absence of all valid awarenesses that contradict it? If the former, even though there is absence at *t* of a valid contradicting awareness there can be a contradicting awareness at $t+n$, so it will be both fit and not fit! If the latter, it will be impossible to determine fitness, since one person's awareness (of incompatibility) cannot be cognized by another.

(ET 7-8) 18-22. Objection: Suppose we say that the mere occurrence of the absence of any valid awareness of incompatibility (not necessarily the awareness of it) is the cause of understanding the injunction.

Prābhākara: No, for then the understanding would not arise when there is illusion about the fitness. But it does arise, since another person may know that it is not fit.

Objector: Suppose we say that when there is no contradicting valid awareness contradicting the compatibility determines a thing as having the form which brings about relation to another meaning?

Prābhākara: That is not possible here (since the "other meaning" is far in the future).

This argument refutes some who say that just as from hearing "Caitra has a beautiful complexion" one does not know just what color he is but knows that his skin has some color, so likewise when one hears "one desiring sacrifice should act", though he doesn't know precisely what to do, knows he should act. Since he doesn't know what to do indifference is likely.

It also refutes what some Bhāṭṭas say. They say that it is not necessary to postulate any *apūrva* (carrying through time to the time of the action), since for one who is desirous of heaven and knows that heaven results from the sacrifice the action of sacrifice exists until the result is produced, just as a strong impression produces memory even after a long time. This position is wrong for several reasons: there will be mutual dependence between being desirous of heaven and being able to get it; further, it is known that sacrifice is momentary.

(ET8-11) 23-31. Objection: To "sacrifice" means to worship, i.e., to pray to a god, which in turn means doing something to cause pleasure to the god. Therefore a sacrifice can be a means to heaven through generating satisfaction in the god. Even though that satisfaction may be momentary, through the production of a memory trace (in the god) the sacrifice can be a means to heaven.

Prābhākara: No. For one thing this appeals to the authority of the grammarians, which is merely (alleged) memory and so not authoritative. There is no other authority to prove that a sacrifice is a cause of satisfaction for a god or that heaven is produced by producing satisfaction in a god. In fact, there is no proof that there even *is* a god!

Objection: But *"yaj" means* that the worship of god is related to his satisfaction, which shows there are gods.

Prābhākara: No, that involves mutual dependency.

(ET11-14) 31-41. Objection: It is simpler to hold that *being the means to what is desired* is the cause of inducement.

Prābhākara: No, for then a person who wants to eat will cook rice again even when the cooked rice is ready to eat, since "cooking" is just the means to what is desired. Or else there will be no inducement to cook at all, since cooking is not what is desired and is (on this alternative) not the means to what is desired.

Objection: But cooking cannot be the instrument to eating through producing cooked rice, since the intermediate factor (cooked rice) is no longer accomplishable (being in existence already). (So it must be that cooking alone is the means to eating.)

Prābhākara: No, for then one couldn't go again to cook rice since one knows that cooked rice is already there!

Objection: Indeed, if rice is known to be cooked no desire to cook it can arise.

Prābhākara: No, since one may cook another kind of rice even when one kind has been cooked, but when a given kind of rice is ready to eat there can be no desire to cook it in that specific form.

(ET14-16) 42-46. Some proud (Naiyāyikas), without refuting the arguments just stated, try to establish that the injunction causes the understanding of effectness (*kāryatā*) associated with the sacrifice by offering inferences, as follows:

> The injunctive suffix in question expresses effectness associated with the action expressed by the root;
> Because it is an element in an instrument of knowledge;
> Like an ordinary injunctive suffix.

Or,

> The effectness understood from the injunctive suffix is related to the action expressed by the root:
> Because it is an effectness known from an injunctive suffix;
> Like the effectness known in "one should cook".

Or

> The sacrifice is related with effectness;
> Because it is expressed by the root having an injunctive suffix;
> Like the action of cooking.

On the basis of such inferences, once the effectness associated with the action (of sacrifice) is understood, *apūrva* can be postulated (since without it, it would not be understood that the sacrifice is to be performed).

Prābhākara: We have already argued that the first of these inferences will never produce knowledge of the conclusion without first knowing the fitness (of the person desiring heaven to perform the sacrifice). Without such knowledge the suffix alone cannot cause the understanding of the relation of effectness to sacrifice. The other two inferences also fail, for they are tantamount to saying that a Vedic injunction conveys what is already known from inference.

(ET16-20) 47-20. Objection: But it can never be known that the injunctive suffix means *apūrva.* Before the sentence ("one desiring heaven should perform the sacrifice") is understood *apūrva* cannot be in our mind, for then it would not be "*apūrva*" (i.e., "not known before") and also it would not be known verbally (being gotten through presumption).

Prābhākara: No. It *is* known verbally. One knows that an injunctive suffix is related to effectness, and that the effect in this case is heaven and the means the sacrifice is known through fitness, since it is not appropriate that the sacrifice should be a means to a pot or anything else.

Objection: But this knowledge is not available since the *apūrva* isn't known yet.

Prābhākara: No, one remembers such a relation from previous experience.

Objection: Since one can only remember the relation between a word one remembers and its meaning, and since *apūrva* is not remembered, the remembrance of the relation in question is not possible.

Prābhākara: No, our explanation is simpler, and indeed necessary. It is not just the memory of the relation between a particular thing and a word designating it that one has, but the memory of the general relationship—so that when one hears "cow" one knows other cows, not just the one cow confronted when he heard the word the first time!

Objection: This has to be explained through reference to the (extraordinary) generic relationship (*sāmānyalakṣaṇa-pratyāsatti*) between all fires and "fire".

Prābhākara: No, that is not required. In whatever manner the pervasion is known in the *h,* in that manner the knowledge of the *h* in the *p* is the cause of inferential cognition. Anyway, if you allow extraordinary generic relationship then we can have our *apūrva* through knowing that relationship to the universal effectness.

(ET21-23) 64-73. Objection: If the reason for postulating an *apūrva* is that the optative suffix requires a result (*kārya*) and the action can't produce the result long after the action occurs, then there shouldn't be any need for *apūrva* in obligatory prohibitive injunctions, since there is no mention of any result there.

Prābhākara: No. The optative meaning in, e.g., "one should cook" doesn't presuppose something other than cooking as a result. The relation between the root-meaning and the result (cooking) is gotten from the root "to cook" (*pac*) through the mere understanding of what that root means. But in the case of the Vedic injunction one must postulate a relation of the optative meaning to something other than the action of cooking now.

Objection: But this "something" might as well be a pot, or anything at all!

Prābhākara: No, for only the relevant thing will be fit to serve.

(The discussion turns to mainly grammatical matters.)

Siddhānta

(ET34-36) 98-103. Naiyāyika: Fitness cannot be what you take it to be, viz., mere relation to some other meaning, since when we already know something contradictory we won't consider the word fit to mean the thing in question. So let "fitness" mean just absence of any contradictory cognition.

Objection: Then the same sentence will sometimes be compatible with another and sometimes not!

Naiyāyika: True, and that's how it should be. Sometimes the hearer understands the sentence in such a way as to involve incompatibility, other times not.

Objection: It is a rule that the universal is known only when some particular is known. If no particular sacrifice is known to be the indirect means to heaven, how can the sacrifice be known to be generally the means to heaven?

Answer: A particular sacrifice is known to be generally the means to heaven, in spite of the fact that it may not be the direct means. But that is all right: if one says "fetch water in a pot" he does not have to add "—a pot other than one with a hole in it", since it is evident that pots with holes cannot carry water.

(ET43-44) 123-127. Your idea might be this: Because of the difficulty of relating the sacrificer who desires heaven to the sacrifice the notion of something to be done is appealed to, and this precludes the relevance of another action now. Though it does not preclude the relevance of (making) a pot, etc. being what is to be done, still the use of the expressions "desirous of heaven" and the optative form of the verb "to sacrifice" making a pot, etc. are excluded since they are not fit to be related to the sacrifice.

But actually the first awareness of difficulty is quite sufficient to exclude the relevance of a pot, etc., since there is already the idea of sacrifice being conveyed which has nothing to do particularly with pots.

Objection: But what is covered by "pots, etc." is innumerable, so everything cannot be excluded as irrelevant!

Naiyāyika: If so we can never understand language at all! For one cannot understand a general term without understanding what things the universal relates too.

(ET47-50) 138-148. Objection: Satisfaction can be a purpose, and so can *apūrva.*

Naiyāyika: No, for it is not experienced that way in ordinary experience. Heaven and liberation are called "purposes" since they belong to the classes of satisfaction or absence of frustration respectively. Even in the case of the Vedas the *apūrva* involved in optional rites is the means to the desired goal, thus is a subordinate purpose. In the other rites, obligatory and prohibitions, it is likewise.

Objection: In obligatory rites, since neither the main or subordinate purpose is known either from ordinary experience or from the Vedas, it must be the optative suffix itself that causes the knowledge of *apūrva* itself as the purpose.

Naiyāyika: Then the optative suffix should cause awareness of an *apūrva* which is desired in itself and not dependent on desire for anything else, but that is not how it is known.

(ET50-53)148-155. Objection: When someone sets out to eat poison and is told what it is and not to eat it, an opposing effort is generated that obstructs the temptation to eat it. The injunction conveyed by the optative suffix is not to eat, and since the result is an effort to avoid eating we say the injunction has power.

Answer: No. There may be awareness of not eating , but no effort to withdraw arises. If it were as you say your supposed injunction to withdraw would be untrustworthy since there will be no relation in the absence of any result.

Therefore one should not suppose that the optative suffix is related to *apūrva.* Being the means to heaven is not a part of the sacrifice. The sacrifice cannot be a direct means to heaven.

(ET53-56) 156-167. Objection: If prohibitions don't produce *apūrva* then atonement for them is useless!

Answer: The atonement does have a purpose—viz., avoidance of undesirable results (like going to hell).

Objection: We prove *apūrva* by disproving your argument. Your argument is this:

Devadatta's body now is preceded by an earlier body of his;
Because it is produced and is the instrument of Devadatta's experiences;
Like a garland prepared by Devadatta.

Now this argument commits the fault of begging the question, since precisely what is at issue is whether Devadatta's body is produced by his earlier body.

Answer: No. Since the earlier body is completely destroyed there is no fault of question-begging: rather, the concomitance between the force of a previous body and the present body is established by positive and negative concomitance.

(ET56-58) 168-176. Objection: The Vedas say that failure to perform an obligatory rite produces frustration. So the prior absence of performance of such a rite causes frustration. Since that prior absence continues it can produce all frustration, and there need be no sins! If you reply that performance of a rite of atonement destroys the prior absence, that's not correct, since the counterpositive of the prior absence is beginningless and endless, so the performance should go on forever!

Answer: Not so. It is the failure to perform the rite at the appropriate time that produces frustration, so when the appropriate time is past there is no longer any failure to perform.

Objector: Then let the posterior absence (of the sacrificing) be the operative cause, for where the posterior absence of something is a cause of *y* the prior absence of *x* is also cause of *y*.

Answer: No. If it were so, you could get milk by destroying curds, or liberation merely by destroying false awareness.

(ET58-59) 159-183. Objection: Look. That the sacrifice is the means to heaven is known from the sentence giving the injunction to sacrifice. But without something (an instrument) to connect them one has to postulate the posterior absence of the sacrifice as the cause of heaven. Thus both the sacrifice and its absence produce heaven!

Answer: No. We know by other means of knowledge that the posterior absence of sacrifice is not the producer of the same effect as is produced by the sacrifice.

Objection: Then let pleasing the gods be the instrument.

Answer: There is no reason to suppose so, and anyway there is no reason to suppose you please a god by taking a bath in the Ganges! It is simpler to take the instrument to be the identity of the performer of the act with the receiver of the result.

(ET59-63) 184-198. Objection: But there's no proof of that—and indeed counterexamples are at hand: the *śrāddha* performed by the son at Gaya benefits the father and the *jāteṣṭi* performed by the father gives merit to the son.

Tentative answer: The merits in each case accrue to the performer himself.

Objection: Then when the son who works to benefit his father dies his merit will be destroyed and his father will not benefit from his efforts. The rule is that merit is destroyed only by its result. If the (tentative) answer is correct the entire performance of *śrāddha*, etc. will become purposeless.

Another tentative answer: Then it must be that it is not whose merit it is that determines who has satisfaction, but rather who has satisfaction is determined by the agent's desire that he should.

Answer: Then the son's merit may as well be the cause of the father's pleasure.

Objection: But that merit, which is the cause of the father's pleasure, must be in the father, not the son.

Answer: No, for it was not produced by the father's action but by the son's. (This discussion continues for several more lines.)

(ET63-67) 199-213. Conclusive answer: The rule is this: An action produces its future result through the connecting link existing in its performer, unless there is some strong opposing cause. And there is no such cause here, e.g., there is a rule that the result (e.g., heaven) mentioned in an injunction to sacrifice is received by the performer of the sacrifice. That it is the father who goes to heaven as a result of his son's *śrāddha*, and the son who becomes pure by his father's *jāteṣṭi*, are made clear by the respective injunctions.

Objection: But the result goes indirectly to the performer, e.g., the son's sacrifice does not result in *anyone's śrāddha.* Only *his* father's, so that the son indirectly gets the result of his own action. So though generally an injunction causes the awareness that the result is gotten by the performer it is not always the case that it causes the awareness that it is gotten *directly* by the performer. Now being the son of a father who will gain heaven is thus not the direct result of the sacrifice, but there *is* an indirect relation between the son and heaven.

Answer: Then the result (the father going to heaven) can be related to anyone at all, if any old relation counts.

Objection: But other relations (than the one intended) are not made known by the Vedic injunction.

Answer: Neither is being this son's father who attains heaven conveyed by any Vedic injuction either. The rule must be that the result goes to that person who is indicated in the injunction as the one who should get the result. So when the son gives a pond desiring that his parents go to heaven as a result, his parents do get the result, heaven, since this is an act enjoined as a means to heaven.

(ET68-70) 214-221. Objection: The attainment of heaven is the result of obligatory acts, but not of optional acts such as the *śrāddha*. There is no reason to think it can be gotten by optional acts, and anyway, one is not able to perform all such acts. What is true is that by the last act (before death) or some act that maintains it heaven (e.g.) is produced.

Answer: No. *Any* act, whether obligatory or optional, if it is performed in a spirit of surrender to God obtains heaven. So the *jāteṣṭi* and the father's sacrifices will also get their result if performed in that spirit.

What does it mean to surrender in a spirit of surrendering to God? Can one surrender just *some* acts, or only optional acts, or only obligatory acts, or does it mean *all* acts? The first four options are wrong. The first makes it too easy to attain heaven, and the next three are impossible. So what has to be understood is that one gains heaven by surrendering *all* acts, and no one performance of a rite or act suffices to gain heaven.

Verbal Potency (II) (*śaktivāda*)

The summary is based on S.C. Vidyabhusana (B and RB: HIL).

(E49-51) The relation that exists between a word and its referent is a special relation called indication (*vṛtti*). It is on account of this special relation that we are, on hearing the word "pot", able to recollect the thing known as a pot. This special relation possessed by a word is generally called its potency (*śakti*). Nice distinctions are, however, often made in this matter. The special relation is described as being of two kinds, viz. (1) signification (*saṃketa*) and (2) implication (*lakṣaṇā*). Signification again is subdivided into (a) permanent and (b) occasional. The permanent signification which a word bears is called in a special sense its potency. This potentiality, which is the capacity of a word to refer to (i.e. produce recollection of) a particular thing, depends upon the will of God manifesting itself in the form "let such and such a thing be understood by such and such a word". For instance, the potentiality of the word "pot" consists in its producing the recollection of an earthen vessel. The occasional signification is called "technicality" (*paribhāṣā*). It depends upon the will of man manifesting itself in the form "such and such a thing is to be understood by such and such a word". A word is said to be "technical" if it produces recollection of a particular thing as desired by man. For instance, *nadī* is a technical word for nouns ending in *i* or *u*. The distinction between permanent and occasional significations is overlooked by those logicians who maintain that words derive their signification, or rather potentiality, not from the will of God but from the will of man. There is according to them as much potentiality in an ordinary word as in a technical one. The potentiality of a word is ascertained from the following sources:

(1) Grammar (*vyākaraṇa*), e.g., in the sentence "*caitraḥ pacati*" ("Caitra cooks") the potentiality of the crude word "*Caitra*", the nominative case-ending ḥ, the root *pac* and the verbal suffix *ti* is ascertained from grammar.

(2) Comparison (*upamāna*), e.g., in the sentence "a *gavaya* is like a cow" the potentiality of "*gavaya*" is ascertained through comparison.

(3) Dictionary (*koṣa*), e.g., the potentiality of the word *pika* to refer to the quality of blueness is ascertained from a dictionary.

(4) Reliable assertion (*āptavākya*), e.g., that the word *pika* signifies a black cuckoo is ascertained from the word of a competent scholar.

(5) Usage (*vyavahāra*), e.g., on hearing "bring a table", "take away a table", etc., and on seeing the table brought and taken away, one understands the potentiality of the word "table".

(6) Context (*vākyaśeṣa*), e.g., if in a sentence the meaning of the word *yava* (which may refer to a piece of corn of a certain seed) is not clear, we can ascertain its true meaning (say, as a piece of corn) by reference to the remaining utterances in which it is spoken of as having ears.

(7) Description (*vivṛti*), e.g., when we describe a belligerent nation as a warlike one, we can understand the potentiality of the word "belligerent".

(8) Association with well known words, e.g. the potentiality of the word *pika* to refer to a bird is easily understood when the word is associated with some well-known words such as "in this mango-tree the *pika* sings sweetly".

We have seen that each word possesses the potentiality of producing the recollection of a thing dependent upon the will of God or man. Now the question arises as to whether the potentiality refers to the genus of the thing or to the thing as an individual. If we suppose that the potentiality refers to an individual, we shall have to assume, say the Mīmāṃsakas, an infinite number of potentialities corresponding to the individuals to which they refer. If, on the other hand, we assume that the potentiality refers to a genus, we shall have to assume only one potentiality corresponding to the genus which will also include individuals without which it cannot stand.

Gaṅgeśa opposes the above view by saying that we could not recollect individuals unless the potentiality resided in them. On the supposition of the potentiality referring to an individual it is not, he continues, necessary to assume an infinite number of potentialities, as one and the same potentiality refers to all the individuals which are comprehended under one genus. Hence, he concludes that the potentiality really refers to the individuals coming under a genus and possessing a form.

Words possessed of potentiality may be specified as follows:

(1) The etymological (*yaugika*) is a word which is understood by the potentiality of its component parts alone, e.g., the word *dātā* (giver) refers to the agent of giving.

(2) The conventional (*rūḍha*) is a word which is understood by the potentiality of its entirety independently of that of its parts, e.g., the word *go* signifies a cow (and not the agent of going, which is the meaning of its part).

(3) The etymologo-conventional (*yogarūḍha*) is a word which is understood by the potentiality of the whole harmoniously with the potentiality of its parts, e.g., the word *paṅkaja* signifies a water-lily which is born in the mud.

(4) The etymological-conventional (*yaugikarūḍha*) is a word which is understood either by the power of its entirety or by that of its parts, e.g. the word *udbhid* signifies a germ, the sprouting of a seed or a sacrifice.

By implication (*lakṣaṇā*) a word refers to a thing which is related to another thing which is the signification of the word, but which does not signify the intention of the speaker, e.g., the word "Ganges" in the sentence "the cow-keeper dwells on the Ganges" does not signify the current which is referred to by the potentiality of the word but signifies the bank which bears to the current the relation of proximity. Similarly the word "crow" in the sentence "protect the curd from the crow" signifies by implication anything that injures the curd.

Section Twelve: Compounds (*samāsa*)
Summary by S.C.Vidyabhusana (B and RB: HIL).

(E727-818) In Sanskrit the compound word (*samāsa*) is of six kinds, viz.,

(1) an attributive compound (*bahuvrīhi*)

(2) a determinative compound (*tatpuruṣa*), including the negative determinative compound (*nañtatpuruṣa*)

(3) a descriptive compound (*karmadhāraya*)

(4) a numeric compound (*dvigu*, including the unified numeral compound, *samāhāra*)

(5) an aggregative compound (*dvandva*) comprising the mutually

aggregative compound (*itaretara*), the unified aggregative compound (*samāhāra*) and the residual aggregative compound (*ekaśeṣa*).

(6) an indeclinable compound (*avyayībhāva*).

In the attributive compound the first word possesses its fixed potentiality and the second word, which through its potentiality points out a thing, refers also by implication to another thing, e.g., *citragum ānaya* (lit. "bring the brindled cow man") signifies "bring the man having a brindled cow". The first word *citra* (brindled) refers through its potentiality to the quality of brindledness while the second word *go* ("cow") besides pointing out, through its potentiality, the thing called "cow", refers also by implication to its owner.

Grammarians maintain that, when two words are combined together to form an attributive compound, the combination possesses the potentiality of referring to a thing which is connected with but lies beyond the things signified by its component words, e.g., *citragu* ("brindled cow") refers to ownership over and above the quality of being brindled and the cow. Gaṅgeśa holds that in an attributive compound all potentialities lie in the words which are combined together to form the compound, and there is no potentiality in the combination itself.

In the determinative compound the second word possesses its fixed potentiality while in the first word there are both potentiality and implication, e.g., *rājapuruṣaḥ* ("a king officer", that is, an officer of the king) signifies an officer belonging to the king in which the word *rāja* refers to a king as well as to connection with him.

In the descriptive compound in which the compound words stand to each other in the relation of identity, there is no special rule for the possession of potentialities by them, e.g., *nīlotpalam* ("blue-lotus"). The same is the case with the numeral compound, e.g., *pañcaguvam* ("five cows").

In the aggregative compound there is no special rule for the assumption of potentiality of implication by the component words, e.g., *yamavaruṇau* ("Yama and Varuṇa").

In an indeclinable compound there are both potentiality and implication in the last word, e.g., *upakumbham* ("near the jar").

Section Thirteen: Verbal Suffixes (*ākhyātavāda*)
Summary by S.C. Vidyabhusana (B and RB: HIL).

(E819-846) A verbal suffix (*ākhyāta—ti, tas, anti*, etc.) used after a root refers to the effort favorable to what is signified by the root, e.g., *caitra pacati* ("Caitra cooks") signifies that Caitra is possessed of efforts favourable to cooking. If the agent is an inanimate thing the verbal suffix refers by implication to the operation favourable to what is signified by the root, e.g., *ratho gacchati* ("a chariot moves") signifies that the chariot is possessed of the operation favorable to moving.

Section Fourteen: Verbal Roots (*dhātu*)
Summary by S.C. Vidyabhusana (B and RB: HIL)

(E847-853) The root (*dhātu*) of a verb refers to the operation favorable to the effect of what is signified by the verb, e.g., the root *gam* ("to go") in the sentence, viz., *saḥ grāmaṃ gacchati* ("he goes to the village") refers to moving, which is favorable to his connection with the village, which is the effect of his going. In the case of an intransitive verb the root refers merely to the operation, e.g., *sa tiṣṭhati* ("he stays") in which *stha* signifies merely staying.

Section Fifteen: Prefixes (*upasarga*)
Summary by S.C. Vidyabhusana (B and RB: HIL)

(E854-859) The prefix (*upasarga*) by itself does not bear any meaning but points out the specialty of meaning borne by the root that follows, e.g. *vi* in *vijayate* ("completely conquers" signifies a completeness of conquest).

Section Sixteen: Validity of the four Instruments of Knowledge (*catuṣṭayaprāmāṇya*)
Summary by S.C. Vidyabhusana (B and RB: HIL)

(E860-866) Some say that a gesture (*ceṣṭā*) is a means of valid knowledge. But this is absurd, inasmuch as a gesture merely reminds us of words which produce knowledge. That a deaf person is sometimes prompted to activity by a gesture must be due to the fact that he infers the desire of the man who makes the gesture. So a gesture is included in either verbal testimony or inference. Similarly tradition (*aitihya*) and rumour (*janaśruti*) are not distinct from verbal testimony while presumption (*arthāpatti*) and nonperception (*anupalabdhi*) are comprised in inference.

2. VAṬEŚVARA

There are a number of writers who are obviously great figures in early Navyanyāya thought in the light of their frequent citation by writers whose works have survived. One of these is Vaṭeśvara Upādhāya, known as the "*Darpaṇakāra*" in both the fields of Nyāya and of *Dharmaśāstra*. He was a relative of a number of famous Naiyāyikas of subsequent generations. His son was named Pakṣadhara, but seems not have been the author of various *Viveka*s (see below, number 25). His grandsons Bhavanātha and Jīvanātha Miśra are to be found discussed below (11 and 12); Bhavanātha was the father of *Śaṃkara Miśra.* Through another grandson, Śivapati (number 14), he is related to Yajñapati, whom we shall meet below as the father of Narahari, who defended his father against Jayadeva Miśra's influential *Tattvacintāmaṇyāloka.* Thus the family of Vaṭeśvara is one of the earliest and most long-lived to carry the Navyanyāya banner from ancestor to descendant.

Dinesh Chandra Bhattacarya[2] has provided an extensive discussion of Vaṭeśvara's family history, tracing it back some 22 generations to around 600 A.D. The family was that of the Mandaras. Through an elaborate analysis Bhattacharya establishes clearly that Vaṭeśvara must have been born around, but not before, 1300. We have therefore estimated him to have flourished around 1340.

At least two works are referred to as having been written by Vaṭeśvara. One is a commentary, *Darpaṇa* on Udayana's *Nyāyanibandha.* This is referred to by Śaṃkara Miśra. The other is a *Darpaṇa* on Vallabha's *Nyāyalīlāvatī,* found cited in Pakṣadhara's *Viveka*s on *Kiraṇāvalī* and *Nyāyalīlāvatī.*

Vaṭeśvara should prove of great importance when a proper account of the history of the development of Navyanyāya gets composed, for, as Dinesh Chandra suggests, the well-known controversy between Yajñapati and Jayadeva may only be an echo of a long-lasting discussion which goes back to Vaṭeśvara's criticism of Gaṅgeśa, criticisms which Jayadeva and possibly others before him seem to have been disposed to respond to. We find references to Vaṭeśvara in the writings of Pragalbha and Mādhava Miśra as well as Śaṃkara Miśra and Jayadeva.

In the field of *smṛti* or *dharmaśāstra* Vaṭeśvara appears to have composed still another *Darpaṇa*; it has been cited by his great-great-grandson Narahari in the *Dvaitanirṇaya.* Vaṭeśvara's son was named Pakṣadhara Upādhyāya, who wrote a work titled *Tattvanirṇaya* on *smṛti* topics a ms. of which is extant in Darbhanga.

3. VARDHAMĀNA

According to Umesh Mishra, Vardhamāna was the eldest son of Gaṅgeśa[1]. As we have seen, he must have written prior to 1360, since a manuscript dating from at least that date if not earlier exists. We estimate his date here as 1345. He is not to be confused with other Vardhamānas: e.g., a grammarian, the author of *Gaṇaratnamahodadhi* (referred to in the *Sarvadarśanasaṃgraha*), or the Vivekakāra of Dharmaśāstra, who was taught by 21 Śaṃkara Miśra and 23 Vācaspati Miśra II.

Vardhamāna is responsible for commentaries on many of the standard works of the Nyāya-Vaiśeṣika system. A problem has been raised over whether he commented on his father's *Tattvacintāmaṇi*. The New Catalogus Catalogorum lists two manuscripts of such a commentary, but Dinesh Chandra Bhattacarya claims that he could not find one of them (in the Banaras Sanskrit University collection) and the other, listed as extant in the Northwest Provinces, has not been further identified. Dinesh Chandra gives a number of reasons to think that Vardhamāna did not compose such a commentary. For one thing, Vardhamāna himself does not refer to any such work, though he is fond of quoting from his own works at a variety of junctures. Secondly, when he does remark on his father's views he does so in such a way as to cast doubt on any more extensive explanation in another place. Finally, Dinesh Chandra argues, if Vardhamāna had composed such a commentary it surely would have been celebrated among subsequent scholars in Mithila and Bengal.

Among the works of Vardhamāna that are available, those in print at the present writing include *Prakāśa*s on *Nyāyakusumāñjali*, on *Nyāyalīlāvatī*, on *Nyāyapariśiṣṭa*, and on the *Kiraṇāvalī*. These are printed in complete editions. A portion of his commentary on *Pariśuddhi* (up to I.1.5) is in print as well. In addition to these, manuscripts of commentaries on the *Nyāyasūtra*s (*Anvīkṣānayatattvabodha*), on the *Ātmatattvaviveka*, and on Śrīharṣa's *Khaṇḍanakhaṇḍakhādya* apparently exist. Furthermore, he must have produced as well a commentary on the *Tarkabhāṣā*, a single manuscript of such a work is cited in New Catalogus Catalogorum. Steinkellner[3] has argued that the *Kiraṇāvalīprakāśa* is an older work than the *Nyāyakusumāñjaliprakāśa*.

Ernst Steinkellner has also analyzed Vardhamāna's commentaries on Udayana and Vallabha with regard to the definitions of pervasion and of *upādhi*. Apart from providing a positive evaluation of Vardhamāna as an expounder of his father's thought, Steinkellner offers the provocative assessment that "the sections on the ... *vyāpti*-definitions which we find in Gaṅgeśa's *siddhāntaḥ*" show "a changed attitude" on Vardhamāna's part which "has had a serious effect on the formation of his *siddhāntaḥ*. The definitions that are rooted in the *anaupādhikatvam* and *avyabhicāritvam* have been put into the *Pūrvapakṣaḥ*, and the definition of Prabhākaropādhyāya has taken the place of the *siddhāntalakṣaṇam* in Vardhamāna's later work".[4]

PRAKĀŚA on Udayana's KIRAṆĀVALĪ, DRAVYA section
Summary by V. Varadachari

"E" references are to the edition by S.C. Sarvabhauma (B2706; RB3997), Bibliotheca Indica 200, 1911-1912.

Introductory Section

(E1-3) While commenting on the benedictory stanza of the *Dravyakiraṇāvalī*, Vardhamāna offers an interesting remark. Udayana here uses a metaphor, likening the Supreme Being to the sun. At the rise of twilight the night vanishes. Knowledge (*vidyā*) is imagined to be twilight, and ignorance (*avidyā*) as night. The commentator remarks that twilight is not part of night. The particular time called "night" is when the sun's rays are removed from this island. The time remains in this island only for a short time. Hence the *Dharmaśāstras* mention night and twilight separately.

Vardhamāna explains *vidyā* as the direct cognition of the self. That itself is the twilight, as it illumines reality. *Avidyā* is erroneous cognition about the self. It is night as it is opposed to knowledge of reality or as it gives to passion.

(E6) In the third stanza of his Introduction Udayana justifies his undertaking the task of writing on Vaiśeṣika by commenting on the *Padārthadharmasaṃgraha*. It is stated that the work is intended to instill fear in those beings of the *tāmasa* kind. Vardhamāna remarks that the beings referred to here are the heterodox (*nāstika*) who have the *tamas guṇa* in preponderance because of their having been misled by wrong arguments. The works of earlier writers are full of mistaken reasoning adduced by Buddhists and others. It is to show that such works are not of help in cognizing reality that Udayana wrote this work. In this context, Vardhamāna reviews an interesting discussion on the propriety of the use of the verb "*vyātene.*" This word means "wrote" or "composed". Some scholars are said to have taken this in the sense of hope, that is, in the sense of "may write".[5] Vardhamāna notes that this *sūtra* applies to the past in a general way, not to that of aorist or perfect. He takes the word *vitene* as a particle (*nipāta*) having the form of a verb. Properly speaking, the use of the perfect tense is justified even when the agent is a witness of the action mentioned. Or it may be due to inadvertence through haste in writing the work. A straightforward explanation would be that this word was not the composition of Udayana.

(E9) Vardhamāna explains that the first stanza of *Padārthadharmasaṃgraha*, containing salutations to God and Kaṇāda, is intended to remove the more powerful obstacles standing in the way of successful completion of the work.

(E13) Obeisance (*namaskāra*) may be primarily mental, according to some scholars; the verbal and physical ones have only secondary significance. Others take obeisance to convey many meanings. Those who stick to tradition do not distinguish obeisance to God from that to the sage. Common to both is the character of obligatoriness.

Modern writers hold that the suffix in "*praṇamya*" refers to an action done before and that there is no harm in referring to obeisance to Kaṇāda, which can intervene between the act of bowing to God and the principal act of composing the work.

(E15-17) That the agent could be the same for many acts may be justified when some acts occur prior to the main act. That a particular act should have taken place before the occurrence of the main act need not be accepted as true in every case. There are two illustrations offered here. (1) He sleeps with his mouth open. (2) He opens his mouth after falling asleep.[6] Vardhamāna refers to the view of his father, who held that priority in time need not be meant here but only that one action follows another.

(E17-18) Udayana explains the preposition "*pra*" as conveying excellence in the form of devotion and faith. Vardhamāna notes that devotion and faith are lower (*apara*) universals of awareness (*jñāna*). Udayana asserts that "*pra*" makes this known. Vardhamāna observes that some scholars are of the opinion that prepositions denote the sense of the root. Udayana rejects this by using the word "*dyotyate*" which means "made known".

(E22) An undertaking begun with the offering of an invocation gets accomplished and makes good progress. Vardhamāna remarks that "progress" consists in the continuity of imparting instruction to the pupil by the teacher.

(E28–29) On the performance of the invocation Vardhamāna notes the opinion of his father Gaṅgeśa. Performance of an invocation is not necessitated by obstacles. It is obligatory to perform it, as its nonperformance entails the rise of the sin of omission (*pratyavāya*). A subsidiary act is to be taken up when a sacred rite is resolved to be performed. This means that when the rite is to be undertaken all the subsidiary acts which form part of it are to be performed. These acts contribute to the successful performance of the main act. They do not have any independent purpose to serve. If they are not done, there is the sin of omission. Similarly, when any work is undertaken, an invocation is required to be performed at the outset. If it is not performed, there is the sin of omission. It does not have any particular purpose to serve. The obstacles, if any, may be removed. Even if there were no obstacles the act is required to be performed. Hence it is said that obstacles do not form the ground for the performance of the invocation.

Vardhamāna refers to an alternate treatment which takes "invocation" to be a technical term. It is held to refer to an act which is invariably employed by the diligent. This practice on their part is like the rise of water in a river. This description shows that performance of invocation forms part of the practise of the disciplined.

So there is no justification in trying to find out the motive behind its performance and the results brought about by it. (However, the text of *Tattvacintāmaṇi* does not contain a reference to this view.) Vardhamāna continues to discuss the matter further. There is no Vedic injunction that one should perform an invocation, but it is possible to frame an injunction in the form that one shall bow to God or offer prayers to God. On the strength of this, the word "invocation" is used, as enjoined in the Vedas, to refer to this act performed with a view to having the obstacles destroyed.

(E35) Udayana explains the sense of word "*mahodaya*", which Praśastapāda uses, to refer to an attribute of Praśastapāda's work *Padārthadharmasaṃgraha*, viz., its giving rise to great knowledge. Vardhamāna says that some commentators take it to mean liberation. All roots which mean motion also mean knowing and so Udayana's taking the word "*udaya*" as knowledge is justified. Its greatness or excellence consists in this knowledge arising about reality.

(E36–37) Udayana describes reality (*tattva*) as a form which is not superimposed. Vardhamāna explains that this meaning of the word *tattva* is conventional, the etymological sense being ignored. The negative particle in *anāropita* ("not superimposed") conveys the sense that superimposition which is the basis of error is ruled out here. Hence correct knowledge has no room for superimpositio: There cannot be reality of a general kind. The classification is merely that in general a thing is either *tattva* (real) or *atattva* (unreal). The latter has the form of something else superimposed on it. Or, in the technical language of Navyanyāya, *x*'s reality is to be taken as *x*'s having a feature which exists in the same locus as a mutual absence whose counterpositive is any different feature.

(E40) Udayana explains that absence is not mentioned as a separate category, as it is to be proved through its counterpositive which must belong to a positive category. On this, Vardhamāna remarks, in the context of treating the categories which are useful for obtaining liberation, that absence also becomes a category (*tattva*). Categories are in general of two kinds, positive and negative. Classification of the categories through verbal expression is confined to the positive categories.

A different interpretation is also offered by Vardhamāna. The Nyāya system adopts a particular mode of treatment according to which an object is studied in relation to another with which it is related. The self is not primarily dealt with here as its study is to be undertaken on the basis of its difference from other objects. This is done through inference. Verbal treatment does not help at all in providing the opportunity for this inferential process. The system therefore shows the instrument of knowledge for the proper understanding of the nature of the self. In parallel fashion this suggests that absence is to be understood to be inferred from the treatment given to the positive categories. Vardhamāna adds further that the Nyāya system depends on the Vaiśeṣika system, with which it is related, for treatment of certain topics, e.g., the internal organ is said to be a sense-organ in Vaiśeṣika, and though that is not mentioned in Nyāya what is stated in the other system holds good here. On like grounds it should be admitted that absence, which is treated in *Nyāyasūtras* 2.2.7–12 and in *Vaiśeṣikasūtra* 9.1, is a category. Vardhamāna adds that this matter is treated by him in his commentary on the Nyāyaprathamādhyāya, first chapter of Udayana's *Pariśuddhi.*

Final Release

(E46) On liberation, Vardhamāna writes that the Naiyāyikas would admit liberation as the utter destruction of positive categories, since the rule is that the knowledge of reality destroys false cognition and itself gets destroyed in consequence.

(E56) Though there may be the prior absence of frustration, that cannot be the aim of life by itself. That aim must be the nonproduction of frustration, which is to be effected by acts of expiation through the destruction of sins.

(E77) Hindu tradition recommends bathing in holy waters, offering of great gifts, death at Kāśi (Banaras) and such other acts as contributing to the obtaining of liberation. Vardhamāna notes that none of these can lead to liberation without dependence on knowledge of reality. The passage "*tameva viditvā*" (*Śvetāśvatara Upaniṣad* 3.8) is cited in support of this contention. Actions also lead to liberation through knowledge of reality. The traditionalists among the Naiyāyikas held the view that knowledge and action are means quite independent of each other. Yet, knowledge and action stand in the relation of grain and barley: unless barley is recommended for use it cannot be taken to be meant by the word "grain". Similarly, action is said to be the means and that statement is to be interpreted as meaning that it is to serve as the means through knowledge.

(E79) Udayana refers to *Vaiśeṣikasūtras* I.1.2[7] and notes that the definition of *dharma* may not have liberation as its immediate end, since the purpose is served without it. Yet this word is necessary in order to show that *dharma* is mediately responsible for liberation.[8] *Vaiśeṣikasūtra* I.1.4 ("*tadvacanādāmnāyasya prāmāṇyam*") must be taken as proving that the Vedas are valid, since they are uttered by God. If it is held that the *sūtra* I.1.2 were to be taken to mean that one *dharma* leads to knowledge and another to liberation, then the definition will not apply to either or both of them. *Dharma* cannot lead to liberation except through giving rise to the knowledge of reality.

Darkness

(E105) Having described what darkness is like, Udayana continues to argue that the yogins who remain within caves in the mountains are not conscious of having apprehended darkness. If they are aware of it, they must have recollection of sunlight. Vardhamāna notes a possible wrong interpretation of this passage. Those who offer this interpretation have taken the awareness of darkness as error. The yogins are admitted to be free from error. How, then, can they be aware of darkness? Vardhamāna meets this objection on the ground that the awareness of darkness is nonerroneous, since *its* content concerns the absence of light. *This* awareness has dark color as its content. In the context, the text passage means that the yogins do not have such an awareness.

Universals

(E119) The word *sāmānya* means a universal, which Udayana explains as a property present in many things. It is a natural feature shared by things of the same kind, not imposed from without. Vardhamāna notes that this should be taken to include imposed properties (*upādhi*). Udayana also says that a universal is eternal and single (*eka*). *Vardhamāna* notes that the word "single" conveys here, according to some commentators, the nature of the universal and does not form part of the definition. Others say that the word "single" means that this is *one* definition. Another definition of a universal is that it is inherent in more than one thing and does not itself have an inherent cause.

(E120) Everything is said to be a cause for some effect or other except the size called "atomic" (*pārimaṇḍalya*). Udayana observes that "cause" here has reference to all effects other than awareness. Vardhamāna says this means *our* (normal) awareness, not that of the yogins which is not produced by objects. Others, it is said, hold that an object is necessary even for the perception of the yogin.

Earth

(E194) Udayana refers to the only-negative nature of definitions and notes that verbal reference is the purpose served by a definition. While illustrating the latter he adopts the only-negative type of inference. Vardhamāna refers to the view of his father. Mutual absence occurs between earth and what is not earth and is also known in the thirteen (five categories plus eight substances) objects such as water, etc. When the only-negative inference is adopted to prove the absence of something the *s* must be something which is not already known. Absence of earthness which pervades water, etc., is known. It is of the nature of absence of water, etc. Hence mutual absence in earth is not well-known and can be the *s*.

(E197) Udayana refers to the view of the Bhūṣaṇakāra, according to whom the words *lakṣaṇa*, *cihna* and *liṅga* are synonyms. Udayana rejects this on the ground that a positive inference has no scope when distinguishing one object from another or making verbal references to it. Vardhamāna remarks on this that the Bhūṣaṇakāra did not realize that *lakṣaṇa* is of the only-negative type.

Color Universals and Color Particulars

(E205–206) While commenting upon variegated-color (*citrarūpa*), Vardhamāna remarks that the word "*citra*" does not denote various colors but variegated color. It refers to the universal present in a single individual unit involving white and other colors. He is against countenancing any awareness of variegated-taste (*citrarasa*) on analogy with variegated-color. If different tastes mingle together and make the composite whole become tasteless, there is no harm. The organ of taste does not apprehend the substance. If the myrobalan is allowed to possess six tastes this could be justified. It can mean that the individual tastes are presented there. The taste of the myrobalan is not then variegated.

(E211) Touch also changes due to the effect of heat. Udayana remarks that if it were not so, then it would not be specifically attached to objects like number, size and others. Vardhamāna observes that the particular kind of contact in the case of snake-bite is the cause for the particular kind of pain produced. Contact with the jewel (which is supposed to control it) is the cause for lessening the pain. Similarly, contact with the cow is held to cause merit. In these cases, touch is not actually helpful. Sipping water (*ācamana*) is enjoined for certain contacts. If touch, effected through heat, is alone meant, then the rules prescribing these acts would become meaningless. Vardhamāna seems thus to suggest that touch effected through heat need not be assumed in all the cases cited by Udayana. He does not make clear whether there can be contact between two objects without the tactile sense operating there and, at least in the case of human beings, giving rise to peculiar sensations. Further, Vardhamāna cites the case of water, which when it is holy is enjoined for purification and when it belongs to the unholy is prohibited, and notes that the effect of heat should be admitted in water also if touch caused by heat is to be admitted to account for the rise of sensations, merit and sin.

Smoothness and roughness of touch are due to the effect of internal heat. They are not to be treated as the result of overly intense contact like cohesion.

Atomic Constituents

(E231) On the nature of the body, Udayana remarks that the bodies of human beings, animals and others may have some common features in the arrangements of the limbs, etc. Yet humanness, cowness, etc., are to be considered as universals. Vardhamāna notes that similarly a man-lion (*narasiṃha*), *hayagrīva* and other forms, made up of features of different natural kinds, should be taken to correspond to specific universals.

(E256) Udayana shows that a particular kind of arrangement of the parts of the body cannot be the reason for becoming viviparous, for cows, elephants, snakes, etc., are also viviparous, though not having the same arrangements of their parts as that of human beings. Vardhamāna tells us that being born as viviparous does not account for the particular arrangement of the limbs, but what does determine it is the particular kind of deeds done by the self.

Gods and others are said to have oviparous bodies. It is scripture (*āgama*, i.e., the Vedas) that is the instrument of knowledge here. When scripture declares that there could not be a body without a womb, the word "womb" (*yoni*) must be taken in the sense of cause, or else in the sense of human body itself.

(E2: 58) Trees and other things are sustained by selves (who experience through them) as they live, die, sleep, keep awake, have diseases and medical cures. On this passage of Udayana's, Vardhamāna remarks that these things are said to be sustained by the selves in the sense that they have contact with the internal organ which gives rise to experiences. Living is the contact with the internal organ which gives rise to a specific quality of the self.

Water

(E2: 69) On variegated taste, Vardhamāna observes that the component parts of a substance may have different tastes. The whole produced out of those parts cannot have any taste corresponding to that of the parts. Hence the Nyāya-Vaiśeṣika tradition holds that the myrobalan is tasteless.

(E2: 74) On viscidity, Udayana offers several remarks, as the quality is noticed in many liquids. In this context, the use of the word *taila* in the case of the viscidity of the oil extracted from mustard is discussed. Vardhamāna notes that Vācaspati Miśra took the etymological import of the word, i.e., being extracted from sesamum. When the word *taila* is used to refer to viscidity in sesamum, it must be taken as having etymological-conventional (*yogarūḍha*) import. The use of the word *taila* in mustard oil and others should be considered as metaphorical.

Time

(E2: 120) Time does not have any specific feature to mark it as having divisions. Yet origination, activity, fruition and destruction become the factors which mark it as varied. Udayana notes that origination refers to prior absence which is adjacent to the beginning of activity. Vardhamāna justifies the use of "adjacent" (*sannikṛṣṭa*) as a property of prior absence. Prior absence as such gives rise to linguistic references to the future. But it cannot be taken note of without apprehending the object which is its counterpositive. Hence, origination means the prior absence which is adjacent or proximate to the effect which is to come into being.

Place

(E2: 125) On the classification of the spatial directions, Vardhamāna says that left (*vāma*) is not a direction. It is, along with right (*dakṣiṇa*), a particular species present in (particular) parts of the body. Down (*adhas*) is the direction which depends on contact produced by a motion having weight as the noninherence cause. Above (*ūrdhva*) is the direction depending on contact produced through the motion in fire, which motion is generated by contact with a self having *adṛṣṭa*.

PRAKĀŚA on Udayana's KIRAṆĀVALĪ, GUṆA section
By Nani Lal Sen and V. Varadachari

"E" references are to the edition by Badrinath Sastri (B3532; RB5561), Princess of Wales Saraswati Bhavana Texts 45, 1933–1936. Sections are numbered following summary of *Padārthadharmasaṃgraha*, Vol. II. This part of the *Prakāśa* is only available up to the section on *buddhi*.

Introductory Section

(E1–2) While interpreting the invocation, the universe (i.e., "the world-all" *viśva*) is said to be a prison, the body, the seat of enjoyment. This body is to be treated as a prison, so that man shall leave off his attachment to the body.

(E2) The appositeness of discussing qualities after substances is explained first as depending on causality—i.e., that substances cause qualities—or as the appropriate time (*avasara*)—since the greatest obstacle to a discussion of quality, viz., an explanation of substance, has been removed in what has preceded.

46. (E2–4) Objection: Praśastapāda says (in introducing the discussion of qualities) "of the qualities, viz., color, etc...." But this is redundant, since the context makes it clear which sense of "quality" is intended.

Udayana: "Quality" means "subordinate" and "color, etc." specifies which subordinates.

Objection: But "subordinate" and "color, etc." have different meanings; so the doubt is not resolved. And if the context is appealed to, then the redundance remains. While if "etc." (in "color, etc.") is restrictive, the expression is likewise redundant.

Vardhamāna: The use of the word "qualities" in "of the qualities, viz., color, etc." shows the causal appositeness referred to above, since a quality is subordinate to a substance. (There is a technical grammatical discussion which we do not reproduce here.)

(E5) Qualityness is not a proper universal, because it is not perceived to belong to several things, unlike cowness.

(E8) The definition Praśastapāda gives of "quality" includes the specification "being other than a motion". Udayana notes that this encourages further such specifications "other than this", "other than that". What is the specific process by which a quality is to be recognized?

Vardhamāna: Just as a particular kind of gem is identified by reference to its specific color, so the presence of qualityness is identified perceptually by reference to its being an instance of a universal and which is not a locus of motion and is not a motion.

(E10–13) In connection with Udayana's rejection of the Bhūṣaṇakāra's attempt to make motions a kind of quality, Vardhamāna explains the general notions underlying Udayana's reasons. That both are caused by substances cannot be a sufficient reason for saying they have the same universal property, for qualities are neither the inherence nor the noninherence cause of contact and disjunction, while motions are.

(E15) Udayana argues that if substanceness were assumed to inhere in colors, etc., then to suppose that qualityness also inheres in them will produce crossconnection. Vardhamāna explains that though there is no crossconnection if qualityness is pervaded by substanceness, still if the noneternal qualities were to occur in all qualities everywhere then liberation would not occur. Then if one were to say that no qualities occur in any qualities, qualityness occurs just where substanceness does and there will be crossconnection. If on the contrary qualities be supposed to be eternal they will be universals, not qualities.

(E15) Qualities are immobile (*niṣkriya*).

Objection: So are destroyed substances immobile.

Answer: Immobility is possession of the absence of the limitor of inherence-causality.

(E16) If qualities were to have qualities, the color of a whole would inhere in the color of the parts, and the whole would then be colorless, says Udayana. Vardhamāna explains that the contingency in question is this: a jar and color will both be inherence causes of color, and if (in a given case) it is color that is the inherence cause, the jar will be colorless.

48. (E18) Udayana says that awareness, etc., are opposed to materiality. Vardhamāna explains that being opposed to materiality is to have a universal that occurs in what is opposed to materiality and is pervaded by qualityness.

49. (E19) Udayana: Number, etc., are pervadable by pervaders of any substance.

Vardhamāna: What he means is that these entities have a universal that is the limiter of the pervaderness whose adjunct (*pratiyogin*) is pervadedness-by-substanceness, which universal is also pervaded by qualityness. Or alternatively, these entities have a universal which, being different from traceness, occurs in the qualities of material things as well as all-pervading things and is pervaded by qualityness.

50. (E19) The word "two" means the locus of duality and so might be also a locus of color, etc. So its referent—a pair—must be explained as having a qualityness which is not the counterpositive of absolute absence and pervades the mutual absence of its locus. Or, alternatively, it is having a qualityness that is not pervaded by unity.

51. (E20) Udayana: All qualities except for numbers other than one and the separateness of a single thing (*ekapṛthaktva*) occur in one substance only.

Vardhamāna: But since even duality, etc., may occur in the locus of unity, and since also mere nonoccurrence constitutes a case of not occurring in many, the definition of "occurring in one substance only" must be specified as follows: it is being the locus of heterolocativity (*vaiyādhikaraṇya*) described (*nirūpita*) by the *dharmin* pervaded by the mutual absence of the locus of the quality. Or, it is being the counterpositive of the absolute absence that pervades mutual absence. Or, it is having a qualityness pervaded by the absolute absence of the mutual absence of the locus of that quality.

52. (E20–21) The "specific" (*vaiśeṣika*) qualities are those that

have specifying (*avāntara*) universals differentiating their loci, says Udayana.

Vardhamāna: This will overextend to include particular contacts (and contacts are not to be counted as specific qualities). So, being a specific quality should be explained as what is pervaded by qualityness and is nonoccurent in any contact other than those that occur in what occurs in earth or water. Then it won't apply to (e.g.) the largest dimension, which is not to be counted as a specific quality. Or, being a specific quality may be defined as being a quality other than weight or liquidity due to cooking, while not being the locus of a universal that occurs in anything occurring in the internal organ other than traces. But being a specific quality should not be defined as a quality having a universal property that promotes difference from what are other than what are limited by the *vibhaktopādhi*s pervaded by substanceness. For, if these *vibhaktopādhi*s are merely pervaded by substanceness, then the definition will overextend to include dense contact (*nibiḍasaṃyoga*), while if the *upādhi*s be of equal pervasion, the definition will exclude satisfaction, etc.

56. (E22) "... perceptible by the internal organ only...." But then an *adṛṣṭa* will be included, and God's awareness excluded. Therefore "perceptible by the internal organ only" means either having a universal property that is pervaded by qualityness and occurs in the specific qualities of the self other than *adṛṣṭa* and traces, or else having a universal property pervaded by qualityness that is not the content of an immediate awareness produced by a propositional awareness produced by the external organs or by yogic merit.

58. (E23) Vardhamāna explains why fluidity, but not (say) dimension are included in the list of qualities discussed here.

59. (E23) An objection which charges that the greatest dimension should be included in this list despite that being objectionable to the Vaiśeṣika is met by pointing out that the greatest dimension is acceptable to the Vaiśeṣika as a specific quality.

63. (E24) "Dependent on our judgments" (in Praśastapāda) means "caused by an enumerative cognition"; otherwise satisfaction, etc., will have to be included in the scope of qualities dependent on our judgements. Being caused by an enumerative cognition means having a universal pervaded by qualityness while not occurring in eternal substances or in any karmic products, though occurring in the qualities of the internal organ.

64. (324) Qualities "which produce their likes" should be understood not to include not-hot touch (*anuṣṇasparśa*), say Udayana and Vardhamāna. The definition of such a quality is that it has a universal pervaded by qualityness which occurs only in what occurs singly in a noninherence cause while occurring in an inherence cause

devoid of any universal pervaded by qualityness that occurs in such a quality.

65. (E26) Praśastapāda says here that satisfaction, frustration, desire, hatred and effort produce their unlikes. Vardhamāna defines the class of qualities that produce their unlikes as those which possess a universal pervaded by qualityness, which only occurs in specific qualities of the self other than awareness, and doesn't occur in anything beyond sensation (*atīndriya*).

66. (E27) "Productive of qualities both like and unlike themselves" means to have a universal pervaded by qualityness that occurs in things that cause things both like and unlike themselves except for nonwarm touch and for God's specific qualities other than His awareness.

Udayana: Awareness, satisfaction, frustration, desire, aversion, traces and sounds produce only things that inhere in the loci of those qualities.

Objection: If this is construed to apply distributively, it fails to extend to individuals that are not causative. And if taken collectively, it overextends to include impetus and elasticity, since those two produce motions in their loci. There is also underextension in failing to apply to God's awareness, which causes our awareness, as well as to language (*śabda*) that causes heterolocative awareness. Vardhamāna provides two ways of defining the class in question that avoid the difficulties. (1) The property in question is possession of a universal pervaded by qualityness and which occurs in what produces a specific quality other than awareness, or (2) the property in question is being a specific quality of an all-pervading (substance) and possessing a universal pervaded by perceptible qualityness (belonging to a quality) other than effort.

68. (E27–28) Udayana: The first five (viz., color, taste, smell, touch and size) produce results in different loci from themselves; those five together with viscidity cause results of the same kinds as themselves in different loci from themselves; and those six together with effort cause results elsewhere that are located in a single substance. Vardhamāna explains this.

70. (E28-29) Here Vardhamāna explains a property common to weight, fluidity, impetus, effort, merit, demerit and a special sort of contact—they possess a universal that occurs in the specific cause of motion other than contactness, which universal is other than traceness and is pervaded by qualityness. Impulsion (*nodana*) has a property that is pervaded by contactness and does not occur in the noninherence cause of sound.

75.(E30) Vardhamāna explains "partial existence" of contact, etc., as their having the same locus with their absolute absence.

Udayana: The partial occurrence of merit, demerit and traces is inferred from their being specific qualities of pervading effects. Vardhamāna dismisses "effects" (*kārya*) as useless, and finds that the inference is vitiated by the obstruction *occurrence in effect alone* (*kāryamātravṛttitva*).

77.(E31) Udayana:The qualities listed in the text are destroyed upon the destruction of their loci.

Vardhamāna: To avoid overextension to the disintegrating contact, and underextension from color, etc., of eternal things, this class of qualities should be understood as demarcated by possession of a universal pervaded by qualityness that occurs only in what is not the counterpositive of posterior absence occurring at the same time as its locus.

78.(E32-33) *Being produced by cooking* (*pākajatva*) is to be defined as possessing a universal pervaded by qualityness that occurs in qualities that occur in one substance only and which have conjunction with fire as their noninherence cause. This avoids overextension to contact with fire, and underextension from color of disintegrating earth.

The specific qualities of all-pervading things that are not destructible by specific qualities are as a rule destructible by contradictory qualities emerging at the moment just following their origination. Otherwise awareness, etc., generated through previous traces will die out at the next moment and will be imperceptible.

Being destructible through destruction of one's instrumental cause is defined as being destructible by destruction of an instrumental cause other than contact, while lacking any universal that occurs only in what occurs in material substances and which universal is pervaded by qualityness.

Udayana: Color, taste, etc., in atoms other than earthy ones are eternal and uncaused.

Vardhamāna: Since elasticity, etc., in earth atoms are eternal the nonearthy-atom-qualities (*apārthiva*) must include the list of qualities up to viscidity.

79. (E34) The names (*saṃjñā*) of objects are of four kinds. (1) Some names involve the universal property under which the object falls as the occasion for their use—e.g., "cow". (2) Some are implicatory (*upalakṣaṇataḥ*)—e.g., "*ākāśa*", which is implied by its being the locus of sound. (3) Some are conditioned (*aupādhikī*)—e.g., "cook" (*pācaka*), a name which is applied to a man in virtue of his having the fitness for volition favorable to cooking. (4) Some names are technical (*pāribhāṣikī*),—e.g., "Caitra"—through which a particular individual becomes the content of awareness through convention (*saṃketa*).

80. (E37) Udayana: Color is that quality which is only visually perceptible.

Vardhamāna: To avoid failure to extend to unmanifested color, being only visually perceptible must be explicated as having a universal property pervaded by qualityness and being visually perceptible only.

Praśastapāda: Color occurs in earth, water and fire only.

Vardhamāna: In order to avoid overextension to touch and fluidity, this property of being occurrent in earth, water and fire only must be explicated as being a universal property pervaded by qualityness that is nonoccurrent in what occurs in air but does occur in the specific qualities of earth, water and fire.

Praśastapāda: Color produces experiences of substances, etc.

Vardhamāna: In order to avoid failure to extend to unmanifest color we must understand the property in question to be a universal pervaded by qualityness and occurring in that specific quality which is the cause of construction-free visual perception.

Since one of the colors is taken to be "variegated color" Vardhamāna explains variegatedness as pervading the property of being produced by cooking.

The relation between substance and color is identity-in-difference (*bhedābheda*). For difference (viz., mutual-absence-ness) is occurrence in what is nonlocuspervading, because it is a property immediately pervaded by absenceness which occurs in absolute absence, like absolute-absence-ness. And this must be accepted, since otherwise we could not have the awareness of collocation as in "the cloth is blue". But of course complete identity-in-difference is not acceptable.

81. (E42-44) Being a taste is defined as a universal which is pervaded by qualityness and is perceived gustatorily, i.e., by no external organ other than the gustatory organ.

Since water is generally taken to be the instrumental cause of nourishment, as taste is grasped by the gustatory organ only in those substances that are soaked in external water, Vardhamāna provides an inference which proves that taste, not water, is the instrumental cause of nourishment, just as light is the instrumental cause of visual experience.

Variegated taste is not accepted. The taste called "*kṣāra*" is not an independent taste but gets included under "salty".

82. (E44) Nonfragrant (*asurabhi*) smell is shown to be an independent kind of smell adopting the *paryudāsa* sense of negation. It is not just the absence of fragrance.

83. (E47) Hot touch is an ordinary cause for cooking (*pāka*) in

general. For specific kinds of heat the causes are manifest color and manifest taste, issuing from fire.

85. (E58-64) Duality and the separateness of two things (*dvipṛthaktva*) do not share the same aggregate of causes, Vardhamāna points out, since the latter requires as an additional cause the cognition of the limit (*avadhijñāna*).

If the number one (*ekatva*) were a universal, argues Vardhamāna, then we should judge "this two is one" just as we do "this two exists".

Vardhamāna offers the following inference for duality: Duality is the result of enumerative cognition, because while being an effect it is necessarily cognized by one cognizer, like satisfaction.

If duality, etc., were a universal, argues Vardhamāna, then there would be no more contradiction in judging "this two is a triad" than there is in "this two is a substance". Again, if duality, etc., were a universal occurring in things insofar as they exist then it would be the same as existence (*sattā*) and so no more a universal than *ghaṭatva* and *kalaśatva* (both meaning potness, and so they can't both be universals).

Praśastapāda says that numbers begin with two and end with *parārdha* (a very large number). Vardhamāna remarks that some explain "*ādi*"—in "*dvitvādi*" as "numbers other than unity", and "*anta*" in "*parārdhānta*" as "absence of any number pervading it". But he says that his tradition "*sampradāya*" explains "*ādi*" as meaning "first," i.e., "beginning with", that firsthood of duality implying that it is pervaded by a number inhering in its loci which is occurrent in more than one. And "*anta*" means "pervasion of all collocative numbers".

Udayana: If duality, etc., are caused by the progressive qualities of their causes, then duality, threeness, etc., will be indistinguishable.

Vardhamāna: Duality occurs where there is prior absence of duality, and threeness occurs only where there is prior absence of threeness, which explains their difference.

Udayana, pursuing further the above argument, says that duality and the separateness of two will fail to have separate manifestors (*vyañjaka*). Vardhamāna attacks the problem from the opposite side: If, as you say, duality etc., are caused by enumerative cognition, then there will be no separate manifestors. But now if you say that the separateness of two is manifested by the cognition of one (*ekabuddhi*), which manifests duality with the help of a cognition of the limit (*avadhijñāna*), then it is all right if duality, etc., be assumed to be manifested by enumerative cognition (which is our position).

(E72-73) While interpreting Udayana's treatment of the difference between a qualifier (*viśeṣaṇa*) and an implicator (*upalakṣaṇa*),

Vardhamāna explains the difference in several ways. (1) A qualifier is that which occurs in the locus of the property which is the limiter of the qualificandness and the awareness of which is related to things other than that locus. Those other things become the content of awareness only as qualified by that qualifier. What is not like that is an implicator. (2) That is a qualifier which distinguishes the object and closely follows it, being related to it, while that which distinguishes the object without closely following it is an implicator. (3) That is a qualifier which distinguishes the object while determining the qualificand which demarcates that object. An implicator does not do so. (A qualifier is that which has for its denotation the property determining the object at a time when there arises the awareness that the object is distinct from others. A qualifier is then the content of an awareness which gives rise to the awareness that the object is qualified by properties. That which distinguishes the object but is other than this is an implicator.

Vardhamāna then offers some remarks. In the case of the judgement "the house of Devadatta with the crow perching on its top shall be approached", "if the crow is on the house at the time when the judgment arises then the crow is a qualifier". If the crow is not there it is an implicator. Hence the expression used is "the penance-doer having matted hair" (*jaṭāvāṃstāpasaḥ*) when he has matted hair and it is "the penance-doer (marked) by matted hair" (*jaṭābhistāpasaḥ*) when he does not have it. So the word "*jaṭabhiḥ*" may be either qualifier or implicator depending on temporal difference. Otherwise, the use of the instrumental case is not justified. Hence, one and the same thing becomes either a qualifier or an implicator at the time of the arising of the judgment that it distinguishes the object by its presence or absence respectively.

86. (E89) Some scholars hold that length (*dīrghatva*) and largeness (*mahattva*) are identical. But if they were so there would not arise judgments of the form "this is large", "this is long", bring something smaller but "longer", etc. Hence the two must be different from each other. Circularity (*vartulatva*) is a kind of largeness and cannot be an independent size.

96. (E140-141) Doubt is defined as an awareness which arises with reference to an object having a single specific feature but presenting several chief qualifiers which are contradictory to one another. Indefinite awareness (*anadhyavasāya*) is awareness with reference to an object having a single specific feature but without presenting several chief qualifiers.

Another set of definitions is then offered. Doubt arises when there is the description of an object having several undifferentiated chief qualifiers and so the object is presented as involving contradiction.

Indefinite awareness is then an awareness having a general presentation of various contradictory alternatives. Some scholars hold that indefinite awareness does not have the presentation, in a specific manner, of various alternatives.

99. (E153) The Bhāṭṭa Mīmāṃsakas hold that enumerative cognition manifests duality, etc. The Vaiśeṣikas take it as producing duality, etc.

(E154) Qualifierness (*viśeṣaṇatā*) has reference to the auditory sense-organ and becomes the cause for the apprehension of the absence of sound. With reference to what is in contact with the sense-organ it becomes the cause of apprehension of any absence.

101. (E159) The *pakṣa* (in an inference) is defined as the property-possessor (*dharmin*) possessing absence of an instrument of knowledge which can prove together with absence of the desire to prove. Others, however, take it as the locus of contentness (*viṣayatā*) related to an inferential conclusion whose chief qualifier limits the pervaderness.

115. (E160) While dealing with the fallacies of the *hetu*, Udayana first points out that once we have established which term is the *h* we can go on to find out whether there are any fallacies in it, but in order to discover fallacies in it we must first know whether it is established (*siddha*) or not. Thus Praśastapāda mentions the *asiddha* or "nonestablished" fallacy first among the fallacies. Vardhamāna observes that the fallacy in the *h* is direct in the case of *asiddha*. This directness lies in the fallacy taking the shape of the absence of the *h*'s being cause of an inferential conclusion. The other fallacies like *viruddha*, have to depend upon *asiddha* and then obstruct the rise of the inferential conclusion. In the Nyāya systen the *savyabhicāra* fallacy is mentioned at the beginning of the list of fallacies (cf. *Nyāyasūtra* I.2.4), while in Vaiśeṣika *asiddha* is mentioned at the outset for the above reason.

(E161-162) In Praśastapāda's section 115 (cf. Vol. II, pp. 296-297) the list of fallacies is provided. This passage is explained by Praśastapāda, citing the *sūtra* of Kaṇāda "*aprasiddho' napadeśo' san saṃdigdhaścānapadeśaḥ*". Udayana notes that the particle *ca* and the word *anapadeśa*, which is repeated, indicate that there are two more fallacies called *kālātyayāpadiṣṭa* and *prakaraṇasama*. Vardhamāna agrees, and in support remarks that Kaṇāda (Kāśyapa) held that the *h* must be well-known in what closely follows it (*prasiddhaṃca tadanvite*). The word *prasiddha* must be taken as meaning established (*siddha*) in an exceptional way (*prakarṣeṇa*). Vardhamāna remarks that according to some, this exceptional way of excellence consists in the *h* not having a counter-*h* (*asatpratipakṣitātva*) and not getting sublated (*abādhitatva*).

(E163) The word *bhūyodarśana* should not be analyzed to mean many observations (*bhūyāṃsi darśanāni*), as this would apply to stream-like cognition (*dhārāvāhikajñāna*). It should not be taken to mean observation in more places (*bhūyassu sthāneṣu darśanam*), as this would not apply to color and taste existing in the same locus preventing inference. Nor can it be taken as the observation of many things (*bhūyasāṃ darśanam*), as this does not apply to an inference involving cowness and substanceness, since only one thing is observed there. And even though many instances are observed of earthness and the property of things capable of being scratched by iron, still they deviate and thus there is no pervasion to be grasped there. Thus we must conclude that pervasion must be grasped by a single observation.

(E165) Pervasion is to be grasped by the awareness that there is no obstruction, not by making more observations. Udayana defines "obstruction" keeping in mind the possibility of equipervasion (*samavyāpti*). When there is unequal pervasion, the knowledge that the *h* and *s* have invariability supported by absence of deviation (*vyabhicāra*) helps in the apprehension of pervasion. Awareness of deviation, whether certain or doubting, arises in certain cases through doubt as to the presence of an obstruction. In other cases it arises through the observation of a general property aided by the failure to observe the specific feature. Absence of obstruction is made known in some cases through an argument involving *tarka*, and in others it is self-established.

(E166) Some scholars hold that certain cases of pervasion are already well-established from beginningless time and known to all people. Causal relations and contradiction come under this head. The newborn baby sucking the breast of his mother, and desisting from evil, respectively illustrate this view.

(E166-170) Regarding the idea of the "third application of the *h*" (*tṛtīyaliṅgaparāmarśa*) the views of some scholars are offered. One view is that recollection of pervasion is the occasion (*karaṇa*) of inference and that this "third application" is the operation (*vyāpāra*). Others say that since the occasion must involve inseparable relation with *s* the "third application" must be the occasion even in the absence of any operation. Vardhamāna observes that, really speaking, pervasion is that in which *h* has its form determined by its relatedness to *s*. He says he has dealt with this in his *Anvīkṣātattvabodha*.

PRAKĀŚA on Vallabha's NYĀYALĪLĀVATĪ
Summary by V. Varadachari

"E" references are to the edition (B2928; RB 4495) by Harihara Sastri and Dundhiraja Sastri (Chowkhamba Sanskrit Series 64, 1927-34). The numbering of sections follows the summary of *Nyāyalīlāvatī* in Vol. II of this Encyclopedia. .

12. (E141-143) Some scholars argue that variegated-taste must be admitted as a distinct kind of taste, since the myrobalan tree (*harītakī*) has such a taste and its parts have distinct tastes. Vardhamāna rejects this argument. Taste is a locus-pervading quality and so occurs in the entire locus in which it inheres. So the parts of the myrobalan cannot have different tastes. The rule is: the quality of a part produces that quality in the whole of which it is the part. Since we perceive visually a whole which is of variegated-color we must assume that its parts have that color too. But we do not perceive the whole myrobalan with our taste organ, and so the parallel inference is inappropriate.

It might be suggested that the taste of the myrobalan is the result of being "produced by heat" (*pākaja*). But change of quality due to heat is only found in atoms. Now if the atoms constituting the myrobalan have different tastes because of heat the rule mentioned above, that the quality of the whole is the same as the quality of its parts, will be violated. So if the parts do have various tastes they should produce a whole with no taste at all.

17. (E262) In connection with the proof of the existence of God Vardhamāna cites *Bhagavadgītā* 15.17, and refers to that text as "scripture" (*āgama*).

27. (E387) The difference between mutual absence (*anyonyābhāva*) and absolute absence (*atyantābhāva*) is this: when a negative judgment is produced through superimposing the counterpositive of an absence, that absence is an absolute absence. But when the negative judgment is produced through superimposing the limitor of the counterpositive, then the absence is a mutual absence. Vardhamāna says he has explained this in the second chapter of his *Nyāyanibandhaprakāśa.*

37. (E488) Recognition (*pratyabhijñā*) is not produced by traces alone; rather, it is produced by the *thatness* (of the object presented) together with the causal collocation (*sāmagrī*) of causal conditions which produce memory.

43. (E543) Concurrence (*sambhava*) is split up into two kinds. An illustration of the first kind is this: that being a Brahmin includes exhibiting understanding and good conduct. An illustration of the second kind is that if there are a thousand present there are a hundred

present. The former is invalid, since it is not always the case, while the latter is a matter of invariable concomitance and so a matter of inference. Thus concurrence is not an additional instrument of knowledge.

5. (E564-565) According to some, one need not suppose a property *absenceness* (*abhāvatva*) present in all absences. Generic absence can be explained with reference to specific absences: e.g., one can define absence as that which has mutual absence with (i.e., difference from) the six positive categories (*bhāva*), or as that which is absolutely absent in the six positive categories. We may be supposed to know the six positive categories on the basis of direct awareness (*anubhava*). Then the four "*kinds*" of generic absence should be understood as four distinct classes deriving from their distinct illustrations. However, the Nyāya tradition is different from this. According to it, *absenceness* possesses a feature which is (generically) opposed to the presentation of existence (*sattā*).

(E573-574) Vardhamāna refers to Gaṅgeśa's view on relational absence (*saṃsargābhāva*). Relational absence is a negation with respect to the superimposition of a relation on the counterpositive and locus, whereas in a mutual absence it is identity (*tādātmya*) which is superimposed.

46. (E588) After explaining how the Advaitin's position on the concept of liberation is criticized by Vallabha, Vardhamāna adds that Brahman, which is intrinsically self-luminous and bliss, is eternal, and so there will be the unwanted result (*prasaṅga*) that there is no difference between the released self and and the bound self. This being the case no human effort will be expended to reach liberation, and it will cease to be a goal of man.

(E588) On the Nyāya view liberation is the destruction of many frustrations at the same time, a destruction occurring in one self and not in others.

48. (E606) *Bādha* and *satpratipakṣa* are included by Vallabha within the fallacy of *asiddha*. In the *bādha* fallacy something *x* is considered to be the *p* which actually lacks the *s*; even though the *h* occurs in *x*, since it lacks the *s* the *s* is "unestablished" (*asiddha*). In the *satpratipakṣa* fallacy even though the *h* is present in both *h* and *s* there is no awareness of that; thus it is likewise a variety of *asiddha*.

61. (E633-637) Weight (*gurutva*) is inferred, but it is sometimes perceptible by the tactile sense with the assistance of *adṛṣṭa*. Does that mean that imperceptible (*atīndriya*) things—such as atoms—must lack weight? No. Atoms are perceptible through extraordinary perception (*yogajapratyakṣa*), and likewise the tactile sense

may be assisted by *adṛṣṭa* to grasp their weight. Some things—e.g., grass—have unmanifest weight.

65. (E717-718) The Prābhākaras say that when an unbaked pot gets baked both the black and red colors (or its constituents) are cognized. Now since one of these colors is eternal, what is produced by baking and destroyed (when the pot is broken up into bits) is a relation between the colors, and it is *this* relation which is inherence.

The view of the Prābhākaras is wrong. What we experience is that the black color is destroyed and the red color arises, and we infer that the inherence (of black color in the pot) is destroyed and that the inherence (of red color in the pot) arises, even though the constituents of the pot are beyond the senses (viz., atoms). Otherwise smells, etc., cognized in a whole will be eternal despite the production or destruction of their inherence there.

66. (E744-745) Objection: The "only-negative" (*kevalavyatirekin*) is not a variety of valid inference, since *pakṣadharmatā* (i.e., presence of the *h* in the *p*) is only possible when there is positive concomitance of *s* with *h* in the *sp*.

Vardhamāna: No. There are general factors which produce an inferential result as well as specific factors producing a specific inferential result. Knowledge of pervasion is required as a general factor for inference. Now even though knowledge of pervasion is present no inference may result when other factors which might produce an inference are absent. Since positive pervasion is grasped by means of ascertaining unobstructed negative concomitance of *s* and *h*, *pakṣadharmatā* merely from such concomitance should be allowed.

67. (E760) The text defines awareness (*buddhi*) as illumination (*prakāśa*) of an object. Vardhamāna notes that this definition as it stands is incorrect because the words *prakāśa* and *buddhi* seem to be synonyms. Hence he treats *buddhi* as meaning the universal *buddhitva*. Then there is no strength in the arguments advanced by some scholars to the effect that *prakāśa* cannot mean awareness in general for then awareness could rise even without reference to objects. Nor can this word mean impressions, as then it will not apply to nonpropositional perception.

70. (E836) Objection: It is a mistake to analyze the destruction of substance as involving destruction of both inherence and noninherence causes. The proper analysis is that the cause of the destruction of a substance is by the destruction of its noninherence cause.

Answer: No, since the destruction of a substance necessarily involves destruction of its inherence cause, and further, since the destruction of a thing's color is found to be produced through the destruction of its locus.

NYĀYANIBANDHAPRAKĀŚA on Udayana's (NYĀYAVĀRTTIKATĀTPARYAṬĪKĀ) PARIŚUDDHI

We are unable to find anyone to summarize either Udayana's *Pariśuddhi* or Vardhamāna's commentary on it. The following remarks in lieu of a summary are by Umesh Mishra, from his History of Indian Philosophy, Vol. II, pp. 277-281, stylistically emended to fit Encyclopedia style. "E" references are to the Bibliotheca Indica edition up to I.1.5 (B223; RB783) by V.P. Dvivedin, 1887. Added information about the content of Udayana's *Pariśuddhi* can be gained by studying the footnotes Ganganatha Jha provides in the notes to his translation of Gautama's *Nyāyasūtra* with Vātsyāyana's *Bhāṣya* and Uddyotakara's *Vārttika* (B242; RB799), Indian Thought 4, 1912-11, 1919. This is also available in a reprinted edition in four volumes from Motilal Banarsidass, Delhi.

Invocation. Following the old tradition of Mithila, Vardhamāna as a seeker after the truth was a devotee of Śiva. So, he bows down to Śiva in the very beginning of his work....He says:

> "I bow down to that Śiva whom devotees perceive (realize) with singleminded and uninterrupted devotion as one who annihilates the delusion of mind towards the world and whose lotus-like feet are bowed down to by a host of gods."

About the aim of his writing this commentary Vardhamāna says:

> "Surrounded by the ignorance (darkness) caused by the forcible wrong reasonings of the rival *darśanas* let good people see the oath of the truth through the growing light, that is, through the *Prakāśa* written by Vardhamāna."

This shows that the influence of the Buddhists was obvious among the scholars of Nyāya even during the days of Gaṅgeśa and Vardhamāna.

(E2) According to Sāṃkhya bondage and release both belong to consciousness (*puruṣa*) and not to *prakṛti*. In support of this Vardhamāna quotes a *kārikā* from the *Sāṃkhyakārikā*s.

(E5) There may be direct connection with the self (*ātman*), but it cannot be called a "contact" (*saṃyoga*) in the ordinary sense.

It is not true to say that one who does an action is its lord (*īśa*), as it is not so in cases like *ṛtvik*, or a cook. Nor is it true to say that he who knows a thing does possess efficacy (*śakti*), nor is it true to say that he who destroys a thing is its agent.

(E18-19) Women and *śūdras* are not fit to achieve liberation.

(E38) There are two types of awareness, one which is produced by effort and another which does not depend upon effort.

(E73) The word "*niḥśreyasa*" means the nonmanifestation in the same self of any type of frustration again once it has disappeared.

(E87) By the powers acquired through the practice of *yoga*, *yogins* who possess knowledge of all things realize the nature of liberation even before it is actually realized.

(E164) Vardhamāna cites Gaṅgeśa as saying that memory is not in conformity with reality (*smṛtirayathārtheti*).

(E169) Gaṅgeśa is cited as saying that that which is knowledge (*pramā*) is not so everywhere, but only at certain places.

(E185) According to Śivāditya Miśra a cause *par excellence* (*karaṇa*) is that which leads to action but is not the cause of it (*vyāpārājanakavyāpārāhetutvam*). So, sense-organs and sacrifices, etc., are not causes *par excellence*, but are only causal factors (*kāraka*).

(E194-195) He refutes the view of the author of the *Ratnakośa*, namely Taraṇi Miśra, that "*vāda*" is taken recourse to without having any gain (*lābha*), devotion (*pūjā*), fame (*khyāti*) in view.

(E291) Vardhamāna explains the term "*nāstika*" as one who does not believe in anything. Given this explanation, Vaitaṇḍikas alone can be called "*nāstika*".

(E341) Vardhamāna refutes Taraṇi Miśra's view that there are two kinds of universals, proper universals (*jāti*) and imposed properties (*upādhi*). The former inhere (*samaveta*) while the latter do not inhere (*asamaveta*).

(E362) The refutation of one's view is not due to any feeling of hatred against him, but in order to propound the truth with compassion on him. Similarly, the desire to achieve victory over someone is to propound the truth with compassion on him.

(E468) He refutes Taraṇi Miśra's view that there are two types of connection (*sannikarṣa*), namely contact (*saṃyoga*) and qualification (*viśesaṇatā*), rather than the generally recognized four kinds of connection, namely, inherence, etc.

(E496) From the line "*yathā viśvanāthāyatane viśvanāthamanubhavataḥ*" it may be concluded that Vardhamāna wrote the *Nyāyanibandhaprakāśa* while he was at Varanasi.

(E589) According to the Buddhists there is no connection of the qualification variety (*viśeṣaṇaviśeṣyābhāva*).

PRAKĀŚA on Udayana's NYĀYAKUSUMĀÑJALI
Summary by V. Varadachari

"E" references are to the edition (B2701; RB3974) by Padmaprasada Upadhyaya and Dundhiraja Sastri in Kashi Sanskrit Series 30, 1956. Sections are identified by paragraphs cited in the summary of the *Nyāyakusumāñjali* in Volume II of this Encyclopedia, pp. 558-988.[9]

I.2 (E12) Some scholars say that the word *apavarga* ("liberation") used here by Udayana has justification, being relevant to the context, but that the word "heaven" (*svarga*) is only used for the sake of illustration. Vardhamāna feels perhaps that *svarga* is illustrative here in the sense that God is known to have been worshipped by many to get heaven. Similarly, liberation will surely be attained by worshipping Him.

I.3 (E22) While explaining why thought should be undertaken relating to God, some commentators say that doubt does not arise regarding God as such. God is the *dharmin* or possessor of properties. Doubt may, to be sure, arise about some of these properties, such as His ability to create the world, etc. "Thought" here means resolving this doubt.

Vardhamāna: This does not stand to reason, since we are advised to give thought to God in the same respects as those in which God is heard about from the Veda. There must be concurrence between hearing (*śravaṇa*) and thinking (*manana*). The Vedas speak of God and His features. There is no feature of God which is not dealt with in the Veda. Where then is there room for doubt?

(E22-23) Objection: Doubt does arise, however, as to whether God is capable of creating the world, etc.

Vardhamāna: No, since that is also settled in the Vedas.

Another objector: Though God is known from Vedas doubt arises regarding the validity of the Vedas and this leads in its turn to another doubt about that God who is dealt with in the Vedas. It is that doubt which needs to be resolved.

Vardhamāna: The words "to be heard" (*śrotavya*) and "to be thought on" (*mantavya*) have grammatical coordination (*sāmānādhikaraṇya*). Now if the Vedas are not known to be valid, how can there be an incentive to listen? Thought must be based upon the validity of the Vedas. Inference to God cannot be treated as inappropriate in the manner argued above.

(E27-28) Doubt does not form part of inference as its cause or its accessory. It relates rather to the desire to know that which is to be inferred.

I. 8-9 (E60) Udayana argues that a limit (*avadhi*) must condition the occurrence of the world, since otherwise it might not exist at all. Vardhamāna notes that perception helps in finding out that an effect takes place when something else preceding it exists, for otherwise it is not produced; thus it is proved that perception is the means of knowing that there is a cause for an effect. Udayana advances in this passage the reasoning necessary to show that cause is an indispensable antecedent in general.

I. 17 (E67) "A jar would be eternal", i.e., it would be beginningless, unless there were a limit.

I. 24 (E80) In connection with the production of an effect from a cause of a different species, Udayana cites the case of the production of curds from milk, where sour taste plays an important part in the component part of milk. Vardhamāṇa notes the view of the author of the *Ratnakośa*, Taraṇi Miśra, in whose opinion curds belong to a species which has a particular taste. The substance may remain intact. It is the taste that determines the identity of the substance. The component parts which produce milk come to possess a particular taste as a result of internal heat and thus produce curds.

I. 29 (E85) On causal relations, Vardhamāna notes the views of his father. Causal efficacy (*śakti*) need not be admitted as the cause, for causal efficacies will have to vary to account for the variety of effects. A universal causality could as well be recognized. Admission of such a universal will not be sublated by nonapprehension of the effect. For example, scorpions are produced from scorpion parents and cow dung. Each must be admitted as the cause, as this is supported by changes in the effect, viz., the scorpions so produced are slightly dark and also tawny.

I. 31-32 (E91) Vardhamāna identifies the opponent, who in *kārikā* 7 argues that only a single cause need be postulated for all effects, as the follower of the *Tridaṇḍimata*, evidently the *Bhedābhedavāda* of Bhāskara.

I. 55 (E109) That absence can be a causal factor is illustrated by Vardhamāna by citing absence of contact with a wall as a cause of motion, nonapprehension (*anupalabdhi*) as a cause of the awareness of absence, nonperformance of an enjoined act as the cause of the sin of omission, absence of defects as a cause of the ascertainment of the validity of the Veda. Vardhamāna notes that there is a wrong conclusion (*apasiddhānta*) in the Mīmāṃsaka's efforts to deny causality to absence, since the Mīmāṃsakas admit absence as a cause in connection with the third of the above-mentioned examples.

I. 61-64 (E117) The Mīmāṃsakas recognize relational absence (*saṃsargābhāva*) when apprehending concomitance and causality established through agreement and difference.

(E118) Regarding the problem of finding a causality which will be applicable to all three of the relational absences (viz., constant, prior and posterior absences), the *siddhāntin* holds that relational-absence-ness could be a property which brings all of them together. Gaṅgeśa, whom Vardhamāna refers to as his preceptor (*asmadguravaḥ*), was of the view that relational absence occurs where the awareness of denial arises through superimposing the counterpositive on the locus, while mutual absence occurs where the awareness of denial arises through the superimposition of that which limits the counterpositiveness.

I. 65-73 (E120) While other Mīmāṃsakas hold causal efficacy to be the cause, Murāri Miśra, also a Mīmāṃsaka, held that the absence of a counteracting agent is not the cause, nor causal efficacy, but rather that some fire other than the one that is counteracted at a particular time is the cause of the heat produced at that time. Hence the absence of a counteracting agent determines causality but is not the cause. This is illustrated in the production of sound. *Ākāśa* is a single entity, while sound is produced at a specific time only and in a particular place. Though the production of sound be counteracted in a particular place, it may be produced elsewhere, say, from a kettledrum which is therefore the cause.

Vardhamāna rejects this, as then there will not be any auxiliary cause, since the wheel-with-the-stick will be the cause. Both the wheel and the stick would be admissable as the cause on the basis of agreement and difference.

I. 82-83 (E140) The Mīmāṃsakas recognize the production of acquired causal efficacy (*ādheya śakti*) in certain cases, e.g., in the cases of the rites called *putreṣṭi* and *pitṛyajña*. *Putreṣṭi* is performed by the father for his son with the result that the son becomes lustrous and possessed of food and cattle, which is evidence that the son has gained acquired causal efficacy. Similarly, the annual ceremonies performed to the departed souls of one's ancestors (*pitṛyajña*) give satisfaction to them.

The Naiyāyikas do not admit this. Karmic traces which are imperceptible (*adṛṣṭa*) and which bear the results are to be taken as resting where the results are to accrue. When a father gets released from worldly bondage, the ceremonies do not create any karmic trace in him, because there is no defect in him then. Vardhamāna refers to absence of defect, following the Nyāya tradition according to which defects usher in bondage for the self; the man who gets release should be free from defects and as such cannot again become the seat of any impression later. This does not invalidate the practice of those ceremonies. Karmic traces are admittedly frequently produced, but in these particular cases they are not produced, since the ground, namely the presence of defects, is not there. Does this ceremonial act produce anything, then? Yes, it produces some connection between the traces and the self of the performer. Does it produce it specified with some imperceptible features? Yes, it does so in the self of the performer, as in the case of offering oblations in the fire.

I. 165-172 (E219) Regarding the validity of the instruments of knowledge, Vardhamāna raises the question of the validity of words uttered by parrots. Parrots reproduce words taught to them. If these words are based on correct meanings the expressions of the parrot must be valid. Similarly the words uttered by a fraudulent fellow seem to be valid and to derive their validity from the merit of the speaker. This should not lead us to conclude that there cannot be invalid utterances. What the parrot and the cheat do is to repeat others' expressions. The valid knowledge which is produced about this must be deemed to be valid. But we cannot declare it to be so. God alone can do that. His cognition which arises about the knowledge so produced must be correct, and the validity of that knowledge depends upon His merit which produces His correct cognitions of the inferential and verbal-authority types.

II. 34-87 (E243-244) Returning to the question of the cognition of absence (see I.55-64 above), the various kinds of absences are further analyzed. Take a case of absence of a jar on the ground. Here there is denial of contact between absence on the one hand and jar and ground on the other. When the jar is denied, the absence of jar on the ground is not of the nature of prior or posterior absences, since these exist at the time their counterpositive exists. Nor can it be constant absence, since the jar may exist on the ground at some other time. Therefore, the proper analysis is that what is absent on the ground is *contact with jar.* When the counterpositive will take place in the future, we have prior absence; when it has ceased to exist, we have posterior absence; and when it does not exist at all we have constant absence.

(E244-245) Other views on absence are mentioned. Some hold that the judgment "there is no jar on the floor" does not have *absence of contact with jar* as its content, but rather has *constant absence of jar* as its content. Cognitions of origination and destruction arise through connection or absence of connection with *contact with jar.* This constant absence has the form of destruction of that contact.

Others hold that absences differ from each other through differences among their counterpositives. This principle applies as well to the absence of jar, which absence is produced and destroyed as conditions change.

Still others maintain that the absence, whose nature is to arise and be destroyed, is to be construed as posterior absence and should be taken to be a fourth kind of relational absence.

II. 104-120 (E278-279) The treatment of universal and individual is clear and brief. The Prābhākara argument for the view that words mean universals is set forth and refuted. That a word has the power to convey a universal is only possible through its power to denote an individual falling under that universal. Gaṅgeśa's view is cited here.

II. 141-172 (E295) The regular sequence of words does not give rise to verbal knowledge. Words should of course have this sequence. They become a cause of verbal knowledge by making it evident that the meaning is not deviant. That is why, even when there is doubt regarding the nature of a syllable being dental rather than retroflex, e.g., the sense of the passage is still available.

The case is different with the verbal knowledge which is gotten from the Veda. The Vedas are inferred to be valid. The necessary conditions for obtaining the sense of Vedic passages are entirely different from the conditions for ordinary knowing. That God composed the Veda is known through the instrument of knowledge which apprehends the property-possessor, viz., God. It is then known that the Vedas are the composition of God who does not have a body (as held in Nyāya). Similarly, the contents of tradition are also representative of practices which prove that they are based on the Veda and are therefore looked to as providing an incentive to take up those practices. Similarly, the Vedas are inferred to enjoin certain rules among these practices. So these pratices are not to be looked upon as baseless, but are in reality based on an independent instrument of knowledge.

(E296) The above-mentioned reasoning is not fully accepted by some of the Naiyāyikas. There is no need to recognize that the Veda, some branches of which are now extinct, should be taken as forming the basis for tradition and practices which have come into vogue later on. On the other hand, it must be admitted that such recensions, however much they were scrupulously adopted for practice by the diligent, have become extinct. A single individual cannot by himself study all the recensions. When those who study some of them cease to exist, those recensions too become extinct. That a particular recension which is omitted by some would have been taken up for study by others is not always necessarily the case. It is also not necessary to hold that Vedic practices have disappeared altogether because the passages in the Vedas pertaining to those practices have become extinct. The enlightened ones take to Vedic practices on the strength of expressions handed down by tradition. Hence those portions of the Vedas which can be inferred from tradition and practice should be admitted as authoritative.

III. 3 (E323) While commenting on Udayana's discussion on the size of the internal organ, Vardhamāna notes that some may argue that the internal organ is a composite whole and account for the sequence or simultaneity of awareness through the expansion and contraction of the internal organ. One can take the baked cake (*śaṣkulī*) and then have the after-cognition that one experiences smell and other qualities at the same time, and this experience cannot be sublated.

Vardhamāna rejects this argument. He argues that the internal organ might as well be given up altogether, and mere contraction and expansion admitted alone. Economy (*lāghava*) would support this. The desire to know one or five objects does not cause contraction and expansion. It is not the cause at all. If it could be the internal organ might as well be admitted as all-pervasive.

III. 4 (E331) There is a subtle discussion of the use of the term "hare's horn" (*śaśaśṛṅga*). In a valid perceptual cognition, contact between sense organ and object is essential for production of the cognition. Contact with no other object is essential in the same way. For example, the jar is not fit to cause valid awareness of something else through its contact with an organ. Now, a hare's horn has no fitness for being the cause of any valid perceptual cognition through contact with a sense-organ. This is what some scholars say. But the *siddhāntin* is of the opinion that the case of hare's horn comes under *asatkhyāti*—i.e., an apprehension of something nonexistent—and the question of validity or essentialness doesn't arise at all.

III. 8 (E336) On the text "*mīmāṃsakaśca toṣayitavyo bhīṣayitavyaśca*" Vardhamāna offers a brief remark. *Apūrva* must be proved to exist, and should not be denied merely on the ground of nonapprehension. The Mīmāṃsakas should be humored thus. Likewise God, who is not apprehensible, cannot be proved not to exist on the ground of nonapprehension.

III. 9 (E345-346) Śrīharṣa criticized Udayana's description of *tarka* and its role in his *Khaṇḍanakhaṇḍakhādya*. Udayana meant that if there is room for doubt regarding the presence of an obstruction then there is scope for inference. If doubt does not have scope, then inference cannot play its role effectively. Doubt persists until *tarka* finds scope for its operation. But it cannot persist when a contradiction is proved to be the result. Śrīharṣa refuted this by holding that if there is contradiction doubt must be admitted to be there. If there is no contradiction, doubt should be there too. Doubt continues until contradiction is *proved* to be there. So how can *tarka* mark the end of doubt?

Vardhamāna observes that contradiction does not depend on doubt, since it prevents the functioning of doubt.

Tarka is declared by Gaṅgeśa not to be capable of apprehending pervasion. It can only grasp pervasion when aided by absence of awareness of deviation. Here by awareness both certain and doubtful kinds of awareness could be meant. Doubt may arise as a result of doubts about the presence of obstructions in some cases, and in others as a result of the apprehension of a common feature together with nonapprehension of specific features. Absence of doubt may come through *tarka* relating to the *vp*; sometimes, it is just naturally there.

(E348-350) Vardhamāna notes many definitions of pervasion. Some of them are found stated as *prima facie* definitions by Maṇikaṇṭha Miśra[10] and some are not noted there. Maṇikaṇṭha's own definition[11] is rejected, though Maṇikaṇṭha's name is not mentioned.

(E351) Doubt regarding the presence of an obstruction does not prevent inference and therefore cannot count as a fallacy.

(E352-362) The definition of an obstruction is discussed in great detail. Many definitions are enumerated and rejected. Some of these are stated and refuted by Maṇikaṇṭha in the *Nyāyaratna*. Vardhamāna notes his father's view which agrees with that of Taraṇi Miśra, author of the *Ratnakośa*. He proves that "obstruction" should be so defined as to apply to cases of equipervasion as well as unequal pervasion.

(E355) An obstruction cannot affect inference by playing the role a counterargument.

(E363-364) As to why an obstruction vitiates pervasion, Vardhamāna first cites the definition of "obstruction" as what does not pervade the *h* and shows that the *h* does not pervade the *s*. Pervasion cannot be proved merely by noting the copresence of *s* and *h* plus the nonapprehension of deviance, since that might be satisified through the absence of favorable reasoning (*anukūlatarka*). *Tarka* alone will determine pervasion. An obstruction is the basis of the fallacy of *asiddha* and so is not itself an independent fallacy. Left to itself it cannot vitiate pervasion and is in this respect like the fallacy of proving what has already been admitted (*siddhasādhana*).

(E367) Regarding the nature of the *asiddha* fallacy, Vardhamāna notes an opinion which treats *asiddha* as having the absence of *siddhi* which consists in the certain knowledge of pervasion plus *pakṣatā*. Knowledge of the qualified-awareness (*viśiṣṭajñāna*) of both is required. Vardhamāna tells us that admission of this would result in the incorporation of *savyabhicāra* and other fallacies under *asiddha*. *Asiddha* does not depend upon the deviant feature to make itself known.

In this context Vardhamāna refers to the view of his father according to whom the three kinds of *asiddha* affect the rise of inferential cognition independently, since each one makes itself known by itself.

Thus the qualified-awareness is not required here. Inferential cognition may be prevented from arising even without such an awareness. The three kinds of *asiddha* are brought together under a common name since they all share the character of vitiating the application, which is the critical cause of awareness of pervasion. Vardhamāna adds that "the sage", meaning Gautama, made this classification.[12]

(E367) A fallacious *h* prevents the rise of inferential cognition only when it is known. Where inferential cognition fails to occur because of the incorrect understanding of pervasion, fallacy plays no part.

(E366-368) The *Nyāyasūtras* (I.2.4) enumerate five fallacies. The basis for enumerating fallacies must lie in the recognition that a fallacy directly prevents the rise of inferential cognition as in the case of sublation (*bādha*) and counterargument (*pratirodha*) as well as in affecting pervasion as in the contradictory *h* (*viruddha*) or deviant one (*vyabhicāra*). Here someone suggests that *bādha* and *pratirodha* may be grouped together, and that *viruddha* and *vyabhicārin* likewise may be grouped together. Gaṅgeśa is here stated to have held that an independent view such as Gautama's cannot be denied credit, as otherwise any axiom or statement dealing with the technical aspects of the system will have to be given up.

(E368) *Āśrayāsiddhi* gives rise to a defective cognition regardingan object whose features prove to be doubtful. That is, this fallacy involves the absence of knowledge in the object itself which is the property-possessor. *Siddhasādhana* is a fallacy, since doubt is aroused by it regarding its *s*. But it is not a fallacy like the deviant one, since it does not affect the efficient cause of inference nor does it prevent by itself the rise of inferential cognition (as the counter-argument does). But there is no need to have these two factors discriminated, viz., a fallacy affecting the efficient cause from the one preventing by itself the rise of inference. It is enough to admit the nature of fallacy as obstructing the rise of inferential cognition through affecting the cause of that cognition.

III. 10 (E373) Vardhamāna takes the opponent referred to by Udayana as a Bhāṭṭa Mīmāṃsaka.

III. 12 (E382) Secondary meaning (*lakṣaṇā*) resorted to when construing the words together becomes inappropriate. For instance, in the sentence "allow the sticks to enter", the context must be taken into account, viz., that of people trying to get into hall to get food, etc. These people are holding sticks, and so the sentence refers in a secondary manner to the people, since the sticks by themselves can't enter.

(E395–396) Arguing for the admission of verbal testimony as an independent instrument of knowledge, Gaṅgeśa points out that verbal testimony cannot be brought under inference. A *hetu* alone cannot give rise to any activity. It is the meaning of a sentence which arouses action. Besides, inferential cognition is concerned only with determining the nature of the *sādhya* and it can take the form "the words (of the sentence) presuppose the knowledge of the relation of their meanings which are then recollected". It will not give any meaning beyond that.

(E400–401) The causes of verbal cognition are expectancy, semantic fitness and contiguity. Expectancy consists in the nonconclusion of what is being stated. "Nonconclusion" means that something is wanting without which the senses of the words do not get mutually related. Mutual relation—e.g., that between nouns, suffixes, roots and verbal terminations, etc.—further requires semantic fitness, which consists in the absence of an instrument of knowledge which could sublate the sense conveyed by the words. Contiguity consists in the recollection of the related meanings without there being an intervention between them.

III. 13 (E422) Vardhamāna gives a clear exposition of the stand the Nyāya system takes on presumption. It is only a case of inference. That Devadatta is not in the house is a judgment concerning an absence, and it is produced by perception. This judgment concerns itself with the counterpositive of that absence, Devadatta, who is remembered. There is no other relation between an absence and its counterpositive. Perception which apprehends the counterpositive of an absence residing in the house, apprehends easily as well the qualification-relation (*vaiśiṣṭya*) of the concomitance of its recollection. Traditional scholars hold that the third subsumptive judgment, regarding Devadatta who is recollected, arises from the internal organ itself assisted by recollection of the relevant concomitance. Recollection is not a distinct instrument of knowledge, since it has no operation.

(E425–426) In the case of Devadatta, who is not present in the house, there are two possibilities: either he is alive and staying elsewhere at that time, or he is dead. Doubt arises about this. That he is alive is assumed through presumption; inference is then brought to bear to prove that he is alive elsewhere. Here *tarka* works on doubt and postulates his existence outside the house. This *tarka* is assisted by presumption. But inference, without the help of presumption, suffices to prove Devadatta's existence outside the house. It is inference of the *sāmānyatodṛṣṭa* type that enables us to prove that Devadatta is alive. This is more easy to prove than that he is dead.

All this is the view of scholars whom Vardhamāna does not identify. The Nyāya tradition considers that inference of the only-negative kind helps in proving the absence of Devadatta in the house. Vardhamāna notes that any other kind of inference, only-positive or positive-negative, could also serve the purpose.

(E438–439) Traces form a relation which helps in the origin of perceptual judgment, and they provide the only relation in the rise of recollection. In recognition, they are brought in through recollection and so do not serve as a distinct relation. If recognition were produced by traces, then it would be recollection.

(E440) Traces cannot be the cause *par excellence* in producing recollection, since such a cause should have an operation.

III.14 (E440) In producing a valid judgment about an absence, the internal organ becomes the cause *par excellence* assisted by a positive specific causal factor.

V.1 (E479) Udayana writes at the beginning of Book Five that the *prima facie* view declaring that no instrument of knowledge is available to prove God's existence cannot be maintained. The mistake of not taking God as existent does not lie with God but merely with the one who fails to discover Him. The passage in this context means that it is not a defect of the pillar that a blind man cannot see it. Vardhamāna writes that the word *sthāṇu*, meaning "pillar", must be taken to mean Śiva. The word *andha*, "blind", refers to the person who cannot find the instrument of knowledge. The word *sthāṇu* is also taken in the sense of a particular kind of wood.

(E484) The interpretation of *kārikā* 1 is detailed and exhaustive. While introducing *kārikā* 2 the commentator offers an interesting note. Udayana says in *kārikā* 2 that the Nyāya argument for God's existence cannot be declared to become defective through sublation. On this, Vardhamāna writes that sublation of the evidence proving God's existence has already been refuted in Book III, and is again stated here.[13]

(E488) The Naiyāyikas offer an inference to prove God's existence through His agency for creation of the world. A counterargument is offered to disprove the creation of the world by any agent, on the ground that the world is not produced by one who has no physical body. Gaṅgeśa (cited by Vardhamāna) makes the following observation in this context: The counterargument seeks to show that the world is not produced by an agent known to us already, on the ground that it is not possible to prove an absence whose counterpositive is not known. But the *siddhāntin's* argument can prove that the agent of the creation of the world is already known on the strength of *pakṣadharmatā*. Since the subject matter of the hypotheses of the two arguments differ, there cannot be any contradiction between them. That the world is produced by an agent cannot be cited as an obstruction, since it does not apply when the agency sought to be proved is to characterize an ordinary agent.

(E491–492) Vardhamāna explains how the definition of "obstruction" offered earlier (E352–362) applies in the case of the present inference involving God as the agent of the creation of the world.

V.5 (E516–518) Regarding the causal relation between the size of the minimal perceptibilium (*truṭi*) and dyad, and that between the size of the dyad and that of the atom, Vardhamāna gives an interesting interpretation. Largeness (*mahattva*) in the minimal perceptibilium is not produced by size, since largeness of the part is the cause of the largeness produced by number and not of that produced by loose contact (*pracaya*). The size of the component parts does not produce the largeness, for then largeness would be produced in the dyad by the size of the atom. Therefore, manyness (*bahutva*) should be taken as the cause. Similarly, the size of the dyad does not produce large size, since its size is small (*aṇu*); otherwise the dyad will have to be taken to have large size. Likewise, the size of the dyad is not produced by that of the atom. The size of an atom does not give rise to any size.

Objection: An atom's atomic size, being eternal, cannot produce anything at all, like the all-pervading-ness of the *ākāśa*.

Answer: No. Other qualities of eternal objects can be causal factors, e.g., number, so there is no reason why atomic size cannot be a cause. Nevertheless, the atomic size in atoms does not make the small size of the dyad atomic. And so the size of the dyad must be produced by number, since the other possibilities are excluded. Specifically, it is the number *two* which produces it. Vardhamāna refers to the Nyāya tradition to this effect.

Objection: The tradition is rather that there are two factors causing the size of the dyad, namely the number and the size of its component atoms.

Answer: No, because of heaviness. It is unnecessary to invoke two noninherence causes for the same effect. Therefore it must be that the number *two* is the noninherence cause.

V.6 (E528) On the relation of desire to verb roots, Vardhamāna's comments are exhaustive and highly informative. In expressions like "the chariot moves", the finite verb "moves" is used even when there is no relevant desire. It is possible to suppose that the sense of the verb is a general activity in the case of insentient agents. But then, the same may be said of the activity of sentient agents also. The use of a verb like "moves" can be taken as having a secondary sense in the case of insentient agents.

(E534) The verb indicates desire only, and not activity. If a particular tense is used at a time when the activity has ceased to exist, then that use must be taken to convey a secondary sense, as in the case of "the chariot goes".

(SUPPLEMENT:) The *Nyāyapariśiṣṭa* of Udayana

In order to provide a summary of Vardhamāna's commentary on Udayana's *Nyāyapariśiṣṭa* we require a summary of the former work, which was missing from Volume Two of the Encyclopedia. The missing summary is here provided. There is no translation of *Nyāyapariśiṣṭa*. "E" references are to the edition by N.C. Vedantatirtha (RB3992). The summary is by Esther A. Solomon.

BOOK FIVE: Portion One
Topic XLVIII: Futile Rejoinders

(E1–8) Twenty-four kinds of futile rejoinders are defined in *Nyāyasūtra* V.1—*sādharmyasama, vaidharmyasama*, etc. The *sama* at the end of each title signifies *likeness* (or parity), which consists in there being no special reason why the original reasoning should be regarded as stronger as proof than the reasoning urged in rejoinder. Udayana indicates here explanations of the term *sama* that were known to him (i) that of Uddyotakara, viz., that a futile rejoinder is put forward for the purpose of neutralizing the force of the original argument; (ii) that of Vātsyāyana, showing that the argument and the rejoinder are on a par; (iii) that of others, who explain it as signifying that the proposer of the rejoinder is *sama*, i.e., not superior, which is to say, inferior to the one who proposes the original argument; and (iv) that the *samatva* of the rejoinder lies in the fact that, while attempting to demolish the argument of the opponent it demolishes itself also. Udayana prefers this last explanation.

(E8–13) 1. Parity through similarity (*sādharmyasama*) and 2. Parity through dissimilarity (*vaidharmyasama*). Each of these futile rejoinders is of three varieties:

(1) Where the argument concerns a correct content (and the rejoinder an incorrect one) (*sadviṣaya*). An example (the one actually provided by Uddyotakara) is:

Argument: Sound is noneternal, because it is produced, like a jar;

Rejoinder: Sound is eternal, because it is immaterial, like *ākāśa*.

Here, since sound really is noneternal according to Vaiśeṣika, the content is correct, the *jātivādin* (the one who offers the rejoinder) defending a false thesis.

(2) Where the argument concerns an incorrect content (*asadviṣaya*).

Argument: Sound is eternal, because it is intangible, like *ākāśa*.

Rejoinder: Sound is noneternal, because it is knowable, like the jar.

Here sound is not eternal, so the content is incorrect.

(3) Where the rejoinder is wrongly expressed (*asaduktika*). The

example is Vātsyāyana's (p. 268 of Vol. II of this Encyclopedia). Here the rejoinder has a correct content (the self is indeed inactive), but is wrongly urged in this connection.

In a case where the argument is based on dissimilarity (i.e., cites a *vp*) and the rejoinder cites an *sp*, the case is to be classified as parity through similarity, not through dissimilarity. So cases of parity through dissimilarity will either be like this:

Argument: Sound is noneternal, because it is produced, unlike *ākāśa*.

Rejoinder: Sound is eternal, because it is immaterial, unlike a jar, where the examples in both argument and rejoinder are negative ones, or like this:

Argument: Sound is noneternal, because it is produced, like a jar.

Rejoinder: Sound is eternal, because it is immaterial, unlike a jar, where the example in the rejoinder is negative even though that in the argument is positive.

Another type of case occurs when an argument based on one instrument of knowledge is opposed by a rejoinder based on another instrument of knowledge which rejoinder is based on a misapprehension. For example,

Argument: This is white, because it is a conch-shell, like other conch-shells;

Rejoinder: This is not white, because it is perceived to be yellow (where the perceiver has jaundice, say).

These futile rejoinders, and all the others to be explained, have two features: (1) they involve some sort of contradiction (*vyāghāta*), and (2) they lack essential components of a correct argument, or are irrelevant, or have superfluous features.

(E15–18) (3) Parity through augmentation (*utkarṣasama*).

Argument: Sound is noneternal, because it is produced, like a jar.

Rejoinder: Sound is not noneternal as the jar is, because if it were it should have color like the jar; but it doesn't.

The finder of futilities (*jātivādin*) here tries to saddle the argument with the fallacy of contradictoriness (*viruddha*).

(4) Parity through subtraction (*apakarṣasama*)

Argument: Sound is noneternal, because it is produced, like a jar.

Rejoinder: Sound is not noneternal as the jar is, because if it were it should be inaudible as the jar is; but it isn't.

This kind of futile rejoinder urges the absence of a certain property associated with *h* or *s* in either the *pakṣa* or the example on the ground of its absence in the other. For instance, in the example just cited sound is argued (in the rejoinder) not to have the *s*-property, but in the following the example is argued not to have the *h*-property:

Argument: Sound is noneternal, because it is produced, like a jar.

Rejoinder: Sound is not something produced, because if it were it would not have color as sound does not; but it does.

In the latter case the finder of futilities alleges contradiction or counterbalance (*satpratipakṣa*) in the argument, while in the former he alleges *asiddha.*

How can the futility-finder question the presence of the *h*-character in *p* when that is a matter of perception? Udayana says that both Vātsyāyana and Uddyotakara have pointed out that what seems to be perceived may not be so—it may be an illusion.

(E18–20) 5. Parity through uncertainty (*varṇyasama*).

Argument: Sound is noneternal, because it is produced, like a jar.

Rejoinder: The noneternality of sound being uncertain (i.e., yet to be proved), the noneternality of the jar must also be uncertain. I.e., the *sp* (the jar) lacks the *s*-property, or if it doesn't, since it may be unlike the *p* (being uncertain) the *sp* may not have the *h*-property, so that either the fallacy of *viruddha* or *asādhāraṇa* are present—so the *jātivādin* claims.

6. Parity through certainty (*avarṇyasama*).

Argument: Sound is noneternal, because if is produced, like a jar.

Rejoinder: If it is certain that the jar is noneternal the *p*, sound, which shares the properties of the *sp*, ought also to be certainly noneternal (so that it can't be the *p*, for a *p* is something in which the presence of the *s*-property is to be proved).

The futility-finder claims to find the fallacy to be that of *asiddha.*

(E20-21) 7. Parity through shuffling (*vikalpasama*).

Argument: Sound is noneternal, because it is produced, like a jar.

Rejoinder: Though sound may be capable of being produced like the jar, sound is produced by disjunction while the jar is not; so, since *p* has properties *sp* hasn't it is quite possible that *p* lacks the *s*-property while *sp* has it.

This is Uddyotakara's example. Vātsyāyana's (p. 269 of Vol. II of this Encyclopedia) goes to the same point, viz., the futility-finder is alleging *anaikāntikatva* in the argument.

(E21-22) 8. Parity through *s* (*sādhyasama*).

Argument: Sound is noneternal, because it is produced, like a jar.

Rejoinder: If sound is like a jar, then the jar is like sound; and so, since sound is to be proved to be noneternal, the jar must also be proved to be noneternal; if not, the *sp* (jar) is not like the *p* (sound) and so is not a proper *sp.*

Here the fallacy of *asiddhi* is being alleged to vitiate the argument.

(E22-25) The solution to (3)-(8) is given by Vātsyāyana (p. 269 of Vol. II of this Encyclopedia, under (3)). A solution specifically applicable to (6)-(8) is that since the *sp* is something which all parties agree has the *s*-property, it could never be like the *p* which has to be shown by argument to possess the *s*-property.

(E25-28) 9. Parity through union (*prāptisama*) and 10. Parity through nonunion (*aprāptisama*).

Argument: Sound is noneternal....

Rejoinder: A cause can establish something either by bringing it about (*kāraka*) or by making it known (*jñāpaka*) either in union with it or not in union with it. But if a cause is in union with its effect it is nondifferent from it and nothing is left to be established. If a cause is not in union with its effect then it cannot establish it, since e.g. a lamp cannot light up an object unless its light reaches that object.

Here "union" may be any one of numerous relations, e.g., contact, inherence, qualifierness, pervadedness, contentness, etc.

The solutions provided by Vātsyāyana (p. 270 of Vol. II of this Encyclopedia) are rehearsed. It is also pointed out that since the rejoinder is supposed to establish the fallaciousness of the argument it falls under its own formulation and is self-condemned thereby.

(E28-34) 11. Parity through continued question (*prasaṅgasama*).

Argument: Sound is noneternal....

Rejoinder: How do you know the jar is noneternal? The futility-finder attempts to refute the argument by alleging that an infinite regress follows from attempts to justify the example, its example, etc., etc. Udayana says that not just continued questioning of the example is meant—one can likewise keep asking for instruments of instruments of knowledge, causes of causes, etc. The futility-finder purports to find *asiddhi* in the *h*, since it needs proof, and he alleges *sādhyavikalatva* or *sādhanavikalatva* with respect to the *sp*.

Solution: We don't need a lamp to see another lamp. Infinite regress is not a problem for things already established.

Udayana says that besides continued questioning of the cause (*kāraka*) of the arising of something, etc., and of the cause which makes us aware (*jñāpaka*) of something, etc., some identify a third kind of *prasaṅgasama* called *viparītaprasaktika* (urging the contingency of the contrary). For example,

Argument: The jar is not on the ground....

Rejoinder: What is not in union (with a locus) cannot be absent there, so the jar must be on the ground!

Udayana finds this not acceptable as an interpretation of *Nyāyasūtra* V.1.9, and remarks further that the example can be classified under 9. Parity through union, citing Uddyotakara.

12. Parity through counterexample (*pratidṛṣṭāntasama*).

Argument: Sound is noneternal....

Rejoinder: The jar exists following (someone's) effort and is noneternal; but *ākāśa* also exists following effort and is eternal; so sound may be eternal also.

This is a different case from 1.*sādharmyasama*, etc., because the futility-finder does not provide any reason to support his counterexample. And that is the solution, to ask the futility-finder to put forward specific reasons for his counterexample.

(E34-38) 13. Parity through nonproduction (*anutpattisama*).

Several kinds of cases of this futile rejoinder are distinguished by Udayana.

A. *Pakṣānutpatti.* Argument and rejoinder as in Vātsyāyana (Vol. II, p. 270). Here the *p* is alleged to be unestablished in a part of locus (*āśrayabhāgāsiddhi*).

B. *Liṅgānutpatti.*

Argument: This is heavy, as it falls.

Rejoinder: Before it starts falling the thing is heavy, so the *h* is unestablished in part of the *p*;

C. *Sādhyānutpatti.*

Argument: This has smell because it is earthy.

Rejoinder: At its first moment of existence it lacks smell, so the argument is either not established or contradicted.

D. *Dṛṣṭāntānutpatti.*

Argument: The self is a substance, because it has qualities, like a jar.

Rejoinder: At its first moment of existence the jar lacks qualities, etc.

E. *Tajjñānotpatti.*

Argument: Air is a substance, because it has touch.

Rejoinder: Even uncognized air is a substance, the *h* is unestablished in the uncognized part of the *p*.

Udayana suggest solutions for (B)-(E) to supplement Vātsyāyana's for (A), e.g., for (B) it must be noted that the pervasion is between falling at time *t* and being heavy at all times. Inference arises from two kinds of situations, from probability (*sambhāvana*) and from certainty (*niścaya*), and an inference has to be judged according to which kind it is.

(E38-40) 14. Parity through doubt (*saṃśayasama*).

Argument: Sound is noneternal, because it comes after effort, like a jar.

Rejoinder: Since sound is perceptible like universals and jars, it is doubtful whether it is eternal like universals or noneternal like jars.

Argument and rejoinder as in Vātsyāyana (Vol. II, p. 270). Udayana provides a general characterization of parity through doubt: it occurs when one raises an objection on the strength of a common factor likely to lead to doubt even when a determining factor is presented. The futility-finder alleges *satpratipakṣa* in the argument.

(E40-41) 15. Parity through neutralization (*prakaraṇasama*). Argument, rejoinder and solution as in Vol. II, pp. 270-71. Vātsyāyana points out, and Udayana reaffirms, that both similarity and dissimilarity are intended by Gautama when he says "through similarity..." in his text.

(E41-44) 16. Parity through lack of *hetu* (*ahetusama*). Argument, rejoinder and solution as at Vol. II, 271. Udayana notes that both *kāraka hetus* and *jñāpaka hetus* are intended to be covered by this kind of futile rejoinder.

Question: How does this (16) differ from (9) parity through union and (10) parity through nonunion?

Answer: A. In (9) and (10) the question is pointedly about the nature of the *h* (whether it is near the *s* or not), while in (16) it is about the causal efficacy of *h* (in relation to whether it is or is not simultaneous with *s*). B. In (9) and (10) the union or nonunion is between the things denoted by the *s*- and *h*-terms, whereas in (16) the question is whether an *h*-term can denote anything. C. In (9) and (10) there are only two alternatives (union or nonunion); in (16) there are three (before, after, simultaneous). D. In (9) and (10) it is the auxiliary causality which is denied (in the rejoinders), while in (16) the rejoinder denies the very nature of an *h*. E. In (9) and (10) it is contended in the rejoinder that a qualifier of the *h* is unestablished, while in (16) a *reductio* (*tarka*) argument is provided.

(E44-45) 17. Parity through presumption (*arthāpattisama*). Argument, rejoinder and solution as in Vol. II, p. 271. Udayana points out that the presumption adduced by the futility-finder is only an apparent presumption, as are (a) sound is noneternal, therefore, by presumption we conclude that nothing else is noneternal, so the jar will lack the *s*-property; (b) that sound is noneternal follows from an inference, so by presumption we conclude that sound should be eternal on the strength of perception; (c) sound is noneternal because it is perceived by the external sense-organs of people like us, so we can presume that sound that is not perceived by people like us is not noneternal.

(E45-49) 18. Parity through lack of differentiating features (*aviśeṣasama*). Argument, rejoinder and solution as in Vol. II, p. 271.

A different interpretation of the *sūtra* (*Nyāyasūtra* V.1.23) has it that the single *h*-property is efficacious, so that if on the basis of it the *p* and the *sp* be taken as possessing the *s*-property in common, then they should be nondifferent in all respects. This nondifference in all respects can be *qua* individual or *qua* universal or *qua* the *s*-property. So e.g. the *h*-property *being produced* which accompanies all the forms such as the color of the jar, etc., while it would establish the noneternality of the *p* would also establish that the *p* is a jar, etc., since otherwise it couldn't prove noneternality either. And again, jarness would be proved. And proving fire on the mountain would also prove the kitchen, since it has been cognized as accompanied by fire in a kitchen, or it would not prove anything.

Udayana rejects this interpretation on the ground that it would make parity through lack of differentiating features indistinguishable from (3) parity through augmentation. He goes on to show how (18) differs not only from (3) but also from (1) and from (7), adding that if the presence of a single property could make two things identical then, e.g., all the nine substances would be nondifferent by sharing substanceness.

The solution to this rejoinder is that pervasion between properties must not be lost sight of. Some similarities are compatible with others, while other similarities are not. This explains why *being an animal* does not entail possession of horns in the case of a hare, etc.

(E50-53) 19. Parity through being equally tenable (*upapattisama*). Argument as before. Rejoinder: there are grounds both for sound's being eternal and for sound's being noneternal—e.g., that sound is intangible.

Udayana cites approvingly Uddyotakara and Vācaspati Miśra's distinction between (19) and (15), which is that in (19) the possibility of the ground for both views is pointed out but the contrary thesis (sound is eternal) is not argued for, whereas in (15) the *jātivādin* tries to prove the contrary thesis.

The solution to this rejoinder is that the opponent cannot deny the argument's thesis, since he admits the presence of grounds for it.

Objection: But both eternality and noneternality have gounds, but they can't both coexist in the same locus.

Answer: True, and likewise the thesis and the *jātivādin*'s contrary thesis cannot coexist.

(E53-56) 20. Parity through awareness (*upalabdhisama*). Argument, rejoinder and solution as in Vol. II, pp. 271-272.

Udayana understands (20) as restricting the intention of the arguer in some way not intended by him, and distinguishes five kinds of futile rejoinders of this type:

20a. The *p* is found in the absence of *s*, e.g., "this mountain has fire, because it has smoke", the futile rejoinder may be "does this mean that the mountain alone has fire, or that the mountain always has fire? Not the former, since the kitchan also has fire, nor the latter, for the mountain sometimes lacks fire. Thus your argument is sublated".

from some obstruction and become manifested to sight. There is no special reason offered by the arguer to show that sound is produced (like the jar) and not simply manifested after effort (following (b)).

This is Vātsyāyana's account (omitted from II, 272 by a printing error). Udayana feels that this rejoinder is correct and so redefines the case as well as widening its scope. His example goes as follows:

Argument: Sound is noneternal....

Rejoinder: It is not established that it is produced after effort. A thing is said to be produced after effort because it is perceived after effort. But a thing may first come into existence from effort and later by perceived, or it may exist but be concealed and then after effort be perceived. So it is not established that sound is produced by effort.

The solution to (24) is that no obstruction is known to be present, so there is no reason to suspect its presence.

30-43. (E74-78) A futile discussion needn't have just six steps, but less or more as the occasion dictates.

BOOK FIVE: Portion Two
Topic XLIX: Ways of Losing an Argument

(*Sūtras* 1-24) Udayana takes I.2.19 to imply the following definition of a "way of losing an argument": When a discussion has started, any behavior indicative of either party's ignorance constitutes a way of losing the argument.

1. (E80-84) Violating the thesis (*pratijñāhāni*). Vātsyāyana's example of this involves the arguer admitting that his *sp* has the property contrary to the *s*-property. Uddyotakara finds this explanation faulty since it doesn't violate the thesis (rather, it violates the example), so he reinterprets it to involve admitting that the *p* may have the contrary property to the *s*-property.

Udayana finds Uddyotakara's explanation too narrow, and proposes understanding it to include both Vātsyāyana's and Uddayotakara's examples or indeed any case where some part of the arguer's position is violated through admission that a contrary property belongs to it, thus abandoing his case.

2. (E85-88) Changing one's thesis (*pratijñāntara*). Udayana says that there are four varieties depending on whether it is the *p* or the *s* or their descriptions which are changed or qualified. Any qualification of one's case constitutes this fault on this interpretation.

3. (E89-90) Reason and thesis contradictory (*pratijñāvirodha*). Uddyotakara offers seven varieties of this way of losing: (1) thesis contradicts reason, being stronger; (2) reason contradicts thesis, being stronger; (3) the words of the thesis are self-contradictory; (4) the example(s) contradict(s) the thesis; (5) the reason is contradicted by the example; (6) the thesis and/or the reason are

contradicted by well-known facts; (7) when the opponent finds the reason inconclusive (*anaikāntika*) since it contradicts some thesis of the proponent.

Udayana, therefore, remarks that the particular contradiction between thesis and reason is mentioned in *sūtra* V.2.4 only as illustration—any contradictoriness of any of the members of the argument constitutes a case of this way of losing. So he adds to Uddyotakara's list the case where the reason or the example is worded in a self-contradictory fashion, or when the hypothesis and the conclusion contradict each other, etc.

4. (E90-92) Renouncing the thesis (*pratijñāsannyāsa*).

5. (E92-93) Changing one's reason (*hetvantara*). Udayana extends this case to cover any change of the probative part of the argument. It has four varieties, according as the reason, the example, the application or the refutation is qualified. Where the thesis, the pervasion or the conclusion are qualified one has a case of violating the thesis, i.e., the first way of losing an argument.

6. (E93-95) Irrelevance (*arthāntara*). Udayana finds four kinds: where the irrelevant statement accords with the speaker's own school of thought, or with the opponent's, or with both, or with neither.

7. (E96-97) Meaningless jargon (*nirarthaka*). Again Udayana finds four varieties: (1) where the proponent carelessly employs a wrong gender, number or case; (2) when he has a wrong conception of the parts of speech and uses one for another; (3) when, say by force of habit, one switches from one language to another (say, from Sanskrit to Apabhraṃśa); (4) when the word's meaning doesn't fit the context.

8. (E97-98) Unintelligibility (*avijñātārtha*). Udayana finds three varieties: (1) where a technical expression is used which is peculiar to one's own school of thought and which the opponent or the audience may not understand—e.g., the Buddhist talking of five *skandhas*, twelve *āyatanas*, four noble truths, etc.; (2) employing words not in current usage, even though they may be explained on, say, the basis of etymology; (3) employment of common words whose meaning cannot be determined from the context.

The rule of "three times" is a very reasonable one in view of the inattentiveness or slow understanding possible in the opponent or the audience. And it saves the proponent from premature defeat by an opponent who, not finding an answer, immediately charges him with unintelligibility.

9. (E99-101) Incoherence (*apārthaka*). Udayana finds three kinds: (1) the sort illustrated in the *sūtra*, where there is no sentence meaning because of lack of connection among the words; (2) where the words are wrongly ordered so that though they might give a sense in a

(19) can only be detected by the audience.

21. (E122-124) Inconsistency (*apasiddhānta*). A debater must stick to the position he has adopted, and not contradict its tenets in the course of argument.

22. (E125-126) Fallacies (*hetvābhāsa*). Udayana says that not only fallacies of the *h*, but also of the example, of *tarka*, and cases where pervasion is not stated or is wrongly stated are cases of this.

Vardhamāna's PRAKĀŚA on Udayana's NYĀYAPARIŚIṢTA

Summary by V. Varadachari

"E" references are to the edition (B2705; RB3992) by N.C. Vedantatirtha, Calcutta Sanskrit Series 22, 1938

(E1-2) In arguments the participants fail because of their incapacity (*aśakti*). Vardhamāna points out that this incapacity consists in lack of correct understanding of cause and effect. The present topic (of Book Five of the *Nyāyasūtra*s) is taken up here since it is necessary to have any obstacles removed which would block acquisition of truth. So such obstacles are studied now.

(E8) Futile rejoinders have denying as their nature, and do not establish anything.

(E21) 7. Parity through shuffling. It is an instance of this futile rejoinder even when the faulty *h* is indicated merely on the strength of the example. Others say that such cases belong to other types of futile rejoinder.

(E38-39) 14. Parity through doubt. Some scholars are said to have held there is a type of futile rejoinder called "parity through not being validly established" (*apramitasama*), which occurs when the rejoinder invokes a cause of false awareness because a determining factor is not present. Vardhamāna responds as follows. If the false awareness is not shown to be about a matter other than the one at hand, it is a case of *nigrahasthāna* (6) irrelevance. If it is shown to apply to one's own argument, then it is a case of *nigrahasthāna* (18) admitting the other party's opinion. In fact, unless the awareness has been sublated the question of its truth or falsity is not the question. So, under these circumstances the authority of previous commentators should be followed, and this sort of case should be classified as parity through doubt. Even if it is held to be a different type of futile rejoinder, it should be classified within the 24 cases enumerated by Gautama, treating it as a case of a list of rejoinders falling under various of the types (*ākṛtigaṇa*).

(E57) 20. Parity through awareness. Udayana notes that items such as parity through what is not desired (*aniṣṭasama*) might be treated as types of futile rejoinder but are not be accepted as such since Gautama didn't define them. Vardhamāna makes this clear by including these within parity through awareness. He cites a grammatical analogue and speaks of the need for a pupil to get instructions from a teacher.

BOOK FIVE: PORTION TWO
Topic XLIX: Ways of Losing an Argument

(E82) A definition of violating the thesis is quoted here: it is the one given by Śaṃkara Miśra in the *Vādivinoda* (p. 30 of that text). It is not refuted, and not explicitly approved either.

(E88) Again, a definition of changing one's thesis corresponding to Śaṃkara Miśra's is criticized.

(E96) 7. Meaningless jargon. An opinion is quoted according to which the present *nigrahasthāna* must be meant to include any case where the speaker does not convey what he intends to say.

(E99-100) 9. Incoherence. Again the view stated by Śaṃkara Miśra is presented without refutation. But a variety of this *nigrahasthāna* that is treated in the *Vādivinoda* (p. 33) is rejected by Vardhamāna.

4. RĀJAŚEKHARA SŪRI

A well-known Jaina author of philosophical works in the Jaina tradition such as *Ratnākarāvatārikāpañjikā* and *Syādvādakalikā*, he is held to have flourished between 1325-1350. He is reported to have written a Nyāya work, a *Pañjikā* on Śrīdhara's *Nyāyakandalī*, but the work has not come down to us.

5. JAYASIṂHASŪRI

A Śvetāmbara Jaina, pupil of Mahendra Sūri, who belonged to the family of Kṛṣṇarṣi. He wrote a *Tātparyadīpikā* on Bhāsarvajña's *Nyāyasāra.* In addition, he is the author of a Jaina *kāvya* in ten cantos titled *Kumārapāla(bhūpāla)carita,* which has been published more than once. This latter work is dated 1366, which establishes his date firmly.

TĀTPARYADĪPIKĀ on Bhāsarvajña's NYĀYASĀRA
Summary by V. Varadachari

"E" references are to Satischandra Vidyabhusana's edition (B2503; RB3790), Biliotheca Indica 188, 1910. Section numberings correspond to those used in the *Nyāyasāra* summary in Volume II of this Encyclopedia.

could be set aside the Buddhist view that erroneous awareness could be knowledge through its relation with its object.

13. (E99) Bhāsarvajña, when he says that the *h* is of three varieties (only-positive, only-negative, positive-negative) uses the word "*ca*" at the end of his remark. Jayasiṃha observes that this "*ca*" shows that the other threefold division of *h*, viz., into *śeṣavat*, *pūrvavat* and *sāmānyatodṛṣṭa*, are also intended to be included here, and that in a work called "*Nyāyasaṃgraha*" the difference between the two sets of three is in name only.[1]

(E101) The *p* is the *dharmin* when its *dharma* is to be known. It becomes *dharma* when invariable concomitance is to be ascertained. And both the *dharma* and *dharmin* are the *p* when it is the *s* that is to be established.

16. (E108-110) Only-negative inference is said to be of two kinds: (1) *prasaṅgonneyin*, an example of which is "this body of a living being is without a self, as it is likely to be without life, like a clod of earth"; (2) *aprasaṅgonneyin*, an example of which is "everything requiring an omniscient agent are effects, because they exist occasionally." Only-negative inference is said to be an instrument of knowledge when it is assisted by *tarka*.

27. (E155) The definition of discussion (*vāda*) contains the word "*pañcāvayavotpannaḥ*", which normally refers to the five-membered form of inference for others. Jayasiṃha says that some interpret these five members as the means for making one's own case (*svapakṣasādhana*), viz., (1) refutation of the means put forward for the opponent's case (*pratipakṣasādhanadūṣaṇa*), (2) justification of the means (*sādhanasamarthana*, (3) justification of the refutation (*dūṣaṇasamarthana*), (4) avoiding defects such as rather too quickly uttering the words (*atidrutoccāraṇa*), and (5) using expressions which are not well-known (*aprasiddhaprayoga*), and others.

(E156) Eight ways of losing an argument have scope in discussion, namely *nyūna*, *adhika* and the five *hetvābhāsas*.

28. (E157-158) Sophistry and cavil come under *vijigīṣukathā*. It involves four participants: the *siddhāntin*, his rival *pūrvapakṣin*, a leader and a questioner. A questioner is said to be one who knows the rules of his system and those of the rivals, born of noble family, attached to both the disputants, having forbearance, diligent in participating in discussion and impartial.

(E161) Reference is made to a certain view according to which cavil can be employed even in *vītarāgakathā*. Aparārka, the commentator on the *Nyāyasāra*, seems to have entertained this view. It is rejected, since if it were accepted the nature of reality may not get determined. *Vītarāgakathā* is undertaken only to determine the nature of reality.

(E168-170) Among the ways of losing an argument, *ananubhāṣaṇa*, *ajñāna*, *apratibhā*, *vikṣepa*, and *paryanuyojyopekṣaṇa* are based on nonunderstanding (*apratipatti*), the rest on wrong understanding (*vipratipatti*).

(E191) Taking the number of futile rejoinders as 24 is not intended as limiting the number of them, for *ananyasama*, which is defined and illustrated, is not included in the list.

(E199-200) *Aprāptakāla* is a way of losing an argument which is to be confined to *niyamakathā* alone; likewise with *adhika*.

(E202) *Ananubhāṣaṇa* applies to the *siddhāntin* if he does not name the fault committed by the opponent's argument.

(E207) The *ca* in *sūtra* V.2 includes fallacies of examples, unconnected and wrongly connected arguments—all lead to ways of losing arguments. Likewise bad ways of speaking, wrong movements, striking the chin and *vāditra* all lead to defeat.

(E208) *Niyamakathā* is conducted through use of expressions composed only in Sanskrit or in the form of *ślokas*. Or, the fifth syllable in each *varga* shall be given up. This is how *apaśabda* becomes a way of losing an argument. On the other hand, in the *aniyamakathā* dropping the subject becomes a way of losing.

CHAPTER THREE

29. (E212) An *āpta* or trustworthy person is one who does not deceive others or one in whom passion and hatred are destroyed.

33. (E226-230) Comparison as the relation of the name and the named is the view of the "*laghunaiyāyikas*". Comparison is listed as a distinct instrument of knowledge for a purpose, just as *hetvābhāsas* are listed in distinction from ways of losing an argument. The purpose in both cases is to develop the faculties of pupils.

38. (E250-251) Of the twelve objects of knowledge listed by Gautama (in NS I.9) the first and last (self and liberation) are to be taken up for study and the intervening ones have to be given up.

39. (E251-252) The body, being the locus of frustration, is treated as frustrating, but it is not frustrating in the primary sense of the term. In its primary sense, frustration is of the nature of affliction, but the body is not frustrating in this sense. Thus the sense is a metaphorical one, i.e., it becomes the cause of frustration.

40. (E254) While interpreting Bṛhadāraṇyaka Upaniṣad IV.5.6 "*ātmā vāre...*" Jayasiṃha observes that "*re*" is addressed to women. The word "*draṣṭavyaḥ*" means that this is to be done through external means like inference.

42. (E256-258) Both inference and verbal testimony are instruments for knowing God. The inference is of the following form: "earth

and others are produced by a specific agent, because they are specific products, like a specific planted figure."

43. (E272-273) Knowledge of God becomes the means to liberation by becoming part of worship of Him. Worship is intended to acquire successful meditation in order to have frustration destroyed. The author cites *Yogasūtra* I 23. Penance is intended to remove madness, passion and other things and is analyzed into the three kinds (internal, external and celestial), following tradition.

6. CINNAM BHAṬṬA or CENNU BHAṬṬA.

A native of the Andhra country, this writer appears to have been patronized by the Vijayanagara king Harihara II, who ruled around 1400. Vidyabhusaṇa dates Cinnam Bhaṭṭa at 1390, which we accept here. Cinnam Bhaṭṭa was the son of Sahajasarvajña Viṣṇubhaṭṭopādhyāya, the *paṇḍita* in the court of King Harihara of Vijayanagar and an Advaita author referred to by the author of the *Sarvadarśanasaṃgraha.* Cinnam Bhaṭṭa taught 15. Viṣṇubhaṭṭa and 16.Rāmeśvara (see below), both of whom commented on their teacher's writings, or in Rāmeśvara's case actually completed one of them.

Two works are extant that seem likely to have emanated from this author's pen: a commentary, *Prakāśikā,* on Keśava Miśra's *Tarkabhāṣā,* and *Vivaraṇa* on Varadarāja's *Tārkikarakṣāsārasaṃgraha.* This last, incomplete at Cinnam Bhaṭṭa's death, was completed by Rāmeśvara.

There are close connections between Cinnam Bhaṭṭa and the Vijayanagara empire. Gopinath Kaviraj estimates that Cinnam Bhaṭṭa was probably a fellow pupil of Vidyāraṇya, the well-known Advaitin of Vijayanagara, as well as of Sāyaṇa, the Vedic commentator. Even more intriguing is the theory of Anantalal Thakur that the *Sarvadarśanasaṃgraha,* the best-known of the classical attempts to summarily expound all the relevant philosophical systems of the age under one cover, was in fact the work of our author Cinnam Bhaṭṭa. The *Sarvadarśanasaṃgraha* is signed by Mādhava, but scholars have argued for years about the identity of this Mādhava with Vidyāraṇya and/or Bhāratītirtha, author of an important commentary on the *Vivaraṇa* of Prakāśatman.

PRAKĀŚIKĀ on Keśava Miśra's TARKABHĀṢĀ
Summary by V. Varadachari

"E" references are to the edition by D.R. Bhandarkar (B3076; RB4789), Bombay Sanskrit and Prakrit Series 84, 1937.

Sections correspond to summary of the *Tarkabhāṣā* in Volume II.

I. Method

(E102) In Keśava's definition of "definition" (*lakṣaṇaṃ tvasādhāraṇadharmavacanam*) the word "*vacana*" must have gotten in through carelessness or a scribe's mistake.

II. Instruments of Knowledge

(E103) Keśava writes: "(Objection): If *pramāṇa* means 'instrument of knowledge' it becomes necessary to point out its result; as it is absolutely necessary for an 'instrument' to have a result...."

(Answer): "True...." Cennu Bhaṭṭa remarks here that the word "true" (*satyam*) implies partial agreement with the principle. That is, the instrument of knowledge is admitted to be the instrument of the result called knowledge (*pramā*), but the remaining part of the objection is not admitted.

(E104) The text defines knowledge as arising with respect to an object which is presented as-the-object-is (*yathārtha*). Cennu Bhaṭṭa gives an elaborate explanation of this.

III. Causality

(E104-105) The causal condition *par excellence* (*karaṇa*) is defined as the one most capable of producing the effect. It is pre-eminently (*atiśayena*) the cause. This explanation, offered by Keśava Miśra, is clarified by Cennu Bhaṭṭa. Appealing to *Aṣṭādhyāyī* 5.3.55 ("*atiśayane tamapiṣṭhinau*") it is explained that the condition *par excellence* is therefore the thing which pre-eminently helps in the successful accomplishment of the activity. Some scholars maintain that it is that condition which accomplishes (*sādhaka*) the action, directly superintended by the agent. At this stage, Cennu Bhaṭṭa offers an interesting remark. An objection can be raised to the condition *par excellence* accomplishing the action, on the ground that the knower alone can accomplish it, as indicated in *Aṣṭādhyāyī* 3.1.133 ("*nvultṛcau*"). Cennu Bhaṭṭa remarks that Keśava Miśra anticipated this objection by explaining *karaṇa* as the pre-eminent (*prakṛṣṭa*) cause. The relation between a noun and a verb in a sentence is called *kāraka*. There are several such relations called by this name, each such relation explaining how the action conveyed by the verb is achieved. Each one could be taken as accomplishing the action. Since the condition *par excellence* may stand in such a relation, it has the capacity of accomplishing the action.

IV. Perception

(E123) Cennu Bhaṭṭa refers to the *anirvacanīyakhyāti* of the Advaitins, whom he refers to as "Vedāntins".

V. Inference

(E133) An obstruction is defined as what is equipervasive with *s* but which does not pervade *h* (*sādhanāvyāpakatve sati sādhyasamavyāptiḥ*), citing Varadarāja. After explaining this with suitable illustrations, Cennu Bhaṭṭa explains the derivation of the word *upādhi* as "fastening its *dharma* to that which is connected with it as if it were its own self."

(E146) After illustrating the only-negative inference, Cennu Bhaṭṭa takes up the question as to whether the *s* in such inference is already known or not. It is already known there is no justification for admitting only-negative inference; and if it is not known, then the fallacy of "unknown qualifier" (*aprasiddhaviśeṣaṇa*) arises. According to some scholars, not identified by our commentator, this fallacy is a strength of only-negative inference and not a weakness. Others hold that the "unknown qualifier" fallacy does not arise here, even when the establishment of the *s* is doubtful, since the *s* is what is to be established.

(E148-151) Cennu Bhaṭṭa justifies the order in which Keśava lists the fallacies. It is the *h* that is established as flawless which can prove the *s*; thus the *h* which is not established is the fallacy which heads the list. The author cites Udayana's explanation of this. Knowledge of *pakṣadharmatā* is establishment (*siddhi*). Its absence is *asiddhi.* Next, the *h* which does not exist in the *sp* but is present in both the *p* and the *vp* is mentioned as *viruddha. Anaikāntika* is mentioned third as it exists in the *p, sp* and *vp,* being a fallacy since it occurs in the *vp.* Fourthly there is *kālātyayāpadiṣṭa* in which the *h* is stultified. Finally, there is *prakaraṇasama,* involving a contrary *h.* The five conditions of a valid *h* bring in one fallacy after the other when they are not fulfilled.[1]

(E152) Cennu Bhaṭṭa notes that, according to some scholars, there is only one fallacy, namely *asiddha,* while others hold that there are three, and still others name six. He does not identify the sponsors of these views.[2] However, he notes that while developing a definition of a thing care must be taken to see that it is in accord with worldly usage. Ordinary usage recognizes more than one, or three, kinds of fallacies; so there must be more. On the other hand, those who recognize six kinds of fallacy[3] distinguish *anadhyavasita* from *savyabhicāra* (i.e., *anaikāntika*), but in fact *anadhyavasita* is a variety of *savyabhicāra,* viz., the *asādhāraṇa* kind.[4]

(E154-156) The topic of obstruction is dealt with at great length during the treatment of *vyāpyatvāsiddha,* discussing two illustrations cited by Keśava and identified by our commentator as stemming from

Buddhists and Jains respectively. Vedic practices are defended against the attack of the latter.

VII. Testimony

(E172) While discussing verbal awareness Cennu Bhaṭṭa refers to a view which declares that the words in a sentence give rise to their meanings which in their turn produce the meaning of the sentence. This view is rejected on the ground that the sentence as such will have no distinct cause. The words must be admitted to give rise to the meaning of the sentence. The meaning of the words is made known by the words and it is this operation which gives rise to the sense of the sentence. But the meaning of the words cannot by itself be the causes.

(E173) The Nyāya school recognizes utterances as valid on the ground that they are spoken by a trustworthy person (*āpta*).Cennu Bhaṭṭa explains a "trustworthy person" as one who offers instruction and whose defects have been destroyed. Trustworthy persons are of two kinds. One, the superior kind, is God. His omniscience encompasses all objects. The other, the inferior kind, is a person who does not know everything, whose awareness does not cover all objects. Such persons may be respectable (*ārya*) or foreigners (*mlecchas*). God is supremely trustworthy as He apprehends all objects as they actually are. He has no defects such as passion, etc. He is filled with sympathy. He acts to provide instruction to others.

VIII. Other Instruments

(E184) Concurrence (*sambhava*) is of two kinds, probable (*sambhāvanā*) and certain (*niścaya*). The former is invalid, e.g., if one declares that because A is a Brahmin he is versed in the four Vedas what he says is invalid, since though one is born a Brahmin he need not be versed in the four Vedas. The latter kind is valid, but is merely a type of inference—e.g., when one infers that there are a hundred things here on the ground that there are a thousand.

IX. Validity

(E189) While the Nyāya school admits complete identity (*tādātmya*) in cognitions such as "the jar exists in itself", the Bhaṭṭa Mīmāṃsakas recognize this cognition as having a relative sense, as involving a kind of identity (*abheda*) compatible with difference (*bhedasahiṣṇu*).

X. Objects of Knowledge

(E200) While dealing with the self, Cennu Bhaṭṭa refers to the view held by the followers of Rāmānuja. In this school, the self is held to be atomic in size. Further, he cites the passage from the Śvetāśvatara Upaniṣad which the Viśiṣṭādvaitins offer to support their concept.[6]

(E211) The Vaiśeṣika school adopts a particular kind of classfication of each under the rubrics of body, sense-organ and object. Cennu Bhaṭṭa offers some information on what an "object" is. Śālikanātha, the famous Mīmāṃsaka of the Prābhākara school, is stated here to have commented on Praśastapāda's *Padārthadharmasaṃgraha.* He is said to have distinguished the object from the body and organ. Udayana described an "object" as a means of enjoyment through being experienced. Śrīdhara's definition is that an "object" is a substance which is a means of enjoyment for the self and which is other than the body and sense-organs.

(E213-214) On gold, Cennu Bhaṭṭa writes that gold's color and touch are manifested (*udbhūta*). Its touch, however, is subdued (*abhibhūta*) because it is not then apprehended as belonging to that which belongs to the same kind and is also powerful. Since the earthy portion, which supports it, subdues the color of gold which belongs to the element fire, the brilliant white color of fire is not apprehended. This does not mean that the color of gold is not manifested. Its color is said to be subdued because its brilliant color is not clearly apprehended like the glow of a lamp. Similarly, a lamp which is lustrous doesn't cease being so because it is cognized in daylight. The author cites a passage from *Kiraṇāvalī* to illustrate this. When some kind of substance is sublimated it appears as red, and that is because the things mixed in subdue the substance. Vādīndra, who commented on this, writes that the color of gold is said to be subdued because it gets mixed up with some other object, i.e., some unmanifested object. Śrīdhara held that the color and touch of gold are unmanifest. Cennu Bhaṭṭa remarks that when color and touch are said to be unmanifest what is really meant is that they are subdued.

(E234-235) Keśava defines number as the special cause for the use of expressions such as "one", "two" etc. Cennu Bhaṭṭa notes that the author of the *Nyāyabhūṣaṇa* did not admit number as a quality, though it is inherent in perceptible substances. Keśava is therefore offering an inference as a proof for the establishment of number. Cennu Bhaṭṭa remarks that the words "one", "two" up to "ten" denote the objects that are numbered, whereas numerals beyond ten denote both the number and the numbered objects. The numerals are used while recollecting something or some persons addressed. In such cases the usage presupposes the knowledge of the object denoted by the words used, and hence the numerals must denote the number which becomes the relevant qualifier in such usages.

(E242-243) Praśastapāda states that sound is opposed to both cause and effect. This is interpreted by some scholars as explaining how a particular sound that is produced gets destroyed. All sounds are destroyed by sounds produced subsequently. The penultimate one is destroyed by the last one and the last one by the penultimate one. This position is not admitted by Cennu Bhaṭṭa. At the moment when the penultimate one is produced the final sound is being produced. The final sound remains when the penultimate one also remains. When the penultimate one is being destroyed, the final sound still remains. Therefore the final sound cannot be destroyed by the penultimate one which does not exist in the third moment since the final one is produced. Hence it must be admitted that the final sound is destroyed by the destruction of the penultimate one.

XXI. Fallacies (again)

(E259) While dealing with the two kinds of *savyabhicāra* (*sādhāraṇa* and *asādhāraṇa*) Cennu Bhaṭṭa writes that absence of concomitance may be due either to the presence of *h* in both *sp* and *vp* or to its absence from both *sp* and *vp*. When it is the former the case is called *sādhāraṇa anaikāntika*, and when it is the latter it is called *asādhāraṇa anaikāntika*.

VYĀKHYĀ on Varadarāja's TĀRKIKARAKṢĀ
Summary by V. Varadachari

The comments on this work, which is unpublished, are made on the basis of transcript copy from the manuscripts of the Government Manuscripts Library, Madras (Ms. No. R.2923).

This commentary was left incomplete by Cennu Bhaṭṭa since he, as his pupil Rāmeśvara tells us, was snatched away by death. The commentary stops with the definition of body under the treatment of earth. Some of the interpretations are similar to those offered by Harihara but since Harihara lived after 1500 A.D. he must have known either the traditional interpretations or Cennu Bhaṭṭa's comments on, for instance, *ālocana*. Vādīndra's view is cited on qualifiers and indicators. He admits *sāmānādhikaraṇya* from the aspect of sense. Then, the cases of Devadatta holding the staff and the penance doer marked by the matted hair apply to the qualifier specifying the object. Names, which are not in the same locus, are indicators. The passage from the work of Vādīndra is then quoted. Others are stated to have held that qualifier excludes the object by being associated with it, while an indicator does the same without being associated with it.

On obstruction the view of Vādīndra, who is also called Śaṃkarakiṃkara, is cited. According to him, the *h* is proved to be perfect through favourable reasoning. Then an obstruction does not get scope, as it could not be proved to pervade the *s*. Others are stated to have maintained that an obstruction is that which has its *h* not pervaded and has pervasion evenly with the *s*. The general definition is that it is an attribute which is related to absolute absence.

The commentator refers to a view on recognition that it is of the nature of two cognitions, namely, recollection and experience, since it is produced by the operation of the impressions. As this is not the view of the Nyāya tradition, this is rejected. Recognition should be known only through (personal) experience.

On darkness, Rāmeśvara refers to five views, as held by Bhaṭṭas, Prābhākaras, Kāśyapa (traditional view), a section of the Vaiśeṣikas (*Śrīdhara*) and another whose name is not mentioned (p. 202).

(Rāmeśvara's commentary, which begins on p. 190, completes the commentary. Towards the end Rāmeśvara pays glowing tributes to his master Cennu Bhaṭṭa as an ardent Śaivite. Cennu Bhaṭṭa is said to be unsurpassed in his proficiency in all the systems of thought.)

7. TVANTOPĀDHYĀYA.

Occasional citations of this Maithila writer indicate his date to be around 1400, and that he wrote at least two works: (1) a commentary on Gaṅgeśa's *Tattvacintāmaṇi* whose title is not known, and (2) a *Makaranda* on Udayana's *Nyāyakusumāñjali.* He is quoted by Bhavanātha Miśra, Śaṃkara Miśra, Jayadeva Miśra, Padmanābha Miśra and Kṛṣṇadāsa Sārvabhauma. Dinesh Chandra thinks he is the earliest commentator on Gaṅgeśa (he is assuming Vardhamāna did not write on his father's work). References to *Makaranda*s in the literature are frequently to the later work of Rucidatta but may not all be such. Jayadeva refers to a *Makaranda* in his *Āloka*, and surely is referring to Tvanta's and not Rucidatta's *Makaranda.* "Tvanta" is probably a pseudonym.

8. GHAṬEŚA UPĀDHYĀYA

All we know of this writer is a name, quite possibly a pseudonym, cited by Vidyānivāsa. Umesh Mishra thinks he probably wrote a commentary on *Tattvacintāmaṇi.* Dinesh Chandra suggests he may even have preceded Gaṅgeśa. *New Catalogus Catalogorum* places him in the 14th century. We guess, with hardly any evidence, 1400.

9. NYĀYALOCANAKĀRA

The author of a *Nyāyalocana*, otherwise unnamed, is cited by a number of later Naiyāyikas as someone who controverted Gaṅgeśa's definition of pervasion. These citers include Śaṃkara Miśra, Vācaspati Miśra II, Vāsudeva Sārvabhauma and Haridāsa Nyāyālaṃkāra.

10. GAṄGĀDITYA

An early commentator on Gaṅgeśa's *Tattvacintāmaṇi*, Gaṅgāditya is mentioned by Vidyānivāsa Bhaṭṭācārya in his *Vivecanā*. Dinesh Chandra Bhattacharya cites a passage in that work which closely associates Gaṅgāditya with Vardhamāna, estimating that the former must have flourished around 1400 in Mithila.

11. JĪVANĀTHA MIŚRA or JAYANĀTHA MIŚRA

Umesh Mishra[1] gives us considerable information on this author. He appears to have flourished around 1400, and was the grandson of 2. Vaṭeśvara, son of Ravinātha, and the eldest brother of 12. Bhavanātha Miśra, who was the father of 21. Śaṃkara Miśra. Jīvanātha taught the *Khaṇḍanakhaṇḍakhādya* to his brother, who in turn taught it to Śaṃkara Miśra, whose commentary on the work is one of the most renowned.

Umesh Mishra also gives us a few bits of information about the tenor of this writer's thought. He was responsible for the definition of *pakṣa* quoted by Śaṃkara Miśra in the *Vādivinoda*.[2] He also criticizes Gaṅgeśa.[3] He seems to have been also a specialist on *dharmaśāstra*, being cited by Narahari and Vācaspati Miśra as well as Gokulanātha Upādhyāya in that regard. We know of none of his works, if there were any.

12. BHAVANĀTHA MIŚRA or DUVE or AYĀCI MIŚRA

Bhavanātha was the younger brother of 11. Jīvanātha Miśra and the father and teacher of 21. Saṃkara Miśra. Thus he is the grandson of Vāṭeśvara. His date is approximately computable, therefore, as 1410. V. Varadachari believes he wrote a commentary on the *Nyāyakusumāñjali*. He apparently wrote on Pūrvamīmāṃsā and Grammar, and Umesh Mishra[1] believes he is the author of the well-known *Nayaviveka*, a prominent Prābhākara work. However, the date of that work is usually estimated as many centuries before—1050, e.g., is the estimate of T.R. Chintamani, who reports that that work must have been written before the time of Vedānta Deśika, who criticizes it.[2]

Bhavanātha, as the father of Śaṃkara Miśra, is the central figure in traditional stories about his famous son. He was known as "Ayāci", Umesh Mishra tells us, because he took a vow, "like so many other Maithila scholars of old, not to accept any gift or anything in any form from any person." At the end of daily *pūjā* there is a passage which says "may we not beg or ask for anything from any person". "*Ayāci*" is the sequence of phonemes in this passage singifying nonbegging.[3]

Bhavanātha came to Vaidyanāthadhāma (modern Devaghara, in the Santhal Parganas, Bihar) "and performed penance at the feet of Lord Śiva, Vaidyanātha. There Bhavanātha Miśra prayed to the Lord for a son, as he, being a Mīmāṃsaka, had full faith in the *Śāstra* that one who did not get a son obtained hell after death. After some days they were told in a dream that the Lord himself would take birth in the form of a son from his wife and fulfil his desires. So they returned home very happy and in course of time, Bhavanātha got a male child from Bhāvanī. It is said that just before the child was about to come out of the womb of his mother, the drum of the *carmakāra* began to sound without being beaten by any stick. It is a custom in India that the wife of a *carmakāra* performs the first nursing at the time of the delivery of a child. The *carmakāra* (shoemaker) told his wife that the particular event was a very auspicious one and it predicted that some great person was to take birth in that village that very day. Just after that she was called to attend to the case of a child birth in the Miśra family."[4] This same *carmakāra's* wife figures in further stories about Śaṃkara Miśra (see below).

13. JINAVARDHANA SŪRI or ĀDINĀTHA JAIN

Jetly refers to this Jain author as "the high priest of the Kharatara Gaccha from 1406 A.D. to 1419 A.D. ... successor of Jinarājasūri of Kharataragaccha...Then he was deposed on account of his having transgressed one of the vows."[1] His *Saptapadārthīṭīkā* must have been written before 1414, since a manuscript exists having that date. He appears to have also written the *Vāgbhaṭālaṅkāraṭīkā*, published in Grantharatnamala, Bombay (cf. NCat II,80).

JINAVARDHANĪ on Śivāditya's SAPTAPADĀRTHĪ
Summary by V. Varadachari

"E" references are to the edition by J.S. Jetly (B2984; RB4601) of the *Saptapadārthī* and Jinavardhana's commentary, Lalpatbhai Dalpatbhai Series 1,1963.

(E1) The word "*guru*" (in "Śambhu (Śiva), the *guru*") is explained as meaning one who speaks (*gṛṇāti*) of *tattva*.

(E5) The categories are not only objects of valid cognition but are also the objects of God's perception.

(E6) Kaṇāda did not enumerate absence as a category. Yet it is to be recognized as the seventh category, since Kaṇāda does not deny it. The evidence of commentators on the *Vaiśeṣikasūtras* supports this.

(E8) The universal of the "highest" (*para*) kind is distinguished in order to account for that which only exists (*kevalānuvṛttihetu*). The "lowest" (*apara*) has the least occurrence (*atyalpavṛtti*) in comparison with the "highest" kind, and the "intermediate" (*parāpara*) has the nature of both.

(E9) Jinavardhana denies the contention of some scholars who consider existence, the universal of the "highest" kind, to be merely the very nature of a category.

(E10) Individuators are things which differentiate the ultimate substances one from another and do not require anything to differentiate themselves. Jinavardhana offers an interesting explanation here. The jar, etc., which are not self-luminous, are illuminated by the lamp, but the lamp does not need anything else to illuminate it. Similarly, atoms and all-pervading substances are differentiated by individuators, but an individuator does not require something else to differentiate it.

(E12) Objection: The atoms of earth are noneternal because they are the locus of colors produced from cooking. For example, the atoms of a jar must be noneternal since color produced from cooking is located in it.

Answer: The opponent's *hetu* is fallacious (specifically, commits the *kālātyayāpadiṣṭa* or "mistimed" fallacy), as atoms are proved by instruments of knowledge to be eternal.

(Inference:) Earthness inheres in eternal substances (among others), since it is a universal property of pots and cloths, like existence (*sattva*). Now since it is impossible for earthness to inhere in *ākāśa*, etc., it must inhere in eternal atoms, i.e., atoms of earth.

(E13) While discussing the noneternal nature of products, the author strikes an ethical note by citing a passage (source not known) which means that the self is distinct from the body since it is destructible like a cloud (*ghanaghana*) tossed by a violent wind and that therefore one should avoid supposing one owns his body.

(E16) The visual organ is of the nature of the element fire. The nature of fire is to burn anything with which it comes into contact. The hot touch of this (ocular) fire is unmanifested, that is, nothing that comes into contact with the eye is consumed by its fire. Otherwise, the eyeball would have been burnt and the rays of light which emerge from the eye would burn the objects on which they are cast. So the visual organ must be admitted to have been created as possessing unmanifested touch, and the basis for this creation is only the *adṛṣṭa* of living things.

(E18) Gold is shown to have the nature of the element fire.

Objection: Gold is of the nature of earth, because it comes from the mine, like salt, etc.

Answer: No, for diamonds and other luminescent substances come from mines too. They are of the nature of fire since they, like lamps, shine (in the dark) without dependence on any other substance to illuminate them.

Objection: Gold is not of the nature of fire, because it has weight, like a clod of earth.

Answer: No. Gold does have earthy parts as well as fiery ones, and the weight arises from the earthy parts. It is these same earthy parts which are responsible for the color and touch of gold to be unmanifested.

Finally, gold is not affected by extreme heat.

(E22) Among the three additional spatial directions mentioned by Śivāditya,[2] Jinavardhana says that *nāgī* is the lower one, *brāhmī* the higher one, and that *raudrī* is the center of all the ten directions.

(E24) By "self" (*ātman*) Jinavardhana means something which is single and has the nature of Brahman. A passage is cited in support of this which says that there is only one *ātman* in each being, and that like the moon in the water it appears to be many due to many imposed properties.

(E25-26) An objector to the hypothesis of variegated color is cited as arguing that if this color is one it is not variegated, and if it is variegated it is not one. The author concludes in favor of variegated color, however.

(E26) While illustrating various tastes the author cites as an example of bitter taste "*rājī*" and for pungent taste "*babūla*". (These words are not Sanskrit in origin.) Lime and the myrobalan are said to have variegated taste.

(E28) The uses of the terms "*aṇu*" and "*hrasva*" with reference to the size of a jar, etc., have to be understood in a secondary sense. These terms apply primarily to atoms and dyads alone.

(E29) The word "perception" (*pratyakṣa*) is derived as that which moves towards *akṣa*, i.e., the sense organ. The explanation of the inferential result (*anumiti*) as thinking subsequent (to perception) is rather strange.

(E33) Of interest are the explanations offered for some of the fallacies. *Anadhyavasita* occurs only in the *p* and is not known to be related by pervasion to the *s* in any instances other than the *p*. *Kālātyayāpadiṣṭa* is what is contradicted by instruments of knowledge. *Prakaraṇasama* proves both the *s* and what is other than the *s*; it is also called *satpratipakṣa*, and some even call it *viruddhāvyabhicārī*.[3]

(E34) In the context of propositional/nonpropositional (*savikalpaka*/*nirvikalpaka*) perception, Jinavardhana interprets the word *vikalpa* as that which differentiates (*paricchidyate*) an object (*vastu*) when it is considered (*kalpyate*) as an individual (*viśeṣa*). It involves understanding a thing's name, etc.

(E35) The word *saṃsārika* is explained as meaning the stage when a self takes (*saṃśṛiyate*) to the source (*yoni*), and the word *saṃśṛiyate* is in turn explained as meaning "revolves" (*bambhramyate*).

(E36) Weight is said to be "of the nature of aggregate" (*samāhārarūpa*) in the sense that many light things such as *arka* grass, cotton, etc., may be bundled up together, and though no one of the things has any weight worth considering, the aggregate has weight.

(E36-37) Viscidity is of two kinds—natural (*svābhāvika*) and conditional (*aupādhika*), i.e., something arising from a condition, in this case contact with a water-atom. This viscidity gets mixed through that contact with the water and is then noticed in earthy things such as ghee, etc.

(E37) As example of elasticity Jinavardhana cites the example of the dog's tail which, though kept straight by force for some months, gets its curved nature back.[4]

(E37) *Dharma* is that which sustains (*dharati*), which protects one from misery (*duḥkhebhyastrāyate*).[5]

(E39) While illustrating the five kinds of motion, Jinavardhana classifies each one as coming under three heads—what is prescribed, what is prohibited and what is neutral. The illustrations are interesting. Under the "lifting up" (*utkṣepaṇa*) kind, the "prescribed" kind is stated to become the cause for increase of merit, and the illustration is the lifting up of the hand in reciting the Vedas. (This is informative of Vedic recitation in the 14th century.) Bowing to a superior person is a motion of the "going down" (*apakṣepaṇa*) kind conducive to increase of one's merit. Stretching forth one's hands illustrates the "going out" (*prasaraṇa*) kind, and the "going" (*gamana*) kind is illustrated by undertaking a pilgrimage which increases one's merit.

(E48) A universal is eternal, single and inheres in many things. Jinavardhana notes that according to some scholars the word "single" does not convey any sense except to refer to the universal's nature; it does not differentiate the universal from anything, and must have been the result of haste.

(E54) Passion (*kāma*), delusion (*moha*), greed (*lobha*), hypocrisy (*dambha*), compassion (*kāruṇya*) and detachment (*vairāgya*) are all kinds of "desire" (*icchā*). Similarly, Jinavardhana takes impatience (*akṣama*), egoism (*ahaṃkāra*), etc., as included under "hatred" (*dveṣa*).

(E55) *Bhāvanā* or "reflection" (a variety of *saṃskāra*) is formed in the self by seeing an object not previously perceived, e.g., when a South Indian sees a camel.

(E59) The hare's horn is cited as an example of absolute absence. The difference between this and the other kinds of absence is brought out here. In this kind of absence, the two objects have no connection—i.e., hare and horn are not denied to exist, but the relation between them is denied. In the other cases an object itself is denied to exist.

14. ŚIVAPATI

The father of 29.Yajñapati, Śivapati seems to have written a work on Nyāya, now lost, on which his son based his own *Tattvacintāmaṇiprabhā.*

15. VIṢṆUBHAṬṬA

A son of Peddi Bhaṭṭa and pupil of 6. Cinnambhaṭṭa, he composed a *Niruktivivṛti* on Cinnambhaṭṭa's *Tarkabhāṣāprakāśikā.* He must have flourished around 1420.

16. RĀMEŚVARA

Pupil of Cinnambhaṭṭa, mentioned earlier as having completed his teacher's *Tārkikarakṣāsaṃgraha.* Should be dated around 1420.

17. NĀRĀYAṆA ĀCĀRYA

He was the author of commentary *Dīpikā* or *Nārāyaṇī* on Udayana's *Ātmatattvaviveka.* V. Varadachari notes that a manuscript dated 1462 exists, and that his style seems to suggest a pre-Śaṃkara Miśra authorship. Prof. Varadachari writes: "The colophon at the end of the first section refers to the author as Nārāyaṇācārya, son of Kṛṣṇācārya of Atrigotra. The author was deeply learned in the system of Nyāya (*nyāyavidyāvipaścit*). The author's father was an ornament (*tilaka*) of Atrigotra. At the end of the second and third sections the author refers to himself as Nārāyaṇa. At the end of the third section his father is stated to have been the chief or head of Atrigotra, and at the end of the last section he himself, as Nārāyaṇācārya, is said to have been the head." The Sanskrit introduction to E by Dundhiraja

Sastri makes the suggestion that the author could have been a southerner, since the manuscript of this commentary is available in the library of the Royal Asiatic society of Bombay. The English introduction declares that he was a Mahārāṣṭra Brahmin. That the author could have been a southerner may be conceded from his name: the word *ācārya* does not generally form part of the names of writers in North India. That he belonged to Mahārāṣṭra is yet to be proved. The manuscript could have been acquired from an adjacent area.

DĪPIKĀ on Udayana's ĀTMATATTVAVIVEKA
Summary by V. Varadachari

"E" references are to the edition (B2678; RB3934) by Dundhiraja Sastri, Chowkhamba Sanskrit Series 85, 1936-1940.

Since the author does not offer any helpful comments on the passages of the text which tolerate Advaita it is not possible to identify his views on Vedānta. This shows that the author's interest, as is evident from the benedictory stanza, is to strengthen knowledge of the self. He presumably did not care to project his own views in a commentary on a work like the *Ātmatattvaviveka*, and does not take advantage of his role through any display of erudition. He is faithful to the context and does not go beyond it.

The virtue of his commentary is that he gives a clear exposition of those passages where Udayana states a corollary to something he has just proved; later commentators largely ignore these passages. The following passage serves to illustrate this.

14. (E56-59) Udayana says "if agreement cannot prove this (invariable concomitance between existence and momentariness), difference cannot either." Suppose the Buddhist argues thus: Whatever is not momentary cannot produce an effect, and so cannot exist: thus momentariness and existence are invariably concomitant. This is an "argument from difference"; as an example the Buddhist may offer the hare's horn. The Buddhist may go on to argue that a momentary existent, efficient at that instant, becomes nonexistent and so inefficient naturally at the next instant. This inefficiency is not a matter of the presence or absence of accessories, he urges, but a natural characteristic of a momentary existent.

Nārāyaṇa gives an effective rejoinder to this. That an effect is produced with the aid of accessories and is not produced when they are not available stands proved on the strength of experience. Even the Buddhist will have to admit it, since he recognizes a momentary existent possessing *kurvadrūpa* as capable of producing an effect only when associated with accessories. A seed, say, produces a sprout only when associated with earth, water, fire and air; it is only when these are present that the seed gains its *kurvadrūpa* or efficiency. Thus efficiency is just the presence of accessories, and so an existent, stable thing may be efficient at time *t*, inefficient at time $t + 1$, and efficient again at time $t + 2$—so efficient things need not be momentary, nor do existents.

13. (E45-46) In another context an opponent's absurd position is exposed by Udayana. A cause is said by the Buddhist to produce an effect at a particular time and not to produce it at another. Does this apply to the production of the effect at all places or only in one place? If the Buddhist says "at all places" the opponent will have to admit that there is no difference between places or else recognize that different causes operate at those places. Nārāyaṇa adds that by admitting that there is no difference between places the objects there will also become one. This would embarrass the Sautrāntika, who admits an external world. If the Buddhist says that different causes operate at different places, then there cannot be even one momentary object in the world.

18. ŚEṢA ŚĀRṄGADHARA

The dating of this writer presents difficulties. He was the teacher of Śeṣānanta, for whom we are told a manuscript exists of one of his works dated 1459. If that is correct Śeṣa Śārṅgadhara must have flourished at least 40 years earlier, say in 1420, which is the date we are assuming here. However, Umesh Mishra reports[1] that Śeṣānanta refers to Prataparāja as his patron, and Prataparāja lived around 1578. The other information supplied by these and other writers does not serve to settle the question, except that Umesh Mishra says that Śeṣānanta makes several references to a "*Tarkasaṃgrahakāra*". If these are references to Annambhaṭṭa it would clearly necessitate Umesh Mishra's dates for Śeṣānanta, and a correspondingly later date for Śeṣa Śārṅgadhara (say, in that case, 1545). Further examination of the relevant works seems called for.

Śeṣa Śārṅgadhara's best-known work is his *Nyāyamuktāvalī* on Udayana's *Lakṣaṇāvalī,* summarized here. *New Catalogus Catalogorum* also lists a *Tarakacandrikā* by him, known from a single manuscript located at Baroda. A doubtful reference in Volume IV of *New Catalogus Catalogorum* mentions a single manuscript of a commentary on Vardhamāna's *Kiraṇāvalīprakāśa* (ascribed on p. 156 of that Volume to "Śeṣa-Gaṅgadhara", which we assume is a misprint).

NYĀYAMUKTĀVALĪ on Udayana's LAKṢAṆĀVALĪ
Summary by Nani Lal Sen

"E" references are to the edition by Surendra Lal Gosvamin

(B2681A; RB3941) in *The Pandit*, new series 21, 1899, reprinted 1900. Section numberings follow the summary of *Lakṣaṇāvalī* in Vol. II.[2]

1. (E1-2) Śeṣa breaks new ground in commenting on the invocation by doubting the propriety of assuming a creator God when everything is governed by irrevocable *karma*. His answer is a mixture of Sāṃkhya and Vācaspati.

2. (E2-3) "Nameable" is offered as a description of the categories, not as a definition. For a definition requires specifying a property which is only-negatively concomitant, while nameability is only-positively concomitant with being a category.

3. (E3-5) "A substance is a thing which is not the locus of an absolute absence of qualities", says Udayana. The point is that a substance at the moment after its production has no quality.

Objection: That first moment of a substance's existence must qualify the substance either as a qualifier or as an implicator, but in either case there must be a relation involved, and on either alternative that relation must be contact. So, the substance has at least the quality of contact at that first moment. Therefore the problem your definition was supposed to meet is no problem at all.

Answer: Since substance is the cause of its qualities it must precede them, since causes invariably precede their effects.

Citsukha: The substance qualified by that first moment is without quality altogether; so the definition underextends.

Answer: But in Vaiśeṣika a moment is not a substance.

Citsukha: Is the absolute absence of quality-possession one or many? If one, self-dependence results. If many, confusion will arise about whether it is all or only some absences that are to be taken into account, and the result will be overextension.

Answer: No, since the locus of absolute absence of possession of one quality may without harm be the locus of the possession of some other quality. As for the first alternative, which is not the Vaiśeṣika view, the self-dependence which results is of no harm since it does not vitiate the origin or apprehension of the substance.

Objection: Not being a locus of the absolute absence of possession of quality = absolute absence of an absolute absence = possession of quality. So the definition still fails to apply to the substance at its first moment.

Answer: We don't accept the equivalence of the absolute absence of absolute absence with the counterpositive.

(E5-7) An alternative definition of substance offered by Udayana is interpreted in two possible ways by Śeṣa. Read one way it appears to overextend to include motion; read the other way it appears to overextend to include both qualities and motions. The definition, properly interpreted, reads "a substance is that which possesses a universal property which inheres in what is free from nonmateriality (*amūrtatva*) and in what is free from inhering in what inheres in what is free from materiality." The first part of the definition excludes motions from the scope of the definition, since a universal that inheres in a substance and doesn't inhere in any quality can't inhere in a motion. The second part excludes qualities, since qualityness inheres in what inheres in what has materiality.

(E7-9) A fourth definition of substance offered by Udayana is that it is what is inhered in by what is inhered in by what is inhered in (*samavetasamavetasamaveta*)!

Objection: The definition overextends to include quality, etc. For colornessness (*rūpatvatva*) inheres in colorness (*rūpatva*) which inheres in color (*rūpa*), a quality.

Answer: Colornessness is not an inhering universal, since to suppose universals of second degree courts infinite regress.

(E9-16) Objection: Sound is an additional (tenth) substance.

Answer: No. For the inferences to prove that are vitiated by obstructions. If sound is held to be a produced substance (*janya dravya*) it must have parts and be noneternal (contrary to the Mīmāṃsaka's belief). If it is held to be atomic it will be nonperceptible by the auditory organ. And if it is supposed to be nonatomic, it will also be nonperceptible, for being an eternal substance it cannot be related by inherence or contact with an unproduced substance.

Mīmāṃsaka objection: Darkness has dark color which cannot inhere in any of the five elements or in quality, etc., so it must be a substance.

Answer: How can darkness be perceived? Perception requires eternal light. Furthermore, is darkness produced or not? Not unproduced, for then it will be visually imperceptible, like *ākāśa*. And not produced, because darkness has no touch.

Objection: We infer that it does have touch from its being visually perceptible.

Answer: But you haven't proved that darkness has color.

The author of a *Tarkasaṃgraha*: Darkness is a substance, for internal-organ-ness, being a universal, must be different from the universal which inheres in what possesses impetus while being absent in things having touch, like cowness.

Answer: This inference is vitiated by an obstruction, viz., universalness inhering in either what has touch or what is without materiality.

Citsukha: The visual organ, like the tactile organ, can grasp colored things even in the absence of external light.

Answer: The example is faulty, as the tactile organ does not grasp colors.

Citsukha: Your inference, viz., that particles of darkness do not generate (*anārambhaka*), because they are without tangibility, like the internal organ, is vitiated by an obstruction, viz., the uselessness of the other organs.

Answer: No, for no matter whether absence of inherence-causality of substance or mere nongeneratingness be taken as the *s* (in the inference), the presence of an obstruction cannot be maintained. For the absence of generation can be inferred in a different way: the locus of the absolute absence of tangibility cannot generate, because it is that kind of locus, like the internal organ.

(E17) Udayana: Darkness is not a substance, because it is visually perceptible while being without a lower universal of substanceness collocative with perceptibility, like color.

Objection: A counterinference (productive of counterbalancing, can be formed by merely substituting a different example—i.e., darkness is a substance, because it is visually perceptible without dependence on external light, like external light (say, the sun).

Answer: No. Perception of external light also depends on external lighting.

4. (E18-19) Objection by the author of a *Tarkasaṃgraha*: The definition of earth (as free from the absolute absence of smell) overextends to water, etc.

Answer: No. Earth lends smell to everything else.

Objection: A flower doesn't produce smell in other things, but its smell is produced from them.

Answer: No. Odorness inheres only in earth, because it inheres only in qualities produced by cooking, like a specific quality produced by cooking.

(E20–23) "...the eternal and noneternal kinds..." Why both kinds? If earth were noneternal only, infinite regress would result. If earth were eternal only, it would be confused with other substances.

The author of a *Tarkasaṃgraha*: Earthness occurs only in noneternal substance, because it only occurs in earth, like clothness.

Answer: No, for the inference is vitiated by the following obstruction: absence of a universal directly pervaded by substanceness. Also there is a counterinference (and so counterbalance), viz., earthness occurs in both eternal and noneternal things, because it occurs in all earthy things, like existence.

Inferences are given for proving universals following old and new Vaiśeṣika theory, and inferences following Vallabha and Vādīndra are offered to prove the noneternality of the minimal perceptibilium, etc.

(E23) In the *Vedāntakalpataru* of Amalānanda the Naiyāyika thesis—that the body is not composed of five elements because then it would not be a substance, like manyness (*bahutva*), and because it would not be perceptible, like the contact between air and the tree, and because it would involve cross-connection of universals—is refuted on the following three grounds: (1) if the thesis were correct the minimal perceptibilium should also be imperceptible; (2) cross-connection is not a fault, since it doesn't preclude speaking of appropriate behaviour following an inference; so cowness and horseness can both overlap earthness inference; (3) verbal testimony.

(E23-27) Answer: (1) That the minimal perceptibilium is imperceptible is incorrect, since there is deviation with respect to sound, etc., which are qualities like contact and yet are perceptible. (2) If cross-connection is not a fault, cowness and horseness may be the same universal.

Objection: But a universal may cover individuals of various sorts; consider variegated color.

Answer: That is irrelevant here, since we are talking of something outside perception...So, the body is not composed of five elements.

(E27-29) "The body is a locus of enjoyment (*bhogāyatana*), says Udayana. What is it to be a locus of enjoyment? It cannot be the *āśraya* (locus) of experience, because the self is that. And it cannot be the producer of enjoyment, for both the self and the internal organ answer to that description. It cannot be the limitorness to enjoyment resident in the self, for that also is satisfied by the internal organ. Furthermore, the produced specific qualities of all-pervading things (*vibhukāryaviśeṣaguṇa*), since they are (spatially) regulated by the noninherence cause, do not reside in the body. The correct analysis is that being a locus of enjoyment is being the locus of contact with self produced by awareness (*jñānajanakātmasaṃyogāśrayatva*) as qualified by being a final whole (*antyāvayavitva*). Vādi Vāgīśvara is quoted as holding that what is material (*mūrta*) and having contact of all its parts with the tactual organ is the body.

8.(E35-39) Vallabha argues that sound is a quality, because while having a universal it is a nonvisually perceptible external content, like smell.

Objection: The *h* in the above argument deviates, since a tactually-perceived jar, etc., and motion are both nonvisually perceptible but are not qualities. If "visually" is interpreted in other ways it still involves either deviation or an obstruction.

Śeṣa answers this argument by *tarka*: if a substance is partless then it is not perceptible by me, but there is no *asiddhi* (i.e., sound can still be nonvisually perceptible external content) of the *pakṣadhar*-

matā since a universal qualifies it insofar as it is other than an existent quality; or if the *h* is taken to be "graspability by a single external sense-organ of mine while possessing a universal, even if not visually perceptible", there is nothing wrong.

Ākāśa is eternal and ubiquitous, as proved by the following reasons: *ākāśa* is a substance uncaused by another substance, and it is a substance without parts. Scripture, which is quoted by the opponent to the contrary, has to be interpreted in as secondary sense; in addition, other scriptural passages are adduced to support the present thesis.

Advaitin: *Ākāśa* is noneternal because it is manifest (*vibhakta*).

Answer: Then you will have to accept duality (since you have admitted something other than Brahman that manifests itself).

Advaitin: Brahman is the material cause of *ākāśa*.

Answer: No, because if Brahman is material it contradicts your school's doctrine, while if it is not material it cannot be the material cause of a substance (*ākāśa*).

Author of a *Tarkasaṃgraha: Ākāśa* does not possess a universal and is not the locus of sound, because it possesses no mark.

Answer: When a property-possessor has been established the establishment that it has a property follows.

9. (E40-43) Author of *Tarkasaṃgraha*: The definition of time (in Udayana's text) overextends to include spatial direction (*dik*). And if emended to exclude spatial direction, it comes to overextend to *adṛṣṭa*. Then if it is further emended—by adding the specification that time is a substance to exclude *adṛṣṭa*—it still overextends to God. And finally, if it is once again emended by adding "being a specific instrumental cause" (*nimittasādhāraṇya*) to exclude God, this will refute your thesis about God and *adṛṣṭa*.

Answer: This argument reveals ignorance of our doctrine (*samaya-maryādā*), and is rebutted by accepting the suggested emendations.

Author of *Tarkasaṃgraha*: The awareness of simultaneity, etc., are likewise contrary to your doctrine. Furthermore, are such things the same as time, or different? If the same, they cannot be used to prove time; if the latter, they need to be separately defined.

Answer: They depend on time conditioned by a limitor. Furthermore, Vādīndra says that simultaneity, etc., are qualities, since they are not the locus of any quality, like farness (*paratva*), etc. Farness, etc., depend on the sun's motions as limitors, while simultaneity, etc., depend on different limitors. Otherwise farness and nearness would either have to be discarded, or simultaneity may be included in farness and nearness. In Praśastapāda farness, etc., are used in the inference to time.

Author of a *Tarkasaṃgraha*: This is wrong. For how is time to be inferred? Not as an inherence cause, for it is not the self. Not as noninherence cause, for it is a substance. Not as an instrumental cause, for it cannot be perceived by the senses. So, time is nothing but *adṛṣṭa*.

Answer: Time is inferred as inherence cause through the method of residues (*pariśeṣa*): there is nothing else which can serve as inherence cause in relation to the noninherence causes (here, contact) of farness, etc.

11. (E45-46) What is the proof of God's existence? "The sprout, etc., have an agent, because they are effects, like pot", says Udayana. Śeṣa shows that there can be no limitor here vitiating this proof.

(E46-49) To prove the multiplicity of ordinary selves Śeṣa refutes the *anirvacanīyatva* of difference in a conventional manner. To say that the counterpositiveness of an absolute absence located in a single substance has the counterpositiveness of the absolute absence located in itself involves contradiction.

12. (E49-51) Śeṣa finds fault with the definition of specific quality provided by Udayana, since (he argues) it overextends to the largest size (*paramamahatparimāṇa*), which cannot reside both in earth and what is other than earth. If, in order to improve the definition, the clause "pervaded by qualityness" is explained as "being directly pervaded by qualityness", then the definition will underextend by failing to cover natural liquidity (*sāṃsiddhikadravatva*) and traces (*bhāvanā*). Śeṣa offers his own definition: a specific quality possesses a universal graspable by the olfactory organ and which is not located in what does not inhere in what has a common locus with the absolute absence of everything. Vādi Vāgīśvara's definition is also cited.

17. (E69-70) Individuators are proved by the following inferences: (1) time is the locus of inherence of what is without universalness and without having something inherent in it, because it is a substance, like a pot; (2) time is the locus of inherence of what is without universalness and without qualityness, because it is a substance, like a pot.

The definition of inherence ("an eternal relation") does not overextend to the qualifier-qualified relation between an eternal counterpositive and its absence. For, being a relation here applies only to presences (*bhāvamātravṛtti*). Absence is not apprehended through any relation. The conditions for awareness of absence are regulated by the collocation of causes of the awareness of its counterpositive.

Vallabha's inference to prove inherence is cited with approval, and the charge of its involving infinite regress is refuted.

19. VĀSUDEVA SŪRI

Vāsudeva is the author of a commentary, *Padapañcikā*, on Bhāsarvajña's *Nyāyasāra*. He tells us he is the son of Sūryasūri of Kashmir. The style of the commentary, and its lack of any trace of Navyanyāya style, suggests it is probably a work stemming from a period preceding that covered in the present volume. Since we are fortunate to have the following summary by Prof. Varadachari we include it here in close juxtaposition to the commentary of Jayasiṃhasūri on the same text.

PADAPAÑCIKĀ on Bhāsarvajña's NYĀYASĀRA
Summary by V. Varadachari

"E" references are to the edition by K. Sambasiva Sastri (B2508; RB3795), Trivandrum Sanskrit Series 109, 1931. Section headings correspond to those in the summary of the *Nyāyasāra* in Vol. II of this Encyclopedia.[1]

CHAPTER ONE

5. (E7-8) Dream awareness is treated by the Vaiśeṣikas as a distinct kind of misconception. This is rejected by Vāsudeva.

6. (E9) While enumerating the instruments of knowledge Bhāsarvajña uses the word "*iti*" after the word for "verbal testimony". This word "*iti*" restricts the number of instruments. Otherwise the number might even be seven.

7. (E15-16) Inherence is not apprehended in all cases. For instace, inherence of color is apprehended in the pot. This is hard for ordinary people to cognize. Those whose understanding is stabilized by training in the *śāstras* will be able to apprehend inherence either as a property or a property-possessor. In this it differs from absence, which is presented in ordinary awareness.

How is inherence perceived? It is inferred that it becomes the content of nonpropositional perception.

Some say that inherence is apprehended in cases that involve contact, inherence in what is in contact, inherence and qualifier-qualificand-relation, unlike absence which may be apprehended through five sense-object connections. Vāsudeva rejects this on the ground that inherence is never perceived as either a property or a property-possessor.

The way that the qualifier-qualificand relation enters into the grasping of inherence is explained thus. The cognition of an object having color arises from the color and from the substance having it. But the difference between them is not actually apprehended.

Therefore inherence is said to be apprehensible through nonpropositional perception.

Objection: What is perceived through nonpropositonal perception is subsequently perceived by propositional perception.

Answer: No, for one who walks along a road is merely aware of the grass but does not cognize it (as grass).

CHAPTER TWO

10. (E22) Objection: The word "mediate" (in "Inference is the instrument of mediate experience...") is superfluous, for since it is specified that inference "works through direct invariable concomitance" the possibility of immediateness is precluded.

Answer: Some scholars hold that mediacy and immediacy are universals which can be perceived. It is to reject this concept that the word "mediate" appears here, they say. Vāsudeva feels that when fire and smoke are cognized as coexisting there arises the direct cognition that smoke does not exist without fire, which is brought about through invariable concomitance. This direct cognition is not inference, and the word "mediate" is used to exclude inference from the scope of the definition.

17. (E49) It is shown that *prakaraṇasama* and *viruddhāvyabhicārin* are distinct from each other. In the former, an *h* becomes counterbalanced when it is not efficient (*asamartha*) in arousing opposing argument. In the latter, the *h* becomes weak (*vikalaśakti*) by arousing an opposing argument.

28. (E60) There is no direction given in *Nyāyasūtra* I.2.2 (where quibble is defined) which requires that quibblers must act with good intentions.

(E62) Cavil is of two kinds, (1) employed by a person free from passion (*vītarāga*) and (2) employed by one anxious for victory in debated.

(E65) In futile rejoinder there is the intention to make the force of the rejoinder equal to the *h* already proposed. The person who employs the futile rejoinder does not intend to show that the *h* proposed is not established. His aim is to refute the view opposite to his and not merely to show that one's position is no better off than the opponent's.

CHAPTER THREE

29. (E93) Verbal testimony brings about correct and direct experience through conventional meanings. Vāsudeva remarks that conventions are created by man to convey the senses of words

in particular contexts and that produces the correct understanding in those contexts.

30. (E97-103) The Vedas cannot be admitted as valid because of their being eternal, for the auditory organ, the internal organ, etc., are eternal (according to you) and yet they are not to be relied on since they give rise to doubt, misconception and so forth. The validity of the Vedas lies in their being the instrument for producing a specific kind of knowledge, and this is done on the basis of conventions, which must be understood. Thus they cannot be intrinsically valid. Otherwise, even those who are not acquainted with grammar should be expected to get the sense of the Vedas merely by listening to their recitation.

Validity cannot be intrinsic, either in respect to the instrument's production or the awareness of it. An effect cannot arise of its own accord; thus, validity too cannot rise of its own accord. And knowledge cannot be known by itself, for whichever be the awareness in question there is always room for doubt about its validity, and so that must be extrinsic.

Objection: The Vedas are eternal, since their author is not remembered and the Vedic tradition goes on unbroken.

Answer: The elders impart the tradition to their children. And activity is found to arise relating to rituals which are chosen by the agent even though the author of the ritual is not recalled. This is because of the faith the agent has in the practice of the disciplined, elderly persons. Human agency presupposes an independent author. His independence lies in his becoming the cause for determining the specific expressions not presupposing some other determination.

If Vedic passages and terms are admitted as eternal, then if they are fit to be apprehended by the sense organs all of them should be conjoined with the senses and so would be apprehended at all times. If they are not fit to be apprehended by the senses, than they could never be apprehended, like the atoms. If there is no condition causing them to be apprehended sometimes and not at other times, then there is no cause which would explain why they are not apprehended at a particular time.

Objection: The nonapprehension of Vedic expressions at a given time is due to the absence of any manifesting factor.

Answer: No, since no such factor is appropriate.

Objector: Yes there is; it is contact with air which causes Vedic expressions to become manifest, and disjunction from air which is the occasion for their nonmanifestation.

Answer: No, since this would imply that all such sounds should become manifested and apprehended at one and the same time, but that doesn't happen.

Objector: But the same fault will arise even if sounds are held to be produced, as you think.

Answer: No, for a cause is one thing, and a manifester another. A cause, such as a lump of clay, gives rise to an effect—say, a jar—according to the desire of an agent. The lamp, however, which is employed to disclose a cloth, discloses also the jar on which its light also falls.

32. (E105-106) Vāsudeva specifically mentions Uddyotakara and others as holding that seeing something like a cow and judging it to be a *gavaya* constitutes a distinct instrument of knowledge. But the instrument here is only verbal testimony. When someone asks the seer how he knew that the animal is a *gavaya* he answers that he knew it from the testimony of the woodsman who spoke to him about it, not through comparison.

Objection: The woodsman's utterance only provides awareness of the similarity of a certain something seen to be a cow. That it is called "*gavaya*" is a different matter.

Bhāsarvajña: Then it should follow that whenever we correctly cognize an animal as, say, a cow we would have to admit a distinct instrument of knowledge.

33. (E106-110) Comparison is mentioned in *Nyāyasūtra* I.1.3 not to say that comparison is an independent instrument of knowledge, but to serve a different purpose, viz., to justify and maintain the validity of verbal testimony. In the same way, example (*dṛṣṭānta*) is mentioned in the list of *tattvas* by Gautama but is not other than one of the members of an argument (*avayava*), and fallacious *h*, mentioned as one of the ways of losing an argument, is not other than one of those ways.

Objection: But at *Nyāyasūtra* II.1.56-59 comparison is not said to be helpful for establishing verbal testimony as valid. "Some say that verbal testimony merely corroborates what is already known through perception or inference, and is therefore not a separate instrument."

Vāsudeva: Of course corroboration is admitted, but that is not sufficient reason to deny independent validity to verbal testimony. An objection could as easily be raised as to why Gautama raised the doubt about comparison's validity at II.1.42-43 and why he establishes its validity.

34. (E110-114) If one argued that since presumption is not a kind of inference involving two examples it is a different instrument from inference, it would follow that only-positive inference would have to be judged a distinct instrument. Likewise, if slight difference in an instrument were to be thought to sanction treatment of the two as distinct, then propositional and nonpropositional perception

would be distinct instruments—so we would have five kinds of instruments (three kinds of inference and two of perception) rather than two.

38. (E119) Some think that memory and intention (*saṃkalpa*) are objects of knowledge by the internal organ. Others classify sleep, laziness (*ālasya*) and passion (*rāga*) under that heading.

39. (E119-120) As to why the body is stated in the text as "pain" (i.e., frustration), Vāsudeva observes that the body is the cause of both satisfaction (pleasure) and frustration (pain). Even satisfaction (*sukha*) is frustrating (painful, *duḥkha*), since it is associated with frustration, and so the word "*duḥkha*" is used with reference to the body. That is, body and the other things must be reflected upon as of the nature of frustration and so become responsible for the rise of nonattachment to their objects.

42. (E122-123) "Selves are of two kinds..." This is intended to set aside the view that monistic knowledge is the means to liberation. Vāsudeva cites Muṇḍaka Upaniṣad III.1.1 and *Bhagavadgītā* 15.16-17.

"The means to the cutting of pain is knowledge of reality...."

(E134-135) In connection with Bhāsarvajña's discussion of yoga, Vāsudeva notes that the three kinds of frustration can be endured by one whose mind has become trained to remain calm. This penance is called "*tapas*" as it leads to the accumulation of the noninstigating (*nivartaka*) *dharma* and to the destruction of *adharma*. Practices like *cāndrāyaṇa* are also penances as they too give rise to the endurance of frustrations caused by abstaining from food. When noninstigating *dharma* gets accumulated, faith in such practices gets strengthened. When *adharma* gets destroyed, the obstacles to concentration such as confusion, passion and *kleśas* get destroyed. Then the mind becomes well-controlled. Vāsudeva quotes from Manu (XI. 234, 239, 241) to support this.

The word *svādhyāya* which occurs in *Yogasūtras* II.1 is taken by Bhāsarvajña as repetition of the calm *mantra* that denotes God. Vāsudeva states that the *mantra* should be a calm one, meaning that the *mantras* of low (*kṣudra*) people are not meant here. By using the word *īśvara* Bhāsarvajña means that the *mantra* should denote only God. As an alternative, Vāsudeva suggests that the study of the *Bhagavadgītā* and other works that deal with yoga could be taken to have been meant here by the word *svādhyāya*.

Meditation on God is constant thinking about God or worshipping Him with praise, flowers, etc., and surrendering all deeds in Him who is the most supreme preceptor.

(E137-138) "*Yama*s and *niyama*s...." Vāsudeva notes the five *yamas* that Patañjali enumerates (YS II.30) and which are causes of purification and development, and that purification here means the destruction of *adharma*, haughtiness and self-conceit. He adds that these are *yamas* when they are unrestricted in terms of space, time and condition and become *niyamas* when such restrictions affect them. *Niyamas*, which are also five according to Patañjali (YS II.32), are enumerated as circumambulating God, adoring *saṃdhyā*, and doing *japa*. Vāsudeva notes that these three illustrate the *niyamas* in point of space, time and condition respectively. With reference to *japa* it is said that "condition" here means only purity of mind.

(E140) On *dhāraṇā*, which is defined as binding the mind to a place, Vāsudeva notes that in the opinion of some scholars the place refers to the navel, the heart and other bodily locations, whereas others say it means the sun, etc. The *ācārya* takes it as meaning the supreme self, since those who seek liberation take to worship of Him.

(E141) Frustrations are of many kinds, for they are produced by wasting one's attention on noticing more prosperous situations than those in which one is oneself placed. A reflection on this would lead to the loss of expectations of acquiring status of Brahmā, etc., and this is what is called nonattachment. Liberation is a state in which relative considerations of superiority and inferiority are absent.

43. (E144) When a man who carries a heavy burden feels refreshed on being relieved of it, his satisfaction does not consist in the absence of frustration. The word "satisfaction" (*sukha*) is used only to denote the sensation arising out of the contact of the body with air currents, etc., and not to convey the sense of absence of frustration. There cannot be any activity for attaining liberation if there is not to be experience of the ordinary kind.

20. GUṆARATNA SŪRI

Bimal Krishna Matilal, in his introductory comments preceding his edition of Śaśadhara's *Nyāyasiddhāntadīpa* with Guṇaratna's *Ṭippaṇī* (L.D. Series 56, 1976) provides the best estimate of Guṇaratna's identity and date. He tells us there were as many as four Guṇaratnas, but that the author of this *Ṭippaṇī* can be identified with the author of a well-known book on grammar titled *Kriyāratnasamuccaya*, written in 1468 *vikrama saṃvat*, i.e., 1412. The same Guṇaratna is also known for his *Ṭīkā* on Haribhadra's *Ṣaḍdarśanasamuccaya*. A biography of this Guṇaratna confirms this identification, and refers to Guṇaratna's "vast learning and great skill in Tarkaśāstra" and debate. Guṇaratna can also be identified as the teacher of 26. Bhuvanasundara Sūri, who commented on Vādīndra's *Mahāvidyāviḍambana* and acknowledges his teacher Guṇaratna's knowledge of texts on *tarka*.

Guṇaratna's *Ṭippaṇī* only deals with four chapters of Śaśadhara's work, those on *Vādavidhi*, *Apūrva*, *Anyathākhyāti* and *Arthāpatti*. These four chapters constitute 98 pages of text, however. Matilal specluates that this was Guṇaratna's last work and was left unifinished.

21. ŚAṂKARA MIŚRA

Śaṃkara Miśra, the son of 12.Bhavanātha Miśra, lived during the second quarter of the 15th century in the village of Sarisava, about 18 miles from Darbhanga, belonging to the important Srotriya family of Mithilā called Śodarapura.[1]

Śaṃkara's importance in the traditions of Nyāya and of Mithilā can be gauged by the stories that have grown up around him. We have quoted above Umesh Mishra's report of the tradition about his birth as an incarnation of Śiva. Another famous legend concerns Śaṃkara's precociousness. "The wife of Bhavanātha Miśra (her name was Bhāvānī) was so poor that she could not give any reward to the shoemaker's wife on that happy occasion (of Śaṃkara's birth), but she made a promise to give to her all that the child would get as his first earning. The newly born babe began to grow like a very precocious child and learnt a good deal of Sanskrit even before he reached his fifth year."

"It is said that once a Rājā of Mithilā, while going on tour, had to stay for a night near the house of Bhavanātha Miśra and saw the young child playing with other children near about." The Rājā sent for the child, and discovering his talent asked Śaṃkara to recite some verses for him. "The child asked the Rājā—should he recite verses of his own composition, or that of others? The Rājā was astonished to hear this and made an enquiry if he could compose himself any verse in Sanskrit. Thereupon the child said—

bālo'haṃ jagadānanda na me bālā sarasvatī
apūrṇe pañcame varṣe varṇayāmi jagattrayam.

(O King! I am a young boy, but my learning is by no means inconsiderable. So I am ready to describe all the three worlds even before I have reached my fifth year in age.)

After Śaṃkara had capped this performance with other even more remarkable verses, "the Rājā was very much pleased at his wonderful genius and ordered him to take away as much gold coins as he could carry from his treasury. The young boy Śaṃkara took as much as he could carry. It is said that as he reached near the outer door of his house his father, who was studying in a room in the outer courtyard, happened to see the boy and guessed some unusual event. So he asked the boy not to enter the house and called his wife to look into the matter. The mother came out and saw the boy with gold coins in his possession. She also asked the boy not to enter the house and to leave all the coins on the ground there. Then she called the father and told him everything."

"Permitted by her husband she sent for the wife of the *carmakāra* who had been promised the gift of the first earning of the boy as her auspicious reward. She came and was asked to carry away the entire amount." The shoemaker's wife demurred but was eventually persuaded to let the mother fulfil her promise and took away the money. "But she spent a large part of it in getting a big tank dug in that very place. This tank exists even today though in a very very mutilated condition and is associated with the name of wife of the *carmakāra*."

"Thereafter the father left that house, as it had become polluted because a gift had been brought into that place. He then constructed another house at a little distance from the old house. Thus, he retained his name Ayāci Miśra, spotless."[2]

Śaṃkara Miśra, besides his voluminous writings on Nyāya and Vaiśeṣika of which seven have been edited and one translated, was also a poet (author of *Paṇḍitavijaya* and *Rasārṇava*), a dramatist (*Gaurīdigambaraprahasana*, a comedy on the marriage of Śiva and Pārvatī), and several important works on *Smṛti* or *Dharmaśāstra*. Vidyābhūṣaṇa tells us he was the guru of the jurist Vardhamāna Upādhyāya.[3] And he must have had many students, since according to tradition "there is a copy of the *Harivaṃśa* preserved in his house which was written by his students in one night!"[4]

It is apparent that Śaṃkara viewed the thought of Gaṅgeśa's tradition as that of a rival, different from his own. Dinesh Chandra speculates that that is because he seems to have commented on a work, titled *Mahārṇava*, which Dinesh Chandra identifies as the Prābhākara Mīmāṃsā work by Vaṭeśvara titled *Mīmāṃsā-mahārṇava*.[5] Though he wrote a commentary (*Mayūkha*) on the *Tattvacintāmaṇi* (D.C. Bhattacharya and Umesh Mishra think this is probably his first work; it disowns any originality and attributes its thought entirely to his father), that commentary was left unrecognized by the followers of Gaṅgeśa, and has yet to be published. His attitude toward Vardhamāna is consistent with this: in this commentary on Vallabha's *Nyāyalīlāvatī* he nowhere mentions Vardhamāna's name, though in several places Vardhamāna's interpretations have been anonymously alluded to and criticized.

ĀMODA on Udayana's NYĀYAKUSUMĀÑJALI
Summary by V. Varadachari

"E" references are to the edition by N.C. Vedantatirtha (B2699; RB3972), Asutosh Sanskrit Series 4, 1954, 1964. Section references are those used in the summary of Udayana's work in Vol. II of this Encyclopedia.

BOOK ONE

179-189. (E120) The words *sahakāriśakti* ("contributing causal factors" in the summary in Vol. II, p. 569) is held by Śaṃkara Miśra to be acceptable to all systems of thought under different names such as *māyā, prakṛti* and *avidyā.* The word *māyā* is favored by "Ekadaṇḍins", i.e., the Advaitins who hold the universe to be a product of *māyā.* Actually, this "*māyā*" is only *adṛṣṭa.* The Sāṃkhyas take *prakṛti* as the ultimate cause, but it too is only *adṛṣṭa.* The Tridaṇḍins hold that the universe springs from *avidyā* which is "afraid of knowledge."[6]

BOOK TWO

121-136. (E179) The commentary on Udayana's proof of the occurrence of creation and dissolution cyclically is clear. Dissolution of the universe need not be questioned, as it is evident that jars, etc., are eventually destroyed.

141-172. (E195) The interpretation of *māyā* indicated in Book One (above) is contracted by the sense of the words *brahmapariṇateḥ* (in Udayana's prose). In commenting on *this* passage, Śaṃkara Miśra says that it is the followers of Bhāskara who are called Tridaṇḍins, and that they hold that Brahman transforms itself into jars and other objects.[7]

BOOK THREE

8. (E221) The passage (in Udayana's prose on III.6) "*mīmāṃsakastoṣayitavyo bhīṣaitavyaśca*" gets an important application to the context. The context is that there are instruments of knowledge which show that God does not exist. The Mīmāṃsakas admit *apūrva* and other things which are not perceptible, but reject the existence of God, who is also not perceptible. The Nyāya contention is that nonperception of what is fit to be perceived (*yogyānupalambha*) may be employed as a means for establishing what does not exist. But

this means has no scope in the case of God, for God is not a thing which is 'fit to be perceived.''

9. (E229) Udayana's definition of an obstruction[8] is applicable to cases of equipervasion (*samavyāpti*). Śaṃkara Miśra adds that indeed it is, strictly speaking, only applicable in such cases; in the cases where pervasion is not reciprocal, obstruction is spoken of only in a metaphorical sense.

(E231) Regarding the failure to mention certain apparent fallacies, such as proving what is already accepted, etc., in the list of fallacious *hetu*s, Śaṃkara Miśra says that the classification and enumeration of fallacies is intended only to stress that the number of fallacies shall be neither more nor less. Otherwise, there is no purpose in enumerating them. Likewise, no faith should be placed in the enumeration of the instruments of knowledge as four. That Gautama rejects presumption and other instruments is no reason for admitting proving what is already accepted in the list of fallacies, for it is not referred to at all. Presumption cannot be even admitted as an instrument of knowledge, while proving what is already accepted can be admitted as a fallacy, but not as an independent one.

BOOK FOUR

4. (E316) While explaining Udayana's definition of instrument of knowledge, Śaṃkara Miśra observes that the derivation of the word *pramāṇa* has grammatical relevance and does not constitute a definition. Other accounts, like Pāṇini's *sūtra* "*svatantraḥ kartā*" (*Aṣṭādhyāyī* I.4.54), will not apply to an agent who acts under another's direction. This is because the person directed by another has no independence in doing the work concerned.

BOOK FIVE

16. (E417) While explaining Udayana's interpretation of the word "*śruteḥ*" in V.16, Śaṃkara Miśra cites passages from the *Puruṣasūkta*, *Rudrādhyāya*, *Nārāyaṇopaniṣad* and other works as illustration.

BHEDARATNA

Summary by V. Varadachari

"E" references are to the edition by S.N. Shukla (B3638; RB5621), Princess of Wales Saraswati Bhavana Texts 49, 1944.

This work is a thorough repudiation of the Advaitin standpoint as conveyed in Śrīharṣa's *Khaṇḍanakhaṇḍakhādya*.

1. (E3) In the introductory stanzas Śaṃkara Miśra contends that those who seek liberation are slack in understanding the sense of the Vedic literature, as a result of their ignoring the value of reasoning (*tarka*), reflection (*vibhāvana*), etc. When difference (*bheda*) is experienced they become indolent and refuse to take note of it. They are sure to fall away from liberation (*kaivalya*) and so are urged to listen to the author's arguments.

2. (E3) The Naiyāyikas (here, *tārkikāḥ*) alone are fit to preserve the "gem of difference" (*bhedaratna*), whereas the Vedāntins are thieves who try to steal this gem. So Śaṃkara Miśra is refuting them.

3. (E3) Difference is real (*satya*), since those who do not realize the difference between the body and the selves cannot get liberation even when they seek it.

4. (E3) There is no awareness which does not involve the presentation of difference. What does not make the world known as it actually is cannot be an instrument of knowledge.

5. (E4-10) The author now quotes a number of Upaniṣadic passages which are held to speak of nondifference, and proves that they actually refer to difference. Passages are drawn from *Bṛhadāraṇyaka Upaniṣad* II.4.5, III.8.8, IV.4.19, IV.5.6; *Kaṭha Upaniṣad* IV. 10; *Chāndogya Upaniṣad* VI; *Tripurātāpinī Upaniṣad* V. 12, IV.17; *Muṇḍaka Upaniṣad* III.1.1; *Śvetāśvatara Upaniṣad* IV.6.

Some of these passages utilize the negative particle (*nañ*) in words like *asthūla*, *anaṇu*, and thus convey the sense of difference. Brahman is stated to be other than what is gross, as well as other than what is subtle. Dissimilarity in features is indicated hereby and so the passage must convey the sense of mutual absence, i.e., difference. This is acceptable only when Brahman is distinct from what is non-Brahman. The pronouns *yuṣmat* and *tat* (in *Chāndogya* VI.8.7) must convey only difference. The same passage denies that there could be a second Brahman. When a king is said to be the only one in the world, what is denied is the existence of another king like him, not the existence of horses, elephants, etc. Again, when the *kiṃśuka* tree is stated to be the only one in the forest, it means that there is only one *kiṃśuka* tree there; it does not deny the existence of other trees!

From the *Tripurātāpinī Upaniṣad* passages one learns that only one self exists in the body, the body undergoing changes from time to time starting with childhood and passing through other stages of growth. This is like the moon, though one only, appearing as many due to its reflections in the water. These passages clearly imply duality.

The *Bṛhadāraṇyaka* passages are supplementary texts conveying praise and blame.

6. (E10) The word for reflection (viz., *manana* as in *śrotavyo mantavyo nididhyāsitavyaḥ*—"hear, reflect, meditate") is a synonym for rational inquiry (*anvīkṣā*). The self is first understood (from scripture) to be different from the body. After that it is to be known that Brahman is different from this. Thus *mantavya* ("reflect") in *Bṛhadāraṇyaka* II.4-5 means the study of the Nyāya system and nothing else, whereas the explanation of the word gives it a sense which is opposed to the knowledge of reality, and so should be rejected.

7. (E10-11) Advaitin: But no such thing as difference is known.

Answer: What do you mean? That difference is not experienced? But clearly we do make judgments based on experience, such as "the pot is different from the cloth", all the time. Or do you mean that there is no *valid* experience of difference? But the discovery of invalidity in experience comes from a thing being sublated by a valid awareness, e.g., by perception, and our perception that the pot is different from the cloth is never contradicted.

8. (E16-17) The Vedāntins, who are hard to tackle, must be handled by critical reasoning alone. E.g., one may ask questions such as: Is difference apprehended or not, and based on what? Both sides of the argument may adopt this method of raising questions.

One such question is: Does nondifference (*abheda*) reside in a Brahman which is different from non-Brahman or in a Brahman which is identical with non-Brahman? What was different cannot become nondifferent. And if there was already nondifference, there is no need to prove its existence.

9. (E18-23) There is now a discussion as to whether difference is the own-nature (*svarūpa*) of a thing, and so the same thing. Now difference is attributed to a thing in reference to another, but one does not have to refer to another in determining the nature of an object. An object may or may not need another to be determined. In general the nature of an object is established through the chief qualifier of an awareness corresponding to the attribute actually possessed by the object of that awareness. The relatedness (*pratiyogitā*) between an object such as jar and another, such as cloth, is not necessary to understand what a jar is. Hence jar and other objects are known to be different from each other on the basis of their own-natures, and thus become known as different from one another. The word "own-nature" is, however, also used to refer to the specific forms of jar, cloth, etc., and it is in this sense that the *form* of the jar is said to be difference.

10. (E24) Advaitin: So, nondifference alone should be admitted as valid, since difference is dependent on nondifference.

Answer: No, since nondifference cannot become the content of an awareness without reference to difference.

11. (E25) Suppose we have the awareness that pot and cloth are not nondifferent—is it real difference (*pāramārthikabheda*) or unreal difference that is denied? In either case difference is established. For if it is real difference that is denied the result is the assertion that difference is admitted.

(E25-26) Advaitin: We do not mean by "nondifference" to deny difference, but we merely say it is another property (*dharmāntara*).

Answer: No, for if this other property is opposed to difference then inasmuch as opposition implies difference difference is proved. But if it is not opposed to difference, then difference must be admitted to exist like other universals such as substanceness, earthness, etc. And in that case it cannot be disproved to exist.

Advaitin: But scripture shows that nondifference alone exists.

Answer: No, since scripture has as its content difference.

12. (E26) Furthermore, where does this nondifference, which the scriptures are alleged to speak of, reside? If it resides in what is not Brahman then difference is proved. If it resides in Brahman alone then there is no dispute: nondifference is just an additional property along with and not contradictory to difference. It cannot reside in both Brahman and non-Brahman, for if that were the case and it is opposed to difference then difference is established, and if it is not opposed to difference then it (nondifference) itself is not established.

13. (E30-31) "The jar is not here" states that there is no contact between ground and jar, while "jar is not cloth" states that the cloth is not of the nature of the jar. If difference is denied to exist, then a cloth may be brought when the jar is asked for. When a cow is prescribed as a gift, a donkey may be given away. When wine is forbidden milk, which is prescribed, may likewise be given up. The Vedic authority on which Advaitins pin their reliance in maintaining nondifference speaks of heaven, *apūrva* and other things as realities; it also speaks of the nondifference of Brahman. The Advaitin should not display a baseless predilection for the latter over the former. Since difference safeguards nondifference, difference establishes itself.

14. (E32-34) Advaitin: Though there is no real difference, since we commonly experience difference it must be admitted on the empirical (*vyāvahārika*) level.

Answer: What is this "empirical level?"

Opponent: To be empirical is to have contents of ordinary usage of the nature of awareness.

Answer: No, for Brahman satisfies that definition.

Opponent: Then, what is "empirical" is what leads to sublation.

Answer: No, since even if difference with respect to some objects at some time be sublated, it cannot be sublated everywhere. Or if it can, then Brahman also should be admitted to be subject to sublation.

Opponent: But difference is shown to be sublated on the strength of Vedic passages.

Answer: No. The very same arguments which you put forward to prove that the immediate experience of Brahman does not admit of sublation are available to prove that difference is real.

15. (E34-36) Opponent: Being empirical, i.e., sublated, is just being nonexistent.

Answer: What does this "nonexistence" mean? If it means being fit for existence (*sattāyogitva*) then we do not believe that difference, which is, after all, mutual absence can be understood as fit for existence. If it means being the counterpositive of a positive thing (*bhāvapratiyogitva*) then difference is admitted.

Opponent: "Difference" means being false (*mithyā*).

Answer: What does this word "false" stand for? Is it determined by convention, or apart from conventional usage? If it is apart from conventions, then words do not mean what they are conventionally taken to mean, and Brahman cannot be spoken of unequivocally. But if the claim is that "false" means difference, it is not supported by dictionaries (*kośa*) or grammar (*vyākaraṇa*).

Opponent: Being empirical is to be of a nature opposed to liberation.

Answer: No. Liberation is the absolute absence of frustration (*ātyantikaduḥkhābhāva*), and mutual absence is different from that.

Opponent: What is empirical is that which does not become the content of an awareness leading to liberation.

Answer: No. Hearing (*śravaṇa*), reflecting (*manana*) and meditating (*nididhyāsana*), which are the awarenesses leading to liberation, have as their contents the difference between the body and the self.

Opponent: Being empirical is being comprised within the world (*prapañca*).

Answer: No, since then Brahman, inasmuch as it can be comprised within the world, would become empirical.

16. (E36) The Advaitins hold that nondifference is real and that it is not known through reasoning. Brahman is then held to be knowable because it is different from empirical things. That is all right. The old Vedāntins held that both Brahman and the world are real as well as empirical, on the principle of the arrow and the fist holding it. The new Vedāntins, however, have become deluded. Really there is no particular feature in either Brahman or the world

which makes one rather than the other valid.

17. (E36-37) It is just because the world is empirical that it is real (*pāramārthika*). Thus difference must be real, because it is empirical. Being empirical means being within the scope of ordinary transactions (*vyavahāragocaratva*), and this is applicable to Brahman also. E.g., the scriptural passage "Brahman is one without a second" means that Brahman is describable in ordinary parlance as being without a second.

18. (E38) Argument: Difference is real, because it is known, like Brahman. To be known means to become the content of an awareness. And you (Advaitins) admit that it is.

Difference, then, is the content of valid awareness, since it is the content of an awareness, like Brahman.

Opponent: But the content of an awareness, say of silverness, is erroneous with respect to a shell.

Answer: No, for even though silverness appears as qualifying the shell, it is valid as qualifying silver. According to Nyāya whatever is knowable is an object of knowledge.

19. (E39) Opponent: Objects cognized in the waking state are unreal, since objects in dreams are unreal.

Answer: No, dream objects are not unreal. In dreams real objects appear unreal.

20. (E41) Argument: The world is real, because it is seen, like Brahman.

Argument: The world is real, because it is nameable, like Brahman. Even the world known in dreams is real.

Argument: Awareness of difference, etc., has a real content, because it is an awareness, like the awareness of Brahman.

21. (E42) Objection: The objects apprehended in dreams cannot be real, since they are sublated when one's head is cut.

Answer: No, when one's head is cut the dream-awareness of the object is sublated (but not the object itself). This does not mean that no events visualized in dreams have ever occurred in reality—they may have occurred in previous births, e.g. But others do not have such visions during that time. Persons who listen to accounts of events may receive experiences of those kinds of events in their dreams.

22. (E43-44) The Upaniṣads declare that direct awareness of Brahman is of assistance in getting the highest aim of man through the cutting off of frustrations; it does not help get direct awareness of the world. That Brahman is not the world is made clear in the Upaniṣads.

Objection: How can inference produce knowledge of awareness, since it is sublated by scriptural proof of nonduality?

Answer: The sublation arising from scriptural sentences involves an awareness quite opposed to what is intended to be proved. Does such an awareness actually occur? If it does then no sublation can take place through it, since it involves the true awareness of difference. If the awareness is not real, then the awareness of nondifference it produces is also unreal.

23. (E45-46) Opponent: Falsity (*mithyātva*), which is being an awareness that is not knowledge, does not prove what it intends to prove. Thus falsity is not expressible as either real or unreal (*sadasadbhyāmanirvacanīyatvam*).

Answer: The defect of nonexpressibility does not lie in the object but in the capacity of the person who cannot describe it. Is this nonexpressibility real or unreal? If real, then the world is admitted to have this real trait of being nonexpressible and thus it is proved to be different from Brahman, which knocks the bottom out of the monistic theory. If it is not real, then it is admitted that the world admits of description.

24. (E46) Opponent: No, what we mean is that the world is not existent, not nonexistent, not both and not neither.

Answer: This only proves the difference of the world from Brahman. Of course in some respects they are similar—both exist, are nameable, objects of valid cognition, knowable—but their specific inner properties are different.

25. (E48-50) Śaṃkara Miśra then shows that Vedic authority cannot be cited in support of nondifference. Since difference doesn't exist, no Vedic passage of the required sort exists, and a nonexistent passage cannot be an instrument of knowledge to prove nondifference. If the Vedas exist then difference is the result, and if they do not, then they do not provide valid cognition of nondifference. So it must be personal predilection that induces the Advaitin to treat nondifference as real and difference as unreal.

26. (E50-51) If the world is unreal and Brahman is real there must be difference between them. So there is difference. If that is not admitted, there is no basis to ascribe reality to Brahman and unreality to the world—they may both be real, or both unreal.

27. (E51-52) Again, if there is difference between Brahman and the individual self, difference is established. If there is no difference between them, Brahman which is consciousness and bliss (*cidānandamaya*) is also full of frustrations (*duḥkhamaya*), which would contradict Brahman's omniscience and emobodiedness.

Opponent: The difference between Brahman and self is due to imposed properties.

Answer: No, since the same kind of problems arise when we ask whether the imposed properties are real or unreal.

28. (E53-55) If you admit as reason (*hetu*) difference at the empirical (*vyāvahārika*) level all appearances are refuted. That in turn will prove difference as ultimately real. As a result seeking liberation on the part of Vedāntins is baseless, knowledge of liberation is unreal, yogic practice is unreal, there is no heaven or *apūrva*, the instruments of knowldege don't exist, and thus Brahman also is nonexistent.

29. (E55-57) An object *x* that is related to another *y* is related not because *x* is different or not different from *y* but because *x* is an entity with an actual nature (*vastusvabhāva*). Then if *x* is apprehended as nondifferent from a different object *y* its difference from *y* is established by the fact that it is related to different objects differently than *y*. This is also the case with objects of erroneous perceptions.

It is the chief qualifier of a cognition which determines the nature of the object known. Thus jar is different from cloth, since the chief qualifiers of the respective cognitions ("this is jar", "that is cloth") are different. The Advaitin, however, treats even the chief qualifier's determination as erroneous. The Naiyāyikas treat it as valid.

30. (E58-59) Objection: (1) Is difference grasped first followed by grasping of the object, or (2) is the object grasped first followed by grasping of its difference? Or, (3) are both object and difference grasped together. If (1) then the Nyāya doctrine stated above is mistaken. If (2), then it will follow that an object *x* though nondifferent from another *y* will have to be admitted to be different from *y*. How can this be? If (3), then there can be no causal relation between object and difference as you (Naiyāyikas) suppose, since they are simultaneous. So there is no grasping of difference.

Answer: No. Awareness of difference arises after the objects have been cognized according to their chief qualifiers. Now in continuous cognition the later awareness is conditioned by previously cognized difference, but in other awarenesses we don't ever come to cognize differences among the objects.

31. (E60-61) It is because of the contrast between jarness and clothness that the jar and cloth are different, but one need not be aware of these universals as such when the difference between jar and cloth becomes known; it is the loci of these universals which become known as different.

32. (E61-62) Objection: But scriptural authority undermines the perception of difference.

Answer: No, for verbal testimony cannot refute perception of the difference between, say, a pot and a cloth.

33. (E64-65) Objection: Scripture speaks of the nondifference of the world, not of the pot and the cloth.

Answer: Even so, scripture cannot refute the numberless instances, like that of pot and cloth, where difference is experienced as objective reality.

34. (E65-66) A person cannot know what goes on in the mind of another, even though he may profess to believe in the nondifference between himself and that other. This is because the selves of the two parties are limited through connection with different physical bodies.

Advaitin: Let us admit that there is difference between the bodies; still, there is nondifference of the Self limited by these bodies.

Answer: No, for if the differences between the two selves is admitted as empirical (*vyāvahārika*), then the adjuncts which limit them will have to be admitted to be really (*pāramārthika*) different, and then the Advaita thesis is abandoned. However, if the difference between the selves is held to be real, then there is no reason why one should not know what goes on in the minds of another. Also, if that is the case the Advaitin cannot appeal to ignorance to explain why a person who cognizes difference doesn't get liberated. A monist should feel ashamed to admit ignorance as different from Brahman.

35. (E67) Only when difference between Brahman and non-Brahman is recognized do hearing, reflecting and meditating have a meaning. Without that recognition undertakings of those kind, as well as yogic practice, will be fruitless.

36. (E68-71) Objection: Brahman cannot be the locus of non-eternal awareness, desires, etc. (as would be implied at best by the Nyāya view), since scripture tells us that "eternal knowledge and bliss is Brahman".

Answer: No, since scripture also says "Brahman is one only, without a second", which shows that Brahman is subject to frustrations, etc. Brahman cannot be both eternally blissful and also frustrated. Actually, the Taittirīya passage ("eternal knowledge and bliss is Brahman") speaks of the lower Brahman, and fits with the *jīvanmukti* stage of the self, in which the highest bliss is experienced directly. If this is not admitted, Brahman could be experienced even during the state of bondage.

Now, if eternal bliss is not produced by ignorance, this means it must be experienced during liberation. It must be proved that this blissful state will not cease, for then there would be bondage again.

Opponent: It will not cease, being like posterior absence.

Answer: Then monism is false, since there is difference from Brahman.

Being nondifferent from awareness this eternal bliss must have some object. If the destruction of ignorance is that object, it is not needed; direct experience which is Brahman will remove it as it removes every thought. And if this direct experience is real, then since it removes something else (ignorance) how can duality not be real? If this direct experience is unreal, how can it remove anything? Therefore "Brahman" and "God" (*parameśvara*) do not differ in meaning.

37. (E71-72) What the Upaniṣads prove is that Brahman is distinct from the selves, that it is the locus of eternal knowledge, desire and volition, is free from pleasure, pain, traces, merit, demerit and hatred, and is the creator and destroyer of the world. Direct knowledge of the self, as distinct from the body, destroys false awareness by arising from a process of listening, reflecting and meditating. This gives rise to the destruction of frustrations in a common locus (the self) and at a different time from the prior absence of frustration in that locus—thus no further frustrations arise. Or else, frustrations are destroyed through the destruction of the *adṛṣṭa* of traces arising from the destruction of the *adṛṣṭa* itself: During the nonpropositional awareness at this time nothing appears other than the self. Upaniṣadic passages (such as *Tripadavibhūtimahānārāyaṇa Upaniṣad* 2.7.9, quoted) which classify stages of understanding as "real" or 'highest' (*pāramārthika*), are meant to convery that what is known at that stage is directly helpful to liberation. This is the view of Śaṃkarācārya and others. Later Vedāntins have created a confusion about this. Therefore duality, difference, are validly known.

VĀDIVINODA

Summary by V. Varadachari

"E" references are to the edition by Ganganatha Jha (Sarman) (B3639; RB5622), Allahabad 1915.

(Śrīharṣa, the author of the *Khaṇḍanakhaṇḍakhādya*, tries to refute the view that words convey meanings or denote objects. Śaṃkara Miśra's aim in writing the *Vādivinoda* is to destroy the haughtiness in opponents such as Śrīharṣa. This is to be accomplished in five steps, viz., through controversy (*kathā*), questioning (*praśna*), understanding the question (*praśnajñāna*), rejecting the questions (*praśnaparāha*), and answering them (*praśnānuttaratā*). So the work has five sections (*ullāsa*).

I. Controversy

(E2) Controversy has three varieties: discussion (*vāda*), sophistry (*jalpa*) and cavil (*vitaṇḍā*). Sānātanī held that cavil should not be included here but treated independently, since one who seeks to know the truth puts forward his standpoint and someone else only notes the objections to it. Wheras the author of *Ratnakośa* held controversy to be of three varieties, viz., the three kinds listed above plus a second kind of cavil, making four in all. The distinction between the two kinds of cavil is that one is intended to win the debate, while the other is intended to get at the truth. Others still hold that controversy is of one kind only, that discussion , etc., are varieties of this one category. Śaṃkara Miśra rejects all these views. One who seeks to know the truth about things (*tattvajñāna*) has to establish his position. One cannot have the desire to know the truth and also to win the debate at the same time. So discussion and the others serve different purposes and thus the classification as given (into three) should be accepted as valid.

The three kinds of controversy might be taken as serving three distinct purposes, respectively, of producing understanding of the nature of reality for one who has not understood that before, safeguarding it when it is attacked by others, and repeatedly considering it and conveying it to others. Or, controversy might be taken to be threefold according to the qualifications of those who adopt them. These qualifications (*adhikāra*) would be a desire to know the nature of reality, a desire to get victory over others, not to talk insultingly of those doctrines which are accepted by everyone on the basis of experience, skill in listening to the views of others, avoidance of arousing strife, being active only to be helpful in taking up a controversy, skill in expressing disapproval, being higly attentive, and already able to find refutations. Those who are qualified for discussion have in addition the following qualifications: not being deceitful, having the right intuition at the appropriate time, not raising unnecessary objections, willing to admit what is arrived at on the basis of reasoning and eagerness to know reality. Such people should enter into debate only with those of similar traits and only then will the intended results follow. Persons who do not possess these qualifications are disqualified from taking part in controversies.

(E2-3) Discussion is controversy taken up in order to come to know the truth. It may be taken up by a pupil with his teacher or by two pupils among themselves. When the positions taken contradict each other it is said to be *vipratipatti.* The defects in such arguments must be shown and resolved.

(E3-4) When one of the disputants has pointed out the defects in the other's arguments, the other shall confine himself to those portions being refuted and make them clear. The five-membered argument form need not be invoked here. Some say that such an argument form must be employed while showing *pakṣadharmatā* within the range of conventions (*samaya*) acceptable to both. But actually what has not been said must be shown by both disputants.

They both must state their positions. The author illustrates by showing how Naiyāyikas and Mīmāṃsakas should argue.

(E4-8) Disputant A should present his case avoiding the faults in it that have been pointed out by disputant B. Then B should state his arguments, eliminating the faults in his own position and establishing those claimed to vitiate A's position on stronger grounds than before. This give and take may proceed for eight turns for each of A and B. However, there is no need to be particular about the number of turns taken. A discussion may extend to the next day. However, when both disputants are well-versed they should not assert more than is necessary for their position and for the refutation of what has been stated by the opponent.

(E8-10) Some of the ways of losing an argument should not be used in discussion: viz., *pratijñāhāni*, *pratijñāsaṃnyāsa*, *nirarthaka*, *avijñātārtha*, *arthāntara* and *apārthaka*. These are used to hide one's own incapacity, and should convince one not to take part in the discussion at all. Seven ways of losing an argument should not be used even if they are relevant. These are: *pratijñāntara*, *hetvantara*, *ajñāna*, *aprātibha*, *vikṣepa*, *matānujñā*, and *paryanuyojyopekṣaṇa*. Seven more should only be raised in a general way: *virodha*, *nyūna*, *adhika*, *punarukta*, *aprāptakāla*, *ananubhāṣaṇa* and *apasiddhānta*. The discussion should only come to an end by appeal to fallacies and defects committed because of delusion. When a defect is pointed out by A and justified then the discussion should end. A discussant should point out a fault in his own argument when it is not noticed by his opponent. In a discussion there is no absolute need for someone to decide the topic, or for an umpire, etc.

(E10-11) In sophistry some conventions will have to be agreed on. There should be regulations about what is to be taken up, and for the disputants to abide by, e.g., that they should abide by the members assembled pointing out ways of losing and by the conventions regarding riddles and regarding when the discussion should conclude. If necessary, one who can record the discussion in writing shall be appointed, one who is acceptable to both parties. The two disputants shall be assumed to be equal to each other, not known as either inferior to the other. Those assembled should be acceptable to both parties, shall understand the positions of both sides, be free from passion and hatred, be skilled in understanding what others say, be able to retain it and reproduce it skilfully. They should total an odd number, since only then can a decision be arrived at on the basis of consensus. The leader of the assembly must be acceptable to both disputants as well as to the others assembled. He should be free from preferences and able to control the situation. Rules need to be arrived at concerning the illustration appropriate to arguments, for pointing out faults in the arguments of others, for what count as ineffectual inferences, concerning the use of pronouns in repeating things, and for other details. Otherwise the discussion will not come to an end, since those assembled may take sides and produce mutual strife.

(E11-13) This is the procedure to be employed in sophistry. When there is a difference of opinion about a doctrine, B should point out reasons for losing even while A is giving his arguments. The reasons for losing to be employed here are *aprāptakāla*, *arthāntara*, *apārthaka* and *nirarthaka*. But B need not elaborate on these, nor need he establish his own position. He need not point out these reasons for losing if he can indicate fallacies (in A's arguments). If he does not do either, his case will be that of *paryanuyojyopekṣaṇa*. But he need not wait till A completes his case. Śaṃkara Miśra shows why only these four reasons for losing should be invoked at the outset.

When A completes his argument, B shall state what is to be refuted and then refute each argument by pointing out fallacies as well as offering arguments of his own and eliminating possible faults from them. Here A may appeal to *apratibhā*, *ananubhāṣaṇa*, *ajñāna* and *vikṣepa*, or he may allude to the four that B invoked. If none of these apply, he may appeal to one of the following eight reasons for losing the argument: *pratijñāvirodha*, *nyūna*, *adhika*, *punarukta*, *apasiddhānta*, *niranuyojyānuyoga*, *paryanuyojyopekṣaṇa* and *matānujñā*. At this state *pratijñāhāni*, *pratijñāntara*, *pratijñāsaṃnyāsa* and *hetvantara* don't apply. If none of the allowable reasons for losing apply, he may reply to the faults alleged in his position and indicate the defects in B's arguments. In sophistry neither A nor B need establish their position, for the purpose here is only to prove their capacity to maintain their position and refute the opponent's. It is a test of strength. Victory cannot be won by refuting the rival position alone, for one's own position has not yet been declared. One deserves to be applauded for one's attack on his rival even at the cost of undermining his own position, like a warrior who strikes at his enemy without caring to protect himself from attack.

This give and take in sophistry may go through six stages, with the *siddhāntin* having the final word.

(E13-16) Cavil differs from sophistry in that, whereas in sophistry skill in both defending a position and attacking the opponent's is valued, in cavil one party is confined to defending and the other to attacking. The procedure is the same as in sophistry except that B needn't maintain his position. Nineteen stages of cavil are described.

(E16-17) Now Śaṃkara Miśra proceeds to show the procedure to be adopted in exposing the opponents' weak points. On the nature of *prakaraṇasama*, he notes the views of Udayana, the author of

Ratnakośa, Maṇikaṇṭha and Gaṅgeśa. According to Udayana, *prakaraṇasama* consists in the presentation of pervasion and *pakṣadharmatā*, which arouses the desire to know which between the *h* and *s* is correct. The author of *Ratnakośa* held that it produces awareness through inference of a doubt regarding which of the two features is correct. Maṇikaṇṭha Miśra takes it to consist in being the instrument of proving the counterpositive of two things, one of which is pervaded by the absence of one of the features at a time and at a place where it is known that the counterpositive has for its object that which is pervaded by one property and also *pakṣadharmatā*. Gaṅgeśa holds that *prakaraṇasama* has an *h* that contradicts its *s* and establishes the opposite with equal strength. Śaṃkara Miśra says it could also be taken as proving contradictory results when it is known that it is strong enough to make a difference to those involved.

The author defines *asiddha* as the fallacy which is not known through pervasion and *pakṣadharmatā*. Some say that applies if it is not known through either or both.[9]

(E18-19) *Bādha* is a fallacy whether or not it is recognized as such. Śaṃkara Miśra distinguishes ten kinds of *bādha*.

(E19-20) After defining *tarka* the author notes the view of some who say that self-residence, etc., are to be included under *aniṣṭaprasaṅga*. Others list six kinds: self-residence, mutual dependence, circularity, infinte regress, contradiction (*vyāghāta*) and obstruction (*pratibandhin*).

(E20-21) Quibble (*chala*) takes place when one intentionally uses it to win when it becomes impossible to refute the opponent's argument.

(E22-29) Now Śaṃkara Miśra takes up futile rejoinder (*jāti*). He does not discuss the relative merits of the definition of the concept as found in Vātsyāyana, Uddyotakara and Vācaspati Miśra. Rather, he defines each kind of rejoinder and offers illustrations. In each case he points out how the reason given by the opponent is found to be at fault.[10]

(E30) Now the ways of losing an argument are taken up. Destruction of another's haughtiness that has so far not been destroyed is the defect called *nigraha*, and since it is accomplished through *pratijñāhāni*, etc., they are called *nigrahasthāna*. Outside the context of debate these things do not have these names. Forgetfulness, confusion and other faults may prevent a person from replying or making the point he needs. These are not in themselves reasons for losing an argument, since the persons involved cannot display their learning. Some say that a way of losing an argument consists in not having the knowledge expected of a participant in a debate, so that, according to them, failure to have knowledge or having a wrong opinion constitute reasons for losing the argument.

(The review of the ways of losing an argument involves citing the views of others at certain points, such as Vardhamāna, Maṇikaṇṭha and the Ratnakośakāra.)

(E39-41) In connection with showing how a position should be maintained Śaṃkara Miśra takes up a number of topics, such as God's existence, the nature of the self, *ākāśa*, satisfaction, validity, darkness, gold, air's perceptibility, nonpropositional perception, *mahāpralaya* and *avāntarapralaya*, and liberation.

The Mīmāṃsakas and Vallabha, author of *Nyāyalīlāvatī* do not admit *sarvamukti*, liberation for all. The Prābhākaras hold that liberation is the prior absence of frustration that does not coexist with frustration. Vallabha agrees. The Bhāṭṭas hold liberation to be the manifestation of permanent satisfaction. The Tridaṇḍins (followers of Bhāskara's *Bhedābhedavāda*) maintain it to be the merger of the self in the highest Self. The Advaitin Śaṃkara holds it to consist in the direct awareness of the nondifference of Brahman. Śaṃkara also reviews the discussion about whether action or knowledge is the means to liberation and comes to the conclusion that knowledge is.

(E43-44) The author offers some tricks to be adopted by a debater. If he has not discovered what he is supposed to be arguing about, he may use his skill in speech and begin with something or other, suddenly mention the matter of sound's eternality (or noneternality) or whatever. To save his position he can employ *mahāvidyā*. *In extremis* he may shout and somehow win the argument. And silence is golden.

II. Questioning

(E44-47) Another way of showing up the opponent is by asking him questions he doesn't know how to answer. For instance, one may ask for definitions of the Vaiśeṣika categories—intricate definitions of categories and subcategories are provided.

III, Understanding Topics Questioned

(E47-51) This chapter discusses methods for putting down B when he questions A's exposition. The upshot is a running review of the tenets of various schools, starting with Nyāya and Vaiśeṣika. Some of the most interesting points mentioned are given here.

(E51-52) Vaiśeṣika tradition holds that the cause of the perceptibility of a whole is its *mahat* dimension and its possession of many substances. Gaṅgeśa held that the latter is included in the former.

Tradition takes manifestness (*udbhava*) as a proper universal and unmanifestness as its absence. Some say both are proper universals, but Gaṅgeśa argues that the latter, being an absence, is not a proper universal.

(E53) The author now enumerates the categories postulated by the different schools and examines each of their doctrines. Kaṇāda and Gautama postulate seven. The Cārvākas say there are four (substance, quality, motion, universal). The Prābhākaras have eight (substance, quality, motion, universal, number, inherence, similarity and power (*śakti*)). Candra, representing a section of the Prābhākaras, holds that there are in addition to those the categories of *krama*, *upakāra* and *saṃskāra*.

The author of the *Mahārṇava* has twelve—the foregoing plus *aupādānika* (effect through material cause).[11] The Pāśupatas admit five categories: cause, effect, *yoga*, *vidhi* and *duḥkhānta*.

The "Vedāntins" hold only Brahman as a category, but for *vyāvahārika* there are five categories as *dharma* and *dharmin*, etc. (*dharmidharmabhāvena*).[12] Murāri Miśra holds the same view as Advaita.

The Prābhākaras admit the same nine substances as Vaiśeṣika. In addition to these, the Bhāṭṭas recognize sound and darkness. The Vedāntins postulate eight substances: earth, air, fire, water, self, internal organ, darkness and sound. They reject *ākāśa*, time and spatial direction.

Of the twenty-four Vaiśeṣika qualities, Prābhākaras recognize twenty-one, leaving out number, disjunction and separateness but distinguishing impetus as a separate quality. The Bhāṭṭas have twenty-four but replace sound by *nāda*. The Vedāntins have twenty: they reject farness, nearness, separateness, merit, demerit, disjunction and sound, and add identity (*tādātmya*), occurrence (*vṛtti*) and *nāda*.

The number of kinds of sense-object connection are taken to be six by the followers of Kaṇāda and Gautama. For the Prābhākaras they are four, viz., contact, inherence, inherence in what is in contact and relatedness (*sambandhaviśeṣaṇatā*). The Bhāṭṭas recognize contact alone. Some hold that there are twelve kinds of connection by adding *yogaja*, *dharma*, *sākṣātkāra*, *utprekṣā*, *jñāna* and *sāmānya* to the Nyāya six.

(E53-57) Now Śaṃkara Miśra summarizes each of several systems: Cārvāka, Buddhism, Pākhaṇḍa, Digambaras, Bhāṭṭas, Prābhākaras.

Cārvāka: One does not need to postulate traces to explain why the baby reaches for his mother's breast; it is a natural desire, just like sex. Inference is not an instrument of knowledge; the activity directed toward fire on seeing smoke is just probability (*sambhā-*

vana), which is thought to be valid (*pramā*) because it is corroborated (*saṃvādana*). The sense organs themselves think, as in evident from our saying 'I see', 'I hear', etc.

Buddhism: After explaining the five *skandhas*, the author goes on to say that Buddhist philosophy takes the world to consist just of smells, colors, tastes, touches and sounds, so that earth is the aggregate (*saṃghāta*) of all five, water of color, touch, sound and taste, fire of color, touch and sound, air of touch and sound. The whole, which is only atoms of color, etc., occurs for only a moment. There are only two instruments of knowledge, perception and inference. There are two kinds of contents of awareness, viz., those that are grasped (*grāhya*) and those that are believed (*adhyavasāya*). Awareness is not different from its content, since they both are experienced together (*sahopalambhaniyama*). The Vedāntins hold *brahmādvaita*; the Buddhists hold *jñānādvaita*. The schools of Buddhism are listed as Vaibhāṣika, Sautrāntika, Yogācāra and Mādhyamika.

The Pākhaṇḍa system is said to be the *somasiddhānta*. Liberation is *svātantrya*. Bondage is *pāratantrya*. Liberation consists in enjoying oneself with wine and sexual intercourse.

Next is the system of the Digambaras. By thc namc "Digambara" is meant that these do not have a covering (*saṃvaraṇa*) in the form of *trayī*. This explanation has a deeper meaning, suggesting that the Digambaras are those who do not conceal themselves under the cover of *trayī*, that is, they do not cite the three Vedas as *pramāṇas*. The categories are seven: *jīva*, *ajīva*, *āśaya*, *saṃvara*, *nirjarā*, *bandha* and *mokṣa*. The *jīva* has awareness as its nature, and its natural conduct is to fly up, i.e., it is always trying to leave this world. But since it is covered by the body, its sense organs do not think truly. Sometimes by those (senses) it sees, just as the light which is kept in a house does not shine outside it but sometimes shines through the window. *Ajīva* is inert (*jaḍa*). The varieties of Digambaras are Kṣapaṇaka, Śvetāmbara, Ārhatas, Nīlāmbara, Raktāmbara, Carmāmbara, Barhāmbara, etc. *Ahiṃsā* is the supreme *dharma* for them, and drinking wine is absolutely prohibited.

The varieties of Buddhists include (Dharma) Kīrti, Dignāga, Bhadanta Jñānaśrī, Prajñākara and others.

Now as to the Bhāṭṭas. Darkness is an independent substance for them, apprehended by the visual organ assisted by the absence of light. Maṇḍana Miśra, representing a section of the school (*ekadeśin*), holds that it is apprehended by the sense organ sprung from the *guṇa tamas*, the *adhiṣṭhāna* of which is the eyeball. *Ākāśa* has color and is visually apprehended. The internal organ is all-pervasive. Contact between the all-pervasive self and the internal organ is due to the *guṇa rajas*. The body is made up of five elements. The auditory organ is the portion of *dik*, not *ākāśa*, circumscribed by the ear-cavity. The relation between substances and their universals and motions is identity-in-difference.

The Bhāṭṭa theory of meaning is outlined. Meanings of words become efficient causes for linguistic apprehension, words being merely the limitors of those meanings. Only by deliberating on the meanings of the words used by poets does understanding of the sense of poetry arise. The meaning of a word is the universal. The sense conveyed by *liṅ* (the verbal form) is *bhāvanā*; thus that is the primary meaning (*abhidhā*). There are two kinds of *bhāvanā*. One is activity (*pravṛtti*), the other is the denoting of that activity through the verbal form. So the activity of a man is denoted by the verbal form, e.g., "*yajeta*" denotes the activity which is the performing of the sacrifice. Knowledge of the relation between the *bhāvanā* and the thing to be brought into existence is the cause of activity. Praise, i.e., instigation (*prarocana*) is intended to arouse faith. *Apūrva* is constructed (*kalpya*), and cannot be denoted. Its form is not fit to be visualized and so it is only the sacrificial act that lasts until the fruit of the act is obtained. Liberation is the manifestation of eternal and unsurpassed satisfaction, as evidenced by (*Taittirīya Upaniṣad* 3.6) "Bliss is the form of Brahman." The Vedas are not of human composition. The recensions of the Vedas, which are taken to be the source of flawless injunctions like *holakā* and *aṣṭakā*, are obscured not lost, since the eternal Vedas can never be lost. Nor are they inferred, since they are eternal. By being "obscured" is meant that they are not presently studied in India.

The Prābhākaras recognize five instruments of knowledge—perception, inference, comparison, verbal testimony and presumption. Perception is "*tripuṭi*", involving cognition, agent and content which are all presented together. In the case of inference also, cognition and agent are perceived while the content alone is apprehended through inference. Nonpropositional awareness is not a kind of cognition; all awareness is from awareness of a chief qualifier whose limitor is a qualifier. Inference does not involve consideration. Awareness of pervasion and of *pakṣadharmatā* function separately. *Upanaya* is not a member of the argument. Pervasion is gotten from a single observation which makes known the absence of obstructions. So no *sāmānyalakṣaṇa* is necessary of, e.g., smokes. Verbal testimony is independently valid, but ordinary speech is not so, since words are the products of persons who are subject to error. The validity of the statements of ordinary persons is arrived at though inference. Such statements presuppose on the part of those who use them knowledge of the connections among the meanings that the words remind us of, and so ordinary usage merely corroborates what has been arrived at through inference.

Earlier Mīmāṃsakas held that comparison brings forth a result in the form of knowledge of similarity between objects at hand. Similarity as a category is to be known by a different instruments of knowledge from perception. Śabara, however, held that similarity with what is not at hand is related to what is so and this is to be known through comparison.

(E57-59) Discussion of pervasion. (The author refers to the view of one Nyāyalocana, who criticized the work of Gaṅgeśa.) This is followed by a discussion of obstruction. Śaṃkara Miśra refers us to his *Anumānamayūkha* for an elaborate treatment of this.

(E59-61) Now the faults of obstruction (*upādhyābhāsa*) are treated.

(E61) And next, the fallacies. (The views of Jīvanātha Miśra, brother of Bhavanātha, are referred to.)

(E61-66) The views of Udayana, Vācaspati and modern writers on expectancy are distinguished.

There are five ways of getting to know the meanings of words: through (1) ordinary usage (*vyavahāra*), (2) being collocative with a familiar expression (*prasiddhapadasāmānādhikaraṇya*), (3) comparison (*upamāna*) (the views of Mīmāṃsakas on comparison are rejected); (4) explanatory or supplementary texts (*arthavāda*); (5) analysis of sentences (*vākyaśeṣa*).

Words operate in five ways to give their meaning. (1) They may operate directly, e.g., "Devadatta". They may operate by (2) *taṭasthopalakṣaṇa*, as with "*ākāśa*", whose meaning is known from the direct meaning of another word "sound", for *ākāśa* is defined as the locus of sound; (3) *antarbhūtopalakṣaṇa*, e.g., "cook" (*pācaka*), since a cook is only a cook when he is preparing food and not at other times; (4) *sapravṛttinimitta*, e.g., "cow" ("*go*") i.e., common nouns; (5) *nimittasaṃkocanīkāro*, e.g., "heaven" (*svarga*") which means satisfaction but whose sense gets limited to absence of connection with frustration.

The Nyāya tradition holds the meaning of a word may be either the individual, the universal or the configuration (*ākṛti*). An example where it is the last is in the application of the word "cow" to cows made of flour. Gaṅgeśa held this to be a case of secondary usage, in distinction from the tradition.

In the case of a word such as "*paṅkaja*" (lotus, literally mud-born), the Nyāya school admits both etymology (*yoga*) and convention (*rūḍhi*) as kinds of meaning—through etymology being born in mud and through convention lotusness are conveyed. The Mīmāṃsakas hold that while it is known from etymology by itself that it is mud-born, that it is a lotus is known from previous traces, and so convention has no scope here.

(E66-70) Sondaḍopādhyāya is stated to have admitted secondary meanings for sentences, whereas the later Nyāya only admits it for words.

The old school takes the sense of the suffix *-ktvā* as indicating past time, and says that in "he goes after eating" both verbs are known to have the same agent through inference. The Mīmāṃsakas hold that the suffix *-ktvā* denotes the unity of the agents and that the sense of past time is gotten through inference. Gaṅgeśa however feels that the suffix *-ktvā* denotes an action taking place subsequently and hence the meaning is the entire complex of going after taking food.

IV. Meeting Questions

(E71-72) Suppose the opponent asks "what is the proof of God's existence?" This should be met by raising the issue whether the question is put by the opponent knowing the evidence concerning God or not. If God is known the question has no scope. If God is not known, the question has no scope either, for a discussion cannot be undertaken about a matter not known before.

V. Answering Questions

(E73) If someone who is neutral intervenes with a question using abusive or sarcastic language, it may be ignored so that his pride may not be shattered. Or one can treat him as an inferior treats his superior by flowery words: "You are a man fit to be honored. You are an eminent disputant. Digression from one section of the topic to another is not objectionable to you. You are huge like a hill and we could not assess you. The divine cow of repute is your mother. Your father is the best among men. Hence you are the most deserving person for reputation. Your learning is traditional." The uproar that may be raised will determine how to proceed. If the way is clear one may then go on to address the president of the assembly in similar modest vain.

KAṆĀDARAHASYA

Summary by V. Varadachari

"E" references are to the edition by V.P. Dvivedin (B3640; RB5624), Chowkhamba Sanskrit Series 48, 1917.

This work is undertaken under the pretext of commenting on the *Padārthadharmasaṃgraha* of Pràśastapāda. Numbering of sections follows that of the summary of *Padārthadharmasaṃgraha* in Vol. II.

1-5. (E3) Substanceness, qualityness, etc., are defined in the terminology of Navyanyāya. For instance, substanceness (*dravyatva*) is the property of that which is not the locus of the absolute absence of a quality. Absolute absence of a quality is that absolute absence whose counterpositiveness is limited by qualityness, which is to say that qualities can never be absent in their loci, namely, substances.

(E4) A clear definition of a "quality" is cited: A quality possesses a universal, lacks a mobile nature, and is not the locus of size.

(E5) The author adopts the "only-negative" method of proving that earth has smell as its specific quality, citing as justification the dictum "the purpose served by a definition is to prove that the object to be defined is distinct from others or to account for drawing references to the object."

36. (E8) Fourteen qualities of earth are enumerated. Some are proved to be apprehended by perception, others by inference. Vallabha (author of *Nyāyalīlāvatī*) is quoted as viewing weight as perceptible, though the Vaiśeṣika school takes it to be apprehensible only by inference.

38. (E20) Fire is said to be of four kinds. One is sunlight whose color and touch are manifested. The second is that of the eye, in which both color and touch are unmanifested. The third kind is the fire in heated oil (*taila*), etc., only the color of which is not manifested. And the fourth kind is the fire of the moon and of gold, where touch alone is not manifested.

(E24) For visual perception both color and touch must be manifested. This is the view of Tātparyācārya (i.e., Vācaspati Miśra).

41. (E26) There are five kinds of names or ways of naming. First is through comprehending each individual falling under a term, e.g., "Devadatta". Second is *pāribhāṣikī*, or *taṭastha*; in the case of "ether" it is known as such by being the faculty by which sound is known. Third is the case of "cook"—the activity of cooking is included in the awareness produced by the word "cook". Fourth is where the name "cow" is given because the thing possesses cowness. Fifthly, a name is given because of a restricted rule (*saṅkocaniyama*) relating to its cause: e.g., the name "heaven" is assigned to something which is caused by pleasure restricted by lack of relation to frustration.

43. (E35) Time (*kāla*) and spatial direction (*dik*) are distinct, though each single; different times and places are due to obstructions. The difference between time and spatial direction is this. The particular divisions of time, such as present, etc., continue to have

the same applicability, that is, present time is the present time for all people at that time. But the eastern direction—or any other direction—is eastern only for the particular person concerned and not for all.

45. (E43-44) Motion in the internal organ must be admitted in order to account for its contact with the various sense organs during the waking state and with the veins (*nāḍī*) to account for deep sleep and for certain activities during the waking state. The desire of the self to know certain things, deep meditation, and *adṛṣṭa* of the self causes this motion in the internal organ. The self's volition causes this motion. The internal organ moves in the tubular vein called *manovahā*. This motion creates speed when there is speed, the internal organ is struck or impelled by its contact with the vein, which has touch and speed. The internal organ then comes into contact with the sense organ which can grasp the desired object. This becomes possible only when the internal organ is admitted to be atomic in size.

(E47-49) Darkness has no objective existence; it is only the absence of light. E.g., darkness is known in a cave through the recollection of light which is that darkness' counterpositive. The absence of light, which is darkness, may be a prior, posterior or absolute absence as the case may be.

(E50) The Prābhākaras are not justified in holding darkness to be absence of awareness—that would only be correct if the notion of darkness were of the sort "I am not aware of anything".[13]

80. (E55) Even when it is possible to prove something by affirmative (*anvayavyatirekin* or *kevalānvayin*) means, the "only-negative" mode may be adopted so that defects, if any, can be avoided.

84. (E61-66) The discussion of the theory of cooking is very elaborate. There is a difference of opinion among Naiyāyikas about the time it takes for a double-atom to change color through cooking. (1) Some say it takes nine moments: (i) through the motion of and consequent disjunction between the constituent atoms the double-atom is destroyed, (ii) the blue-color inherent in each atom is destroyed, (iii) a red-color is produced in each atom, (iv) motion in the atoms is produced, (v) which in turn produces disjunction of the atom from the particular portion of space, and so (vi) disjunction of the atom from that portion, and (vii) contact between the two atoms, which yields (viii) the double-atom and (ix) the red-color of the double-atom. (2) A second account introduces a moment, between (iii) and (iv) above, at which the motion of the atoms mentioned under (i) is terminated, leading then to (iv), the motion of the atoms leading to renewed contact. Thus the total number of moments taken on this second view is ten. (3) Still a third account

finds eleven moments. (4) On still another account there are five moments in the process—(i) the process leading to the destruction of the double-atom through the disjunction of one atom from the other, (ii) destruction of the blue-color in one atom, together with the destruction of the previous contact between the two atoms, (iii) production of the red-color in the atom together with contact with the other atom, (iv) production of the double-atom, (v) production of the red-color in the double-atom. A fifth counting involving six moments, a sixth involving seven moments, a seventh involving eight or nine moments, and an eighth involving two, three or four moments are further distinguished.[14]

Application of heat must not be taken to be uniform, as in that case the effect of heat will also be only of one kind. Heat travels fast. One kind of fire is impelled to move on by another. If a particular kind of fire is admitted to destroy a color and is also taken to continue to function then the atom which has lost its color through that heat would remain colorless when that heat is lost. If the same heat were to give rise to a color, that color might not be red.

87. (E75-76) The author maintains that separateness is distinct from mutual absence. Neither *vaiśiṣṭya* nor *vaidharmya* can be treated as equal to separateness.

88. (E80) Contact resides in more than one substance and does not pervade its loci (the conjoined substances). Or, contact may be admitted to be pervasive of its loci. Its loci appear to be conjoined only in certain of their parts, and that is what is meant (in the first option) by absence of locus-pervasion. Or, while contact between the parts is apprehended contact between the composite whole is also apprehended; but when those parts which are not in contact are found to be not in contact the composite wholes are likewise discovered not to be in contact, and it is in this sense that contact is said to have partial pervasion.

(E81-82) The views of Śrīdhara and Udayana on contact produced by contact are noticed. Also, the view of Śrīdhara that destruction of contact in a thread would give rise to the destruction of contact in some other thread is criticized by citing the view of Udayana.

89. (E87) Whether the destruction of the effect is the destruction of substance is discussed with reference to the views of Śrīdhara and Udayana.

99. (E90-91) The nature of the connections (*sannikarṣa*) in the three kinds of extraordinary perception is explained. In the case of *sāmānyalakṣaṇa* perception the connection is a particular qualifierness (*viśeṣaṇatāviśeṣa*). Yogic perception is a different sort of connection. In the case of *jñānalakṣaṇa* perception the connection is

being a qualifier of what is inhered in by what is in contact (*saṃyukta-samavetaviśeṣaṇatā*).

100-104. (E94-97) Several definitions of pervasion are offered. Some of them are as follows: (1) Pervasion is a relation that does not wander (*avyabhicārataḥ sambandhaḥ*). (2) It is a relation between one thing and another which does not exist without it (*avinābhāva-sambandha*). (3) Or, it is a relation insofar as it is complete (*kārtsnyena sambandha*). (4) Or, it is the having a common locus with that *s* which is not counterpositive of an absolute absence which has a common locus with an *h* whose locus is other than the countepositive (*pratiyogiviruddhasvasamānādhikaraṇātyantābhāvāpratiyogisādhya sāmānadhikaraṇya*). (5) Or, it is an obstructionless relation (*anaupādhikasambandha*).

(E98-100) On the definition of obstruction, the author reviews the views of the author of the *Ratnakośa*, of Maṇikaṇṭha and others. Udayana's definition is held to apply to cases of equipervasion.

115. (E101-103) Fallacies are classified into three kinds: (1) unestablished (*asiddha*), (2) contradictory (*viruddha*), and (3) deviation (*saṃdigdha* or *savyabhicāra*). *Āśrayāsiddhi* is subdivided into two types: *āśrayasvarūpāsiddhi* and *āśrayaviśeṣaṇāsiddhi*. The first is illustrated by "the sky lotus is fragrant, being a lotus", where the nature of the locus of the *h* is not established. An example of the second is adopting inference to prove something which is established through perception; here there is neither doubt regarding the qualifier of the locus of the *h*, nor a desire to prove it. This type of case is known as proving what is already accepted (*siddhasādhana*). The author of the *Nyāyalīlāvatī* held the uncertain (*anadhyavasita*) *h* to be an independent (fourth) fallacy.[15] Śaṃkara Miśra equates (3) deviation (*saṃdigdha*) with *anaikāntika*, and shows that there is room for doubt in each of the three cases of deviation.

The fallacy called "sublated" (*bādha*) is shown to come under either deviation (*anaikāntika* = *saṃdigdha*) or unestablished (*āśrayāsiddhi*). Counterbalanced (*satpratipakṣa*) gets included under *vyāpyatvāsiddhi*. So they are not independent fallacies. *Aprayojaka* is not an independent fallacy; it falls within *vyāpyatvāsiddhi*. Śaṃkara Miśra refers to his *Tattvacintāmaṇimayūkha* and *Vādivinoda* for details.

(E104-115) Śaṃkara Miśra shows that verbal testimony, comparison, presumption, negation, tradition, probability and "script" (*lipi*) are not independent instruments of knowledge but are to be brought under inference. Incidentally, the author refers to the concept of *upamāna* as held by Śabarasvāmin, as well as his concept of similarity, and rejects both of them.

(E115-116) While dealing with ignorance or nonknowledge

(*avidyā*), the author discusses the nature of doubt, which is of only two kinds—one rising from things having the same features, the other from things having opposed features—and not three or five kinds.

(E117-120) Under the topic of error (*viparyaya*), Śaṃkara Miśra explains the various theories of error and supports *anyathākhyāti*. In general, teachers (*ācārya*) say, erroneous cognition is said to be of two types: in one, what is remembered is superimposed, and in the other, the superimposition is of something directly experienced. They (or he?) are (is) stated to have held the view that similarity between the object superimposed and its locus is grasped by bringing the object superimposed in the first type. The Nyāyācārya (i.e., Udayana) is stated to have held that this view of "teachers" is available also in the second type.

132. (E131-132) A single impetus is present in the arrow shot into the air, and it continues until the arrow falls down. The Naiyāyikas hold that impetus produced in the arrow by an act gives rise to motion which in its turn produces another impetus, which produces a further motion which again produces another impetus, and so on.

(E132-133) A trace (*bhāvanā*) is a dispositional tendency produced by the experience of objects seen, listened to and experienced. It is a specific quality of the self, and produces recollection and recognition. In some cases, it is removed by a judgment opposed to the particular judgment which gave rise to it. Sometimes, those who get drunk lose the dispositional tendencies already formed in them. Intense misery also removes them. Tendencies produced in previous births get aroused in subsequent births at the sight and thought of things similar to those which had given rise to their formation.

133. (E135-141) Merit is defined and illustrated with a number of examples. It is destroyed by knowledge of reality. It must be admitted here that those dispositional tendencies which have not borne fruit in the case of an enlightened self can be made to bear their fruits through the creation of additional bodies by yogic power. They are to be experienced at any cost.

134. (E135-143) Demerit is gotten rid of by experiencing pain (frustration, misery), as well as by proclaiming it and by acts of expiation. Prior absence of frustration must be admitted, as that is borne out by the steps taken in advance to avoid frustrations. Otherwise those precautionary steps to ward off future evils could not be explained. Some scholars hold that expiatory acts are undertaken with a view to get fully qualified for enjoying the fruits of merit.

UPASKĀRA on Kaṇāda's VAIŚEṢIKASŪTRAS
Summary by Karl H. Potter

"E" references are to the edition by Sri Narayan Misra, Kashi Sanskrit Series 195, 1969. "T" references are to Nandalal Sinha's translation (B43; RB499), Sacred Books of the Hindus 6, Allahabad 1911, 1923, 1974. In the references below, the first number in parentheses refers to the numbering of the *sūtras* given in the summary in Vol. Two.

Introduction

(E3-5; T1-2) The invocation pays respects to the Lord (Hara), to Kaṇāda and to Bhavanātha (Śaṃkara Miśra's father), who taught Śaṃkara Miśra Vaiśeṣika.

Discriminating persons, looking for the cause of the three afflictions (*tāpatraya*), gathered from scriptures, *smṛtis*, *itihāsas* and *purāṇas* that direct awareness of the nature of the self (*ātmatattvasākṣātkāra*) is that cause. So they approached Kaṇāda with a desire to know the path to self-knowledge. Now Kaṇāda had the knowledge of the natures of things, as well as nonattachment and lordliness; he reflected that knowledge of the six categories constituted the path, and that that knowledge would be easily gained by the disciples through that merit marked by turning away from action; so he resolved first to teach them merit and then the six categories.

I.1.1 (E5-10; T3-5) (*Sūtra:* "Now, therefore, we shall explain merit.") The import of the introductory words "now, therefore" is explained in a manner reminiscent of commentaries on the *Brahma-* and *Mīmāṃsāsūtras*, indicating why the inquiry is useful.

Objection: Why has Kaṇāda not himself provided an invocation?

Answer: He has, in the word "*atha*", which indicates auspiciousness.

Objector: We think it is merely because he has noticed that invocation and result desired are not necessarily related.

Answer: No; if an act, preceded by an invocation, does not yield its desired result it must be that either the results will come in another birth, or else that the invocation was defective.

Objection: An act must produce its result in this life only.

Answer: No; for example, one performs a sacrifice for the rain, or the birth of a son, in this life, not the next, since that is the temporal reference of his desire; other sacrifices result in heaven after this life, for that is their intent. Now here the desire is for completion, and so it is like the desire for heaven in being otherworldly; the difference is, however, that while there the result depends on *apūrva*, here the removal of hindrances is what is desired so that completion may be reached.

Objection: Then the result of the invocation is merely the removal of the hindrances; completion will follow from its own cause.

Answer: No, the mere removal of hindrances is not itself a human end, while liberation is.

Objection: Then the destruction of demerit is the end.

Answer: No, for that is attainable by other means, and the rule is that an invocation is needed only for that which it can uniquely produce.

Objection: We mean that it is specific demerits which obstruct the disciple's getting to liberation which must be destroyed.

Answer: But they can be destroyed by giving gold, bathing at Prayāga (Allahabad), etc. An invocation is an act (*karman*) which brings about completion as its result by means of removing obstacles; it is of the form of saluting the deity. And even where no obstacles are present in the nature of the case (and thus no invocation needed), still the idea of invocation is there because of the general relevance of the notion of gaining completion by removing obstacles.

I.1.2 (E11-14; T5-6) (*Sūtra*: "Merit is that from which comes the attainment of *abhyudaya* and *niḥśreyasa*". "*Abhyudaya*" means knowledge of the nature of things, and "*niḥśreyasa*" means the absolute cessation of suffering (*ātyantikī duḥkhanivṛtti*). This merit is the result of meditation (*nididhyāsana*) and *yoga*, and is the same as *adṛṣṭa*.

The Vṛttikāra, however, explains "*abhyudaya*" as pleasure, and "*niḥśreyasa*" as the simultaneous destruction of all the specific qualities of the self. Superficial readers object to this account on technical grounds, but in fact both happiness and absence of frustration are ends of man, indeed, the two great ends.

Objection: Scripture is the instrument for learning that merit is as described. But we doubt the authority of scripture, since it includes falsehoods, contradictions and repetitions. (Examples are given.) And there is nothing to substantiate scripture's authority. Since it is not eternal, and is probably the product of human thought, there is no reason to trust it.

I.1.3 (E14-16; T7) Answer: (*Sūtra*: "The authoritativeness of scripture is due to its being the word of *tat*—that.") Here the "that" may refer to God, so that the authority of scripture is due to its being God's word. Or it may refer to merit, and the meaning be that scripture's authority is due to its speaking of merit.

As for the allegations addressed against scripture, these are refuted in order. The "falsity" is explained by resort to other meanings or better explications of text; the "contradictoriness" is likewise to be explained away; and "repetition" is not always a fault.

(1) I.1.4 (E17-27; T8-11) Having explained merit, as the disciples wished, Kaṇāda now turns to explain the subject-matter (*abhidheya*) and relationship (*sambandha*) of knowledge of the nature of things. This knowledge is dependent on Vaiśeṣika doctrine (*śāstra*); thus that doctrine is likewise a means to the cessation of suffering. And the relationships are these: by understanding the categories the Vaiśeṣika doctrine is demonstrated; that doctrine is constituted by knowledge of the nature of things; and that knowledge is the means to the cessation of suffering.

The "absoluteness" of that final cessation of suffering which is liberation consists in its nonsimultaneity with the prior absence of frustration in the same locus, or in its simultaneous existence in the same locus with the annihilation of the specific qualities of the self. Or, liberation is the prior absence of frustration up to the moment of the remainderless specific qualities.

Objection: Since it is an absence, then, liberation cannot be a goal of man.

Answer: Yes it can, since even prior absence can be produced by means of destroying its cause; it is still a prior absence even under such conditions, since it is the absence of its counterpositive-producer (*pratiyogijanakābhāva*), and to be such a producer mere fitness (*svarūpayogyatā*) is all that is required. In *Nyāyasūtra* I.1.2 the "annihilation" of each of the five items mentioned is properly understood as their prior absence.

Objection: Liberation is just the absolute absence of suffering. Even though it may not be located in the self, but in a stone (say), it is yet related to the self just by being a posterior absence of suffering which does not accompany a prior absence of suffering. Since when that is the case there arises the idea of the absolute absence of suffering, Vedic passages such as "he moves about absolutely free from suffering" (*duḥkhenātyantaṃ vimuktaścarati*) are justified.

Answer: No, for absolute absence is not an end of man, since it cannot be attained. The Vedic text merely implies that by destroying the causes of suffering, the prior absence of suffering may amount to an absolute absence.

Objection: Still, this prior absence cannot be an end of man, since one only seeks to destroy suffering in order to obtain pleasure.

Answer: No, since one can equally well say that pleasure is only sought in order to obtain absence of suffering; indeed, we see that men in despair kill themselves in order to obtain absence of suffering.

Objection: Even if it is an end of man, it is only so as something to be known; but liberation as absence of suffering is not even something known. And if liberation is not knowable men would try to attain it by fainting, etc.!

Answer: No. A thing knowable from scripture and from inference can hardly be held to be unknowable. It can also be known by perception at the final moment before death and by *yogis*.

Objection: Liberation is the manifestation of eternal pleasure, not the absence of suffering.

Answer: No. There is no proof that pleasure can be eternal. And if there were there would be no difference between a liberated and a bound man. Furthermore, manifestation being a product, on its cessation *saṃsāra* would recur.

Objection: Liberation is the dissolution (*laya*) of the individual self into the self which is Brahman.

Answer: No. If "dissolution" means that two things become one, that is impossible. Or if "dissolution" means the removal of the subtle body, then since this subtle body is the cause of suffering its removal, viz., absence of suffering, is liberation, which is our view.

This also refutes the Ekadaṇḍins, who hold that liberation consists in the Self, having consciousness and bliss as Its nature, remaining after ignorance has ceased. There is no proof that the Self consists of consciousness and bliss.

Objection: The proof is the scriptural passage "Brahman is eternal, knowledge, bliss" (*nityaṃ vijñānamānandam brahma*).

Answer: All this text proves is that the self has knowledge and bliss—we perceive "I know" and "I am happy", but not "I am knowledge" or "I am happiness". Brahman exists now, so there will be no difference between a bound and a liberated person. Further, the cessation of ignorance is not an object of human action. Brahman, being eternal, is not something which can be attained.

Objection: Liberation is the pure flowing of the stream of consciousness (*citśānti*).

Answer: If by purity you mean the absence of suffering, then that is what is an end of man, and there is no proof of the pure flowing, the survival of consciousness. Furthermore, the maintenance of the stream is only possible when the body, etc., are present; thus your definition will entail the maintenance of *saṃsāra*.

(E27-31; T11-13) The categories are enumerated to be six, and this has been taken as a rule, viz., that the categories are *only* six in number. But this is not proved, since if another category exists the rule is wrong, and if no such category is known the specification is unnecessary.

Objection: What the rule indicates is that everything in the world is excluded from belonging to any other category than these six.

Answer: No. This commits the fault of proving what has already been proved, and also wrongly implies that nothing else is known (other than these six kinds). What the rule actually means is that for each perceptible object in the world one or another of the six categories applies.

The *sūtra* says that knowledge of the nature of things is produced by a certain merit: this "certain merit" is in fact *nivṛtti* or turning away from worldly actions. If it is held that "knowledge of the nature of things" refers to Kaṇāda's *sūtra*s, then this *sūtra*'s "certain merit" must mean the injunctions and grace of God (*īśvaraniyogaprasāda-rūpa*). But "knowledge of the nature of things" here indicates direct awareness of the nature of the Self, since only such awareness can root out false awareness combined with traces. Upaniṣadic passages are quoted in support.

(9) I.1.6 (E35-37; T18-19) In this *sūtra* (listing the qualities) the words for color, taste, smell and touch are compounded to show that none of them have a common locus with contemporaneous instances of others of them. The words for number and dimension, however, are not so compounded and are given in their plurals to show that they can coexist with contemporaneous numbers and dimensions. The peculiarities in grammar in the rest of the list are likewise explained, and alternative explanations are offered.

(10) I.1.7 (E38-43; T20-21) Objection: There are not five kinds of motion, but only four, since "going" (*gamana*) is just a synonym for "motion".

Answer: It is true that "going" is a synonym for "motion". Still, it is mentioned here to comprehend a number of kinds of motion which do not fall under the first four kinds. Or else, goingness is a fifth kind of motion, thus pervaded by motionness, and the motions of the first four kinds are not really cases of going, but are called so in only a secondary sense.

Entering and exiting are not proper universals or kinds, since one motion may be considered by one person entering and by another exiting, and thus there will be cross-connection.

In the case of the first four kinds of motion, however, precise definitions can be given which do not allow cross-connection. E.g., throwing upwards (*utkṣepaṇa*) is a motion caused in the hand by the desire to throw the pestle upwards, where the noninherence cause is contact with the self which possesses the desire; then from the noninherence cause of motion in the hand thrown up, the upward motion of pestle results. The other kinds are defined in relevant fashion.

In the case of prescribed rituals, bathing, giving, etc., the motions involved are produced by contact with a self whose efforts are devoted toward merit, while in motions involved in going to a forbidden place, killing, tobacco-chewing, etc., the soul's efforts tend toward the production of demerit.

(13) I.1.8 (E43-46; T21-22) Substance, quality and motion are said to be noneternal in the sense of having posterior absence as their relatum (*dhvaṃsapratiyogitva*); thus, though atoms are not noneternal in the ordinary sense, still all members of these three categories share as distinguishing condition (*vibhājaka upādhi*) the function of tending toward annihilation.

Likewise, "substance-possessing" (*dravyavat*), though it doesn't literally apply to atoms, means that which has a substance as its inherence cause, i.e., all members of these three categories share this function as distinguishing condition. "Effect" (*kārya*) indicates the distinguishing condition of functioning as the counterpositive of a prior absence. "Cause" (*kāraṇa*) indicates the distinguishing condition of being the invariable antecedent of all kinds of effects except for awareness. The clause excludes awareness from the relevant class of effects so that a self, or cowness, etc., will not fall into the definitions of these three categories.

"Genus-and-species-possessing" (*sāmānyaviśeṣavat*) means that the members of these categories possess universal properties like substanceness, qualityness, motionness which, though universals, still mutually demarcate (*vyāvarttaka*) their particulars (*viśeṣa*).

Objection: The specification of being a cause overextends to include universals; e.g., in scriptural texts like "Give a cow" or "A cow should not be touched with the feet" cowness is the cause of merit or demerit.

Answer: No; universal properties have as their only function delimitation (*avacchedakatā*).

Objection: Praśastadeva says "causality occurs elsewhere than in the atoms, etc.", implying that only things which have causes can be effects and noneternal.

Answer: Then the *sūtra* must mean that these properties cannot be viewed as qualified by their being distinguishing conditions of categories.

(14) (E48; T23) "No motion is originated by (another) motion." If a motion could produce another motion, it would have to produce it immediately after its own production. Now when a motion is produced in *x* which was in contact with *y* disjunction is effected in *x* from *y*. Disjoined through the first motion, there is no contact from which *x* can be disjoined by the second motion. But the definition of motion involves its being a cause of contact and disjunction.

Objection: Then the second motion need not immediately follow the first one.

Answer: No, since there is no occasion for its not being produced immediately, since the first motion has (according to the hypothesis) the ability to produce another motion.

The same line of argument applies if one thinks of motion as producing contact—then how can the second motion produce contact?

(2) I.1.15 (E51-53; T25-26) The *sūtra* states a conclusion which is proved by the following argument: Substance is different from quality, etc., because it possesses quality.

Objection: This argument suffers because its *s* is not proved.

Answer: No; *difference from quality, etc.* (the *s* in the above inference) is perceived in the water pot, etc.

Objection: Then the argument commits the fault of proving what has already been established.

Answer: No, for although *difference from quality, etc.* has already been proved with respect to water pots, etc., it has not yet been proved with respect to substances in general.

(3) I.1.16 (E53-55; T26) Qualityness (*guṇatva*) is defined as possession of a universal property pervaded by existence-which-resides-in-something-eternal which has eternal function. (Thus, qualities reside in eternal substances like atoms, which go on functioning forever.)

(16) (E62; T29) Substances are not the effects of motions, according to the *sūtra*, because of being different (*vyatirekāt*), which Śaṃkara Miśra says means because the motion has terminated before it could be causally effective in producing the substance. If motion could be a cause of substance it would have to be either a noninherence cause or an instrumental cause. It can't be a noninherence cause, since it would follow that when the motion ends the substance will be destroyed, as the rule is that an effect is destroyed by the destruction of its noninherence cause. It can't be an instrumental cause of substance, for we see that after a large piece of cloth has been torn up small pieces are still produced by the contacts remaining, even though those parts are motionless.

(17) (E63-67; T30-31) A substance may be the effect of more than two substances—e.g., many threads make up a single cloth.

Objection: But we find that a single thread can be woven to make a cloth.

Answer: No, since there is no contact to supply the noninherence cause.

Objector: Well, the contact is between the thread and the fibres (making up the part which curls around and touches the thread).

Answer: No, for that relation is inseparable. In any case, what you think is evident on perception is wrongly analyzed: where you think there is one piece of thread wound around on itself, in fact the long thread has been destroyed by the loom, etc., and it is small resulting pieces which combine to produce the thread.

Sūtra: "No motion is a common effect of substances...."

Objection: The motions of the body and its parts are surely produced by many substances—otherwise how could we have the awareness that our body is moving and thus our hands, feet, etc.?

Answer: The reason for our awareness here is that the causal collocation of motions in the parts of the body is pervaded by the causal collocation of motions of the whole body, but the reverse is not the case. Otherwise the anomaly will result that when a causal substance collides with another substance contact between them will not result since there is no motion in the second substance.

I.2.1 (E72-77; T35-37) "From the absence of the cause (there follows) the absence of the effect." The notions of cause and effect are required in order that we explain what conditions what in the world. If causality were not operative there could be no activity or withdrawal (*pravṛtti/nivṛtti*); for only if we know that by doing *x* we can get *y* will we be moved to act, and only if we know that by refusing to do *x* we can avoid *z* will we be moved to withdraw from activity.

Objection: Only what exists arises, and not what does not exist, as the Vedas say ("In the beginning there was only the existent"). And if it were not so a cloth might arise from potsherds.

Answer: If so, those who believe in transformation (*pariṇāmavāda*) will have some difficulty in explaining why pots only arise from potsherds and not cloths, etc. Furthermore, if the idea of the opponent is that the effect already exists before its production, then causality is merely the development (*āvirbhāva*) and envelopment (*tirobhāva* of things. But even so, development and envelopment depend on causes, and are processes which bring about states not present prior to the process.

Thus causality (*kāraṇatva*) can be defined as (1) the possession of a natural kind (whose members are the regular antecedents of members of the effect class), where the relation is otherwise unexplainable. Or it may alternatively be defined as (2) the property of possessing the absence of the effect produced by a deficiency in the accessory conditions.

These definitions are intended to encompass plurality of cause. "One should perform the sacrifice with either barley or rice" (where one can get the same effect using either foodstuff) technically lacks "regular antecedence", but nevertheless constitutes a case of causality according to the second definition. (2) in the previous paragraph provides a definition of causality which suffices in both ordinary (*laukika*) and scriptural (*vaidika*) contexts, while (1) is satisfactory only in the former context; the reason for this is that in a scriptural context such as provided by the sentence quoted ("One should perform the sacrifice...") positive concomitance is sufficient to show causality, negative concomitance is unnecessary. So it has rightly been said that one who follows Vedic practices in all their parts will necessarily get the results. When the Teacher (*ācārya*, viz., Udayana) says "because it is rooted in the scriptures, nonconcomitance is not a fault in this case" he has in mind (scripturally) authenticated objects (*ṛjvartha*) (i.e., that in the case of such objects it is not necessary to show negative concomitance to prove causality). But in the case of objects such as grass, wood and jewel (each of which can cause fire) it is necessary to show that when the cause is absent the effect is also. If that were required also in the case of scriptural objects one would have to suppose that different effects were produced by different sacrifices (*rājasūya*, *vājapeya*, etc.).

I.2.3 (E78-80; T38-40) The *sūtra* reads "*sāmānyaṃ viśeṣa iti buddhyapekṣaṃ*"). The meaning is that awareness (*buddhi*) is the mark of genera (*sāmānya*) and species (*viśeṣa*). There are two kinds of genera, (1) Being (*sattā*), the higher, and (2) lower universals, such as substanceness. A genus is responsible for reidentification (*anuvṛtta*), a species for differentiation (*vyāvṛtta*) of things. A genus is that something eternal which occurs in many individuals (*nityamanekavyaktivṛtti*). Or, a genus is that which, being eternal, has a common locus with the mutual absence of its own locus. A lower universal is also a species, as it results in both reidentification and differentiation.

Buddhist objector: Universals don't exist, since reidentification can be explained merely by absence of differentiation. "This is a cow" has as its content differentiation of *this* from what is not a cow. Even the believer in universals admits that the notion of cowness arises in this way, since being a specific kind of entity is nothing other than not being differentiated from what is so specified. Furthermore, where does this "universal" *cowness* allegedly reside? Not in the cow, since there is no cow before *cowness* occurs in it. Not in noncow, obviously. Where was the universal before the piece of flesh, etc., became a cow?! Not there, since then the place would have already been bovine! And you say the universal is eternal, so it cannot have a beginning someplace. Furthermore, since it has no parts it cannot occur in many distinct individuals.

Answer: A universal is eternal and pervasive (*vyāpaka*). Pervasiveness consists in something's being related to all places naturally (*svarūpatas*). But places themselves can't be bovine, since the relation involved is inherence, and times (and places) don't have shapes, colors, etc. So the *cowness* which pervades a particular place where the piece of flesh is situated at a particular time, constitutes the cow. As for "where does the universal reside?", the answer is, where it is cognized. You say that the reidentification "this is a cow" means differentiation from what is not cow, but this can't explain "this is a cow or an ox", for a disjunction presupposes single properties as disjuncts.

The Prābhākaras say that universals are manifested just in their instances. If its mark is reidentification, then what is the fault in saying that universals are merely qualities and motions (and not a separate category at all)? For we reidentify colors, tastes, etc., and thus recognize a property. Just as there is a property *ākāśa*-ness in a single kind of thing, *ākāśa*, so colorness resides in a single kind of thing, viz., color—thus our theory does not violate the requirement of (1) identity of individuals (*vyaktyabheda*) (among Udayana's six requirements of universals). Nor does it violate the requirement that the putative universal not be (2) equipollent (*tulya*) with any other property (as, e.g., *ghaṭatva* and *kalaśatva*, both potness), since colorness is not equipollent with any other property. And there is no (3) crossconnection (*jātisaṃkara*), for the same reason. Nor is there (4) infinite regress, for no other universals are contained in colorness. There is not (5) giving up a thing's own nature (*rūpahāni*), because our universals also have the nature of being species (*viśeṣatva*): such species which reside in substance will be either qualities or motions, and those residing in all-pervading substances will be qualities only, and though this may repudiate the category of individuators (*viśeṣa*), it does not affect anything critical. Finally, our theory does not violate the requirement of (6) relation (as inhering in something does): we accept inherence as residing in the relevant items (as you do). Even though inherenceness is not a universal (on the standard theory), because of violating the first requirement of *vyaktyabheda*, still one should also consider the view of those who think that there are many inherences (which would allow inherenceness to qualify many loci, viz., the inherences).

The author of a *Vṛtti* is quoted in favor of the notion that universals are proved to exist by the fact of reidentifying awarenesses.

(5) I.2.5 (E86-89; T41-42) "...genera such as substanceness, qualityhood and motionhood may be regarded as species (as well as genera)..."

Objection: Substanceness cannot be satisfactorily defined.

Answer: Yes it can: substanceness is what limits the inherence causality of an effect limited by contactness: The contact occurs between atoms, etc. Qualityness is that which limits the causality in a thing having a universal property and which is not inherence or noninherence cause of contact or disjunction. A similar definition is provided for motionhood. There is a discussion of our inference that the sun moves—although we can't directly perceive the sky, etc., with which the sun is in contact and disjunction, still as the rays of the sun can be perceived to be in contact with the solar zone (*maṇḍala*), the sun's movements can be inferred. Uddyotakara is quoted.

BOOK TWO, CHAPTER ONE

(19) II.1.1 (E99-109; T48-51) "Earth possesses color, taste, smell, and touch." And its possession of smell is its differentiating mark.

Objection: That is, earth is different from other things because it has smell, according to you. But is this property of being different from others already accepted or not? If it is not already accepted, then there can be no desire to infer anything involving it. But if it being different from others is already accepted, does the *h* (possessing smell) pervade it or not? If it does not, then the fallacy of "too-specific" is committed, as no *sp* or *vp* can be provided. But if it does pervade that property, the inference is a positive (*anvayin*) one, and does not provide a differentiating mark.

Answer: Our thesis is supported by perception—differences from other things such as water, etc., are evident in a pot. Thus it does not depend on inference, and your objection is without point.

(Nevertheless, Śaṃkara Miśra goes on to discuss the technicalities of the inference which the objector attributes to him.)

(E109-115; T51-53) The color of water is white, its taste is sweet and its touch cool.

Objection: But we find blueness in the river Jumna, bitterness in the juice of berries and warmth in water at midday. Furthermore water cannot be naturally fluid and viscuous (as II.1.2 states) since ice is not fluid, and viscidity is not always perceived in water. Finally, *waterness* is not a proper universal since it has no differentia. Viscidity is found in butter, etc., and so cannot be the differentium.

Answer: The blue color, bitter taste and warm touch in the cases mentioned are due to the conditions of the locus of the water in each case, and are thus adventitious. Thus specific qualities listed are differentia of water as claimed. Viscidity is found in water: the evidence is that when it is mixed with barley or sand, etc., a compound (cohesive ball) of stuff results; this does not result when these things are mixed with ghee (butter), etc. Indeed, the viscidity found in butter is adventitious there, due to the water in the butter; viscidity is natural to water. Finally, waterness is a proper universal directly pervaded by substanceness, since it has been proved that it is a property which is found in the ultimate atoms and which limits the inherence causality of contact occurring just among objects having viscidity.

II.1.18 (E141-144; T65-66) "Names (*saṃjñā*) and actions (*karman*) are the mark of existence of beings distinct from us," viz., God, (II.1.19) "because name and action presuppose perception", i.e., one cannot name things without perceiving them, and the effects of actions must have agents. This last point is meant to specify that objects like earth, etc., must be caused by something other than an *adṛṣṭa*.

II.1.20-23 (E144-147; T66-68) (which do not appear in Candrānanda's *sūtrapāṭha*) present a Sāṃkhya argument to the effect that *ākāśa* is to be inferred from the motions of going in (*praveśana*) and going out (*niṣkramaṇa*). This is rejected, since a motion can have only one substance as its inherence cause, and *ākāśa* cannot be a noninherence cause; *ākāśa* is not the instrumental cause of motion either, since the instrumental causes of motions are the contacts between substances, and *ākāśa*, being all-pervasive, is always in contact with everything.

BOOK TWO, CHAPTER TWO

(22) (E156-160; T73-75) When color, taste, smell and touch are produced from the corresponding qualities in the inherence cause of their locus the qualities are natural (*svābhāvika*), but not otherwise. Thus the *sūtra* (II.2.1) says that the smell of a certain flower (the golden *pandanus odoratissimus*, says Sinha) found in a cloth which has been in contact with the flower does not belong naturally to the cloth, because it is not produced from any smell in the yarns which are the inherence cause of the cloth. If the smell were natural, then it would be perceived in the cloth before the yarns are brought into contact with the flower. So smell is natural in earth, hot touch in fire, and cold to water.

(24) (E160-165; T75-77) Time is inferred from the use of (e.g.,) "later" with respect to something which is later (than something else), "simultaneous", etc. That is, with respect to a young man the notion of "older than" arises with respect to an old man, in virtue of the fact that his birth is separated from us by a larger number of revolutions of the sun. This priority (of being older than) must depend on some noninherence cause. But color, touch, size, etc., cannot be the noninherence cause in question; by elimination it is concluded that that cause must be contact between the sun in its revolutions and some other substance, indeed, some substance which is also in contact with the body of the individual man in question. Now, that substance cannot be *ākāśa*, for if it were then when one

beat a drum at one place every place would resound with drumbeats! So the substance *time* must be inferred.

Objection: Time is not uniform but manifold, since it comes in moments, hours, days, etc.

Answer: The appearance of difference is due to limitors such as the motions of the sun, etc., as well as the limits imposed by the effects of such limitors. Thus the moment (*kṣaṇa*) is a limitor of time which does not pervade another limitor of time, or else it is that time which is not the locus of the counterpositive of either the prior or posterior absence of what is located in it—that is, something is produced and destroyed at every moment.

Objection: Yet time must have at least three kinds—past, present and future.

Answer: No, for the distinction is due to the distinction between the existence, prior absence, and posterior absence of a thing, e.g., time limited by a thing's existence is its present; time limited by a thing's prior absence is its future; time limited by its posterior absence is its past.

(25) (E166-170; T78-81) Place (*dik*) is inferred as the substance which makes possible that there be more or less contacts among a few conjuncts, thus explaining judgments of spatial direction and extent.

Objection: Why not let time be this substance. Why do we not need still another substance?

Answer: Time was inferred in order to establish fixed motions (*niyatakriyā*). If it is also supposed to establish nonfixed (i.e., subject to differences of degree) properties such as "farness" (*paratva*) then it would establish Kashmiri saffron paste on the breasts of Karṇāṭaka women! For the same reason one would not suppose that *ākāśa* or the self can function in place of place. Time supports motions, while space supports contacts between simultaneously existing substances.

Another difference between time and place is this: the limitors which qualify time are such that if *x* is present with respect to *y*, *y* is present with respect to *x*, but in the case of space, if *x* is east with respect to *y*, *y* is not east, but west, with respect to *x*.

"East" is the name given to that direction where the first contact of the sun took, takes, or will take place as it circles around Mt. Meru, says the *sūtra* (II.2.14). The reason for putting it thus is that the observer may be thinking of "east" at different times of the day or night.

(26) (E172-177; T82-84) In our kindred system (i.e., Nyāya) indefinite knowledge (*anadhyavasāya*) is not recognized as a distinct kind of awareness, and so they mention the too-specific property as a cause of doubt. Contradictory propositions are also said in Nyāya

to produce doubt. Thus in Nyāya works doubt is said to be of five kinds. But all the five kinds are really of the same sort, answering to our "perception of the generic character of an object." Again, in (Uddyotakara's) *Nyāyavārttika* there are said to be three kinds of doubt according to difference in the cause of doubt. But the three kinds (mentioned in this *sūtra*) cannot be distinct but sufficient conditions for doubt, since they are not heterogeneous (*vaijātya*) —they all operate together. Thus the idea is that perception of the universal property, together with nonperception of its specific character along with a memory of the specific character, combine to produce doubt in all cases.

Objection: Doubt is awareness which produces the desire to know.

Answer: No, for this definition overextends to include indefinite knowledge.

Now, doubt is actually of two kinds—that having to do with external objects (*bahirviṣayaka*) and that having to do with internal objects (*antarviṣayaka*). The first kind in turn has two varieties: that where the object is visible, and that where it is not. Examples of each are given.

Doubt may arise from perception of a universal whether it is found in one object or more than one object, e.g., the height of a post is similar to that of a man, thus doubt; but Caitra with hair and without hair being the same Caitra, doubt arises when one sees him with a piece of cloth on his head—the doubt "is Caitra bald or not?".

(27) (E180-181; T86) Objection: In order to explain the judgment "this is a single word" or "this is a single sentence" we must postulate a *sphoṭa* which causes these judgments and becomes manifested in the final syllable or letter (respectively) of the word or sentence.

Answer: The *sphoṭa* is not needed to explain our understanding of the meaning, since that is provided through convention. As for the judgment "one word" or "one sentence", this is a mere manner of speaking (*vyavahāra*) through which we indicate that a number of syllables (or words) convey a single sense. If we could perceive some inner meaning of a word in addition to its syllables we might denominate it "*sphoṭa*", but as we can't, Gautama has ignored the *sphoṭa* doctrine as pointless.

BOOK THREE, CHAPTER ONE

(28) (E206-217; T102-106) Objection: What is pervasion? Not (1) a nonwandering relation (*avyabhicāratas sambandha*); nor (2) being a necessary condition (*avinābhāvatva*); nor (3) a relationship with the whole (*kārtsnena sambandha*); nor (4) an essential or natural relation (*svābhāvika sambandha*); nor (5) an obstructionless relation

(*anaupādhika sambandha*); nor (6) merely being any relation; nor (7) having a common locus with the *s* which is not the counterpositive of the absolute absence residing in the *h*; nor (8) being the locus of that which does not have a common locus with *s*; nor (9) having a form limited by being related to *h*. These are all rejected for technical reasons by the opponent.

Answer: No; pervasion is (5) an obstructionless relation, more specifically, having a common locus with that *s* which co-varies with the *h* (*yāvatsvavyabhicārivyabhicārisādhyasāmānādhikaraṇya*), or alternatively, having a common locus with that *s* which has a common locus with the absolute absence whose counterpositive is the counterpositive of the absolute absence having a common locus with the *h* (*yāvatsvasamānādhikaraṇātyantābhāvaprayogipratiyogikātyantābhāvasamānādhikaraṇasādhyasāmānādhikaraṇyam*).

Udayana's definition of "obstruction", is given, viz.: An obstruction is that which pervades the *s* but does not pervade the *h*.

Objection: The definition fails to include an obstruction which is merely nonpervasive of *s*, e.g., in the inference "air is perceptible, because it is the locus of perceptible touch", *possession of manifested color* is an obstruction which fails to pervade the *s*, since self is perceptible though it lacks manifested color.

Answer: No, for the rule only applies after the proper extent of the *s* is finally determined. In the example offered, possession of manifested color does pervade the *s* perceptible as the limitor of external substancehood.

Objection: Still, this is not what the word "obstruction" means primarily. An obstruction is a property which appears elsewhere than where it belongs, e.g., the redness of the flower in the crystal.

Answer: We admit that the use is a secondary one, at least where there is unequal pervasion (*viṣamavyāpti*). Still, a rule of debate allows a disputant to bring forward an obstruction relevant to the *s* as finally determined even though it may not pervade the *s* as proposed by the speaker, as a way of showing counterbalance (i.e., to show that an equally weighty argument proves the opposite of the conclusion the speaker is arguing for).

(29) (E219-226; T107-110) A "contradictory" (*aprasiddha*) *hetu* is one which fails to be pervaded, where the pervasion is not known, and that where the pervasion is contrary. Thus it includes what others have called "*vyāpyatvāsiddha*" and "*viruddha*". "Unreal" (*asat*) means an *h* which does not reside in the *p*, either because of the nature of the form attributed to the *h* or because of absence of desire to prove something, as in proving what is already accepted. "Doubtful" (*sandigdha*) includes whatever produces doubt whether the *s* exists in the *p* or not. Sometimes this arises from perception

of common property (*samānadharmadarśana*), sometimes from the observation of an uncommon property (*asādhāraṇadharmadarśana*), and sometimes from finding that the *h* accompanies both the *s* and its absence. The first of these three may be called *sādhāraṇaikāntika*, the second *asādhāraṇaikāntika*, and the third *anupasaṃhārin*.

There are three kinds of unestablished *h*: (1) *vyāpyatvāsiddha*, (2) *svarūpāsiddha*, and (3) *āśrayāsiddha*. The first, *vyāpyatvāsiddha*, occurs when pervasion has not been perceived—either because it doesn't exist, or because though it is there, it is not perceived. Thus there are myriad kinds of this fallacy.

Putting matters positively, we can say that there are three kinds of *h*—only-positive, only-negative, and positive-negative. The only-positive *h* has four properties: residence in *p*, residence in *sp*, nonsublatedness, and not being subject to counterbalance by being shown to prove the opposite of *s* as well. These four properties, plus absence in *vp*, are the properties of the positive-negative type. The first, third, fourth and fifth are the properties of the only-negative type. A putative *h* which lacks one of the appropriate properties is a fallacious *h*, and doubt whether these properties apply obstructs inference, except that in the case of only-positive inference the absence of the fifth property, or in the case of the only-negative inference the absence of the second property, do not count against the validity of the inference. Śaṃkara Miśra shows how each of the fallacies previously identified fails one or more of these tests. The same procedure is used to show why self-dependence (*ātmāśraya*), mutual dependence (*anyonyāśraya*), circularity (*cakraka*) and infinite regress (*anavasthā*) involve fallacies of the *h*.

The Vṛttikāra is inclined to follow Gautama rather than Kaṇāda in his classification of fallacies into five (including sublation and counterbalance) rather than three.

More details on these points can be found in the *Mayūkha*.

(30) (E228-231; T111-113) What is produced from the contact between self, sense-organ, and object is awareness (*jñāna*), which is thus an *h* to prove the existence of self. This proof follows from two considerations, first, that awareness must have a locus, and second, our recognition that it is the same thing which both saw *x* and touched it.

Buddhist: Recognition is due to the causal relation between consciousness and its effect, awareness.

Answer: Then the pupil should recognize his guru's awarnesses as his own.

Buddhist: No, since there is no relation between material and form (*upādāna-upādeya-bhāva*) there as there is in genuine recognition.

Answer: Talk of "material", i.e., substance (*dravya*), is senseless with respect to awareness. Anyway, under your hypothesis of momentariness recognition is impossible.

Buddhist: The stream of abode-consciousness (*ālayavijñāna-santāna*), which is different from the stream of consciousness of objects (*pravṛttivijñānasantāna*), is what remembers and recognizes.

Answer: If this abode-consciousness is a continuant (*sthira*), our position is established, but if it is momentary, the difficulties have not been solved. Furthermore, what proof is there that it is different from the stream of consciousness of objects?

Buddhist: The proof is the stream of awareness "I", etc.

Answer: Let it be; but then, if the "matter" of the stream of consciousness, of objects is only what is provided by the abode-consciousness, the stream of conciousness of objects cannot operate even as instrumental cause, since an instrumental cause must be pervaded by "materiality" (*upādānatva*).

Buddhist: Then it is not an instrumental cause either.

Answer: Then the stream of consciousness of objects doesn't exist at all, since (according to you) the mark of existence is causal efficiency (*arthakriyākāritva*).

Buddhist: Both the abode-consciousness and the consciousness of objects streams are material jointly for each other.

Answer: Then you cannot argue against us (as you do) that wholes made up of parts cannot contact each other, since you too admit that a cause can be *vyāsajyavṛtti* (i.e.,operative at a place other than the one it occupies).

An alternative explanation of the *sūtra* is provided according to which it refutes the Sāṃkhya.

BOOK THREE, CHAPTER TWO

(32) (E233-236; T114-115) The internal organ is proved from the correlation of its contact with the self and the presence of awareness.

Objection: The internal organ is all-pervading (*vibhu*), because, like time, it lacks specific qualities (*viśeṣaguṇa*), because, like the self, it is the locus of a contact which is the noninherence cause of awareness, and because, like *ākāśa*, it has absolute absence of touch.

Answer: No. If the internal organ were all-pervading it would be in contact with all the sense-organs, and there would be only one kind of perception, namely, omnisensuous.

Objection: That doesn't happen, since the effects are of different sorts (i.e., visual, auditory, etc.).

Answer: A sufficient condition (*sāmagrī*) produces an effect which comprehends contrariety of that sort (otherwise we couldn't specify causes in general at all).

Objection: Then what is produced is of variegated-form, analogous to variegated-color, as when we eat some pudding (and have multisensory experience).

Answer: No, since even there we can attend to one kind of sensation at a time.

Objection: But we also cognize that we are simultaneously perceiving colors, tastes, smells, touches—how is that possible?

Answer: Because the internal organ moves swiftly and we remember the several sensations and produce a complex judgment.

III.2.3 (E237-239; T116-117) "Internal organ is one in each organism...". If there were many internal organs in a single body, awarenesses and efforts would be simultaneous.

(33) III.2.4 (E239; T117) The ingoing and outgoing breathing in the body requires the existence of a self to explain them.

Objection: But breathing goes on in deep sleep!

Answer: True; and though there is no fit effort (*yogyaprayatna*) at that time on the part of the self, there is another kind of effort then.

(34) III.2.6-9 (E245-250; T120-122) Objection: You think that the self can be inferred to exist. But there is no mark (*liṅga*) perceived by which to infer it, since when there is contact of the senses with Yajñadatta one does not perceive a self.

Counterobjection: The inference can be by analogy (*sāmānyatodṛṣṭa*), so that no perceived mark need be present.

Objector: Then one could not infer the self in particular but only that desires, etc., must have some locus or other. For this reason we conclude that the self must be proved by scripture, e.g., from hearing the Upaniṣads.

Answer: No, the self can also be proved by inference from the fact that the word "I" must have a referent, and none of the other substances, etc., are appropriate as referents of that word. Granted, this is an inference by analogy, but nevertheless a particular thing can be inferred thereby, since the word "I" indicates the property of egoity or selfhood by its nature. Furthermore, merely hearing scriptural statements about the self is not enough, for without reflection (*manana*) and meditation (*nididhyāsana*) mere hearing will not guarantee self-knowledge.

Objection: How can one know the self by inference when the self is imperceptible?

Answer: We never said the self was imperceptible. It is directly known in such experiences as "I am happy", "I desire", "I feel pain", etc.

(E250-258; T122-127) Objection: If the self is perceived, no inference to its existence is necessary.

Answer: Though the self is present in perception, it is frequently obscured by confusing it with the body ("I am fair", "I am lean"), and so inference is needed to arrive at a proper conception of the self. It has been said "skillful logicians wish to understand through inference even what is grasped by perception". Anyway, if thinking and meditating on the self is specified in scripture as requisite the self must be the object of inference—otherwise those activities would be impossible.

Objection: If "I am Devadatta" refers to the self, then the statement "Devadatta goes" must be an error.

Answer: It is not error, but a metaphorical extension. This is indicated by the fact that we use the word "I" to refer to oneself and not anyone else's; if the primary reference of that word were to the body we should not speak the way we do. Again, we know that a blind man or one with his eyes closed is still aware of his self, we realize that the referent of "I" is not the perceptible body but something nonperceptible.

(E258-261; T127-128) Objection: Just as when we speak of hot, fragrant water, though heat and fragrance don't belong to the water but are superimposed on it, so when we speak of ourself we superimpose on the body qualities, such as awareness, pleasure, etc., which do not belong to it. The real locus of those qualities must be gleaned from scripture, and is not perceptible.

Answer: No. Experiences such as "I feel pleasure" arise from perception alone, and do not need scripture or inference; we have as a primary idea egoity through immediate awareness.

BOOK FOUR, CHAPTER ONE

IV.1.10 (E279; T140) Objection: Weight is inherent in many substances, and has a common locus with color and size—so why is it not (visually) perceptible?

Answer: Because there is absence of manifested color, etc., in weight.

BOOK FOUR, CHAPTER TWO

(42) IV.2.5 (E288-289; T145-146) "Bodies not born from the womb" include watery, fiery and airy bodies, and also the bodies of gods and sages like Manu; these are not produced by sexual union at all. Of those bodies produced by sexual union there are two kinds, womb-born and ego-born.

Trees and plants are also bodies, since they are the seat of experiences; that is shown by their being alive or dead, propagating seeds, woundable, etc., and by passages from scripture which indicate that they get liberated, etc.

BOOK FIVE, CHAPTER TWO

(50) V.2.18 (E323-324; T170) Direct intuition of the nature of the self is produced by the power of yoga; thus false awareness is destroyed, and so faults like passion, hatred, delusion disappear; so activity stops, birth does not take place, and thus frustrations cease. Now a *yogin* wears away the karmic residues produced by previous merit and demerit earned in various bodies—horse, elephant, snake, bird, by taking up those kinds of bodies and experiencing the results of those former acts; thus his faults are removed, and no further merit and demerit being produced, no future body is produced.

(55-56) (E330-332; T175) "In the Vedas the composition of sentences is preceded by awareness" (*sūtra* 1). This shows that Vedas have an author, an independent Person (*svatantrapuruṣa*). And the distinguishing feature of the Vedas is that they are verbal testimony (or, language) whose authoritativeness is not produced from understanding of the meanings of sentences composed of words, while the scope of its meaning is not produced by any instrument of knowledge other than that involving verbal testimony.

(E335-342; T177-181) Jaimini's *sūtra* "the result (of an act) indicated by the *śāstra* belongs to the one who performed that act" (*śāstradeśitam phalamanuṣṭhātari*) is justified.

Objection: No, since such a rule is violated when we sacrifice for birth of a son, or perform *śrāddha* for our ancestors. The fruits of a father's sacrifice accrues to the son, or of the son to his departed ancestor.

Counterobjector: Then let it be that *apūrva* (*adṛṣṭa*) is the result for the agent, and vigorousness (or heaven) for the son (or the ancestor, respectively).

Objector: No, since there is the rule that the operation (*vyāpāra*) must inhere in the same locus as the result of the act—and if the son is liberated before he gets a chance to perform *śrāddha*, the ancestor will not get to heaven.

Counterobjection: Likewise, if the ancestor is liberated before the *śrāddha* is performed heaven will not result, even if the performance is perfect—so the anomalies are equivalent.

Answer: Jaimini's rule, being general, admits of exceptions where there is a strong sublating factor: in these cases scripture is the sublating factor.

Objection: In the case of the *mahādānas* ("great gifts") heaven results for whomever is declared to be the beneficiary of such an act.

Answer: That is absurd. Here there is no strong sublating factor; so kings, etc., still must practice ritual acts and cannot merely depend on others to bring about beneficial results by prayer, etc.

The Vṛttikāra, however, says that Jaimini's rule is without exception of any kind. In the case of sacrifice for a son, or *śrāddha*, the results which accrue to the son, or the ancestor, come from the *mantras* recited by Brahmins at the rites, which remove obstructions to those results just as *mantras* chanted by foresters over one who has been bitten by a snake remove the poison.

If an impure Brahmin presides at *śrāddha* the wished-for result (heaven) will not accrue to the ancestors and sin will result, while if the rite is presided over by a pure Brahmin, one whose conduct follows scriptural injunctions, it will be efficacious and no sin will result. One should always give preference in honor to the pure Brahmin over an impure one, even when one has invited an impure one and only later received a purer one, or even where the impure one is of a higher status than the pure one.

(57) (E342-345; T181-183) Merit arises from receiving from a virtuous person of whatever status. If a Brahmin is denied sustenance he may even kill the other, provided the other is inferior in status to him—or if the refusing donor is superior to him, he should commit suicide.

BOOK SEVEN, CHAPTER ONE

(62) (E365-367; T196-197) Objection: Colorness is (not a proper universal but) an imposed property, viz., being graspable by the visual organ.

Answer: No, for then we wouldn't necessarily have experience of color when the visual organ fell upon an object, as an imposed property will not produce the relevant experience since it is not present already. Thus colorness, viz., perceptibility by the visual organ only, is a proper universal.

Objection: Shades (blue, yellow, etc.) are individual eternal things; there is no universal colorness or blueness, etc.

Answer: No, for then we could not explain our notions of "deeper blue", etc.

Objector: These notions are due to the blue being relatively unmixed with e.g., white.

Answer: No. Mixture (contact) will involve inherence, and inherence is eternal.

(E371-376; T199-202) A discussion over the theory of cooking takes place. The *piṭharapākavādins* say that the whole pot—from atoms up to the whole—is baked. The *pīlupākavādin* holds that it is only the atoms which are burnt. Their view entails that the pot must break down into its ultimate components while in the kiln, that the pot will be destroyed. Indeed, only if it is can the heat get to the inside parts of the pot and change their color.

Piṭharapākavādin: If the pot is destroyed, how is it that we say of the pot coming out of the kiln "this is the same pot I put in?" Why does it have the same form as before, and in the same place on the pan in which they were inserted? Why should there be the same number of pots on the pan, and of the same size, with the same markings?

Answer: When one removes a few "molecules" (*trasareṇu*, triple-dyads) from a pot one can still recognize it as the same, even though in a sense it has been destroyed. At least, this is what the Mīmāṃsakas say. But they should be asked how it is that with a smaller number of constituent parts the same recognizable arrangement can be maintained? Pots are not like cloths, contractible in size.

There is an extended and highly technical discussion of different views about the number of moments involved in the cooking process—whether it involves nine, ten or eleven moments. The author says he has also explained the points in his *Kaṇādarahasya*.

BOOK SEVEN, CHAPTER TWO

(68) (E398-399; T215) Objection: Separateness (*pṛthaktva*) is nothing but mutual absence (*anyonyābhāva*).

Answer: No. When we speak of separateness we use a different locution ("This is separate *from* that", but "This is not that").

Objector: But consider: "This is distinct *from* that", "this is separate *from* that"—here both involve the "from".

Answer: No. "Maitra is distinct from the stick he holds" is consistent with his not being separate from the stick. Likewise, substances are separated from each other, but not from qualities, etc., though a substance is certainly distinct from a quality, etc.

(E404-411; T219-223) Noneternal unity and separateness-of-a-single-thing have as their antecedents qualities of their causes; other numbers and separateness are produced by enumerative cognitions. An elaborate discussion shows that it takes eight moments to produce duality, e.g., beginning with the contact between object and organ and ending with a trace, and likewise eight moments to destroy it. Some intricate objections to this account are considered.

A difference of opinion between Śrīdhara and Udayana is reported, Śrīdhara holding that the processes reviewed can explain the generation of our idea of multiplicity, but not of specific large numbers such as "one hundred" or "one thousand". Udayana retorts that in that case one could not entertain the doubt whether there be a hundred or a thousand in the army. The question here is, our author says, whether "multiplicity" denotes in general all numbers above three to the highest number, or whether it denotes a different number from any of those. Neither answer is satisfactory, according to the two writers under discussion.

However, Śaṃkara Miśra says that multiplicity (*bahutva*) is actually a different number which coexists in the same locus with three, four, etc. That it is different is shown by its having a different prior absence as its antecedent from each of the cardinal series, i.e., when we say "there are many", we don't know precisely how many. Thus, threeness is produced by enumerative cognition accompanied by twoness, fourness by enumerative cognition accompanied by threeness, etc. One can have doubts about which of these is present, but when we are speaking of multiplicity there are no alternatives available about which to doubt.

(69) (E412-424; T228-232) Objection: There is no proof of the existence of disjunction, for it is just the absence of contact.

Answer: If it is supposed to be absolute absence, then the term "disjunction" would also apply to qualities and motions as well as disjunct substances. Further, it would apply to the Vindhya and Himalaya mountain ranges (which are not disjuncts, but just distinct).

Objection: Disjunction is just the destruction (posterior absence) of contact.

Answer: But if something with several parts loses the contact of one part with *x*, it has not become disjoined with *x*.

Objector: Then disjunction is the destruction of all contacts between *y* and *x*.

Answer: Then when one part of *y* leaves *x* there will be no disjunction.

Motions produce contacts and disjunctions, but motions cannot destroy contacts, since a quality can only be destroyed by its opposite quality. Thus it is disjunction of *x* and *y* which destroys the contact between *x* and *y*, as is observed.

Sarvajña is quoted as holding that the motion of, say, a finger can produce destruction of contact between the hand and the tree, but since it is generally observed that destruction of a quality is brought about only by the opposite quality his opinion should not be accepted without some further argument against the principle. Examples are discussed in detail, both of destruction of contact and of disjunction.

(70) (E430-432; T236-238) The "convention" is God's, causing us to understand which object is meant by which word. The con-

vention is learned sometimes from ordinary usage, sometimes from testimony directly, sometimes from comparison, sometimes from abusive language, sometimes from something's having a common locus with something else already known. The Tautikas say that convention only applies in learning general terms, not of individuals, while the Prābhākaras allow it for both general and individual terms. But the ancients (*vṛddha*) say that convention is the power (of words) (*śakti*) and that the meanings of the words involve individuals, universals and configurations (*ākṛti*). As is explained in the *Mayūkha*, words designating qualities and motions do not involve forms.

(71) (E433-439; T238-242) A lengthy section details the process by which nearness and remoteness are produced and destroyed.

(E445-446; T246) Inherence is one, since there is nothing which differentiates it into parts. The Prābhākaras say that it is many and noneternal, but that is not right, for we say that a thing's color is destroyed, but not that the inherence of color in it is destroyed. The Naiyāyikas say that inherence is perceptible, but that is wrong: inherence is supersensible, since it is not inhered in.

BOOK EIGHT, CHAPTER ONE

(72) (E447-449; T247-248) Śaṃkara Miśra explains why *Nyāyasūtra* (I.1.15), which says that *jñāna, upalabdhi, buddhi* and *pratyaya* are synonyms, refutes the Sāṃkhya.

(E450-453; T249-250) Awareness born of the senses is of two kinds—omniscient and nonomniscient. The omniscient kind is born of the merit accruing from yoga, and it allows yogis to perceive objects—such as the atoms—which are normally beyond the scope of vision by grasping properties indicative of those objects.

Objection: How can that be? There are no properties such as size, which belong to atoms which yogis can grasp by their senses.

Answer: Yogis can grasp properties by their internal organs only; their merit is so strong that no auxiliaries are required for them to see things.

Nonomniscient awareness is of two kinds, construction-filled and construction-free. Dharmakīrti and Dignāga hold that construction, filled awareness is not an instrument of knowledge because it involves relationship with words, universals, etc., and thus cannot be related to the momentary particular (*svalakṣaṇa*). But we say that even though construction-filled awareness involves a relation with words, still, since it is produced by contact between object and sense-organ it is at least open to question whether it is an instrument of knowledge. Furthermore, a thing distinguished by a name can be an object of awareness, the connection being furnished by memory. And we have shown that universals are present qualifying existing things. So both construction-filled and construction-free are instruments of knowledge.

Objection: What is the proof of construction-free awareness?

Answer: It has to be inferred from the fact of construction-filled awareness, for the materials of construction must be provided somehow.

BOOK NINE, CHAPTER ONE

(75) (E467-480; T262-271) An effect is absent prior to its production, and this absence is called its prior absence. It is the perception of this prior absence which enables us to say, as the clay is on the potter's wheel, that there will be a pot produced there, etc. And this prior absence is a causal condition in the production of its counterpositive (the pot). The author goes on to distinguish posterior absence, mutual absence and absolute absence, and shows that they are all perceptible.

Objection: The absence of pot in the room is not an absolute absence, since the pot may be there at some other time; it is neither a prior nor posterior absence, for they occur only in inherence causes; it is not an absolute absence undergoing production and destruction, for that is impossible. So what kind of relational absence is it?

Answer: "The absence of pot in the room" means that there is absence of contact of pot with room. This is an absolute absence if no such pot ever has existed, does exist or will exist; it is prior absence if the pot will exist later, and posterior absence if the pot existed in the past.

Objection: Then the judgment should have been "There is absence of contact of pot with room" (and not "there is absence of pot in the room"). And then it would follow that the pot is always there, at least that would not be denied.

Answer: No. The only two ways the pot could be in the room are through contact or inherence; the judgment denies the former, and the latter is impossible.

(76) (E482-483; T274) *Sūtra* IX.1.13 speaks of those whose internal organs (*antaḥkaraṇa*) are not involved in meditation (*samādhi*), who have given up meditation, and says that they too have yogic powers of perception along with other *siddhis*. They realize that they must experience all the karmic residues they have acquired in previous births, and so they use their enhanced powers of perception to bring about those experiences.

BOOK NINE, CHAPTER TWO

(77) (E485-489; T277-278) Jīvanātha Miśra is cited as holding that the *p* (in inference) is that in which there is an absence limited by the property of preventing the arising of doubt, which absence is terminable by ascertainment of a producible *s*. Others say that the *p* is that in which there is absence of the property of proving accompanied by a desire to prove.

The cause *par excellence* of inferential awareness is the *liṅga* (or *hetu*) alone, and not its consideration, since once a properly qualified *h* is known to be there consideration has no function.

Objection: How can there be inferential awareness when the *h* is past or future?

Answer: The *s* which is inferred is also past or future.

Objection: How, on your view, can there be inference of fire from a cloud of dust mistaken for smoke?

Answer: Because the cloud of dust is taken to be pervaded by fire—how is it any better on the view that consideration is the cause?

Objection: Suppose the *h* is beyond the scope of the senses; how can it function to produce an inference, since no consideration can occur?

Answer: It can if there is a saving (?) argument (*kṣaimika sādhanatā*) showing the *h*'s existence—otherwise the funtioning of inherence in cases of hearing, etc., would not be possible.

(E492-493; T280-281) The property of being pervaded (by the *s* in the *h*) is the possession of a natural relation (*svābhāvikasambandha*), where naturalness means being without obstructions (*anaupādhikatva*). This relation is sometimes grasped directly from perception, sometimes (in the case of supersensible objects) through other inferences. The doubting devil (*śaṅkāpiśācin*) who says "but still there may be some obstruction after all" should be rejected, as he undermines all injunctions and prohibitions, for there is the possibility of ascertainment.

(E496-501; T282-285) Verbal testimony (*śabda*) is included within inference. (The inference goes as follows: "These objects possess interconnection, because they are remembered as possessing expectancy, etc., like the words "drive away the cow".)

Objection: Verbal testimony is not inference in a case where the words are spoken by an untrustworthy person.

Answer: No, for the words must have the qualification of being spoken by a trustworthy person. Trustworthiness means knowing that one's sentence corresponds to the way things are within the scope of the meaning of that statement, not merely that he isn't a liar.

Objector: How can we detect the presence of such a property in the speaker's words before we understand their meaning?

Answer: Well, those (Naiyāyikas) who hold that verbal authority is distinct from inference appeal to trustworthiness to detect false statements.

Objector: But there verbal awareness (*śabdajñāna*) is produced whether or not the property of trustworthiness is discerned in the speaker, whereas in your case the *h* must necessarily be known to have that property.

Answer: No, since we can have the awareness "he is infallible as regards this sort of thing".

Objector: But we don't know what sort of thing prior to hearing the sentence!

Answer: No, we can know that in general this speaker is trustworthy with regard to this sort of thing, even though in a given case we may be mistaken, in which case the inference proceeds as in the instance (above) of inferring fire from a cloud of dust mistaken for smoke.

Objection: In this alleged inference of yours, what is the *s*? Is it that the meanings of the words are connected, or that that connection is possible? Not the first, since in the case of the untrustworthy speaker the connection is absent. And the second doesn't prove enough.

Answer: It is the regularity of interconnection of objects that is the *s*, and this is not dependent on trustworthiness.

Objection: Expectancy is the prior absence in the hearer of awareness of the interconnection (of the objects of the words). Only as long as this expectancy exists can there be a relevant *h* in an inference of the sort you have in mind. But since according to you awareness of the interconnection of the object must occur before awareness of expectancy, your inference is useless.

Answer: No. Expectancy is qualified by the possession of an inseparable relation between what is remembered and what is presented now. It is not a prior absence as you say. Or else, expectancy may be defined as the desire to know the objects denoted by the words, or as the comprehending of the meaning. Whichever definition is accepted, in any case awareness of expectancy is necessary in the words, as well as semantic fitness and contiguity, as contrasted with what is to be proved, the interconnection of the objects.

(E502-504; T285-286) Some say that gesture (*ceṣṭā*) is an additional instrument of knowledge. There are two kinds of gesture—conventional and nonconventional. The conventional sort calls to mind words which are thus the instruments of knowledge (through inference).

Objection: Then how can a deaf person understand gestures, since he does not know the convention.

Answer: But he must know regular connection between the gesture and ideas and their conventional meanings—i.e., he must be aware of inseparable relationships, pervasion, which allows him to make inferences, and so inference is ultimately the instrument of knowledge.

Now as for nonconventional gestures—they are not instruments of knowledge at all, but merely remind the hearer of the speaker's intentions, etc.—there is no regular relation with interconnected objects, but merely doubtful notions, intuitions or instinct operating.

(78) (E514-515; T291-292) Dreams are conditioned in three ways: (1) from the force of impressions left by ideas and actions in waking just prior to sleep, (2) from derangement of the humors—wind, bile and phlegm, (3) from *adṛṣṭa.* Examples are provided.

BOOK TEN, CHAPTER ONE

(81) (E520-521; T296-297) Śaṃkara Miśra interprets the first *sūtra* as saying that pleasure and pain are different from each other. When Gautama says (in *Nyāyasūtra* IV.1.58) that pleasure is another kind of pain he is teaching nonattachment (and not speaking seriously).

KALPALATĀ on UDAYANA'S ĀTMATATTVAVIVEKA

Summary by V. Varadachari

"E" reference are to edition by V.P. Dvivedin and L. S. Dravid (B2676; RB3932), Bibliotheca Indica 170, 1907-1939. Section references are geared to the summary of the *Ātmatattvaviveka* in Vol. II.

INTRODUCTION

2 (E10-11) While interpreting the text "knowledge of reality of the self alone is the means for obtaining relief" (*ātmaiva tattvatojñeyaḥ*) Śaṃkara Miśra remarks that "alone" precludes death in Kāśi (Banaras) and other means from becoming the direct means to liberation. He means that knowledge of reality is essential and is the only means to liberation, and that death in Banaras may perhaps help one who has knowledge of reality of the Self in getting liberated.[16]

KṢAṆABHAṄGAVĀDA

21 (E253) While explaining that a particular absence cannot have

another absence as qualifier, Śaṃkara Miśra remarks that the absence and its counterpositive are opposed to each other. Since an absence is the absence of its counterpositive, then, no purpose is served by assuming that an absence has another absence of the same counterpositive; then a third one can as well be assumed, and a fourth, etc., ad infinitum.

BĀHYĀRTHABHAṄGA

50-51 (E524-529) Śaṃkara Miśra does not hesitate to expose the hollowness of Advaita. Udayana rejects the Buddhist Yogācāra theory that awareness and its object are identical; he argues that if that were so an awareness would have to have mutually contradictory properties such as blue, white, etc. Śaṃkara Miśra comments that this rejection applies as well to the Advaitin, who cannot explain how a single cognition can be of one kind, then of another and so on.

53 (E534) Udayana illustrates, with examples, how a sentence becomes meaningless if it transgresses the limits of worldly experience, and prescribes expectancy, appropriateness and contiguity as required for a sentence to "convey its sense". In this context Śaṃkara Miśra notes that, according to Udayana, expectancy is the cause of meaningfulness by its very presence or existence, while the other two become causal only when they are known. Other scholars, he remarks, hold that all three become causes only when they are known.

73 (E699) Udayana discusses the method of apprehending the validity of an awareness. To determine validity in an awareness one must notice a property the awareness has. But to do this one must have a different awareness which apprehends both the first awareness and its property as nondifferent from each other. That is why the Nyāya tradition holds validity to be extrinsic. Vācaspati Miśra I, however, held that in such cases validity is intrinsic, as there is no room for error. Udayana admits this as the easier method. Extrinsic validity is to be adopted only when validity is questioned. Śaṃkara Miśra notes this last explanation, and remarks that Vācaspati meant by intrinsic validity only that which does not give scope for doubt regarding invalidity.

ESTABLISHMENT OF GOD AND OF THE AUTHORITY OF THE VEDAS

108 (E906) Udayana proves the validity of the Vedas on the ground that they are God's compositions. In spite of creations and dissolutions, an omniscient God is able to reproduce the Vedas intact at

each creation. The Mīmāṃsakas, on the other hand, take the Vedas to be eternal, there being no creation or dissolution to intervene. Udayana rejects this, since if that were the case objects such as a jar might equally well be eternal, but experience disproves that. Further, on the Mīmāṃsā view it doesn't matter whether God is admitted or not. Śaṃkara Miśra clarifies this passage by explaining that what is meant is that even if God be admitted nothing can be proved to help the Mīmāṃsaka's case. The jar and other objects are always objects of God's knowledge and so could be reproduced by Him like the Vedas. This is what the Nyāya system admits as the eternal stream. Thus the explanation that the Mīmāṃsā position might be justified by admitting God does not stand to reason.

FINAL RELEASE

112 (E939-940) Udayana describes the stages of realization through which one has to pass. He mentions the Nyāya method as characterizing the final stage, and Advaita as fitting the penultimate stage. During this Advaita stage the self alone shines. Udayana says even this stage should be given up, as is enjoined in the passage "not nonduality, not also duality" (*nādvaitam nāpidvaitam, Dakṣiṇāsmṛti* 7.48). Instead of taking this passage as directed against Advaita, Śaṃkara Miśra says it is cited here to avoid this stage getting misconstrued according to the Bhāskara doctrine of *Bhedābhedavāda.* It is not therefore to be taken as opposed to Advaita. What is meant is that the self should be intuited with the help of the mind that is not involved in investigations of dualism or monism. The impressions (*vāsanā*) in the self are then annihilated, and the self has only construction-free awareness. This stage is thus that of Advaita, the one represented in the Upaniṣadic passage which says that thought and mind do not reach that final stage. Śaṃkara Miśra remarks that this passage is correct, since at this point there is no object for the self to be aware of. Udayana says this stage should not be given up, since it is the principal gate leading to the city of liberation. This (Advaitic) stage becomes extinct by itself, not by anything being opposed to it, but by the passage of time involving the complete destruction of all impressions.[17]

KAṆṬHĀBHARAṆA on (Śrī) Vallabha's NYĀYALĪLĀVATĪ
Summary by V. Varadachari

"E" references are to the edition by Harihara Sastri and Dundhiraja Sastri (B2928; RB4495), Chowkhamba Sanskrit Series 64, 1927-1934. Sections are numbered according to the summary of *Nyāyalīlāvatī* in Vol. II of this Encyclopedia.

1 (E2-5) The author does not himself refer to Puruṣottama as the name of Śrī Vallabha's father, but tells us that this is the view held by some scholars. Līlāvatī was the name of Śaṃkara Miśra's wife.

(E10) A category (*padārtha*) is said to be a relation between the form of an object and awareness of it. This relation exists through the cognition of God, or His will, which takes the form "this (object) is to be known from this word."

2. (E69) Nyāya terms the relation between sense-organ and an absence *viśeṣaṇaviśeṣyabhāva*. Śaṃkara Miśra remarks that the relation between an absence and its locus is a self-linking connector, which may also be taken as *vaiśiṣṭya*, a specific kind of knowledge relation.

14. (E179-180) The cause of the external perceptibility of substances is manifested color. Where it is not present, perceptibility is not found. Manifested touch is not such a condition, since moonlight lacks it and is yet perceptible. Vācaspati Miśra, on the other hand, says that both manifest color and manifest touch are required, and that moonlight is not perceptible since it lacks the second of these.

39 (E498) Śaṃkara Miśra notes that Vallabha does not agree with Vācaspati Miśra in defining pervasion as a relation free from obstructions.

(E511) Taraṇi Miśra's definition of "obstruction" is stated and refuted.

46 (E580) There is no instrument of knowledge to prove Brahman to have a blissful nature or to prove that the world is false.

(E512) The Upaniṣadic passages which speak of nonduality are metaphorical and mean only that those who seek release should meditate on Brahman alone.

(E594) To illustrate that there cannot be pleasure in the world without at least some tinge of pain, Śaṃkara Miśra offers the following. Some men are born or become kings and are said to be leading a life of happiness, but they too have to spend a somewhat frustrating time in their mothers' womb before they are brought forth into this world.

48 (E606-609) Counterbalance, which involves doubt about pervasion, therefore belongs under the rubric of *vyāpyatvāsiddhi*. Sublation, in which the *pakṣa* is doubtful, is a kind of deviation.

22. HARI MIŚRA

Authorities conflict on this personage. Phaṇibhūṣaṇa Tarkavāgīśa[1] reports a tradition that Hari Miśra was the uncle and teacher of Jayadeva (also called Pakṣadhara) Miśra, and that Hari was a teacher of the famous Maithila poet Vidyāpati Ṭhakkura. Now Vidyāpati flourished in the first half of the 15th century, but Jayadeva a number of decades later, and so D.H.H. Ingalls[2] doubts that Hari Miśra was the teacher of Jayadeva. In fact, the solution is simply to recognize that the Pakṣadhara who is the nephew and pupil of Hari Miśra was not Jayadeva but another Pakṣadhara, perhaps the one known as the Vivekakāra. Indeed, our evidence that Hari was the uncle and teacher of some Pakṣadhara is a *Viveka* on *Nyāyalīlāvatī*, the work of Pakṣadhara, presumably not Jayadeva, despite the common identification of the two. If we place Hari Miśra around the beginning of the 15th century, we should be close.

23. VĀCASPATI MIŚRA (II)

One of the great Maithila scholars of the period, Vācaspati came from a family of Mīmāṃsakas and made his fame as an authority on that topic, on which he says himself he wrote at least 30 treatises.[1] He was, as well, the teacher of Smārta Vardhamāna, author of *Daṇḍaviveka* and most famous name in jurisprudence in India after the ancient authorities.

Vācaspati Miśra's family appears to have lived in several different villages of Mithilā during these days. Vācaspati himself had four wives, at least two of whom were related either by blood or through marriage to Śaṃkara Miśra. One of his sons was 39. Narahari, who commented on *Ātmatattvaviveka* and is discussed below.

D.C. Bhattacharya[2] provides some telling textual arguments proving that Vācaspati preceded most of the other early great Maithila Naiyāyikas such as Yajñapati, Pakṣadhara and Jayadeva the Ālokakara. He argues that it is likely that Vācaspati wrote his Nyāya works in his youth, suggesting that when he found his own stature in this field eclipsed by that of Yajñapati and Jayadeva he retired from Nyāya and spent the rest of his life writing on Mīmāṃsā.

Some of these early Nyāya works appear to have been written in the North, where Vācaspati must have spent some of his early days. A manuscript of one of his works, the *Nyāyaratnaprakāśa*, indicates the work was written at the behest of Padmāvatī, Pratāparudra's queen of Pañcālabhūmi. However, Vācaspati spent the greater part of his days in his native Mithilā. Estimates of his date by D.C. Bhattacharya, Umesh Mishra[3] and B.K. Matilal[4] place Vācaspati's Nyāya works in the first half of the 15th century, though he seems to have lived to an advanced age. He was the court pandit of Bhairavasiṃha, king of Mithilā, who also patronized Vācaspati's pupil Vardhamāna. Vācaspati was also the paṇḍit of Bhairavasiṃha's successor Rāmabhadradeva, and both also patronized Vardhamāna, Vācaspati's pupil, and as all can be shown on the basis of an inscription to have lived before 1495 we must assume that Vācaspati was born between 1400-1410 and was still alive late enough in the century to serve Bhairava and Rāmabhadra.

In the same passage where Vācaspati tells us that he wrote thirty books on Mīmāṃsā he also mentions that he wrote at least ten works on Nyāya. Dinesh Bhattacharya[5] has spent much scholarly effort in attempting to track down which these ten works are and the order in which they were written. His findings:

1. Vācaspati wrote a large commentary on the *Nyāyasūtras* called the (*Nyāya)Tattvāloka*, of which no complete manuscript is known. It seems to have been remarkable in that it includes summaries of the views of some of Gaṅgeśa's section of *Tattvacintāmaṇi* under the relevant *sūtras*. D.C. Bhattacharya points our that after this commentary the commentarial literature on the *Nyāyasūtras* tails off in frequency and length, suggesting that the increasing popularity of *Tattvacintāmaṇi* threw study of the *Nyāyasūtras* into decline.

2. *Nyāyasūtroddhāra*, which Umesh Mishra believes may itself be Vācaspati's first effort, is merely a reconstructed text of the *Nyāyasūtras* numbering 531 *sūtras* (as contrasted with the 528 identified by Vācaspati Miśra I in *his Nyāyasūcīnibandha* many centuries earlier).

3. A *Prakāśa* on Maṇikaṇṭha Miśra's *Nyāyaratna*, which exists in manuscript in full at the Bhandarkar Library in Poona. This is the work noted above as written while abroad.

4-6. Three independent works dealing with the topics of the three important chapters of *Tattvacintāmaṇi* (i.e., excluding *upamāna*). These are called respectively *Pratyakṣanirṇaya*, *Anumānanirṇaya* and *Śabdanirṇaya*. A fragmentary MS. of the *Anumānanirṇaya* exists in Nepal, according to Bhattacharya and Miśra.

7. *Khaṇḍanoddhāra*, summarized below, is a refutation of Śrīharṣa's *Khaṇḍanakhaṇḍakhādya*.

8-10. Commentaries on the three main chapters of *Tattvacintāmaṇi* itself, the entire thing titled *Cintāmaṇiprakāśa*. Only partially extant in MS.

As Umesh Mishra points out, counting the *Cintāmaṇiprakāśa* as a single work, which makes the most sense, leaves us two works short. Bhattacharya suggests there might be a lost commentary on the *Nyāyalīlāvatī*.

KHAṆḌANODDHĀRA

Summary by V. Varadachari

"E" references are to the edition by V.P. Dvivedin and Vamacarana Bhattacarya (B3644; RB5657), first published serially in The Pandit new series 25, 1903-30, 1908, and then reprinted at Banaras in 1910.

(E3-5) Śrīharṣa's argument: Must the instruments of knowledge be admitted in order for discussion to take place? Materialists and nihilists engage themselves in discussions without admitting them, so clearly it is possible. Worldly practice does not require the instruments of knowledge; there is no proof that it does.

Answer: The older school of Nyāya meets this objection by noting that the instruments of knowledge have to be admitted to be available, as otherwise what is apprehended cannot be assumed to exist—it might be like a sky lotus, or sublated like the judgment that the self is the body or like the notion of red color in a crystal which is near a red flower. These are mistaken judgments, and thus presuppose valid judgments, known by instruments, which are contrary to these. Knowledge based on an instrument of knowledge is never sublated. The Advaitin has to admit the instruments of knowledge to explain empirical experience. It is for this reason that the materialist, who refuses to admit inference, is not generally taken as a participant in discussions. That the world is illusory is no argument for rejecting the instruments of knowledge, for this illusory nature is not established by any instruments of knowledge. So the instruments of knowledge must be admitted, since without them disputes could never be conducted.

(E5-7) The modern Naiyāyikas answer thus: In order for Śrīharṣa to prove that instruments of knowledge are not needed for participation in debate, he must use an instrument of knowledge! Or to put it another way, if the instruments of knowledge are sublated then Śrīharṣa's argument must also be sublated, and so cannot prove that instruments of knowledge are not necessary for arguments.

Objection: Discussion can proceed without referring to the instruments of knowledge.

Answer: No, since a discussion must begin with a statement of the *pūrvapakṣa* and go on to its refutation in order to establish one's own position, and these steps necessarily involve consideration of validity, i.e., of the instruments of knowledge.

(E7-8) Śrīharṣa: But the instruments of knowledge need not be mentioned at all.

Answer: Nevertheless their relevance cannot be denied.

Śrīharṣa: A debate can proceed according to the conventions of debating alone, without reference to instruments of knowledge.

Answer: No; the conventions may not be known to everyone. In any case, conventions can only obtain where the śāstraic rules (involving validity) do not apply. For example, a convention may be established requiring participants to avoid labial sounds.

(E10-11) Śrīharṣa: Still, all your argument shows is that a discussion requires people to speak and think of the instruments of knowledge, but it doesn't require that their judgments be valid. The so-called "instruments of knowledge' may be merely invalid judgments, yet discussion can perfectly well proceed. A nonexistent thing can be a cause, and an existent thing may not be a cause—so the reality of the instruments of knowledge cannot be insisted on as providing a cause for the discussion.

Answer: A nonexistent, having no feature of its own, cannot control production of an effect, for there would be nothing such that when it occurs, the effect occurs.

Objection: It is the occurrence of its form (*svarūpasattā*) that makes it a cause.

Answer: Then it is something existent, with a form, and the view is no different from our (*Nyāya*) view. Furthermore, if the existence of a jar is held to arise from nonexistence, past and future jars should arise now.

Objection: Still, a cause need not actually occur at the time of its causal functioning; it is enough that it be in the mind of somebody. An idea of *x* may cause *y* even though *x* does not actually occur then (though it may occur at some other time).

Answer: Then you would be in the absurd position of saying that a person who thinks of or imagines sweetmeats in their absence should get the same satisfaction as one who actually tastes them! There is no alternative: the cause must actually occur at the time it produces its effect, or at the moment just prior to that.

(E14) We agree, however, that positive existence (*sattā*) is not necessary in the causal factors for some effects, e.g., the nonobservation of a certain feature may lead to erroneous cognition. Absence of defects leads to validity of awareness. Nonperformance of what is obligatory causes a sin of omission (*pratyavāya*). The absence of erroneous awareness causes liberation. Udayana says[6] that absences may be causes inasmuch as they can be effects.

Śrīharṣa (taking the standpoint of Yogācāra): Awareness is self-luminous.

(E16-17) Answer: No. Every awareness requires its independent content.

Objection: Since it takes time for an awareness to reach an independent object, we could never know an object to exist at the present (if the Nyāya position were correct).

Answer: This is no argument. The intervals between moments are very small, so it is not impossible to know that something exists at the present, especially since the awareness which arises directly after a given awareness is not different from it—if it were different, we could never achieve liberation.

Objection: The object of an awareness is insentient (*jaḍa*); but on your view one awareness can have another as object; thus awarenesses must be insentient, which is absurd.

Answer: No. We do not say that every awareness becomes the object of another awareness of a similar kind arising about the same object at the same time. Rather, awarenesses are apprehended in several ways: they are known by worldly activity or verbal references, logical marks, after-cognitions (*anuvyavasāya*), extraordinary perception of universals (*sāmānyalakṣaṇa*) or yogic perception. So awarenesses can be known by other awarenesses, but it does not follow that they are known in the same way as objects and thus are insentient.

(E17-18) And awareness is not self-luminous; what an awareness illuminates is its object, not itself. And that object may be inert, as, e.g., a jar is. Now since an awareness depends on its object, and the object may not be luminous, it follows that the cognition is not self-luminous, i.e., it depends on something which is not luminous.

(E18-19) Awareness of objects always stems from sense perception; since awarenesses are not grasped by sense perception there is no awareness which is the object (in that way) of another awareness. There is, to be sure, recollection, aftercognition, etc., which grasp cognitions, but not as objects in the same way the sense grasp them.

(E19) Eternal consciousness (*nityacaitanya*), which is nondifferent from Brahman, cannot have the jar as its supporting object (*ālambana*), and so cannot be known at all. So clearly it cannot be self-luminous! Thus nondualism cannot be proved on the basis of that self-luminosity. Indeed, if this self-luminosity does not arise without its property included, then it cannot be spoken of, even under the influence of *avidyā*, using expressions which can only apply by referring to properties. Futhermore, you can't cite the Upaniṣad here to support nondualism, for that would preclude other means of knowing. Nor can implication (*upalakṣaṇa*) give nondualistic knowledge of Brahman, since its operation requires that it makes known something with graspable properties.

(E19-22) Objection: The Upaniṣads advise one to see, listen, consider and meditate on the Self—construed in mutual coordination such passages prove that the Self alone exists and is the single thing that needs to be known.

(E23) Answer: Verbal authority cannot produce direct apprehension which Advaitins hold to be required for liberation. The Upaniṣads do not support nondualism; they eulogize it. Again, what is the relation between the Brahman known from the Vedas and Brahman Itself? If the Advaitin says that it cannot be described as either identity or difference, this indicates a defect in the knower, that he is beset by ignorance. It is really strange that what does not lie within the province of an instrument of knowledge is taken by the Advaitin as the real object, and what is supported by the instruments of knowledge is treated as an unreal object. And a nondualist should not admit concepts such as action, object, etc.

(E23-25) How can a nondualist admit a distinction between an act (*kriyā*) and its object (*karman*)? Yet, how can he fail to admit it, since the object is what is produced (*kārya*) and so determines the action?

Śrīharṣa: Actions are not determined by their objects—if that were so there could be no actions is the future, since their objects would not exist yet.

Question: What *is* an "object (of action)", then?

Śrīharṣa: It has been defined as (1) that which is the sphere of the operation of the instrument, or (2) that which receives the result of the action, where the action itself inheres in something else. Neither of these definitions leads us to think that the object is that which determines or produces the action. In any case, the distinction cannot apply in such an action as is reported in "I know myself"—knowledge cannot have the self as its object. Grammarians coin technical terms for their special purposes, but there need be no definition of "object of action", and indeed none is satisfactory.

Vācaspati: An "object" is the recipient of the result of an activity which inheres in a different locus (*tatkriyānadhikāraṇatve sati tatkriyāphalaśālinaḥ karmatvāt*). There is a difference between the older and the new Naiyāyikas about the meaning of the verbal root (*dhātu*). The latter say that some roots have, and some don't have, the sense of activity (*kriyā*), and that the accusative case does not necessarily signify an object of an action, as in "he goes to the village", where 'the village,' in the accusative case, is nevertheless not a direct object of the verb. There are likewise cases where the accusative case is employed metaphorically, and "I know myself" is such a case. Vācaspati says he has treated this in greater detail in his *Tattvāloka.*

(E26) Śrīharṣa: Everything except pure consciousness cannot be considered either real or unreal (it is all *anirvacanīya*).

(E27-34) Vācaspati: The Vedas do not deny duality; where nonduality appears to be conveyed the texts are probably speaking of the commonality among things engendered by their sharing universal properties. And our cognition of diversity is not the product of ignorance, because one can only speak of delusion if he has had nondelusive cognition, which we have not had according to the Advaitin. The Advaitin tells us that duality is unreal and yet allows that his scripture issues injunctions and prohibitions about that unreality.

Again, how can nondifference be supposed to be conveyed if there is no difference between the teacher and the taught, between word and its meaning, etc. If as wrangler (*vaitaṇḍika*) the opponent merely denies difference argumentatively, he must then have been citing the Veda as an instrument of knowledge for nondualism under the influence of ignorance, whether nondifference be taken as the absence of difference or what is opposed to difference, difference must be taken as real either as counterpositive or proper opposite.

The Advaitin should not suppose that the Vedas say that the world and Brahman are nondifferent, for this is opposed to Śaṃkara's statement that Brahman alone is real, and the world not. Again, if Brahman and the world are nondifferent, Brahman will become inert, and a liberation-seeker will have no interest in it. Indeed, if the Vedas really do deny the world the question of nondifference between the world and Brahman will never arise.

Objection: What the Vedas declare is nondifference between the self and God.

Answer: No, that is contrary to perception; everyone knows that he is not God.

It is absurd to use expressions to prove that Brahman is beyond expressions. It is equally absurd to hold that what is not proved by the instruments of knowledge is real and what is proved by them is unreal. Therefore the word "*brahman*" must be taken to mean the creator of the world. Udayana's *Nyāyakusumāñjali, kārikā* V.1 is the evidence for this. Passages in the Vedas which appear to teach monism must be understood as intended as a basis for meditation. Thus the world is different from Brahman.

(E34) The author of the *Bhāmatī* says that *avidyā* has each self (*jīva*) for its locus. But this cannot be right. It involves mutual dependence: the self's distinctness is caused by *avidyā*, and yet it is the seat of *avidyā*. If one tries to avoid the dependence by asserting that the difference among the selves is beginningless, then it will follow that the selves' distinctness is not caused at all, and therefore is not caused by *avidyā*.

(E35-36) As for the view of the Vivaraṇa school: If *māyā* is indescribable, it is foolish to maintain it by speaking about it! Brahman cannot remain transcendent and suffer the changes involved in being conditioned by *māyā*.

(E36-40) Vācaspati now offers an exposition of the concept of God in the Nyāya system. He proves God's existence in the manner of Udayana.

Mīmāṃsā objector: All creators have bodies; you say God is the creator of the world, but he does not have a body, so he cannot be the creator of the world.

Answer: There is a distinction. Human creatures require embodiment to act, while God is not subject to such a requirement. The *Mahārṇava* and Vaṭeśvara held that one who has the will, the desire and knowledge still will not create, lacking a body. Narasiṃha and Hariśarman questioned the generality of this formulation. But actually the question of embodiment is irrelevant in the present context.

(E42-45) Śrīharṣa: You say that the nature of a thing is the mutual absence or being other than what is nonidentical with it. But one doesn't have to bring in the notion of cloth to cognize a pot. So difference cannot be mutual absence, or even separateness. Therefore nondualism cannot be sublated by perception. Difference exists, but it is unreal, i.e., illogical.

Vācaspati answers this by appealing to Udayana's *Ātmatattvaviveka* to show that difference is what Śrīharṣa denies it to be.

(E46-49) Śrīharṣa: Sophistry (*jalpa*) is not an independent kind of controversy (*kathā*), but consists of two steps involving cavil.

Vācaspati: No. Sophistry involves two steps, viz., pointing out the faults in the opponent's argument and rejecting that argument, perhaps by putting forth a counterargument. Sophistry is thus not entirely cavil.

Śrīharṣa's account is that sophistry involves two steps. The old Naiyāyikas interpret him as taking as the two steps the establishing of the position by the opponent and the criticism of the opponent's position. But the new Naiyāyikas understand him to be referring to the critique of the opponent's position and the establishment of the proper position. Śrīharṣa is saying that both steps involve destructive reasoning, intially by the opponent, subsequently by the *siddhāntin*. Still, the truth is that this process is both positive and negative, in contrast to cavilling, which is entirely negative.

(E49-50) Śrīharṣa next turns to the Nyāya definition of knowledge (*pramā*) as the direct awareness of reality (*tattvānubhūti*). He points out that the word *tattva* must be construed as *tasya bhāvaḥ*, that is, "the nature of it" but that the "it" has no antecedent. *Tattva* cannot be merely a synonym for "essence" (*svabhāva*), since it would have to be the essence of something and nothing but the Self exists. And it cannot mean "that which is experienced as it is", since something experienced as F at one time would be real even though it was actually only F at some other time or place, etc. Furthermore, experience or direct awareness (*anubhūti*) has no proper universal (*jāti*) since various things—pleasure, frustration, inference as well as perception—count as awareness, and not all awarenesses are valid, even if they appear to be "direct".

Vācaspati: The "reality" (*tattva*) of a thing is its "highest form" (*pāramārthika rūpa*), e.g., the *tattva* of a pot is potness. Knowledge (*pramā*) is awareness of the properties belonging to a thing which has those properties.

(E50-53) Śrīharṣa: Still, awarenessness is not a proper universal, since direct awareness cannot be distinguished from memory. Recognition (*pratyabhijñā*) involves both direct awareness and memory, and thus there is crossconnection (*saṃkara*).

Vācaspati: Recognition is a kind of awareness even though it is produced by a combination of memory-traces and sensory givens. It is not merely a combination of two different kinds of cognition as you have asserted. The author of some *Nibandha* (perhaps Udayana) understands recognition as that whose qualifiers are connected with the sense organ and arranged by traces. Uddyotakara is quoted also. The traces (*saṃskāra*) being activated in sequence explain memory of past experiences. Knowledge can also be defined as awareness of the object as it is (*yathārtho'nubhavaḥ*), i.e., as an experience which does not wander.

(E53-61) An instrument of knowledge is defined as the cause *par excellence* of knowledge (*pramāyāḥ karaṇam*). After discussing the significance of the *kārakas,* the cause—the instrument of knowledge—is described as "not free from noncontact with activity", i.e., that it is what is inseparably associated with the main activity. Thus that is an instrument of knowledge without which the knower and the knowable object would not give rise to knowledge.

(E63-64) Now, God's knowledge and yogic perception are the two kinds of supernormal (*alaukika*) perception. In the *sāmānyalakṣaṇa* kind of perception that perception of smoke, etc., which occurs in the locus which is in contact with the sense organ is taken to be 'normal' (*laukika*), while that perception of it which is not in such a locus is supernormal. Determinative (*vyavasāya*) perception and aftercognition (*anuvyavasāya*) belong to the "normal" variety.

(E70) Immediacy (*sākṣāttva*) in the case of God's knowledge depends on the instrument of knowledge by which He grasps the property-possessor (*dharmin*). The functioning of sense-organs is only required for immediacy in the case of normal people's perception; it is not present in God's or the yogi's immediate awareness. Or, God's knowledge is immediate in that it does not have any cognition as its instrument.

(E72-73) While dealing with inference, Śrīharṣa questions Udayana's concept of reasoning (*tarka*) and its role in determining the nature of invariable concomitance (*avinābhāvatva*). Two definitions of invariable concomitance are mentioned by him, and criticized. One is that invariable concomitance is "natural relation" (*svabhāvabhāva*); the other that it is a relation "free from limitors". Udayana's defintion of "limitor" (cf. Vol. II of this Encyclopedia, p. 582: "what pervades the *s* but does not pervade the *h*") is questioned and criticized.

While rejecting Śrīharṣa's contentions, Vācaspati Miśra defines invariable concomitance as a relation which does not wander (*avyabhicārasambandha*), a relation which holds between two things which are invariably concomitant whether they coexist in the same substratum or not: e.g., earth's having smell. Vācaspati ridicules Śrīharṣa for professing to be unable to distinguish mutual absence (*anyonyābhāva*) from absolute absence (*atyantābhāva*). Śrīharṣa appears to think that mutual absence involves denial of *x*'s occurrence in the same substratum as *y*, while relational absence (*saṃsargābhāva*) involves the denial of *x*'s occurrence in a different substratum from *y*, but Vācaspati says that Śrīharṣa "in his old age" is offering an opinion opposed to what is held by all schools of thought.

The reason for the clause "whether they coexist in the same substratum or not" in the characterization of *avyabhicāra* (in the previous paragraph) is as follows. The old Naiyāyikas used the term "coexistence in the same locus" (*sāmānādhikaraṇya*) to refer to invariable concomitance which exists between relata which exist in the same substratum. But this notion must not be taken to apply to all cases of invariable concomitance. Hence the "nonwandering" which is defining of invariable concomitance must be specifically identified as covering noncoexisting relata as well. The author of the *Ratnakośa*, for example, left them out.

(E74-75) Invariable concomitance, or pervasion (*vyāpti*), does not necessarily involves spatial and temporal relationship. "*Vinābhāva*" means the deviating relation (*vyabhicāra*), and thus "*avinābhāva*" or invariable concomitance means the opposite of deviation. This relationship must be "*aikāntika*", that is, such that it does not coexist with its absence. Thus, pervasion is that relation of *x* with a *y* such that the relation does not determine the counterpositiveness of the mutual absence of *y* coexisting in the same substratum (viz., *x*).

(E76-77) Since pervasion is a relation which is opposed to deviation it was called a "natural" relation (*svābhāvikasambandha*) by the author of the (*Tātparya*)*Ṭīkā*, i.e., by Vācaspati Miśra I. Uddyotakara (the author of the *Vārttika*) called it a nondeviating relation, and the author of the *Nibandha* (Udayana) termed it a relation free from adjuncts (*nirupādhisambandha*). Vallabha, the author *Nyāyalīlāvatī*, says it is a "complete relation" (*kārtsnyena sambandha*). Later writers who introduce the notion of "coexistence in the same locus" (*sāmānādhikaraṇya*) are speaking with regard to the specific and well-known example of smoke and fire—they do not mean that pervasion is based on or requires coexistence in the same locus. Therefore Vardhamāna wrote in his *Khaṇḍanoddhāra* that Udayana did not attach any significance to the idea that pervasion should be through coexistence in a common locus only; otherwise it would be difficult to prove that earth has smell because of its difference (mutual absence) from the other thirteen (nonpsychic qualities, since their loci are different from earth).

(E77-83) Pervasion is grasped through *sāmānyalakṣaṇa* perception. While developing his arguments in support of this contention, Vācaspati refers to Udayana and in conclusion draws the attention of the readers to his own work *Anumānanirṇaya.*

(E93-94) While rejecting Śrīharṣa's treatment of comparison, Vācaspati refers to Jayanta Bhaṭṭa's view that comparison determines the condition inasmuch as its occasion is an awareness of similarity. Vācaspati rejects this view.

(E101) Absence (*abhāva*) becomes known by nonawareness of what is fit to be known (*yogyānupalabdhi*), which may be either an instance of inference or of perception.

(E113-114) Vācaspati makes some useful observations in defending the Nyāya view of the fallacies of the *h*. For example, he says that the "too specific" kind of deviating *h* is a defect only under certain conditions, whereas the other varieties (viz., too-general, inconclusive and counterbalanced) are always defects in inferences.

(E118) Counterbalanced *h* and futile rejoinder (*jāti*) are alike in that in both there are two parties, one proposing an argument and the other opposing it. Yet there is a difference: in the case of counterbalance the rejoinder of the second party is made on good grounds, while in the case of futile rejoinder the rejoinder is wrong.

(E124-125) While criticizing Śrīharṣa's views on the ways of losing an argument, Vācaspati refers to Maṇikaṇṭha Miśra's treatment of *pratijñāntara.*

Śrīharṣa holds that *pratijñāvirodha* can be illustrated by using the negative particle *nañ* in connection with a noun such as "*ghaṭa*" (pot), instead of with the verb *asti* (is). Vācaspati controverts this. When the negative particle is used with the word *ghaṭa*, it cannot convey the sense of "is not" (*nāsti*). This way of losing an argument, which is admitted by one of the parties, is distinct from *apasiddhānta*, which is attributed to an argument on the basis of the authorities on the *śāstras.*

(E132) In the third part of his work Śrīharṣa raises an objection to the Naiyāyikas' use of pronouns, and questions on such grounds the validity of Nyāya arguments for the existence of God. In refuting this Vācaspati explains the sense of some of the most important pronouns. *Kim* conveys the sense of the desire to know; it may also convey the sense of objection implied and raised against a contention, and at times means open objection. It may also mean censure, or the provision of alternatives. Seven pronouns such as *yat, tat,* etc., are confined in signification to property-posssessors (*dharmin*). *Idam, etat,* etc., refer to perceived objects, while *adas* refers to objects which are beyond the range of the senses.

(E133) The categories (*padārtha*) can be classified under three headings: (1) those which exist (*sattā*), such as substance, quality and motion; (2) those which involve the notion of existence (*sattādhī*), such as universals, individuators, and inherence; and (3) those which do neither, as, e.g., absence. Or, absence may also be classed under the second heading.

(E167) Fallacies of *tarka* are of five kinds: Each of the five lead respectively to (1) *svarūpāsiddhi,* (2) *siddhasādhana,* (3) *vyāpyatvāsiddhi,* (4) *bādha,* and (5) *satpratipakṣa.*[7]

24. MALLINĀTHA

Umesh Mishra tells us that this author was a "famous commentator of *kāvyas*"[1] known as "Kolācala Mallinātha".

NIṢKĀNTIKĀ on Varadarāja's TĀRKIKARAKṢĀ
Summary by V. Varadachari

"E" references are to the edition by Arthur Venis (B2986, RB 4609) published serially in *The Pandit* new series 21, 1899–25, 1903, and reprinted as a single volume at Banaras in 1906. The text is only available through Book One.

2 (E6) *Kārikā* 2 says that an instrument of knowledge is a means to knowledge, "or" it is the locus of valid knowledge and pervaded by it. Mallinātha denies that the "*vā*" in this stanza means "(exclusive) or", and thinks rather that is must mean "and". It is not that an instrument of knowledge is either a means or the locus, since it is both, and to suppose that the two options are exclusive of each other will produce a wrong conclusion.

(E8) However, Varadarāja actually states that one of the two descriptions can be accepted as the definition. Mallinātha says that "an instrument of knowledge is pervaded by knowledge" is the definition, and the rest is illustration.

(E10) Traces are the exclusive conditions for memory. This sets aside recognition, etc., which have a relation to the traces, as causal conditions of memory. A passage is cited to indicate the difference between memory and awareness (*grahaṇa*). While contact with traces gives rise to memory, awareness is produced by contact with the object apprehended.

3 (E12-13) While commenting on the passage describing God as the locus of eternal knowledge, Mallinātha cites two passages in support. One is *Nyāyasūtra* 2.1.69, the other *Nyāyakusumāñjali* 4.6 (*tan me pramāṇaṃ śivaḥ*).

Objection: What proves that God's awareness is true?

Answer: To be a knower of truth one must be such that true awareness inheres in one. One need not produce that awareness. Now though God does not produce His true awareness He is nevertheless the knower, since it inheres in Him. And since an instrument of knowledge is what is pervaded by true awareness (see under E8 above) God is an instrument of knowledge as well.

4. (E19) While discussing perception Varadarāja states that the name of an object, even if it is remembered, does not affect the perceptual nature of the object. It only occupies a neutral position, and does not screen the color or form of the object. Mallinātha sees this as explaining what is involved in corroborating a judgment. According to his interpretation, the name is said to occupy a neutral position in the sense that it acts like an accessory, with the help of memory, in producing the propositional awareness of the objects having that name. It does not occupy a position parallel to the sense organ in producing it. If it did the result would have the nature of a mixture of memory and direct sensation, a result which would be both mediate and immediate, which is impossible. Hence it must play a role like that which memory plays in the case of recognition; it assists without overriding the operation of the primary cause (which is direct perception in both cases). The name of the object may be remembered but does not in any way affect the individuality of the object. Mallinātha offers another example of this. On beholding sandalwood from a distance, the man who looks at it gets the awareness that the sandalwood is fragrant. This awareness of fragrance helps determine the identity of the object, but does not in any way affect the nature of the visual or tactual awareness of that objects; it is neutral with respect to that.

5 (E19-20) Concerning the use of the expression "instrument of knowledge" (*pramāṇa*) Mallinātha remarks that this word has the sense of an instrument when used in a discussion concerning sense-object connection, and it has the sense of the root *mā* itself when treating perception as an instrument of knowledge.

6. (E44) While interpreting Udayana's passage "perception of the object as it is the instrument of knowledge" (*Nyāyakusumāñjali* 4.1) Mallinātha remarks that perception is by itself a valid awareness, since it does not require anything else to indicate the object. Memory is not a valid instrument because it is always dependent on perception.

7. (E55) As for the order in which the instruments of knowledge are enumerated by Gautama in *Nyāyasūtra* I.1.3, Mallinātha justifies it, saying that perception forms the basis for all instruments of knowledge and so is listed first. Inference comes next, since all other instruments depend on it except perception. Comparison is enumerated before verbal testimony in order to show its individual validity.

8 (E57) The text defines perception as pervaded by immediate (*aparokṣa*) validity. Mallinātha explains the sense of the word "immediate". He cites three words of negative construction—*avighna*, *abrāhmaṇa*, and *adharma*—to explain the significance of the word "immediate". The negative particle *(n)a(ñ)* in the first two cases signifies the absence of *vighna* and *brāhmaṇa* respectively. But the same particle in the word *adharma* denotes something which is opposed to *dharma*. In the case of validity it is the latter kind of negation which is appropriate, not the former, so that "immediate" means what is opposed to mediate. Thus it is equivalvent in sense to "directness" (*sākṣāttva*).

9. (E68) Mallinātha notes a mistake committed by some scholars in locating the source of the definition of *upādhi* cited in the text. They locate it as coming from *Kiraṇāvalī*, while in fact it stems from *Ātmatattvaviveka*. Mallinātha remarks that these scholars display their inability to look into the source of these passages.

10. (E71) The text interprets the word *tatpūrvaka* in *Nyāyasūtra* I.1.5 as presupposing the knowledge of pervasion plus observation of the *h*. These two are presupposed by inference which is the consideration of the *h*. Mallinātha remarks that "observation of the *h*" is awareness of the *h* arising for the second time. "Consideration of the *h*" is the third subsumptive awareness of the *h*. Hence the word *tatpūrvaka* should be taken to mean that inference is the subsumptive awareness or consideration of the *h*. The word "*pūrvavat*" in the *sūtra* means the positive kind, as it precedes the negative one. The word "*śeṣa*" means what remains and therefore refers to the negative kind. The word "*sāmānyataḥ*" refers to the positive-negative kind, since it is noticed to have both features together. Mallinātha refers to the view of some scholars who take the word *pūrvavat* in the sense of inference having *hetu* as cause, *śeṣavat* as having *hetu* as effect, and *sāmānyatodṛṣṭa* as what is different from both. He notes that this interpretation is questionable, as it does not agree with what was stated above.

11. (E77) Mallinātha refers to the definition of definition as given by Udayana in the *Nyāyakusumāñjali* and criticizes those who trace it to the section in *Kiraṇāvalī* where the self gets treated. He tries to show that this definition can be traced to the influence of Vācaspati Miśra's *Tatparyaṭīkā*.

12. (E85-86) In treating comparison in this section Mallinātha shows that an alternative interpretation proposed by others is wrong. Varadarāja describes comparison as perception effected through recognition. Mallinatha explains the word *upamāna* (comparison) as the instrument of the resultant comparative awareness (*upamiti*). It is the perceptual awareness obtained through recognition or identification. But some scholars hold that the name of the object to be known becomes pertinent only through being remembered, and thus that comparison consists in the recognition of the sense of the proposition in which the memory is reported, not just merely through recognition of the applicability of the name. Mallinātha puts a question here: if the word *gavaya* is eliminated from the sentence "*gavaya* is similar to a cow" is there any sentence remaining whose sense could be recognized? Therefore the interpretation proposed is not based on adequate reflection and need not be given any credence.

13. (E106) While treating nonapprehension (*anupalabdhi*) Varadarāja observes that knowledge of the absence of an object arises for one the defect of whose senses affect it. That is, the senses do not cognize the object because they are defective. Consequently, the awareness which arises then is also defective in the sense that it arises concerning the absence of that object. If this is not admitted there will be overextension. Mallinātha remarks that awareness is defectless by nature. Thus apprehension of a locus, memory of a counterpositive and nonapprehension cannot be associated with defects. Hence the sense-organ alone should be admitted to be defective. Otherwise the defects which appear in awareness, etc., must be admitted to have come into being without a cause (which is absurd). In this context the commentator refers to the view of Udayana who maintained that the sense-organ is an instrument of knowledge of absences, because it is the instrument of the knowledge of the counterpositive.

14. (E122) The text explains the word *bhogāśraya* as meaning the locus of enjoyment or experience. That is, the self derives experience through the body's dependence on it. Mallinātha observes that only within the limits of the body can the self be the locus of experience. Experience, which is a feature determined by the self, is secondarily referred to as belonging to the body which sets a limit to it.

15. (E127) Defects give rise to activity. Mallinātha notes that by implication they are also to be taken as causes for the cessation of activity as well.

16. (E128) Varadarāja represents death as the separation of the self from the body in which it was till then resting, and birth as the contact between the self and the body into which it will get hereafter.

Mallinātha remarks that separation here means the departure of the internal organ, which the self has acquired through its deeds, from the body where it was till then staying.

17. (E129) The Nyāya system conceives liberation as the final cessation of frustration. Varadarāja describes finality as the nonproduction of frustration of the same kind in any subsequent time in the same self. Mallinātha remarks here that liberation means the total extinction of all frustrations present in a single self. Since those who aspire for release are each individuals in themselves, this definition applies to them also. This is the definition offered by the Vilāsakāra.

18. (E133-134) Varadarāja refers to a particular view regarding darkness, according to which darkness is the black color of the subtle parts of earth spread out in the sky. Mallinātha remarks that some scholars mistakenly suppose this to be the view of the Prābhākaras, but that they do not properly understand Prābhākara doctrine. The Prābhākaras hold that darkness is the absence of light but that it is not negative in nature; rather, it is another positive object. They say that darkness is a portion of the earth where sunlight does not fall. Thus Varadarāja here is referring rather to a view held by some of the Naiyāyikas.

19. (E155) The Bhāṭṭas hold that the dark color of a substance gets destroyed though contact with heat in the substance which remains intact, the red color being produced there. On the other hand, the Prābhākaras hold that color, etc. are eternal like universals. Things related to them are destroyed and produced through contact with heat.

20. (E161) The Prābhākaras hold there are many inherences, since we speak of inherence of jar, inherence of cloth, etc. The Nyāya concept is that inherence is single. Varadarāja says that, like the universal existence inherence is differentiated through the variousness of its instances. Mallinātha says that such differentiation is "accidental" (*aupādhika*).

21. (E167) Varadarāja says that some scholars hold that apprehension (*upalabdhi*) and nonapprehension (*anupalabdhi*) are independent causes of doubt. Mallinātha remarks that this refers to the view of Bhāsarvajña, according to whom doubt is of five kinds according to five causes. These two causes are causes of a general nature, and thus should be included under the *samānadharma* of *Nyāyasūtra* I.1.23.

22. (E211) The nature of reality is made known in three ways—making known what is not yet known, strengthening what is already known, and removing doubt—so says Varadarāja. Mallinātha remarks that the first of these applies to the discussion between

teacher and pupil, the second to that among students, and the last to discussion among the disciplined and those who seek liberation.

23. (E230) Mallinātha remarks that mistimed (*kālātīta*) is not a fallacious reason according to the followers of Kaṇāda. It is a fallacious statement of the hypothesis (*pratijñābhāsa*) since the stating of the *pakṣa* alone is involved.[2]

25. PAKṢADHARA the Vivekakāra

There is considerable confusion about how many Naiyāyika Pakṣadharas there were and which works they wrote. We know that there was a famous scholar Jayadeva Miśra (our 31 below) who was also called "Pakṣadhara" and who wrote the *Āloka* on Gaṅgeśa's *Tattvacintāmaṇi*. This *Āloka* becomes the most important commentary on Gaṅgeśa prior to Raghunātha's *Dīdhiti* half a century later, and we know a lot about its author Jayadeva Miśra. A number of other works are also ascribed to a Pakṣadhara, however, and it is not entirely clear whose works these are, as some of them exist only in damaged copies from which the introductory and concluding pages are lost.

Among the works ascribed to Pakṣadhara are a number called *Vivekas*. There is a *Viveka* on Vardhamāna's *Dravyakiraṇāvalīprakāśa*, a *Viveka* on the *Nyāyalīlāvatī*, another on the *Nyāyalīlāvatīprakāśa*, and one on Udayana's *Nyāyakusumāñjali*. There is also a *Viveka* on Gaṅgeśa's *Tattvacintāmaṇi*; it is a different text from the *Āloka*. Dinesh Bhattacharya starts out by identifying the author of these *Vivekas* as Jayadeva Miśra, but it occurs to him as he proceeds that it would be unlikely (though not altogether impossible) that the same author who wrote the highly successful *Āloka* should have also written another commentary on the same text. Furthermore, the common titles of these several works suggests the possibility of those works being by the same author. So, several pages into his discussion, Bhattacharya comes to this point: "The identity of this Vivekakāra Pakṣadhara as distinguished from the Ālokakāra is now a great puzzle before us difficult to solve."[1] His main reason for separating the two Pakṣadharas is that the first verse of the *Āloka* uses language which normally implies that the work—the *Āloka* in this case—is its author's first book, making it even less likely that the two works are by the same author.

Dineshchandra Bhattacharya[2] conjectures that Pakṣadhara the Vivekakāra is identical with an author known as "Śrīmat-Pakṣadhara" of Amarāvatī (in South India) who translated the *Viṣṇupurāṇa*. He notes that Satischandra Vidyabhusana, who identifies this Vivekakāra with Jayadeva Miśra, the Ālokakāra, also takes Jayadeva to be this Pakṣadhara of Amarāvatī. But the reasoning here is not very firm. Nevertheless, what Bhattacharya has said seemed enough to convince Umesh Mishra[3] that "the author of the *Viveka*s was most probably a distinct scholar who was also called Pakṣadhara, but not Jayadeva".

There is also some evidence to be gleaned from which works quote which other works. Notably, the *Dravyaviveka* is once referred to in the *Līlāvatīviveka*, and these two works are (Dinesh Bhattacharya has concluded) from the same pen. Furthermore the author of these works refers to his commentary on *Tattvacintāmaṇi* as *Viveka* and not *Āloka* and does so a number of times. Surely, given the fame of the *Āloka*, he would have used that name when referring to it if he were in fact Jayadeva. All of this evidence suggests even more strongly that there was an author who wrote a number of *Viveka*s and who was not the same person as Jayadeva Miśra.

Having tentatively concluded this, however, there is not much more we can say. The *Viveka* on the *Tattvacintāmaṇi* is not at present known to exist. All the other *Viveka*s are available in manuscript, but none has as yet been edited, much less translated. We are forced to conclude, then, that this author, who may have flourished around the middle of the 15th century, wrote the *Viveka*s on Gaṅgeśa's *Kiraṇāvalīprakāśa*, on the *Nyāyakusumāñjali*, the *Nyāyalīlāvatī* and *Nyāyalīlāvatīprakāśa*. However, the reasoning is tenuous, and further investigation may change our thinking entirely.

26. BHUVANASUNDARASŪRI

Bhuvanasundara was a pupil of Somasundarasūri of the Tāpagaccha sect, who became the fifty-second head of the sect in 1404. Bhuvanasundara also studied under Guṇaratna, the author of *Ṣaḍdarśanasamuccayavṛtti*, who is known to have flourished in 1409. One of Bhuvanasundarasūri's pupils was Ratnaśekhara, who wrote a *Śrāvakapratikramaṇasūtraṭīkā* in 1440. Thus Bhuvanasundarasūri's dates can be fixed at around 1390-1450.

This author seems to have written three works, all on *mahāvidyā* inference. All three are published in M.R.Telang's edition of various *mahāvidyā* works in Gaekwad's Oriental Series 12, 1920. The major work is *Vyākhyānadīpikā* on Vādīndra's *Mahāvidyāviḍambana.* This commentary seems to have been composed in the temple of Śrī Pārśvanātha at Harshapura, and is concerned with refuting the *mahāvidyā* method of inference. It is a good-sized work, totalling about 150 pages in the edition cited above. A second work, *Laghumahāvidyāviḍambana*, is brief (2 page) summary of the first. Finally, also edited under the same cover is a *Ṭippaṇa* on an unknown author's *Mahāvidyāślokavivaraṇa*, a work of about 32 pages, which Telang tells us is a commentary on an exposition of the rules laid down to frame the *mahāvidyā* syllogism.

Besides these three works Bhuvanasundarasūri appears to have written at least one other. One of these was titled *Parabrahmotthāpanasthala*; we find it mentioned in the Gujarati work *Jainagranthāvalī*, which is a list prepared from a number of catalogues belonging to the Jain *bhāṇḍāras*.

27. ŚEṢĀNANTA

Śeṣānanta was the son of 18.Śeṣa Śārṅgadhara who flourished around 1420. A manuscript of Śeṣānanta's *Padārthacandrikā* gives its date as 1459 A.D. We can therefore estimate this author's date at about 1455. Two of his works are extant, a commentary on the *Saptapadārthī* and a *Prabhā on* Śaśadhara's *Nyāyasiddhāntadīpa*. Both have been published, though we have only found a summarizer for the first.

PADĀRTHACANDRIKĀ on Śivāditya's SAPTAPADĀRTHĪ
Summary by V. Varadachari

"E" references are to the edition by Narendra Chandra Bagchi Bhattacharya (B2981, RB4598), Calcutta Sanskrit Series 8, 1934.

(E105) It must be admitted that if a cause has opposed qualities (e.g., several colors) inhering in it the result also has opposed qualities inhering in it—otherwise even variegated color would not exist. Likewise, there would be no doubting if there were no mutual opposition among the collection of causal factors which get superimposed. And variegated smell may arise from pleasant and unpleasant smells. So, admission of variegated taste (*citrarasa*) would only show that the qualities are opposed to each other. Thus, either variegated color should be given up or else variegated taste must be admitted.

(E112) Śivāditya maintains that *qualifiedness* (*vaiśiṣṭyam* or *viśiṣṭatva*) is not an additional category but only a relation. But Śeṣānanta says that it is another category.

(E118) Śivāditya says that to be a universal property is to be eternal, single, and to inhere in many things. Śeṣānanta says that the word "single" is not a part of the definition. He says that according to some who follow the *Dravyakiraṇāvalīprakāśa* (of Vardhamāna) the words "inheres in" mean "occurs in" and the word "single" functions to preclude overextension to the definition of apply to absence and inherence.

(E123) In the course of discussing the definition of weight ("Weight has the universal *weight-hood* (*gurutvatva*), occurs in a single thing, and is the noninherence cause of the first moment of falling") the question is raised whether this definition does not overextend to inertia (*vega*), since inertia is a noninherence cause of falling. Some say (says Śeṣānanta) that inertia is only an instrumental cause of falling. Others read the phrase in the definition to say "is the specific (*asādhāraṇa*) cause of falling", and that inertia is a cause different from both the specific and the generic causes of falling. This view is endorsed by Śeṣānanta.

28. NARAHARI, father of Vāsudeva Sārvabhauma

This Narahari seems to have been regularly confused with Narahari Upādhyāya (=Maheśvara Viśārada), who was the son of Yajñapati. Yajñapati's son is a well-known author of several Nyāya works, but must have lived not far before the beginning of the 16th century. However, another Narahari is referred to as both the father and teacher of Vāsudeva. This Narahari is quoted by Jayadeva as well as by the later Narahari.

Gopinath Kaviraj informs us that the father of Vāsudeva was a "Brahmin of the Rāḍhi class, born in a noble family at Vidyānagara in the city of Navadvīpa."[1] According to Gopinath, this Narahari wrote a commentary on the *Tattvacintāmaṇi*, part of which is at the Government Sanskrit Library at Banaras. He adds that Narahari moved to Banaras later in his lifetime. Gopikamohan Bhattacharya has discovered that Vāsudeva quotes Narahari some fifteen times, sometimes differing from his father in his interpretations.[2]

We do not know of any extant works of this author. The manuscript that Gopinath refers to in Banaras seems to have been the work of the later Narahari (=Maheśvara Viśārada).

29. YAJÑAPATI UPĀDHYĀYA

Thanks to the work of Gopikamohan Bhattacharya we are well-acquainted with the available data about this author. His dates are given as c. 1410 to 1470. Prof. Bhattacharya considers his commentary to be the "earliest extant commentary on *Tattvacintāmaṇi*"[1]. He is cited by subsequent authors as "Upādhyāyamata", and appears to have been the teacher of Jayadeva, whose *Āloka* soon became the most famous commentary of the time. The *Āloka* is rife with criticisms of Yajñapati, as are Pragalbha and Vāsudeva's commentaries (see below), and the criticisms of these authors are answered by Yajñapati's son Narahari Upādhyāya in his *Dūṣaṇoddhāra* on the inference section of *Tattvacintāmaṇi*.

Yajñapati, Gopikamohan Bhattacharya tells us, was born in the Mandara family of Kāśyapagotra in Mithilā, a family which goes back to at least the 7th century and featured many great Naiyāyikas. He was the son of 14.Śivapati and the grandson of Paśupati, the son of 2. Vāṭeśvara.

PRABHĀ on Gaṅgeśa's TATTVACINTĀMAṆI

The section on perception and inference of Yajñapati's *Prabhā* on the *Tattvacintāmaṇi* are known to be extant: we do not know the whereabouts of his commentary, if he wrote one, on the last two books. However, only the inference (*anumāna*) section has been published so far. The summary which follows is based on the synopsis provided by Gopikamohan Bhattacharya in his edition of the work.[2] "E" references in the summary refer to that edition.

BOOK TWO: INFERENCE

Section One: Inferential Awareness

(E54-56) Objection: One awareness, that might be produced by the awareness that the qualification of the *p* is qualified by pervasion (D1), is the aftercognition of consideration.

Answer: No, since no such aftercognition exists.

Objection: D1 fails to cover a false inferential awareness of, say, smoke in a lake.

Answer: No, since there is no awareness of being qualified by fire that is a property of a lake.

Traditionally the reason why the second "awareness" (by which in D1 the inferential awareness is said to be produced) is held to be required is to avoid the fault of overpervasion of traces by consideration. But this is not why that second "awareness" is included. Rather it is given to avoid overpervasion into desire to know (*jijñāsa*) (which is produced by the qualification but not when the conclusion has been arrived at.

Refutation of the Cārvāka view.

Section Four: Absence Limited by a Property whose Loci are Different from its Counterpositive

(E61-63) Objection to Gaṅgeśa's solution: The cognition of the counterpositive which takes the kind of property we are speaking of (one whose loci are different from its counter-positive) might be a case of error.

Answer: If it is error then the absence of such a property cannot be only-positive.

As for the problem about "on the cow there is no hare's horn",

Sondāḍa's theory which is under consideration here violates the condition of fitness: the counterpositive must be apprehended, and a hare's horn isn't.

Section Seven: General Absence

(E69-71). Opponent: Although the specific absences of all known colors are ascertained in air, these absences are not known as limited by absencehood of color, and that is why the doubt whether there is color in air or not arises. So a distinct generic absence need not be postulated.

Answer: If "absencehood of color" means "absencehood of which the counterpositive is limited by colorhood" it is known. If it means "absence of color as such" it must be known because, in the opponent's view, generic absence is nothing but the collection of specific absences.

Objection: But there may be the possibility of more types of color. The above doubt relates to those types of color not known to us.

Answer: Even so, the doubt whether there is color in air or not arises.

Opponent: The specific colors known to us cannot be the object of doubt. Nor can any color other than those known to us, since there is no such color.

Answer: The counterpositiveness of the absence of all known colors in air is not limited by colorhood, but it is the generic absence of which the counterpositiveness is limited by the universal *colorness.* The doubt relates to this generic absence.

Yajñapati now criticizes the view that generic absence is the logical product of the collocation of specific absences. The argument is that there would be no perception of color in two differently colored pots since the specific absence of one color will be perceived in the other pot and vice versa, and the collocation of these two specific absences will generate perception of the absence of color as such in the two pots.

Objection: No, because in the case in question the two specific absences do not share the same locus.

Yajñapati: Is this "sharing the same locus" the nature of general absence, or is it just a qualification of the collocation of specific absences? If the former a color, being the absence of absence of color, would share contradictory natures. If the latter the same charge of nonperception of any color in the pots holds good.

However, we hold that general absence is not just a collection of particular absences. Suppose we perceive a blue pot and a red pot side by side. We cognize the particular absence of red in the blue pot and the particular absence of blue in the red pot. The collection of these two pots will result in a joint perception of colorlessness in the two pots.

Objection: No. The two specific absences do not share the same locus.

Yajñapati: If sharing the same locus is the nature of general absence, color would be the general absence of absence of color, which would mean that it would have both a positive and negative nature—a contradiction. If sharing the same locus is merely a property of a collection of particular absences, the problem of colorlessness remains.

Section Eight: Particular Absence

(E72-77) Why must the notion of a limitor (*avacchedaka*) be appealed to in the definition of pervasion? Pervasion is a thing's nature of being related with another thing which being related has for its limitor the universal feature of the first thing. Otherwise the definition will overextend to include false inferences, e.g., "it has smoke because it has fire", since fire is also sometimes related to smoke, e.g., in a mountain or courtyard.

Yajñapati's own view, however, is that the interpretation of limitorhood as no wider in extension than the limited property need not always be applied, e.g., the relation between being known and being named, which have the same extension, presents problems when taken to concern *ākāśa*, which has no locus. So it must be concluded that being known and being named are not limitors of each other *simpliciter*, but only as qualified as applying to things which have a locus.

Section 8A: Three Definitions of Obstruction

(E77-78) Yajñapati attributes the first definition to Prabhākara Upādhyāya.

Section Nine: The Means of Grasping Pervasion

(E78-79) Repeated observation can assist neither the external sense-organs nor the internal organ in establishing pervasion, because if they could they would themselves be instruments of knowledge. Inference arises from knowledge of pervasion. The knowledge of an imposed property does not enter into the causal conditions of pervasion.

Objection: If specific attributes are not observed, even the perception of coexistence together with knowledge of absence of deviation will still merely produce doubt, not assertion of pervasion.

Answer: When both the two possibilities are remembered doubt will arise, but when they are not both remembered pervasion will be asserted.

Section Ten: Reductio Ad Absurdum

(E79-83) Objection: If the causal relation (between fire and smoke) is ascertained before *reductio* is applied the *reductio* will be useless. If, however, the relation is not ascertained before *reductio* is applied then *reductio* will be overpowered by doubt whether, e.g., smoke has a cause different from fire or not. So both ways *reductio ad absurdum* cannot assist ascertainment of the causal relation between fire and smoke.

Answer: *Reductio ad Absurdum* is generated from a twofold awareness.

(a) Smoke does not arise in the absence of fire. This is known through positive and negative concomitance.

(b) An effect has a cause.

With both (a) and (b) present there is no room for doubt.

Objection: Even if positive and negative concomitance is observed, doubt whether smoke is produced even in the absence of fire may still persist.

Answer: If we go on doubting like this our practical behavior will be undermined. When we see that fire is absent, but all other conditions of smoke are present and smoke does not arise, all doubt is removed.

An objection posed in Śrīharṣa's *Khaṇḍanakhaṇḍakhādya*: Knowledge of contradiction removes doubt. But contradiction is just the absence of the coexistence of doubt and behavior. This contradiction is a case of negative concomitance, and doubt may arise about it too. To remove it one must appeal to contradiction—and thus we are led to an infinite regress.

Answer: But *reductio* is precisely that which removes doubt.

Does repeated observation play any role in the ascertainment of pervasion? Gaṅgeśa thought it did not *per se*, but through its traces it helps in ascertaining pervasion. Yajñapati's own view is that repeated observation helps in eliminating doubt about deviation, and that this elimination contributes to the ascertainment of concomitance between cause and effect.

There are two types of doubt regarding alleged deviation, which is supposed to undermine pervasion: (a) "Maybe this smoke is accidentally caused in this case by fire, but not generally", (b)

"Maybe sometimes smoke will exist without fire". The first type of doubt may be eliminated by a second observation of concomitance, the second doubt by a third observation, and so on. In this way the ultimate doubt will be removed by *reductio*. So sometimes repeated observation and sometimes *reductio* contributes to the ascertainment of pervasion by removing doubt concerning the possibility of deviation.

Section Twelve: Perception Through Connection with the Universal

(E84-88) Yajñapati denies Gaṅgeśa's reasons for the necessity of postulating this kind of perception. Gaṅgeśa argues that this extraordinary kind of perception is required since without it one cannot explain the emergence of doubt in cases where *reductio ad absurdum* is absent. But his explanation, says Yajñapati, supposes that the doubt that arises is about *all* cases of smoke. In fact no such awareness of *all* cases of smoke can occur, and thus no doubt about it either.

Gaṅgeśa argues that one can only explain the emergence of desire for something not yet cognized, e.g., satisfaction, by postulating this kind of perception through connection with a universal. Gaṅgeśa says it is the identical character of the adjective, not that of the substantive, which determines the causal relation between knowledge and desire. Yajñapati responds that both are essential factors in determining a causal relation.

However, the argument that preceded Gaṅgeśa, that desire for satisfaction presupposes the prior awareness of satisfaction, does indeed require this kind of perception.

Section Thirteen: On Obstruction

(E89-92) Those proposing D3 (in Gaṅgeśa's text) are identified by Yajñapati as "*sāmpradāyikāḥ*", "the tradition". (Gopikamohan's summary attributes the view to Sondāda.) But "some" construe D3 as meaning "that the absence of which does not pervade the *s*." This is criticized by Yajñapati as involving infinite regress, since the definition so construed involves the notion of pervasion which presupposes knowledge of the absence of obstruction.

(E92-97) A definition of obstruction is attributed to Prabhākara Upādhyāya, which reads as follows: An obstruction is a qualifier which has common locus with the *s* and is thought to be the *h*.

(E97-99) "Being other than the *pakṣa*", which was discussed above, may be classified under the "doubtful obstruction" (*saṃ*-

digdhopādhi) rubric.

Some say that sometimes there may be cases of fallacious inferences which are vitiated by an obstruction that even pervades the *h*. So, for example, an obstruction vitiates inference not always through pointing out deviation but also by raising an equally strong counter-inference.

Section Fourteen: Being the Pakṣa

(E101-102) Objection: The desire to infer ceases to exist with the emergence of consideration. So, the desire to infer plays no part in the emergence of inference.

Gaṅgeśa's answer: A distinct desire emerges again after consideration, and this, generating another awareness, immediately precedes inference.

Yajñapati: Actually, remembrance of pervasion produces emergence of desire to infer, which produces consideration, which then produce the inference.

Section Fifteen: Consideration

(E102-106) Mīmāṃsaka: Our view is the more economical. In inference what is required is the ascertainment of pervasion, not the knowledge that *p* is pervaded by *h*, since this latter knowledge presupposes pervasion. So there is no need to admit the consideration (i.e., the combining together of the two in thought) as the peculiar condition of inference.

Furthermore, where an *h* that is beyond our senses is remembered one would infer pervasion by *s* and inference will follow. So the need for consideration is excluded.

Objection to the Mīmāṃsaka: Even after cognizing smoke on the mountain if one doubts whether this (smoke) is pervaded by fire or not the inference should still occur because the causal conditions of inference that are proposed by the Mīmāṃsaka are present.

Mīmāṃsaka answer: No, inference does not occur because it is opposed by doubt. (This reply supposes that the opponent's position is provisionally admitted. In fact, on the Mīmāṃsaka's view, in such cases the inference will occur but not doubt.)

Nyāya answer: If it is asserted, or even doubted, that the property of the *p* is different from the thing that is pervaded then inference will not take place. It is the assertion that what is pervaded by fire is identical with the property of the *p* (e.g., smoke on the mountain) which causes inference to occur, and this is precisely consideration.

Yajñapati's own view: Knowledge of pervasion cannot be the

immediate cause of inference through the mediation of consideration. When one remembers both the absence of deviation and the coexistence of *h* and *s* and then has the mental awareness of both, the awareness of pervasion does precede inference. Awareness of the pervaded is separated from this conclusion in that it is its trace that functions, not the memory itself. So the awareness of pervasion cannot be the immediate cause of inference. The internal organ, in fact, is that immediate cause.

Section Seventeen: Only-Negative Inference

(E109-120) Yajñapati's own view is that only-negative inference commits the fallacy of "too-specific".

In the text it is said "some say" that in an only-negative inference such as "earth is different from everything else, because it smells", the kind of absence that is the *s* here is constant absence, not mutual absence, i.e., what is to be shown is that earth has at all times absence of identity with everything else. Yajñapati's response is that the constant absence of identity *is* mutual absence.

Section Nineteen: Members of an Inference

(E121-133) Why is the application (*upanaya*) needed? To meet the condition of expectancy. Indeed, the first three members of an inference generate expectancy which is fulfilled by the last two.

Yajñapati's definition of a member of an inference: A member of an inference is the cause of verbal awareness which generates awareness of the meaning of a whole sentence which conditions consideration.

Why is a conclusion necessary (since it is stated at the outset of the inference)? Without it an inference for others is not possible. It is necessary for ascertaining that there is not contradiction or counterbalanced *h*.

Objection: It is merely the absence of contradiction, not awareness of that absence, that is required. Thus the statement of the conclusion is not necessary. Furthermore it involves heaviness, because if the awareness of the absences of contradictory or counterbalancing, etc. are considered to be causes of inference there will be two different limitors of their causalities.

Answer: No. If the awareness of X thwarts the emergence of Y, then the awareness of the absence of X facilitates the emergence of Y.

Section Twenty: Fallacies
Part One: General Definition

(E134-39) A "fallacy" may mean either of two things: a fallacious *h* or the fallacy of *h*. The fallacies called "sublated", "inconclusive" and "unestablished", etc., are determined according to the second definition. Yajñapati's own view is that the term *hetvābhāsa* really means a fallacious *h* and the varieties just mentioned are factors whose presence promotes an *h*'s being fallacious.

Objection: By the same reasoning as you give (in answer to the objection raised against Gaṅgeśa) it would follow that the too-general fallacy would have to be actually known before it stops the inference from going through. So it should be added to the other two (viz., sublated and inconclusive) as "occasional" fallacies.

Answer: No, it is different in this way. The too-general fallacy blocks inference whether known or not. But that is not true of the inconclusive and sublated fallacies, which is why they are called "occasional". I.e., we must know that the *sp* occurs in both *h* and non *h* for inconclusive to apply; we must know that the *s* does not occur in the *sp* for sublation to apply.

Objection: Then the types of unproved fallacy called *ajñānasiddhi* and *pakṣāsiddhi* also cannot be counted as fallacies since they are not considered by Gaṅgeśa to be fallacies.

Answer: No, a fault when cognised becomes a fallacy.

(E135-137) Objection: D2 underextends by failing to include the fallacy called "sublated", since that fallacy is constituted simply by the awareness of the absence of the *s* in the *p*, no matter whether that awareness is in itself true or false.

Answer: No. It is not simply the awareness of the absence, but rather that knowledge of truth of that awareness that inhibits an inference. Otherwise, mere absence, and not even the awareness of it, of the *s* in the *p*, would constitute the sublated fallacy. This is so also in the case of counterbalance: it is the awareness of a countervailing cognition that blocks inference. And again in the too-specific fallacy it is the awareness of the *hetu*'s being absent in both *sp* and *vp* (and not merely that absence itself) which blocks the inference. So counterbalance is an "occasional" (*anitya*) *h*.

Objection: Then so should the too-specific be an "occasional" *h*, but it isn't (according to Nyāya tradition).

Answer: Nevertheles, since it is the *awareness* of the too-generalness of the absence of the *s* in the *sp*, that inhibits inference.

Objection: Then the types of unestablished *h* called "*ajñāna*" and *pakṣāsiddhi* cannot be fallacies either.

Answer: They are not fallacies according to Gaṅgeśa. A faulty *h* only becomes a fallacious one when it is apprehended to be such.

Objector: Let a fault which is too-specific to an inference be considered a fallacy; then these two (*ajñāna* and *pakṣāsiddhi*) will be fallacies.

Answer: No, for then being sublated, which is found also in perception, will not be a fallacy.

Objection: Then being unestablished (*asiddhi*) is neither a fallacy nor a way of losing an argument.

Answer: No. It is said in the *Nyāyasūtra*s to be a way of losing an argument.

Objection: If a fault specific to inference alone (and not to the other instruments of knowledge) is to be called a fallacy, then sublation and counterbalance cannot be considered fallacies.

Answer: A fault is a fallacy if it is either common to other instruments of knowledge or specific to inference, as long as it is known to occur.

Part Two: Deviation

First Section: Definition of Deviation

(E139-142) Objection: D10 is faulty, since it does not include the too-specific case. If "possessing the *sādhya"* in D10 means agreeing in examples the definition will be overpervasive to a valid *h*. Further, it will not include the inconclusive case, where both the agreeing and disagreeing examples are absence, e.g., when "being an object of knowledge" is the subject of the inference.

Answer: D10 is based on the assumption that an *h* of which the *s* is everpresent is not to be considered inconclusive. D10 is free from the defect of being nonpervasive, while D8 involves the fault of overpervasion.

Second Section: Too-Generalness

(E142) Since contradiction is not included in the scope of the general definition of deviation, the question of its being covered by the definition of too-general-ness doesn't arise.

Third Section: Too Specific

(E142-145) Yajñapati agrees with an objection which affirms that the too-specific and counterbalanced fallacies are the same and should not be listed as separate fallacies. However, there is a difference between them: in the counterbalanced fallacy there are two *hetus* which respectively prove the *sādhya* and its absence, whereas in the too-specific fallacy there is only one *hetu*.

Fourth Section: Inconclusive

(E145-147) Why is D13 given in addition to D12? D12 involves absence of conclusiveness, which shows that inconclusiveness by itself, not the knowledge of it, blocks ascertainment of pervasion. But a fallacy should be actually known before it inhibits assertion of pervasion. Hence D13 is proposed.

Objection: This fallacy of inconclusiveness is not a separate fallacy. It is a type of too-general fallacy.

Answer: Then inference will not be possible, since if one knows the *h* in the *p* and still has doubt about the *s* pervasion will not be ascertained.

However, in the fallacy of inconclusiveness what is needed is the absence of knowledge of coexistence (of *s* and *h*), which coexistence helps in ascertaining pervasion. It is the knowledge of this absence, not that of inconclusiveness, that blocks ascertainment of pervasion. Thus D13 is not correcct.

Part Three: Contradictoriness

(E147-148) Objection: A contradictory *h* does not block inference by preventing consideration, as sublation and inconclusiveness do. Nor does it do so by contradicting knowledge of pervasion, if it is to be maintained that it blocks inference directly.

Answer: This is why Gaṅgeśa gives D18-20. It is the awareness of the nonoccurrence of the *h* in the locus of the *s* that is the root cause of contradiction being a fault, since that awareness contradicts awareness of pervasion.

Part Four: Counterbalanced Hetu

(E148-153) Objection: Counterbalance is not a fallacy, since the root cause of fallacy, viz., absence of pervasion together with consideration, is not present there. Nor can one say that a fallacy occurs whenever the argument fails to lead to a conclusion, since that failure may also be due to the ignorance of the addressee.

Answer: The counterbalanced *h* is a fallacy because it blocks the emergence of a conclusion through the contradiction between two opposing reasonings of equal strength. Or if you prefer, the fault consists in one reasoning's contradicting the assertion of pervasion in the other reasoning.

Objection: Then when perception is sublated by a valid contradictory inference it will not be fallacious, since perception is not an inference.

Answer: Perception is not contradicted by inference.

Objection (of the author of the *Ratnakośa,* according to Gopikamohan Bhattacharya): Only the knowledge of the absence of the *s* in the *p* inhibits inference. So where the *h* is known to be pervaded by the absence of the *s* no inference is possible. But in this counterbalanced case it is not necessary to *know* that the awareness of the two contradictory *h*s is valid. Therefore in a counterbalanced argument the awareness of two opposing *h*s does not inhibit inference.

Answer: Simple awareness, but not knowledge of its validity, blocks inference. Otherwise there will be heaviness and absence of proof.

Objection: In this counterbalanced case the absence of memory of either pervasion is what brings about the vitiation of inference.

Answer: No. It is rather the awareness of the *hetu* qualified by opposing pervasions and considerations that vitiates inference. The statement of the contestants brings about the awareness, so it can't very well be absent.

Part Six: Sublated

(E157-169) Gaṅgeśa postulates sublation as a separate fallacy from the others discussed here, in opposition to Dharmakīrti and others. Yajñapati agrees but criticizes Gaṅgeśa's argument for thinking so. Dharmakīrti argues (end of *pūrvapakṣa* section) that "... knowledge of validity which confers superior strength on the awareness of the absence of the *sādhya* from the *pakṣa*... becomes the basis of the fault of deviation (*savyabhicāra*)." But deviation is the occurrence of *h* in the locus of the absolute absence of *s*, and so, in the false inference "the pot limited by prior absence of color possesses color, because it is a pot", the *p* does not have an absolute absence but rather the prior absence of *s*. So it is not a case of deviation, but rather of sublation.

Objection: But here the *p* is qualified and one in which the absolute absence of color occurs, and so it *is* a case of deviation.

Yajñapati: No, since it is the qualifier, not something qualified, which is the *p*. Actually, even if the qualified *p* is the subject of the inference, it will be a case of unestablished, not of deviating *h*. Furthermore, since there is prior absence of color there can't be any absolute absence of color. And awareness of nonestablishedness depends on awareness of sublation.

Objection: If the *p* is taken to be qualified by prior absence of color, then knowledge of absence of color cannot inhibit the inference. So it cannot be an example of a sublated inference.

Answer: For any inference, knowledge of the absence of the *s* is contradictory to it and cannot occur.

Objection: If so, then if the awareness of the absence of the *s* is erroneous inference will not be inhibited!

Answer: We have only claimed that knowledge of the absence of the *s*, being contradictory to inference, brings about actual sublation. Actually cognition of the absence of the *sādhya*, whether it is correct or incorrect, undermines inference.

Yajñapati's own view: Knowledge of the absence of the *s* in the *p* precludes inference, but the absence in question is absolute, not prior, absence. "A jar qualified by prior absence of color possesses color, because it is a jar" is a case of proving what is already proved, not of sublation.

Objection: Proving what is already proved consists in the occurrence of the *s* in the *p* delimited by the limitor of subjectness. So it is a case of sublation, like the example "in the jar qualified by prior absence of color color does not exist".

Yajñapati: Then "a jar qualified by prior absence of contact possesses contact, because it is a substance" will also be a case of sublated inference, because contact does not exist in a jar delimited by the constant absence of contact. Again, "the mountain possessing a horn has fire, because it has smoke" will also be a case of unmixed sublation.

Objector: No, this last inference is a case of the *svarūpāsiddhi* kind of unestablishedness, since smoke does not occur on a mountain possessing a horn.

Answer: Then the inference "the jar possessing constant absence of contact is a substance, because it possesses contact" will also be this kind of unestablishedness, since there too the *h* does not occur in the *p* delimited by the limitor of *pakṣa*ness.

Part Seven: Fallacies are Serviceable as they Point out Inefficiency

(E169-174) A fallacy has a twofold purpose: Contradicting the opponent's inference and showing that the reason advanced by the opponent is ineffective to prove his standpoint. That is why definitions of incompetency to prove the desire object must be discussed.

Section Twenty-One: The Inference to God's Existence

(E174ff.) Yajñapati's commentary follows the text straightforwardly.

No commentary by Yajñapati on the remaining sections of the *Anumānakhaṇḍa* has come down to us.

30. PRAGALBHA MIŚRA or ŚUBHAṄKARA

An important author, Pragalbha's works are as yet not available except in bits and pieces. He seems to have been the author of four commentaries. Most important is his commentary *Prāgalbhī* on all four books of the *Tattvacintāmaṇi.*[1] His commentary on the third book, on *Upamāna,* seems to have been one of the few such commentaries; most of those who commented on Gaṅgeśa's work did not bother with this book, the shortest of the four. The *Upamānakhāṇḍa* commentary has recently been edited from three manuscripts by Gaurinath Sastri.[2] Besides this the only other portion of *Prāgalbhī* that has been published is a small introductory section of the *Pratyakṣakhāṇḍa.*[3]

Besides the commentary on Gaṅgeśa Pragalbha appears to have written a commentary on the *Nyāyalīlāvatī*[4] and a commentary on Vardhamāna's *Kiraṇāvalīprakāśa.* Neither work has been published. Finally, there is a *Darpaṇa* on Śrīharṣa's *Khaṇḍanakhaṇḍakhādya* a few pages of which are printed as Chowkhamba Sanskrit Series 82.

Pragalbha's father's name was Narapati Miśra, his mother's Jāhnavī. Umesh Mishra, following V.P. Dvivedin, considers him a Maithila, but Dinesh Bhattacharya and Gaurinath Sastri have argued that he hails from Bengal, not Mithila, and was in fact a Varendra Brahmin. He mentions Divākara and Jagadguru as his teachers, and was also "a reputed teacher of Vedānta, being a disciple of Anubhavānanda"[5].

From the evidence we can surmise that Pragalbha was a near contemporary of Vāsudeva Sārvabhauma. Bimal Matilal thinks he was a junior contemporary, but Gaurinath shows that Vāsudeva criticizes Pragalbha's view on the *vyadhikaraṇa* section and is thus likely to have been slightly junior to Pragalbha. We estimate his date as around 1470.

31. JAYADEVA or PAKṢADHARA MIŚRA

Umesh Mishra[1] provides us with mountains of information about this author, and we have already considered some questions of his authorship in connection with several works attributed above, after consideration, to the earlier Pakṣadhara the Vivekakāra. We summarize here the voluminous findings of Umesh Mishra. Dineshchandra Bhattacharya[2] has also devoted several pages to this author's history, but as Umesh Mishra's treatment is subsequent to and corrective of certain features of Dineshchandra's conclusions we shall report it here.

Jayadeva Miśra belonged to the Sodarapura family of Mithilā, of

Śāṇḍilya *gotra*. His father was Guṇe Miśra, and he lived in a village named Yamasama. He had a son named (Mahāmahopādhyāya) Mādhava (our 40 below), who is said to have defended his father's views against the works of Narahari, presumably Narahari Upādhyāya (39 below). Tradition holds that Jayadeva studied with 29. Yajñapati Upādhyāya.[3] Jayadeva frequently criticizes Yajñapati's views.

Gopikamohan Bhattacharya gives Jayadeva's dates as 1430-1490, but Ingalls points out he must have still been alive aound 1500.[4] Ingalls provides a careful review of the evidence about Jayadeva's date. The most conclusive evidence concerns his relation to his pupil Bhagīratha Ṭhakkura, as Bhagīratha says he studied with Jayadeva up to when he was 20 year old. We know that "Bhagīratha's younger brother, Maheśa Ṭhakkura..." became Rājā of Mithilā in A.D.1557, and did not die until 1569.[5] Making a few obvious assumptions one can see that the Rājā would have been very old indeed unless his elder brother studied with Jayadeva not far before 1500. Ingalls also adds evidence from the stories about Raghunātha Śiromaṇi's youth which support the estimate adopted here, that Jayadeva flourished around 1470 but lived to see the very end of the 15th century.

Jayadeva had many illustrious pupils. They included 39. Narahari Upādhyāya, his son 40. (Mahāmahopādhyāya) Mādhava, 43. Vāsudeva Miśra (who was his nephew), and 44. Rucidatta Miśra. If old stories can be trusted, one who was not a pupil of Jayadeva for very long was Raghunātha Śiromaṇi. If Raghunātha was a pupil of Jayadeva he was a most disrespectful one. Ingalls recounts the story of Pakṣadhara's insults to Raghunātha, the pupil's threats in return and eventual triumph.[6] Although by no means a believer in this story, Ingalls admits the possibility that Raghunātha did in fact study with Jayadeva.

Just which, besides the famous *Āloka* on the *Tattvacintāmaṇi*, are the other works of Jayadeva is a troublesome problem. If we assume that works called "Viveka" can be attributed to 25.Pakṣadhara the Vivekakāra, we are left with a few works of doubtful authorship. The most firm of these is the *Pramāṇapallava*, referred to by Jayadeva's nephew Vāsudeva. Dineshchandra Bhattacharya says it "seems to have been an independent treatise rather than a commentary."[7] There is also reason to believe he wrote a *Śaśadharavyākhyā* on Śaśadhara's *Nyāyasiddhantadīpa*—Umesh Mishra says there is a manuscript of this work in the Sarasvati Bhavana Library in Banaras.[8] New Catalogus Catalogorum also cites a work of Jayadeva's called *Nyāyapadārthamālā*.[9]

Portions of the *Tattvacintāmaṇyāloka* are available in print. Separate editions of the *Maṅgalavāda* and *Prāmāṇyavāda* sections are available, and in addition certain portions of the first book (the sections on *Samavāya*, *Anupalabdhi*, *Abhāva*, *Pratyakṣakāraṇa*, *Mano'ṇutva*, *Anuvyavasāya* and *Nirvikalpaka*). These works are, unhappily, no longer studied and we have been unable to find summarizers for them, with the exception of the *Prāmāṇya* section.

ĀLOKA on the *Prāmāṇyavāda* Section of Gaṅgeśa's TATTVACINTĀMAṆI

Summary by Jitendranath Mohanty

"E" references are to the 1974 version of Kamakhyanatha Tarkavagīsa's edition of *Tattvacintāmaṇi* with various commentaries (B3379; RB5287). Numbered sections correspond to the summary of Gaṅgeśa's *Tattvacintāmaṇi*, above.

Part One

6-13 (E121-122) "(A1) The truth of an awareness J is grasped...." The awareness referred to in this passage by Pakṣadhara means that only known validity (*jñānaprāmāṇya*) is to be considered here, for unknown validity is not apprehended in the manner indicated by (A1). Also, Pakṣadhara parses (A1) to say that truth of J is grasped by any awareness K which is produced by the same collection of conditions as give rise to the awareness of J without producing awareness of J's falsity. Pakṣadhara adds the proviso that only those awarenesses K of J apprehend J's validity which, *qua* awareness of J, apprehend its objects. Such a merely verbal apprehension of an awareness as arises upon merely hearing the words "awareness of a pot" does not apprehend validity even on the Mīmāṃsā view. Pakṣadhara's provision seeks to exclude such cases.

26-29. (E215-221) Gaṅgeśa says "Furthermore", there is no universal property of defectness (*doṣatva*) present whenever there is doubt." Pakṣadhara interprets this to mean that there is no generic character called "being born of unfamiliar circumstances" (*anabhyāsadaśājanma*); this has reference to the fact that doubts about truth—on the possibility of which Gaṅgeśa's argument rests—take place generally in the case of those awarenesses which are yet unfamiliar. Now, lest the Mīmāṃsaka might count this unfamiliarity as itself a defect which is responsible for the occurrence of the doubt in spite of an initial certainty, Pakṣadhara takes Gaṅgeśa to mean that there is no generic character of that description, so that no definite causal law could be formulated in this matter.

Part Three

3 (E184ff.) To Gaṅgeśa's account of truth Pakṣadhara adds that J must entertain its content in the same relation to the qualifier as it is in reality.

32. ŚRĪNĀTHA BHAṬṬĀCARYA CAKRAVARTIN

Śrīnātha was the younger brother of Vāsudeva Sārvabhauma's father Narahari, which makes it relatively easy to estimate his date as around 1470. He appears to have written a commentary on the *Tattvacintāmaṇi*, at least the first two parts of it. Tarasankar Bhattacarya reports "three definitions of Cakraborti"[1] that are discussed by Raghunātha Śiromaṇi among the 14 definitions in his section on such definitions.

33. VĀSUDEVA SĀRVABHAUMA

This famous teacher appears to have flourished around 1480. He taught a number of famous people, not by any means confined to Naiyāyikas. Raghunātha Śiromaṇi studied with him. So did Raghunandana, generally held to be "the best authority on the Bengal school of Hindu law"[1]. Another pupil was Kṛṣṇānanda, who wrote works on tantric charms and other kindred subjects.[2] Last and most celebrated of all, toward the end of his lifetime Vāsudeva was an instructor of Caitanya, the father of *Acintyabhedābheda* Vaiṣṇava philosophy.

Vāsudeva was born into "one of the greatest Brahmin families in Bengal, the Akhaṇḍala Banerjees (Bandyopādhyāya). This was a family of Rārhī Brahmins."[3] Umesh Mishra speculates that either Vāsudeva or his father must have studied with Pakṣadhara Miśra, since visiting Mithilā for instruction was the only way at the time a Bengali could have learned Nyāya. Stories exist about the difficulties of the tests that Vāsudeva had to pass, having, according to one of these, to learn by heart the entire *Tattvacintāmaṇi*, the *Nyāyakusumāñjali* and the notes of his teacher's lectures. Having jumped these hoops he returned to Navadvīpa and founded his own school. Late in life he apparently left Bengal and moved to Purī, where he associated with Caitanya and is reputed to have abandoned Nyāya. It is at this time that he is reputed to have written a commentary on Lakṣmīdhara's *Advaitamakaranda* as well as various hymns (*stotra*). He is held to have died after 1510 in Orissa.

Dinesh Bhattacharya questions parts of the above story. According to him[4] Vāsudeva's parents were named Narahari and Bhagīrathī; he was a grandson of Svapneśvara and father of Vāhinīpati. He was a nephew and pupil of Jayadeva Pakṣadhara, whom he defended against Narahari. He was a classfellow of Caitanya's maternal grandfather, who must have been born about 1420, though Dinesh estimates that Vāsudeva himself was born about 1450. He doubts that Vāsudeva introduced Navyanyāya into Bengal, and believes he must have left Bengal for Orissa before 1500. He also thinks that Vāsudeva left Purī before Caitanya's death and ended his life in Banaras. Operative in these differences of opinion one can discern a certain amount of contentious bias.

Vāsudeva wrote a commentary on at least part of the *Tattvacintāmaṇi.* Gaurinath Sastri tells us it was called *Sārāvalī,* and that it "runs from *anumiti* to *bādha* omitting avayava,.."[5] Gopikamohan Bhattacharya differs: he states that the work is titled *parīkṣā,* and that only the *anumāna* chapter is known.[6]

In his commentary Vāsudeva quotes his teacher Narahari Viśārada "at least 15 times",[7] and sometimes differs from him. According to Gopikamohan "some of the peculiar doctrines introduced by Vāsudeva are (a) qualified is something more than non-qualified; (b) bothness is one qualified by the other."[8]

Gopikamohan Bhattacharya in one of his articles[9] gives a generous resume of how much Raghunātha Śiromaṇi owed to his teacher Vāsudeva. He finds that Raghunātha refers to Vāsudeva some 52 times. Notable among the references are his authorship of one of the 14 definition in the *Vyadhikaraṇa* section of *Dīdhiti,* a definition which Raghunātha discusses in two different versions, and Raghunātha's attribution to Vāsudeva of the two original views mentioned in the preceding paragraph here that are set forth in the *Siddhāntalakṣaṇa* section.

34. KṚṢṆĀNANDA VIDYĀVINODA or VIDYĀVIRIÑCI

"Kṛṣṇānanda Vidyāviriñci is one more commentator on the *Tattvacintāmaṇi.* His commentary goes by the name of *Kṛṣṇa,* to be more precise, *Pratyakṣakṛṣṇa.* He is described as a younger brother of Sārvabhauma."[1]

35. JANĀRDANA of Mithilā

This author came originally from Tirhut or Mithilā. He is the author of *Prakāśa* on the *Tattvacintāmaṇi,* which was wrongly ascribed to Timmabhūpāla.[1] His probable date is 1490.

36. TIMMABHŪPĀLA

See the previous paragraph. The work by Janārdana was wrongly ascribed to this author, who must be contemporaneous.

37. MISARU MIŚRA

Another author who flourished around 1490, he was the author of *Padārthacandra*, a work on Vaiśeṣika categories, as well as a work on *smṛti* titled *Vivādacandra*. "But the actual authorship of (both) work(s) is attributed to Lacchma Devī, who was the chief queen of Candrasiṃha, the younger brother of Bhairavasiṃha Deva."[1] This author is a different person from the author of a work titled *Nyāyadīpikā*.

38. VIRŪPĀKṢA MIŚRA

New Catalogus Catalogorum, p. 121, dates this writer at 1494, the date of a unique, incomplete manuscript extant in Bikaner. The work is a commentary on the *Tarkabhāṣā*.

39. NARAHARI UPĀDHYĀYA or MAHEŚVARA VIŚĀRADA

Not to be confused with 28. Narahari the father of Vāsudeva, this Narahari is a rather better-known Naiyāyika, the son of Yajñapati and great-great-grandson of Vāṭeśvara. This Narahari studied under Yajñapati as well as Jayadeva, and wrote several works on a variety of topics. Available in manuscript is his *Dūṣaṇoddhāra*, a commentary (or at least based on a commentary) on the first two chapters of the *Tattvacintāmaṇi*[1] in which Narahari defends his father's views against Jayadeva's. The author is aware, in addition to these two forebears, of Pragalbha Miśra, whom he quotes 9 times.

In addition to the *Dūṣaṇoddhāra* Narahari seems to have composed a commentary on Udayana's *Ātmatattvaviveka*.[2] Umesh Mishra tells us that he is the author of a *Dvaitanirṇaya* "on *dharmaśāstra* which has been published from Darabhanga".[3]

40. MĀDHAVA MIŚRA

Umesh Mishra tells us that this writer was a son of Pakṣadhara Miśra and wrote a commentary on the *Tattvacintāmaṇi* defending his father against Narahari. The title of the commentary is not known.

41. ŚRĪKĀRA KUBJAŚAKTIVĀDA

Umesh Mishra[1] informs us that *Jāgadīśī* attributes to Raghunātha Śiromaṇi the refutation of this writer's arguments. That would suggest a date around 1500.

42. ŚŪLAPĀṆI MIŚRA

Another figure who must have flourished about the beginning of the 16th century, Śūlapāṇi is quoted in the *Padārtharatnamālā* by Jānakīnātha Bhaṭṭācārya. No works, or even titles of works, on Nyāya are known. Umesh Mishra[1] guesses he may be the same as the author of a *Prāyaścittaviveka* that is quoted by Jānakīnātha in his *Padārtharatnamālā* as well as by Laugākṣi Bhāskara.

43. VĀSUDEVA MIŚRA

Vāsudeva was Jayadeva's nephew, and wrote his *Nyāyasiddhāntasāra* to defend his uncle's views. He must have flourished around 1500. The work is available in manuscript.

44. RUCIDATTA MIŚRA

This prolific commentator was one of Jayadeva's pupils, placing him around 1505. He belonged to the Sodarpura family of Mithilā, and was also known as Bhaktū. The date of 1505 is substantiated by a manuscript of a transcription by him of his teacher's *Āloka* dated that year.

We know of at least five of Rucidatta's works. These are all commentaries. A *Prakāśa* on Gaṅgeśa's *Tattvacintāmaṇi*, a *Makaranda* on Udayana's *Nyāyakusumāñjali*, and a *Vivṛti* on Vardhamāna's *Dravyakiraṇāvalīprakāśa* have been published. A *Vibhāsa* on the *Nyāyalīlāvatī* of Vallabha and a commentary on Vardhamāna's *Tarkabhāṣāprakāśa* are available in manuscript.

PRAKĀŚA on Gaṅgeśa's TATTVACINTĀMAṆI
Summary by V. Varadachari

"E" references are to the edition by N.S. Ramanuja Tatacarya (RB 5346), Tirupati 1973. The remainder of the work is only available in manuscript.

Section One: Invocation

The invocation at the beginning of the *Tattvacintāmaṇi* contains expressions which illustrate the figure of speech called *virodhābhāsa*. The commentator explains every expression. The word *triguṇasaciva* is explained as the attribute to the lord having knowledge, desire and volition as the three qualities.

(E21-22) While interpreting the passage in the text summarized above as "Though no such Vedic statement can be found, it can be inferred from the fact that an invocation is performed by cultured people", the commentator gives an inference supporting this passage. It runs thus: an invocation is based on the Vedas, as it is the object of the super-worldly practise of the disciplined people. The author justifies every word in this proposition.

(E28) There is in fact no Vedic passage to declare that the practise of giving an invocation is obligatory. Rucidatta says that a passage, "one who desires to complete the work without any hindrance shall practise *maṅgala*", will have to be assumed as having the status of scripture.

(E85) The author elucidates his position by showing that the invocation is declared by the Vedas to bring about a particular kind of completion. Then when the particular case is taken up, it is understood that the nature of completion is related to the sphere where obstacles have scope to play.

(E87) Disciplined persons take to the practise of giving invocations when there is room for doubt regarding obstacles or certainty that there are obstacles and one wishes to avoid them. Even when there is the desire that the work which is undertaken should be completed, the doer's thoughts center round the destruction of the obstacles. Otherwise, there will be the need to accept the position that an invocation is undertaken even by one who is bereft of the knowledge that obstacles may hinder his activity.

(E88) There is no need to accept the position that if enough invocations are performed completion is bound to be achieved, for irrespective of the number of invocations, completion is still found unrealized. So, destruction of obstacles should not be taken as determining the completion of the act undertaken. Some scholars are reported as treating the nonproduction of obstacles as the result brought about by an invocation, like the act of expiation which is undertaken in order that misery may not rise.

(E99) The text speaks of an injunction to give an invocation. This injunction takes the form "He who is desirous of completing the work without any obstacle should offer praise to god." But according to Rucidatta that one should perform an invocation is not an injunction. He remarks that this is the view held in the Nyāya tradition.

Section Two: Truth

(E115-124) The text discusses the validity of an instrument of knowledge in two aspects, namely, how it is grasped (*jñapti*) and how it arises (*utpatti*). While treating the first aspect, the text states the *prima facie* position which maintains intrinsic validity. The author remarks in connection with (A1) that the nihilist (Mādhyamika) objects to the undertaking of a discussion of this kind, as it is impossible to find out whether an awareness satisfies (A1), dependent as it is upon the nature of reality. Gaṅgeśa takes up the discussion on intrinsic validity which is maintained by the school of Mīmāṃsā. He seeks to reject the positions of both at one stroke.

(E124-149) While discussing (A1) the commentator notes the purposes served by every word. In the course of this discussion, the author refers to the views of Jayadeva and Pragalbhamiśra.

(E166-183) (A3), otherwise put, says that validity is apprehended by the mode (*prakāra*) of the awareness.

(E174) (A4) makes truth ascertainable through its locus, that is, through the awareness that is true. (A5) makes the truth of the awareness "this is a jar", ascertainable by awareness of it by any means which apprehends this cognition. All of definitions (A1-5) are shown to apply to the concept of validity maintained by each of the three schools of Mīmāṃsā.

(E234-235) Udayana's argument for extrinsic validity runs thus: the validity of an awareness which is subjected to repetitive study is ascertained extrinsically, like invalidity (cf. *Nyāyakusumāñjali* Book Two). This is upheld by Gaṅgeśa who notes also the view that validity is ascertained extrinsically since intrinsic ascertainment is sublated. Rucidatta holds that this view is to be discarded.[1]

(E243, 248) While commenting upon the arguments for admitting extrinsic truth, the author states that truth has to be inferred, since activity is found occasioned even by doubt regarding validity.

(E287) Awarenesses differ from each other because of their content. Contents differ because of the difference in their qualificands. Qualifiers differ from each other and create distinctions in their qualificands, but qualifiers cannot by themselves distinguish content.

(E301-302) Gaṅgeśa remarks that aftercognition is invariably admitted to be true and so doubt does not arise about its validity. Rucidatta notes that though aftercognition is held to be valid, it is not known to be so. Otherwise it cannot remove doubt when that arises. He does not therefore agree with this statement of the author of the text.

(E357-360) The Nyāya stand is that merit is the cause for truth and defect for falsity. Regarding the question of the difficulty of finding a uniform characteristic for merit in all cases of instruments of knowledge, differences of opinion are entertained by writers. Gaṅgeśa held that for the different instruments merits should also differ from each other. Rucidatta notes the views of Jayadeva in the case of each instrument. Correct consideration is the merit in the case of inferential awareness, and knowledge of similarity in case of comparison. Narahari's (the son of Yajñapati's) view is also noted.

(E381) While the text mentions fitness, etc. as constituting merit in the case of verbal awareness, Rucidatta insists that fitness alone should be meant here. It is only when this is available that a true awareness will be produced even if expectancy, etc. are not properly made out in the given passage.

(E434-436) The text defines knowledge as the experience of *x* at the particular place where *x* is. Another definition makes knowledge the experience of an object that has a qualifier as having it. Rucidatta notes that in the first mentioned definition, experience should help to apprehend the same relation between the qualifier and the qualificand as one which exists really between the qualifier and the qualificand. The same qualificand and qualifier shall be presented in the helping experience. The second definition means that experience should arise about the same qualificand and qualifier which involves the same relation, all of them really existing. The two definitions do not seem to be different from each. Yet, the distinction is noteworthy. The former is with reference to being qualified (*vaiśiṣṭya*) which it has on account of the governing qualifier, while the latter shows that truth is produced by the knowledge of that particular qualifier.

(E437) The definition of false awareness is likewise given in two ways which are the reverse of those given for knowledge. A similar explanation is given for these two by Rucidatta.

(E441-454) The text notes that nonpropositional awareness cannot be referred to by expressions and as such is outside the scope of true or false awarenesses. Rucidatta, however, notes that nonpropositional awareness also gets included in a definition which the text offers in a negative way.

Section Three: Error

(E542-547) While discussing the theory of error, Rucidatta notes the stand taken by the Prābhākara school of Mīmāṃsā. The Prābhākara cites the case of recognition of the form, (A) "This is that Devadatta." He says it is not a case of perception. (A) is a single awareness and similarly the awareness "this is silver" is a single awareness. Gaṅgeśa notes that for the Naiyāyika recognition is produced by the sense-organ and so is a case of perception. Traces can serve as the relation in the production of this awareness. Rucidatta observes that the case of error should be treated on a different footing. Here what is not near (connected) presents itself due to defects.

(E544) Actually, the relation with the qualifier is also in a general way a cause in producing perception. That is, silverness is not present in the shell. Yet its relation to silvery things acts as the cause for giving rise to the awareness "this is silver." This explanation is given in reply to the Prābhākaras who do not admit knowledge as a relation. The correct position, Rucidatta states, is that knowledge, traces or memory serve as the relation. This applies to the perception of the correct type. The contact with the correct type of qualificand will have to be recognized as causing the perception of that qualificand.

(E550-551) Gaṅgeśa remarks that perception is an instrument of knowledge in cases of error. The aftercognition "I know this to be silver" is the instrument of knowledge for one thing in presenting itself as another. Rucidatta observes that by admitting this position intrinsic truth need not be supposed to take the place of extrinsic truth, which the Nyāya school maintains, because the aftercognition gives guarantee to the truth of an awareness only in the sense that it reveals itself and also that awareness.

Section Four: The Definition of Perception

(E567-585) Gaṅgeśa does not approve of the traditional definition of perception as given in *Nyāyasūtra* 1.1.4, as it is necessary to admit God's perception. Connection (*sannikarṣa*) is not uniform in every case of perceptual awareness. Hence he defines perception as immediate. The difficulty arises in explaining whether this applies only to ordinary perceptions or to eternal ones also. Rucidatta therefore remarks that Gaṅgeśa was not satisfied with that traditional definition and so framed a definition which could apply only to ordinary perceptions.

(E590) The internal organ is also a sense-organ. Yet, it cannot have any contact in the real sense of the word. Rucidatta therefore says that conjunction (*yoga*) with the internal organ is meant here and not any relation (*pratyāsatti*).

(E595-599) Gaṅgeśa offers his own definition (D6 in the summary of *Tattvacintāmaṇi* above). Rucidatta remarks that this definition is applicable to ordinary perceptions and also to (God's) perceptions. He adds further that this definition does not apply to yogic perception, which is produced by an efficient cause in the form of knowledge of reflective thinking (*manana*) brought forth through constant meditation (*nididhyāsana*).

Objection: (D6) does not apply to the perception of an absence, since that is produced by the awareness of its counterpositive.

Answer: No, there is no evidence to prove that, since the awareness of a counterpositive is required to cause the rise of perceptual awareness of an absence. Even without this intermediate cause the perceptual cognition of absences is known to rise.

(E602-605) Gaṅgeśa states that memory of the object as it is is the cause of recognition. Hence in a case of error memory of the superimposed object is stated to be the cause. Therefore direct awareness (*anubhava*) of it, which is past, cannot be the cause for recognition through traces.

Section Five: Sense-Object Connection

(E613-621) The number of connections for the rise of perceptual awareness is held to be six, which could be brought under the common head of qualifierness (*viśeṣaṇatā*). That is, each connection serves as a qualifier; otherwise the connections, which are different for the specific kinds of perceptions, could not be brought together under a common group. To the question as to where sensory connection is located, Rucidatta observes that the object, for example, odor, is to be treated as the locus for the contact between itself and the sense-organ apprehending it. Otherwise, the object will not be perceived because of the absence of any connection with the sense-organ to serve as the qualifier.

(E633-634) A problem is posed in the case of perception of sound. Inherence is the relation between sound and *ākāśa*, which is the auditory organ when it is delimited within the auricular orifice. Since *ākāśa* is all-pervasive, all sounds will have to be admitted to be heard everywhere. It is therefore held that the relation of inherence with sound is nonpervasive. When it is restricted to the particular region of the organ of hearing, there is absolute absence of sound elsewhere. Inherence of sound is of course present there, but there is the absence of sound in the particular region of the *ākāśa* bound by the auricular orifice, and so sound is not audible there. Therefore any kind of inherence cannot be a relation, but only that with reference to the sound that is delimited by the contact with the auditory organ.

(E640) The spread of sound is explained to take place in two ways, namely, like the little wave and big wave (*vīcītaraṅganyāya*) and like the *kadamba* buds (*kadambamukulanyāya*). Rucidatta observes that the former applies in the case of the motion of sound in regions where its absence is uniform, and the latter where it is not uniform.

Consequently, when the absence cannot be uniform in the ten directions, the sounds produced should be not the same one but two or three others. Hence the same sound may give rise to more than one series of sounds.

(E640-41) One and the same sound can give rise to several sounds because of different air currents. An alternative explanation is also referred to. It is due to differences in the prior absences of sounds. The latter is given greater importance. The nature of prior absence determines the differences in the effects. For instance, potsherds and threads are different from each other. The effects to be produced are pots and cloths, and their prior absences differ from each other, and as such these alone determine the differences in the effects, and the differences in the inherence causes have no scope to play here.[2]

Section Nine: Connection of Content and Illumination

(E770) Apart from connections (*sannikarṣa*) of six kinds, the contact between the object and external light (*āloka*) is also a cause of perception. Even if only a particular part of the object has contact with external light, that part could be perceived only when it comes into contact with the eye.

(E771-772) Some scholars appear to have held the view that the text does not contain the statement denying contact between the eye and the external light as causing the rise of perceptual cognition, and so both contacts (eye and external light and object and external light) could be admitted as causes. Rucidatta rejects this on the ground that the contact between the eye and external light is superfluous here. The contact between the object and external light is established as necessary for the production of perceptual cognition through agreement and difference.

Section Ten: Perceptibility of Wind

(E799) While discussing the several conditions which give rise to perceptual awareness, Rucidatta remarks that possession of manifested color in the case of an object is essential for the perception of that object produced by an external sense-organ. This applies to all the kinds of perception. However, in the case of visual perception, the causal apparatus which is needed for apprehending color is required also, in order to distinguish it from perceptions arising from the function of other sense-organs like nose and tongue. It is because of this that gold is not perceived in darkness.

(E801-802) Upādhyāya held the view that number is perceived in fire but not in its radiance. This is because possession of manifested touch is also the cause for the perception of certain substances. If both wind and heat were perceptible, then their number would be perceived. It is not, in fact, perceived, and so wind is not perceptible.

Rucidatta does not admit this position. No number is perceived in the sun's radiance though it has manifested color. If on this account, number could be said to be perceptible, then wind also can be stated to have number which could be perceived, and on this ground wind also can be taken to be perceptible. That is, if an object having manifested color could be perceived on account of having manifested touch, then the reverse can also hold good, as in the case of wind.

Section Eleven : The Fieriness of Gold

(E817) Rucidatta states that there is no instrument of knowledge to give us knowledge of variegated taste.

Section Twelve : Atomicity of the Internal Organ

(E823) While commenting upon the size of the internal organ Rucidatta identifies an argument in the text as the one advanced by Bhaṭṭa Bhāskara, in whose opinion the internal organ has no touch and is partless. It does not give rise to the perception of smell, color, taste and touch, one after the other, and so must be taken as one of the substances like earth, etc.

Section Thirteen : Aftercognition

(E850) The Nyāya school recognizes aftercognition which is a case of mental perception. Awareness is not therefore self-luminous, and it itself becomes knowable. The relation here is awarenessness. God's awareness is however self-luminous, that is, luminous to Himself. Rucidatta remarks here that connection (*sannikarṣa*), whether it is needed for external or internal perception, is to be considered with reference to ordinary perceptual awarenesses. God's awareness, though perceptual, is not ordinary (and has no limitations of any kind) and arises concerning all objects. Hence it is self-luminous.

Section Fourteen : Nonpropositional Awareness

(E859) Awareness of the qualifier is responsible for the awareness of a qualified awareness. This principle applies also to the awareness of absences, where the qualificand serves as the qualifier. One may not object here that the qualificand and the absence are distinct from each other, and that what is different and so disconnected from the other cannot serve as the other's qualifier. In the case of positive objects, awareness of the qualifier forms the causal apparatus for the awareness of the propositional awareness. The same causal apparatus is available for the rise of perceptual awareness of an absence. A different kind is not needed. Or, the qualificand serving as the qualifier can be taken as a specific case.

(E861) Rucidatta refers to the view held by some thinkers who take being qualified as a relation. According to them, awareness of it arises from the awareness of the objects which are related. In the case of an absence, the relation involves only the counterpositive and not the qualificand also. In positive objects, both the qualifier and the object are known since contact pervades partially the thing in contact.

Rucidatta questions this interpretation. If the counterpositive can itself prove the relation between an absence and the ground where that absence is located, then the qualificand cannot be taken to play its part. When an absence is not ascertained to be present there, then the propositional awareness that the ground has no jar on it will not be produced.

(E867) Some scholars are said to maintain that the awareness of the qualificand need not be admitted as the cause for the awareness of an absence. This is only a statement of general applicability. It does not apply in apprehending the absence of sound.

Section Fifteen: Qualifier and Indicator

(E880) Rucidatta takes up the definition of "qualifier" which Gaṅgeśa gives as (D12) and offers a note by way of illustration. In the passage "bring the person having a staff", the staff is a qualifier, because it is related to the person having it. On the other hand, in the passage "go to Devadatta's house on which a crow is perching", the crow is not related to Devadatta and so is an indicator. Similarly in the passage "visual perception arises of a substance having color", color is a qualifier, while it is an indicator in the passage "taste in the colored object", as it is related to taste. After offering seventeen definitions of "qualifier" and "indicator" Gaṅgeśa concludes with the words *alam vistareṇa*, meaning that further elaboration is not necessary. On this, Rucidatta remarks that Gaṅgeśa took up a discussion on this matter mainly to find out what a qualifier and an indicator are. This discussion has relevance only to other systems when the sense of the Vedas gets discussed (e.g., in interpreting *Brahmasūtra* I.1.2).

Section Sixteen: Propositional Awareness

(E887) Gaṅgeśa says that memory cannot be true to the object about which it rises. A memory presents the object as though it exists at the time of the memory's occurrence, because it does not present it as related to the past and future times. In this respect, it behaves like recognition. Awareness is confined in respect of the object related to a specific time. Memory, however, can arise referring to a particular time even when it is about an object which is not now experienced. This is because of the materials which produce the awareness. In this case impressions have no role to play. Hence the awareness of a jar as red after it is baked black is stated to be a case of error, though ordinary people take it to possess the black color. Rucidatta identifies this as the view of the old school.

(E888) A question arises here regarding the memory of the meaning of words. Can this memory be treated as erroneous? No! Here the thatness which belongs to the object is not lost. This means that this kind of memory is not erroneous.

BOOK TWO: INFERENCE

Section One: Inferential Awareness

The compound (in D1) is *vyāptiviśiṣṭapakṣadharmatājñāna* is taken as *karmadhāraya* compound. It is not to be taken as a *dvandva* compound.

Section Six: The Conclusive Definition

While commenting on the definition of pervasion, Rucidatta discusses the several meanings that are offered for the words *sāmānādhikaraṇya* ("having a common locus") and *atyantābhāva* ("absolute absence"). The word *atyantābhāva* must be taken to be what is opposed to the *hetu.* This means that the *h* must not have any common locus with the counterpositives of absences. In this sense, pervasion may be spatial or temporal. In the former, absence of common-locusness is with reference to place and in the latter to time.

Sections Seven and Eight: General and Particular Absences

Rucidatta discusses the difference between the general and particular absence. In the former, all those things which are delimited by the determinant of the *s* have pervasion through having a common locus with anything that is determined by the *s.* In the latter, there is pervasion only between those (*s* and *h*) that have the same locus.

Rucidatta makes it clear that mutual absence should have been included under absolute absence. According to some scholars, to be a limitor is a particular self-linking connector. This is applicable in the cases of contact and a tree's branches where the branches are inhered in by the tree.

Section Nine: The Means of Grasping Pervasion

What operates in the apprehension of pervasion is the awareness of coexistence of *s* and *h*, not repeated observation. The coexistence of difference is helpful in apprehending pervasion. What prevents the use of inferential awareness is the same thing that produces the awareness of nondeviation, that gives rise to inferential cognition.

Section Ten: Reductio Ad Absurdum

Regarding the scope for *tarka*, Rucidatta makes it clear that the causal relation between smoke and fire must not be taken to be apprehended through *tarka*. Doubt may not rise at all in certain cases where the other alternative does not come into the picture. *Tarka* cannot therefore be admitted to help in the apprehension of pervasion, but it is to be employed for setting aside the doubt that there may be room for straying.

Section Eleven: Comprehensiveness of Pervasion

Rucidatta discusses the relative advantages of absolute absence's and mutual absence's having the same locus as the *h*. Logical economy is shown to favor absolute absence in preference to mutual absence. Some scholars prefer mutual absence on the grounds of logical economy and conveying the sense quickly. Rucidatta rejects this and indicates that absolute absence has advantages over mutual absence. The traditional view and Gaṅgeśa's view are stated to be in favour of recognizing absolute absence.

Section Twelve: Perception Through Connection with the Universal

Regarding the universal application of pervasion the Nyāya school recognizes inference as the connection for the extraordinary perception. Rucidatta observes that the universal that is connected with the sense-organ is alone the relation here.

Section Thirteen: On Obstruction

The definition of "obstruction" is taken up for detailed discussion by Gaṅgeśa. Some hold that an obstruction does not pervade that which is held to be the *h*, while it has pervasion with what is held to be the *s*. This definition is applicable to what is other than the *h*. The word *pakṣetara* is explained by Rucidatta as that which has the *h* in the form of something else. That is, an obstruction has pervasion of the *s* when something other than the *h* is held to be the *h*. Rucidatta remarks that this has overpervasion to what is other than the *p*, which when considered would mean the *h* is sublated.

The definition that an obstruction does not pervade the *h* when it has equal pervasion with the *s* is identified as given by Udayana, according to Rucidatta, while Gaṅgeśa does not identify it. Gaṅgeśa notes that this does not apply to the cases of deviating pervasion. He further notes the treatment of obstruction in the *Ātmatattvaviveka*, where it is described as a feature which helps in the mention of the *s*, and in the *Nyāyakusumāñjali*, where the apprehension of the reflection of the china rose in the crystal is treated as illustrating the concept of obstruction.[3]

Section Fourteen: Being the Pakṣa

Rucidatta refers to an interpretation of the definition of *pakṣatā*. Even if the desire to infer were to rise and continue to be entertained for two or three moments, inferential awareness does arise. Hence the words "desire to infer" must be taken to refer to a time when the proving of an object has not taken place, but a time subsequent to that of the object's production. Rucidatta offers his comments upon this by stating that inferential awareness will not rise at that moment on its closely following the rise of desire to infer, even if consideration is to intervene. The desire is only with reference to the inferential awareness.

Section Sixteen: Only-Positive Inference

Only-positive is discussed at length, drawing attention to two views of predecessors. Then Rucidatta offers his definition. It consists in the *h*'s being a characteristic that does not determine counterpositiveness of a mutual absence.

Section Twenty: Fallacies

Sublation and counterbalance are shown by the opponents of the Nyāya system as nondifferent from *asiddhi* since consideration, which is the cause of the inferential cognition, is not applicable to these two cases. They do not directly affect the rise of the inferential awareness.

Rucidatta refers to the view of some scholars who bring *anupasaṃhārin* under deviation, and some others correct the *prima facie* view by pointing out that it is to be brought under the unestablished *h*.

Rucidatta gives an interesting survey of the fallacy of deviation. A discussion is taken up to examine whether the too-specific kind of deviation could include the contradictory fallacy also. On this, Rucidatta remarks that the definition of deviation may be given as providing a condition for the declaration of the fallacy which vitiates the certainty of the knowledge of the presence of the *h* in *sp* and *vp*, an *h* which is present only in the *p*. Then this condition applies to all the three kinds of deviation. This condition is present also in contradiction. This is common to more than one fallacy, but it does not mean that there is no difference between too-specific deviation and contradiction. Presence of this condition in the *vp* does not mean that the fallacy should be of the too-specific kind. Otherwise, sublation and counterbalance could be considered as identical with each other, as they directly affect the rise of the inferential cognition.

Rucidatta remarks further that the above explanation, which he had offered, is in the line of the tradition. According to Gaṅgeśa, the reason for calling deviation a fallacy is that it is opposed to the certain presence of the *h* in the *p* alone. This definition brings contradiction within counterbalance. Yet, an objection cannot be raised against the enumeration of contradiction as an independent fallacy. Otherwise, contradiction can be included even within unestablishedness. Rucidatta adds further that the basis for the sublation fallacy is that it makes known the absence of the *sādhya* and that this applies to contradiction as well.

The unestablishedness fallacy is taken to be of three kinds. Other kinds are also available. For instance, the *h* may not have contact with the *p*, and the *p* may not be related to the *h*. There may not be a common locus shared between pervasion and *pakṣadharmatā*. This does not suggest that the number of fallacies would become greater than that enumerated by the author of the *sūtra*s. The common factor among these is the absence of the object for subsumptive reflection.

Rucidatta notes the definitions offered by various scholars for fallaciousness. Some hold that the fallaciousness arises about a reason whose correct cognition prevents the inferential awareness. Others hold that it arises about an object whose knowledge determines action counter to the inferential awareness. Rucidatta's view is that the fallacious *h* is one perceptual awareness of which prevents the rise of the inferential awareness.

Section Twenty-one: The Inference to God's Existence

Rucidatta states that the exhaustive treatment given to inference till now must be taken to find its ultimate purpose served in employing it for proving the existence of God.

While commenting on the objections raised against the Nyāya argument for proving God's existence, Rucidatta makes some interesting observations. God is taken by the Nyāya school as the agent for the creation of the universe. To set aside man's agency from consideration, the contention is that God is the agent, not man through his *adṛṣṭa*. Some scholars hold that man's *adṛṣṭa* brings about certain effects and God cannot be included for the purpose. Some others maintain that even heaven, which is reached by people with *adṛṣṭa*, need not be taken as obtained through God's endeavour. In either case, God is the agent, not the merit of individual selves.

Some others say that the white color in the body of Kālī is produced by volition in the the form of doing penance related to Kālī's body. This volition is due to *adṛṣṭa* and is with reference to the body of Kālī, which is the material cause for the white color of Kālī's body. The clause in Inf3a "not due to the merit and demerit of individual selves" is intended to avoid underextension here and also in getting heaven.

In the case of the inference adduced to prove God's existence, being produced by a body (*śarīrajanyatva*) is shown to be an obstruction. Some scholars suggest, according to Rucidatta, that there is heaviness in admitting this, and so *being produced* (*janyatva*) could be the obstruction due to logical economy.

Others declare that it should first be admitted that the world is produced by an agent, and *being produced* must be admitted to determine this.

Rucidatta takes up the opponent's argument disproving the agency of God on the ground that the world could not be a product, as it is not produced through (possession) of the body. The qualifier "bodily" in the *h* "not being produced by bodily movements" does not serve any purpose. This is illustrated by the case of the *h*, blue smoke, in the inference that the hill is fiery. The qualifier "blue" does not serve any purpose here. This is treated elaborately by the commentator. The early school of Nyāya held that if nonproduction is intended to serve as the *h* in the argument of the opponent, the qualifier *bodily* is not necessary, as nonproduction pervades absence of agency. Rucidatta does not approve of this. "Nonproduction" has no meaning unless it has a reference to its counterpositive. So either the qualifier "bodily" should be used, or the *h* shall not be used at all with this qualifier.

Some scholars are stated to have held the view that the inference of the Nyāya school which is put forward to prove God's existence shows that the makers of the earth and of the sprouts and others are identical. Yet, whether this maker is the same as the maker of oceans and so on is not made clear and, as such, the doubt does arise that such makers are many or varied. Hence, the explanation for this inference should show that the production of these kinds is beginningless and as such gets included here, though the things that are created are many.

The view of the modern school that the world's creation is due to the eternal nature of the knowledge of its agent does not stand. Therefore something more will have to be provided in their *p*. That is, the *p*, its material cause and something beyond these have to be postulated here.

Section Twenty-Two: Causal Efficacy

Rucidatta explains that causal efficacy cannot be admitted, even if the production and destruction following it are to be admitted as a case of absence of a fourth kind (*utpādavināśaśālin*), which is neither a qualified nor an absolute absence. Some scholars hold that qualified absence consists in its determining its object as made known by the denial which presupposes the superimposition of its counterpositive. According to Rucidatta, the absence of mutual absence is not a qualified absence. An absence whose counterpositive is an absence is not distinct from its locus.

Some scholars hold that there is a common (single) causal efficacy in blowing the wind through dried grass (*tṛṇaphūtkāra*), germ and others. Yet, fire is produced only through the grass, churning the sticks and others. Rucidatta rejects this interpretation, as "causal efficacy" means only cause here.

The author of the *Nyāyalīlāvatī* is said to have held that fire of the digestive kind has unmanifested touch.

The commentary on this topic of causal efficacy is elaborate and, like the text, is based fully on the treatment of this topic in the *Nyāyakusumāñjali*. Similarly, the topic of cause is found treated under the influence of the *Nyāyakusumāñjali*. Some scholars are stated to treat a particular self-linking connector as a cause.[4]

BOOK FOUR

Section One: Language as Instrument of Knowledge

Language is taken up for treatment after comparison, as the latter depends upon an assimilative proposition (*atideśavākya*), which comes in the form of linguistic expressions.

Rucidatta offers his own definition of linguistic knowledge as that which is limited by the limitors of the results of that knowledge of reality which is knowledge of its own sense. The modern school, Rucidatta notes, holds linguistic knowledge to be produced by the knowledge of the real nature of its own sense, which is qualified by everything that is helpful in producing it. Vardhamāna is stated to have defined the language instrument in his *Pramāṇatattvabodha* as the extraordinary cause for linguistic knowledge.

After commenting upon the textual passage which introduces and rejects the views of the Buddhists and Vaiśeṣikas, Rucidatta identifies some of the objections of Vaiśeṣikas as those stated by Śrīvallabha, the author of the *Nyāyalīlāvatī.* The author proves that language is a distinct instrument of knowledge by itself. If a strong objection is raised against the validity of linguistic knowledge, then the awareness arising out of the relation between the meanings of words could as well be treated as merely mental.

Some scholars hold that the utterances of parrots, children, Vedic passages and other worldly utterances are distinct from each other. Yet all these could be treated as having the same verbal potency and thus could be classed as providing linguistic knowledge. Rucidatta does not agree with this view. What brings all these under one common head is that they have fitness to provide knowledge of the true sense of a passage. The unsublated nature of the meaning determines this fitness.

Rucidatta raised a point regarding the Vedas from the opponents' position. Why does not doubt arise regarding the meaning of the Vedas? "Meaning" cannot here mean intention, as there is no speaker for the Vedas. If "meaning" means what gives rise to understanding, it must be said that this is due to language's very nature. Direct and simple sense is available in those portions of the Vedas which are not involved in conceptual construction. In this respect, there is parity between linguistic knowledge on the one hand and inference and perception on the other. Rucidatta corrects this position by drawing attention to the unsublated nature of the sense as determining the cause which produces such awareness.

Section Two: Expectancy

Knowledge of expectancy is held to be helpful for giving rise to linguistic knowledge. Some scholars are stated to distinguish *yogyatā* from *ananubhāvakatva.* The former implies the absence of obstructions, while the latter denotes the absence of a specific kind of obstruction in the form of words.

Rucidatta shows that the knowledge of intention is the first cause for expectancy. The modern school is stated to hold that expectancy represents the stage of delay which makes the relation (between the words) known through the delay caused by another. According to Rucidatta, expectancy helps the words bring about the experience of their sense. Really speaking, expectancy helps in linguistic knowledge. Its knowledge does not help by itself. Hence expectancy should be associated with intention. Knowledge of intention is by itself an independent cause. It must therefore be admitted that expectancy makes known that sort of relation which is not produced. It does not certainly involve the absence of some other word.

Section Three: Semantic Fitness

Fitness consists in the object of the linguistic awareness remaining unsublated.

Section Four: Contiguity

Contiguity is defined as the presence of those which have the fitness to be related to each other. This is a cause by its very nature and not through awareness of it. The moderns are stated to have treated it as the presence of the meanings that are produced by particular words. There is no need to state that the words should be used in close contiguity.

Section Five: Speaker's Intention

Knowledge of intention is also a cause for giving rise to linguistic knowledge. It becomes the cause by the utterance of words without a break in some cases, by connecting the words in others and by some other means in others.

Section Seven: Sounds Destroyed, not Concealed

The nonhuman origin of Vedas, as held by the Mīmāṃsakas, is discussed. In this connection Rucidatta states that the Veda, in all the thousand recensions, conveys only the idea of *apūrva*. The passage "the Vedas produce feeling (*vedanā*)" has the word *vedanā* in the sense of *apūrva*.

Regarding the identity of a sound the author refers to certain views. Two sounds (say, two *gas*) can be cognized in two different ways. In one of them, the two sounds are inhered in at different times by the same universal of *ga*-ness (*gatva*). In that case, when two *ga* sounds known to be different are uttered at different intervals, the sound uttered later becomes recognized as the same kind of sound as that which was uttered earlier. The second way of understanding involves the two *ga*s both simultaneously being inhered in by *ga*-ness. Here also recognition occurs. But while difference is noted between them in the former case, it is not so in the latter.

Other scholars observe that the nondifference between the two sounds is noted in the individual units of sounds, and even though the relation is not direct, the resulting apprehension takes the form "this is that". If the features present in the two sounds are presented, then the resulting cognition is "this is of that form".

Yet others feel that when the nondifference between the individual sounds is apprehended by its nature in either or one or the other of them, then recognition results as "this is that."

On the contention of some scholars that the Vedas are eternal and intrinsically true and that the utterances of those who had realized the truths or contents of the Vedas are also true in themselves, Rucidatta notes that in the opinion of these scholars God need not be admitted to have anything to do with the Vedas. Some scholars hold that the Vedas can be admitted to be eternal, like a running stream, as there is no break in the Vedic tradition. Gaṅgeśa remarks that such a stream is not available. The stream is found to have become interrupted.

Some scholars express here the view that the recensions of the Vedas, which are inferred on the basis of the *smṛti* texts and of conduct, both of them having been inspired by the Vedas, are unbroken in their continuity. Hence what exists is sometimes obscured by the traditions presented in the Vedānta and other systems.

Rucidatta adds that *pralaya* which sets in periodically brings about the destruction of created products. The Vedas also then get destroyed. This is the proof for admitting the Vedas as noneternal.

In this context, Rucidatta refers to the Vedic authority for performing an invocation. That the Vedas are the authority for this is known only from inference. What is needed is to know whether the Vedas convey the knowledge that an invocation is to be performed. To that extent, this inference serves the purpose.

The *smṛtis* are valid, as what they preach is already stated in the

Vedas. The code of conduct laid down by them must be admitted to be based upon the portions of the Vedas which are composed by God and which are now lost.

In the case of *pralaya*, substances, qualities and motions get destroyed one after the other. Some scholars hold that all produced objects get destroyed at the same time. That there must be a time when *pralaya* takes place cannot be questioned, as deeds which create experiences for the self get themselves destroyed when that experience is over. Whatever deeds are left, the fruits of which are not experienced, are at *pralaya* prevented from bearing their result. This is done by that time. Gaṅgeśa claims that there is a Vedic passage in support of *pralaya*. Rucidatta notes that the Vedic passage in question (Ṛgveda X.129) means that at that time there is neither night nor day, neither sky nor earth.

Section Eight: Injunction

This section is concerned primarily with the nature of Vedic injunctions. Merit (*dharma*) is held as the best aim in life (*puruṣārtha*). Not only is it difficult to understand but it is also beyond the reach of the senses. It is therefore denoted by the words *apūrva*, *adṛṣṭa*, *atiśaya*, etc.

The nature of merit cannot be ascertained from any person, however eminent and enlightened he may be, or any source of human origin. It is to be known through the Vedas, which represent a collection of sentences and passages.

Merit is defined by Jaimini as having the trait of prompting a person to do a ritual act. Such promptings take the shape of passages with their predicate in the optative mood. No person, including God, is held to have the direct grasp of merit. So the Vedas, which are not treated as of human origin and are held as valid in themselves, are considered as containing the directions for undertaking those means which are necessary to achieve merit. The Vedic passages are treated as containing directions, which are technically called "injunctions" (*vidhi*), conveyed through sentences whose predicates take the optative mood.

The Nyāya, Mīmāṃsā, Vedānta and Grammarian systems are found to have evolved their own concept of an injunction. Their concepts differ mostly from each other, not only from one system to another, but also among the exponents of the same system at different periods. The Nyāya system in particular is justified in developing the treatment of injunction under the heading of language.

Quite often, the Nyāya system is opposed to the Mīmāṃsā system in several respects, and this section in particular refers to the concepts of both the Prābhākara and Kumārilabhaṭṭa schools of Mīmāṃsā, noting down minute aspects of such views.

The Prābhākara school holds that the optative mood (*liñ*) conveys the sense of prescription (*niyoga*). That is, it enjoins action that should be undertaken categorically. It shall not be questioned. It is also called *kārya* and *apūrva*.

There is difference of opinion among the followers of Kumārila Bhaṭṭa. Maṇḍana Miśra held that the optative mood conveys the means of accomplishing what is desired. A section of thinkers in the Bhaṭṭa school take it to mean action or deed, which the sense of the particular roots convey when used in the optative mood. Yet, another section of the same school considers that the optative mood means denotative power of the primary kind (*abhidhā*), which makes its meaning clear. Pārthasārathi Miśra held that the optative conveys the sense of the means of achieving what is desired in its aspect of giving rise to activity for that purpose. Bhaṭṭa Someśvara, Khaṇḍadeva and others held that the optative denotes a specific merit which is not of thc worldly kind and is called inciter of activity (*pravartana*), and which is distinct from the means which achieves the desired end.

The modern Nyāya school takes it that the optative conveys three senses: (1) the means of achieving the desired end, (2) that which does not give rise to a powerful evil (or undesirable result) and (3) that which is to be effected through volition. The ancient school holds that there is only one meaning of the optative.

Taraṇi Miśra, the author of the *Ratnakośa*, held that the optative mood conveys only the sense of getting achieved through volition. Udayana, however, held that the optative conveys the intention of the speaker.

While commenting upon the text on the view of the Bhaṭṭa school, Rucidatta makes clear the roles played by *śabda* and *artha bhāvanā*. The early school held cessation from activity as the absence of activity. That is, the definition is negative. Rucidatta notes that Gaṅgeśa follows the ancient school in this respect.

Gaṅgeśa notes that the view of Udayana is not the same as maintained in the tradition of the Nyāya school. According to Udayana, what incites a person to the undertaking of a rite is his getting the knowledge of the means to achieve the desired object, and the optative conveys the sense of a credible person (*āpta*). So, that activity which is to be carried out by volition must also be taken as accomplishing the desired object without having any trace of a powerful undesirable factor. This is inferred.

Udayana's view of injunction differs from that of the Nyāya traditionalists. Rucidatta seeks to prove that the two views are not opposed to each other. The tradition means that though the optative is held to convey a sense which does not lead to an undesirable end, it is necessary to hold that this will not apply to all cases. Where it applies it must be a specific case by itself. In that case, it will be difficult to have a uniform definition of "injunction" which could apply to all cases. Besides, in cases like taking food mixed with poison, there is no desire to be happy, and as such it cannot illustrate that an injunction conveys the sense of a means for achieving what is desired. Again, an excess of hatred and of liking must be admitted to lead to activity and cessation from activity respectively, even though their objects may remain the same. This must be understood as admissible with reference to different agents and different times. An awareness about an object which arouses an excess of hatred prevents activity. Awareness of its absence does not prevent activity. When understood in this sense, there is no difficulty in treating all the three senses as having uniform applicability as the definition of "injunction". When activity is said to be prevented, the conditions for refraining from activity should be taken to operate. This is not directly opposed to the production of an awareness which in turn creates the awareness regarding activity. It is only an awareness which is not opposed to the creating awareness that could oppose it. It is for this reason the knowledge that an *h* has no counter *h* is not treated as an *h* giving rise to inferential awareness.

"Injunction" must therefore be taken to mean that an awareness about an object where it has applicability will incite one to act. This does not change with reference to time or agent. Hence the injunction enjoining the *śyenayāga* is held to be capable of inciting to activity. This also admits of one's having awareness of the means of achieving an object which arouses excess of desire. Hence excessive liking and excessive hatred lead to activity and cessation from activity respectively. In this context, the injunction "one shall not eat *kalañja*" must be examined. Really speaking, being the means to a desired end and being a thing one wants to accomplish are not opposed to the prohibitory nature of this injunction. Yet activity and cessation from activity regarding the same object could be explained on grounds of differences among the agents and at different times. So the instance cited above may give rise to activity in some cases. The negative particle *na* in the injunction may be taken to have the *paryudāsa* significance as in *asura*, *avidyā* and others, and as such may be taken to mean that it achieves an undesirable thing opposed (to the agent). In cases like "one who desires heaven should sacrifice", the undertaking of a sacrifice is enjoined for one who likes to go to heaven, or the sacrifice may be taken to achieve the desire. Here the sentence expressing the injunction suppresses sense of possession on the part of the agent. Similarly, an explanation could be given to passages which prohibit certain undertakings. Here secondary denotation has no scope. It can be said that prohibition has no propriety, and so personal intention (*abhiprāya*) shall be taken to be the sense of an injunction. It is in this sense that Udayana's definition of "injunction" as given in *Nyāyakusumāñjali* v.15 is justified and is not opposed to the traditional view.

Rucidatta notes that each of the three senses of "injunction" are conveyed through three verbal potencies, one for each. He rejects the view of the modern school which holds that the passage of an injunction has only one significative potency. Rucidatta illustrates several kinds of injunctions.

Section Eleven: *Apūrva*

After an injunction is proved to be the means of achieving the desired object, what that desired object is is now discussed. The Mīmāṃsā school takes this to be *apūrva*, a word which means literally that which is brought into existence afresh, that is, which did not exist before. If this is not the meaning, there would be no attempt to follow the injunction.

The author discusses the question of the sin of omission in its relation to obligatory and other rites. He expresses his view to the effect that by not performing what is ordained one commits the sin of omission. This principle of becoming a sinner does not apply to a person who does not do a rite for which he is merely qualified.

In this context, the author explains the stand taken by the Prābhākaras in treating the meaning of the optative as justifying the actual performance of an act, which is different from the act itself, and which deserves to be the means of getting heaven. This is rejected by Rucidatta.

Section Twelve: Verbal Potency (II)

An objection is raised by the Prābhākaras against the Nyāya theory of injunction. An injunction, according to them, has the power to convey a sense only when it has relevance to the performance of a rite enjoined by the Vedas. Supplementary passages cannot therefore be authentic, as they deal only with matters that are already established.

This is rejected by Rucidatta on the ground that an injunction conveys only the awareness that the particular rite is to be done and not the awareness that it is related to what is to be done. The potency of the words lends support only to the Nyāya concept. Likewise, *apūrva* cannot be admitted as inciting a person to acquire the means which would accomplish his wish. Thus it is clear that the optative denotes the means of getting what one desires. Words, too, convey the sense of an object having definite arrangement of parts, the individual and the universal which inheres in it. The Mīmāṃsakas hold that a word denotes the universal only, and the individual becomes available through inference or presumption.

Gaṅgeśa refers to the view of Śrīkara, a Mīmāṃsaka who maintained that the universal and the individual function only through action. The individual serves the purpose by being the seat for the verbal potency of the word and the universal as determining it. Thus the word gives rise to the experience of the universal from its verbal potency. The individual is merely the material for the use of the word. Rucidatta applies Śrīkara's concept and explains this passage.

The derivative etymologo-conventional method of denotation is illustrated by the instance of *paṅkaja.* This kind of meaning has to be admitted to explain the memory of the lotus. The lotus that is thus remembered is experienced through the parts of the word *paṅkaja* as being the agent for being produced from mud. Therefore neither the apprehension nor usage of this word rise with reference to a lily. It cannot be urged that the word *paṅkaja*, which denotes the lotus by convention, may be taken to denote a lily by secondary usage. Secondary usage is invoked only when the cognition rising from derivative significance stands obstructed. There is no problem here in taking the intention of the speaker to refer to the lotus and not to the lily. The modern school, however, holds that the word *paṅkaja* can give rise to awareness of a lily only when the lotus which is remembered is found to be inappropriate in its syntactical relation. Secondary meaning then applies.

Rucidatta discusses the question of God's convention that a particular word should convey a particular sense. Does this apply to Apabhraṃśa words too? It is contended that Apabhraṃśa is the name of a language that is impure or which has fallen from its perfect state. Yet, such expressions convey sense. As there is no reason to deny it, there is no harm in admitting God's wish as the basis for the convention that a word conveys a sense. Some scholars do not admit this argument. That a particular word conveys a particular sense cannot apply to the expressions of Apabhraṃśa, as those expressions are not uttered by God. Rucidatta observes that to be uttered does not mean that sounds are made audible by issuing from the bodily places of articulation. It may be taken to have been produced by God. Verbal potency really consists in the relation between a word and its meaning, which takes the form of a desire resembling that.

Though desire may be proved to be available in such cases, that relation cannot be shown to exist in the Apabhraṃśa expressions.

Section Twelve: Compounds

While commenting upon Gaṅgeśa's treatment of compounds of the attributive kind, such as *citragu*, *lambakarṇa* and others, the author identifies the views which Gaṅgeśa refers to as those held by the traditionalists, grammarians and others. Rucidatta justifies the use of the plural number in words like *apas*, *dārāḥ*, etc., and cites the view of Vardhamāna in support of his interpretation.

Section Thirteen: Verbal Suffixes

Some scholars seem to hold the view that usages like "a chariot moves" are correct, and do not involve secondary usage of the case-suffixes, so do not involve secondary meaning. Rucidatta remarks that the rule must be taken to apply to cases where the sense conveyed is contradicted. In the present case what is meant is that a person goes by (seated in) the chariot. Since there is contradiction of the use of the word "chariot" meaning a person, secondary meaning will have to be admitted here. In cases like *puruṣavyāghra*, secondary meaning is assured.

MAKARANDA on Vardhamāna's NYĀYAKUSUMĀÑJALIPRAKĀŚA

Summary by V. Varadachari

"E" references are to the edition by Padmaprasada Upadhyaya and Dundhiraja Sastri (B2701; RB3974), Kashi Sanskrit Series 30, 1956.

I.3. 4-5 (E33) While dealing with the concept of agency, Rucidatta says that awareness produces effects in a general way through *adṛṣṭa*, whereas desire produces effort in specific cases.

"The Upaniṣadists worship him as he whose nature is pure consciousness...." Rucidatta notes that the sense of the word "consciousness" (*buddhi*), viz., self-luminous knowledge, is acceptable to both the Vedāntins, that is, both to the Tridaṇḍins and Ekadaṇḍins. Some scholars say that what is common to both Vedāntas is that *buddhi* and *ātman* are conceived as one awareness, while other scholars say that it is sense of ego (*ahaṃkāra*).

I.82-83. 108-110 (E163) Vardhamāna defines cause as that which invariably precedes the effect provided it is not dispensable (*anyathāsiddhi*). Rucidatta notes an objection. Does the "invariability" (*niyatatva*) refer to spatial or temporal invariability? A donkey may be regularly present nearby prior to the production of a pot or a cloth, and yet be a dispensable cause, so it is not spatial invariability that is in question. But *adṛṣṭa*, etc., are not invariably connected directly with the place where their effects are to be produced, so that there is no particular time that can be specified during which *adṛṣṭa* has to be present so that the effect will occur.

Answer: Rucidatta clarifies the matter by limiting "invariability" to a necessary spatial relationship which is direct (*sākṣāt*), sequential (*paramparasādhāraṇa*) or belonging to the same genus as the effect (*ekajātīya*). Thus, since the donkey is not regularly related to the pot by any of these specific kinds of relationship, it is not a cause.

I.82-83 (E140) With respect to the "acquired causal efficacy" (*ādheyaśakti*) Rucidatta adds this comment. When grains are sprinkled with water (in the ancestral rites) the grains are referred to subsequently as having become "well-formed" (*saṃskṛta*) or as having received impressions or "traces" (*saṃskāra*). Similarly, a boy after having been invested with the sacred thread is said to have received impressions. His body gets them. But the relation between the impressions and the grains, or the impressions and body, is only a sef-linking connector.

145-158 (E189-190) Rucidatta offers an interesting account of the presence of universals in individuals. A problem is posed by the difficulty of finding some feature common to all the individuals comprised within the class which the universal is claimed to pick out. The arrangement of the composite parts may not be uniform in such a class—e.g., not all jars are made of parts arranged in the same way. Because of this, some scholars are reported as having held the view that potness is present only in clay pots; when potness is said to be present in golden pots and pots made of other materials, they say the reference is metaphorical. This is supported by pointing out that when one asks for a pot to be brought the natural response is to bring a clay pot, and only to bring a golden pot if it is specifically asked for. Similarly, when the words "cow made of flour" are used, the word "cow" is used there in a secondary sense, since the cow made of flour has a form which is similar to that of a real cow.

BOOK TWO

5-33 (E220) Udayana is arguing that to trace the causes of validity and invalidity respectively to the presence of merits and demerits in the knowers should lead one to admit the extrinsic-truth-and-falsity thesis of the Nyāya. Rucidatta remarks that there may be cases where we cannot discern any special meritorious feature nor any fault in the knower; in such a case we shall have to treat *absence of merit* as a fault. In the case of the utterances of a parrot this does not apply. For example, inferential awareness that results from consideration may be erroneous, since it may become sublated. It is to be treated as valid until it is sublated. Then the correct awareness that is not sublated becomes the merit, and the erroneousness the fault. In the case of linguistic awareness incorrect understanding of the meaning of a passage is a fault, and correct understanding the merit. Again, erroneous understanding of fitness is a fault, and correct understanding is merit.

(E228) The Nyāya school denies that an instrument of knowledge is intrinsically true either with respect to its arisal or to awareness of it. Yet, Rucidatta notes, sometimes a fault may arouse doubt about truth, a doubt grasped by the internal organ and which is not sublated. Since it thus has fitness to be grasped by the internal organ, it will have as its intrinsic nature both a fault and its absence. For instance, when a shell is grasped as silver the knower is not aware of his having an erroneous awareness, and silverness, which is not present there, becomes fit to be grasped by the visual organ; here both the fault and its absence are present, and so awareness of silverness arises.

II.86-98 (E279) Efficacy (*śakti*) which is ineffective is called *kubjaśakti*. Rucidatta says that according to one set of scholars this name is given to that power which does not function to produce verbal awareness (*śābdabodha*). According to others it is the cause of verbal awarenesses by nature, but we are not aware of its being so.

BOOK THREE

9 (E344) Objection: Udayana declares that doubt is ended by *tarka*. Now, the awareness that a particular means will produce a desired result gives rise to desire to produce that result. Doubt, however, which is not positive in nature, cannot produce a desire to know. How can *tarka* be said to end a doubt, since doubt produces a desire to know?

Answer: No, doubt can produce a desire to know, and *tarka* can end doubt as well as the desire to know. It can remove the desire to know by showing that inquiry will not lead to the desired result. It may remove doubt in the following sort of case: where there is doubt caused by equally likely alternatives, and there is no awareness of a specific feature which would resolve it, then *tarka* may become relevant to resolve the issue.[5]

11. (E380-382) Udayana argues that the statement "a *gavaya* is

like a cow'' does not require appeal to secondary meaning—it means what it says.

Objection: The statement ''a *gavaya* is like a cow'' cannot mean that a *gavaya* is a cow, so it must refer to some animal which is like a cow. Therefore, the word ''*gosadṛśa*'', (''like a cow'') must mean, not any animal having likeness to a cow, but an animal which is called ''*gavaya*'' through secondary usage.

Rucidatta: The whole statement ''*gavaya* is like a cow'' cannot have secondary meaning—that is a feature of single words. It may be that the single word ''*gosadṛśa*'' together with the other words would justify the application of secondary meaning. Now, the Nyāya view is that secondary meaning is not to be appealed to when the words in the sentence yield a straightforward sense construed together in their primary meanings. Where some lack of fitness occurs these appeal to secondary meaning is appropriate. Rucidatta notes that Vardhamāna cites his father's (Gaṅgeśa's) view on secondary meaning. He remarks that even if one accepts this view on the nature of secondary meaning, still it cannot be proved that in this particular case the words in the sentence are construed together in their primary meanings to yield a straightforward sense: indeed, since ''like a cow'' primarily applies to any animal similar to a cow it seems to him that secondary meaning is appropriate here. Therefore Rucidatta concludes that the reason why Vardhamāna cites Gaṅgeśa's dictum on secondary meaning must be to set aside the view of opponents that impropriety of intent (*tātparyānupapatti*) can form the basis for an appeal to secondary usage.

BOOK FIVE

1 (E482) Vardhamāna notes that when ''the universe'', i.e., earth, etc., are stated to be effects, they are to be understood as effects produced by a volition which relates to the inherence cause of a product not influenced by *adṛṣṭa*. Rucidatta adds that the word *adṛṣṭa* is used here to set aside overextension of the definition to the body of Kālī, whose penances give rise to the white color of her body, or to the nourishment of their bodies gained by people who bathe at Prayāga, etc.

V.16 (E570) Udayana mentions results gotten by worshipping God: they are ''*sālokya*, *sāyujya*, etc.'' Vardhamāna interprets these as omniscience and attainment of the *siddhis*. Rucidatta remarks that ''*sāyujya*'' cannot here mean contact. One's body is always in contact with God and so contact is not brought about by worshipping God. There is no contact between an individual self and God.[6]

VṚTTI on Vardhamāna's DRAVYAKIRAṆĀVALĪPRAKĀŚA

Summary by V. Varadachari

"E" references are to the edition by S.C. Sarvabhauma, continued by N.C. Vedantatirtha (B2706; RB3997), Bibliotheca India 200, 1911-12, 1956.

(E6) Rucidatta does not approve of Vardhamāna's alternative explanation of the use of the perfect as due to inadvertence.

(E22) A "disciplined person" is explained to be one who is not deluded.

Final Release

(E77) Because understanding of the categories (*tattvajñāna*) is authoritatively recognized as the means to liberation, it must also be admitted that it can destroy the residues of past *karma* and provide for taking on several bodies at the same time. To suppose these all to be results effected by understanding of the categories might appear overly complex, but since it is supported by authority the heaviness is not defective.

(E80-81) Only understanding of the categories leads to liberation (not *dharma*). It leads to the destruction of *karma* through experiences had in several bodies, since it is stated that *karma* that is not experienced is not destroyed. This statement does not contradict another authoritative statement that the fire of knowledge destroys all *karma*, since the correct view is that whatever *karma* that is not destroyed by ordinary experiences is destroyed by understanding of the categories.

Darkness

(E85-114) Rucidatta examines the views of the other schools on this topic in detail. Nyāya-Vaiśeṣika takes darkness to be the absence of light. Apprehension of darkness only takes place through apprehending night time when there is no light. But to know what night is one must know what day or light is.

Universals

(E119) An imposed property is, unlike a universal, not related to another imposed property, since each imposed propery is independent of any other.

(E120) Yogis can have perceptual awareness of an object without that object's being present—e.g., of objects that have ceased to exist.

Color Universals and Color Particulars

(E206-207) Variegated taste cannot be admitted because of the perceptual nonapprehension of e.g., the myrobalan. Variegated touch, however, may be admitted, since the sense of touch does apprehend an object with various tactile properties. Manifested touch is required to account for the rise of the perceptual awareness of the substance that has it. There is nothing objectionable in recognizing this touch to be variegated.

Water

(E274) On Udayana's speaking of the use of "*taila*" to speak of cohesion as "conventional", he means that the primary meaning is to be attached to the oil extracted from mustard; in others, it has secondary meaning.

45. RATNĀKARA or VIṢṆUDĀSA VIDYĀVĀCASPATI

This Naiyāyika was the younger brother of 33. Vāsudeva Sārvabhauma, referred to by his son Vidyānivāsa Bhaṭṭācārya. Gopinath Kaviraj tells us he was a court pandit of the King of Gauḍa and was later converted to Caitanya's Vaiṣṇavism as his brother was. His commentary on the *Tattvacintāmaṇi* combined with Jayadeva's *Āloka* is preserved in manuscript. Gopinath Kaviraj presumes that a MS. of the commentary on *Śabdakhaṇḍa* by Vidyāvācaspati is preserved in the Sarasvati Bhavana Library at Banaras.

46. PURUṢOTTAMA BHAṬṬĀCĀRYA

Gaurinath Sastri reports that Raghunātha Vidyālaṃkāra identifies this author as the *kaścit* ("some say") of *Dīdhiti*'s "taṃ nirasyati tac ce'ty api kaścit".[1] We thus date him around 1510, slightly ahead of Raghunātha Śiromaṇi.

47. JANEŚVARA (or JALEŚVARA) VĀHINĪPATI

Janeśvara was Vāsudeva Sārvabhauma's son, according to Umesh Mishra[1] and *New Catalogus Catalogorum*, as well as a pupil of Vāsudeva's. Gopinath Kaviraj favors instead the traditional ascriptions to him of being the brother of Vāsudeva. Both Umesh Mishra and Gopinath Kaviraj take Vāhinīpati to be a Bengali—the first to comment on Jayadeva's *Āloka*. The commentary, available in manuscript form, is titled *Uddyota*. Vāhinīpati may be dated around 1510.

48. BHAIRAVENDRA

This writer's *Śiśubodhinī* on Śivāditya's *Saptapadārthī* is partly available in printed form. He must have flourished about the beginning of the 16th century.

49. GADĀDHARA MIŚRA

According to V. Krishnamacharya Gadādhara, to be dated around 1510, wrote a *Prakāṣa* on the *Nyāyabhūṣaṇa*. The work exists in manuscript.

50. RAGHUNĀTHA ŚIROMAṆI

After Gaṅgeśa himself Raghunātha Śiromaṇi is the arch Navyanaiyāyika. Reading Raghunātha's works provides an experience both exhilarating and exasperating. Raghunātha's writings, especially the *Dīdhiti* on Gaṅgeśa's *Tattvacintāmaṇi*, constitute the quintessential source for the "new" Navyanyāya. The literature of Navyanyāya after Raghunātha is dominated by commentaries on his *Dīdhitis*; it is a literature that is vast and constitutes the most difficult material to read in all of Indian philosophy. Our summaries (below) of this material can hardly do justice to its complexity—rather than summary, the material requires expansion, with further commentaries on it, in order that its delicate distinctions be properly grasped. Our summaries inevitably do an injustice to Raghunātha's style, and can hardly begin to capture the elegance of his comments.

Raghunātha's birthplace is disputed: Umesh Mishra, Gopinath Kaviraj and others report the tradition that he came from Sylhet—modern Assam. Ingalls disagrees, citing Phanibhusana's introduction to his (Bengali) *Nyāyaparicaya.*[1] The traditional stories place him in a family of Maithila Brahmins who migrated to Assam in the seventh century. Raghunātha's father, the story goes, died early, and his mother, unable to support her young son, came to Navadvīpa and found work in Vāsudeva's *ṭol.* Raghunātha grew to study first with Vāsudeva[2] and later went to Mithilā to study under Jayadeva.[3]

Many stories are traditionally told about Raghunātha's brashness. A few of them are recounted by Ingalls. He comes over as a very proud man as well as quick. He was apparently blind in one eye,[4] which undoubtedly added to his powerful impression. Tradition has it that he committed the whole of the *Tattvacintāmaṇi* to memory. He was in the thick of every issue surrounding Gaṅgeśa's work, and such issues were rife in his time. "He refuted Jayadeva's view almost at every step, but showed sympathy and tolerance for Yajñapati's views".[5] Ingalls rates him "a brilliant but disrespectful pupil in youth, and in his maturity a great scholar, perhaps overly proud''.[6]

After studying in Mithilā Raghunātha returned to Navadvīpa and started his own school. Many famous scholars "flocked to Raghunātha's schools"[7]. He lived a long and productive life. Ingalls writes "If we assign his death to A.D. 1550 we shall probably not be more than 20 years wrong''.[8]

Raghunātha's works, almost without exception, are known as *Dīdhiti*. The *Dīdhiti* on the *Tattvacintāmaṇi* is his great triumph. Apparently it covered all four books, though the *śabda* portion is unavailable. It is the quintessential Navyanyāya work.

Besides this *magnum opus* Raghunātha wrote *Dīdhitis* on many of the major Nyāya and Vaiśeṣika works. Most of these are available in print, several in translation. We summarize below those that are available in print. The three that have so far not been printed are (1) *Dīdhiti* on the *Nyāyakusumāñjali* of Udayana, (2) *Dīdhiti* on Vardhamāna's *Nyāyalīlāvatīprakāśa*, and (3) a *Vibhūti* on Vallabha's *Nyāyalīlāvatī* itself. In print, and summarized below, are (4) *Dīdhiti* on Udayana's *Ātmatattvaviveka*, (5) *Dīdhiti* on Vardhamāna's *Kiraṇāvalīprakāśa*, and (6) *Dīdhiti* on the *Tattvacintamaṇi*, plus the independent works, each of them brief but fiercely complex in its implications, (7) *Padārthatattvanirūpaṇa*, (8) *Ākhyātavāda* and (9) *Nañvāda*.

DĪDHITI on Udayana's ĀTMATATTVAVIVEKA
Summary by V. Varadachari

"E" references are to the edition by V.P. Dvivedin and L.S. Dravid (B2676; RB3932), Bibliotheca Indica 170, 1907-39.[9]

(E684-685) Experience of the world shows that the object presented in a judgment should be different from it. The Buddhist attitude towards this object is discussed. The relation between an awareness and its content is discussed in detail. Being a content (*viṣayatā*), being a chief qualifier (*prakāratā*), being a counterpositive (*pratiyogitva*) and other factors which enter into the discussion on this matter get a clear treatment. *Viṣayatā* is treated as a distinct category with *prakāratā* and others forming its shades. Regarding the nonmention of this in the metaphysical treatment of the categories in the system as such, the commentator writes that the references made to the categories as seven in number is in conformity with the doctrine of categories held in the Vaiśeṣika school. Some scholars are stated to maintain *viṣayatva* and *viṣayitva* as distinct categories.

(E697) The second illustration is noticed in the treatment of the Buddhist doctrine that an object is presented together with its qualifiers in an awareness and so are not different from each other.

Udayana dismisses this on the ground that this assumption cannot explain why certain objects appear distinct and also indistinct at times. The commentator notes that nonpropositional awareness can create bare sensation of objects but cannot determine the nature of the objects. Besides, the awareness of the one qualifier may give rise to the propositional awareness of another qualifier, since there is no restriction based on the individuality of the qualifier to be presented in an awareness. The author explains the Buddhistic terms *adhipatipratyaya* and *ālambanapratyaya.*

(E695-697) While discussing how an awareness is made out to be true, the commentator gives a lucid exposition of views held by the Bhāṭṭas, Prābhākaras and Murāri Miśra.

(E689) On the question of variegated color, getting admitted as the seventh color, the commentator notes three views. One of them refers to this color as created by the instrumental cause in the form of a color of quite a different species present in the component parts. According to the second view, this color is produced by the color of the component parts. The third view explains the awareness of variegated as arising from the aggregate of several colors belonging to different species.

(E651) The gross size of objects establishes that those objects are enduring. Udayana remarks that this is proved on the basis of *adhikaraṇasiddhānta.* The author explains this by citing the relevant passages from *Nyāyasūtra*, *Bhāṣya*, *Vārttika* and *Tātparyaṭīkā.* He refers to a different concept of *adhikaraṇasiddhānta* which is held by some scholars. It is held to be got on the strength of *pakṣadharmatā.* This concept is referred to in the commentaries of Śaṃkara Miśra and Bhagīratha.

(E688) After noting the meanings of *svarūpa* and *vaidharmya* as held by other scholars, the author states that absolute absence could be admitted to be available for another absolute absence. Absence of absence is an independent absence. Prior and posterior absences are to be admitted for posterior and prior absences respectively. Some scholars are stated to hold that absences differ from each other on account of attributing contradictory features to them, as it is done in the case of positive objects. The view of some scholars on the nature of absenceness is noted. Those scholars hold that absenceness, in each one of the four kinds of absence, is an undivided condition (*akhaṇḍopādhi*).

(E875) While commenting on the passage of text which states that the misery of the world created by God does not indicate the absence of compassion in Him, the author interprets the word *kāruṇya* as the desire to remove others' distress or to bring about happiness for them. The former sense is to be admitted. A man in distress will not be satisfied if his misery is got rid of, and would hope for obtaining happiness. The second explanation should have been given with this end in view. Further, it is said here that *kāruṇya* should not be taken as the desire not to give rise to distress for others. When the materials are available to give rise to an effect, the production of that effect cannot be prevented. Hence there cannot be a desire not to produce this particular effect.

(E880-881) Raghunātha shows that God cannot be admitted to have atoms for his body, as it would amount to admitting countless bodies for God. It would be proper to treat eternal knowledge as His body.

(E925-933) While commenting on the textual passage which rejects the view that eternal happiness characterizes the state of liberation, Udayana discusses what exactly is the cause of liberation. He takes up a serious discussion on the interpretation offered by some scholars who cite passages from the Upaniṣads to show that knowledge of God is not essential for obtaining final liberation. It is said by them that the impressions of false awarenesses which a self is suffering from can be destroyed by the direct perception of one's own self, and so this is the cause for liberation and not the knowledge of God. Udayana rejects this position. Neither by knowledge of the categories nor by undergoing the results of past deeds can liberation be acquired. That traces get destroyed, when merit and demerit no longer are produced, may be conceded, but this will not lead to liberation. That knowledge of the self is essential is borne out by the passage in the *Bṛhadāraṇyaka Upaniṣad* 2.4.5. Udayana then offers interesting comments on some passages like *Chāndogya* 6.1.3, which he says convey the sense that the self would become omniscient by directly perceiving itself. *Taittirīya Upaniṣad* 3.1.1 and *Chāndogya* 6.8.7 show that reflection upon the self that it is nondifferent from God would lead to liberation. Udayana makes it clear that according to Vedānta the self and God are nondifferent and knowledge of this is knowledge of the truth, but that according to the Nyāya system reflection on nondifference between self and God, though they are different from each other, is the cause of liberation. He thus reveals his Advaitic leanings. Raghunātha demonstrates with a series of arguments that destruction of frustrations is the aim of life. This is justified by interpreting the *Muṇḍaka Upaniṣad* 2.2.8 to mean that knowledge of the self leads to the destruction of sins. Liberation is not obtainable through experiencing the results of the deeds leading to their extinction. Udayana then discusses what kind of sins would be destroyed by the prescribed courses stated in the Upaniṣads. The opinions of scholars are noted down and explained in this connection.[10]

DĪDHITI on Vardhamāna's GUṆAKIRAṆĀVALĪPRAKĀŚA
Summary by Nani Lal Sen and V. Varadachari

"E" references are to the edition by Badrinatha Sastri (B3532; RB5561), Princess of Wales Saraswati Bhavana Texts 38, 1932.

Introductory Section: (E1) Causality cannot be the proper explanation of the appositeness of discussing qualities after substances, since a discourse on a property may perfectly well precede that on its possessor. So Vardhamāna's alternative explanation in terms of appropriate time is meant as a better alternative. And that the property-possessor should be discussed first is quite apposite, since the self, knowledge of which leads to liberation, is a substance.

(E2) The reason for the specification of "qualityness" is so that color, etc. can figure in inferences as delimited by the limitor of causeness, viz., qualitynessness.

Vardhamāna's inferences must be supplemented by two qualifications to read as follows: Qualityness is not a proper universal, because being inherent in the self and not occurring in the sense-organs only it is not perceived to belong to several things, unlike cowness. The qualifications are required so that there will be no deviation in the case of selfness and internal-organ-ness.

(E2-3) Colorness, etc. are *akhaṇḍa* imposed properties, not universals, as also qualityness, sweetness, contactness, inherenceness, etc.

(E4-7) Udayana: "A motion produces two opposite results—contact and disjunction of bodies." Vardhamāna adds: "*directly* produces". Raghunātha: The specification of "directly" is to avoid overextension, and it means "nondependence on any positive entity born at the moment that is the locus of destruction of the moment that is the locus of the motion." So consider the following case: Contact between a twig and the fingers caused by the motion of the fingers is a "direct" cause of contact between the hand and the twig as well as of the disjunction between the twig and the fingers effected by the twig's motion simultaneous with the first contact. To avoid this, "directly" is to be defined as "kindredness of the cause of contact which is dependent on disjunction effected by itself (the cause) without dependence on what is produced after it." Then the disjunction of the forward part of the hand, which helps effect contact of the hand with the tree caused by contact of fingers with the tree, is not the effect of that cause. Hence there is no overextension here. In the ultimate analysis "direct causation" resolves itself into a noninherence-cause-ness which is independent of any other noninherence cause. So, it can be defined as "the limitorness of the noninherence-cause-ness of both contact and disjunction", or as "the kindredness of the noninherence cause of the disjunction that occasions contact."

When the whole is in motion, the parts cannot be at rest. So according to the ancient Vaiśeṣikas, with the onset of motion in the whole all the parts are necessarily activated. Others say, to the contrary, that the motion in the whole is regulated by the motion of the parts, and Praśastapāda confirms this by saying (in his section on disjunction) that the motion first starts iṇ fibre (*aṃśu*), then in the thread (*tantu*). Both these views are based on wide experience. If the dyad is destroyed, or if the motion in the potsherd, etc, is blocked, there may be no motion in the pot, etc. But one cannot rule out the production of motion in a jar, etc. through the collection of conditions sufficient for it. This is the view of the Naiyāyikas. In all three views the motion of the whole may die out before it comes into contact, for the locus of the motion may be destroyed just at the moment of posterior contact through the motion of the parts generated at the same time. On the latter two views (of Praśastapāda and the Naiyāyikas) the motion generated in the whole just at the time of the emergence of the causes of its destruction ceases without producing any disjunction or contact—or, if the motion has been produced in the preceding moment, it ceases after contact occurs. There is no bar to production of motion in a dying inherence cause. This has also been asserted by Praśastapāda while speaking of the destruction of twoness, farness, etc. occasioned by the destruction of their loci.

Here Raghunātha sets forth a demonstration that a motion does not necessarily last for four moments. For if (as some maintain) the word "contact" and "disjunction" here designate specific kinds, then the definitions of motion given above will read as follows: "Motion is the limitorness of the noninherence-causeness of contact or disjunction that is not produced by an earlier contact or disjunction respectively", and that shows how a motion may last for two or three moments. And a motion that produces a disjunction that blocks arising (*ārambhaka*) contact lasts for five moments.

To take a detailed example: The body, while moving, loses its prior contact and at the same time a twig moves. The motion in the twig produces disjunction between the twig and *ākāśa*, while the contact of the body with the twig is produced through the motion of the body. Disjunction of the body from the twig cannot occur at that moment, for that moment is the one when they are in contact. On the other hand, through the disjunction of twig from *ākāśa* their contact no longer exists. And through the motion of the twig disjunction between twig and body is produced. That a motion may without harm depend on a posterior contact has already been shown.

And so the contact between twig and body ceases. At that moment the twig cannot have any posterior contact, since that is obstructed through its contact with the front of the body. Otherwise one must assume the simultaneous occurrence of an atom in the front and rear portions of space. The disjunction of twig from body cannot destroy this obstructing contact since it does not occur in the locus of that contact. Otherwise, something *x* which is disjoined through the motion of some other thing *y* will be capable, even without moving, of destroying contact with bits of *ākāśa*, etc. So at the next moment the twig has posterior contact, and finally the motion ceases. This is a case where a motion lasts five moments. (Raghunātha goes on to demonstrate how it might last for six moments in a different case.)

(E7-9) Vardhamāna says: Directness (*anapekṣatva*) is defined as not producing a contact depending on a positive entity generated a moment following the moment of its origin.

Raghunātha: If Vardhamāna had not specified "following the moment of its origin" the definition would have overextended to substance, since a substance does not produce a contact depending on a positive entity generated at the moment of its (the substance's) destruction.

Vardhamāna: If color, etc. be taken as the noninherence cause it would have a universal in common with motions.

Raghunātha: Because a motion, by generating a trace, is a noninherence cause.

Vardhamāna: The causeness in color, etc. is limited by the universal qualityness.

Raghunātha: This is debatable. An effect that inheres in many things is regulated by a cause which is many. So, if we assume a limitor of such a causeness, it turns out to be a universal unless there is an obstruction. But there is such an obstruction, since there is no effect whose effectness can determine causeness that has qualityness as the universal delimiting it. If despite this one postulates a universal to limit that causeness anyway, an infinite number of such universals may have to be postulated.

Objection: Qualityness is a universal that limits what is denoted by the word "quality".

Answer: No. A word denotes a thing as having certain properties, which presupposes the occurrence of those properties there. But here qualityness is not denoted nor is it known as qualifying anything. If we still go on assuming a universal in situations of this sort there will be no end to it.

For example, moonness can be adduced as the limitor of denotingness of "*hari*", etc., and then the moon will not be made known by the word "moon". Thus, too, color will not be made known through the word "color", etc. Furthermore, a word like "*guṇa*" means other things besides quality, and is not normally used to apply to something like farness (*paratva*), etc. Its use in this context to mean quality is a metaphysician's (*tāntrika*) convention (*paribhāṣa*), but that does not justify assuming a universal qualityness.

The notion of "instrumental cause" intended here, viz., a kind of cause that is different from the inherence or noninherence causes, is a distinct notion from that utilized earlier, which was a notion of a cause that has the same locus with the absences of each of the other two kinds of cause. For the notion as it is used here applies to something not in the same locus with either of the two absences.

(E9-10) If a thing is a substance it cannot be a quality; otherwise there will be crossconnection, says Vardhamāna. That is, if substanceness is pervaded by qualityness it would be a *vibhājakopādhi* of quality like colorness, etc. If on the other hand qualityness be pervaded by substanceness, qualityness would be a *vibhājakopādhi* of substance like earthness, etc. Finally if the two are mutually exclusive, crossconnection certainly occurs.

"...if noneternal qualities were to occur in all qualities everywhere then liberation would not occur." There would be a series of qualities standing in the relation of locus and located. And though one destroyed a locus-quality its located-quality might still exist. In any case, *adṛṣṭa*, which is such a located-quality, may still exist.

"If on the contrary qualities be supposed to be eternal, they will be universals, not qualities." The supposedly "eternal qualities" will inhere in produced (*janya*) things. But any eternal thing which inheres in a produced thing must be a universal.

(E11) Udayana: Color, etc. are not material (*mūrta*), because color, etc. are occurrent in the same locus (*samānadeśa*).

Raghunātha: Occurrence (of *x*) in the same locus (as *y*) is for *x* to be inherent in something occurring at the same time as *x* and in which another substance (*y*) inheres. It is essential that the relation in question be inherence—thus, e.g. a thread and a ray of light may occur in the same locus through contact without vitiating the argument. And the specification "at the same time" is likewise essential.

Vardhamāna's explanation of immobility (*niṣkriyatva*) is independent of Udayana's, since the *Kiraṇāvalī* definition in itself suffers from overextending to material substances as well as all-pervading entities. Vardhamāna's definition ("immobility is possession of the absence of the limitor of inherence causality") is expanded by Raghunātha as follows: Immobility is being the inherence-locus of any property other than existence that occurs in what possesses the absence of the limitor of inherence-causeness to motion. The word "limitor" excludes substanceness, etc. occurrent in a substance whose parts are immobile and are destroyed. And so a quality's not possessing any quality has to be explained as its being the inherence locus of any property that is always occurrent in what is nonoccurrent in what possesses the quality.

PADĀRTHATATTVANIRŪPAṆA

In this work Raghunātha sets out to demolish certain of the classical Vaiśeṣika categories and introduce new ones. The summary is by Karl Potter. "ET" references are to his (B3719; RB5943) *The Padārthatattvanirūpaṇam of Raghunātha Śiromaṇi* (Harvard Yenching Press: Cambridge, Mass., 1957).

1 (ET21-24) After a salutation to the "supreme self" (*paramātman*) (a salutation found in other works of Raghunātha's as well) the author identifies place, time and God as comprising a single category. Since the older school explains the variety of judgments about spatial and temporal directions by reference to a single substance (viz., place (*dik*) or time (*kāla*) respectively), and since there is no proof that place and time are different from God, it is simpler to identify the three.

2 (ET26-28) Furthermore, God, who is accepted to be the instrumental cause of (each) sound, is also its inherence cause, not *ākāśa*, which is eliminated along with place and time from Raghunātha's ontology.

Objection: A sound is caused by the individual self, since a sound is produced by the *adṛṣṭa* of such a self, like satisfaction, etc.

Raghunātha: This argument does not affect me, for even if I admit it, it doesn't prove that the self is the inherence cause, and if I (e.g.) were the inherence-cause of a sound we should judge "I am sounding" just as we judge "I am satisfied". But we don't. Thus the auditory organ is just God limited by the oral cavity rather than *ākāśa* so limited.

3 (ET29-30) The next passage concerns the internal organ. Commentators differ on what it means. Raghunātha identifies the internal organ as the noninherent element (*asamavetaṃ bhūtam*), and says that this definition doesn't overextend since he agrees with old school that the merit and demerit of the individual self are necessary.

4 (ET31-32) There are no imperceptible substances—no atoms or double-atoms as in old Vaiśeṣika. The smallest substance is the minimal perceptibilium (*truṭi*). The standard argument to prove the existence of an atom, alleging infinite regress if the atom is not accepted, is rejected on the ground that the regress may as well stop with the *truṭi*.

Objection: An element (such as a *truṭi*) inheres in its parts, because it is a visible substance, like a pot, and the double-atoms that are thus inhered in inhere in their parts, because they are the inherence causes of visible substances.

Raghunātha: If so there will be an infinite regress, since there should be the inherence cause of the inherence cause of the double atom, the inherence cause of that, and so on. And a term like "small" doesn't refer to any definite size, but is a comparative notion (smaller than).

5 (ET33) So there is no proof that God has a size.

Objection: All substances have a size.

Answer: No. Being a substance no more requires having a size than it requires being an element. Even to say that God has "unlimited occurrence" (*aparimitavṛttitva*) is not established.

6 (ET36-38) There are no unmanifest colors. Every color is fit for perception. In the first place, no one believes there are (unmanifest) colors in wind, etc. Secondly, if you were right, the generic absence of color would be as imperceptible as a hobgoblin (*piśāca*), since its counterpositive would be beyond the senses. And thirdly, rather than holding that the inherence cause of a substance has an endless series of supersensory touch qualities, it is simpler merely to hold that being the inherence cause of a substance is to be material (*mūrta*).

7. (ET38-39) *Being material*—i.e., the universal that limits the inherence causality of motions—is the same universal as *being elemental.*

Objection: *Being elemental* is possessing a universal pervaded by substancehood residing in a thing that possesses a quality perceptible through a sense-organ that is inherent in its parts.

Answer: But you agree with me that the final whole (*antya-avayavin*) is not an inherence cause of substances (and, given my revisions in the system, the descriptions "material" and "elemental" otherwise describe precisely the same things).

8 (ET40–41) Separateness is not a distinct kind of quality, since separation of *x* from *y* can be explained as mutual absence of *x* from *y*. Awareness of separateness does not involve its content's having a limit (*avadhi*)(as the old theorists thought), for there is no proof of that. (A limit is relevant only when there is movement away from something, but not all ablatives involve that.)

9 (ET42) Farness and nearness aren't distinct qualities either, since the awareness of farness and nearness can be explained through appeal to spatial and temporal relations without postulating such qualities.

10 (ET43) Individuators are not a separate category, since diffe-

rentiation between eternal substances is a natural fact, just as according to the old school the differences between the individuators ia a natural fact. Raghunātha doubts that yogis see individuators.

11 (ET44-49) The old school held that each kind of quality (e.g., color, taste touch) as well as motions must be either locuspervading or non-locuspervading. Raghunātha sees no reason to suppose that. For example, seeing a baked pot as red is not a mistaken judgment, even though when we break the pot open we see that it is black on the inside; it merely means that the pot's color is non-locuspervading. Furthermore, there is no need to postulate a distinct kind of color called "variegated", once we admit non-locuspervading qualities.

Some tactual qualities, such as soft and hard touch, are likewise non-locuspervading.

Objection: These are kinds of contact.

Raghunātha: No, since then we could perceive them visually. Likewise, some taste and smell qualities are also non-locuspervading. Again, some motions are non-locuspervading, e.g., when the branches are moving but the roots are not.

Objection: No, there the branches have a locuspervading motion and the roots lack such a motion.

Answer: But you must then believe the tree is motionless, which contradicts perception and common usage.

(Objector: On your view the differently-colored parts cannot combine to form a variegated-colored whole. But then by parity of reasoning a number of parts of the same color cannot combine to form a whole of one color.)

Raghunātha: Just as in a collective (*samūhālambana*) awareness one has a single awareness of various different individuals of whom one is distributively aware as well, so it is here: since there is no conflict among the colors of the parts they combine to produce a single color that fills the locus of the whole produced.

12 (ET50-51) The noninherence cause is not really a cause. Unity has no noninherence cause. Still, the destruction of the noninherence cause is always the cause of destruction of a substance, since I admit that it is the cause of the destruction of any substance that inheres in eternal components.

13 (ET52-58) Possession of a touch-quality alone is the necessary condition for a substance to be tactually perceived, and not possession of color (as the old school held).

Objection: But a minimal perceptibilium has no touch qualities.

Raghunātha: If so, add to the necessary conditions the further requirement that the substance have a size larger than an element.

Number and other qualities of wind are preceptible by touch.

On the other hand, possession of a color is the condition of a substance's being visually perceptible, not possession of touch, e.g., the motion of a beam of light that lacks touch is visibly perceptible.

The necessary condition for a substance's perceptibility is that it has either perceptible color or perceptible touch inhering in it.

14. (ET60) Can the absence of a universal be perceived? Raghunātha rejects the old view that existence is a perceptible universal residing in all substances, qualities and motions. Existence can't be perceptible since it belongs to imperceptible things such as merit. Furthermore, it cannot be a universal at all, since universals are also spoken of as existent, and no universal inheres in a universal. Raghunātha identifies existence with the property *being positive*. *Being positive* is explained as not being an absence, and *being an absence* is held to be an indivisible property (*akhaṇḍopādhi*). So it is all right to hold *being positive* to be a single property. Now *being positive*, like knowability, the absence of a pot, etc., is self-occurrent (*svavṛtti*), for *being positive* is itself a presence, just as knowability is knowable, etc.

16. (ET64-65) Qualityness (*guṇatva*) is not perceptible, since it belongs to qualities such as God's awareness, merit, demerit, etc., which are not perceptible. It does not belong to just the twenty-four qualities in the standard Vaiśeṣika list, since it also is used to refer to the swiftness of a horse's movement and the faultlessness of a Brahmin, etc. Finally, it is not a universal at all. Since there is no single limitor of the effectness (of a quality as cause) there will result overextension (*atiprasaṅga*) and crossconnection of universals (*jātisaṃkara*).

17. (ET66-67) When it is said that knowledge gained by instruments of knowing such as verbal testimony, etc. is "experience" (*anubhava*) no universal is being referred to; rather, what is meant is that the piece of awareness in question is other than memory. There is, to be sure, a universal which can be referred to when the term "experience" is used; it is the universal otherwise called "directness" (*sākṣātkāritva*), but it only occurs in sense-perception, not in the other instruments of knowledge. Otherwise I should say, when I infer that someone is satisfied, that I am experiencing satisfaction—and we don't say that.

18. (ET67-69) A double absence—the absence of an absence—being an absence, is not the same thing as a presence or positive entity. But no regress results, since a triple absence—absence of an absence of an absence—*is* identical with a single absence. The mutual absence of a mutual absence is not another mutual absence, for that would lead to an infinite regress, but is the property of *being present* (*bhāvatva*) as well as of being a relational absence (*saṃsargābhāvatva*).[11]

Likewise, the prior absence of a posterior absence, as well as the posterior absence of a prior absence, are distinct kinds of absences, since there is nothing to cause us to find our cognitions of them as absences faulty. However, some say that prior absence is not real (not *pāramārthika*).

19. (ET70-71) The old school holds that the cause of recognition (*pratyabhijñā*) is the trace (*saṃskāra*) of the item recognized.

Advaitin objection: That cause is a memory of the item, since it is an awareness born of a trace.

Raghunātha: The correct position is that memory is the cause of recognition, since when the trace is not excited or is obstructed recognition of the item does not arise; therefore memory is the (immediate?) condition of recognition.

20. (ET72-75) Raghunātha now begins proposing new types of entities. First, he suggests that the category of moment (*kṣaṇa*) should be added. A moment is a momentary (*kṣaṇika*) condition upon time (*kālopādhi*).

Objection: A moment is just a motion qualified by the prior absence of disjunction.

Raghunātha: No, since such a motion is not necessarily momentary—it could last a long time.

Objector: Then let's say that a moment is a motion qualified by the prior absence of disjunction produced by that motion itself.

Raghunātha: No, for a moment must be the locus of a repeatable property, viz., momentariness. But the motion qualified as proposed is unique.

21. (ET75-76) As an aside, Raghunātha asks us to consider how people come to identify individuals they've never met before just from hearing their names.

22. (ET76-77) Another new category is possessedness (*svatva*).

Objection: That is nothing but being fit for use as one wishes.

Answer: Not precisely, for one may "use" food, i.e., eat it, even when it belongs to others.

Objector: One is enjoined not to eat food belonging to others.

Raghunātha: You see, you must already understand possessedness in order to understand such an injunction. Possessedness is a property that belongs to people when they receive gifts and that they lose when they give things away.

23. (ET78-80) Causal efficacy (*śakti*) is another new category. This type of individual belongs to certain connectors (*sambandha*), e.g., contact between our breath and the grass we blow on to produce fire. It is argued that it is simpler to postulate an added category than to suppose that there are three different universals in the three causes of fire—grass, wood, a jewel. There can't be just one universal

in all three, since that involves crossconnection of universals. Or if one argues that causality inheres in these three causes (rather than the connectors) the postulation of causal efficacy is still a simpler view than that.

24. (ET81-84) The theory about doubt (*saṃśaya*) (associated with Vātsyāyana) that doubt arises directly from there being mutually contradictory ascriptions, is defended against the later theory (associated with Vācaspati Miśra I) that doubt only arises in connection with perception and relating to the other instruments of knowledge. The analogy is with a blue pot. Just as a blue pot is not produced as an individual entity, but rather a pot is produced and blue-color is produced, just so doubt is not an individual entity resulting from a single kind of cause. Again, just as potness is free from blueness, so belief (*niścaya*) is free from limitation by doubt. So doubt is not a category.

25. (ET84-85) Causality (*kāraṇatva*) is another new category (belonging to individual causes whereas causal efficacies belong to the connectors). It is differentiated by its different effects and its different limitors, just as the one absence is differentiated by different counterpositives and loci. And like absence also, each such differentiated causality possesses the imposed property *causalityness* (*kāraṇatvatva*), just as each differentiated absence possesses the imposed property *being an absence*, i.e., *absenceness*. We sometimes become aware of causality through perception supporting agreement and difference (*anvayavyatireka*), sometimes through inference, sometimes through language (*śabda*), etc.

26. (ET85) In the same fashion effectness (*kāryatva*) is another added category, explained in a parallel fashion. We need both causality and effectness just as, it was argued (in section 15), we need both *being present* and *being absent*.

27. (ET86-87) Number (*saṃkhyā*) is not a quality (as tradition holds) but an added category in its own right. For we do enumerate qualities, etc., not just substances, and these cognitions about (e.g.), the number of colors in something are not found to be false.

Objection: A judgment that "there are two colors in *x*" is to be explained as based on the connections called "inherence of two qualifiers in one locus" (*ekārthasamavāya*).

Raghunātha: Then, if inherence and inherence of two qualifiers in one locus are different connectors, we can't explain why we report both cases as the locus' possessing its qualifier(s) (in the words "*tadvat*"). Furthermore, if "*x* possesses *y*" means that *x* and *y* co-inhere in *z* (as argued, viz., that "this (these) quality (qualities) possess(es) the number one (two)", then "potness is one" will express the co-inherence in the same locus of unity and potness, and likewise, "colorness possesses twoness" should express the coinherence in the same locus of twoness and colorness—but that's absurd.

28. (ET87) There is not just one inherence as the old school holds, but as many inherences as there are pairs related by inherence. Otherwise water would smell. What is common to all the many inherences is the simple imposed property *inherenceness* (*samavāyatva*).

29. (ET87-88) Another added category is one called "being qualified" (*vaiśiṣṭya*) that causes us to become aware of absences, in a fashion parallel to the way that an inherence causes us to become aware of colors, etc.

Objection: The connector in question is a certain sort of self-linking connector.

Raghunātha: Then we can get along without inherence, since the self-linking connector can stand duty for it as well.

30. (ET88) A final new category is contentness (*viṣayatā*). It is the cause of awarenesses of objects in a way parallel to the way in which *vaiśiṣṭya* operates.

ĀKHYĀTAVĀDA

This summary by Prabal Kumar Sen specifies passages as "E" which refer to pages in his own edition of the work from Calcutta, 1979.

1. (E1-2) Raghunātha begins this work with an account of the traditional Nyāya doctrine concerning the meaning of verbal endings (*ākhyāta*). According to this view, a verbal ending primarily means conscious effort (*yatna*), and a paradigmatic use of verbal ending occurs in a sentence where the word in the nominative case denotes some conscious agent. This claim is fortified by the interchangeability of expressions such as "(one) cooks" (*pacati*) and "(one) performs cooking" (*pākaṃ karoti*)—the latter expression being a paraphrase of the former.[12]

There are, however, cases where the verbal ending cannot mean effort. Thus, for example, in sentences like "the chariot moves" (*ratho gacchati*) the word in the nominative designates something unconscious, and so the question of effort does not arise. In such cases the verbal ending stands for an "operation conducive to a certain result" (*anukūlavyāpāra*), this being its secondary meaning (*lakṣyārtha*).

2. (E3) According to Raghunātha, the traditional Nyāya doctrine about the meaning of the verbal ending is inadequate. While he supports the view that a verbal ending primarily means effort, he points out at the same time that the range of a verbal ending's

secondary meaning is not exhausted by "operation conducive to a certain result". Thus in the expression "(one) cognizes" (*jānāti*) no conscious effort is indicated, nor is there indicated any operation conducive to some result (since the act of cognizing does not produce any result in its object). The same holds in cases like "(one) desires" (*icchati*), "(one) sleeps" (*nidrāti*), etc. In these cases the scope of the secondary meaning should be extended to encompass locushood (*āśrayatva*), for in such instances the verbal endings merely indicate that the nominatives associated with the verbs are loci of the acts denoted by the respective verbs.

Old Naiyāyika: Such an extension of secondary meaning is unnecessary, since in the counterexamples cited above by Raghunātha locushood may be apprehended though *saṃsargamaryādā*, i.e., through awareness that the verbal stem and the verbal ending are syntactically related through expectancy (*ākāṃkṣā*).[13]

Raghunātha: Then consider "(one) perishes" (*naśyati*), where the understood nominative associated with the verb is the counterpositive of the destruction (i.e., the person who perishes). Now the property of being a counterpositive cannot be apprehended through *saṃsargamaryādā*. Furthermore, if locushood could be apprehended through *saṃsargamaryādā* then ungrammatical and inadmissible sentences like *caitraḥ pacati taṇḍulaḥ* (where both nouns are in the nominative) should be capable of producing verbal cognition (and they aren't).

3. (E5-8) Raghunātha now proceeds to justify the traditional Nyāya view that the verbal stem "*kṛ*" primarily means effort. He proves this by showing that the use of the expression "*kṛta*" (formed by combining the verbal stem "*kṛ*" and the verbal suffix "*kta*", a participle) and "*akṛta*" (formed by combining the negative participle *nañ* with *kṛ* and *kta*) is governed by the presence of effort and absence of effort respectively. A further reason in favor of the view is the fact that the word "*kartṛ*" ("agent") (formed by combining "*kṛ* and the verbal suffix "*tṛc*", which indicates locushood) means "the locus of effort", just as the word "*jñātṛ*" (which is derived similarly from the verbal stem "jñā", to be aware of or cognize) stands for "the locus of awareness". Some philosophers maintain that "*kṛ*" stands for action *simpliciter* (=*kriyā*), or for an operation conducive to a certain result (the context being the determining factor in particular instances). Raghunātha points out that these philosophers would have to admit in the long run that all cases (e.g., accusative, instrumental, dative, locative) would coalesce into the nominative case, an undesirable outcome.

Objection: The traditional Nyāya view is untenable because it fails to account for instances where unconscious things are indicated by the verbal stem "*kṛ*" (as in, e.g., "*ratho gamanam karoti*", "the chariot performs motion"). Consequently it is better to admit "operation" as the the primary meaning of "*kṛ*", since such operation characterizes all such nominatives (whether conscious or unconscious) associated with this verbal stem. In some cases (e.g., when "*kṛ*" occurs as a constituent of "*kartṛ*") effort may be admitted as the secondary meaning of the verbal stem "*kṛ*" when usage so demands. Moreover, if we accept "operation *producing* a result' (*janakavyāpāra*) instead of "operation conducive to a result" (*anukūlavyāpāra*) as the primary meaning of a verbal ending, we can also successfully maintain the distinction between the nominative case and the other cases. The fact that one is aware of effort after listening to expressions like "*pacati*" does not pose any problem, because the result (in this case, cooking), which constitutes the meaning of the verbal stem, is produced by conscious effort. The result, being an effect, is invariably related to its cause, i.e., conscious effort, and hence it enables us to infer the latter. Where such explanations are not tenable (as in expressions like "*śobhanam pacati*", "he cooks propitiously"), one may suitably expand the range of the secondary meaning of the verbal ending so as to include in it "effort producing the result" (*janakayatna*).

Raghunātha: This view unduly violates the law of parsimony. (Other objections are considered.)

4. (E9-11) Raghunātha now presents the view of the Grammarians, which differs sharply from that of the Nyāya. The Grammarians base their theory on the difference in the rules governing active voice (*kartṛvācya*) and passive voice (*karamavācya*).[14] According to the Grammarians, the Nyāya theory that verbal endings stand for effort cannot explain why different rules pertain to the formation of active voice and passive voice, because in both cases the awareness of effort features in the cognitions generated by the sentences.[15] The Grammarians suggest that the verbal endings in the active voice signify the item in the nominative case, while those in the passive voice signify the item in the accusative case. Unless this is admitted, one cannot explain the fact that the nominative (of the active) and the accusative (of the passive) are presented in the verbal cognition as related through identity. (On an alternative interpretation: one cannot otherwise explain how the different words in the sentence could make us understand a single thing characterized by properties.) Moreover, according to the rules of grammar, when the verbal ending does not stand for the nominative, the agent gets the third case-ending (the instrumental), and when the verbal ending does not stand for the accusative, the objects gets the second case-ending. (This is, so to speak, the negative version of the Grammarian's view.) Unless

this is admitted, one has to admit the possibility that in the active voice the agent may have the third case-ending, and that in passive voice the object may have the second case-ending (and such a possibility is not admitted by anyone).

One may point out that this position of Grammarians is vulnerable to an objection which is similar to their own objection against the Nyāya theory, because in Sanskrit the active and the passive voices need not be indicated by verbal endings: that purpose may be served by verbal suffixes as well. Thus, instead of using the sentence *caitraḥ pacati* ("Caitra cooks, in the active voice) one may say *caitraḥ paktā* ("Caitra (is a) cook", and instead of saying *Caitreṇa ghaṭo dṛśyate* ("the pot is seen by Caitra", passive voice) one may say *caitreṇa dṛṣṭo ghaṭaḥ ("the pot (is a) thing seen by Caitra")*. In both the alternative usages no verb with a personal ending has been used, and hence verbal endings do not play any role in the presentation of nominative or accusative. The critics now say that the factor determining the usage of active and passive voice is whether or not the number (singular/dual/plural) associated with the verbal "postfix" (*dhātūttarapratyaya*) is the same as the number associated with the agent or object. When the verbal postfix does not have the same number as that of the object, the object has the second case-ending (i.e., the sentence is in active voice), and when the verbal postfix does not have the same number as that of the agent, the agent has the third case-ending. (A "postfix" (*pratyaya*) may be either a case ending or a verbal suffix.) The Grammarians reject this theory by pointing out that verbal suffixes do not indicate number in any way, and that consequently one cannot claim that postfixes as such can indicate number.

(The critics may point out yet another defect in the Grammarians' theory. According to rules of Sanskrit grammar, verbal endings are of two kinds, (1) *parasmaipada* and (2) *ātmanepada*. Passive voice can be expressed though the *ātmanepada* form alone, but the reverse does not hold, because in the case of some verbs the *ātmanepada* form is used in active voice as well. Accordingly the Grammarians have to admit the queer situation that verbal endings in the *ātmanepada* form stand at times for the nominative and at times for the accusative. As a consequence, they have to admit that even pseudo-sentences such as *caitraḥ pakṣyate taṇḍulaḥ* (where both the agent and the object have the first case-ending and the verb has an *ātmanepada* ending) can be meanigful.)

The Grammarians now introduce further refinements into their theory, and maintain that a verbal ending, insofar as it is a verbal ending, primarily means the nominative, while an *ātmanepada* verbal ending, insofar as it is an *ātmanepada* ending, primarily means the accusative. This, they think, effectively rules out the chance of any confusion while explaining sentences that contain verbs with *ātmanepada* endings. They also point out that grammatical rules (e.g., Pāṇini 3.1.67-68) do not permit pseudo-sentences such as *caitraḥ pacyate* or *taṇḍulaḥ pacyate.*

The critics may now ask how the Grammarians can account for the fact that the use of active and passive voices is characterized by agreement between the number associated with the verbal ending and the number associated with the nominative or accusative. The Grammarians reply that this is due to the fact that the case (i.e., nominative or accusative) and the number associated with the verbal ending is presented by the same word (viz., the verbal ending). In this connection they also admit that singular endings mean unity, dual endings mean duality, and so on.

5. (E12-18) The Grammarians' view is now rejected on two counts. First, it unduly violates the law of parsimony. (The Naiyāyika admits only *one* entity, viz., effort, as the primary meaning of the verbal ending, whereas the Grammarian has to admit *three* entities, viz., nominative, accusative and number.) The prolixity cannot be condoned on the ground that this is the only way of maintaining the distinction between active and passive voices, because one may reasonably hold that active or passive voice is determined by the agreement between the number associated with the verbal ending and the number associated with the agent or object. The Grammarians rejected this view on the ground that sentences like *caitraḥ taṇḍulaṃ pacati* (where the agent, object and verbal ending are *all* characterized by singular number) may, on this theory, be interpreted as a case of *both* active voice and passive voice. This, however, results in their second mistake, because this difficulty can be overcome by stating the rule concerned in terms of *bhāvanā* (which comprises the primary as well as the secondary meaning(s) of verbal ending, e.g., effort, operation, locushood, property of being a counterpositive, feasibility, conduciveness to something desirable, etc.). *Bhāvanā* has the meaning of the verb as its qualifier and has the nominative or accusative as its qualificand according as the sentence is in the active or passive voice. Raghunātha now suggests that the number associated with the verbal ending is related with the qualificand of *bhāvanā.* The qualificand of *bhāvanā* is expressed by the word that has the first case ending, and that does not feature as the accusative, instrumental, etc. (This prevents the possibility of treating sentences like *caitraḥ taṇḍulaṃ pacati* as an instance of both active and passive voice. In active and passive voice the agent and the object respectively are characterized by the first case ending. (Thus we can maintain the distinction between active

and passive voices without subscribing to the view of the Grammarians.) An exception has to be made, however, in the case of verbs ending in *bhāvyavācya* (e.g., where the agent has the third case-ending and the object is either not mentioned or is ruled out altogether in the case of an intransitive verb), because here no word has the first case-ending, and consequently there can be no qualificand of the *bhāvanā.* In such cases, one has to admit that the number associated with the verbal ending is not related to any qualificand, and that its use serves the sole purpose of making the sentences grammatically correct.

The introduction of *bhāvanā* helps us to distinguish between active and passive voice in another way as well. In active voice the *bhāvanā* is related through locushood (*āśrayatva*), but this does not hold in the case of the passive voice. There is, however, some dispute among the Naiyāyikas as to how the *bhāvanā* is related in the passive voice, and Raghunātha gives an account of this dispute. He deals with the meaning of verbal suffixes like "*tṛc*", "*kta*", etc., which may be employed to indicate active and/or passive voice without using any verbal ending; and the manner in which sentences containing words formed by such suffixes are to be understood.

6. (E19-22) Raghunātha discusses and rejects the following alternative solutions.

1) All verbal postfixes primarily mean effort, though this does not hold in the case of words like "*pācaka*", where the postfix has *locus of effort* as its secondary meaning.
2) Verbal postfixes like "*tṛc*" primarily mean effort, while they have *locus of effort* as their secondary meaning.
3) The meaning of a verbal stem is a certain kind of operation, and the meaning of the case-ending indicating accusative, etc., is the property of being the cause of the result (*phalajanakatvam*) or result *simpliciter* (*phalamātram*), the property of being the cause being understood through *saṃsargamaryādā.*

7. (E22-29) Raghunātha now discusses how sentences in passive voice like "*gamyate grāmaḥ*" ("the village is being reached", where the agent is not mentioned) are to be understood. In this connection he also mentions some alternative solutions. Some allied problems (e.g., what is the "object" of a transitive verb? When is a verb regarded as transitive?, etc.) have been discussed with respect to specific cases.

8. (E30-34) Raghunātha now states the theory maintained by the followers of Maṇḍana Miśra. According to them, the meaning of a verbal stem is a certain result, while the meaning of a verbal ending is an operation conducive to a result, or the operation *simpliciter*,

the causal relation between the operation and the result being grasped through *saṃsargamaryādā.* Other properties indicated by verbal endings (e.g., temporal features, feasibility, conduciveness to something desirable, etc.) are related to the operations, since they are expressed by the same word (viz., the verbal ending). Though operation is accepted as the meaning of a verbal endings in the active as well as the passive voice, the distinction between active and passive voice is not thereby obliterated. In active voice, the operation is the qualificand and the result is the qualifier; while in passive voice, the result is the qualificand and the operation is the qualifier.

A refined version of this theory maintains that in the passive voice the third case-ending (associated with the agent) means operations, while the verbal ending means *locushood determined by the result indicated by the verbal stem.* Verbal suffixes in *kartṛvācya* (e.g., *tṛc*) mean locus of operation, while verbal suffixes in *karmavācya* (e.g., *kta*) mean locus. Alternatively, one may also say that the verbal ending primarily means operation and locus. Raghunātha rejects this view as it fails to explain why expressions like *pacati* make us aware of an effort conducive to cooking.

9. (E35) The Prābhākara Mīmāṃsakas maintain that the verbal stem means an *operation conducive to a certain result.* The nominative stands for the locus of such an operation, while the verbal ending means number, temporal features or locushood, as the case may be. The criticism levelled against the view of Maṇḍana's followers is applicable to this view as well.

NAÑVĀDA

This summary was initially prepared by Janakivallabha Bhattacharya, with revisions by Potter. The work is edited and translated by Bimal Krishna Matilal in his (RB5341) *The Navya Nyāya Doctrine of Negation.* Section numberings follow Matilal.

1. (E189; T148-149) The negative particle *nañ* has two meanings, (a) relational absence (*saṃsargābhāva*) or (b) mutual absence (*bheda* or *anyonyābhāva*).

2. (E189; T149-150) In either case the counterpositiveness of an absence referred to by *nañ* must be limited by a property which also limited the property of being-syntactically-connected-to-*nañ* (*anvayitā*). Thus we do not say "a blue pot is not a pot", but we do say "a yellow pot is not a blue pot".

3. (E189; T150) Just as in a positive sentence a term denoting the object *x* is syntactically related to a term denoting *x*'s locus, so in a negative sentence the term denoting the absence of *x* is similarly related to a term denoting *x*'s locus. Thus in "Caitra cooks"

Caitra is related by the locus-located relation (*ādhārādheyasambandha*) to his effort of cooking; so in the sentence "Caitra is not cooking" Caitra is related to his effort by the same relation.

4. (E189; T151) In parallel manner, "this is Caitra's" and "this is not Caitra's" likewise involve the same relation. Since the relation must always be an occurrence-exacting relation the proper analysis of "this is Caitra" is "this (object) possesses the property of being-possessed, a property which is conditioned (*nirūpita*) by Caitra". Likewise, for "this is not Caitra's" we must read "this object possesses an absence of the property of being-possessed, which property is not conditioned by Caitra", rather than "this (object) does not condition the possessorship resident in Caitra", since this last relates the object to the absence by a non-occurrence-exacting relation.

5. (E189-190; T152) Indication of the locus of an absence may be either through using the locative case or because of some other natural indication in the language. The intention of the speaker may also determine the indication of which item is the locus—e.g., "there is smell in earth and not in water" can mean either "smell occurs in earth and absence of smell occurs in water" or "smell occurs in earth and possesses absence of occurrence-in-water". According to the latter, the judgment has one qualificand and two qualifiers.

6. (E190; T153-154) Objection: No, a negative judgment must always express the absence of a qualifier in a qualificand. That is why there is the grammatical rule that the qualificand term and the qualifier term must agree in number; the rule directly corroborates our view that in "there is not a pot" (*ghaṭo nāsti*) the qualificand is "a (=one) pot", while in "there are no pots" (*ghaṭa na santi*) the qualificand is (more than one) "pots".

Raghunātha: Then how will you explain the true judgment "there is no existence in a universal" (*jātau na sattā*)? Here the qualifier should be (according to you) "absence of the property *occurrence-in-universal*:, but there is no such absence, since its counterpositive *occurrence-(by-inherence)-in-universal* is unexampled (nothing inheres in universals).

7. (E190; T155) Someone else has said: the absence must be construed as its counterpositive's qualifier and then taken as the qualifier.

8. (E190; T156) Where (as in "this pot is a blue thing") the relation between a qualifier and qualificand is identity, the negation is a mutual absence, and the two terms must have the same case-ending. For example, in the Mīmāṃsā rule "in sacrifices one utters *ye yajāmahe*, but not in an *anuyāja* sacrifice" since the qualifier and the qualificand of the (unnegated) sentence have the same case-

ending we can construe the rule in the way the Mīmāṃsā wishes to, viz., "one should utter *ye yajāmahe* in sacrifices other than the *anuyāja*" (rather than the odd "in sacrifices one should utter *ye yajāmahe*, but one should not utter it in *anuyāja* sacrifices"). Thus the sentence alludes to a mutual absence.

11. (E191; T159) Mīmāṃsaka: The reason why the Mīmāṃsā rule involves a mutual absence is that otherwise it would allow an alternative (*vikalpa*) (since the odd interpretation above requires both that one utter *ye yajāmahe* at sacrifices and not do so).

Raghunātha: No, that's not the reason. No such alternative needs to be allowed. Consider "Yogurt should be given to brahmins but not to Kauṇḍinya"; here it is perfectly clear that one should give yogurt to all the brahmins except Kauṇḍinya.

15. (E191-192; T161-162) Generally, if one has a general prescription (e.g., "one must sacrifice to the *manes* on the calends of a lunar month") together with a specific prohibition ("one must not perform the funeral ceremony at night"), one is not allowed to conclude the possibility of option (e.g., performing the funeral ceremony at night on the calends of a lunar month), since the natural meaning of the prohibition rules that out.

16. (E192; T162) Mīmāṃsaka: If there is no such possibility of an option why should there be any such prohibition? One only prohibits something he thinks would otherwise occur.

Raghunātha: One might as well say, then, that the truth of "there is no fire in a lake" should lead us to expect a fire to occur on a lake! In any case, the reason for offering the prohibition (in the case discussed in 15) is because of the possibility of misunderstanding a general prescription of the sort specified (not because one is disposed to perform funeral ceremonies at night).

17. (E192; T63) (Mīmāṃsaka: Then there is no chance of options occurring at all.)

Raghunātha: An option arises when we find two scriptural statements which directly conflict, e.g., that one is to use a certain kind of cup (called *ṣoḍaśin*) in a certain kind of ceremony (called *atirātra*), and that one is not to use that kind of cup in that kind of cermony, and there is no other way out.

18. (E192; T163-164) One can in fact find a way out even in this case. Construe "one should use the *ṣoḍaśin* in the *atirātra*" to mean "in the *atirātra* ceremony, using the *ṣoḍaśin* is a means to the desired end", and then construe "one should not use the *ṣoḍaśin* in the *atirātra*" to mean "in the *atirātra* ceremony, non-use of the *ṣoḍaśin* is a means to the desired end". These do not contradict each other.

19. (E192; T165) That is why the Prābhākaras construe "one must

not eat *kalañja*" as "the non-eating of *kalañja* is enjoined" (or, on Nyāya grounds, "...is a means to the desired end").

20. (E192-193; T166) (Objection: The *ṣoḍaśin* cup cannot be a means to the desired end, since it is only a subsidiary item in the ritual.)

Raghunātha: Well, we can say that use of the cup assists the ritual in producing the desired result by strengthening the *apūrva* which connects the act with its eventual result.

DĪDHITI on Gaṅgeśa's TATTVACINTĀMAṆI
BOOK ONE: PERCEPTION
Section Two: Truth
Summary by Jitendranath Mohanty

This is the only section of Book One of Raghunātha's *Dīdhiti* to have been published to date. It is available in an edition by P.B. Ananthachariar (B3388; RB5296), Sastramuktavali Series, Conjeeveram 1908. We have been unable to procure a copy of this work to establish page references. Section numberings correspond to the numberings in the summary (above) of *Tattvacintāmaṇi*.

1-5. "*Svatas*" (in the phrase "*svataḥprāmāṇya*, intrinsic validity), may be construed either as *svasmāt*, "from oneself", or as *svakīyāt*, "from one's own". On the former reading, the validity of an awareness is apprehended by that awareness itself; this is the Prābhākara view. On the latter reading, the validity of an awareness is apprehended by the aftercognition of that awareness (this is the Miśra view) or by an inference depending on knowness as *hetu* (this is the Bhāṭṭa view).

6-13. Gaṅgeśa's (A1) is construed by Raghunātha so that J refers to a particular awareness. Its validity (if it is valid) is a property peculiar to it. This is in contrast to Pakṣadhara's interpretation.

Similarly, Raghunātha differs from Pakṣadhara over the interpretation of "the same conditions as give rise to the awareness of J" in (A1). For Raghunātha, the sentence means that validity is apprehended by all those awarenesses which are produced by the same conditions as give rise to the awareness of J and which do not apprehend the invalidity of J.

Why does Gaṅgeśa list (A4), which only applies to the Prābhākara thesis? Raghunātha explains this procedure of Gaṅgeśa as due to the fact that one cannot take up an issue with all the three at one time, so that a statement of what is common to all three would in fact be useless.

15. "Relatedness" in (e) should be taken to mean merely the property of being related as property and possessor (*dharmadharmi*-

bhāva), not as the relation of inherence which is either not admitted by the Mīmāṃsakas or, if admitted, is held to be imperceptible.

16-21. "... Since an awareness is determined (*nirūpya*) by its content ...." *Dīdhiti* explains "determined" here as perception. Awareness being a perception of a content, aftercognition of that awareness would amount to a perception of the content of that awareness, which amounts to a perception of the truth of the awareness. Further, an awareness of a relational entity such as chief-qualifierness (*prakāratva*) implies awareness of the relatum, i.e., the thing determined by the chief-qualifierness. If, therefore, in aftercognition an awareness is seen to have potness as its chief qualifier, this necessarily implies that its substantive must also be seen as determined by potness. But all this amounts to perceiving the truth of the awareness "this is (a) pot". In fact, as Gaṅgeśa points out, the aftercognition of the awareness "This is (a) pot" takes the form "I know the yonder object and the pot." Commenting on this, *Dīdhiti* appeals to the rule that an extraordinary presentation of an object through *jñānalakṣaṇasannikarṣa* would have necessarily the same form in which that object was originally apprehended. It is well-known that in the aftercognition the original content is presented through *jñānalakṣaṇa*: both the primary awareness and the aftercognition must therefore apprehend the original content in the same way, in this case, as determined by the appropriate chief-qualifierness.

Though the above argument suits the Miśra point of view—since the Miśras accept an aftercognition of an awareness—still, it can also be used by the other two schools. On the Prābhākara theory, the primary awareness which (according to Prābhākaras) perceives itself should perceive its own content in the manner stated above. On the Bhāṭṭa theory, the very knownness from which an awareness is inferred would be apprehended as qualified by the content in question, so that the awareness that is thereby inferred is the concept-bound awareness having this determinate object.

25. Raghunātha rejects Gaṅgeśa's contention in (2) here that the relative strength of the alternatives (*koṭyutkaṭatva*) is a decisive consideration in this matter. He argues that the so-called *koṭyutkaṭatva* is not a proper universal. Furthermore, Raghunātha points out that if doubt were just the joint predication of a property and its opposite, there would be no proper universal of doubtness (*saṃśayatva*). He admits, however, that sometimes from the same conditions, viz., joint predication of opposite properties, there may ensue contradiction (*virodha*).

27. As to Gaṅgeśa's contention that there is no proper universal of defectness, Raghunātha reads this literally as it stands, in contrast

to Pakṣadhara's more complex interpretation. Raghunātha takes Gaṅgeśa to mean that there is no universal defectness, a thing that is common to all those cases where prior certainty about something stands frustrated by an error or doubt about the very same thing.

BOOK TWO: INFERENCE

Section One: Inferential Awareness

Summary by Madhusudana Nyayacharya as translated by Sibajiban Bhattacharya. "E" references are to the edition by Gurucaran Tarkadarsanatirtha (B3394; RB5302), Bibliotheca Indica 194, 1910-12, 1963.

1. (E4-24) Raghunātha begins his work by saluting the Supreme Self (*paramātman*), which is of the nature of infinite bliss and consciousness.[16]

The different chapters of a book must be interrelated to form one organic whole. This interrelation of the chapters is due to the interrelation of the things or objects discussed in the chapters. "Relevance" (*saṃgati*) is this interrelation of the objects, and is thus a property of objects. This relevance has been classified into six kinds, and is relative to our desire to know. When a cause has been discussed we may want to know its effect, and the relevance here is the objective property of being the effect. When an effect has been discussed first, we may then want to know its cause, and the relevance is the property of being the cause. Gaṅgeśa opens this chapter by saying that he takes up inference after perception because inference is caused directly or indirectly by perception. Thus the relevance is here "being the direct or indirect effect of". Some commentators before Raghunātha have interpreted this to mean that according to Gaṅgeśa the cause has to be discussed first always, and the effect discussed in the next chapter. But Raghunātha rejects this interpretation by pointing out that Gaṅgeśa himself has discussed the effect *anumiti* (inference) and then its cause (*anumāna*) (the instrumental cause of inferential awareness). So according to Raghunātha, Gaṅgeśa cannot accept the rule that the cause has to be discussed before the effect.

(E27—51) Gaṅgeśa's definition of inferential awareness ("The conclusion of an inference is an awareness produced by an awareness of the qualification of the *p* as qualified by pervasion") is ambiguous. It is not clear which noun is qualified by the phrase "qualified by pervasion". Many commentators of Gaṅgeśa have taken it to qualify the (unexpressed) term "*hetu.*" But Raghunātha, following his teacher Jayadeva, says that the phrase qualifies "awareness" in "awareness of the qualification." To support this he has to interpret the phrase "qualified by pervasion" in a different way, for literally only the *hetu* can be qualified by pervasion, not awareness. So to make it an adjective of "awareness" he interprets "qualified by pervasion" to mean "of which pervasion is chief qualifier". Thus interpreted "qualified by pervasion" obviously becomes an adjective of "awareness", for only awareness has a chief qualifier. Raghunātha's interpretation makes the definition applicable to invalid as well as valid inference. If we accept the literal meaning of the definition, inference cannot be invalid. For if the *h* actually occurs in the *p*, and is actually pervaded by the *s*, then the resulting inference cannot be invalid. On Raghunātha's interpretation, however, an *h* which is merely believed to occur in the *p* and to be pervaded by the *s* need not actually occur there or be pervaded thus. Hence it can be a defective *h* giving rise to an invalid inference.

(E54–78) This definition of inference as it stands may appear to be overextensive. For (1) it applies to perception of a special sort. When, for example, we perceive that this is a tree, after doubting whether it is a tree or not, to resolve the doubt it is necessary to perceive the specific features of the tree, i.e., to perceive this as possessing branches, etc., as pervaded by treeness. This perception, which has the form "this possesses branches pervaded by treeness", is of the same form as consideration (*parāmarśa*). Hence the resulting awareness, which is of course perceptual, should be regarded as inference since it is produced by consideration, as the definition specifies.

The answer to this objection is that the perception of the specific features, although of the same form as consideration, nevertheless produces perception inasmuch as it cancels the opposite awareness "this is not (or may not be) a tree", whereas consideration, which produces inference, does not cancel any opposite awareness. Hence the definition of inference should be interpreted to mean that awareness which is produced by the sort of consideration that doesn't cancel an opposite awareness.

(2) (Second objection to Gaṅgeśa's definition of the conclusion of inference:) The definition of inference overextends to cover the conclusion of comparison (*upamiti*) of a certain sort. When, for example, one knows that a kitchen is the denotation of the word "kitchen" by remembering that the thing denoted by the word "kitchen" is similar to the hill possessing smoke pervaded by fire, the awareness of the relation between the kitchen and the word "kitchen" is produced by consideration, viz., awareness of the hill possessing smoke pervaded by fire.

The reply to this objection is that this *upamiti* is caused by the awareness (which has the same form as consideration) *qua* awareness, whereas inference is caused by consideration *qua* certain knowledge. So the definition must be understood in that fashion and no overextension arises.

(3) Objection: Gaṅgeśa's definition overextends to cover verbal awareness (*śabdabodha*) concerning a sentence containing the names of the five members of an argument, since this verbal awareness results from *upanaya* (the fourth member) and has the form of consideration.

Answer: So, the definition should be further modified, as follows: The conclusion of an inference is an awareness *x* produced by consideration (= awareness *y* of the qualification of the *p* as qualified by pervasion) but where *x* does not have pervasion as its content. According to this revised definition, pervasion cannot be the content of the conclusion of an inference. From the consideration "the mountain possesses smoke pervaded by fire" we cannot infer any conclusion containing "pervaded by fire". As a result of the modification, the verbal knowledge resulting from the five-membered sentence cannot be regarded as inferential since it mentions awareness of pervasion.

But even this modified definition cannot be the correct one. For there is no rule that the conclusion of an inference cannot contain pervasion. For example, since we can surely infer "the hill possesses fire as well as smoke pervaded by fire" from the consideration "the hill possesses smoke pervaded by fire" the modified definition of the previous paragraph is too narrow. Raghunātha, therefore, gives up the attempt to define the conclusion of an inference by specifying its instumental cause (as Gaṅgeśa attempts to do) and falls back on introspective evidence. He says, let us first find one case of inferential conclusion to which Gaṅgeśa's definition as given applies; then by introspection let us find out the peculiar feature of this awareness. Inference in general will be the kind of awareness in which we find this peculiar feature.

(E87–93) Gaṅgeśa says the cause of inference is the consideration of the *hetu*. Others hold that awareness of pervasion is the cause. Raghunātha rejects that view, because every awareness of pervasion does not produce inference; although every such awareness is capable of producing an inference, only some actually do. To avoid this difficulty, Raghunātha says that the term "*anumāna*" should mean "the instrumental cause of that awareness which is produced by consideration", as Gaṅgeśa has it.

Gaṅgeśa adds that it is the consideration of the *h*, not the *h* as considered, which is the cause of inference. Raghunātha explains that the *h* as the object of the awareness called "consideration" is an object and a different thing from the awareness of it. Gaṅgeśa asserted, in discussing relevance in section 1 above, that inference is always caused (directly or indirectly) by perception, and perception is a kind of awareness, not the object perceived.

Section Two: Five Definitions of Pervasion

Summary by Madhusudana Nyayacarya as translated by Sibajiban Bhattacharya. "T" references are to Daniel H.H. Ingalls (B3417; RB Ingalls), op. cit. "E" refers to the edition by Gurucaran Tarkadarsanatirtha (B3394; RB5302), op. cit.

(E101–108; T154–161) Without first determining the nature of pervasion, we cannot determine how pervasion can be known. Thus Gaṅgeśa first tries to determine the nature of pervasion.

The first definition of "nondeviation" fails because it does not apply to cases where the *s* is non-locuspervading.

The second definition of "nondeviation" says that nondeviation is the nonoccurrence of the *h* in a locus of the absence of *s*, which absence occurs in something which is not a locus of *s*. It fails because there is no reason to think that an absence of contact occurring in motion is different (from absence of contact occurring in something else).

The third definition of "nondeviation" underextends, since *h* may occur in examples of locus of *s* which are different from the *p*.

The fourth definition of "nondeviation" is ambiguous. It may mean (1) *h*'s being the counterpositive of an absence which resides in a locus of all absences of the *s*, or (2) *h*'s being the counterpositive of an absence which resides in all loci of absence of the *s*. Interpreted as (1) the definition will not overextend to include a false *h* that is the counterpositive of an absence residing in some loci of absence of *s*. Interpreted as (2) the definition will not fail to cover a correct *h* which proves an *s* consisting of several particular things. If we interpret "locus of *h*" as "locus of *h* which is not a locus of absence of *h*", and "locus of *s*" as "locus of *s* which is not a locus of absence of *s*", the definition will not include false *h*s and exclude correct *h*s (in the kinds of cases mentioned). Still, even so the definition (on either interpretation) fails to cover cases where *s* is a single particular, or where the locus of absence of *s* is a single particular. It also fails to cover an inference where *s* is *what is pervaded by absence of smoke* and *h* is *fire*, since no single locus of absence of *h* will occur throughout the locus of absence of *s*.

The fifth definition raises a problem about the meaning of "other than". Raghunātha's view is that "other than the locus of *s*" in the definition means "other than *any* locus of *s*". Otherwise, he argues, a blue pot might be other than a pot.

Section Three: Lion-Tiger Definitions

The summary is based on T.S. Bhattacharya (RB9381), *Nature of Vyāpti*, op. cit., pp. 104-12. "E" references are to G. Tarkadarsanatirtha's edition (B3394; RB5302).

(E112–124) In order that (6) and (7) not be identical, Raghunātha says that the expression "not-having-a-common-locus-with-*s*" in (6) should mean having a locus different from the *sādhya*.

Objection to (6): Then (6) overextends by making "it has smoke, because it has fire" true.

Answer: No, for "not-having-a-common-locus-with-*s*" means not having a common locus with *any* locus of the *sādhya*.

Now both (6) and (7) fail to cover only-positive inferences, since no locus where the *sādhya* is absent is available. Further, in an inference where the *s* is specific (e.g., kitchen-fire), the locus which does not determine the existence of this specific *s* may not be excluded by the *h*, and so the inference will fail to be covered. And there will even be overextension sometimes. Finally, if "having a locus different from *s*" alludes to mutual absence (*anyonyābhāva*), then there will be underextension where the loci of *s* are many.

Now some say (Jagadīśa says this refers to Vāsudeva Sārvabhauma) that (6) means that the relation in which the *h* stands to the *p* should be the relation limiting the absence of the locus of *s* (in the definition). Then (it is claimed) there will be no difficulty merely because the locus of *s* is absent from specific bits of smoke, since the relation between smoke and its parts is inherence, not contact. Nor is there any difficulty because the *h* is not located in what possesses fire by inherence, since inherence is not the relation between *h* and *p*.

Objection to Vāsudeva Sārvabhauma: Consider "it is a substance, because it possesses existence." Now the *s* and *h* inhere in substance, and inherence is the relation between *h* and *p*. Yet the inference is invalid.

Answer (by Vāsudeva Sārvabhauma): But in this, or any, fallacious inference the *s* is not present in every locus of *h*: we perceive that there is no substanceness in some existents, viz., qualities.

Objector: Then there is underextension to a valid inference such as "it is a substance, because it has specific existence other than quality or motion."

Sārvabhauma: No, since the specific is additional to the general. And notice that on (6) interpreted my way there is no underextension to only-positive inferences (though there is on (7)).

Raghunātha: The perception of the absence of common-locusness of substanceness and existence in qualities is like the perception of the absence of common-locusness of earthness and substanceness in qualities. Nevertheless, despite these perceptions qualities and earthness coexist in substances. So, it doesn't follow that substance has no common locus with existence; indeed, we perceive that substances exist. And since that is so, the invalid inference: "it is a substance, because it exists" becomes valid after all! Likewise, there is perception of both monkey-contact with the tree and the absence of that contact with the tree.

Returning to (6) and (7), consider an invalid inference with supersensible *s* and *h*. Since here the absence of what has common locus with the *s* is not perceived in *h* (6) or (7) are satisfied, and there is overextension.

Finally, there will be underextension where the limiting relation (connecting *h* and *p*) is the temporal relation and the *p* is, say, *eternity* (*nityatva*), since in eternity there cannot be the absence of time in the temporal relation.

Section Four: Absence Limited by a Property whose Loci are Different from its Counterpositive

The summary is based on T.S. Bhattacharya (RB9381), Chapter III, pp. 113–121. "E" references are to G. Tarkadarsanatirtha's edition (B3394; RB5302).

(E132-248) In the only-positive inference "it is nameable because it is knowable" the jar can be a *vp* since the *s*, nameability, is absent in the jar as limited by being a locus of inherence. But how about "it is knowable because it is nameable"? Just as the absence of absence as limited by presenceness is present everywhere, so the absence of knowability as limited by nonknowability is present everywhere. Or, again, the absence of nonfire as limited by fire is everywhere. Or, etherhood (*gaganatva*) is absent everywhere insofar as that absence is limited by *being related by any relation other than inherence.* Or, the absence of knowables as limited by the relation of contact with clothhood or jarhood is present everywhere.

Now the following is a (apparently successful) definition of pervasion (of the *vyadhikaraṇa* sort): (D1) Pervasion is the *h*'s having a common locus with every absence whose counterpositive has a common locus with it when that counterpositive is the limitor of the pervaderness limited by the limitor of the *s*-ness. This definition covers "it is nameable because it is knowable", since a jar is the *sp* (being a nameable and knowable) as well as the *vp* (being a locus of the absence of jar in the relation of inherence).

Objection: This will overextend to include the invalid inference "it is both material (*mūrta*) and elemental (*bhūta*), because it is material."

Answer: No, since the internal organ is material but not elemental. The principle is that when *s* as such and its absence as limited by another limitor of the counterpositiveness always have a common locus then there is pervasion, but here that is not the case. The "as such" is important: otherwise no inference will be valid, e.g., in "the hill has fire because it has smoke" the absence of kitchen-fire on the hill as limited by another limitor does not have a common locus with the *s*, fire (since kitchen-fire doesn't occur on the hill); nevertheless, this does not invalidate the inference since the *s* as such is not kitchen-fire but fire *per se*. And it is the coexistence of that *s* with the *h* which insures pervasion.

And the relation between the *h* and the common locus of *s* as such and its absence as limited by another limitor has to be through the relation which determines *s* as such. Thus D1 does not fail to cover the valid inference "it is the self, because it has awareness in the relation of inherence", since, e.g., a jar, which is not a common locus of *s* as such and its absence as limited by another limitor, is not related to awareness by the relation of *contentness* (*viṣayatā*), which is the relation which determines the self as such.

Objection: Then there is overextension in the invalid inference "this has earthness, because it is either eternity or a pot-half", since the *h eternity-possessing* is related to the *s* in the relation of temporality (*kālikasambandha*), the relation which determines the *s* as such, and the *p*, *this*, has both the *s* as such and its absence as limited by another limitor.

Answer: No, since the relation in which the *s* pervades the *h* should be the relation in which it is related to the locus of absence of *s* by another limitor. Since *earthness* is a universal it should be related to its loci by inherence, and not by temporality; thus there is no overextension. And there will be no underextension with respect to the valid inference "it has generic absence of color, because it is an earth atom", since at *pralaya* or at the time just before the color's arising in the atom there *is* absence of color.

Objection: There is overextension to the invalid inference "this moment is one in which a cow exists, because it is a moment in which cowness exists", since both the *s* as such (cow) and its absence as limited by another limitor have a common locus with *h*.

Answer: No, that is not the case at *pralaya*.

The definition does not fail to apply to the valid inference "it has absence of monkey-contact, because it is known", since *every* place is a locus of absence of monkey-contact.

Raghunātha now formulates an improved definition of pervasion of the present sort as follows:

(D2) Pervasion is the *h*'s having a common locus with all the absences whose counterpositives have a common locus with it, when those counterpositives are limited by the nature (*rūpa*) which limits the pervaderness limited by the limitor of the *s*-ness.

Section Five: Fourteen More Faulty Definitions of Pervasion

Summary based on T.S. Bhattacharya (RB3981), op. cit., Chapter III, pp. 122-95. "E" references are to the edition by G. Tarkadarsanatirtha (B3394; RB5302).

(E15–16) Raghunātha discusses fourteen definitions of pervasion in all, starting with D1 and D2 above. These are not the same as Gaṅgeśa's fourteen definitions. D3–D5 are identified by commentators as those of Cakravartin. (Tarasaṃkar Bhaṭṭacharya suggests this may be 32. Śrīnātha Bhaṭṭācārya Cakravartin, the uncle of Vāsudeva Sārvabhauma.)

(D3) Pervasion is *h*'s having a common locus with what is limited by that limitor of the *s*-ness which is not a limitor of the counterpositive of an absence of *s*, which absence is locus-pervading and shares all loci with *h*.

(D4) Pervasion is *h*'s having a common locus with all that is limited by that limitor of *s* which is not the limitor of anything having a common locus with the counterpositive of the absence which is locus-pervading and shares all loci with *h*.

(D5) Pervasion is *h*'s having a common locus with all that is limited by that limitor of *s* which is not the limitor of all that has a common locus with the counterpositive of the absence which shares all loci with *h* but whose counterpositive is *vyadhikaraṇa*, i.e., occurs in places other than the loci of *h*.

Raghunātha thinks these three definitions do not fail to apply to cases of pervasion, such as the pervasion of smoke by fire, since the definitions imply that the limitor of *s* must not have a common locus with the counterpositive of any absence residing in *h*, and since *fireness*, which is the limitor of the *s*, is not the limitor of kitchen-fire (which does not occur on the mountain) by the *paryāpti* relation, which is to say that though there are many fires there is only one *fireness*.

These definitions do not overextend to fallacious inferences, e.g., "it has contact, because it has existence", since even though absence of *s*, viz., absence of contact, has a common locus with existence (e.g., in qualities), since absence of contact is locus-pervading it is excluded by the definitions.

Likewise, D3–5 do not overextend to include such a fallacious inference as "it has contact, because it has existence other than that of quality", since the *h* has a common locus with the absence of contact, viz., motion.

(E173–195) (Now, say the commentators, Raghunātha discusses three definitions of Pragalbha Miśra.)

(D6) Pervasion is *h*'s possessing an absence of the *s* which has a common locus with *h* and which is the limitor of that generic property of *s* by which is limited the limitor of *s*-ness.

(D7) Pervasion is that (state) in which there is no obstruction (*pratibandhaka*) of awareness of the locus of an *s*, when there is veridical awareness that the absence of that *vyadhikaraṇa s* shares its loci with absence of *s per se.*

But these are not accurate definitions, since in both of them the term "absence of *s*" is superfluous.

(D8) Pervasion is that state in which there is no contradiction of an inference proving *h* to occur in the locus of the absence of *s* (as *vyadhikaraṇa*).

This is not right, since it is too extensive.

Next Raghunātha takes up three definitions which the commentators ascribe to Pakṣadhara Miśra.[17]

(D9) Pervasion of *h* by *s* is that absence of the *s* which is collocated with *h* and is also the determinant constituting the general characters of the *s* by which every instance of *s* is determined.

The meaning is that the absence of *s* may be either *qua* its own nature or *qua* having loci different from the essence of its counterpositive; in either case we must find a locus of an absence of the appropriate kind, and the absence of these loci in the *h* is a sufficient condition for pervasion. This definition does not underextend (e.g., in the case of the monkey-contact example) since *absence of s* must be understood in a locus-pervading fashion. Nor does it overextend provided again we specify that the locus of absence of *s* must be a pervasive (i.e., not numerically specific) and not a specific (numerically) locus; thus in "it has smoke because it has fire", one may not take as a locus of absence of *s something nonsmoky which is specific to earth* (which would satisfy the definition otherwise and make this fallacious inference valid). Likewise, one cannot pick as the locus two nonsmoky things. Finally, the locus of absence of *s* that is chosen must be determined by the relation limiting the *h* so that the valid inference "this has fire, because it has smoke" will not fail to be included merely because both smoke and fire have smoke-particles as their loci (since they are related to those particles by different relations).

(D10) Pervasion is *h*'s having a form which is pervaded by the limitor of the counterpositive whose locus-pervading absence pervades all the loci of absence of *s*, which absences may be either *qua s*'s own nature or through having loci different from those of its counterpositive.

The application of this definition to "it is a substance, because it has specific existence other than that of quality and motion" and to "it is knowable, because it has knownness" is explained.

(D11) Pervasion is *h*'s having a form which is pervaded by the limitor of the counterpositive of the relevant absence of locus-pervading *s*, where the *s* is taken in the nature in which it pervades the *h*.

(E196–248) Next, Raghunātha explains some version of definition ascribed to Vāsudeva Sārvabhauma by the commentators.

(D12) Pervasion is *h*'s being characterized by the absence of every existent which is an absence of *s*.

This definition has to be understood as requiring that each existent in question must be absent in the relation by which the *h* is related to the *p*.

(D13) Pervasion is *h*'s being characterized by the absence of every existent locus of all absences of *s*.

Here the entire locus of the absence of *s* is what is to be taken as the counterpositive of the absence characterizing *h*. Again, the counterpositive must be limited by the relation in which the *h* is related to *p*. And it should be understood that *s* must pervade the counterpositive of *absence of s*, and that the limitor of the counterpositive must pervade the *s*. Thus, e.g., there is no overextension to the invalid inference "it possesses earthness, because it has a universal property." Nevertheless, (D13) is not correct, says Raghunātha. Consider "it has both substanceness and earthness, because it has substanceness" (an invalid inference). Since there is absence of substanceness in the absence of both *s* and *h*, the definition overextends to include this inference. Or else, take "it possesses substanceness of something other than earth, because it possesses substanceness"—again the definition overextends, because quality, a locus of absence of *s* (viz., substanceness) is absent from *h* (substanceness). Other overextensions of this definition are to "it possesses absence of quality inhering in this earth, because it is air," and "it possesses absence of inherence of this earth which is different from existence, because it is different from the locus of color," as well as "it is other than eternity, because it is the jar in temporal relation."

(D14) Pervasion is *h*'s being characterized by all absences of the loci of all locus-pervading absences of *s*, which counterpositives are limited by a nature which pervades *h* and is limited by the limitor of the *s*-ness.

This definition is intended to meet problems about locus-pervasion, but it is ultimately defective, as its predecessor was.

All these definitions involve admitting the possibility of an absence limited by a property whose loci are different from its counterpositive. But no one is validly aware of any such absence. If someone perceives, say, a jar as being a cloth, we unhesitatingly judge it to be false perception, an error. Likewise with an absence of jar: if one perceives it under some description of its counterpositive (jar) other than its essence (jarness) then that would amount to perceiving the absence of an illusory jar. But no valid inferences can come from such a notion.

Section Six: The Conclusive Definition
Summary by Kali Krishna Banerjee

"E" references are to G. Tarkadarsanatirtha's edition (B3394; RB5302).

(E310–363) Raghunātha uses Gaṅgeśa's conclusive definition as a starting point, but has changed it beyond recognition.

1. In Gaṅgeśa's definition, hereafter called the "original definition", the *sādhya* is said to "differ from what is limited by the limitor of the counterpositiveness", i.e., it is said that *s* is different from the counterpositive. This is not accepted by Raghunātha. Instead of saying that *s* is not the counterpositive he says that the limitor of *s*-ness is not the limitor of the counterpositiveness.

2. After asserting that the limitor of *s*-ness is not the limitor of the counterpositiveness (specified in Gaṅgeśa's definition), Raghunātha declares that having a common locus with whatever is limited by this limitor is pervasion. That is, Raghunātha's formulation of Gaṅgeśa's definition involves the following:

(1) An absence residing in a locus of *h* should be available.

(2) This locus of *h* should be different from any locus of the counterpositive of the absence.

(3) The limiting relation and the limiting property of the *s* should not be both the same as those of the counter-positiveness of the absence described in (1) and (2).

(4) Pervasion is having a common locusness of such an *h* with such an *s*.

3. Next, Raghunātha suggests that the "having a common locusness of such an *h* with such an *s*", which in Gaṅgeśa's original definition

is a property of the *hetu*, instead should be thought of as *whatever is limited by the limitor of hetu*ness.

4. Raghunātha also declares that pervasion is described (*nirūpita*) by everything which is limited by the limitor of *sādhya*ness.

5. Now the definition together with the insertions made so far cannot cover a case of inference which has "staff-owner" as its *sādhya*, since by using "sifting" (*cālanīnyāya*) it may be shown that the limitor of the *s*-ness is not different from the limitor of the counterpositiveness in the case of an absence residing in the locus of *h*. So Raghunātha maintains that inferences with *owner of staff*, etc., as their *sādhya* have *staffness*, etc., as their limitors of *s*-ness, the limiting relation of *s*-ness being an indirect one.

6. The expression "has a common locus with *h*" occurs in the original definition. Raghunātha replaces it with "has a common locus with *h* as qualified by its (*h*-) form". In other words, Raghunātha contends that the absolute absence spoken of in the definition should have a common locus with, not the *h* as such, but the *h* as limited by the limitor of *h*-ness. The reason for this is that otherwise the definition will fail to apply to "This is a substance, because it possesses an existence that is different from the existence qualified by quality or motion."

7. Pervasion is said to be a case of having a common locus, and the having of a common locus is a particular. So, since the individuals that may be said to have a common locus will differ, the particular property will also differ. And this will imply that pervasion, at least when the pervaded thing is smoke or the like, will be many in number. But this is against Nyāya doctrine. It has been clearly stated in the section on consideration that there is only one pervasion that is common to all smokes. So Raghunātha asserts that though the property of *having a common locus* is a particular and there are many such particulars, yet in view of the fact that the limitor to the describerness (*nirūpakatva*) as well as the limitor to the locusness is one, pervasion is also one. That is, to take an example, though there are many smoke and fire individuals, the relation of pervasion holding between smoke and fire is one that the limitor of describerness, viz., fireness, is one and the limitor of locusness, viz., smokeness, is also one.

8. But this is not consistent with Raghunātha's own views, for he does not believe in sense-contact through general features and so merely from what has been said cannot rule out the possibility of a consideration of the form "the hill possesses a donkey which has a common locus with such fire as is a pervader in relation to smoke." So he observes that the said *having a common locus* as qualified by *smokeness*, or *smokeness* as present in the said *having a common*

locus, gives the definition of pervasion. And it may be said, he observes further, that if one adopts the first view one comes to hold a pluralistic view on the nature of pervasion, but if one adopts the second view one becomes a monist.

9. In the original definition it is stated that (A) "absolute absence has no common locus with its counterpositive." Raghunātha observes that it will cover a case such as "This possesses contact with monkey because it is this tree."

10. Then he considers the suggestion (of Pragalbha, say commentators) that the insertion (A) has been made to cover cases like "This possesses contact, because it is a substance", and rejects it, after considering at some length a view on the nature of generic absence of contact, on the ground that there is no evidence in favor of the view that there is generic absence of contact, or that substance (or a tree) may be the locus of such an absence.

11. Lastly, Raghunātha observes that the insertion of (A) has been made to account for inferences where the *sādhya* is nonlocus-pervading. But then, he notes the view of the "new school" that the common view on the nature of this kind of inference is ill-defined. Thus, it is not the commonly accepted view that the inference "it possesses fire because it possesses smoke" is an example of the nonlocus-pervading kind of inference. But in fact it is an example of that kind of inference, the new school says. So likewise are the inferences "it possesses quality, because it is a jar", and "it possesses contact, because it is the sky." Then, Raghunātha concludes the discussion by making a reference to the view that the insertion of (A) is unnecessary when the *s* is in every respect locus-pervading.

12. The expression (A), which occurs in the original definition, Raghunātha takes to mean "has no common locus with what is limited by the limitor of the counterpositiveness." The reason for this is that if it is not interpreted this way it will fail to exclude nonpervasion in cases such as "It possesses such existence as is different from the existence qualified by quality or action, because it possesses generic attributes" and "It possesses both elementness and limitedness, because it possesses limitedness."

13. The interpretation in (12) is necessitated by the fact that the most widely held Nyāya view is that qualified *x* is not different from bare *x*, and so qualified existence is not different from bare existence, and limitedness as qualified by elementness is not different from (unqualified) limitedness. Now the followers of Vāsudeva Sārvabhauma do not accept this view. They take (A) to mean "nonoccurrentness in the locus of the abode of counterpositiveness." So Raghunātha examines the view of the followers of Sārvabhauma and rejects it.

14. Absence of jar is different from absence of cloth. So absence of jar is the locus of a mutual absence, i.e., it is not identical with absence of cloth. And when the locus of an absence is itself an absence the two absences, to avoid infinite regress, are said to be identical. So, absence of jar is identical with the mutual absence of cloth, and absence of cloth is as legitimate a counterpositive to the absence of jar as jar itself is. This logic of absence is used by a school of thinkers to argue that the term "absolute" which occurs in the original definition and qualifies absence has been used to indicate (1) that the property *not having a common locus* is of such a counterpositive as is a describer of constant absenceness, and (2) that the counterpositiveness of which the limitor of *s*-ness is not a limitor is a describer of constant absenceness. Raghunātha does not subject the first proposition to any critical examination. But neither does he approve of it, the reason for this being the insertion that he intends to make in what follows below. As against the second proposition he mentions an old objection that it makes the definition apply to illegitimate cases such as "time possesses cow because it possesses cowness."

15. This objection rests upon the assumption entertained by earlier Naiyāyikas that the relation between posterior absence and absolute absence is one of opposition. Raghunātha does not subscribe to this view. In the section on *vyadhikaraṇābhāva* (Part Four of this Book) he has opined that such a view cannot be substantiated. He will also observe later that time may be the locus of both posterior absence and absolute absence. Anyway, the objection of this school of thinkers is an old one. Pakṣadhara Miśra did not think that one could overcome it, and so took the term "absence" (in the definition) to stand for relational absence (only).

This view of Pakṣadhara's is held by Raghunātha to be defective. In his opinion, it fails to exclude illegitimate cases such as "When there is vibration, then there is dyad," or "When there is person's moral desert, then there is his awareness." Besides, time may be the locus of both posterior absence and constant absence.

16. Raghunātha now considers the proposition that since absolute absence is a form of relational absence and since relational absence is the object of a negative awareness that has been conditioned by the superimposition of the counterpositive in some relation other than identity and accordingly takes the form of reductio and presupposes pervasion, there is a circularity in this definition. Some think that the difficulty may be overcome by defining pervasion presupposed in relational absence in a different way, that is, in terms of mutual absence. Raghunātha makes mention of this view. But he holds that relational absence may be defined independently

of relational superimposition (that is, as an absence other than mutual absence), and so independently of pervasion also, and there is no circularity here. Besides, he observes, relational absence is not indispensable for the definition, and if it be held to be a constituent of the definition, the definition will fail to cover those cases of legitimate inference where the limiting relation of *sādhya*ness is identity.

17. The definition as it presently stands fails to exclude cases such as "It possesses awareness, because it is a substance", or "It possesses a specific quality, because it is a substance other than internal organ", or "It possesses universals, because it is a positive entity," etc. So Raghunātha observes that not being the locus of the counterpositive means not being so in the limiting relation of counterpositiveness. Further, it is to be understood that "locus" is not used in its strong sense. Instead it may be used to mean any relatum, and so mutual absence will be included in the scope of "an absence that has no common locus with its counterpositive." It may also be noted that the property of *being an absence which has no common locus with its counterpositive* has for its locus what is the locus of *h* and is not the locus of its counterpositive. So the definition will not fail to cover those legitimate cases of inferences where the *s* is nonlocus-pervading. It will also be able to exclude illegitimate inferences of the form "It possesses contact because it possesses existence" (i.e., an illegitimate inference where *s* in nonlocus-pervading).

18. Objection: What does the expression "not the locus of the counterpositive as limited by the limitor of counterpositiveness" mean, exactly? Does it mean (1) not being the locus of any one of the counterpositives as limited by the limitor of counterpositiveness? or (2) not being the locus of such counterpositives in general? or (3) not being the locus of what is limited by any limitor of counterpositiveness? Not (1), for then the definition will fail to cover cases where *s* in nonlocus-pervading. Not (2), for then it will fail to exclude cases like "It possesses generic absence of contact because it possesses existence." Not (3), for then it will fail to include a case such as "It possesses absence of contact with monkey, because it is a self." The position seems precarious.

Answer: There is no cause for despair. The expression means that the limitor of *s*-ness is not the limitor of that kind of counterpositiveness which limits such a counterpositive as is not present in the locus of the *h*.

19. In consideration, *s* is apprehended as having in a certain relation a common locus with the limitor of the *p*-ness. And there is also the awareness that the *s* in a certain relation will have a common locus with the *p*-ness. These relations may respectively be called

the limiting relation of *h*-ness and the limiting relation of *s*-ness. Now Raghunātha makes it clear that by "locus of *h*" should be understood a locus in the limiting relation of *h*-ness, and that the locus of the absence specified in the definition is such a locus of *h*. Moreover, the counterpositiveness in respect of this absence, i.e., the counterpositiveness of which the limitor of *s*-ness is not a limitor, should be limited relationally by the limiting relation of *s*-ness. If these insertions are not made the definition will not even cover "it possesses fire because it possesses smoke".

20. Objection: It was said before that "not the locus of the counterpositive" means "not so in the limiting relation of counterpositiveness." Now you are saying that the counterpositiveness which has such a counterpositive as its abode should be limited relationally by the limiting relation of *s*-ness. This violates the law of parsimony.

Answer: Then one need only hold that the limiting relation of *s*-ness does not hold between the locus of *h* and counterpositive.

21. Thus, "not in relation with" replaces "not a locus of". "Locus" is not used in its strong sense in this context. Raghunātha now recommends that this interpretation be placed on all uses of the word. That will enable one to hold that a possessor of a property may be either a pervader or a pervaded in relation to another property-possessor, or in relation to a property. Raghunātha enumerates some of these cases and makes a reference to view that contact may be a nonoccurrence-exacting relation.

22. Then Raghunātha mentions the case "the jar possesses temporal relation, because it has this dimension."[18] It is an inference where *s* is nonlocus-pervading and the limiting relation of *s*-ness is the temporal relation. And as either (1) the counterpositiveness, which has as its abode a counterpositive that is not a relatum of the locus of *h* in the limiting relation of counterpositiveness, will not be limited relationally by the temporal relation, or, (2) there is no counterpositive between which and time this relation will not hold, the absence required by the definition will not be available and the definition will fail to cover the case under discussion.

23. After mentioning this difficulty, Raghunātha considers the attempt made by Vāsudeva Sārvabhauma to overcome it.[19] This way out goes as follows: By an absence which has no common locus with its counterpositive is meant an absence all the counterpositives of which are limited by the limitor of their counterpositiveness and is the possessor of absence of occurrentness which is limited by the limiting relation of *s*-ness and is described by any individual locus of *h*. Thus, absence of *ākāśa* is the required absence. In view of the fact that "limited by the limiting relation of *s*-ness" has been inserted,

the definition will not fail to exclude "It possesses awareness (or, it possesses contact), because it possesses existence." Again, since "limited by the limitor of their counterpositiveness" has been inserted, it does not fail to exclude inferences like "It possesses both elementness and limitedness because it possesses limitedness" and "It possesses such existence as is different from the existence qualified by quality or motion, because it possesses universal properties." Lastly, since "all" has been inserted to qualify "the counterpositives" it will not fail to cover the case of "It possesses contact, because it is a substance."[20]

24. Raghunātha finds Sārvabhauma's formulation of the above way out of the difficulty insufficiently precise. So he reformulates it as follows: The absence required for the definition is a conjoint absence (*ubhayābhāva*), in every limiting relation of *s*-ness, of (a) an individual locus of *h* which is not a subjunct (*anuyogin*) of this relation (the subjunct-character being taken in its entirety), and (b) of such a counterpositive as has been limited by the limitor of counterpositiveness and is not an adjunct (*pratiyogin*) of this relation (the adjunct-character also being taken in its entirety). Since the contact which has smoke as its adjunct does not have the red-hot iron ball, a locus of fire, as its subjunct—or, as the contact which has as its adjunct this staff as qualified by the property of being other than Caitra has not as its subjunct Caitra who is a locus of this staff—or, again, as the inherence which has qualified existence as its adjunct has not as its subjunct a quality, which is a locus of a universal property, the definition is not overextensive.

25. Now the above way out (of Sārvabhauma as reformulated) assumes that *ākāśa* is not present in any locus. But this may be challenged. It may be said that though *ākāśa* cannot be an adjunct of a relation like contact or inherence, it may be a relatum in self-linking relation (*svarūpasambandha*). Indeed this alone explains the accepted Nyāya view that time is the abode of the universe. So the definition is to be reformulated further thus: When there is a conjoint absence, of the state of being limited by a particular property and of the state of being limited by a particular relation, in every counterpositiveness in respect of the absence which abides in a locus that is the locus of an *h* as limited by the limitor of *h*-ness as well as the limiting relation of *h*-ness, but is not the locus of its counterpositive as limited by the limitor of counterpositiveness as well as by the limiting relation of counterpositiveness, then what is limited by that particular attribute is in that particular relation a pervader in relation to that *h*. The definition is applicable to a case like "It possesses an object of veridical awareness, because it possesses the property of being a nameable thing", in that the state of being limited

by the attribute of being an object of veridical awareness is available in some counterpositiveness in respect of an absence if the absence of an object of veridical awareness in the relation of inherence be taken into account, the state of being limited by a self-linking relation is also available, and in the counterpositive in respect to absence of pot there is a conjoint absence of them. It may also be stated that as the conjoint absence has for its possessor, not a relation, but a counterpositiveness, it can exclude cases like "It is a substance because it has universal properties" and "It possesses both fire and smoke, because it possesses fire."

26. In this definition, counterpositiveness, limitorness, locusness, etc., are specific forms of self-linking relations and have not been introduced as regular relations. The relation of having a common locus is to be reduced to contact and similar relations. Absenceness also is a form of self-linking relation. Or, one may treat them as additional categories instead.

Examination of Limitorness
(*avacchedakatvanirukti*)

This section by Raghunātha is added. Our summary of it is based on an unpublished translation (part of his doctor's thesis at the University of Poona) by Yusho Miyasaka. "E" references are to the edition by Jivananda Vidyasagara (B3377; RB5285), Calcutta 1872.

(E41-42) Objection: Limitorness (*avacchedakatva*) cannot be either a self-linking connector or an additional entity. The first possibility involves overapplication of the definition of pervasion to an invalid inference where the *sādhya*-ness is limited by a heavy property, e.g., "that mountain has knowable smoke because it has fire". And the second possibility is ruled out by consideration that it applies to the valid inference "this has fire because it has smoke", since fireness cannot be a limitor of the counterpositiveness of an absence existing in *any* locus of smoke. The "two-fold absence" (*ubhayābhāva*) of fire-and-pot exists on the mountain even when absence of fire does not, so there will always be *some* locus of smoke having an absence of counterpositiveness limited in the required way.

(42-43) Answer: No. The definition of limitorness is this:

(D1) Being a property which does not occur in any locus of an absence of the limitor of the counterpositiveness of an absence sharing a locus with *h*.

Here the limitor must be understood as occurring in its own locus, i.e., as occurring completely in it by the completeness (*paryāpti*) relation.[21]

Now fireness (in "this has fire because it has smoke") satisfies the thus-formulated definition of a limitor.

What is this completeness relation? It is a self-linking connector itself, linking the number *one* with the complete pot despite the fact that a pot is made of parts, and the number *two* with a pair of pots, etc. And since *threeness* cannot occur in that which has the completeness relation to *twoness*, etc., there is no danger of the definition of pervasion vitiating the proper *hetu* in a valid inference.

The limitorness involved here is itself a self-linking connector. By our definition of limitorness the second possibility raised by the objector above is ruled out by interpreting (D1) in either of two ways:

(D1a): Being a property of all the loci one of which, being qualified by that property, is connected with any locus of an absence whose counterpositiveness is limited by a property limiting the counterpositiveness of an absence coexisting with the *hetu.*

(D1b): Being a property which qualifies that which is connected with some locus of an absence whose counterpositiveness is not limited by the property which limits the counterpositiveness of an absence coexisting with the *hetu.*

D1b is provided to deal with the possible use of the definition of pervasion to apply to the valid judgment "it has existence because it possesses a universal property", which fails D1a.

(E43-44) Objection: The part of D1 which specifies that the absence of the limitor not share a locus with *h* is unnecessary.

Answer: It is required, since anything at the first moment of its occurrence could not otherwise occur, e.g, in contact with a kitchen. However, one can avoid that specification if we assume that the counterpositiveness specified in D1a or D1b is limited by the same connector or by a particular qualificative relation. Again, D1b precludes the overpervasion of the definition of pervasion to any argument with a self-contradictory *h.*

Even an unduly heavy property can be a limitor of absential counterpositiveness. E.g., in "nothing has a conch-shaped neck", having a conch-shaped neck should be admitted as a limitor of the counterpositiveness, where the absential counterpositiveness is not a particular thing but rather all pots having a conch-shaped neck. If heavy properties are not admitted as limitors D1 will fail to apply in cases where a heavy property is concomitant with a simpler one. Also, substanceness *qua* substanceness could not be known as, e.g., pervaded by *quality-possession,* since everything has its own particularity (*svatva*), making any generalization "heavy".

Section Seven: General Absence

Summary by Madhusūdana Nyāyācārya as translated by Sibajiban

Battacharyya. "E" references are to the edition of G. Tarkadarsanatirtha (B3394; RB5302).

Gaṅgeśa's answer to the problem of this section is to postulate an absence of fire in general, a generic absence of fire. His argument is that without postulating such an entity we could not explain the doubt as to whether air has color, which doubt persists even when we have perceived the absence of all colors known to us.

Now some members of the tradition say that there are two distinct kinds of doubts about whether air has color, one stemming from awareness that all known colors are absent in air, the other stemming from the awareness that air is different from the locus of known colors. Raghunātha finds this tradition confused, since awareness of difference does not necessarily lead to doubt. Rather, the new school says that doubt occurs when two opposing properties seem to reside in the same locus, though really they cannot.

Some say that doubt is just the awareness of color's either residing or not residing in air, since if either alternative is known for certain no doubt will arise. Otherwise, they say, even when one knows, e.g., that a jar is on the ground, one might still have a doubt about it. So, in the case in question the doubt arises just when (1) we have no certainty about the absence in air of all colors, (2) we do not have certainty about the possible ways in which color may be absent in air, (3) we have no certainty that air is absent from all things which have color, and (4) we have no certainty about the location of absences of color.

But all of these kinds of doubt give way before the certainty that something (say, a jar) is absent because of its nonperception there. So these references (in (1)-(4)) to "all" are misleading.

Objection: If one is certain that absences of all known colors occur (in air), together with the certainty that there are no other colors, then one does not need generic absence as an additional entity.

Raghunātha: This argument is heavy. Even when one is certain about the absence of known colors and when there is no possibility of any other colors, still one has doubt about whether there is generic absence of color in air. But if one is aware of an absence whose counterpositive is general, then the doubt is removed. So generic absence must be an additional kind of absence to the specific absences.

Universal absence is distinct from the sum of particular absences, but characterizes the locus of every particular absence.

Objection (the view of Pakṣadhara Miśra, according to commentators): The different kinds of absences are not distinct entities, but involve different limiting relations of the one absence of, say, a jar. Thus universal absence of jar is such as has its counterpositive limited by inherence, mutual absence has a counterpositive limited by identity, prior and posterior absence have a counterpositive that is temporally limited.

Answer: No. The various kinds of counterpositives of relational absences do not have the same limitor, and because there is no proof that the limitor of the counterpositive of, say, posterior absence must always be limited by prior existence. Indeed, absences differ from one another, not because their counterpositives are not the same, but because their loci are incompatible, e.g., the absolute absence of things pervading the same space and time is the same; again, the prior and posterior absences of things which arise and are destroyed at the same time are the same, providing there is no incompatibility with regard to their spatial location. And if one accepts the *vyadhikaraṇa* absence, then the counterpositive of one such absence is limited by all the natures of all the opposed loci, as well as by all the relations of such loci.

Now if the generic absence is identified with the collection of specific absences, the difference between absences is undermined, since there may clearly be absences of universals as well as of particulars. Indeed, the counterpositive of a generic absence is not a *vyāsajyavṛtti* property,[22] i.e., it is not limited to a specific number of particulars. If it were, there would be undesired difficulties: e.g., through contact of the senses with a jar and a cloth simultaneously, one would have awareness of generic absence. One does not have to perceive every specific absence of *x* to perceive generic absence of *x*.

Objection: The postulation of two ideas—a generic absence and its locus—is no simpler than postulating the two ideas of generic absence and its *vyāsajyavṛtti* extension.

Answer: No, since generic absence is related to its locus by a self-linking relation, unlike the *vyāsajyavṛtti* absence.

Objector: Even so, it is more complex to postulate a single absence with an infinite number of counterpositives than to postulate a generic absence whose counterpositive is some specific number of instances.

Answer: No, since we do in fact perceive generic absences as *general*—i.e., as negating an in(de)finite number of counterpositive particulars.

Section Eight: Particular Absence

Summary by Madhusūdana Nyāyācārya as translated by Sibajiban Bhattacharyya. "E" references are to the edition by G. Tarkadarsanatirtha (B3394; RB5302).

(E49-50) Gaṅgeśa's defintion (23) fails to extend to cover "it has color, because it possesses earthness", since specific pieces of earth have different colors, and each color is the counterpositive of a constant absence which shares a locus with a possessor of earthness and differs in locus from its counterpositive.

Objection: The *s* here is meant to be *possession of colorness* (not *possession of (some one or another) color*).

Answer: No, since colorness is not absent from earth in the relevant relation (since it is not located in a substance at all, but in a quality, viz., color).

Furthermore, (23) fails to cover "it has existence, because it has substanceness", since existence occurring in quality or motion is absent in earth, etc. If this is not allowed, then there will be overextension of (23) to a fallacious inference such as "it has specific existence (*viśiṣṭasattā*), because it possesses a universal property."

Objection: Since "that which is not the counterpositive of an absence" means the absence of that counterpositive, in "it has color, because it has earthness" the counterpositive of the absence of earth is not perceived to be *colorness* and so color, which is the absence or the counterpositive of the absence of earth, pervades earth, so (23) is satisfied.

Raghunātha: No. When we perceive color as not the counterpositive of the absence of earth, what we perceive is that color is not the limitor of the counterpositive absent from earth. Indeed, we know that a color is the counterpositive of the absence of earth, and that no color possesses the absence of that counterpositive. Otherwise, things would be counterpositives through natures which do not belong to them. And then there will be an overextension into "it has knowable smoke, because it has fire," since smoke is not perceived to be absent in some locus of fire, and therefore smoke as knowable can be held to be never absent in any locus of fire.

Objection: The overextension does not arise, since knowable smoke is not the limitor of the common-locusness (of *h* with *s*) because of overcomplexity (since "knowable" is unnecessary).

Raghunātha: Then there will be underextension to "it has fire, because it has smoke", since fireness may be said not to be the limitor of the common-locusness, inasmuch as fire occurs in the red-hot iron bar where smoke does not exist. And the valid inference "it is a jar, since it has a conch-like neck" will not be covered, since being the locus of a conch-like neck is more complex than mere jarhood.

So the phrase "not the counterpositive of a constant absence", in D23 means *possessing* the property which is the nonlimitor of the counterpositive of the constant absence. And the difference between D23 and the conclusive definition of pervasion is that the conclusive definition specifies that *h* in general has common loci with *s* in general, whereas in D23 the common-locusness of two specific things, mountain-fire and mountain-smoke, is pervasion. Some say that the difference is that absence in one case is mutual absence, in the other constant absence.

Gaṅgeśa's definitions (24) and (25) are stated in terms of mutual absence. However, (24) fails to cover an inference in which *s* occurs in several loci, since one or another of those loci may have mutual absence with the locus of *h*, e.g., "it has fire, because it has smoke": here a locus of *h*, kitchen, has mutual absence with a locus of *s*, mountain. So (24) should be revised to read as follows:

(24') There is pervasion of A by B if, and only if, A shares a locus with B in such a way that the loci of B have a nature which is not the limitor of the counterpositive of mutual absence of A.

Thus "it has fire, because it has smoke" is covered, because the mountain, which is a locus of fire, has a nature (*mountainness*) which is not the limitor of the counterpositive of mutual absence of smoke. This will work also when the *s* is, say, *contact with fire*: there, the nature of the locus of *s* is *fire-contactness*.

"The tree is not the locus of monkey-contact in its root" only appears verbally to refer to an absence restricted to a part of the tree, but really doesn't do so, any more than if one cuts off a man's topknot the man is not killed. And there is no overextension because of this to a fallacious inference such as "it possesses contact, because it exists", since it is well-known that there is mutual absence of the locus of contact with a locus of existence (viz., motion).

In the case of constant absence, when there is definite awareness of something (say, jar *qua* jarness) being the counterpositive of a constant absence, then, even though we are aware of the absence of its absence somewhere, we are still aware of the constant absence. Likewise, when there is definite awareness of something (say, monkey-contact) as the counterpositive of a mutual absence with something else (say, the tree), then, even though we are aware of the absence of monkey-contact with the root, we are still aware of the mutual absence between monkey-contact and tree. Our perception is that the tree is the locus of monkey-contact in respect of its top; so, the absence of mutual absence of locus of monkey-contact must be taken in respect of the top, not the root. And again, we are not aware of the mutual absence of locus of monkey-contact as absent from the tree, since we perceive monkey-contact there. Likewise, we do not have the awareness of mutual absence of mutual absence of monkey-contact in the tree, since it is no contradiction for one part of the tree to be in contact with the monkey and another not. Furthermore, we are not aware of the root as being the locus of monkey-contact in the root, since monkey-contact's existence there is precluded on the principle that the mutual absence of what is different from the locus of something is that something itself. So, the mutual absence of what is different from jar is not something over and beyond the jar, just as the absence of the absence of *x* is nothing other than *x*.

"The topknot is destroyed" means (not that the man is dead but) that that part qualified by possession of hair is destroyed, not the whole locus of contact. If awareness of the absence of one locus of contact involved the mutual absence of the entire qualificand, then how could we ever be aware of the constant absence of a qualifier? Not by a hundred perceptions of silver can it be established that a thing is a shell. Mutual absence is itself nonlocus-pervading; otherwise, why should we suppose that the baked jar is not dark-colored, or to take Caitra to be a nonholder of a stick when the stick is destroyed.

Objection: Mutual absence of the locus of contact requires the absence of relationship (*saṃsargābhāva*) with the qualifier.

Answer: No, since the absence of relationship is not perceived without the perception of the locus of the absence. The awareness that the ground is not the jar doesn't require the constant absence of jar on the ground, and if the nonperception of the locus of a constant absence produces the perception of that constant absence, then we would perceive the constant absence of a jar in the jar itself.

To perceive a relational absence its locus must be presented. But the awareness "Caitra does not cook" does not require awareness of locus; indeed, it refers to the difference (mutual absence) of *Catira* from *one who cooks*, not to any absence of relation between Caitra and cooks. Likewise, "the jar is not now black" refers to the mutual absence now between the jar and anything black, based on the difference between (say) redness and blackness; it doesn't mean that the jar (or any red thing) is separate (*pṛthak*) from black things.

(E54-56) Given the awareness that the jar and the cloth do not exist on the ground, there still may be doubt whether the jar exists on the ground. Actually the awareness of absence of pairs occurs when one thing is absent in one place and another in another place, e.g., "the jar and the cloth do not exist." It cannot be supposed that this awareness has to do with a counterpositive of these absences which is the locus of duality, for we do not necessarily perceive the absences of jar and cloth in a locus of duality.

Objection: Then we may say that the perception that the jar and cloth do not exist has for its content an absence whose counterpositive is limited by either *jarness* or *clothness.*

Answer: No, for even without such an alternating perception we can be aware that the jar and cloth don't exist.

Objection: Then the content of the perception that the jar and cloth don't exist is the generic absence of dualty residing in the jar and cloth through the relation of contact.

Answer: No, for one doesn't have to be aware of the duality residing there to be aware that the jar and cloth don't exist.

(*Re* (26):) The term "all" governs only the limitors of counterpositiveness to constant absence sharing a locus with A. Any objection which tries to introduce such a general quantifier at some other point in (26) is baseless.

The constant absences referred to in (26) must never be, or be equivalent to, positive entities (*bhāva*). That is why there is no failure of (26) to cover, e.g., "it is water, because it is the locus of oiliness", even though all colors fail to share a common locus with waterness, these colors being the absences of the counterpositives limited by the absences of *colorness*, which last absence limits the counterpositive of an absence which shares a locus with the locus of oiliness. Likewise, there is no overextension for the same reason in "Here there is destruction of jar, because here there is destruction."

The proper meaning of (26) is this:

(26') Pervasion is *h*'s sharing a locus with a generic absence of a pervasive constant absence, whose counterpositive is limited by the limitor of the pervasive *s*.

Section 8A: *ata eva catuṣṭayam*
Three Definitions of Obstruction

Summary by Madhusūdana Nyāyācārya as translated by Sibajiban Bhattacharyya. "E" references are to the edition by G. Tarkadarsanatirtha (B3394; RB5302)

(E520-542) Gaṅgeśa says that an obstruction is something different from the limitor of the *h*. Here Raghunātha points out that the obstruction does not limit the limitor of the *h* either. Otherwise there will be underpervasion. As example, consider "it is (uncooked) curd or cooked curd, as it is made of curd-atoms". *Being uncooked or cooked curd* is not the limitor of the *h*, but it limits the limitor; if it were itself the limitor *being made of curd-atoms* there will be underpervasion.

Section Nine: The Means of Grasping Pervasion
Summary by Kishor Kumar Chakrabarti

"E" references are to the edition by G. Tarkadarsanatirtha (B3394; RB5302).[23]

(E560-573) Prabhākara has held that lack of awareness of deviation together with the awareness of concomitance are the means of ascertainment of pervasion. If deviation is the same as 'being present where the *s* is absent', then lack of awareness of deviation cannot be regarded as a necessary causal condition for the ascertainment of pervasion. For, if, as it sometimes is, the *s* is only-positive (*kevalānvayin*), it is not absent anywhere; in such a case there can be no such fact as being present where the *s* is absent—hence there cannot take place the awareness of the *h* being present where the *s* is absent—hence one cannot also speak of the absence of such an awareness.[24]

Objection: Although "the *h* being present where the *s* is absent" cannot be a fact where the *s* is only-positive, there could still in those cases be the mistaken awareness that the *h* is present where the *s* is absent, for the constituents of the said complex are real entities; hence the absence of such awareness could also be a fact.

Reply: Even if this were conceded, it cannot be shown that in every such case the said kind of mistake would take place, and therefore it cannot be shown that in every such case the said absence would be a fact.

Nevertheless, absence of the limitor of the *s*-ness being the content of the awareness that something is the limitor of the counterpositiveness of an absence belonging to the locus of the *h*, as possessed by a certain person, may be said to be a causal condition of the ascertainment of pervasion by that person.

As a matter of fact, pervasion becomes different as and when *h* or the *s* become different: hence the causal condition must be determined with reference to the specific cases. Thus deviation may be construed as the *h*'s belonging to the locus of absence of the *s*; it may also be construed as that the limitor of the *s*-ness is the limitor of the counterpositiveness of an absence belonging to the locus of the *h*, etc. In a particular case awareness of only one kind of deviation may be a fact: in that case absence of that awareness as belonging to a certain person would be a causal condition of ascertainment of pervasion. In another case awarenesses of more than one kind of deviation may be facts: in that case absence of all of them as belonging to a certain person would be a causal condition. That is why, although there is absence of awareness of deviation of one kind, awareness of pervasion becomes obstructed if there is awareness of deviation of another kind.

Pervasion may be identified with smoke-ness, etc., belonging to what is co-located with fire which pervades smoke, etc. Pervasion should not be construed as merely being co-located with fire which pervades smoke, etc.; for the latter characteristic is possessed also by a thing which is merely co-located with fire in one or more cases (but is not pervaded by fire).

It may be noted in this connection that lack of awareness of deviation is the causal condition of the awareness of being the pervader. On the other hand, the awareness of co-location is the causal condition of the awareness of belonging to that which is co-located. However, lack of awareness of deviation and the awareness of co-location taken severally should not be thought to be the cause of ascertainment of pervasion; rather, lack of awareness of deviation as qualified by the awareness of co-location is the cause of such ascertainment.

Section Ten: Reductio Ad Absurdum
Summary by Kishor K. Chakrabarti

"E" references are to the edition by V.P. Dvivedi and Vamacarana Bhattacarya (B3400; RB5308), Chowkhamba Sanskrit Series 42, 1913-27.

(E675-734) After observing that smoke is co-present with fire, donkeys, etc., and also observing that smoke is absent when some of these are absent, it is ascertained that some of these factors are the causes of smoke. The question naturally then is: which one or ones are the causes of smoke (from among these factors)?

The question may be answered as follows. When it is found that smoke is produced in spite of the absence of some of these factors, it becomes known that the latter are not the causes of smoke; for this reason, for example, donkeys cannot be the causes of smoke. When, however, it is found that smoke is not produced when one of these factors is missing although all others are present, it is known that the former is a cause of smoke; on this ground fire is ascertained to be a cause of smoke.

When it is doubted whether something is the cause of something, the doubt is set aside (or confirmed) by the above kind of reasoning.

Is it proper to investigate how causal connections are known when the subject is to enquire how general propositions may be known to be true? The answer must certainly be in the affirmative, for generalization (of a certain kind) are based on causation.[25]

Gaṅgeśa has posed the question whether smoke is caused by what is concomitant with fire or not. It should be noticed in this connection that even what is not caused by fire may be caused by something concomitant with fire (but different from fire), just as it may be that something not caused by fire is not caused by anything which is not concomitant with fire. Hence the proper import of Gaṅgeśa's question is whether smoke is caused by fire or not. Further, "not being caused by what is concomitant with fire'' should be construed as ''being caused by a sum total of causal conditions which does not include fire.''

In order to show that all smokes are caused by fire various kinds of considerations of parsimony may also be brought in support.

Some prefer to show that absence of fire should, on the ground of economy, be regarded as the cause of the nonorigin of all smokes.

Some others prefer to state the *tarka* (of Gaṅgeśa) in a different language as follows: If it were the case that smoke is neither originated in a place where fire is not located nor originated in a place where fire is located, smoke would have been uncaused.[26]

In the view of Vācaspati Miśra the *tarka* shows that the sceptic's doubt would stultify his own action of regularly using specific causes for producing specific effects.

(We have been unable to locate anyone to summarize Section Eleven: *Vyāptyanugama* of the *Dīdhiti*.)

Section Twelve: Perception Through Connection with the Universal
Summary by Kishor Kumar Chakrabarti

''E'' references are to the edition by V.P. Dvivedi and Vamacarana Bhattacarya (B3400; RB5308), Chowkhamba Sanskrit Series 42, 1913-27.

(E773-780) The expression *sāmānyalakṣaṇā* may be construed as that which by nature is a common character; then the common character itself turns out to be connection (*pratyāsatti*). Alternatively, the said expression may be construed as that of which a common character is the specifier (*nirūpaka*), then the awareness of a common character turns out to be the connection. Upon the first construal the common character (serving as the sensory connection for such nonordinary perception in which all particulars of a kind are perceived) must be understood as a character which is the qualifier of that which is in contact with a sense organ; for example, when a sense organ is in contact with a smoke, the universal *smokeness* which is the qualifier of the awareness having 'smoke' as the qualificand, is such a common character.

The sense organ must be in contact (with the particular of which the universal is the qualifier) through one of the ordinary means of sense-object connection. The resulting extraordinary perception arises from the same organ (which is in contact with the given particular).[27]

Accordingly, though, when a cloud of dust is mistaken for smoke and taken to be pervaded by fire, smoke is not thereby (correctly) known to be pervaded by fire, smokeness being absent in dust, it cannot be objected that there can be no inference of fire from the perception of smoke. Nor can it be objected that when smokeness is not visually perceived due to some defect or when smokeness is remembered, there could still be such (extrordinary) visual perception (of all smokes).

Universals are of two kinds: simple or complex. In the case of a complex (*sakhaṇḍa*) character a simple character which is indirectly related serves as the connection. Moreover, such a character serves as the connection for (the perception of) those things to which it is related by the same relationship through whih it is known to be related to what is (directly) in contact with sense organ.

Objection: When a noneternal individual which is connected with many loci, such as a pot, serves as the connection, there can be such perception (of all the loci) when the individual happens to be nonexistent.[28]

Reply: In such cases also potness, etc., serve as the connection by means of their being connected with those individuals. (That is, an indirectly related eternal universal would serve as the connection in such cases.) Alternatively, it is because of this difficulty that the second view has been advanced. In view of the fact that thc universal may belong to the past or the future, the awareness of the universal which is related (in the specified way) with the sense organ should be regared as the connection (for such extraordinary perception).[29]

(E780-798) This (*sāmānyalakṣaṇā*) is an awareness having the character as the object and serves as the connection for (the perception of) those possessing that character. The other (*jñānalakṣaṇā*), however, is the connection for the perception of the object of the awareness. This is why, in such cases as the visual perception that the sandalwood is fragrant, fragrance is also known.[30]

The pervasion of smoke (by fire which, as said in Gaṅgeśa's text, is first perceived and then remembered, leading to the inference to fire) is one and common to all smokes. If, however, the said pervasion were many, then on the one hand concomitance (*sāmānādhikaraṇya*) with the fire on the hill could not have been apprehended without contact with *that* smoke, and on the other hand, if concomitance with the fire belonging to something else (i.e., other than that on the hill) is predicated of the smoke on the hill), that would be a mistake.[31]

The significance of "words like cow also", etc. (in Gaṇgeśa's text), is that the awareness of meaning and remembrance of what is meant—these two are the causes of understanding the meaning of a sentence. This does not involve any conflict with the view that universals constitute the meanings of words. Both universals and individuals are meant (by words); however, individuals are brought before thought only by way of being the seats of universals.

Gaṅgeśa speaks of the precedence of the awareness of the qualifier, etc. It cannot be objected that since the said inference presupposes the awareness of the limitor of the *p*-ness (*pakṣatāvacchedakatā-jñāna*), it proves what is already known; for what is implied is the general proposition that that which is the awareness of being qualified by something presupposes the awareness of that thing.[32]

(E799-813) As a matter of fact a perception of that kind (e.g., the perception that this possesses someone holding a stick) takes place from the simultaneous sensory connection with the limitor of qualifierness, etc. (i.e., with that limitor along with the qualifier and the qualificand). An inference of that kind takes place from the awareness of pervasion in terms of that property (viz., the property of being someone holding a stick: *daṇḍitva*). Hence there is no need to admit *sāmānyalakṣaṇa* connection to account for the awareness of the limitor of the qualifierness where there happen to be many limitors of the qualifierness.[33]

Gaṅgeśa speaks of the known cases of smoke, etc. It should be noted in this connection that awareness of the subject (*dharmin*) is not a causal condition of doubt. Still *sāmānyalakṣaṇa* perception should be admitted to account for the awareness of the subject in doubt. There is no controversy that the awareness in which the limitor of subject-ness (*dharmitāvachhedaka*) features as the qualifier, does serve as a sensory connection. It is accepted that an awareness in which a property is featured as the qualifier serves as the sensory connection for those having that property.

In this connection some say the following. Are the known cases of smoke known to be pervaded insofar as they are characterized by smoke-ness, or insofar as they are particular smokes? If the first, doubt is ruled out. ("Smoke as characterized by smoke-ness" means all smokes. If it is known that all smoke is pervaded by fire, there is no room for the doubt as to whether some smoke is not pervaded.) If the second, since only the knowledge that 'what is limited by smoke-ness'(i.e., all smokes) is pervaded is opposed to that doubt, the doubt is not ruled out. Otherwise, although it is known that earthen and other colors do not belong to air, how can there be the doubt as to whether air has color or not? (More literally: although it is known that earthen color, etc., are pervaded by absence of airness, how can there be the doubt whether color deviates from absence of airness or not?) It cannot be said that the doubt arises from the possibility that there may be other colors and that *sāmānyalakṣaṇa* connection should be admitted to account for the awareness of these others. For the possibility of other colors is ruled out by the knowledge of the special nature of color. Since neither smoke nor color have been known to be pervaded insofar as they are characterized respectively by smokeness and colorness, the doubt regarding deviation is not unaccountable.

(E813-24) It has been argued that *sāmānyalakṣaṇa* has to be admitted to account for the awareness of generic absence (e.g., the awareness that there are no pots here), which signifies that every particular of a certain kind is absent. For without *sāmānyalakṣaṇa* perception the cognition of all the counterpositives is impossible. But this contention is not acceptable. Awareness of the counterpositive is not a necessary precondition of the awareness of an absence. For example, when one has the awareness "this is dark" the awareness is not preceded by the awareness of light, though "this" refers to darkness which is nothing other than absence of light. Secondly, even if it were conceded that awareness of the counterpositive is a necessary precondition of the awareness of an absence, it still does not follow that awareness of all the counterpositives is a necessary precondition; for it is possible that such awareness may take place from the awareness of some of the counterpositives only.

Incidentally, darkness is the 'generic absence' (*sāmānyābhāva*) of a specific kind of light. It is not (as held by Miśra) the totality of all the particular absences of the specified kind of light. The latter view fails to give a unitary account where one is possible; it also lacks parsimony.

With regard to prior absence it is to be noted that its awareness does not presuppose awareness of the counterpositive, but rather such awareness follows upon the awareness of the limitor of the counterpositiveness and other factors.[34]

It may be held that such a perception as that a pot will be produced has as its object a pot that is yet to be produced; a past or present pot could not be the object of such perception; even if it were so, the perception would be erroneous. The contact with a future pot, however, can be effected, not by any ordinary kind of sense-object contact, but only through *sāmānyalakṣaṇa* perception. It may, however, be the case that when one has such an awareness as that a pot will come to be, prior absence is not perceived, but inferred. The sum total of causal conditions (*sāmagrī*), insofar as it is that which is immediately followed by the origin of the effect, may be regarded as the basis for the inference of prior absence.[35]

(E824-831) Coming to be (in the future) does not mean being the counterpositive of a prior absence which is now present, because that involves the consequence that even with respect to something which will come to be tomorrow one could have the awareness that it will come to be today (prior absence of what will be produced tomorrow being available today also). On the other hand, since "will come to be" and "will be originated" are synonymous, (future) coming to be means being originated at a time after the present time. In an awareness such as "a pot will be produced here today" a particular place and a particular time are apprehended as the locus of origin, and not as the locus of prior absence. If in the above case, a particular place were apprehended as the locus of prior absence one could have had the awareness with reference to a pot-half, the destruction of which will be the cause of the destruction of the pot, that 'this will be the locus of the destruction of the pot.' On the other hand, if in the above case a particular time were apprehended as the locus of prior absence, the defect already mentioned would ensue, viz., that even with respect to something which will be produced tomorrow, one could have the awareness that it will be produced today.

Within the expression "will be" (*bhaviṣyati*), the root verb "be" (*bhū*) signifies origin and "will" (*syati*) signifies belonging to the time after the lapse of the present time.[36]

The awareness of absence of the effect before its origin has as its object the absolute absence of that temporal period (i.e., the absolute absence belonging to the time before the origin of the effect).[37]

It cannot be objected that there is no evidence for saying that the absolute absence of the specified temporal period belongs to the inherence cause of the effect; for even in the cases where a pot will be produced or has been destroyed we have such an awareness as "there is no pot in this pot-half". The absence of a particular pot cannot be the object of the awareness, for then this awareness could take place also with reference to a locus where a pot is present. Hence the absence of all pots must be the object (literally: an absence the counterpositiveness of which is limited by potness). Neither prior nor posterior absence is so (i.e., signifies the absence of all objects of a kind). Even if either prior or posterior absence were so, that is not the case for this pot-half, for many pots are yet to be produced as well as yet to be destroyed.[38]

(E831-849) Just like the awareness that a pot has come to be, so there is the awareness that the destruction of a pot has taken place. On the strength of such latter awareness posterior absence may be admitted additionally (over and above absolute absence), but not prior absence. Temporal priority (*pūrvatva*) need not be explained as "belonging to the period of time when there is prior absence", but may be explained as "belonging to past time". "Being temporally prior to that" may be explained as "belonging to a time the cessation of which exists at the moment of the origin of that." The problem regarding further production may be resolved by making the more economical assumption that the effect, etc., function as the obstruction.[39]

For those who do not believe in *mahāpralaya* (the total dissolution of all noneternal things), origin may be defined as being related to that moment in which there does not occur the cessation of any of the moments during which a thing is existent.

For those who believe in *mahāpralaya*, origin (*utpatti*) may be defined as being related to that moment in which occurs the cessation of a moment during which the thing is not existent.[40]

A moment is that which does not become the locus of what ceases to exist during its being.[41]

The fact that a piece of cloth is not produced, except where there are the threads out of which it is made, is explained more economically by supposing that a numerically single prior absence of cloth belongs to all those threads rather than by supposing that each of the thousands of threads is separately related to each particular cloth as a cause.[42]

(E849-862) There is no conclusive evidence for admitting prior absence as a cause. Moreover, the cloth is not produced when a few threads are not in contact.[43]

Others surmise that just like the common awareness that a pot has been destroyed here and now, there is also the common awareness that there is prior absence of the pot here and now. On the latter's strength they admit both prior absence and *sāmānyalakṣaṇa-sannikarṣa*.[44]

It may be asked: how can it be known that awareness is the cause of desire (*icchā*) and desire is the cause of volition (*kṛti*)? Since these do not occur simultaneously, awareness cannot be perceived together with desire; nor can desire be perceived together with volition. If, however, *sāmānyalakṣaṇa* perception is admitted, the awareness causing the desire may be apprehended through that means and the causal connection be ascertained thereby.

But this argument for admitting *sāmānyalakṣaṇa* perception is not acceptable. Two things cannot be known to be causally related merely by knowing what they are, but without knowing that they are related by way of temporal precedence and succession. Further, just as twenty volitions in twenty fingers may be produced simultaneously, so also it cannot be denied that cognition may arise simultaneously with desire or volition.[45]

Cow-ness-ness (*gotvatva*), the property of being the common property of all cows, incorporates the idea of not belonging to what is not a cow, but does not incorporate the idea of belonging to all cows; the latter could not be apprehended even through *sāmānyalakṣaṇa* perception.[46]

(E862-872) It has been stated by Gaṅgeśa that an awareness having a qualifier produces a desire having the same qualifier. But the causal relation between awareness and desire cannot be determined in terms of having the same qualifier alone to the exclusion of the factor of having the same content. For then there would have been no restriction to a certain kind of desire having, say, silverness as its qualifier being produced, but another kind of desire having the same qualifier being not produced. Further, how could something which is not silver be the object (erroneously) of a desire having silverness as the qualifier? It is not a good explanation to say that such desires are produced, because it has not been apprehended that the qualifier does not belong to the presented object. As a matter of fact, compared to "nonapprehension of lack of belonging" "having that the same content alone" is more economical. That is to say, it is more economical to suppose that a cognition having *that* as a content produces a desire having *that* as the qualifier.

Alternatively, if it becomes established that an awareness produces a desire having the same qualifier as itself, still "having the same content" should be added as a condition, just as it has to be added as a condition in order to avoid absurdities that both the awareness and the desire should belong to the same person. Compared to "nonapprehension of lack of belonging" it is still more economical to add "having the same content" as a determinant of the causal relation. The truth or falsity of the effect state is dependent on the truth or falsity of the causal state. Accordingly, it should not also be admitted that while, on the one hand, in the case of a congruent (*saṃvādinī*) desire an awareness having the same qualifier together with absence of defect (*doṣa*) is the cause, on the other hand, in the case of a noncongruent (*visaṃvādinī*) desire an awareness, having the same qualifier together with nonapprehension of the fact that the qualifier does not belong to the presented object, is the cause.

The awareness of fulfilment of all pleasures of a kind, and not simply fulfilment, is the obstruction to desire. Otherwise, how could a man who has been away for a long time and is not aware of his wife's passing away, have the desire of seeing her?

It may be said that on grounds of economy awareness of nonfulfilment rather than absence of awareness of fulfilment, should be regarded as the cause of desire; further it may be held that one should have recourse to *sāmānyalakṣaṇa* perception to account for the awareness of nonfulfilment.

But this is not so. Awareness of nonfulfilment cannot possibly be acquired through *sāmānyalakṣaṇa* perception. On the other hand, awareness of a pleasure that is yet to be realized, as well as the awareness of the fact that it is yet to be realized, may be obtained through inference. This will be explained more fully in the commentary on Book Four.

Gaṅgeśa speaks of the awareness "that is a pot," etc. An ascertainment (*niścaya*) having the same form (*ākāra*) as a doubt becomes the obstruction to the latter. In the doubt "is this a pot or not" pot-ness appears as a limitor which is not further limited by any othe property. But the awareness "this is characterized by a knowable" (where knowable = potness) is not so. (Thus the resultant awareness from a *sāmānyalakṣaṇa* perception having knowability as the connection cannot be the obstruction to the said doubt.) Hence although one has the ascertainment "this is characterized by a universal" (where universal = potness), one may still have the doubt as to whether this is a pot or not. However, the ascertainment "this is characterized by pot-ness" (in spite of not being of strictly the same form), which comprises the idea of having a property which does not belong to what is not a pot, is opposed to the doubt as to this being different from a pot, just as the ascertainment of possessing holes, etc., which do not belong to a person, is opposed to the doubt of being a person.

As said in the *Tattvacintāmaṇi* the requisite conditions for the ascertainment "this is a pot" are not available at the time of *sāmānyalakṣaṇa* perception. For the ascertainment that this is a pot the nonpropositional perception of potness is a causal condition; such ascertainment does not indeed arise if potness is presented merely as a universal. However, in the case of *sāmānyalakṣaṇa* perception an awareness having a common character as the qualifier becomes the cause.

Section Thirteen: On Obstruction
Summary by K.K. Chakrabarti

"E" references are to the edition by V.P. Dvivedi and Vamacarana Bhattacarya (B3400; RB5308).

(E713) In D1 Gaṅgeśa speaks of the "putative" *h* and *s*, for these cannot really be the *h* and *s* if an obstruction is involved. What the definition amounts to is: that which pervades something and does not pervade something else is an obstruction with reference to them.[47]

(E729) With reference to the acceptance of being other than the *p* as an obstruction some have held that it cannot be an obstruction, for an obstruction is a defect not for the reason that it proves deviation, but for the reason that it leads to counterbalancing; just as the existence of the *s* would follow from the existence of the pervaded *h*, so also the absence of the *s* would follow from the absence of the obstruction which pervades the *s*; it is thus that an obstruction leads to counterbalancing. "Being other than the *p*" however, does not lead to counterbalancing; for its absence is absent from all *sp*s and *vp*s and hence cannot prove the absence of the *vp*s.

The above, however, may be disputed and "being other than the *p*" too may be said to lead to counterbalancing. Further, it may be said to lead to the doubt that the *h* is deviant, which too may be said to be the reason for which an obstruction is a defect.

(E772) With reference to Gaṅgeśa's own account that an obstruction is that because of deviation from which the *h* becomes deviant from the *s*, another account may be suggested as follows: an obstruction is that which is the counterpositive of an absence which belongs to a locus where there are both the *h* and absence of the *s*. An obstruction may also be said to be that because of the absence of which or because of difference from what possesses it, it follows that there is absence of the *s* where the *h* is present.[48]

(E782-786) With reference to Gaṅgeśa's definition that an obstruction is that which pervades what amounts to the *s* as specifed by that character with the specification by which the *s* is known to be present in the locus of the *h*, this amounts to pervasion of relation between the *s* and the *h*. Alternatively, what may be intended is: pervasion of the *s* as specified by that character which pervades the *h*.

In this connection some say the following: The character by being co-located with which the *s* is pervaded by the obstruction should be the same as that character by being co-located with which the *h* is not pervaded by the obstruction. This helps to show why food will not be an obstruction in the correct inference of fire from smoke; just as food pervades fire co-located with kitchen-ness (i.e. kitchen-fire), so also it pervades smoke co-located with kitchenness; hence it will not be an obstruction. It would be a mistake to replace the expression "being co-located with which" in the above by "being specified by which" (i.e., *sāmānādhikaraṇya* by *avacchedakatva*); for then although food will not be an obstruction in the above inference, "being different from that pot" will turn out to be an obstruction in the inference "that pot is colored because it is an earthen object." It so happens that color is absent in that pot in the moment of its origin, but even in that moment the property of being an earthen object is present there. Thus it is clear that *being different from that pot* pervades color as specified by the property of being contemporaneous with the moment of origin of that pot, but *being different from that pot* does not pervade *being an earthen object* as specified by the property of being contemporaneous with the moment of origin of that pot.[49]

Alternatively, an obstruction may be said to pervade the *s* as specified by the character which belongs to that locus of the *h* which is not a locus of the obstruction.[50]

(E790-804) Again, an obstruction may be defined as that which possesses the character which belongs to what is co-located with the *s* which is the limitor of the counterpositiveness of an absolute absence (which is such that it is not co-located with the counterpositive as specified by the limitor of counterpositiveness) belonging to that locus of the *h* which is the locus of what is not co-located with *s*.

It may be noted in this connection that in the view of Pakṣadhara Miśra Gaṅgeśa's account, to the effect that an obstruction is that because of deviation from which the *h* becomes deviant from the *s*, is what gives the definition of an obstruction. The other account of Gaṅgeśa to the effect that an obstruction is that which pervades what amounts to the *s*, etc., does not give the definition of an obstruction, but vindicates what is conducive to proving the fact of deviation.

Gaṅgeśa has said that if the *h* deviates from what is qualified, then, if the *h* does not deviate from the qualifier, it follows that the *h* deviates from the qualificand. This is in accordance with the view of the earlier thinkers that deviation from what is qualified is the same as deviation from either the qualifier or the qualificand. Then if it is given that the *h* does not deviate from the qualifier and still deviates from qualified, it follows that the *h* deviates from the qualificandum.

With reference to the inference of deviation (*vyabhicārānumāna*), viz., that the property of being the locus of perceived touch deviates from the property of being perceived, etc., it may be noted that this represents Gaṅgeśa's own view. Here "perceived" should be construed as "perceived by an external sense organ," or "substance" should be construed as "external substance", and *mahattva*, as "originated *mahattva*." "Deviation from the pervader" should be construed as "belonging to the locus of absence of what is specified by that character which is the limitor of pervaderness."[51]

(E804-811) With reference to the definition that an obstruction is that which establishes the fact of deviation directly or indirectly, etc., it may be noted that this covers both the obstructions which pervade the *s* itself and the obstructions which pervade the *s* as qualified. The fact of deviation from the *s* itself may be inferred (in the manner indicated above) from the fact of deviation from the obstruction which pervades the *s* as qualified. It is leading to the fact of deviation, irrespectively of whether this is done directly or indirectly, which is the characteristic nature of an obstruction. That an obstruction is a defect may be recognized even if it leads to deviation indirectly. The qualification "what is co-located with the *s*" should be added to leave out the opposed (*viruddha*) pseudo-*h*.

One may first state the fact of deviation from the *s* itself; then as the ground for that one may state either the fact of deviation from the obstruction which pervades the *s* itself or the fact of deviation from the obstruction which pervades the *s* as qualified together with the fact of nondeviation from the qualifier. Further, just as deviation is opposed to pervasion, so also is possession of what is pervaded by deviation. Hence, alternatively, one may also state that the putative *h* is possessed of deviation from the obstruction, which deviation is pervaded by deviation from the *s*.

Some held that if "being other than the *p*" were accepted as an obstruction all inferences will be vitiated by it, including the inference of deviation; hence its acceptance as an obstruction is self-stultifying. But this is not correct. That *being other than the p* pervades the *s* has to be ascertained with the help of a supportive *tarka*. This will be possible in cases of *bādha* and may also be possible in some other cases. But this cannot be done in every case, and certainly not in those cases where the fact of pervasion of the *h* by the *s* has been ascertained with the help of a supportive *tarka*. Thus *being other than the p* cannot be an obstruction in those cases where it is uncertain, due to lack of supportive *tarka*, that it pervades the *s*. On the other hand, if it can be ascertained with the help of a supportive *tarka* that it pervades the *s*, it will be a certain obstruction; indeed, the fact of deviation from the pervaded follows necessarily from the fact of deviation from the pervader.[52]

(E827) The definition that an obstruction is that because of the absence of which the *h* becomes dissociated from the *s* would amount to the following by way of adding the word "subject": an obstruction is the counterpositive of that absence through which absence of the *s* in the subject may be ascertained. This account is in accordance with the view that an obstrction is a defect basically for the reason that it leads to counterbalancing. On the other hand, if the word "locus" is added, the definition would amount to the following: an obstruction is the counterpositive of that absence through which absence of the *s* in the locus of the *h* may be ascertained. An obstruction may lead to the ascertainment of absence of the *s* in the subject in some cases and in some other locus of the *h* in other cases.

(E846-868) With reference to the probable obstruction it may be noted that doubt about the pervaded is a ground for doubt about the pervader. In this connection it is obvious that if it is doubtful whether the obstruction does not pervade the *h*, then if it were doubtful whether the *h* deviates from the pervader of the *s*, then it would be doubtful whether the *h* deviates from the *s*. On the other hand, if it is doubtful whether the obstruction pervades the *s*, then if it were doubtful whether the *s* is pervaded by what does not pervade the *h*, then it would be doubtful whether the *s* does not pervade the *h*. It is also said that if it is doubtful whether the obstruction pervades the *s*, then it would be doubtful whether the *h* deviates from the pervader of the *s*, and then it would be doubtful whether the *h* deviates from the *s*.

The new scholars hold that the *h*'s deviation from the *s* is inferred from the *h*'s deviation from the obstruction which pervades the *s*, and further, that the *s* does not pervade the *h* is inferred from the *s*'s being pervaded by the obstruction which does not pervade the *h*.

It may be noted that if what deviates from the pervader were nondeviant from the pervaded, that would contradict the nature of the pervaded and the pervader.

It may be pointed out that in some cases an obstruction may lead to counterbalancing if it is an equal match of the *h*. In some cases an obstruction may also lead to *bādha* if, with the aid of *tarka*, etc., it proves to be stronger.

Section Fourteen: Being the Pakṣa
Summary by Kishor Kumar Chakrabarti

"E" references are to the edition by Jivananda Vidyasagara (B3377; RB5285), Calcutta 1872.

(E123-124) The discussion of being the *p* after discussing pervasion is quite in order since both are conducive to the same effect, viz., the inferential result.

(1) The first definition discussed by Gaṅgeśa makes it applicable to the doubt which has *p* as the qualificand as well as to the doubt having the *s* as the qualificand. Furthermore, it serves to exclude doubt about the *s* having some other relation to the *p*. Finally, it shows how being the *p* can operate in such an inference as that *ākāśa* belongs to darkness through inherence.

(2) The second of Gaṅgeśa's definitions says that being the *p* consists in the absence of both (a) (*siddhi*) certainty that *s* belongs to *p*, and (b) (*bādha*) sublation, or the certainty that *s* does not belong to *p*. Sublation is possible even if the *s* is only-positive, since it can be apprehended to be the counterpositive of an absence located in the *p*.

(3) Gaṅgeśa has criticized the third definition on the ground that,

e.g., the desire to infer may have ceased to exist before the consideration occurs. But this criticism can be met by supposing either that the desire occurs one moment before the occurrence of consideration or by supposing that the desire occurs a moment after one remembers the consideration and realizes that the inference will serve one's purpose. Nevertheless, Gaṅgeśa's criticism is correct, since, e.g., an inference of clouds from hearing thunder may take place without being accompanied by any desire.

Objection: Then we shall suppose that at least inference is always accompanied by God's desire, since that is a common causal condition of all effects.

Answer: But since God's desire is always present there will be *pakṣatā* even when there is certainty.

(E124-125) Gaṅgeśa's definition is that being the *p* is absence of certainty-qualified-by-absence-of-desire-to-infer. The qualification is needed to account for cases such as these: (a) when inference arises from remembering that the *s* as well as what is pervaded by the *s* belonged to the *p*, where that memory is preceded by the desire to infer; (b) inference arises from the desire to infer which is preceded by the memory that (1) the *s* and what is pervaded by the *s* belonged to the *p* and (2) that the inference has served one's purpose.

When the desire to infer is spoken of it must be understood as the desire to infer that the specific *s* in question belongs to the specific *p* in question. Otherwise someone with a desire to infer something or other and who is certain that *p* has *s* should be able to infer (according to Gaṅgeśa's definition), whereas in fact he isn't. On the other hand, the desire to infer includes any desire amounting to a desire to infer; it is not required that it be a desire of which inferenceness is the chief qualifier.

Raghunātha tries to bring all relevant desires (amounting to desires to infer) under a common description, but concludes that it can't be done, and that "absence of desire to infer" should be understood as the absence of all those kinds of desires which lead to inference.

Consider an instance where, although there is no certainty that there is fire on the mountain, the desire to infer fire there from smoke is followed by the consideration of the concomitance of light (*āloka*), which is also pervaded by fire, and so no inference occurs), then the desire to infer through a different *h* should be taken as an obstructor (*pratibandhaka*). On the other hand, if inference does occur in the above situation, the desire to infer through a different *h* (is not an obstructor, but it isn't a stimulator (*uttejaka*) of inference either, since it) doesn't lead to inference when there *is* certainty. The stimulator is the desire to infer through the same *h*—or rather, the desire which is different from a desire to infer through only a different *h*.

(E125) When one believes that what has fireness (*tejastva*) belongs to what is made of stone, the inference that fire is on the hill still takes place. Therefore it is necessary to understand the *s* as being limited by the *sādhyatā*-limitor and the *p* as being limited by the *pakṣatā*-limitor.

One may believe that the *s* belongs to some *p* and so infer that it belongs to what is limited by *p*'s limitor. Therefore it is the belief that *s* belongs to what is limited by *p*'s limitor which should be taken as an obstructor to the inference that *s* belongs to what is limited by *p*'s limitor. As for the inference that *s* belongs to some *p*, either kind of belief is an obstructor of it. Similar distinctions as made earlier need to be made here too.

If, though there is belief having *s* as its qualificand, there is an inference having the *p* as its qualificand, then only the belief which has the *p* as qualificand can be taken as obstructing an inference having *p* as the qualificand. But a belief having either *s* or *p* as qualificand obstructs an inferene having *s* as its qualificand—or the obstructor may be taken to be simply belief about the *s*, in which case only an inference having the *p* as its qualificand can take place where belief about *s* is present.

(E125-126) Now consider the case where the desire to infer is followed by memory of the pervasion followed in turn by the consideration that *p* has *s*. There the desire has ceased to exist and belief that *p* has *s* is present, and even so inference takes place. (Yajñapati) Upādhyāya says that one should explain this by assuming that another desire occurs before the conclusion is drawn.

Others (commentators say Pakṣadhara Miśra) propose the theory of desire-potency (*anumitayogyatā*) to explain the above case. This is a technical term referring to the period after the initial desire and up to the time the consideration arises, or it may be taken to refer to the time period within which inference takes place after the desire ceases even though belief that *p* has *s* be present, and marked (*upalakṣita*) by the desire. Furthermore, if the inference does not originate within two moments after cessation of the belief unless there is desire, then the period of time in question is to be considered marked by the belief.

(E126-end) Suppose one remembers that the *s*, what is pervaded by the *s*, and what is pervaded by what is pervaded by the *s* belong to the *p*, as well as that inferring *s*, etc., is beneficial. Suppose this memory is followed by desire to infer that the *s*, etc., belong to the *p*, and in due course by the inferential conclusion that the *s*, what is pervaded by the *s*, etc., belong to the *p*. One would have to admit that the inference that *p* has *s* will also occur, unless we require that the desire (or desire-potency) must be specified to be one whose content is not already believed.

The causal efficacy of *pakṣatā* for a particular inference will vary as the *p* and *s* are differently specified. Therefore it is sufficient to take absence of belief that *p* has *s* as the *pakṣatā* for those cases where such belief is never followed by initiation of inference. In such cases reference to desire to infer is superfluous. Again, if no one has ever entertained the desire to infer that a certain *p* has a certain *s*, it is unnecessary to bring in God's desire to explain this case.

Another view is that belief whose absence qualified by absence of desire is regarded as *pakṣatā* should be further specified as follows viz., as the belief which is different from a belief which is followed by the origin of inference at the moment immediately following that moment in which there is belief without desire to infer. But this is not right, for it fails to account for *pakṣatā* in a case where the consideration is preceded by a perceptual belief which is itself preceded by cessation of the desire. Even this objection can be met if one specifies that the belief (in the definition of *pakṣatā*) must be one which is not a belief followed by the origin of inference in the first or second moment immediately following. But still the view in question remains unsatisfactory; there is a collection of causal conditions to differentiate a belief which will be followed by inference from one which will not.

(Summaries of Raghunātha's commentary on sections 15-19 have not been obtained. We hope to be able to include them in the next volume on Nyāya-Vaiśeṣika.)

Section Twenty: Fallacies

This summary is based on Nandita Bandyopadhyaya's summaries of sections of Raghunātha's commentary in her *The Concept of Logical Fallacies* (Calcutta 1977). That work is referred to as "B" below. 'E' references are to the edition of Gaṅgeśa with Raghunātha and Gadādhara by Vamacharana Bhattacharya and Dhundiraja Sastri (B3400; RB5308) in Chowkhamba Sanskrit Series 42, 1913-27.)

Part One: General Definition (*sāmānyanirukti*)

(E1580; B6-11) "Inferential awareness" (*anumiti*) in Gaṅgeśa's D1 may be construed either as the awareness of the conclusion or as an awareness that operates as a cause of it. Or if secondary meaning is viewed as inferior "inferential awareness" should be taken to mean the *p*'s possesing the *s*-pervaded *h*, or its equivalent.

(E1585-1588; B25-27) Objection: The components of a valid inference,e.g., "lake" and "absence of fire" (in "this mountain has fire because it has smoke, like kitchen and unlike lake") also satisfy D1, being contents of a veridical awareness as described in D1. So D1 overextends to them as well.

Raghunātha: Only the negation of the entire valid awareness stating a true state of affairs comprises a fallacy. Awareness of mere parts of such a total awareness does not block a valid inference. That being so, the term "veridical" (in D1) is redundant, since its intent is already guaranteed. For that reason Gaṅgeśa passes on to D2.

(E1591; B38-39) In the invalid awareness "this mountain has smoke because it has fire" fire is qualified by knowability. So, isn't "this mountain has smoke because it has knowable fire" also an invalid inference? No, says Raghunātha, because that is heavy.

(E1603; B47) Some propose

D2a: A fallacious *hetu* is something which has the nature of something such that awareness of its having that nature contradicts the inferential awareness.

(Raghunāṭha's style suggests he disapproves of D2a.)

(E1621; B59) The following definition is better:

D2b: A fallacious *hetu* is what is different from what is other than as many faults as are (held to be) possible in that kind of *h*, that kind of *p* and that kind of *s*.

This definition is applicable in all five kinds of fallacy to be discussed.

Part Two: Deviation (*savyabhicāra* or *anaikāntika*)
Second Section: Too-General-Ness (*sādhāraṇatva*)

(E1705-1706; B93-95) What does *vipakṣa* mean? Jayadeva holds that it refers to what is known (*niścita*) to lack the *sādhya* property. But Raghunātha disagrees: it just refers to something that lacks the *sādhya* property, since pervasion is defined that way (without the *niścita*).

(Pakṣadhara: Then the definition of pervasion overextends to include doubt.)

Raghunātha: No. Knowledge of pervasion is required for an inference to be known to be valid. Once such knowledge is possessed no suspicion of deviation of *s* from *h* can arise. A mere doubt about this will block knowledge of pervasion.

Third Section: Too-Specific (*asādhāraṇa*)

(E1728-1729; B96) Raghunātha disagrees with Gaṅgeśa about the absence of *vp* being redundant. The joint absence of both *sp* and *vp* constitutes the fault of too-specific-ness.

Fourth Section: Inconclusive (*anupasaṃhārin*)

(E1747-1768; B101-109) What does "inconclusive" mean, exactly? Consider

(A) "Everything is nameable because it is knowable. (A) is traditionally inconclusive since there is nothing other than its *pakṣa* that has the *sādhya* and *hetu*, and there is nothing that lacks the *s* and *h*. But if "inconclusive" means that the *h* is always found with the *s*, (A) is conclusive. Or, if "inconclusive" means merely that somebody lacks knowledge of *sp* or *vp* the fallacy is not a fault of the argument but of the person whose knowledge is lacking. Raghunātha says this is why Gaṅgeśa offers D13 as an alternative to D12.

Raghunātha suggests another way of thinking about the inconclusive *h*. He defines it as an inference where the absence of the *s* is pervaded by the absence of the *h*. That is, where there is absence of negative pervasion (*vyatirekavyāpti*) of this kind the judgment—e.g., (A)—though true is not valid, since the conclusion merely repeats what is already contained in the premisses.

Part Three: Contradictoriness (*viruddha*)

(E1764; B117-118) While Gaṅgeśa treats D17 as equivalent to the definition of the too-specific (*asādhāraṇa*) and thus rejects it here, Raghunātha, who has a different definition of too-specific, defends D17.

Part Four: Counterbalanced (*satpratipakṣa*)

(E1792-1793; B128-129) Clarifying Gaṅgeśa's D21 Raghunātha explains that a counterbalanced *h* is the content of a consideration which has the capacity to establish the *s*, which consideration is present in the speaker's mind at the same time as a consideration having the capacity to establish absence of *s*. It is not, as Pakṣadhara supposed, merely that the two considerations have equal strength as true in the mind of the speaker. It is sufficient if the speaker has not ascertained the falsehood of either.

Part Five: Unestablished (*asiddha*)

(E1855-1867; B153-156) Consider

(B) "This mountain has fire because it has blue smoke".

Classically (B) was considered fallacious because "blue smoke" is unnecessarily heavy. Raghunātha disagrees. The essential requirement for a limitor is that its occurrence not overreach what it limits, irrespective of whether the limitor is lighter or heavier than what it limits. Although not a fallacy, Raghunātha admits *vyāpyatvāsiddhi* as a reason for losing an argument (*nigrahasthāna*) not expressly mentioned in the *Nyāyasūtras* but intended to be covered in its last *sūtra.*

Part Six: Sublated (*bādha*)

(E1885; B158, 165-167) Raghunātha defines sublation as the direct inhibition of an inferential conclusion where the contradictory of it is accepted without doubt as known.

Gaṅgeśa argues that not mere awareness of the absence of *s* in *p* but awareness of the truth of that awareness is required for an inference to be sublated. Raghunātha disagrees. The way it needs to be put is this: the contradicting awareness must be valid and there must be no (false) awareness that it is false.

(E19817; B177) Sublation need not also involve a *vyabhicāra* or unestablished *h.* Consider "the pot at this moment of its production has smell, because it is made of earth".

NOTES

INTRODUCTION TO THE PHILOSOPHY OF NAVYA-NYĀYA

1. M.R. Bodas' notes to Y.V. Athalye's edition and translation (B3910; RB6383) of Annambhaṭṭa's *Tarkasaṃgraha.* Bombay Sanskrit and Prakrit Series 55, 1897, p. xlvi.

2. Ibid

3. See below, p. 77 and Daniel H.H. Ingalls (B3417; R.B. Ingalls), *Materials for the Study of Navya-Nyāya Logic.* Harvard Oriental Series 40 (Cambridge, Mass. 1951), pp. 9-17.

4. See Vol. II of this Encyclopedia, pp.410-424.

5. Cf. pp.307-308 of Vol. II of this Encyclopedia.

6. A point noted by D.C. Guha (RB9368), *Navya Nyāya System of Logic* (Varanasi 1968), pp. 23 ff. But Guha has failed to explain the use of "limitor" as referring to the mode of presentation of an object in an awareness. (SB)

7. Cf. Vol. II of this Encyclopedia, p. 524. See Sadananda Bhaduri (B6048, RB9277A), *Studies in Nyāya-Vaiśeṣika Metaphysics* (Poona 1947), pp. 66-69.

8. Cf. Vol. II of this Encyclopedia, p. 437.

9. Ibid., p. 87.

10. Ibid., pp. 87.

11. Cf. Vol. II, pp. 434-435.

12. Umesh Mishra's (B6026; RB9275) *Conception of Matter according to Nyāya-Vaiśeṣika* (Allahabad 1936; Delhi 1987), pp. 293-295, reviews the issue and some of the arguments.

13. *Mahattvādanekadravyatvāt rūpaviśeṣācca dravyaṃ pratyakṣam.* Vaiśeṣikasūtra IV.1.6.

14. Cf. Volume II, p. 91.

15. Umesh Mishra (B6026; RB9275), pp. 137-159 reviews most of the arguments.

16. Cf. John Vattanky, *Gaṅgeśa's Philosophy of God* (Madras 1984), pp. 123-129.

17. *Ātmattvavivekadīdhiti,* section 8 of the summary below.

18. Vol. II of this Encyclopedia, p. 287.

19. Cf. section 89, p. 106 of the edition by J.S. Jetly (RB1975) of Udayana's *Kiraṇāvalī* in the Gaekwad's Oriental Series 154, 1971, p. 106.

20. Sadananda Bhaduri (B6048; RB9277A), pp. 112-116.

21. Ibid., pp. 115-116.

22. Ibid., p. 126.

23. The reader may find these arguments outlined and explained in Umesh Mishra (B6026; RB9275), pp. 163-166.

24. Ibid., p. 44.

25. Ingalls (B3417; RB Ingalls), p. 38.

26. Section Seven of Book I of *Tattvacintāmaṇi* below, pp. 136-142.

27. See the relevant sections of the summaries of Raghunātha Śiromaṇi's *Ātmatattvavivekadīdhiti, Tattvacintāmaṇidīdhiti* and *Padārthatattvanirūpaṇa* below.

28. See Karl H. Potter (B3719; RB5943), *The Padārthatattvanirūpaṇam of Raghunātha Śiromaṇi* (Harvard-Yenching Institute Studies 17; Cambridge, Mass., 1957), p. 69.

29. On this see J.L. Shaw, "The Nyāya on Cognition and Negation", *Journal of Indian Philosophy* 8, 1980. pp. 279-302.

30. Erich Frauwallner (RB5952), "Raghunātha Śiromaṇi", Wiener Zeitschrift für die Kunde Südasiens 10, 1966, 86-207; 11, 1967, 140-208; 14, 1970, 161-208.

31. See Tarasankar Bhattacharya (RB9381), *The Nature of Vyāpti according to Navya-Nyāya* (Calcutta 1970), pp. 252-262.

32. Cf. Vol. II of this Encyclopedia, p. 63.

33. Ibid., p. 50.

34. The next fourteen paragraphs are taken from K.H. Potter, "Does Indian epistemology concern justified true belief?", *Journal of Indian Philosophy* 12, 1984, pp. 307-328.

35. "*Tathāpi tadvati tatprakārakajñānatvaṃ tadvati tadvaiśiṣṭyajñānatvaṃ vā prāmāṇyam*".

36. "*Avisaṃvādakaṃ jñānaṃ saṃyagjñānam. Loke ca pūrvam upadarśitam arthaṃ prāpayan saṃvādaka ucyate...Pradarśite cārthe pravartakatvameva prāpakatvam. Nānyat. Tathā hi na jñānaṃ janayadarthaṃ prāpayati. Api tvarthe puruṣaṃ pravartayat prāpayatyartham. Pravartakatvamapi pravṛttiviṣayapradarśakatvameva.*" P. Peterson (ed.), *The Nyāyabinduṭīkā of Dharmottara Ācārya to which is added the Nyāyabindu* (Reissue, Calcutta 1929), p. 3. Potter's translation.

37. E.g., Dignāga and Dharmakīrti use this term in defining perception. See ibid., p. 103, third sentence of the text.

38. Jitendranath Mohanty (RB5338), *Gaṅgeśa's Theory of Truth* (Visvabharati, Santiniketan 1966), p. 6.

39. Ibid.

40. And once again considering Mohanty's excellent review of their views, ibid.

41. Mohanty (RB5338), p. 12.

42. Mohanty renders the expression "*arthaparicchedasāmarthya*" differently than I do, taking "*artha*" as meaning "object" here and elsewhere.

43. Mohanty (RB5338), p. 42 *et passim.*

44. In the Prābhākara and Bhāṭṭa versions of the *svataḥ* theory we do not become aware of the *prāmāṇya* of an awareness through an aftercognition, but rather, in the case of the Prābhākaras, the awareness itself vouchsafes its own *prāmāṇya*, and for the Bhāṭṭa, we draw an inference from the knownness (*jñātatā*) which characterizes the content as a result of our cognizing it.

45. Pradyot Kr. Mandal, "Some problems of perception in Navya-Nyāya", *Journal of Indian Philosophy* 15, 1987, p. 139.

46. Bimal Krishna Matilal, *Nyāya-Vaiśeṣika.* A History of Indian Literature Volume VI, Fascicule 2 (Wiesbaden 1977), p. 102. This point does not appear from the summary of the *Nyāyaratna* in Vol. II of this Encyclopedia.

47. Umesh Mishra (B1026; RB9275), p. 312.

48. The editors of this Encyclopedia offer a large vote of thanks to Jadavpur

University for helping to defray the expenses involved in copying the text, and to Gopinath Bhattacharya for allowing his book to be copied.

49. V.N. Jha points out that this section of Gaṅgeśa derives from Śaśadhara's *Apūrvavāda* section of his *Nyāyasiddhāntadīpa* and summarizes the argument of that section. Cf. V.N. Jha's introduction to his translation of this section in 49. *The Logic of the Intermediate Causal Link* (Sri Garib Dass Oriental Series 46: Delhi 1986), pp. xv-xxiv.

50. Book Four goes into a number of further issues relating to language. We shall be content not to discuss them further in our introductory essay here, not because they aren't important, but because their importance is more grammatical and comparatively less philosophical than what precedes them.

51. We presuppose in this section that the reader is acquainted with corresponding section on logical theory in the Introduction to Vol. Two of this Encyclopedia.

52. Materials for such an introduction are to be found in various places, notably Ingalls (B3417; RB Ingalls); Sibajiban Bhattacharya, "Some aspects of the Navya-Nyāya theory of inference", *Journal of the Indian Academy of Philosophy* 22.1, 1981, 36-56; 23.1, 1984, 37-68, and "Some principles and concepts of Navya-Nyāya logic and ontology", *Our Heritage* 24.1, 1976—25.1, 1977, 56 pp.; D.C. Guha (RB9368); B.K. Matilal (RB5341), *The Navya-Nyāya Doctrine of Negation.* Harvard Oriental Series 46 (Cambridge, Mass., 1968).

53. In several of the papers reprinted in Frits Staal, *Universals. Studies in Indian Logic and Linguistics* (Chicago 1988).

54. Sibajiban Bhattacharya, op. cit.

55. B.K. Matilal (RB5341)

56. See pp. 200-203 of Vol. II of this Encyclopedia.

57. C. Goekoop (RB5339), *The Logic of Invariable Concomitance in the Tattvacintāmaṇi* (Dordrecht 1967), pp. 19-21.

58. See Vol. II of this Encyclopedia, p. 184.

1. GAṄGEŚA

1. Mahadeva Rajaram Bodas (B3910; RB6383), p. xlv.

2. A. Berriedale Keith (B6002; RB9248), *Indian Logic and Atomism* (Oxford 1921); Satischandra Vidyabhusana (B and RB: HIL), *History of Indian Logic* (Calcutta 1921). See also *New Catalogus Catalogorum* Vol. 5, p. 226.

3. Gopinath Kaviraj (GK), *Gleanings from the History and Bibliography of the Nyāya-Vaiśeṣika Literature* (Calcutta 1962); Ingalls (B3417; RB6383); Umesh Mishra (RB: UM), *History of Indian Philosophy*, Vol. Two (Allahabad 1966); Dineshchandra Bhattacharya (RB6105), *History of Navya-Nyāya in Mithilā* (Darbhanga 1958).

4. B.K. Matilal, *Nyāya-Vaiśeṣika*, op. cit.; Gopikamohan Bhattacharya, *Navya-Nyāya: Some Logical Problems in Historical Perspective* (Delhi 1978).

5. Ingalls (B3417; RB Ingalls), p. 4.

6. Ibid., p. 6.

7. It is controversial whether the *Maṅgalavāda* is a part of the *Tattva-cintāmaṇi.* A *resumé* of the contents of the *Maṅgalavāda* is provided in Gaurinath Sastri's edition, Bibliotheca Indica 308, Calcutta 1979.

8. The understood premiss is: Whatever activity is not denounced and is practiced by cultured men (*śiṣṭa*) is fruitful. The commentators have taken a lot of pains to explain the significance of this premiss.

9. Inf1 refers to the well-known example of error where a piece of shell is perceived as silver and sought to be acquired by the perceiver. The acquiring of the shell mistaken for silver is preceded by the activity (*pravṛtti*) toward acquiring silver mistakenly directed towards the shell. Thus the shell becomes the intentional object of the activity of someone looking for silver. This is possible only if the shell is taken for silver. Hence it is said that there must be an awareness having silverness as its qualifier. The argument has been stated with being the intentional object of (the activity of) someone looking for silver as its *pakṣa*, being pervaded by the property of being the content of a direct awareness having silverness as its chief qualifier as its *sādhya*, and being a property that belongs only to the intentional object (of the activity) of someone looking for silver as its *hetu*, with a property belonging only to silver as the *sapakṣa* or corroborative example for the suppressed universal proposition that all properties which belong only to the intentional object of someone looking for silver are pervaded by the property of being the content of a direct awareness having silverness as its chief qualifier. The application (*upanaya*) is: all intentional objects of the activity of someone looking for silver possess a property which belongs only to the intentional object of someone looking for silver. The conclusion (*nigamana*) is: all intentional objects of the activity of someone looking for silver are pervaded by the property of being the content of a direct awareness having silverness as its chief qualifier. A property belonging only to silver serves as *sapakṣa* for the pervasion because both the *h* and the *s* are found together in (things having) this property. A property belonging only to silver, such as silverness, is a property which belongs only to the intentional object of someone looking for silver; it is also pervaded by the property of being the content of a direct awareness having silverness as its qualifier.

Alternatively, being the content of a direct awareness having silverness as its qualifier may be taken to be the *sādhya*. Then the argument reads as follows: all properties which belong only to the intentional object of the activity of someone looking for silver are contents of a direct awareness having silverness as the qualifier; all intentional objects of the activity of someone looking for silver possess a property which belongs only to the intentional object of the activity of someone looking for silver; therefore, all intentional objects of the activity of someone looking for silver are contents of a direct awareness having silverness as its qualifier.

10. The *pakṣa*, *sādhya*, *hetu*, and *sapakṣa* of the above inferences may look inordinately complex. Different commentators, however, have explained how any deletion or simplification would lead to difficulty.

11. If qualifications are added to the *hetu* and its application is thereby narrowed, normally it itself will not be acceptable as an *upādhi*, for the

presumption is that it would fail to pervade the *sādhya* which is taken to be pervasive of the *hetu*. As a matter of fact *being an activity towards a desired object* also does not pervade the *sādhya being caused by the awareness of the desired intentional object of activity*.

12. The Prābhākara's view is that the activity towards the shell is caused by three factors—(1) awareness of *this*, (2) awareness of silver, and (3) lack of awareness of the difference between *this* and silver. He rejects Gaṅgeśa's view that the said activity is caused by the awareness of *this* as silver, i.e., the awareness of *this* as qualified by silver.

13. If instead of the shell there is silver itself in front of one, and an awareness having silverness as its qualifier is followed by desire for and activity towards silver, there is no possibility of there being an awareness of the difference between the desired object and the object in front. Since the desired object is actually in front and is also being cognized as such, it is impossible that the awareness of the difference between what is desired and what is in front should take place in such a case. It is a well established dictum of Nyāya philosophy that the absence of something impossible is not a "real" absence and therefore cannot function as a cause. Thus, contrary to what the Prābhākara seems to claim, absence of the awareness of difference cannot be the cause in all cases of volitional activity. Can it then be regarded as the cause of activity in the error situation?

14. The absence of the awareness that this is not silver or of the awareness that this is not the desired object turns out to be unavailable in the case cited. Hence the absence has been restated in such a way that it becomes available in every case and that every constituent of the complex counterpositive is an existent entity in accordance with the Nyāya-Vaiśeṣika ontology.

15. According to the Prābhākara the activity towards the shell is caused by the lack of awareness that this is not silver. The objector seeks to press home the point that something more is involved for the activity to take place, namely, that *this* should be taken *as* silver, i.e., as identical with silver. In other words, the activity is caused by the awareness "this is silver", not merely the absence of the awareness "this is not silver".

16. The Prābhākara seems to hold that, like cognition, desire and activity of the kind in question do not have as their qualifiers properties not belonging to their intentional objects. Just as (according to Nyāya) a unitary and erroneous awareness is split into two separate parts, so also the seemingly unitary desire is split into two parts, viz., *this* and identity with silver. The lack of connection between these two is not apprehended. Hence the common way of speaking implies their identity.

17. Like the so-called false awareness, true awareness too should be split up into two independent parts, so that it is not the case that one qualifies the other.

18. In the case of recognitive perception such as "this is that man", the content of the trace(s) and the content of perception are the same. This is not so in erroneous perception: while the object with which the sense organ is in contact is the shell, the trace's content is the silver.

19. This amounts to the acceptance of *anyathākhyāti*, for the lake is being cognized as having fire.

20. The relational awareness "the lake has fire" is not accepted to be the cause of the activity. Instead, the memory of fire, unrelated to the lake, together with the absence of awareness of absence of fire are accepted as the causes.

21. After showing that there is no need to accept *anyathākhyāti* to account for the impulse to act in a case of so-called erroneous perception, it is shown that there is no need to accept *anyathākhyāti* to account for withdrawal from an "erroneously perceived" object either.

22. There should simultaneously be attraction to the silver and repulsion from the foil with reference to the silver, and similarly again, *mutatis mutandis*, with reference to the foil since both absence of awareness of difference from silver and absence of awareness of difference from foil as well as the independent presentations of silver and foil are present.

23. The defect which is responsible for our taking the foil to be silver should obstruct the repulsion from the foil; similarly, the defect which is responsible for taking the silver as foil should obstruct the attraction towards silver. Hence there will take place only the attraction to silver directed towards the foil and the repulsion from foil directed towards the silver.

24. When the awareness "this is silver" is followed by the sublating awareness "this is not silver (but shell)", the former awareness is an instance of *anyathākhyāti*, i.e., it is an awareness in which something (silverness) features as the qualifier which does not belong to the qualificand (this).

25. Just as "this is not silver" is opposed to "this is silver", so is the latter opposed to the former so far as the mere logical relationship between the two awarenesses is concerned. If *anyathākhyāti* is accepted and the latter is regarded as a case of error, so can the former be also. How can it then be decided which awareness is sublated by which?

26. According to *anyathākhyāti* what is sublated is an erroneous relational awareness. But according to *akhyāti* (the Prābhākara view) an awareness can never be sublated, for an awareness by its nature reveals the nature of things. What instead is sublated is the usage resulting from the so-called error. The latter, moreover, is not an awareness at all; rather it is lack of awareness of difference between what is presented and what is remembered. So what happens in correcting an error is that the lack of awareness of difference is replaced by an awareness of difference.

Although awarenesses of satisfying and frustrating things are attended by usage of acquiring or rejecting them, there is no ostensible usage arising from the awareness of an object to which one is indifferent. What will then be sublated in such a case of error? The Prābhākaras answer to this too above.

27. The contents of a so-called erroneous awareness are either existents or nonexistents. If they are existent, the awareness cannot be false and Gaṅgeśa should accept the position of *akhyāti*. If the contents are nonexistent Gaṅgeśa should side with the Buddhists. *Anyathākhyātivāda* has to be given up in either case.

28. Nothing can be the *sādhya* of a correct inference if it is totally unknown; in order to be proved to belong to the *pakṣa* it must at least be believed to pervade the *hetu*. It could be objected to the inference in the text that

its *sādhya* is unknown (*aprasiddha*). Since no awarenesses are false, the property of having something as a qualifier which does not belong to the qualificand is not possessed by anything. Hence it cannot be known. So it is pointed out that the said property belongs to some desires, so that the objection that the *sādhya* is unknown cannot be justified.

29. The referent of a contentness is of course some awareness. So what is inferred is that awareness does not belong to any awareness which is false, i.e., no awareness is false. This is more or less the same as what is being proved in the previous inference. But the most complicated formulation is not without a purpose. Various objections that may be raised against the previous inference cannot be raised against the present one.

30. This is not strictly a case of *satpratipakṣa*, because the subjects of the two inferences are different. Still the aim of this inference is to thwart what is sought to be proved by the previous inference. Hence it is described as an obstruction (*pratirodha*). *Being the cause of an awareness which is other than a true visual awareness* pervades the *sādhya*. Since the Prābhākaras do not accept any false visual awareness, it is true that whatever is the cause of an awareness which is other than a true visual awareness is also the cause of an awareness which is other than visual awareness. But *being the cause of an awareness which is other than visual awareness* does not pervade the *hetu*, for it is not true that every sense organ is the cause of an awareness which is other than true visual awareness. Hence it is an *upādhi* and vitiates the pervasion between the *hetu* and the *sādhya*. Thus it becomes clear that the so-called obstructive inference contains a false premiss and hence fails to obstruct.

31. According to the ontology accepted by both parties heat does not belong to water but to fire. So the awareness that the water is hot should be false. In fact so far as *anyathākhyātivāda* is concerned the qualified entity, viz., the water qualified by heat, is unknown (*aprasiddha*) or nonexistent. Still, according to popular belief, the awareness is true. The Prābhākara suggests that this is so because the said awareness has produced a usage which terminates in success, i.e., in getting hot water. From the point of view of the Prābhākara the truth or falsity of an awareness does not depend on whether the qualified entity that has become the content is existent or not, but on whether the awareness produced successful usage.

It is obvious that the Prābhākara has adopted a strong pragmatic line. In his view we find the rather unusual combination of faith in infallibility of cognition with a staunch pragmatism. It is this commitment to pragmatism which prompts him to hold that even those cognitions which do not produce any usage can be regarded as true or false insofar as they have the potentiality for producing usage.

32. It is accepted by the Prābhākara also that in the awareness that this is silver when there is silver, relatedness (the fact of *this* being qualified by silverness) too becomes a content. Furthermore, it is apparent that having relatedness as a content is simpler than having lack of awareness of difference. It is a well established rule of procedure that when something has been established as the cause, then, as between two contenders, that which is simpler should be regarded as the limitor of causality. Hence Gaṅgeśa

proposes that having relatedness as content is the limitor of the fact that the awareness that the desired object is in front of one is the cause of activity when an awareness is true. Once this is accepted, it will have to be conceded by the Prābhākara that relatedness becomes a content also when such awareness is false; for nothing can function as a cause which is not possessed of the limitor of causality.

33. Once false relational awareness is admitted as the cause of unsuccessful activity, the question arises: what are the causes of such awareness? The reply is that the defective sense organs, defective sense-object contact, etc., are the causes. Such defects may be imperceptible. Still, they have to be hypothesized as the cause, because the situation is inexplicable in any other way.

34. From Gaṅgeśa's account it can be explained how there is unwavering repulsion from foil resulting in withdrawal from silver and unwavering activity toward the foil from impulsion toward silver. But it cannot be so explained from the Prābhākara account, because the resultant awareness should be of the nature of doubt which does not lead to any activity. This is so because from the Prābhākara's point of view doubt consists in an awareness having two independent (*svatantra*) and opposed (*viruddha*) alternatives (*koṭi*) as its qualifiers and lack of awareness of difference of the subject from either.

35. From the awareness of, say, the sheen of the silver the foil will be remembered, because the person may have previously seen the particular kind of sheen to belong to foil. For similar reasons, from the awareness of the sheen of the foil the silver will be remembered and not the foil. Hence there will be only impulsion from silver and repulsion from foil.

36. If defects cannot be regarded as the cause of attraction and repulsion on the ground that they do not share any identical property, how can defects be regarded as the cause of erroneous awareness? Gaṅgeśa's answer is that in the case of error just as defects are not of the same kind but are of different kinds, so also their effects, viz., erroneous perception, erroneous inference, etc., are of different kinds. But in the case of attraction and repulsion there is no ground for holding that impulses are of different kinds.

37. The property of being strong cannot be regarded as a universal. On the other hand, if it is regarded as an additional category that will invite many complications.

38. Since the view that lack of awareness of difference is the cause of all activity leads to the difficulty of there being simultaneous attraction and repulsion in the above case, the Prābhākara may try this way out. The alleged lack of economy in Gaṅgeśa's view is due to the fact that it would be necessary to hypostatise a false relational awareness before each unsuccessful activity. It is also unsubstantiated, because it has not been established that every unsuccessful action is invariably preceded by a relational awareness.

39. This is the advantage of specifying the cause of successful and unsuccesful activity separately.

40. The "evidence" is the pervasion stated above. Gaṅgeśa's point is that there is good evidence, as indicated above, in favor of the pervasion, but no sublating evidence in the form of a clear counterexample.

41. Although stickness belonging to the stick which is a cause of the pot is inevitably related to the pot by way of positive and negative concomitance, it is not a cause, but is *anyathāsiddha.*

42. It is a widely accepted principle of the Naiyāyika's that anything which is independently, and not by virtue of something else, related to the effect by way of positive and negative concomitance is a cause. Stickness and the color of the stick are related to pot by way of positive and negative concomitance, but not independently: it is rather by virtue of their relationship with the stick. Hence they are not causes of the pot.

43. Though the difference is there it is not apprehended due to some defect.

44. If the above view were true, attraction should not have taken place merely from the awareness "this is silver", for then there is no awareness that is not counterpositive of the difference belonging to what is in front.

45. Even if it were conceded that the awareness "what is desired is not the counterpositive belonging to what is in front" is invariably found in cases of true awareness, it would still not follow that it could be regarded as the cause in preference to or equally with the said relational awareness, for the former is more complex than the latter. Another application of this principle is the following: although all perceptible substances are both of large (*mahat*) size and are made of many parts, only large size is regarded as a causal condition of perception, because the latter is more complex than the former.

46. In recognitive perception the sense organ produces a perception which has an X for its qualificand and a Y for its qualifier which are also respectively the qualificand and qualifier of a trace. How can the trace having silver as its qualificand and silverness as its qualifier then combine with a perception having the shell as its qualificand and silverness as its qualifier?

47. If the awareness "this is silver" is regarded as partly perceptual and partly recollective, it would have to be regarded as characterized by both direct awarenessness (*anubhavatva*) and memoryness (*smṛtitva*). But then a difficulty would arise if *anubhavatva* and *smṛtitva* are both universals, for neither of these two pervades the other and no two universals which are not related as pervader and pervaded can be copresent, for that would lead to overlapping (*saṃkara*). This difficulty does not arise if the awareness is regarded as exclusively perceptual.

48. In the erroneous perception of the shell as silver, silver too is visually perceived according to Gaṅgeśa's view. The silver, however, is a silver which has been perceived earlier elsewhere. Since the silver does not occur at the time of the perception the connection between it and the visual organ cannot take place through ordinary means. Gaṅgeśa holds that the connection is established through the trace or the revived memory of the previously experienced silver.

49. The implict objection is that even if the connection with silverness is dispensed with, at least the contact of organ with silver should be required for the perception of silver. To meet this objection Gaṅgeśa reformulates the causal connection. Instead of saying that contact with silver is a cause of the perception of silver, he says that contact with silver is a cause for the perception having silver as its qualificand. This clears the way for the perception of the shell as silver without contact with silver.

50. The usual list of six different kinds of sensory connection is given here. The different cases of qualifierness (*viśeṣaṇatā*) may be unified insofar as they are all characterised by qualifiernessness (*viśeṣaṇatātva*); hence it is not necessay to admit more than six kinds of sensory connection.

51. The self is partless, so the question of contact with a part of it, whether big or small, does not arise. One could still say that for perception of substances having parts contact with a big part is necessary; hence Gaṅgeśa supplies the futher counterexample of the minimal perceptibilium. The minimal perceptibilium is composed of double atoms (*dvyaṇuka*) which have atomic size, i.e., are extremely small.

52. In all cases except that of the self (which is disputed, since the self is held to be imperceptible by many Naiyāyikas), a substance which is perceived as a whole (*avayavin*) is inherent in its parts. Hence the objection.

53. Contact should be preferred to inherence in what is in contact with the organ as the sensory connection even if for perception of substances the self were held to be imperceptible.

54. This objection obviously is made by the Prābhākara, according to whom universals are admitted corresponding to substance only. The Prābhākaras do not agree with the Nyāya-Vaiśeṣika view that awareness of sameness is the proper basis for the admission of universals.

55. Although inherence is one and the same everywhere, inherence as specified by contact with the auditory organ is limited only to that and difference from inherence as specified by something else.

56. Prior absence is necessarily missing once the effect is produced. Hence if prior absence is accepted as a causal condition, the totality of causal conditions can never be available once the effect comes into being.

57. Gaṅgeśa has indicated above why perceptual evidence in favor of inherence is not available. Next he disposes of an attempt to prove the existence of inherence through inference.

58. A "relational" awareness may be construed as an awareness which is preceded by the awareness of the qualifier, or alternatively, as an awareness which leads to the awareness of differentiation of the qualificand from others. Differentiation (of the qualificand) from others implies differentiation from what lacks the qualifier in a specific relation. The latter is possible only if the relation is a content of the relational awareness.

59. The argument seeks to prove the existence of inherence as the relation between the qualificand and the qualifier in such an awareness as "the pot is blue", where the qualificand is a substance and the qualifer is a quality. The argument is intended to be supplemented by further eliminative arguments showing that other accepted relations, such as contact, which are distinct from their relata do not suffice for the purpose of accounting for the ontic bond between a substance and its qualities, a universal and its loci, etc. Gaṅgeśa objects that the argument is inconclusive, because it fails to rule out the possibility that a substance and its qualities, etc., could be self-connected, i.e., related to each other without the aid of any relation distinct from them.

60. This argument too is intended to be supplemented by eliminative arguments. The objection to it is also similar: there are cases of true

awareness of something being the substratum of some other thing where the substratum and the substrate are self-connected. The text supplies an analysis of the concept of substratum (locus). Not only what is required for origination or continuation in existence, but also what is required for making known, is a subtratum. This is why the ground may be described as the locus of absence of pot, for awareness of the ground is required for the awareness that there is no pot on the ground. The ground and absence of pot, however, are held to be self-connected, without the mediation of any distinct relation. The same could be the case with a whole and its parts, etc.

61. This view is held by the Prābhākaras. Gaṅgeśa holds that though color is noneternal, it is related to the colored thing through inherence which is eternal. The Prābhākara holds the opposite view. Though color is eternal, it is related to the colored things through inherence which is noneternal.

62. Inherence is proved to be single, Gaṅgeśa claims, by virtue of the nature of the awarenesses, i.e., by the awarenesses of being qualified by quality or motion or universal having an identical nature. Though those awarenesses are admittedly different as individual occurrents, they all have the same relation as their content. So, the thesis is that the relation between a substance and its qualities is the same as that betwen a substance and its motions as also is that betweeen a universal and its loci. Since the relation in all these innumerable relational situations is the same relation, it must obviously be different from the relata themselves. Hence it cannot be a case of self-linking connection; though a self-linking connector is admittedly a relation and becomes both a content and a cause of relational awareness, it is ontologically nondifferent from its relata. If a substance and its qualities and motions were to be regarded as self-connected, one would also be compelled to give up the thesis that the relation between a substance and its qualities is the same as that between it and its motions, etc. The argument from parsimony works in more than one way and some light is thrown on it in the following passage.

63. That effects of the same kind are to be explained by a cause of that kind is a well-known application to the law of parsimony. Effects of a given kind could conceivably be produced either by causes of the same kind or by causes of a different kind. The former supposition is prefered on the ground of economy. A kind of *reductio* argument called *anukūlatarka* has beed added to justify the truth of the supposed universal premiss, viz., every (true) relational awareness that has relation with its qualifier as a content is caused by the relation with its qualifier. The second argument may be reformulated as: every true perceptual relational awareness is caused by the relation with its qualifier; the chosen perceptions of being qualifed by quality or motion or universal are true perceptual relational awarenesses; therefore each said perception is caused by its relation with its qualifier.

64. The qualification "which is different from the relata of that relation" has been added to the *sādhya* to exclude self-linking connection. The portion "not detemined by a determination of the other" has been added to the *hetu* to exclude relational awarenesses is which the qualifier is an absence, etc.

65. This is where Gaṅgeśa disagrees with the Vaiśeṣikas, who maintain that inherence is imperceptible. In Gaṅgeśa's view the single inherence connecting the innumerable relata is perceived where the relata are not perceived and perceived when the relata are not perceived.

66. This objection, raised by the Bhāṭṭa Mīmāṃsakas, is due to the fact that in Gaṅgeśa's view negative entities are related to their loci by way of self-linking connection. Since Gaṅgeśa admits absence, holds that they qualify their loci and that our awarenesses to that effect are true, why should he not also hold, in the manner he regards all qualities, motions, etc., to be related to their loci by the single same inherence, that all absences are related to their loci by that same relation?

67. Since the numerically single relation called *vaiśiṣṭya* would relate all absences with their loci, the relation through which a given locus is related to absence of pot is the same relation as that through which the locus would be related to absence of cloth. Thus the requisite relation between the given locus and absence of cloth is already available. Further absence of cloth is also available, for there are without doubt many places, except the given locus, where there are no cloths. Since absence of cloth is available and the relation between it and the given locus is already accomplished, one should have the awareness that the locus is qualified by absence of cloth even though the cloth is there.

68. This difficulty arises in the same manner as that from supposing that there is only one *vaiśiṣṭya.*

69. Inherence of color belongs to air because as inherence it is the same as inherence of touch which undoubtedly belongs to air. Still it would not follow that air is colored, because air, by virtue of its own nature, is colorless. Could it not also be said that for the same reason, although *vaiśiṣṭya* is numerically one, absence of cloth does not belong to a locus where there is cloth? But obviously absence of cloth on a given locus, say a table, cannot be due to the nature of the table, for then there could never be any cloth on the table. On the other hand, in the case of the relata of inherence, if something lacks a quality, motion or universal it lacks it forever; hence the lacking may be attributed to its nature.

70. I.e., the sense organs do play a role in the direct awareness of absence; they are required for the awareness of the locus. But their function is exhausted thereby and cannot extend to awareness of the absence itself, for there is no way in which they could conceivably be connected with the absence.

71. The cause of a cause is regarded as dispensable (*anyathāsiddha*) and not admitted as a cause. But an exception has to be made for the operation (*vyāpāra*); otherwise the cause *par excellence,* which functions as a cause through its operation and is regarded as the most efficient among the causes, could not be regarded as a cause.

72. According to Gaṅgeśa, air is not perceived but inferred from its touch.

73. Memory is a mediate awareness, but not a direct (*anubhava*) one. Perception is a direct awareness, but not a mediate one. Inference, etc., are direct and also mediate awarenesses; thus there is overlapping.

74. Matilal in his notes to T points out the close connection between this

exposition and Śrīharṣa's discussion of the same matter in his *Khaṇḍana-khaṇḍakhādya.*

75. The beginning portion of this discussion concerning *anugama* is obscure, and we have omitted summarizing it. T provides one possible interpretation.

76. In Gaṅgeśa's view liberation is the absolute absence of frustration. Such absence belongs to the liberated self, which is the locus of the absence. If the absence were the same as the locus, liberation would turn out to be the same as the self.

77. In the Nyāya view the outer visible eyes are only the seat of the visual organ, which itself is imperceptible.

78. According to Nyāya-Vaiśeṣika there is an internal sense organ (*manas*) which is different from both the self and the external sense organs. This internal sense organ is required for the perception of internal states such as satisfaction, frustration, etc. The concept of an internal sense organ is not common in Western thought; Western thinkers usually attribute the functions discharged by the internal sense organ either to the mind or, in more recent times, the brain. (This difference between Western and Indian positions is partly due to some difference between the common Western and Indian approaches to the notion of the self.) But the doctrine of an internal organ is popular in Indian thought and the different schools have advocated a wide variety of views regarding its nature and constitution. The main objective of this chapter is to defend the traditional Nyāya-Vaiśeṣika view that the internal organ is atomic in size and not ubiquitous (*vibhu*) as held by the Mīmāṃsakas. Gaṅgeśa has discussed the issue more thoroughly and elaborately than any other Nyāya thinker; hence the chapter deserves special attentions.

79. The nose can apprehend smell, but not color. Similarly, *mutatis mutandis,* the other external sense organs apprehend their respective qualities. But the internal organ is involved, in Gaṅgeśa's view, in all perceptions. The self first comes into contact with the internal organ, which is then connected with an external sense organ, which latter is then connected with its appropriate object.

80. The contact between the self and the internal organ is regarded as a noninherent causal condition of the origin of any awareness.

81. In Gaṅgeśa's view an awareness is not self-illuminating (*svataḥ-prakāśa*). Like every other object an awareness too must be cognized only through another awareness distinct from the one it cognizes. So an awareness J_1 taking place now would reveal its content (say, the pot) but not itself, and the awareness of it, J_2, does not take place at the very moment of J_1's occurrence. J_2 may, however, take place at the following moment; it is an aftercognition with the internal organ functioning as the sensory instrument.

82. This last argument may require some amplification. Nothing can be a content of a perception arising through a sense organ unless it is connected with that sense organ. To say that a visual awareness is self-revealing amounts to saying that it is its own content, i.e., a content of a visual awareness. But in order to be a content of a visual awareness the awareness too must be connected with the visual organ, which is impossible.

83. In Gaṅgeśa's view internal states like satisfaction (*sukha*), etc., are perceived through contact between the self and the internal organ. Thus awarenesses grasped through that same contact are perceived in the same manner as they are produced.

84. That is, when J_1 is cognized through an aftercognition different from itself, J_2, the latter J_2 will have as contents both J_1 and J_1's content. Then when J_2 is cognized through another aftercognition, J_3, this J_3 will have as its contents J_2 as well as J_1 and J_1's content, and so on. A succeeding member in such a series will thus be burdened by having all the previous members as its contents.

85. For an extended analysis of this section see Sukharanjan Saha, "A study in Gaṅgeśa's theory of *Viśeṣaṇa*", in Pranab Kumar Sen (ed.), *Logical Form, Predication and Ontology*. Jadavpur Studies in Philosophy 4 (Delhi 1982), pp. 109-165.

86. Visvabandhu Bhattacharya suggests reading "*...jātāder sattva...*" for "*...jātāderasattva...*" in line 5 of p. 869 of E.

87. Visvabandhu Bhattacharya suggests reading "*...svārthasāmyāt...*" in line of 2 of p. 871 of E.

88. The question is: what is the cause of the direct awareness of pervasion? The numerous observations cannot be the cause, for they cannot all be present before the occurrence of the direct awareness. The difficulty is circumvented by supposing that the observations can be the cause through the impression produced by them which could be regarded as their operation. A thing may be regarded as the cause even if it is not present immediately before the origin of the effect, provided the operation produced by that thing is present.

89. This is Udayana's definition, according to Tarasankar Bhattacharya (RB9381), p. 156.

89A. Vallabha's definition, says Tarasankar Bhattacharya (RB9381), p. 159.

90. Vācaspati Miśra I's definition, says Tarasankar Bhattacharya (RB9381), p. 160.

91. This is the definition of Vātsyāyana and Kumārila, according to Tarasankar Bhattacharya (RB9381), p. 161.

92. "In the *Tattvacintāmaṇi* this section is entitled 'The four *ata evas*' (*ata eva catuṣṭayam*), because the phrase *ata eva* ('that is why') occurs four times in it. But the third *ata eva* does not introduce a new corollary; we have only three corollaries." Goekoop (RB5339), p. 19.

93. The question is: what is the cause of the direct awareness of pervasion? The numerous observations cannot be the cause, for they cannot all be present before the occurrence of the direct awareness. The difficulty is circumvented by supposing that the observations can be the cause through the impression produced by them which could be regarded as their operation. A thing may be regarded as the cause even if it is not present immediately before the origin of the effect, provided the operation produced by that thing is present.

94. Regarding (1) the intended generalisation is not "whatever has taste has color" but something like this: "whatever has the taste of this particular

thing has the color of this particular thing" (where both taste and color are taken to be particular qualities of particular things). The fact that in some cases pervasion may be ascertained without numerous observations proves that the latter cannot be the cause of the former: there is lack of negative concomitance (*vyatirekavyabhicāra*).

95. Gaṅgeśa now states his own thesis regarding the means of ascertaining pervasion. This is also intended to be a rebuttal of the Cārvāka view.

96. If smoke is caused by anything, it must be either that the latter is concomitant with fire or that the latter is not concomitant with fire: there is no third possibility. Hence if it is the case that neither what is concomitant with fire nor what is not concomitant with fire is the cause of smoke, smoke must be uncaused.

97. Whenever one wants to produce smoke, one lights a fire, including the skeptic who may profess any one or more of the above three kinds of doubt. The skeptical position thus is open to the charge of belief-behaviour contradiction.

98. There would have been an infinite regress if a *tarka* to remove skeptical doubt had itself to be supported in every case by another *tarka*. But this is not so. Since the skeptic's own action amounts to a surrender of his own thesis, no further *tarka* is called for.

99. If *tarka* were a kind of knowledge, the said impression would have been regarded as an additional source of knowledge: it is not reducible to any of the recognized four instruments of knowledge.

100. This is another reason why there is no infinite regress of a generalisation being supported by *tarka*, and the latter being supported by another *tarka*, and so on. *Tarka* is not required as the basis of the knowledge of pervasion in every single case. It is, however, required as the support of the most basic source of the knowledge of pervasion, viz., perception. Knowledge of pervasion through inference or testimony is ultimately based on knowledge of pervasion through perception.

101. The doubt as to whether the object in front of one is a man or a statue is resolved when one notices that the thing has some feature which belongs only to a man, or to a statue, but not to both. If the awareness of such an exclusive feature is itself false, the resultant awareness, such as that the object in front of one is a man, may be false too. Similarly in the case of a generalization and the *tarka* brought in its support.

102. This beginningless regress of previous cognitions of pervasion is not a fault, because it is taken to be based on sound reasoning. This way of stopping the skeptical regress does not seem to have Gaṅgeśa's full approval, for he refers to it as the view of others.

103. That the awareness of the qualifier precedes the corresponding relational awareness is a widely accepted dictum in the Nyāya tradition and provides the principal basis for the acceptance of nonpropositional awareness. Since the mountain-fire has not been perceived by any ordinary instrument of knowledge and since its awareness must be there before any inference to it can take place, the only possible recourse is to *sāmānyalakṣaṇa* awareness through which all cases of fire are perceived.

104. In the text here the doubt is raised as being "whether there is potness

or not." But later (below), while replying to this objection, Gaṅgeśa puts the doubt as "whether that thing is a pot or not". The latter makes better sense.

105. An example of an obstruction which pervades the *s* as limited by a property of the *p* is found in the following inference: air is perceived because it possesses perceived touch. Here *possession of manifested color* is an obstruction although it does not pervade the *s being perceived*, but pervades the *s* as limited by a character of the *p*, viz., *being a substance which is an object of external perception*. In other words, it is not true that all that is perceived has manifested color, but it is true that all substances which are objects of external perception have manifested color. Air cannot be a counterexample to the latter generalization, for the case of air is disputed.

106. For example, take the inference "the hill has fire because it has smoke." The property of being other than the hill pervades the *s* fire, for the former belongs to all the *sapakṣas*; but it clearly does not pervade the *h*, for it does not belong to the hill where smoke is present. Thus it appears to fulfil the definition of an obstruction and would seem to vitiate the above inference.

107. For example, take the inference "fire is hot, because it is a substance." The property of being other than fire pervades the *s*, for all things which are not hot are different from fire.

108. In such cases it is not certain that the *p* is devoid of the *s*. Hence the said property cannot with certainty be said to pervade the *s*: the property does not belong to the *p* while the *s*, for all we know, may be present.

109. The above is meant to be an objection to the thesis that an obstruction may be said to pervade the *s* without being co-extensive with it.

110. It appears that Gaṅgeśa is willing to accept the definition suggested by the author of the *Ratnakośa*, but only after removing the vagueness in the notion of what amounts to the *sādhya*.

111. Destruction is endless according to the Naiyāyikas. *Possession of manifested color* too would be an obstruction in the inference "air is perceived because it is the locus of perceived touch." Air is not perceived, but inferred, according to many Naiyāyikas.

112. Thus in the inference "the hill has fire because of smoke" *being other than the hill* is a fallacious obstruction and would fail to nullify the pervasion.

113. Anything whatsoever is a fallacious obstruction in such cases for nothing could fulfil the twin conditions of pervading the *s* and yet not pervading the *h*.

114. The last four are meant to be fallacious obstructions in some cases but not in all cases.

115. The world is created from eternally existing atoms. At the first stage of creation, two atoms are formed into dyads, then at the next stage, three dyads into triads, and the triads then give rise to gross material objects. Now whatever objects are created are created for the enjoyment of the selves which themselves are embodied at the right moment. This teleological nature of creation is explained by the theory that all selves have accumulated merit

and demerit as a result of performing good and bad deeds in previous cycles of creation. Nothing is created uselessly, i.e. which is not for the enjoyment of some self in accordance with its store of merit and demerit. Thus whatever object is created will be created in accordance with the merit and demerit of selves. So the collective merit and demerit are causes of creation. Only natural phenomena like storms, earthquakes, etc. are not created by the merit and demerit of selves. So God can be proved as a creator of the world only in the sense that He creates the natural phenomena. All other things are created by God in accordance with the collective merit and demerit of selves, so the selves are as much causes of these things as God. So the *p* in the argument must not be the world as such, but the world minus those things which are created by merit and demerit of persons. This is the first restriction on *p*.

The second restriction on *p* is due to the fact that many things are created by humans or animals. For example, a pot is made by a potter. Now those things which are created by finite creatures are already accepted by all parties in the debate as having a creator. So to prove this over again is pointless. Therefore the world which is the *p* in the inference must be further restricted in this way. The world which is the *p* of the inference must exclude things which are created by bodily movements which are the effects of mental effort.

The third restriction on *p* is that it must exclude destruction of things (though in a sense it is also an effect and has therefore a cause). For Gaṅgeśa gives an *h* for this inference which is not present when things have been destroyed. To avoid this defect, Gaṅgeśa imposes a third restriction on *p*, that it must include all and only those objects which inhere in anything. Destruction, according to Nyāya, does not inhere in anything, so that is excluded in the *p*.

116. We shall have to understand here the psychological theory of human production as propounded by Nyāya. For producing a pot, the potter has first to have immediate knowledge of the material (the clay in this case). According to Nyāya a blind potter will not engage in the activity of producing the pot because he will not have the necessary immediate knowledge of the material, unless of course he happens to touch the material. Then, when the potter has seen the appropriate material he has the desire to produce the pot. Then he becomes eager to produce the effect, this eagerness being his mental effort, and he makes the appropriate bodily movements to produce the effect. Thus in this process of creation each of the following factors has a causal role: (i) immediate awareness of the appropriate materials, (ii) desire to produce, (iii) mental eagerness (effort), the self which makes the effort. All these are included in the total collection of causal factors. As we have already seen in the first stage of creation of the dyads the collective merit and demerit are causes, which presuppose the performance of good or bad deeds by human beings existing in the previous cycles of creation, and for the performance of these deeds those men had to have immediate knowledge of the material, desire to produce, effort and thus all the factors required for production of the effect would have to be there. Yet in this creation of the dyads, as we have already seen, human agency being involved,

although very indirectly, God is not the sole creator. In the inference what is to be established is the presence of a creator who is omnipotent and omniscient. So there is need to exclude human agency from what is to be proved by the inference, that is, from the *s* of the inference. For this purpose Gaṅgeśa imposes restrictions on *s*.

He does this in several alternative ways. Here is the first way. The *s* is: being created by a self which has effort, desire to infer, and immediate knowledge of the appropriate material which are not the counterpositives of any prior absence pervaded by the prior absence of merit and demerit. Let us explain how this restriction excludes the very indirect agency of human beings existing in the previous cycle of creation. Merit and demerit are caused by human beings performing rituals or other good or bad deeds. But this performance of rituals and deeds presupposes on the part of human beings knowledge of the material without which no one can perform any action. So if all these are not yet there, then necessarily merit and demerit are not yet there, i.e., the prior absence of merit and demerit pervades the prior absence of immediate knowledge of the material, etc. Thus human knowledge of the material, etc. are the counterpositives of prior absence pervaded by the absence of merit and demerit. By excluding this sort of immediate knowledge Gaṅgeśa therefore excludes human agency of the creation of dyads, etc. But divine agency is not excluded, for God has no merit or demerit, so there is no prior absence of merit and demerit in God, and therefore it cannot pervade His knowledge. So His knowledge is not a counterpositive to any prior absence pervaded by the prior absence of merit, etc.

117. An alternative way of excluding human agency from the creation of the world is to hold that the immediate knowledge, etc. must exist after the merit and demerit. Now in the case of human beings of an earlier cycle of creation, their knowledge of material, etc. for the performance of rituals, etc. must precede their merit and demerit as their causes, and will cease to exist when the merit and demerit start the process of creation. (According to Nyāya, human knowledge, etc., are momentary.) So by stipulating that the knowledge, etc. concerning the material must exist after merit and demerit, human agency is excluded, but not divine agency, for God's knowledge, etc., being eternal, will exist always even after human merit and demerit have created the worldly objects.

118. Gaṅgeśa has a still simpler restriction of the *s* of the inference. This is to hold that the *s* will be *being the object of immediate knowledge, desire to infer, and effort*, for even though human beings existing in the earlier cycles of creation had immediate knowledge, etc. of material for performing rituals, etc., their knowledge, desire to create, and effort did not have the dyads (the first created entities at the beginnings of this cycle of creation) as their objects.

119. S.C. Vidyabhusana (B and RB: HIL).

120. This summary has been prepared by the editor using V.N. Jha's translation, *The Philosophy of Injunctions* (New Delhi, 1988). The following footnotes are by Professor Jha.

121. Suppose a person goes to perform a particular sacrifice. The imme-

diate cause of his inducement is the understanding generated by a Vedic injunction, since without such an injunction he won't perform that particular sacrifice. Thus, by positive and negative concomitance we establish a cause-and-effect relationship between that understanding and the inducement and between the understanding and the injunctive sentence. Therefore, the sentence is called the indirect cause (*sākṣātkāraṇasya kāraṇam*) or inducer with reference to that inducement.

122. According to Mathurānātha, *abhidhā* is a synonym of *bhāvanā*. *Bhāvanā* is accepted by the Bhāṭṭa school of Pūrvamīmāṃsā as a property of the injunctive (*vidhi*) form, to be more precise, of the form in potential mood. Take for instance the injunction "one desirous of heaven should perform the new moon and the full moon sacrifices" (*darśapūrṇamāsābhyām svargakāmo yajeta*). Here, in the optative form *yajeta* the suffix -*ta* has two properties, namely *ākhyātatva* and *liṅtva*. *Ākhyātatva* is a property which is found in any personal suffix, whereas *liṅtva* is a property which is found only in the personal suffix in the optative mood. This very property in the personal suffix of an optative form conveys a *bhāvanā*, i.e., the intention of the speaker, namely, A wants the hearer to undertake a particular activity. If such an optative form occurs in a Vedic injunction, this *bhāvanā* is accepted as existing in the suffix itself, since there is no speaker of the Veda according to the Mīmāṃsakas; but in an ordinary sentence it is accepted as the property of the speaker, i.e., the self.

According to the Bhāṭṭas *abhidhā* or *bhāvanā* is the *vyāpāra* (function) of the personal suffix.

123. The word *saṃkalpa* stands for desire (*icchā*). It is not clear exactly whose doctrine is referred to here. Mathurānātha also does not specify and simply says "others say".

124. Some others hold the view that the awareness born of *apūrva* is the inducing factor. *Apūrva* means unseen merit (*adṛṣṭa*). In the case of Vedic sacrifices *apūrva* is accepted as the connecting link between the sacrifice and heaven, etc., produced by sacrifice.

But there are some Vedic rites called "obligatory rites" which do not produce any result over and above *apūrva*. This *apūrva* arising out of the performance of obligatory rites destroys sins, it is assumed. Therefore, to include all Vedic injunctions they propose that awareness of *apūrva* causes inducement.

125. *Bhāvanā* is paraphrased as volition (*prayatna*). Those who hold the view that the awareness of volition is the inducer put forward the same type of argument as in the preceding case. That is, since not all Vedic injunctions mention a result, we cannot say that the knowledge of a thing's being the means to a desired goal is the inducer. On the other hand, all injunctive forms convey some sort of activity to be undertaken. Thus, awareness of volition is the inducer.

126. *Iṣṭasādhanatā* means the property of being the means of obtaining the desired result. In other words, the awareness that *x* has the potentiality to generate the desired result *y* induces a person to go for *x*. This is what the Naiyāyikas mean when they say that *iṣṭasādhanatājñāna* is the inducer. However, the four above-mentioned views do not accept this.

Gaṅgeśa points out the defect of violating the cause-and-effect relationship (*vyabhicāra*) in those four views. Here, the *vyabhicāra* is of both types, i.e., positive and negative *vyabhicāra*.

A is said to be the cause of B if and only if in the presence of A (+A) there is presence of B (+B), and in the absence of A (−A) there is absence of B (−B). But if this relation is violated, the following two situations are possible:

(i) In spite of +A there is −B, and

(ii) In spite of −A there is +B.

(i) is called the case of positive *vyabhicāra* and (ii) is called that of negative *vyabhicāra*. Gaṅgeśa has pointed out both defects here.

127. Here "awareness that something is to be done" (*kāryatva-jñāna*) is to be understood in the sense of *kṛtisādhyatājñāna*, the knowledge that it is possible for one to undertake that particular activity. If someone knows that he can do a particular act he may proceed to perform it, but not otherwise. It is for this reason that a person does not try to catch the moon.

128. Awareness produces desire and desire produces volition. Now if volition is to be produced by awareness, awareness must produce desire first. In other words, through desire awareness will produce volition. Thus, the desire to do (*cikīrṣā*) is a link (*vyāpāra*) between cause and effect. There is nothing else to be done by awareness than to produce the desire to do.

129. "Other causal factors" includes two types of causes:

(1) The ordinary perception of material causes, say stick, clay, etc., in the context of producing a pot, and

(2) The absence of obstruction.

Therefore, in the presence of (1) and (2) and the desire to do volition is bound to occur. This is what the Prābhākaras think.

130. Awareness, desire and volition are treated as having objects and they have a particular structure of qualifier and qualificand. Since the desire to do is a desire it is presented in this structure of qualifier and qualificand. Here, Prabhākara wants to point out that the object of this desire is the activity to be accomplished by the agent. Thus, whatever is the object of the awareness which has produced the desire is also the object of that desire. In other words, *kṛtisādhyatvaprakārakajñāna* has produced *kṛtisādhyatva-prakārikā icchā*.

131. If some action is known as feasible to be perfomed, a desire to perform that action comes into existence. Thus, the chief qualifier of the desire corresponds to the chief qualifier of the awareness which has produced that desire.

132. Thus, whatever is the object of the awareness, the same thing is the object of the desire and of the volition.

133. Prabhākara categorically denies that the awareness of a thing's being a means to a desired goal is not the cause of inducement. Had it been so, then a person would try to capture the moon just because he knows it would give him immense pleasure. But that never happens, nobody makes such an attempt. Why? Simply because it is not possible for him to do it. What does that imply? Prabhākara concludes that it is the

awareness that a certain act is feasible to be performed or not that decides whether inducement to act occurs or does not occur, not mere awareness that an object is a means to a desired goal.

Thus, the cause-and-effect relationship is between awareness of a thing's being what one wants to accomplish and subsequent action, not between an action's being a means to a desired goal and subsequent action, because there will be the fault of positive *vyabhicāra* since in spite of an action's being a means to a desired goal there is no action in the above-mentioned case.

134. The objector argues: let the awareness that something is a means to a desired goal be the cause of inducement. Nonoccurrence of the inducement in some cases can be explained by the presence of an obstructor. In the case of any effect the absence of an obstructor is required as the general cause. *Pratibandhakābhāvaḥ kāryasāmānyaṃ prati kāraṇam* is the generally accepted dictum.

In the present case since the performer knows that it is not possible on his part to perform some activity, it implies that there is an obstructor and so naturally the effect, i.e., the inducement cannot take place.

135. In comparison to awareness of capability (to perform the action) awareness of the absence of capability is cumbersome so far as the cause-and-effect relationship is concerned. Naturally, it is clear from this that Prābhākaras do not regard absence of obstruction as the general cause for each and every effect. Most probably, since Mīmāṃsakas accept *śakti* as an independent category they can avoid absence of obstruction as a general cause.

136. Prābhākaras argue that the awareness of one's capability induces a man to act. But if the awareness of one's capability is the cause of inducement it must be there (*siddha*). But, it is not ready before the desire to do, since desire to do cannot arise if there is absence of definite awareness of capability. Naturally, how can the awareness of a thing's being what one wants to accomplish be the cause of inducement?

137. The Prābhākaras try to argue that the awareness of a thing's being the thing one wants to accomplish is the inducing factor, which is obtained from the optative suffix. If one knows that an act can be undertaken by him, he may do it, but if he is sure that it is not possible to do it he won't undertake it. This implies that the awareness that a thing is what one wants to accomplish is the inducing factor through producing a desire to do the act. An awareness of an obstructor is that which destroys the awareness which produces the result, and not mere being the counterpositive of an absence (*kāraṇībhūtābhāvapratiyogitvaṃ pratibandhakatvam*). An obstructor is better defined as the counterpositive of the absence of an inducer (*prayojakībhūtābhāvapratiyogitvam*).

138. To the opponent's argument that the awareness of the thing one wants to accomplish is the obstructor, the Prābhākaras reply that in that case not only being the thing one wants to accomplish should be postulated as obstructor, but in addition *aniṣṭasādhanatva*, etc. as well. *Aniṣṭasādhanatva* should be understood as *balavadaniṣṭānubandhitva*, i.e., being the producer of unwanted hurdles more than necessary. *Upekṣaṇīyatva* should be interpre-

ted as being bereft of the limitor of being the means to the desired goal (*iṣṭasādhanatāvacchedakaśūnyatva*) and *niṣphalatva* as being bereft of the capacity of producing a result (*iṣṭaphalopadhānaśūnyatva*).

139. The Naiyāyikas insist that being a means to a desired goal should be the meaning of the optative suffix. Taking into account the derivation of the word *cikīrṣā* they argue that if the word *cikīrṣā* is treated as a derivable word, it should mean the desire to do what is conveyed by the root to which the desiderative ending is added. If, however, the word *cikīrṣā* is treated as indivisible, it has to be understood as the desire in *kṛti.* In comparison to *kṛtisādhyatvaprakāraka icchātva, kṛtīcchātva* is a simpler *pravṛttinimitta* for the word *cikīrṣā.* Thus, the *pravṛtti* occurs in spite of the awareness of *kṛtisādhyatā* as without it one desires rains.

140. Gaṅgeśa gives here an account of *kāryānvitaśaktivāda* (which we would like to render as the context theory of the imperativist) against the background of the rival doctrine of *anvitābhidhānavāda* (which we would like to render as the nonimperativist context theory). The two theories are held by the Prābhākara philosophers—the former doctrine by the neo-Prābhākaras who according to some flourished in the period preceding Gaṅgeśa's and the latter by many earlier Prābhākara philosophers including Śālikanātha Miśra. Both theories are opposed by Kumārila Bhaṭṭa and his followers, and also by Gaṅgeśa, who differs from the Bhāṭṭas. The salient feature common to the two theories under reference is this: A word gets its meaning only in the context of a sentence, i.e., in association with other words used in the sentence. Expressed in the manner in which it is traditionally expressed in the writings of the supporters of the theories, a word in a speaker's utterance can be said to have meaning only if it can generate an awareness in the hearer of a proposition (*vākyārtha*) embodying a relationship (*anvaya*) between the denotations of the several words used in a sentence. Gaṅgeśa does not accept the thesis, though he starts with an account of the context theory of the imperativist.

141. The example discussed in the *Abhāvavāda* section of the *Pratyakṣa-khaṇḍa*, cf. p. 136

142. The title of this section suggests that Gaṅgeśa records here his own views (*siddhānta*) on the theory called *kāryānvitaśaktivāda*, an account of which has been given in an earlier chapter. In other words, the chapter gives a refutation of the imperativist context theory. But a refutation has been presented in a manner that will give the impression that the refutation has been given by the nonimperativist context theorist. If it is a fact, as some scholars think, that the imperativists Gaṅgeśa had in mind were Prābhākara philosophers who flourished immediately before Gaṅgeśa, then the refutation that Gaṅgeśa offers is his own construal of the nonimperativist Prābhākara position. But Gaṅgeśa's construal of the nonimperativist rufutation of the imperativist thesis is not simply polemical in nature, for Gaṅgeśa couples this refutation with a thorough defence of the positive thesis of the nonimperativist context theory. Gaṅgeśa wants to achieve a purpose by this coupling effort and the purpose is finally to offer a refutation of the positive thesis of the nonimperativist context theory by following a similar approach that has been taken by the nonimperativist in criticizing the

imperativist thesis. Therefore, in a sense, while criticizing the imperativist position through the dummy of the nonimperativist context theorist Gaṅgeśa himself is offering a refutation of the imperativist thesis and is preparing the ground for his refutation of the nonimperativist context theory. The first part of the present section has thus been concerned with the criticism of the imperativist thesis by the nonimperativist context theorist and also with a defence of the positive thesis of the nonimperativist. The second part is concerned with Gaṅgeśa's refutation of the positive thesis of the nonimperativist context theory from the point of view of Nyāya philosophy. Gaṅgeśa also develops here the positive Nyāya thesis regarding sentential understanding and defends it against objections that can be raised from the standpoint of the Prābhākaras. In the third and final part of the chapter Gaṅgeśa defends his theory against charges that can be raised by the Bhāṭṭa philosophers.

143. The Sanskrit equivalent of our term "the imperativist context theory" is *kāryānvitaśaktivāda.* If in our rendering we retain the component word *kāryatā* the theory means that the meaning of an utterance consists in generating in the hearer an understanding of a relationship involving reference to *kāryatā.* In our rendering without that Sanskrit term the theory means: the meaning of speech consists in generating in the hearer an understanding of a relationship involving reference to what ought to be done. Our use of the word "ought" is not intended in its ethical sense. Given that the end involved in a particular case is accepted by the speaker and the hearer as desirable (for example in "one desiring heaven ought to perform the *agnihotra* sacrifice" which, at least in Nyāya theory, is an example of conditional imperative and most of the imperatives are explicitly or implicitly conditional imperatives), the important question is whether the speaker as well as the hearer think that what is being enjoined is capable of being performed by the hearer. As ought implies can, the natural presumption is that the hearer is capable of performing what has been enjoined on him. Keeping this meaning of "ought" in mind, i.e., treating "ought" not so much in its sense of "desirable" but more in its sense of "capable", we would like to give a presentation of the contents of this subsection in the following manner.

Gaṅgeśa here makes use of the results he has earlier established in the *Vidhivāda* above. Our presentation presupposes those results.

144. It would be wrong to infer from this that according to Gaṅgeśa the understanding of the qualificand is a mere unconnected idea about a discrete thing. We shall shortly see that the apprehension of a relation as involved in the qualified understanding which is what in such a situation actually takes place is treated by Gaṅgeśa as a contribution from or function of some conditions (other than words) that are considered necessary for the taking place of the qualified understanding.

145. The purport involved here is the purport behind use of a sentence and not purport behind use of a word. Gaṅgeśa quotes the following verse from Daṇḍyācarya's *Kāvyādarśa*:

Gaccha gacchasi cet kānta panthānaḥ santu te śivāḥ
Mamāpi janma tatraiva bhūyād yatra gato bhavān.

(A lady is trying to refrain her husband from going to a far-off place as pangs of separation seem intolerable to her. She addresses her husband in the above words, whose meaning is:)

Go where thou art going, my beloved. Let thy journey be blessed (and free from troubles). On your reaching the place thou art going I shall be reborn (?) there (to meet thee again).

In Sanskrit the rhetoric involved is called *ākṣepa* (implication), because the purport behind this speech is that the husband of the lady should not leave his home leaving her behind. This is not a part of the literal meaning of the verse, though it is implied by it. The husband takes the sentence to mean (as is evident from the use of the word "reborn" (*janma*)) that his going abroad will be the cause of the death of his beloved wife. That he should not go abroad is the purport here which the husband arrives at not through consideration of the meaning of the utterance but through employment of a reasoning process like this: if I go abroad, my wife will die. Therefore, I should not go abroad.

146. Sanskrit lacks articles.

147. See above, Section ..... of the *Pratyakṣa* book of the *Tattvacintāmaṇi.*

148. *Cowness* plays such a role in respect of the term *dhenu* which is conventionally used for a milch cow. Etymologically, however, it means any milch animal; thus a milch buffalo or a milch ass should, etymologically speaking, constitute the denotation of the term *dhenu.* Similarly, an ox that is not a milch animal should not constitute the term's denotation. Strictly speaking, even a cow that is not an ox but is not giving milk in case it is too young or did not give birth to any offspring in the recent past will not constitute the term's denotation. The problem is how to collect and assimilate all that actually constitutes the denotation of the term *dhenu.* The identifying mark cannot be *cowhood* for that would make an ox or a non-milch non-ox cow its referent. It cannot be the property of being a milch buffalo or a milch ass for that would make a milch buffalo or a milch ass its referent. It is therefore widely accepted that in the absence of any property that can be found in *all* the referents of *dhenu* and in all such referents *only* we shall have to treat cowhood as such a mark, perhaps in association with the mark of milk-giving which naturally varies with varying *dhenus* in relation to quality and quantity of milk each one gives. Cowhood then plays the logical role of *upalakṣaṇa* in our use of the term "*dhenu*".

149. For doing justice to the position defended here we are offering a free construction. Confining our attention to testimonial knowledge resulting from a sentence containing the general word "cow" we shall try to make out a case for the position. The recollection and the resultant testimonial awareness, if they are to be about a particular cow as qualified by cowhood cannot be about all cows or a specific cow. Even if they were about all cows, the recollections involved could not be said to be based on perception since

no one can be credited with perception of all cows. But if it is contended that they are about a specific cow traceable as a content of a definite previous perception then, as this also has been shown earlier, there is no guarantee about the correctness of this identification of the content of perception, recollection and testimonial awareness. In fact the awareness of this difficulty affords justification for the Prābhākara thesis that it is only the universal that should be taken as related to the word through the meaning-relation. Given the truth of the insight behind this thesis we can well understand why the conditions sufficient for the awareness of the universal is considered sufficient also for the awareness of the particular involved in testimonial knowledge and the antecedent recollection.

2. VĀṬEŚVARA

1. D.C. Bhattacharya (RB6105), p. 165.

3. VARDHAMĀNA

1. Umesh Mishra (RB: UM), p. 275.
2. D.C. Bhattacharya (RB6105), p. 111
3. Ernst Steinkellner (RB5562), "Vardhamāna als Kommentator Gaṅgeśa's", Wiener Zeitschrift für die Kunde Sud-und Östasiens 8, 1964, 182–223.
4. Ibid.
5. They cite Paṇini's *sūtra* "*āśaṃsāyāṃ bhūtavacca*" (*Aṣṭādhyayī* 3.3.132) in support.
6. Vācaspati Miśra gives these in the *Tātparyaṭīkā* while dealing with *pretyabhāva* (I.1.19).
7. *Yato'bhyudayaniḥśreyasasiddhiḥ sa dharmaḥ.*
8. Vardhamāna notes that the word *abhyudaya* stands for the knowledge of reality.
9. The commentary of Vardhamāna is more detailed and more informative than that of Varadarāja. It is erudite, providing all the available details on almost all the topics discussed in the text. As the illustrious son of Gaṅgeśa, Upādhyāya Vardhamāna had to his credit a rich inheritance of traditional information on fundamental doctrines. This commentary provides scholars with a rich feat and could be considered, in a way, as a dissertation.
10. See Vol. II of this Encyclopedia, p. 671.
11. Ibid., p. 672.
12. But the *Nyāyasūtra*s do not contain it.
13. There appears to be a difference in the two treatments, however. Sublation in Chapter III was chiefly based on nonapprehension when suitable factors were present (*yogyānupalabdhi*). In Chapter V it is sublation based on inference which is refuted.

5. JAYASIṂHASŪRI

1. This *Nyāyasaṃgraha* is clearly a commentary on the *Nyāyasāra*, and

from the *maṅgalaśloka* of the *Nyāyabhūṣaṇa* it can be concluded that it is the name of the *Nyāyabhūṣaṇa* itself. However, it should be noted that the text of the *Bhūṣaṇa* as we have it does not identify *pūrvavat* with *kevalānvayin*, etc., as this passage implies.

6. CENNU or CINNAM BHAṬṬA

1. See the edition of Jayanta Bhaṭṭa's *Nyayamañjarī*, Vol. One (RB3723) by K.S. Varadacarya, Mysore 1969, pp. 283-284.

2. Maṇikaṇṭha (p. 163 of (B3268) the edition by V. Subrahmanya Sastri and V. Krishnamacharya, Madras Government Oriental Manuscripts Library, 1963) also mentions the view that *asiddha* is the only one and explains the reasoning that leads to that view. An *h* becomes fallacious when a defect arises affecting either pervasion, *pakṣadharmatā* or its valid cognition. Maṇikaṇṭha, like Cennu Bhaṭṭa, does not identify the proponents of this view.

3. Bhāsarvajña and Śivāditya.

4. Sarvadeva mentions *asādhāraṇa* as one of the six fallacies he enumerates in *Pramāṇamañjarī*.

5. The Navyanyāya school admits that the knowledge of the words gives rise to the meaning of the words leading to verbal knowledge.

6. This is proof that the doctrines of the Viśiṣṭādvaita were known in Vijayanagar and neighouring places in the 14th century A.D.

11. JĪVANĀTHA or JAYANĀTHA MIŚRA

1. Umesh Mishra (RB: UM), pp. 287-289.

2. At p. 288 of the edition of *Vādivinoda* by Ganganatha Jha (B3639; RB5622).

3. Ibid., p. 288.

12. BHAVANĀTHA MIŚRA or DUVE or AYĀCI MIŚRA

1. Cf. RB: UM, pp. 143, 301.
2. Cf. RB: TRC.
3. Cf. RB: UM, p. 303.
4. Ibid., pp. 303-304.

13. JINAVARDHANA SŪRI or ĀDINĀTHA JAIN

1. Cf. J.S.Jetly's Introduction to his edition of the *Saptapadārthī* and *Jinavardhanī* (B2984; RB4601), Lalpatbhai Dalpatbhai Series 1, Ahmedabad 1963.

2. Cf. the summary of *Saptapadārthī* in Vol. II of this Encyclopedia, p. 643, 4.

3. Cf. Varadarāja's *Tārkikarakṣā* (B2986; 4609), reprinted from the *Pandit*, 1903, p. 122.

4. The commentator here seems to disagree with Śivāditya's definition

of elasticity, viz., *ṛjutvapādakaḥ saṃskāraḥ sthitisthāpakaḥ*.

5. This is inconsistent.

18. ŚEṢA ŚĀRṄGADHARA

1. Cf. RB: UM, p. 466.

2. Śeṣa Śārṅgadhara evinces a spark of originality here and there in his aggressively pedantic and polemical commentary. At least he dishes out to us a banquet of stimulating arguments and ideas that might otherwise have been irretrievably lost. At times he finds fault with Udayana and suggests emendations, while at others he lapses into puerile, though conventional, dilemmatic arguments that cut little ice. (NLS)

19. VĀSUDEVA SŪRI

1. The identity of this writer is not ascertainable, and his date is not known. His style is simple and free from neologisms. This itself suggests an early date. The mention of "Bhūṣaṇabhūṣaṇa" on p. 81 may be taken to suggest that he commented on the *Nyāyabhūṣaṇa.* Vāsudeva refers to himself as the son of Sūryasūri of Kashmir. In the Poona edition (by Vāsudeva Sastri Abhyankar and C.R. Devadhar) there is a *śloka* after the colophon which states that this commentary was written for the sake of those who cannot take to the study of the vast *Nyāyabhūṣaṇa.*

Vāsudeva refers to the author of the *Nyāyasāra* as "Saṃgrahakṛt", i.e., the author of *Saṃgraha.* This suggests that the *Nyāyasāra* was also known as *Saṃgraha.* The colophon of the text of the *Nyāyabhūṣaṇa* reads the name of that commentary as *Saṃgrahavārttika*, which reinforces the view that the *Nyāyasāra* was also known as *Saṃgraha.* The text of the *Nyāyabhūṣaṇa* refers to the work as *Nyāyapadārthasaṃgraha*, and simply as *Saṃgraha.* The absence of such a reference in other commentaries on the *Nyāyasāra* suggests an early date for the *Padapañcikā.*

21. ŚAṂKARA MIŚRA

1. Umesh Mishra has a detailed account of the background of this family. Cf. RB: UM, op. cit., pp. 302 ff.

2. Ibid., pp. 304-306.

3. S.C. Vidyabhusana (B and RB: HIL), p. 459.

4. D.C. Bhattacharya (RB6105), p. 135.

5. Ibid., p. 136.

6. It is of interest to note here that Varadarāja takes *māyā* to refer to the nihilistic approach (p. 217).

7. There is no justification for holding that Śaṃkara Miśra is referring to two classes of Tridaṇḍins, one holding *avidyā* to be the cause of the universe, the other *māyā.*

8. Cf. the summary of *Nyāyakusumāñjali* V.1, Objection 5, on page 582 of Vol. Two of this Encyclopedia.

9. This view seems to have been held by Maṇikaṇṭha Miśra. Cf. p. 180

of B3268.

10. Without mentioning him by name, Maṇikaṇṭha's definitions of *ahetusama*, *apakarṣasama*, *anutpattisama*, *prakaraṇasama* and *sādhyasama* are alluded to. Likewise, Vardhamāna's views are noted on pp. 23 and 33. Śivāditya's view on *kāryasama* is specified under that author's name on p. 30, but no work of Śivāditya's on *jāti* has come down to us.

11. Mahārṇavakāra is said to have been the father of Pakṣadhara Miśra. As a Naiyāyika he could not have maintained twelve categories.

12. Śaṃkara Miśra only mentions these two. In *Nyāyasiddhāntamālā* the five are given as *dharmin, dharma, ādhāra, pradeśa* and *viśeṣa*.

13. This view of darkness is not held by Prābhākara school as such. Only a section of that school holds this view.

14. Cf. Umesh Mishra, *Conception of Matter* (B6026; RB9275), op. cit., pp. 84-89.

15. In this context it should be noted that the author of the *Nyāyalīlāvatī* was not the only writer who treated *anadhyavasita* as a fallacy. Praśastapāda was the earliest to take note of it. He enumerated it in the list of fallacies and defined it as present in the *pakṣa*, and not as existing in the *sapakṣa* and *vipakṣa*.

Bhāsarvajña held it to occur only in the *pakṣa* and interprets (in the *Nyāyabhūṣaṇa*) as well as noting its varieties. Śivāditya recognizes this fallacy which he defines in expressions which are identical with those offered by Bhāsarvajña.

Sarvadeva's definition of this is almost the same as that given above. This fallacy is said by (Śrī) Vallabha to be present in a portion of the *pakṣa*. It is clear that Vallabha's definition does not agree with the tradition. In later years, *anadhyavasita* was given the name *asādhāraṇa anaikāntika*.

16. It is interesting to note in this context the view of Kālidāsa, who says that the death of a person at the confluence of the Ganges and Jamuna rivers will lead him to final release even without the knowledge of reality (*Raghuvaṃśa* 13.58).

17. Śaṃkara Miśra refers frequently to the view of others, many of which have not been identified. He appears to have had access to other (now lost) commentaries on the *Ātmatattvaviveka*. Credit should be given to him for identifying the authors of some of the *prima facie* positions stated in the text such as Dharmakīrti, Prajñākaragupta, Jñānaśrī and others. Ratnakīrti's arguments are identified. The name "Kaṇikākāra" occurs in connection with an objection raised against God's creation of the world. The alternate reading is "Kāśikākāra"; evidently he refers to Sucarita Miśra. He quotes the works of Udayana, and also his own works.

It is interesting to note here that the line *parasparavirodhe hi na prakārāntarasthitiḥ*, which forms part of *Nyāyakusumāñjali* 3.8, is treated as a general statement. This passage is looked upon as a maxim by Vedānta Deśika in his *Śatadūṣaṇī*, *vāda* 24.

Two things are worth noting about Śaṃkara Miśra and his commentary on the *Ātmattvaviveka*. One is his concept of deity. The benedictory stanza depicts God as a weaver producing the cloth of the world and as a potter producing the pitcher of the world. He wears a garland of white and dark-blue flowers in the form of creation and *pralaya*. This is reason, then, to take Śaṃkara Miśra as a thoroughgoing Naiyāyika who looks upon God as the creator and destroyer of the world and the instrumental cause for effects. The second point is that he reports what he was taught by his father Bhavanātha. In fact, his father was teaching his son the commentary of his elder brother Jīvanātha. It is not clear whether Jīvanātha wrote the commentary or simply gave an oral exposition to his brother Bhavanātha.

Another aspect worth noting here is that Śaṃkara Miśra does not take any personal responsibility for any merit or shortcoming in his commentary, saying he is only repeating what his father taught him. Finally, he avows that anyone who attempts to comment on the *Ātmatattvaviveka* cannot claim to display any skill in his attempt unless her reads through his father's commentary along with his own. Once again, it is not clear whether his father too wrote a commentary or gave an oral exposition.

22. HARI MIŚRA

1. Cf. his *Nyāyaparicay* (in Bengali), Calcutta 1934, 1940, p. 17 according to Ingalls (B3417; RB Ingalls), p. 8.
2. Ibid.

23. VĀCASPATI MIŚRA II

1. Cf. D.C. Bhattacharya (RB6105), p. 143.
2. Ibid.
3. U. Mishra (RB: UM), pp. 296-297.
4. B.K. Matilal, *Nyāya-Vaiśeṣika* (A History of Indian Literature, Vol. 6), Wiesbaden 1977, p. 106.
5. D.C. Bhattacharya (RB6105), pp. 144-153. See also U. Mishra (RB: UM), pp. 291-294.
6. *Nyāyakusumāñjali, kārikā* 10. Cf. the summary in Vol. II of this Encyclopedia, p. 564, 565.
7. The work *Tattvāloka*, mentioned on p. 25, is lost. It was written by Vācaspati Miśra on a grammatical aspect of the Nyāya system.

While criticizing the view of opponents that God's agency of the world cannot be supported since this creation is not produced through the possession of a body, Vācaspati Miśra cites the view of some scholars in support of this contention of the opponents and offers *ākāśa* as example. Mahārṇavavāseśvara and Narasiṃha Hariśarman are mentioned here (p. 40) as offereing this example. Vācapati notes that the weak point which was raised by Śrīharṣa has not been answered by these writers. *Mahārṇava* is the name of a work whose author is known to have postulated twelve categories—substance, quality, motion, universal, number, inherence, similarity, potency, sequence, assistance, impressions and condition. This list of categories suggests that this writer was a follower of the Mīmāṃsā system. Since Kumārila Bhaṭṭa did not admit these, the author the *Mahārṇava* might have been a follower of the Prābhākara school of Mīmāṃsā. But this is only a surmise, because Bhavanātha, a Prābhākara and author of the *Nayaviveka*, criticizes the view of *Mahodadhi* who held the same view on verbal construction as did the Bhāṭṭas and Naiyāyikas and whose name may be taken as equivalent to *Mahārṇava* (p. 270).

Śrīharṣa's vindictive and insinuating suggestions that inference and memory too could be claimed to be immediate are shown to be opposed to the *Bṛhadāraṇyaka* passage prescribing *darśana*, *śravaṇa*, *manana* and *nididhyāsana*, which involve mediate and immediate aspects of awareness. Worldly practice is also based on a clearcut division between mediate and immediate kinds of awarenesses. Śrīharṣa flouts both and pursues a wrong course (p. 62). Śrīharṣa is represented as having spent all his life proclaiming that mutual absence consists in the denial of objects having the same locus, while relational absence is their denial in different loci. Even in the evening of his life he uttered nonsense, opposed to the understanding of the exponents of all system of thought. Yet he is neither ashamed of his utterances nor afraid of others (p. 73). What is apprehended by the eye and mind is denied existence and that which is reflected there is noted by Śrīharṣa, who is therefore addressed as ignorant (p. 90). The opponent is asked to get away from the *siddhāntin*, since by maintaining nondifference between what are opposed to each other he has given up the Nyāya system and does not know how to get to understanding of the Vedānta system (p. 103). With severe vehemence the author asks the opponent to give up his faith in the existence of Brahman that represents the purport of the Vedas, then to study the texts of the nihilists and to take up nihilist doctrines (p. 130).

24. MALLINĀTHA

1. U. Mishra (RB: UM), p. 188.

2. Mallinātha quotes Śālikanātha frequently, describing him as fully conversant with system of the Prābhākaras (p. 22).

Mallinātha refers to the *Niṣkāntaka*, his own commentary on the Praśastapāda *Bhāṣya*. *Nikāśa* occurs as the name of a work on Nyāya-Vaiśeṣika. It appears to be his own work. But it is not clear whether it is identical with the *Niṣkāntaka* referred to.

His knowledge of grammar is evident in his commentaries on the *Mahākāvyas* and *Ekāvalī* from disucssions of certain forms such as *kṛtaṃ vistareṇa* (p. 39). Mallinātha cites *Nyāsoddyota* and cites his own explanation of the passage *alam mahīpāla* (*Raghuvaṃśa* 2.34). This work, which is not extant, is his own commentary on Jinendrabuddhi's *Nyāsa*.

Mallinātha's commentary stops where this summary ends, and the further portion of it was not available to the editor. However, Mallinātha commented upon the entire text.

25. PAKṢADHARA, the Vivekakāra

1. D.C. Bhattacharya (RB 6105), p. 119.
2. Ibid., p. 121.
3. RB: UM, pp. 334-335.

28. NARAHARI, father of Vāsudeva Sārvabhauma

1. G. Kaviraj (B and RB: GK), p. 50 of the 1961 edition.
2. Gopikamohan Bhattacharya, *Navya-Nyāya*, op. cit., p. 5.

29. YAJÑAPATI UPĀDHYĀYA

1. Yajñapati Upādhyāya's *Tattvacintāmaṇiprabhā (Anumānakhaṇḍa)* edited by Gopikamohan Bhattacharya. Österreichische Akademie der Wissenschaften, Philosophisch-Historische Klasse, Sitzungsberichte 423. Band, Veroffentlichungen der Kommission für Sprachen und Kulturen Südasiens Heft 17. Wien 1984, p. 13.
2. Ibid., pp. 19-50.

30. PRAGALBHA MIŚRA or SUBHAṄKARA

1. Though Bimal Matilal, citing D.C. Bhattacharya's *Vaṅge Navya-Nyāya Carcā*, estimates he wrote "about eight commentaries (Bimal Krishna Matilal, *Nyāya-Vaiśeṣika*, Vol. VI of *A History of Indian Literature* (ed. Jan Gonda), Wiesbaden 1977, p. 108.
2. M.M.Sivakumarasastri-Granthamala Vol. 7, Varanasi 1983.
3. Sarasvati Bhavan Texts 78, 1939.
4. Referred to by Umesh Mishra (B and RB: UM), p. 327.
5. Gaurinath Shastri in Bibliotheca Indica 308, 1979, quoting a manuscript from Calcutta.

31. JAYADEVA, PAKṢADHARA MIŚRA

1. B and RB: UM, pp. 328-341.
2. D.C. Bhattacharya (RB6105), pp. 115-128.
3. Umesh Mishra (B and RB: UM), pp. 330-331.
4. Daniel Henry Holmes Ingalls (B3417; RB Ingalls), *Materials for the Study of Navya-Nyāya Logic* (Cambridge, Mass., 1951), pp. 6-9.
5. Ingalls, Ibid., p. 9.
6. Ingalls, Ibid., pp. 13-14.
7. D.C.Bhattacharya, op. cit., p. 119.
8. U. Mishra (B and RB: UM), p. 333.
9. New Catalogus Catalogorum VII, 178.

32. ŚRĪNĀTHA BHAṬṬĀCĀRYA CAKRAVARTIN

1. T.S. Bhattacharya (RB9381), pp. 288-289.

33. VĀSUDEVA SĀRVABHAUMA

1. Bodas, Introduction to B3910; RB6383, p. xlvi.
2. Bodas, ibid.
3. Ingalls (B3413; RB Ingalls), p. 9.

4. D.C. Bhattacharya (RB5676), "Vāsudeva Sārvabhauma", *Indian Historical Quarterly* 16, 1940, pp. 60-69.

5. Gaurinath Sastri's Introduction to his edition of Gaṅgeśa's (*Tattvacintāmaṇi*) *Maṅgalavāda*, Bibliotheca Indica 308, 1979, pp. 13-14.

6. G. Bhattacharya, Introduction to the edition of Gadādhara's *Vidhisvarūpavicāra* (RB6627), p. II.

7. Ibid.

8. Ibid., p. iv.

9. Gopikamohan Bhattacharya, *Navya-Nyāya*, op cit., pp. 19-26.

34. KṚṢṆĀNANDA VIDYĀVINODA

1. Gaurinath Sastri, Introduction to *Maṅgalavāda*, op. cit., p. 16.

35. JANĀRDANA of Mithilā

1. Cf. New Catalogus Catalogorum VIII, p. 23.

37. MISARU MIŚRA

1. S.C. Vidyabhusana (B and RB: HIL), p. 460.

39. NARAHARI UPĀDHYĀYA or MAHEŚVARA VIŚĀRADA

1. Gopikamohan Bhattacharya's article in the Gaurinath Sastri Felicitation Volume, p. 210.

2. Cf. U. Mishra (RB: UM,) p. 343.

3. Ibid., p. 343. We assume the reference is to this Narahari. Umesh Mishra conflates the two authors.

41. ŚRĪKĀRA KUBJAŚAKTIVĀDA

1. RB: UM, p. 353.

42. ŚŪLAPĀṆI MIŚRA

1. RB: UM, p. 346.

44. RUCIDATTA MIŚRA

1. The subcommentary *Nyāyaśikhāmaṇi* identifies this view as Jayadeva's. This identification is perplexing. Jayadeva flourished after Gaṅgeśa, who could not therefore refer to the former's view in his work. It appears that Jayadeva quarreled with his preceptor Yajñapati and found fault with his writings. It would therefore be prudent to identify this view as that of some other Naiyāyika who was a predecessor of Gaṅgeśa.

2. This kind of argument seems to be perplexing. What determines the course of the motion of sound is the air current. When the latter is uniform,

the principle of the wave holds good, and when it is not, the principle of *kadamba* buds holds good. In the system of Nyāya and Vaiśeṣika, which maintains the *ārambhavāda*, the nature of the effect cannot be precisely stated, though it is predetermined on the strength of the causal relation. In the present case the nature of sound together with its varieties cannot be known beforehand and so cannot be described or assumed through their prior absences. It is therefore proper to admit air currents as modifying the cause of sound.

3. Rucidatta does not explain the portion of the text which discusses the passage from the *Ātmatattvaviveka*.

It is worth noting here that Gaṅgeśa's treatment is close to that of Maṇikaṇṭha (cf. the edition of *Nyāyaratna* (B3268) by V.S. Sastri and V. Krishnamacharya, pp. 80-83) in all the aspects of the treatment given to Udayana's definition and treatment of the topic. The order of treatment is also the same and is suggestive of Gaṅgeśa's indebtedness to Maṇikaṇṭha's treatment.

Gaṅgeśa refers to a definition which also aims to apply only to even cases of pervasion. Rucidatta explains this accordingly. Maṇikaṇṭha (ibid., p. 82) notes that this view was held by modern Naiyāyikas. He states that his comments on the text follow the treatment of this topic in the *Nyāyakusumāñjali*.

Rucidatta observes that some scholars hold that the definition alone is not meant to be derived here, but it is to be derived in the way of knowing it. It does not mean that it is known only in the way indicated. What is not known in that manner also happens to be an obstructor.

The view of Taraṇi Miśra, the author of the *Ratnakośa*, is identified by Rucidatta. Gaṅgeśa does not mention his name but cites a *śloka* which is also cited by Maṇikaṇṭha (ibid., p. 86) associating its authorship with the author of the *Ratnakośa*.

4. Special mention must be made of the treatment the author gives to repeated observation (*bhūyodarśana*), pervasion (*vyāpti*) and *tarka*. The views of several writers are cited and criticized. Most of these writers must have been commentators on the *Tattvacintāmaṇi* preceding Rucidatta.

Apart from Udayana, referred to as "Ācārya", and other well-known writers, Śaśadhara's view is quoted under "*liṅga*". The *Parimala* is mentioned by Rucidatta as the work of Jagadguru. Divākara Upādhyāya is known to have written the *Parimala*, a commentary on the *Nyāyakusumāñjali* (see D.C. Bhattacharya (RB6105), pp. 72-73). From other sources it is found that Jagadguru commented upon the *Nyāyakusumāñjali* and *Kiraṇāvalī* (ibid., pp. 93-94), but these commentaries do not appear to have been called by the name *Parimala*. Rucidatta's specific reference to the *Parimala* as the work of Jagadguru raises a problem. Rucidatta refers to the *Parimala* a number of times in his commentary upon Vardhamāna's *Kusumāñjaliprakāśa*, but no mention is made there as to the name of its author. In his commentary on the *Tattvacintāmaṇi* Rucidatta does not refer to the *Parimala* as a commentary on the *Nyāyakusumāñjali*, but that it could be on this work is borne out from his references made to the work in his commentary upon Vardhamāna's *Nyāyakusumāñjaliprakāśa*. Rucidatta's reference must therefore be admitted to treat the *Parimala* as Jagadguru's commentary on the *Nyāyakusumāñjali.* This goes against the attribution of the *Parimala*'s authorship to Divākara Upādhyāya made for certain reasons (given in D.C. Bhattacharya (RB6105), pp. 72-73). Two conclusions could be drawn on the strength of the data available on this problem. There must have been two works with the same name *Parimala* upon the *Nyāyakusumāñjali* by two different writers, Jagadguru and Divākara Upādhyāya. This conclusion has to face the objection that Rucidatta would not be referring to both, associating one of them with the name Jagadguru and leaving out the other without mentioning the author. The second conclusion is that the *Parimala* referred to by Rucidatta in his two works should be one and the same. Reference in one of the two works to the *Parimala* as the work of Jagadguru and the other references made to the *Parimala* in the evidence cited by D.C. Bhattacharya should somehow be reconciled. Divākara Upādhyāya and Jagadguru must be treated as identical. Perhaps "Divākara Upādhyāya" was the name of the commentator upon the *Nyāyakusumāñjali* and "Jagadguru" was his title. Admission of this conclusion raises another difficulty. Divākara Upādhyāya is known to have commented upon Udayana's *Kiraṇāvalī* from the evidence cited by D.C. Bhattacharya. If Divākara's commentary upon the *Nyāyakusumāñjali* is the *Parimala*, what was the name of his commentary on the *Kiraṇāvalī*? Was it also known as *Parimala* like the name *Prakāśa* given to Vardhamāna's commentaries on the works of Udayana and Vallabha? Further information must be obtained about the contents of the works of Jagadguru and Divākara Upādhyāya to decide the authorship of the *Parimala.*

5. Rucidatta cites the passages from the *Pramāṇatattvabodha* of Vardhamāna to support his argument. It is worth noting that Bhagīratha also cites these very same passages noting the same source, except for the difference that Bhagīratha mentions the name of the work of Vardhamāna as *Prameyatattvabodha.*

6. Rucidatta questions the interpretation of the text offered by Vardhamāna in a few cases. He does not justify the use of the word *utpatti* for a second time in Vardhamāna's explanation.

46. PURUṢOTTAMA BHAṬṬĀCĀRYA

1. Gaurinatha Sastri, Introduction to his edition of Gaṅgeśa's *Maṅgalavāda*, op. cit., p. 15.

47. JANEŚVARA VĀHINĪPATI

1. U. Mishra (RB: UM), p. 336.

50. RAGHUNĀTHA ŚIROMOṆI

1. Ingalls, op. cit., p. 10.
2. Ibid., pp. 10-12.
3. Ibid., pp. 14-15.

4. Ibid., p. 13.
5. Cf. Matilal, *Nyāya-Vaiśeṣika*, op. cit., p. 108.
6. Cf. Ingalls, op. cit., p. 9.
7. Ingalls, ibid., p. 15.
8. Ingalls, ibid., p. 17.
9. The commentary on the *Ātmatattvaviveka* is called *Dīdhiti*, and the colophon at the end in the printed text reads the name of work as *Ātmatattvavivekabhāvaprakāśa* and the name of the author as Mahāmahopādhyāya Śrīmadbhaṭṭācāryaśiromaṇi. Perhaps *Bhāvaprakāśa* is the actual name, as suggested in the introductory verse, where the words are *ātmatattvavivekasya bhāvamudbhāvayatvayam*. The title *Dīdhiti* given at the top of the commentary is perhaps suggested by the word *dīdhiti*, which is the name of his well-known commentary on the *Tattvacintāmaṇi*. This word, which means "ray", fits with *maṇi*, "a gem", and has no relevance to *viveka*, a word which forms part of this text of Udayana's.

This commentary is complete except for the concluding passage in the *Bāhyārthabhaṅga* and for the two concluding *ślokas*.

Raghunātha Śiromaṇi reveals his Advaita leanings in several places. The benedictory stanza bears testimony to this. It is also not improper to take this *śloka* as conveying the author's concept of deity as based on the Upaniṣads. While commenting upon Udayana's treatment of the Mādhyamika theory vis-a-vis Advaita, the author notes that the rejection of the nihilistic doctrine is based on the Vedantic plane (p. 503). The word *vedanaya* in the text (p. 529) is interpreted by the author as the doctrine based on the Upaniṣads (*aupaniṣadanaya*), and this is supported by him with citations from the Upaniṣads (p. 530). While commenting on the textual passages which deal with the stages of realization (pp. 935-36), the author cites passages from the Chāndogya Upaniṣad 6.2.1, 7.15.4, 7.25.2 and notes down the commentary on them. The author's writing is clear enough to show that he had Advaita doctrines in his mind. Vide: *advitīyasaccidānandātmakabrahmabodhikānāmupaniṣadām prapañcamithyātvasya siddhāveva pravṛtteśtatsādhakānāṃ dvāratvam* (p. 945). The term *carama vedānta* is interpreted by him thus: *śuddhasvaprakāśa-citsvarūpa-brahma-pratipādakavedāntānām upasaṃhāraḥ pratipādyāntaravirahāt* (p. 946). These show unmistakably that the author was a follower of the Vedānta school of Advaita.

10. The author refers frequently to the views of others. Their names are not mentioned, but are simply stated and not generally controverted. In some of these references the views of Śaṃkara Miśra seem to be referred to. (Cf. pp. 16, 44, 99, 173, 231, 238.) Some of Śaṃkara Miśra's views are stated and questioned, without explanation or refutation. (See pp. 235, 420.) Repeatedly the author mentions the views of Bhagīratha without mentioning his name (cf. pp. 22, 80, 132, 143,150, 174, 231, 437, 547, 734). He does not question these views. Yet he uses the words "others" (*pare, anye, kecit*) while referring to the views of Bhagīratha. So the author must have lived not exactly when Bhagīratha flourished but a little later. He refers to the opinions of others who cannot be easily identified (cf. pp. 208, 229, 277, 312, 537, 565, 760, 893). The commentary contains citations from

several sources, Buddhistic and non-Buddhistic. In Nyāya, the *sūtras*, the *Vārttika* and the *Ṭīkā* of Vācaspati Miśra are cited. A *śloka* from Kumārila Bhaṭṭa is also quoted (p. 892). Pāṇini's *sūtras* and passages from the works on grammar are also cited. Besides, passages from the Upaniṣads are profusely quoted.

11. Cf. B.K. Matilal, 'Double negation in Navya-Nyāya' in *Sanskrit and Indian Studies. Essays in Honour of Daniel H. H. Ingalls* (ed. M. Nagatomi et al.), Sltudies in Classical India 2 (Dordrecht, 1980), pp. 1—10.

12. The expression *pacati* is formed by combining the verbal stem *pac* (to cook) and the verbal ending *ti* (third person, singular number, present tense), while *pāka* is formed by combining the verbal stem *pac* and the verbal suffix *ghañ* which belongs to the type called *bhāvavihita*, which merely expresses the fundamental notion of the verb to which it is adjoined. According to the Naiyāyikas, a verbal stem means a certain result or operation (*phalavyāpārau dhātvarthau*), and the verbal stem *pac* and the noun *pāka* mean the same thing, viz., cooking. By the method of residues the verbal ending *ti* and the verb *karoti* should mean the same thing. the verbal stem *kṛ*, when conjugated, yields the form *karoti*, and *kṛ* stands for effort (*kṛnaśca yatnavācakatvam*). It thus follows that the verbal ending primarily means effort.

13. This counterargument invokes the so-called *tadagamanyāya*, viz., a word cannot mean something that can be indicated by anything else, because a word means something only if the latter cannot be meant by anything else (*ananyalabhyaḥ śabdārthaḥ*).

14. When transitive verbs are used in the active voice, the agent (*kartṛ*) occurs as the nominative, and has the first case-ending; while the object (*karman*) occurs as the accusative, and has the second case-ending. In the case of passive voice, the object occurs as the nominative and has the first case-ending, while the agent occurs as the instrumental and has the second case-ending.

15. In active voice, the agent appears as the locus of the effort, while in passive voice, the object appears as something toward which the effort is directed.

16. Although this seems to suggest a Vedāntic conception of the Self, yet commentators on Raghunātha like Gadādhara have interpreted it from the Nyāya point of view. Still at times Raghunātha has rejected Gaṅgeśa's solutions in favour of Vedānta and even Mīmāṃsā theories.

17. They are not put in precisely the way Pakṣadhara put them.

18. Raghunātha's own formulation of the case is rather complex and requires reformulation. The reformulation is Bhavānanda's, though those of Jagadīśa and Kṛṣṇadāsa, though different, cannot be said to be substantially so. They reformulate it as: Time possesses a jar, because it is infinite time. And *Siddhāntamuktāvalī* formulates it as "time possesses a jar, because it possesses temporal dimension."

19. There was also another well-known attempt, though who made it is not known. It consists in holding that the absence of cloth (the commentators say "absence of a jar", but as Vāmācaraṇa Nyāyācārya points out, if *s* be a jar, the absence of jar cannot be the definition constituting the absence)

as qualified by its nonidentity with infinite time is the definition constituting absence in that cloth as qualified by its nonidentity with infinite time cannot be in time. This way out is considered by all the commentators on Raghunātha except Kṛṣṇadāsa, and is judged to be insufficient. Even *Siddhāntamuktāvalī* takes it into consideration and gives it up in favour of a better alternative. But Raghunātha does not mention it.

20. Raghunātha subjects this way out to critical examination. But before this is explained let it be mentioned that he has not formulated the Sārvabhauma thesis in the way in which its author would have liked. For in the opinion of Sārvabhauma "the qualified one" or "the superstratumness as described by the qualified one" is something additional, and so he would not have felt the necessity of making the insertion "limited by the limitor of its counterpositiveness." This has been pointed out by Jagadīśa and he has observed that Raghunātha's formulation in this respect is rather irregular. Gadādhara has made a similar observation. Anyway, the first objection of Raghunātha is that as the qualified one, that is, as the superstratumness described by the qualified one, is not something additional, the definition as construed by Sārvabhauma cannot exclude an inference like "it possesses qualified existence, because it possesses generic attributes". Even if the distinctive contention of Sārvabhauma that the qualified one is additional be admitted, his construction cannot be said to be valid since it fails to exclude inferences like "it possesses generic attribute (the limiting relation of *s*-ness being inherence), because it is an object of knowledge", and "it possesses contact, because it is something other than a quality or motion".

A perusal of Raghunātha's examination will make it clear that the refutation is not as conclusive as he might have expected it to be. For the definition fails to exclude the first case as it is held that the qualified one is not something additional, and it fails to exclude the other two cases as such loci of *h* as generic attribute or what follows it in the list of categories cannot be the describer of occurrentness in the limiting relation of *s*-ness. So if the qualified one be held as something additional, and if again in place of "the limiting relation of *s*-ness" some well-defined essential relation be substituted, the definition will be successful in excluding the cases which it has been alleged it cannot exclude. Accordingly Jagadīśa following his preceptor has reformulated it; and in recent times Vāmācaraṇa Nyāyācārya has given it a formulation that overcomes these objections.

21. See for *paryāpti* Ingalls (B3417; RB Ingalls), op. cit., pp. 76–77, and D.C. Guha (*RB9368), op. cit., pp. 225–270.

22. Cf. Ingalls, op. cit., pp. 77-78.

23. The earlier portion of the this section giving an exposition of Prabhākara's thoughts has not been summarized. Only some of the various critical remarks contained in the later portion have been touched upon in the summary.

24. The point is that in some cases there is ascertainment of pervasion without there being absence of the awareness of the *h* being present where the *s* is absent. In some cases absence of the awareness that *h* is present where the *s* is absent cannot be a real entity: it is usually held that an absence cannot be accepted as real unless the counterpositive is real; it is also held

that only real entities can be cognized. If the said absence cannot be a real entity in some cases of ascertainment of pervasion, it cannot precede such ascertainment in every case, and hence cannot be a causal condition.

25. Raghunātha is well aware of the fact that true generalizations may be based on noncausal connections as well.

26. The reader is expected to assess the relative philosophical merits and demerits of the different formulations of the *tarka*.

27. A universal may serve as a connection for such extraordinary perception of all particulars of a kind only when it is the qualifier of that which is in contact with a sense-organ through one of the six ordinary kinds of sense-object connection. In other words, such extraordinary perception of all particulars of a kind may take place only when a sense-organ is actually in contact with a given particular of the said kind.

28. This objection springs from the fact that not only eternal properties, such as universals like cowness, may be regarded as universals, but also eternal individuals, which are connected with many loci, may be regarded as universals. This notion of an individual serving as a universal is not found in old Nyāya. According to the view under consideration, the universal itself serves as the sensory connection for the extraordinary perception of all the loci of that sort. If the notion of a universal is extended to cover individuals which are noneternal, obviously no such perception of all the loci of the said character may take place when the universal is not there. This objection prepares the ground for the other view that it is not the universal, but rather the awareness of the universal, which serves as the sensory connection for the perception of all the loci of that sort.

29. If the awareness of a universal rather than the thing itself be regarded as the connection for *sāmānyalakṣaṇa* perception, the question arises as to how it differs from *jñānalakṣaṇa* in which also an awareness serves as the connection. This question is answered in what follows.

30. In the visual perception of the *jñānalakṣaṇa* variety that the sandalwood is fragrant, awareness of fragrance (*saurabhatva*) serves as the connection, and fragrance itself is featured as a content of the perception. But in *sāmānyalakṣaṇa* perception, though awareness of the property serves as the connection, the property itself does not become a content of the perception.

31. If pervasion of smoke by fire were not regarded as one and common to all smokes, but rather were regarded as many, pervasion of smoke in the kitchen by fire in the kitchen would have to be regarded as different from pervasion of smoke on the hill by fire on the hill. Raghunātha shows the difficulty in accounting for the inference to fire from smoke (and thereby of any inference of the same kind) if the latter view were advocated.

32. The objection springs from the fact that the inference that this has fire not only presupposes the awareness of fire, but also the awareness of this-ness which, too, is a qualifier and happens to be the limitor of the fact that *this* is the *pakṣa*. There is, of course, no need to appeal to *sāmānyalakṣaṇasannikarṣa* for the cognition of this-ness.

33. Gaṅgeśa has argued that it is more economical to say that a relational awareness is caused by the awareness of the limitor of the qualifierness, rather than saying that the awareness is caused by the awareness of the

qualifier. Since the limitor of the qualifierness is usually one although the qualifiers are many, this dispenses with the need to appeal to *sāmānyalakṣaṇa* perception to account for the awareness of a qualifier with which there has been no prior acquaintance. Raghunātha shows that the case for *sāmānyalakṣaṇa* perception cannot be reopened even if one takes into consideration cases where the limitors of the qualifierness happen to be many, so that the limitors of the qualifierness may not be previously known. A common example of such a case is the awareness "this possesses someone holding a stick" where the limitor of the qualifierness is the stick, which happens to be multiple (i.e., if some stick, not one particular stick, that is referred to).

34. After disposing of the view that *sāmānyalakṣaṇa* perception is needed to account for the awareness of generic absence, Raghunātha proceeds to consider whether *sāmānyalakṣaṇasannikarṣa* is needed to account for the perception of a prior absence.

35. If prior absence is inferred and not perceived, there is no need to have recourse to *sāmānyalakṣaṇa* perception to account for the awareness of a counterpositive belonging to the future. Next Raghunātha proceeds to deny that the awareness that something will come to be, which awareness has traditionally been regarded as providing the evidence for the admission of prior absence, refers to prior absence at all.

36. The awareness "the effect will be produced here (in the inherence cause)" does signify absence of the effect. If prior absence is not admitted, what would be the object of this awareness? Next Raghunātha suggests that the absolute absence (*atyantābhāva*) of the effect is now the object of this awareness.

37. According to the traditional view, absolute absence cannot be the object of this awareness because absolute absence and prior absence are incompatible and absolute absence does not belong to the effect's inherence cause, which is the locus of the prior absence of the effect. Next Raghunātha anticipates and answers this objection.

38. The awareness "a pot will be produced here" does not signify that all pots will be produced here, but rather that a particular pot will be produced here; similarly with the awareness that a pot has been destroyed. This fact is expressed in the technical language by saying that the counterpositiveness of prior absence and posterior absence is not limited by a general property. But the awareness "there is no pot in this pot-half" signifies the absence of all pots. Hence, Raghunātha suggests, that is not the awareness of prior absence, but of absolute absence.

There are two exceptional circumstances under which prior or posterior absence may signify the absence of all pots: before any pot has been produced, one might speak of the prior absence of all pots; similarly, after all pots have been destroyed one might speak of the posterior absence of all pots. Hence, Raghunātha adds, although this may be possible in exceptional cases it is not so in the present case.

Just as Raghunātha dispenses with prior absence, so one may except him to dispense with posterior absence by replacing it with the absolute absence belonging to the time after a thing ceases to exist. But he does not do so, as may be seen from following passage.

39. An argument which has been advanced for admitting prior absence is that otherwise one cannot explain why there is never further production of a thing after the thing has been produced. Since the thing has been produced, the sum total of its causal conditions must exist at the moment preceding the moment of the thing's origin. Further, the same sum total may remain available at the moment of the origin of the thing. But that would not explain why in no case whatsoever is the thing ever reproduced. The problem is resolved by admitting prior absence, which may then be regarded as a causal condition, which is necessarily missing once the thing is produced.

Raghunātha suggests that the problem may be resolved without admitting prior absence and in fact by supposing that the thing itself acts as the obstruction to its further production.

Next Raghunātha explains the notion of origin which is crucial for his rejection of prior absence.

40. Thus origin amounts to being related to the first moment, which alone can answer to the above descriptions.

41. This definiton rules out the possibility of a moment being contemporaneous with the previous moment as well as the succeeding moment. Raghunātha has given four other definitions of a moment.

42. The Naiyāyika does not subscribe to *satkāryavāda* (the view that the effect is potentially existent in the cause) and accounts for the fact that an effect is produced only in its inherence cause by holding that the prior absence of the effect belongs only to the inherence cause and to nothing else. Raghunātha, next, rejects this too.

43. Since the cloth is not produced until all the threads have been woven together, the totality of all the contacts has to be regarded as a cause. Then it is superfluous to admit prior absence to account for the above fact.

44. Raghunātha seems to imply that although the awareness of posterior absence is common and universal, the supposed awareness of prior absence is not.

45. The above argument in favour of *sāmānyalakṣaṇa* perception is attributed to "Miśra". Raghunātha rejects it on the ground that temporal precedence and succession cannot be known through *sāmānyalakṣaṇa* perception. All that can be known through *sāmānyalakṣaṇa* perception about a particular is that it is the locus of a common property. Raghunātha also disagrees with the traditional Nyāya position that no two introspectible qualities of the self can arise at the same time.

46. To the question "what is cownessness?" the common reply is "it is 'belonging to all cows together with not belonging to what is not a cow.'" Raghunātha rejects the first part of this analysis. He further points out that it would be futile to build a case for *sāmānyalakṣaṇa* perception on the ground that it is through such perception that we acquire the knowledge of belonging to all cows; for the idea of a totality could not possibly be apprehended through *sāmānyalakṣaṇa* perception.

47. Raghunātha's reformulation achieves complete generality by way of replacing the expressions "putative *h* and *s*" by pronominal variables.

48. The difference between these accounts and Gaṅgeśa's account is not

merely verbal. Raghunātha has also suggested several refinements and modifications in Gaṅgeśa's account in this connection.

49. Although *being different from that pot* pervades color as specified by the said property, it does not pervade color as co-located with that property.

50. The qualification "which is not a locus of the obstruction" is required to prevent food, etc., from turning out to be obstructions in the inference of fire from smoke, etc.

51. The given analysis of "deviation from the pervader" is in preference to other similar analyses like "belonging to the locus of absence of what is specified by pervaderness" or "belonging to the locus of the pervader", for the latter lead to certain difficulties.

52. Gaṅgeśa has accepted "being other than the *p*" as an obstruction in cases of *bādha*. Raghunātha goes further and accepts it as an adjunct in every case where it can be ascertained with the help of supportive *tarka* that the *s* is pervaded by it.

INDEX

ābhāsa, see finding fault where none is committed
abhāva, see absence
abhāvīyaviśeṣaṇatā, see qualification, absentuial
abheda, see nondifference
abhibhūta, see subdued
abhidhā, see meaning, primary
Abhyankar, Vasudeva Sastri 617
abhyudaya, see liberation (*abhyudaya*)
ablution (*prokṣaṇa*) 232-34
absence (*abhāva*) 16, 32, 46-48, 62, 66, 104, 122, 127-28, 133-42, 171, 198, 202-03, 207, 219-20, 228-29, 254, 317, 339-40, 365, 388-89, 413-14, 419, 448, 450-51, 453, 457, 464-65, 472, 475-76, 478, 482-85, 519, 528, 532, 534-35, 542, 549, 551-56, 559-60, 563-64, 572, 583, 587, 590, 602
absential qualification (*abhāvīya*), see qualification
absolute or constant (*atyanta*) 39, 47-8, 72, 99, 128-29, 139, 172-73, 176-77, 181, 187, 195, 202, 210, 229, 237-38, 324, 326, 328, 333, 340-41, 374, 380, 383, 385, 388, 402, 418-19, 425, 437, 439, 445, 447, 463, 484-85, 497, 501, 506, 523, 557-59, 561, 568, 570, 575, 629
awareness of an 94, 126, 130-32, 134-36, 140, 163, 341, 365, 468, 497, 499-500, 576
conjoint (*ubhaya-*) 562-63
generic/specific 47-8, 61, 334, 475, 501-02, 523, 570, 577, 629
limited by a property whose loci are different from its counterpositive (*vyadhikaraṇāvacchinnābhāva*) 102, 172, 474-75, 551-56, 559, 566
locative (*vyadhikaraṇa*) 138
mutual (*anyonya-*), see difference
-ness (*-tva*) 129, 140, 334, 475, 532, 534
of pairs 177, 569
particular (*viśeṣa-*) 176-78
(*paryudāsa*) 328
posterior (*dhvaṃsa*) 47, 130, 190, 214, 216, 229, 237, 263, 306, 322, 327, 335-36, 340-42, 406, 419-20, 428, 435, 445, 447, 452, 523, 531-32, 559, 566, 577, 606, 630
prior (*prāg-*) 47, 62, 125, 130, 148, 214-15, 221, 229, 235, 237-38, 245, 277, 306, 318, 322, 329, 340-41, 407, 419, 422, 425, 428, 435, 445, 447, 449, 484, 523, 532-33, 566, 576-78, 600, 608, 629-30
qualified 506
relational (*saṃsarga-*) 334, 339-40, 342, 463, 532, 541, 559-60, 569, 620
triple 47, 532, 551
universal 565-66
ācārya, see teacher
Acintyabhedābheda 4, 489
act, action (*karman, kriyā*) 115
bodily 218
cause of 468
ceremonial, see rite, ritual
congruent/deviant 106-10
incitement to/prevention of 512, 598
invocative, see invocation
mental 20-21, 53, 151-52, 215, 315
object of 459
optional or desired (*kāmya*) 277-79, 308
purposive 55, 237
required or obligatory or prescribed

(*nitya*) 269, 277-79, 308
subsidiary 316
successful 56, 94-5, 598
unwavering (*niṣkampa-*) 88, 94, 96-7, 105
verbal or speech-act, see language
volitional/nonvolitional 101-02, 219, 248
(positive) activity (*pravṛtti*) 103-07, 113-14, 415, 430
actual, see real
ādhāra, see substratum
ādhāratva, see located in, being
adharma, see demerit
ādheya, see superstratum
ādheya śakti, see causal efficacy, acquired
adhika, see redundancy
adhikāra, see qualification for a role
adhikaraṇa, see locus
-*tā*, see located in, being
Ādinātha Jain, see Jinavardhana Sūri
adjunct, see (1) counterpositive, (2) obstruction, (3) referent admitting the other party's opinion (*matānujñā*) 361-62, 409-10
adṛṣṭa (see also merit and demerit) 44, 149, 211-14, 223, 225-27, 234, 322, 325, 334-35, 340, 378, 387, 397, 407, 419, 424, 434, 442, 450, 505, 510, 515-16, 518, 528, 609
advaita, see nonduality
Advaita Vedānta 8, 33, 36, 38, 44-5, 54, 60, 334, 368-69, 381, 397-407, 413-14, 451-52, 456, 458-59, 486, 524, 533, 625-26
Advaitamakaranda of Lakṣmīdhara 489
affirmative, see positive-negative
affliction (*tāpa*) 367, 423
aftercognition (*anuvyavasāya*) 56, 60, 89-92, 95, 107, 115, 150-55, 166, 343, 365, 458, 462, 474, 494, 496, 544, 592, 604
āgama, see Veda
agent (*kartṛ*) 222-23, 225, 391, 415, 442, 515
embodied/bodiless 220, 222
insentient 348
aggregate (*saṃghāta, samāhāra*) 379, 414
agnihotra, see sacrifice, *agnihotra*
agreement and difference, or agreement in presence and absence, see concomitance
aham, see ego
ahaṃkāra, see egoity
āhāryajñāna, see awareness, contrary-to-fact supposition
ahiṃsā 414
air or wind (*vāyu*) 33-5, 40, 45, 47-8, 66, 125, 128, 132-36, 145, 163, 328, 353, 386, 413, 444, 475, 530-31, 565, 602, 606, 622
perceptibility (*pratyakṣa*) of 143-45, 412, 437, 498-99
ajīva 414
ajñāna, see (1) failure to understand, (2) ignorance
ākāṃkṣā, see expectancy
ākāra, see shape
ākāśa 37, 45, 124-25, 145, 147, 195, 216, 327, 340, 348-49, 353, 377, 384, 387, 412-13, 415-16, 432, 434-35, 439, 476, 497, 526-27, 529, 561-62, 584, 619
akhaṇḍa, see partless
Akhaṇḍala Banerjees 489
akhaṇḍopādhi, see imposed property, *akhaṇḍa*
ākhyāta, see suffix, verbal
Ākhyātavāda of Raghunātha Śiromaṇi 13, 522, 535-41
akhyāti(vāda) 364
ākṛti, see configuration
a type of word-meaning 416, 446, 514
akṣama, see impatience
ākṣepa, see implication
ālasya, see laziness
alaukikārthakhyāti 364
alaukika perception, see perception, ordinary/extraordinary
Allahabad, see Prayāga
all-pervading, see size, ubiquitous
ālocana 373
āloka, see light, external
alternative position (*vipratipatti, koṭi*) 88-91, 408, 598
strength of (*koṭyutkaṭatva*) 515
(*vikalpa*), see (mere) construction

Amalānanda (1255) 386
Amarāvatī 470
ambiguity 261-62
anadhyavasāya, see knowledge, indefinite
anadhyavasita (a fallacy) 370, 378-79, 618
anaikāntika, see deviation
ānanda, see bliss
Ananthachariar, Prativadi Bhayankara 544
ananubhāṣaṇa, see feigned failure to reproduce the other party's argument
ananubhāvakatva 508
ananyasama 367
ananyathāsiddhi, see invariable connection
anavasaragrahaṇa, see finding fault at a time other than the proper time for doing so
anavasthā, see infinite regress
Andhra 368
anirvacanīya (in Advaita) 459
anirvacanīyakhyāti 364, 367
anirvacanīyatā 388, 404
anityatā, see noneternity
fallacy, see fallacy, occasional
Annambhaṭṭa (1575) 382, 591
answering the questions (*praśnuttaratā*) 407
aṇu, see (1) size, small; (2) atom
Anubhavānanda 486
anubhūti, see experience
anugama, see comprehensiveness
anuktagrāhya, see (a fault) detected by the debater not speaking
anumāna, see inference
Anumānamayūkha of Śaṃkara Miśra 416
Anumānanirṇaya of Vācaspati Miśra II 11, 455, 464
anumiti, see inference, inferential result
anupalabdhi, see nonapprehension or nonperception
anupasaṃhārin, see inconclusive
anutpatti, see nonproduction
anuvṛtta, see reidentification
anuvyavasāya, see aftercognition
anuyāja, see sacrifice, *anuyāja*
anuyogi, see referend
-*tā*, see referend, being the
anvayavyatirekin, see positive-negative agreement
anvayin anumāna, see inference, positive
kevalānvayin, see only-positive
anvīkṣā, see inquiry, rational
anyathākhyāti(vāda) 102, 105-06, 111, 115, 422, 595-97
anyathāsiddha, see dispensable
a fallacy 111
anyonyāśraya, see mutual dependence
āp, see water
Apabhraṃśa 260, 359, 514-15
apakarṣa, see subtraction
apakṣepaṇa, see going down
Aparārkadeva (1125) 35, 42, 366
aparatva, see nearness
apārthaka, see incoherence
apaśabda, see ungrammaticality
apasiddhānta, see inconsistency
apauruṣeyatva, see authorlessness
apavarga, see liberation, *apavarga*
apekṣābuddhi, see enumerative cognition
apohavāda 159, 166
application (*parāmarśa*), see consideration
third (*tṛtīyaliṅga*-) 332
(*upanaya*) 415, 480, 594
apprehension (*upalabdhi*), see awareness
appropriateness, see fitness
apramita, see not being validly established
aprāptakāla, see inconsequentiality
aprāpti, see nonunion
aprasiddhaviśeṣaṇa, see unknown qualifier
apratibhā, see lack of ready answer
apratipatti, see nonunderstanding
aprayojaka, see support, lack of adequate
āpta, see reliable
apūrva, see traces, karmic
ārambhaka, see generating
ārambhavāda, 623
argument, five-membered 216, 408
Ārhatas 414
āropa, see superimposition

artha, see purpose
arthāntara, see irrelevance
arthāpatti, see presumption
arthavāda 278
asādhāraṇa, see (1) property, specific, (2) too specific
asaduktika, see wrongly expressed
aśakti, see incapacity
asatkhyāti, a fallacy 343, 364
-*vāda* 106, 115-16
asamavāyikāraṇa, see cause, noninherence
āśaya 414
ascertainment (*niścaya*), see belief
asiddha, see unproved
āśraya, see locus
Assam 521
assimilation (*āvāpa*) 288
Aṣṭādhyāyī (of Pāṇini) 369, 398
aśvamedha, see sacrifice, *aśvamedha*
atadvyāvṛtti, see awareness of *x* as distinct from things other than itself
Athalye, Y.V. 591
atīndriya, see imperceptible
ativyāpti, see overextension
ātmakhyātivāda 374
ātman, see self
Ātmatattvaviveka (of Udayana) 461, 467, 491, 503, 618, 623
-Commentary (of Narahari Upādhyāya) 454
-Commentary (of Vardhamāna) 10, 314
-*Dīdhiti* (of Raghunātha Śiromaṇi) 12, 381, 522-24, 591, 625
-*Dīpikā* (of Nārāyaṇācārya) 11, 380-82
-*Kalpalatā* (of Śaṃkara Miśra) 11, 450-52, 618-19
atom (*paramāṇu*) 146, 529
atomic constituents 321
atomic theory 217-18, 333, 419, 444, 606
contact between, see contact
double atom (*dvyaṇuka*), see dyad
eternality of 377, 428-29
(yogic) perception of 130, 391, 446
properties of 40, 327, 334-35, 377, 434, 552
size of 348, 378
attraction 105, 108, 111-12, 599
augmentation (*utkarṣa*), parity through 350, 355
authority (see also testimony) 248-49
speaker's 245, 247-48, 251-53, 256, 259, 261
authorlessness (*apauruṣeyatva*) 253, 442
scripture's 424-25
avacchedaka, see limitor
avacchedya, see limited
avadhi, see limit
avagītatva, see not being a condemned object
āvāpa, see assimilation
avarṇya, see certainty
avayava, see (1) awareness, part of, (2) members of an inference
aversion (*dveṣa*) 43, 219, 326, 337, 407, 442
avidyā, see ignorance
avijñātārtha, see unintelligibility
avinābhāvatva, see invariable connection
āvirbhāva, see development
avyabhicāra, see nondeviation
avyāpti, see underextension
avyāpyavṛtti, see relation, non-locus-pervading
awareness (*jñāna, buddhi, grahaṇa*) 19-26, 29-33, 43, 53-67, 94, 100-03, 106, 109, 117-18, 137, 139, 141, 149, 151, 154, 160, 215, 219-20, 265, 316, 324, 327, 335, 337, 386, 389, 401, 405-06, 415, 428, 430-31, 438-41, 446, 451, 458, 465, 474, 488, 494, 522, 535, 544-45, 571, 577, 594-97, 604, 610
collective (*samūhālambana*) 99, 107, 197, 531
contrary-to-fact supposition (*āhārya*) 77
correct (*pramā*), see knowledge
direct (*anubhava, sākṣātkāra*) (see also perception) 117, 133, 138, 334, 423, 462, 497, 599, 602
eternal/noneternal 188, 220-22, 224

God's, see God's awareness
immediate, see perception
indefinite (*anadhyavasāya*) 330-31
inferential (*anumiti*), see inferential result
initial (*vyavasāya*) 151-52
linguistic or verbal (*śabda-*) 249, 251, 256, 261, 297, 371, 449, 480, 517
mode of 494
-ness (*-tva*) 139-40, 152, 220-21, 334, 462, 499
of a qualified qualifier (*viśiṣṭavaiśiṣṭya*) 156-57, 186
of an awareness 135, 153-54, 241-42, 391, 403-04
of bare locus 140-42
of *x* as distinct from things other than itself (*atadvyāvṛtti*) 159
(*upalabdhi*), parity through 355-56, 362-63
propositional/nonpropositional (*savikalpaka/nirvikalpaka*) 24-25, 33, 59-60, 66, 81, 92, 94-95, 100, 118-21, 163, 164-65, 169-70, 185, 325, 328, 335, 365, 379, 389-90, 392-93, 407, 412, 415, 446-47, 452, 466, 495, 499-501, 523
qualified (*viśiṣṭa*) 25, 103, 106-17, 122, 125-28, 156-58, 159-68, 182, 344-45, 499, 600, 605, 628
quality/quantity of 32
relational, see qualified
right (*samyak-*) 54-55
self-revealing or -illuminating (*svaprakāśa*) 60-61, 141, 151-54, 165, 180, 377, 457-58, 499, 515, 603
stream of (*dhārāvāhika*) 179, 332
Ayāci Miśra, see (1) Bhavanātha Miśra, (2) Śaṃkara Miśra
āyatana 359

bādha, see sublation
bahutva, see manyness
Banaras 12, 318, 337, 450, 473, 490
Sanskrit University 314
Government Sanskrit Library 473
Sarasvati Bhavana Library 487, 520
bandha, see bondage
Bandyopadhyaya, Nandita 197-211, 587-90
Banerjee, Kali Krishna 556-63
Barhāmbara 414
barley 232-34
Baroda 382
bathing, ceremonial 237, 318
beginninglessness (*anāditva*) 237, 506, 605
Being, see existence
being the means to a desired goal (*iṣṭasādhanatā*) 264-81, 300-02, 512, 609-12
being a thing one wants to accomplish (*kṛtisādhyatva*) 264-81, 300, 512, 610-11
being the thing to be named (*uddeśya*) 269-70
being something that is to be done (*kāryatva*) 264, 283
belief (*adhyavasāya*) 414
belief (*niścaya*) 22, 30, 53, 88, 534, 580
Bengal 4, 251, 314, 486, 490, 520
Bhaduri, Sadananda 33, 42, 591
Bhagavadgītā 333, 393
Bhagīratha Ṭhakkura (1550) 487, 523, 724-25
Bhagīrathā, mother of Vāsudeva Sārvabhauma 489
Bhairavasiṃha, King of Mithilā 454-55, 491
Bhairavendra (1510) 12, 521
Bhaktū, see Rucidatta Miśra
bhaṇḍāras, Jain 472
Bhandarkar, D.R. 368
Bhandarkar Library 455
Bharatītīrtha (1350) 368
Bhāsarvajña (the Bhūṣaṇakāra) (900) 5, 38, 41-45, 320, 323, 364-66, 389, 392, 445, 469, 616-18
Bhāskara (750) 339, 452
Bhaṭṭa Bhāskara 499
Bhāṭṭa Mīmāṃsā 8, 33, 56, 66, 131-35, 293-94, 299, 301, 331, 345, 371, 374, 413-15, 469, 511, 523, 545, 592, 602, 609, 612-13
Bhattacharya, Dinesh Chandra 313-14, 374-75, 396, 454-55,

470-71, 486, 489-90, 593, 615, 617, 619-22, 624
Bhattacharya, Gopika Mohan 86, 473-74, 478, 484, 490, 592, 621-22
Bhattacharya, Gopinath 5, 593, 622
Bhattacharya, Janakivallabha 541-44
Bhattacharya, Narendra Chandra Bagchi 472
Bhattacharyya, Sibajiban 69, 193-96, 211-38, 549-50, 564-70, 593
Bhattacharya, Tarasamkar 489, 550-53, 592, 604, 621
Bhattacharya, Vamacarana 187, 197, 226, 235, 455, 572-73, 580, 587
Bhattacharya, Visvabandhu 604
bhāva, see positive entity
bhāvanā, se (1) reflection, (2) trace, (3) volition
  sense of the word 415, 539-40, 609
Bhavānanda Siddhāntavāgīśa (1600) 626
Bhavanātha Miśra (1050) 619
Bhavanātha Miśra or Duve (1400) 10, 313, 375-76, 395, 416, 423, 616, 619
Bhavanī, wife of Bhavanātha 376
Bhavanī, wife of Śaṃkara Miśra 395
bhāvatva, see presence
bheda, see difference
bhedābheda, see difference and non-difference
Bhedābhedavāda (of the Tridaṇḍins) 397, 515, 617
  of Bhāskara, see Bhāskara
Bhedaratna (of Śaṃkara Miśra) 11, 398-407
bhoga, see experience
bhramatva, see falsity
Bhūṣaṇakāra, see Bhāsarvajña
bhūta, see elemental
Bhuvanasundarasūri (1450) 11, 394, 471-72
bhūyastva, see manyness
bhūyodarśana, see observation, repeated
Bihar 4, 376
bile, see humors
birth (*janma*) (see also origination)
  previous 86, 403, 422, 447
  subsequent 423
blind 67, 133, 441
bliss (*ānanda*) 334, 404, 406, 415, 426, 453
blocking
  mutual 204-05
  theory of 75-78, 81, 88
Bodas, Mahadeva Rajaram 85, 591, 593, 621
body (*śarīra*) 118, 218, 223, 306, 322, 367, 372-73, 377, 386, 393, 399, 406, 415, 430, 441-42, 461, 468-69, 519
  bodilessness 220-21
  God's, see God's body
  subtle (*sūkṣma*) 426
bondage (*saṃsāra, bandha*) 141, 336, 340, 379, 414
Brahman 378, 387, 399-407, 413, 415, 426, 453, 458, 460, 620
  as God, see God as Brahman
  brahmādvaita, see Advaita
Brahmasūtras (of Bādarāyaṇa) 423, 500
Brahmin (*brāhmaṇa*) 333, 371, 443, 532, 543
breath (*prāṇa*) 118, 440
Bṛhadāraṇyaka Upaniṣad 367, 399-400, 524, 620
Buddhism (see also Madhyamaka, Yogācāra, etc.) 8, 36, 54-56, 62-63, 80, 86, 106, 115, 159, 166, 239-40, 315, 336, 357, 359, 371, 381-82, 413-14, 431, 438-39, 507, 522, 596, 626
butter, clarified, see ghee

Caitanya (1520) 4, 489-90, 520
Caitya 272
cake, baked (*śaṣkulī*) 343
cakṣus, see eye
Candra (820) 413
Candrānanda 434
Candrasiṃha 491
cāndrāyaṇa 393
carmakāra, see shoemaker
Carmāmbara 414
Cārvākas 75, 80, 357, 413-14, 474, 605
case (*kāraka*) 262, 369, 536-39, 626
  accusative 459
  locative 542

nominative 262, 309, 535
case-ending (*vibhakti*) 262, 538-40, 542-43, 626
category (*padārtha*) 15, 48-51, 224, 299, 377, 383, 412-13, 425-28, 453, 465
knowledge of, see reality, knowledge of
causal efficacy (*śakti*) (see also power) 9, 49-50, 226-34, 252, 297, 337, 339-40, 413, 446, 506, 517, 533-34, 611
acquired (*ādheya*) 340, 516
ineffective (*kubja*) 517
causality, causal factors (*kāraṇa, kāraka*) 16, 50, 77-80, 97-98, 105, 110, 121-25, 156, 161, 219-28, 232-34, 264, 288-89, 323, 332, 337, 339-40, 348, 352, 354, 369, 373, 392, 397, 413, 428, 430-31, 447, 457, 472, 477, 502, 515, 525, 527, 534, 571-73, 578, 585, 602, 604, 610-11, 623
auxiliary 149, 221, 340
causal condition *par excellence* (*karaṇa*) 44, 59, 116-19, 133-34, 148, 163, 170, 239, 337, 347, 369, 448, 462, 602
complete collection of causal factors (*sāmagrī*) 139, 175, 181-82, 191-92, 225, 329, 333, 388, 430, 439, 472, 576, 600, 607, 630
general/specific 232
inherence cause (*samavāyikāraṇa*) 125, 139, 213-14, 217-18, 221, 324, 335, 385, 387-88, 428, 432, 434, 447, 528-30, 577, 610, 629
limitor of causality (*kāraṇatāvacchedaka*) 107, 109
noninherence cause (*asamavāyikāraṇa*) 147-48, 218, 221, 322-23, 326-27, 335, 348, 388, 427, 429, 433-34, 439, 443, 525-28, 531
instrumental cause (*nimittakāraṇa*) 218, 221, 227, 327, 345, 87-88, 415, 429, 434, 439, 473, 523, 528-29
plurality of causes 231, 430
cavil (*vitaṇḍā*) 366, 390, 407-08, 410, 460-61
Cennu Bhaṭṭa, see Cinnam Bhaṭṭa
certainty (*avarṇya*)
(*niścaya*) 353, 371, 546, 565
parity through 551
(*siddhi*) 584-85
cessation of activity, see withdrawal from activity
ceṣṭā, see gesture
Chadana 85
Chakrabarti, Kishore Kumar 86-88, 100-06, 122-55, 178-92, 570-87
chala, see quibble
Chāndogya Upaniṣad 399, 524, 625
changing one's reason (*hetvantara*) 410
changing one's thesis (*pratijñāntara*) 409-10, 464
channel, see vein
characterization (*nirūpaṇa*) 7
charity 234
chief qualifier, see qualifier, chief
Chintamani, T.R. 375
Cinnam Bhaṭṭa (1390) 10, 34, 44, 368-74, 380, 616
circle, vicious (*cakraka*) 132, 164, 175, 187, 216, 222-23, 228, 295, 411, 438, 559-60
circularity (*vartulatva*) 330
citra, see color, touch, etc., variegated
Citsukha (1295) 33, 384-85
co-contentness (*ekavittivedyatā*) 296, 298
co-existence in the same locus, see locus, having a common
cognition, see awareness
enumerative, see enumerative cognition
logic of 23-24
valid, see truth
cohesion, see viscidity
co-inherence (*ekārthasamavāya*) 42, 534-35
co-location (*sāmānādhikaraṇya*) 17, 71-73, 172-73, 338, 373, 437, 446, 463-64, 501, 528, 550-54, 561, 563, 567-68, 570, 572, 574, 581-82

collocation (*sāhacarya*)
color (*rūpa*) 601-02, 605, 631
absence of 48, 475
change of, see cooking
manifested/unmanifested 34-35, 124, 142-46, 191, 328-29, 372, 378, 418, 432, 437, 441, 453, 498-99, 530, 606
-ness (*-tva*) 40, 124-25, 143, 384, 432, 443, 475, 525, 528, 567, 570, 576, 581
locus-pervading/nonlocus-pervading 531
of air 48, 163, 565
of earth 566-67
of water 570
natural 434
perception of 123, 126, 132-33
shades of 124, 443
's relation to its substance 128-29, 432-33
variegated (*citra*) 39, 41, 320, 328, 333, 378, 386, 440, 472, 523, 531
common property, see property, common
comparison or comparative awareness (*upamāna*) 9, 116, 156, 170, 210, 238-39, 309, 367, 392, 415-16, 421, 446, 464, 467-68, 495, 507, 518
result of (*upamiti*) 238, 468
compassion (*kāruṇya*) 225, 337, 380
God's, see God's compassion
completion
desire for 123
of a text, cause of 87, 315, 493
complexity, see simplicity/complexity
compositeness, see property, composite/noncomposite
(grammatical) compound (*samāsa*) 280, 310-11, 501, 515
comprehensiveness (*anugama*) 603
of pervasion 184
conceptual construction (*kalpanā, vikalpa*) 55, 379, 415, 507
conclusion of an inference 480, 587, 594
concomitance (*sahacāra*), positive and negative (see also co-located) 78, 86, 98, 110-13, 142, 150, 219-20, 222-23, 236, 274, 306, 340, 431, 477, 534, 599, 611
invariable, see pervasion
universal, see pervasion
concurrence (*sambhava*) 333-34, 371
condition
(a category) 219
undivided, see imposed property, *akhaṇḍa*
conditioned, see determined
conductor, conducive (*prayojaka*) 101
configuration, see shape
confusion 393, 411
conjunction (*yoga*) 496
connection, see relation
sense-object, see relation, sense-object
syntactic (*anvayitā*) 541
connector, see relation
self-linking (*svarūpasambandha*) 15-17, 32, 126-29, 167, 173, 217, 453, 502, 506, 516, 535, 562-64, 601-02
consciousness
abode-consciousness (*ālayavijñāna*) 439
eternal (*nityacaitanya*) 458
pure (*cit, buddhi*) 404, 426, 459, 515
puruṣa in Sāṃkhya 336
(mere) consideration (*vikalpa*) 159-62, 543
consideration (*nirdeśa*) 356
consideration (in logic) (*parāmarśa*) 117, 170, 175, 193-200, 223, 415, 448, 467, 479-80, 495, 503, 517, 560, 585-86, 589
construction, see conceptual construction
construction-filled/-free, see awareness, propositional/ nonpropositional
contact (*saṃyoga*) 15-17, 35, 39, 43, 50, 99, 114-18, 122, 126, 129, 132, 136, 142, 144, 167, 185, 320, 323, 325, 327, 336-37, 341, 365, 413, 420, 429, 439, 443, 445, 465, 468-69, 485, 518, 525-27, 531, 533, 549-52, 554, 558, 560, 562-63
atomic, see atom

dense (*nibiḍa*) 325-26
loose (*pracaya*) 327, 348
-ness 326, 432
sense-object contact 113, 122-25, 160-61, 218, 296, 343, 383, 386, 388-89, 394, 413-14, 434-35, 438, 444, 446, 496-98, 502, 557, 573, 575-76, 598, 628
content of an awareness (*viṣaya*) 21, 23, 61, 92, 107, 115, 121, 124-25, 128, 152, 403, 414-15, 494, 498, 545, 570, 579
correct/incorrect (sad/asad-) 349
having content (*viṣayitva*) 16, 522
-ness (-*tā*) 51, 92, 106, 273, 331, 522, 535, 552, 597
context (*vākyaśeṣa*) 255, 261-62, 309, 359
imperativist theory (*kāryānvita-śaktivāda*) 65-66, 282-94, 612-13
contiguity (*saṃnidhi, āsatti*) 64, 240, 244-47, 249-50, 263, 346, 449, 451, 508
continuant (*sthira*) 439
contraction 149, 343
contradiction (*viruddha, virodha*) 21-22, 77, 81, 129, 140, 171, 204-08, 240, 248, 273, 304, 332, 343, 359, 388, 424-25, 437, 451, 477, 480, 482, 545, 583
practical (*vyāghāta*) 183, 250, 411
self-contradiction 359, 364
(*virodha*), a way of losing an argument 409
(*viruddha*), a fallacy 200-04, 331, 345, 350-51, 421, 437, 451, 477, 480, 482, 545, 583
contraposition (*vyatireka*), see pervasion, negative
contrapositive (*vyatirekin*) 202
-ness 388
controversy (*kathā*) 407-12, 461
convention (*saṃketa, rūḍha, samaya*) 327, 390-91, 402, 408, 416-17, 436, 445-46
in debate 409-10
(*paribhāṣā*) 528
conventional meaning, see meaning, conventional
cooking or baking (*pāka*) 272, 302, 325, 327, 385
being produced by cooking (*pāka-jatva*) 327-29, 333
cook (noun) (*pācaka*) 416, 418
theory of cooking (*pākavāda*) 33, 126, 129, 335, 377, 419-20, 443-44, 469, 531
corroboration (*saṃvādana*) 414
cosmological argument for God's existence 36-37
counterargument (*pratirodha*) 345
counterbalance (*satpratipakṣa*) 198, 201, 204-06, 334, 351, 354, 379, 385, 390, 421, 437-38, 453, 464-65, 480-84, 503-04, 580, 589, 597
counterexample (*pratidṛṣṭānta*), parity througth 352-53
counterfactual 77-79
counterpositive of an absence (*prati-yogin*) 7, 46, 48, 62, 97, 99, 102, 111-12, 129, 132-34, 137-42, 163, 167, 171-76, 180-84, 195, 198, 202-03, 215, 221, 228-29, 306, 317, 322, 324, 327, 333, 340-41, 346, 383, 388, 411, 421, 425, 437, 447, 451, 474-75, 497, 500-01, 522, 530, 534, 542, 549, 553-60, 566-68, 576, 582-84, 599
-ness, being the counterpositive (*pratiyogitā*) 7, 16, 176, 418, 503, 541, 552, 556, 560-64, 570-71, 576, 582, 629
creation 211-13, 217, 224-26, 397, 451
cycles of 607-08
God's, see God's creation
creator, see God
cross-connection (*jātisaṃkara*) 38, 50, 323, 386, 427, 432, 528, 532, 534, 599
cumbrous (*gaurava*), see simplicity/complexity

D = definition
Dakṣiṇāsmṛti 452
dambha, see hypocrisy
dāna, see giving

Daṇḍaviveka (of Smārta Vardhamāna) 454
Daṇḍyācārya 613-14
Darbhanga 10-11, 85, 313, 395, 491
darkness (*tamas*) 145, 319, 384-85, 412-14, 419, 469, 519, 576, 584, 618
Darpaṇakāra, see Vaṭeśvara
Dasgupta, Surendranath 86
Dāyabhāga 4
death 450, 468
  final moment before, see moment, final
debate (*vāda*) (see also discussion) 201, 360, 408, 437, 456
defect (*doṣa*) 97-98, 104-08, 113-15, 217, 228, 253-54, 339, 409, 468, 495, 579, 598-99
  absence of 340
  having a different object (*arthāntara*) 126-27
  -ness 91, 488, 545-46
  sense-defect 139, 468
deficient formulation (*nyūna*) 360, 366, 409-10
definition (*lakṣaṇa*) 6, 164, 320, 364, 369, 383-84, 388, 418, 467, 473, 549, 553-54
  conclusive (*siddhānta*) 71-72, 176, 501, 556-63
  lion-tiger, see lion, tiger
  underextensive (*avyāpta*) 122, 173
deity, see god
delusion (*moha*) 380, 409, 442
demerit (*adharma*) 44, 235-38, 276-79, 318, 339, 393-94, 407, 413, 422, 424, 428, 442-43, 505, 516, 524, 529, 532, 607-08
dependence
  mutual (*anyonyāśraya*) 138, 241, 267, 277, 301-02, 411, 438
  self-, see self-dependence
describer, described (*nirūpaṇa, nirūpita*) 324
  -ness 557
designated (*uddeśya*) 169
designative capacity (*śakti*) 185, 254, 282-300, 308-10, 513-15
desire (*rāga, icchā, saṃkalpa*) 43, 106, 150-51, 186, 219-20, 244, 265, 269, 273, 282, 289, 307, 326, 348, 380, 392-93, 406-07, 413, 423, 440, 461, 478-79, 512, 515, 536, 578-79, 586-87, 610
  congruent/noncongruent (*saṃvādin/visaṃvādin*) 579
  awareness of what is desired 108-10, 280
  God's desire to create 213-17, 585, 587
desire to do (*cikīrṣā*) 264-70, 273-75, 281, 610, 612
desire to infer 585-86, 608
  potency for inference (*anumitayogyatā*) 585-87
desire to know (*jijñāsā*) 246, 408, 419, 436, 465, 474, 517
destruction, see absence, posterior
  awareness of 341
  creation and 225
  final 373, 607
  of sounds (*ucchanna*) 263-64, 373
detachment (*vairāgya*) 380, 394, 423, 450
  (a fault) detected by the debater not speaking (*anuktagrāhya*) 361
  (a fault) detected even while the debater is speaking (*ucyamānagrāhya*) 361
  (a fault) detected after the argument has been stated (*uktagrāhya*) 361
determination (*nirūpaka*) 127
determined (*nirūpya, nirūpita*) 127, 545
deva, see god
Devadhar, C.R. 617
Devaghara 376
development (*āvirbhāva*) 430
deviant (*visaṃvādinī*) 102
deviation (*vyabhicāra*) 72-73, 76-78, 126, 170, 188, 199, 209-10, 212, 243, 332, 344-45, 386, 463, 477-78, 571-72, 576, 582-84
  (*asādhāraṇa*) 618
  as a fallacy (*anaikāntika, savyabhicāra*) 192, 198-202, 212-13, 331, 351, 359, 370, 373, 421, 438, 453, 482-84, 504, 580-81, 588
devotion, see worship

dhāraṇā 394
dhārāvāhika jñāna, see awareness, stream of
dharma, see (1) merit, (2) property
Dharmakīrti (640) 208-09, 414, 446, 484, 592, 618
Dharmarājādhvarīndra (1615) 183
dharmaśāstra 312-13, 315, 375, 396, 491
Vivekakāra of 313
dharmin, see property-possessor
Dharmottara (770) 54-55
dictionary (*kośa*) 309, 402
Dīdhiti, see *Tattvacintāmaṇidīdhiti* (of Raghunātha Śiromaṇi)
difference, diversity (*bheda*) 18, 42, 47-48, 72, 102-13, 129, 139-40, 171, 173, 176-77, 181, 317, 319-20, 324, 328, 333-34, 371, 388, 399-404, 407, 420, 431, 433, 444, 447, 459, 461, 463-64, 480, 502, 506, 530, 532, 541-42, 550, 559-60, 565-66, 568-69, 581, 598, 620
and nondifference (*bhedābheda*) 129, 328
(*vyatireka*), see pervasion, negative
differentiator, differentiation (*vyāvartta(ka)*) 164, 168-69, 431, 433, 469
(*viśeṣa*), see individuator
Digambara, see Jain, Digambara
Dignāga (480?) 356, 414, 446, 592
dik or *diś*, see space
dimension, see size
Dinesh Chandra, see Bhattacharya, Dinesh Chandra
directness, see immediacy
(*anāpekṣatva*) 527
dīrghatva, see length
discourse, scientific (*śāstra*) 188, 389, 425, 464
discussion (*vāda*) 337, 366, 407-08, 456-57
disjunction (*vibhāga*) 15, 35, 39, 43, 144, 323, 413, 419-20, 432, 445, 525-27, 533
dispensable (*anyathāsiddha*) 602
disposition, see trace, mental
dissimilarity (*vaidharmya*), parity through 349-50
dissolution (*laya*) 397, 426, 451
distinctness, revealed (*pratiyogyavyāvṛtti*) 166
Divākara, teacher of Pragalbha Miśra 486
Divākara Upādhyāya (1250) 623
doṣa, see defect
doubt (*saṃśaya*) 22, 30, 57, 75-81, 90-92, 96, 103-05, 139, 180-83, 187, 191, 195-96, 201, 206, 211-12, 216-17, 247, 249, 251, 253, 258, 260-61, 263, 330, 338, 344-46, 364, 391, 411, 422, 436-37, 448, 453, 469, 475, 477-79, 488, 493, 502, 517, 534, 545-46, 565, 569, 572, 575, 580, 583-84, 588, 590, 605
doubting devil (*śaṅkāpiśācin*) 448
doubtful (*sandigdha*), a fallacy 437-38
parity through doubt 353-54, 362
dravatva, see fluidity
Dravid, L.S. 450, 522
dravya, see substance
Dravyakiraṇāvaliprakāśa (of Vardhamāna) 10, 472
Dravyakiraṇāvaliprakāśaviveka (of Pakṣadhara), see *Kiraṇāvaliprakāśa-dravyaviveka* (of Pakṣadhara)
dream 365, 389, 403, 450
dṛṣṭānta, see example
-*amutpattisama* 353
dualism (*dvaita*) 452, 459
duality, the number two (*dvitva*) 42, 107, 119, 324, 329, 331, 348, 372, 387, 444, 490, 564
duḥkha, see frustration
Dvaitanirṇaya (of Narahari Upādhyāya) 313, 491
dveṣa, see aversion
dvitva, see duality
Dvivedin, Vindhyesvara Prasada 187, 226, 235, 336, 417, 450, 455, 486, 522, 572-73, 580
dyad (*dvyaṇuka*) 189, 212, 217-18, 225, 348, 378, 419-20, 526, 529, 600, 606-07
triple dyad, see minimum perceptibilium

ear, the auditory organ 124, 148-49, 331, 384, 391, 415, 497, 600
earth (*pṛthivī*) 33, 145-46, 211-17, 222-23, 319-20, 327-28, 373, 378, 385, 388, 413-14, 418, 433-34, 464, 469, 567
-ness 377, 551, 555, 566
economy, see simplicity
effect or result (*kārya*) 211, 220, 304, 327, 413, 428, 447, 518
being the effect, or effectness (*kāryatva*) 16, 50, 278, 302-03, 532, 534
parity through being the effect 357-58
effect of a material cause (*aupadānika*) 413
efficiency (efficacy)/nonefficiency (*sāmarthya*) 381-82, 390 (*arthakriyātva*) 439
effort (*yatna, prayatna*) 43, 212, 218, 220-21, 235, 305, 326, 357-58, 440, 515, 535-39, 608-09
God's effort 212-19, 224, 226
egg-born, see oviparous
ego (I) (*aham*) 439-41
egoism, egoity (*ahaṃkāra*) 380, 515
Ekadaṇḍins 397, 426, 515
ekadeśin 414
ekatva, see one, the number
Ekāvalī 620
ekavittivedyatā, see co-contentness
elasticity (*sthitisthāpakatva*) 43, 326-27, 379, 617
elemental (*bhautika*) 552
elements, see material
eliminative inference, see inference, eliminative
empirical level (*vyāvahārika*) 401-06, 413
ending, verbal, see suffix
enjoyment (*bhoga*), see experience
(actual) entity (*vastu, bhūtārtha*) 158, 239
enumerative cognition (*apekṣābuddhi*) 20, 42, 325, 329, 331, 444-45
envelopment (*tirobhāva*) 430
epistemology 53-67, 235
equally tenable (*upapatti*), parity through being 355
equipervasion (*samavyāpti*), see pervasion, equi-
equipollent (*tulya*) 432
equivocal, see ambiguous
error, see falsity
theories of error (*khyātivāda*) 364-65
essence (*svabhāva*) 461
establishment (*siddhi*) 370
eternal(ity) (*nitya(tva)*) 220-21, 224, 327, 385, 387, 391, 431, 472, 551
God's, see God's eternality
etherhood (*gaganatva*) 551
ethics 377
etymology (*yoga*) 359, 416
etymological-conventional meaning (*yogarūḍha*), see meaning, etymological-conventional
eulogizing (*stuti*) 88
evasion (*vikṣepa*) 361, 367, 409-10
example (*dṛṣṭānta*) 392
(in inference), see *sapakṣa, vipakṣa*
excellence (*guṇa*) 97
exciter (*udbodhaka*) 157, 160-61, 226-29
existence (*sattā, sattva*) (see also presence) 140, 214, 329, 334, 377, 381, 431, 457, 465, 469, 532, 550, 562, 567
notion of (*-dhī*) 465
specific (*viśiṣṭa*) 567
expansion (*prasaraṇa*) 149, 343
(mutual) expectancy (*ākāṅkṣā*) 63-64, 240, 243-52, 257-62, 283-87, 292, 346, 416, 448-51, 480, 508
experience (*anubhava, anubhūti*) 461, 532
(*bhoga*) 386, 468
expiation 235, 237, 318
eye, the visual organ (*cakṣus*) 34, 106, 123, 130, 132, 142, 250, 377-78, 384, 414, 418, 443, 498, 603

failure to understand (*ajñāna*) 361, 367, 409-10
feigned, see feigned failure to understand
fallaciousness (*ābhāsatva*) 504-05

fallacious obstruction, see obstruction, fallacious
fallacy of the example (*dṛṣṭāntābhāsa)* 367
fallacy of the *hetu* (*hetvābhāsa*) 197-211, 331, 345, 360, 366-67, 373, 392, 398, 416, 421, 464, 479, 481-85, 503-05, 550, 553-54, 587-90, 616
  fallacy of redundant qualifiers of the *h* 220
fallacy of the hypothesis (*pratijñābhāsa*) 470
falsity, error (*apramā, mithyā(tva), viparyaya*) 22, 27, 29, 53-58, 64, 91-92, 100-06, 111, 114-15, 140, 181, 209, 225-26, 236, 240, 246-58, 261, 317, 364-66, 389, 402-05, 422, 424, 427, 442, 449, 453, 456, 474, 476, 485, 495-97, 516-17, 546, 579, 594, 596-99
  absence of, see truth
  (*bhramatva*) 91, 156
farness (*paratva*) 39, 387-88, 413, 435, 444, 528, 530
fault, see defect
feigned failure to be able to reproduce the other party's argument (*ananubhāṣaṇa*) 360-61, 367, 409-10
finding fault at an improper time (*anavasaragrahaṇa*) 361
finding fault where none is committed (*ābhāsa*) 361
fire of light (*tejas*) 33-34, 147, 327-28, 372, 377-78, 413-14, 418-20, 568
  digestive fire 506
  gold's, see gold
  invisible fire 220
fireness 146
fitness, semantic (*yogyatā*) 64, 240, 243-50, 261-63, 300-04, 346, 449, 475, 495, 507-08
  mere fitness (*svarūpayogyatā*) 425
fluidity (*dravatva*) 43, 146, 325-26, 328
  instrumental 39
  natural (*sāṃsiddhika*) 388, 433
  of gold 145-46
foil, silvery 104-13
foreigner (*mleccha*) 371
forgetfulness 411
form, material (*upādeya*) 438
  (*ākāra*), see shape
  highest (*pāramārthika rūpa*) 462
  variegated 440
fragrance, see smell
fraudulent fellow, see liar
Frauwallner, Erich 48, 592
free from passion (*vītarāga*) 390
frustration, unhappiness, misery (*duḥkha*) 43, 118, 147, 214, 218-19, 225, 236-38, 281, 306, 318, 334, 336, 367-68, 379, 393-94, 404, 407, 416, 422, 425-26, 442, 453, 469, 524, 603
  cessation of, see liberation
futile rejoinder (*jāti*) 349-58, 361-62, 367, 390, 411, 464, 618
future, see time

Gadādhara (1700) 6, 9, 18, 57, 626-27
Gadādhara Miśra (1510) 12, 521
gain (*lābha*) 337
Gaṇaratnamahodadhi (of Vardhamāna the grammarian) 313
gandha, see smell
Gaṅgāditya (1400) 10, 375
Ganges river 618
Gaṅgeśa (1320) 3, 6, 8-10, 18, 34-37, 40, 44-49, 53-67, 70-73, 81, 85-314, 316, 334, 336-37, 340, 342, 345, 347, 374-75, 411-13, 416-17, 470, 474, 477-81, 484, 486, 488-89, 494-97, 500-04, 509-11, 514, 518, 521, 544-46, 549, 553, 556, 565-66, 568, 570, 572, 574-75, 579-90, 593-615, 622-31
Gangopadhyaya, Mrinalkanti 178
Gauḍa, see Bengal
gaurava, see simplicity/complexity
Gaurīdigambaraprahasana (of Śaṃkara Miśra) 396
Gautama (150 A.D.?) 88, 299, 336, 345, 354, 357, 362, 364-65, 367, 392, 398, 413, 436, 438, 450, 467
gavaya 238-39, 392, 517-18

generating/nongenerating (*ārambhaka, anārambhaka*) 385
generic property, see property, common
genus, see universal
gesture (*ceṣṭā*) 449
conventional/nonconventional 449-50
ghaṭa, see pot
Ghaṭeśa Upādhyāya (1400) 10, 374
ghee 145-46, 300, 379, 433
giving, gift (*dāna*) 318
great (*mahā-*) 442-43
goal, see purpose
god (*deva*) 424, 441
God (*īśvara*)
as author of (e.g.) the Veda 244, 318, 424, 442
as Brahman 407
as establisher of conventional meanings 445-46, 453, 514
identified with space and time 35, 529
proof of (see also cosmological argument) 37, 211-26, 388, 417, 451-52, 460, 485, 505-06
's awareness or knowledge 36-37, 100, 116, 118, 159, 213-15, 217, 325-26, 341, 452-53, 462, 466, 499, 532, 608-09
's body 36-37, 211, 222, 225, 524
's compassion (*kāruṇya*) 523-24
's creation of the universe 230, 348, 383, 387, 505, 607-08, 618-19
's desire, see desire to create, God/s
's eternality 37
's existence 9, 37, 215, 333, 347, 397-98, 412
's grace 427
's infallibility 242, 341, 371
's merit 341
's nonapprehendability 343
's omnipotence 225, 608
's omniscience 201, 242, 351, 341-52, 466
's perception 152-53, 218, 224, 377, 496
's size 43, 530
's will 308-09
's worship 368, 393-94, 518
salutation to 315, 317, 338
specific qualities of 326
surrender to 308
three-faced (*trimūrti*) 86
Goekoop, C. 71-73, 170, 593, 604
going (*gamana*) 379, 427
going out (*prasaraṇa*) 379
going up (*utkṣepaṇa*) 379, 427
Gokulanātha Upādhyāya (1710) 375
gold (*suvarṇa*) 34, 145-46, 372, 378, 412, 498-99
Gosvamin, Surendra Lal 382
grace, God's, see God's grace
grammar (*vyākaraṇa*), 309, 375, 402
Grammarians (*vaiyākaraṇa*) 25, 60, 62, 302, 459, 510, 515, 537-40
grammatical coordination, see collocation
grasped (*grāhya*) 414
pervasion, means of, see pervasion, means of grasping
greed (*lobha*) 380
Guha, D.C. 591, 593, 627
guṇa, see (1) quality, (2) excellence, (3) in Bhaṭṭa Mīmāṃsā 414
Guṇakiraṇāvaliprakāśa (of Vardhamāna) (see also *Kiraṇāvaliprakāśa* (of Vardhamāna) 10, 38, 322-32
Guṇaratna, author of *Ṣaḍdarśanasamuccayavṛtti* (1409) 471
Guṇaratna Sūri (1420) 11, 394-95
Guṇe Miśra 487
gurutva, see weight
gustatory organ, see taste

h, see *hetu*
happiness, see satisfaction
hare's horn, see horn, hare's
Haribhadra Sūri (750) 394
Haridāsa Nyāyālaṃkāra Bhaṭṭācārya (1530) 375
Harihara 373
Harihara II 368
Hari Miśra (1430) 11, 453-54, 619
Hariśarman 461
harītakī, see myrobalan tree
Harivaṃśa 396
hatred, see aversion
haughtiness, see pride
having the same locus, see coordination

having its occurrence obstructed (*pratibandhitva*) 16
hayagrīva 321
hearing (*śravaṇa*) 338, 406-07, 448, 620
heart (*hṛdaya*) 394
heat (see also cooking; warmth) 142, 144-45, 320, 378, 420, 441, 499
internal 321
heaven (*svarga*) 225, 233-34, 281-82, 305-08, 388, 401, 405, 416, 423, 442-43, 505, 512-13, 609
one who desires heaven 300
hell 237, 278
heterolocativity (*vaiyadhikaraṇya*) 324, 326
heterodox (*nāstika*) 315, 337
hetu (*h*) (see also reason) 36-37 69-76, 93, 106, 110, 117, 120-21, 126-27, 146, 158, 162, 170-82, 187-217, 220, 222-23, 241-44, 249-52, 260, 270-71, 331, 334-35, 344-45, 350-56, 362, 366, 370, 373-74, 377, 386-87, 390, 411, 421, 433, 437-40, 448-49, 458, 463-64, 467, 479-84, 501-04, 544, 549-64, 567, 570-71, 580-83, 588-89, 594-97, 604, 616, 627
fallacy of the *h*—see fallacy of the *h*
lack of an *h*, parity through 354
Himalaya 445
hiṃsā, see violence
hindrance, see trace, mental
horn
hare's (*śaśaśṛṅga*) 343, 380-81, 475
horse's 219
hṛdaya, see heart
humors 450
humped-dwarf theory of meaning (*kubjaśaktivāda*) 297
hymn (*stotra*) 489
hypocrisy (*dambha*) 380
hypothesis (*kalpanā*) 106
(*pratijñā*), see thesis

idealism, see *sākāravāda*
identity (*tādātmya*) (see also nondifference) 17-18, 30, 102, 334, 371, 413
-in-difference, see difference and nondifference
ignorance (*avidyā*) 235, 315, 397, 406, 421-22, 458-59, 617
illumination (*prakāśa*) 335
immediacy (*sākṣāttva*) 98, 462, 532
immobile (*niṣkriya*) 324, 528
impatience (*akṣama*) 380
imperativist, see context, imperativist theory of
imperceptible (*atīndriya*) 334
impetus (*vega*) 39, 43, 326, 384, 413, 419, 422, 473
implication (*ākṣepa*) 614
implicator, see indicator
imposed property (*upādhi*) 38, 40, 45, 267, 319, 337, 378, 404, 443, 519, 534
akhaṇḍopādhi 523, 525, 532
vibhājaka or *vibhakta* 325, 528
impression, see trace
impulsion (*nodana*) 326
incapacity (*aśakti*) 362
inciter, see inducement
incoherence (*apārthaka*) 207-08, 359-60, 363, 409-10
inconclusive (*anupasaṃhārin*) 198, 200-02, 464, 481, 483, 504, 589
(*anaikāntika*), see deviation
inconsequentiality (*aprāptakāla*) 360, 367, 409-10
inconsistency (*apasiddhānta*) 362, 409-10, 464
indication (*lakṣaṇā, vṛtti*) 308
indicator (*upalakṣaṇa*) 164-69, 266-67, 295, 329-30, 373, 383, 458, 500, 586, 614
indifference (*upekṣā*) 135
individual, see particular
individuator (*viśeṣa*) 46, 184, 295, 377, 388, 432, 530-31
parity through lack of 354-55
indriya, see organ, sense
-*artha* relation, see relation, sense-object
-*sambaddhaviśeṣaṇatā* 126
inducement, inducer (*pravartana, pravartaka*) 511
to activity 264-65, 269, 279-81, 512, 609-11

induction 77
justification of 70-71, 73
paradox of 80
problem of 75-76, 79
inert (*jaḍa*) 414, 457-58
inertia, see impetus
infallibility, God's, see God's infallibility
inference (Inf) (*anumāna*) 23, 27, 34, 56-57, 64, 69-81, 86-87, 91, 96, 98, 116-20, 133-36, 155-56, 170-242, 245, 248-49, 255-60, 317-18, 338, 341, 343, 346, 364-67, 370-71, 385-92, 403, 413-15, 419, 421, 426, 433-35, 440, 448-50, 456, 467, 474-85, 501-06, 525, 534, 546-90, 605
desire to infer 503
eliminative (*pariśeṣa*) 153
for oneself (*svārtha-*) 93, 200-01
for others (*parārtha-*) 175
inferential result (*anumiti*) 335, 378, 474, 495, 501, 517, 525, 534, 546-90, 575, 586-87, 605
mahāvidyā, see *mahāvidyā* inference
mistimed, see mistimed inference
negative (*uyatirekin*) 93
positive (*anvayin*) 93
pūrvavat 80, 366, 467, 616
sāmānyatodṛṣṭa 80, 346, 366, 440, 467
śeṣavat 80, 366, 467
too specific, see too specific
inferiority 394
infinite regress (*anavasthā*) 33, 47, 49, 63, 96, 136, 139, 151-53, 158, 161-62, 179-83, 230, 241, 296, 352, 385, 388, 411, 432, 438, 477-78, 529-30, 532, 559, 605
inflection 261
inherence (*samavāya*) 15-17, 30, 46, 50, 116, 123-30, 132, 167, 215, 296, 335, 337, 365, 372, 379, 384, 388-90, 413, 432, 443, 446, 469, 472, 497, 527, 530, 534-35, 545, 550-52, 563, 566, 584, 600-02
inherence cause, see causal factor, inherence
in what inheres (*samavetasamavāya*) 50
in what inheres in what is conjoined (*saṃyuktasamavetasamavāya*) 50, 122-23, 153, 413, 421
in what is conjoined (*saṃyuktasamavāya*) 50, 114, 132, 387
in what is inhered in by what is inhered in (*samavetasamavetasamaveta*) 384
-ness 432, 535
of two qualifiers in one locus (see also co-located) 42, 534
Ingalls, Daniel Henry Holmes 7, 46, 69, 85, 454, 487, 521-22, 549, 591, 593, 621, 624-25, 627
injunction (*vidhi*) 44, 65, 233, 264-82, 291, 305, 339, 413, 415, 448, 460, 493, 510-13
one who is enjoined (*niyojya*) 300
Vedic injunctions 87, 232-34, 304, 307-08, 317, 609
inquiry, rational (*anvikṣā*) 400
insentient (*jaḍa*), see inert
instigation (*prarocana*) 415
instrument of knowledge (*pramāṇa*) 8, 55, 58, 88, 134, 170-71, 180, 193, 197, 223, 235, 239-40, 249-50, 256, 318, 321, 331, 347, 350, 365, 369, 375, 389, 391-93, 398-99, 405, 413-16, 442, 446-50, 453-57, 459, 462, 465-67, 476, 494-95, 499, 507, 517, 532, 534, 605
instrumental cause, see cause, instrumental
intention (*saṃkalpa*) 241, 393
personal intention (*abhiprāya*) 513
speaker's intention (*tātparya*) 64-65, 213, 243-44, 254-63, 292- 93, 508, 514, 518, 542
intercourse, sexual 414
interest, selective 149
internal organ (*manas*) 35, 60, 116, 118, 120, 134, 146-54, 218, 318, 321, 325, 343, 384-86, 391, 393, 413-14, 419, 439-40, 446-47, 469, 476, 480, 496, 498, 517, 529, 552, 603-04
introspection 27-29, 219, 296
intuition, yogic, see perception, yogic
invariable connection (*avinābhāvatva,*

ananyathāsiddha) 91, 115, 515-16, 599
invocation (*maṅgala*) 86-88, 316-17, 322, 364, 383, 423-24, 492-93, 509
irrelevance (*arthāntara*) 189-90, 359, 362, 409-10
iṣṭasādhanatā, see being a means to a desired goal
itihāsa 423

jaḍa, see inert
Jadavpur University 592-93
Jagadguru, teacher of Pragalbha Miśra 466, 623
Jagadīśa (1620) 6, 9, 18, 57, 550, 626-27
(*Tattvacintāmaṇidīdhiti*) *Jāgadīśī* (of Jagadīśa) 492
jagat, see universe
Jahnavī, mother of Pragalbha Miśra 486
Jaimini (25 A.D.?) 442-43, 510
Jaina 363, 371
Digambara 413-14
Jainagranthāvalī 472
Janakīnātha Bhaṭṭācārya Cūḍāmaṇi (1540) 492
Janārdana (1490) 12, 490-91, 622
Janeśvara Vāhinīpati (1510) 12, 489, 520, 624
janya, see (being) produced
japa 394
jargon, meaningless (*nirarthaka*) 359, 363, 409-10
jāteṣṭi, see sacrifice, *jāteṣṭi*
jāti, see universal property
-*saṃkara*, see cross-connection
-*vāda*, see futile rejoinder
jaundice 22
Jayadeva or Pakṣadhara Miśra (1470) 4, 12, 48, 313, 374, 453-54, 470, 473, 486-95, 521, 544, 546, 554, 559, 565, 582, 586, 588-89, 618, 621-22, 626
Jayanātha Miśra, see Jīvanātha Miśra
Jayanta Bhaṭṭa (870) 8, 464, 616
Jayasiṃhasūri (1366) 10, 363, 365, 389, 615-16
Jetly, J.S. 376, 616
Jha, Ganganatha 336, 407, 616
Jha, V.N. 264, 300, 593, 608
Jīmūtavāhana 4
Jinavardhana Sūri (1412) 10, 34, 36, 41, 376-80, 616-17
jīvanādṛṣṭa, see preservation, instinct for
Jīvanātha Miśra (1400) 10, 313, 375, 416, 448, 616, 619
jñāna, see awareness; cognitive act
(Bhadanta) Jñānaśrī (Mitra) (1025) 414, 618
jñātatā, see knownness
jñeyatva, see knowability
judgment, see awareness
Jumna (Jamuna) river 433, 618
jurisprudence 69, 454, 489
jyotiṣṭoma, see sacrifice, *jyotiṣṭoma*

kaivalya, see liberation, *kaivalya*
kāla, see time
kalañja, see poison
kālātyāpadiṣṭa, see mistimed
Kālī 505, 518
Kālidāsa 618
kalpanā see (1) conceptual construction, (2) hypothesis
kāma, see passion
kāmya, see sacrifice optional
kāmyakarman, see act, optional
Kaṇāda (100 A.D.?) 34, 315-16, 331, 377, 413, 423, 425, 427, 438
Kaṇādarahasya (of Śaṃkara Miśra) 11, 35, 70, 417-22, 444
kāraka, see (1) case, (2) cause
kāraṇa, see cause
Karion 85
kārīri, see sacrifice, *kārīri*
karma (karman), see act
karmic results 65, 325
Karṇāṭaka 435
kāruṇya , see compassion
kārya, see effect
Kashmir 11, 435
Kāśi, see Banaras
Kāśyapa 374
gotra 85, 473
kathā, see controversy
Kaṭha Upaniṣad 399
Kauṇḍinya 543
Kaviraj, Gopinath 368, 473, 520-21, 593, 621

Kāvya 465
mahākāvya 620
Kāvyādarśa (of Daṇḍyācārya) 613-14
Keith, A. Berriedale 593
Keśava Miśra (1250) 6, 368-72
kevalānvayin, see only positive
kevalavyatirekin, see only negative
Khaṇḍadeva (1640) 511
Khaṇḍanakhaṇḍakhādya (of Śriharṣa) 6, 53, 81, 85, 343, 375, 398, 407, 455, 477, 603
Khaṇḍanakhaṇḍakhādyaprakāśa (of Vardhamāna) 10, 314, 464
Khaṇḍanakhaṇḍakhādyadarpaṇa (of Pragalbha Miśra) 12, 486
Khaṇḍanoddhāra (of Vācaspati Miśra II) 11, 58, 455-65
Kharatara Gaccha 376
khyātivāda, see error, theories of
killing 443
Kiraṇāvalī (of Udayana) 38, 372, 467, 528, 591, 623-24
Kiraṇāvalīprakāśa—Commentary (of Pragalbha Miśra) 12
Kiraṇvalīprakāśa (of Vardhamāna) (see also *Dravya-*, *Guṇa-*) 314, 382
Kiraṇāvaliprakāśadravyaviveka (of Pakṣadhara) 11, 314-22, 479-82
Kiraṇāvaliprakāśa—Commentary (of Śeṣa Śārṅgadhara) 11
Kiraṇāvalīprakāśadīdhiti (of Raghunātha Śiromaṇi) 13, 35, 522, 525-29
Kiraṇāvaliprakāśavivṛti or *-Vṛtti* (of Rucidatta Miśra) 12, 492
Kiraṇāvalīviveka (of Pakṣadhara) 313
kleṣa 393
knowability (*jñeyatva*) 188, 404, 476, 532, 551, 588-89
knowledge (*pramā, pramiti*) 54, 66, 116, 207, 238, 257-58, 337, 369, 414, 461-62, 495
condition of 250-52
eternal 406-07
immediate, see perception
indefinite (*anadhyavasāya*) 435-36
instrument of, see instruments of knowledge
of another's mind 406
of the truth (*tattvajñāna*) 408, 424-25, 427
of what ought to be done 283-86
self-knowledge 37, 423, 440
theory of, see epistemology
(*udaya*) 317
(*vidyā*) 238, 315
(*vijñāna*, in Advaita) 426
(*yātharthya*) 369
knownness (*jnātatā*) 151, 592
kośa, see dictionary
krama 413
Krishnamacharya, V. 616, 623
kriyā, see (1) motion, (2) verb
Kriyāratnasamuccaya (of Guṇaratna Sūri) 394
Kṛṣṇācārya of Atrigotra 380
Kṛṣṇadāsa Sārvabhauma (1575) 374, 626-27
Kṛṣṇānanda 4, 489
Kṛṣṇānanda Vidyāvinoda (1485) 12, 490, 622
Kṛṣṇarṣi family 363
kṛti, see volition
kṛtisādhyatva, see being a thing one wants to accomplish
kṣaṇa, see moment
kṣapaṇaka 414
kubjaśaktivāda, see humped-dwarf theory of meaning
Kumārapāla(bhūpāla)carita (of Jayasiṃhasūri) 363
Kumārila Bhaṭṭa (660) 56, 604, 612, 619
's school, see Bhāṭṭa Mīmāṃsā
kurvadrūpa 381-82

lābha, see gain
Lacchmā Devī 491
lack of ready answer (*apratibhā*) 361, 367, 409-10
lāghava, see simplicity
Laghumahāvidyāviḍambana (of Bhuvanasundarasūri) 11, 471
laghunaiyāyika 367
lakṣaṇa, see definition
lakṣaṇā, see implication
lakṣaṇārtha, see meaning, secondary
Lakṣaṇāvalīnyāyamuktāvalī (of Śeṣa Śārṅgadhara) 11, 382-83
Lakṣmīdhara (1440) 489
language, linguistic awareness (*śabda*)

(see also testimony) 69, 116, 161, 165, 182, 225-26, 239-312, 326, 507-15, 593
abusive 446
and thought 26, 29-30, 59-60, 305
as instrument of knowledge (*śābdaprāmāṇya*) 239-62
-free 55
higher order 32
rules of interpretation of 232
theory of language 66, 283-91, 294, 391
Laugākṣi Bhāskara (1660) 492
laukika perception, see perception, ordinary
law, see jurisprudence
laya, see dissolution
laziness (*ālasya*) 393
length (*dīrghatva*) 330
liar, lying 63-64, 239, 242-43, 245, 247, 252, 254, 341, 448
liberation (*mokṣa, mukti*) 9, 37, 88, 141, 235-38, 305, 317, 323, 334, 336-37, 367-68, 394, 399, 402, 405-07, 412-15, 426, 442, 450, 452-53, 457-60, 469-70, 519, 524-25, 528, 603
(*abhyudaya*) 424
(*apavarga*) 338
(*kaivalya*) 399
(*niḥśreyasa*) 337, 424
while living (*jīvanmukti*) 406
light or fire (*tejas*) 132, 142, 385, 576
absence of, see darkness
eternal (*āloka*) 498, 585
likeness, see parity
Līlāvatī, wife of Śaṃkara Miśra
limit (*avadhi*) 338-39, 530
awareness of 329
limited (*avacchedya, avacchinna*) 437
-ness 17, 562
limitor (*avacchedaka*) 26, 31-32, 66, 71, 129, 194, 222-23, 229, 233, 273, 324, 333, 387-88, 415, 435, 463, 476, 502, 525, 532, 534, 551-57, 562-63, 570-71, 575, 580, 586, 590, 627
liṅga, see hetu
linguistics 69
link, see operation
lion (*siṃha*) definition 70, 171, 550-51
liquidity, see fluidity
lobha, see greed
(being) located in (*ādhāratva, adhikaraṇatā*) 16
locus (*āśraya, adhikaraṇa, āyatana*) 138, 386, 560-61, 601
having a common locus, see collocation
-hood or -ness 536, 540-41, 563
locus-located relation 528, 542
locus-pervading, see quality, locus/nonlocus-pervading
logic 69-81
epistemic 76
Western 18
lordliness 423
lotus (*paṅkaja*) 416-17, 514
sky-lotus 421
lying, see liar

Mādhava, see Vidyāraṇya
Mādhava Miśra (1500) 12, 313, 487, 491
Mādhava Sarasvatī (1515) 41
Mādhyamika 414, 494
madness 368
Maharashtra 381
(*Mīmāṃsā) Mahārṇava* (of Vaṭeśvara) 269, 396, 413, 461, 618-20
mahat, mahattva, see size, large
mahāvidyā inference 471-72
Mahāvidyāviḍambanavyākhyānadīpikā (of Bhuvanasundarasūri) 11, 394, 471
Mahāvidyāślokavivaraṇaṭippaṇa (of Bhuvanasundarasūri) 11, 471-72
Mahendra Sūri 363
Maheśa Ṭhakkura (1540) 487
Maheśvara Viśārada, see Narahari Upādhyāya
maintenance (*sthiti*) 322
Maithila, see Mithilā
Mallinātha (1445) 11, 465-70, 620
manana, see reflection
manas, see internal organ
Mandal, Prodyot Kumar 592
Maṇḍana Miśra (690) 299, 414, 511, 540-41
Mandara family 313, 473-74

maṅgala, see invocation
manifest (*vibhakta*) 387
-ness (*udbhava*) 413
/unmanifest (*udbhūta/anudbhūta*) quality, see quality, manifest/ unmanifest
manifested (*vyakta*) color, touch, etc., see color, touch, etc., manifested
manifestor (*vyañjaka*) 329, 391-92
Maṇikaṇṭha Miśra (1300) 61, 86, 344, 411-12, 421, 464, 616-18, 623
man-lion (*narasiṃha*) 321
manovahā, a vein 419
mantra 232, 393, 443
Manu (and *Mānavadharmaśāstra*) 226, 251, 393, 441
manyness or multiplicity (*nānātva, bhūyastva, bahutva*) 43, 179, 348, 386, 445
matānujña, see admitting the other party's opinion
material(ity) or element/nonmaterial (*mūrta/amūrta*) 324, 384, 386, 528, 530, 552, 562
(*upādāna*) 438-39
materialists 456
Mathurānātha Tarkavagīśa (1650) 9, 609
Matilal, Bimal Krishna 61, 69, 86, 136, 169-70, 394-95, 454, 486, 541, 592-93, 602, 619, 621, 625-26
māyā 44, 397, 617
meaning (*artha*) (see also designative capacity) 26-27, 239, 415
as established by God's will, see God's will as establisher of conventional meanings
conventional (*rūḍha*) 390
etymological-conventional (*yoga-rūḍha*) 322, 514
secondary meaning (*lakṣaṇā*) (see also metaphor) 166, 255, 261, 285, 293, 298, 300, 345, 387, 416-17, 513-15, 518, 529, 536, 587-88
sentence-meaning (*vākyārtha*) 23, 66, 185, 239-62, 297-98, 371, 442, 451, 468, 574, 614
word-meaning (*padārtha*) 240, 283, 286, 291-99, 303, 342, 371, 407, 415-16, 442, 450, 501, 574, 612
mediacy or mediateness (*parokṣatva*) 121, 133, 156-57, 365
medicine 69, 233
meditation 368, 393, 419
(*nididhyāsana*) 402, 406-07, 424, 440-41, 497, 620
(*samādhi*) 447
members of an inference or argument (*avayava*) 197, 360, 392, 480
memory (*smṛti*) 55, 59-60, 89-90, 98, 103, 109, 116-19, 122, 133, 135, 138, 150, 156-61, 169-70, 178-81, 184-85, 194-95, 241, 245, 263, 292-98, 301-03, 308-09, 337, 346-47, 372, 479, 484, 497, 501, 532-33, 574, 585-86, 596, 599, 602, 614-15
memory free 55
memory-trace 20, 122
mental act, see act, mental
merit (*dharma*) 44, 307, 318-19, 364, 379, 407, 413-14, 422-27, 442-43, 494-95, 505, 510, 516, 519, 524, 529, 532, 607-08
absence of (as a fallacy) 517
and demerit (*-adharma*) 65, 214-16, 25, 321, 326, 327
God's, see God's merit
noninstigating (*nivartaka*) 393
yogic 214, 325, 446
Meru, Mount 435
metaphor 244, 441, 453
metaphysician (*tāntrika*) 528
middlesizedness 34-35
Mill, John Stuart 77, 80
(Pūrva) Mīmāṃsā (see also Prābhākara, Bhāṭṭa, Miśra Mīmāṃsā) 8, 34, 37, 42, 44, 49, 53-54, 74-75, 86, 94, 98, 181, 185-86, 194-95, 197, 214, 217, 227-34, 238, 251, 263, 309, 339-40, 343, 375-76, 384, 397, 409, 416-17, 444, 452, 454-55, 460-61, 479, 488, 494, 508, 510, 513-14, 542-43, 545, 603, 626
Mīmāṃsāsūtras (of Jaimini) 423
mind 452
another's, knowledge of 406
minimal perceptibilium (*truṭi, trasa-*

reṇu) 33, 122, 348, 385-86, 444, 529-31, 600, 606
Misaru Miśra (1490) 12, 491, 622
misconception, see falsity
misery, see frustration
Mishra, Umesh 45, 61, 86, 313, 336-37, 374-76, 382, 395-96, 454-55, 465, 471, 486, 489, 491-92, 520-21, 591-92, 615-24, 632
Miśra Mīmāṃsā 8, 56, 544-45
Misra, Sri Narayan 423
mistimed (*kālātyayāpadiṣṭa*) 1, 331, 377, 379, 470
Mithilā 4, 10-12, 85, 314, 336, 374-76, 395, 454, 473, 487, 489, 492, 521-22
mithyā, see falsity
Miyasaka, Yusho 563
mleccha, see foreigner
moha, see delusion
Mohanty, Jitendranath 98-100, 488, 544-46, 592
moment (*kṣaṇa*) 49, 419-20, 526-27, 533, 578
  final moment before death 426
  first moment 383
  interval between moments 457
momentariness (*kṣaṇika*) 49, 270, 381, 435, 439, 444, 533, 608
  kṣaṇabhaṅgavāda 450
monism (see also Advaita) 558
  (sentence) mood 264
  imperative 283, 613
  indicative 283
  optative or potential (*liṅ*) 304, 510-14, 609
moon 34, 378
  double moon 364
  fire of the moon 418
  new- or full-moon sacrifice, see sacrifice
    moon-stone 227-30
motion (*kriyā*) 17, 35, 39, 45, 49, 122, 125, 127, 144, 323, 326, 379, 383, 386, 413, 419, 427-32, 434-35, 445-46, 510, 526, 531-32
  bodily motion (*ceṣṭā*) 213, 221, 226
  fixed motion (*niyata*) 435
  -ness 428, 432-33
Mukhopadhyay, Prodyot Kumar 116-22, 239-62
mukti, see liberation
Muṇḍaka Upaniṣad 393, 399, 524
Murāri Miśra 340, 413, 523
mūrta, see materiality
mutual dependence, see dependence, mutual
myrobalan tree (*harītakī*) 41, 320, 333, 520

nāda 413
nāḍī, see vein
Nadia(d) 4
nāma, see stem
namaskāra, see salutation
name (*nāman*, saṃjñā) 327, 418, 434, 466
  (*abhidhā*) 54
  nameable (*abhidheyatva*) 383, 403-04, 476, 551, 562, 589
  conditional (*aupādhika*) 327
  implicatory (*upalakṣaṇatas*) 327
  technical (*pāribhāṣika*) 327
nānātva, see manyness
Nañvāda (of Raghunātha Śiromaṇi) 13, 522, 541-44
Narahari (1455) 11, 375, 473, 489-91
Narahari Upādhyāya or Maheśvara Viśārada (1495) 4-5, 12, 313, 454, 473, 487, 490-91, 495, 498, 622
Narapati Miśra 486
narasiṃha, see man-lion
Narasiṃha 461, 619
Nārāyaṇācārya (1420) 11, 380-82
Nārāyaṇa Upaniṣad 398
nāstika, see heterodox
nature (*rūpa*) 553
  essential or "own" 400
Navadvīpa 4, 11, 473, 489, 522
navel 394
Nayaviveka (of Bhavanātha) 375, 610
nearness (*aparatva*) 39, 413, 446, 530
negation (see also absence)
  as instrument of knowledge 421
  double negation 626
  negative concomitance (*vyatirekāvyabhicāra*) 605
  negative particle (*nañ*) 317, 399, 464, 467, 512, 536

neutralization (*prakaraṇa*) 333, 370, 379, 390
parity through 354-55, 410-11
New Catalogus Catalogorum 314, 374, 382, 487, 491, 520, 593, 621-22, 632
Nibandha (of Udayana?) 462-63
nididhyāsana, see meditation
nigamana, see conclusion of an inference
nigrahasthāna, see way of losing an argument
nihilism 456, 494, 617, 620
nihsreyasa, see liberation, *nihsreyasa*
Nikāśa 620
Nīlāmbara 414
nimittakāraṇa, see cause, instrumental
nimittasaṃkocanikāra 416
nipāta, see particle
niranuyojyānuyoga, see wrongly finding fault
nirarthika, see jargon, meaningless
nirjarā 414
nirūpaka, see determination
nirūpaṇa, see characterization
nirūpita, nirūpya, see determined
nirvikalpakajñāna, see awareness, nonpropositional
niścaya, see belief
niśkriya, see immobility
nitya(tva), see eternality
nityakarman, see act, required
nivartaka, see precluder
(*Praśastapādabhāṣya) Niṣkaṇṭaka* (of Mallinātha) 620
nivṛtti, see withdrawal
niyama 393-94
invariable precedence 515-16
sahopalambhaniyama 414
niyāmaka, see regulator
niyoga, see prescription
niyojya, see injunction, one who is enjoined
nodana, see impulsion
nominative case, see case, nominative
nonapprehension (*anupalabdhi*) 66-67, 131-36, 138, 219, 339, 468-69
of a nonexistent difference (*avidyamānabheda*) 98
of what is perceptible (*yogyānupalabdhi*) 131, 135, 398, 464, 615
parity through 356-57
nonattachment, see detachment
nonawareness, nonperception, see nonapprehension
nondeviation (*avyabhicāra*) 70-71, 116, 171, 174, 203, 314, 421, 436, 502, 549
viruddhāvyabhicāra 390
nonconcurrence (*sahānavasthāna*) 140
nondifference (*abheda*) 46, 128-29, 400-02, 405-06, 432, 460, 509
nonduality (*advaita*) 452-53, 459
noneternality, parity through 357
noneternity (*anityatā*)
of products 377, 384-85
of sounds, see sound, noneternality
nonexistence, see absence
(*bhāvapratiyogitva*) 402
(*sattāyogitva*) 402
nonexpressibility 404
nonimperativist (*anvitābhidhāna*) theory 65-66, 282-94, 612-13
noninherence cause, see cause, noninherence
nonperception, see nonapprehension
nonpervasion 482
nonproduction (*anutpatti*), parity through 353
nonpropositional, see awareness, propositional/nonpropositional
nonunderstanding (*apratipatti*) 367
nonunion (*aprāpti*), parity through 352, 354
nonwandering, see nondeviation
Northwest Provinces 314
nose, see smell, the olfactory organ
not being a condemned object (*avagītatva*) 272
not being validly established (*apramita*), parity through 362
number (*saṃkhyā*) (see also unity; duality) 17, 39, 41-43, 50, 144, 320, 324, 372-73, 413, 427, 444-45, 498-99, 531, 534, 538-39
cardinal number 445
the highest number (*parārdha*) 329, 445

NV, see awareness, nonpropositional, (believer in)
Nyāsa (of Jinendrabuddhi) 620
Nyāsoddyota (of Mallinātha) 620
nyāya, see reasoning
Nyāyabhūṣaṇa (of Bhāsarvajña) 6, 41, 264, 372, 616-18
Nyāyabhūṣaṇprakāśa (of Gadādhara Miśra) 12, 521
Nyāyabinduṭīkā (of Dharmottara) 54
Nyayacarya, Vamacarana 626-27
Nyayacharya, Madhusudana 193, 549-50, 564-70
Nyāyadīpikā (of Misaru Miśra) 491
Nyāyakandalīprakāśa (of Rājaśekhara Sūri) 10, 363
Nyāyakusumāñjali (of Udayana) 466-67, 489, 494, 503, 506, 513, 617-19, 623
Nyāyakusumāñjalidīdhiti (of Raghunātha Śiromaṇi) 13, 522
Nyāyakusumāñjaliparimala (of Divākara Upādhyāya) 623-24
Nyāyakusumāñjaliparimala (of Jagadguru) 623-24
Nyāyakusumāñjalimakaranda (of Tvantopadhyāya) 374
Nyāyakusumāñjalyāmoda (of Śaṃkara Miśra) 11, 397-98
Nyāyakusumāñjaliprakāśa (of Vardhamāna) 10, 85, 314, 338-48
Nyāyakusumāñjali (prakāśa) makaranda (of Rucidatta Miśra) 12, 374, 492, 515-18
Nyāyakusumānjali—Commentary (of Bhavanātha Miśra) 375
Nyāyakusumāñjaliviveka (of Pakṣadhara) 470-71
Nyāyalīlāvatī (of Vallabha) 6, 8, 396, 421, 455, 463, 506-07, 618
Nyāyalīlāvatīkaṇṭhābharaṇa (of Saṃkara Miśra) 11, 452-53
Nyāyalīlāvatī—Commentary (of Pragalbha Miśra) 486
Nyāyalīlāvatīprakāśa (of Vardhamāna) 10, 314, 333-36
Nyāyalīlāvatīprakāśadhiti (of Raghunātha Śiromaṇi) 13, 522
Nyāyalīlāvatīvibhāṣā (of Rucidatta Miśra) 12, 492
Nyāyalīlāvatīvibhūti (of Raghunātha Śiromaṇi) 13, 522
Nyāyalīlāvatīprakāśaviveka (of Pakṣadhara) 11, 313, 470-71
Nyāyalīlāvatīprakāśa—Commentary (of Pragalbha Miśra) 486
Nyāyalīlāvatīviveka (of Pragalbha Miśra) 12
Nyāyalīlāvatīviveka (of Pakṣadhara) 11, 454, 470-71
Nyāyalocana 10, 375, 416
Nyāyamañjarī (of Jayanta Bhaṭṭa) 8, 616
Nyāyanibandhadarapaṇa (of Vaṭésvara) 10, 313
Nyāyanibandhaprakāśa (of Vardhamāna) 10, 333, 623
Nyāyapadārthamāla (of Jayadeva Miśra) 12, 487
Nyāparicaya (of Phaṇibhūṣaṇa Tarkavāgīśa) 521, 619
Nyāyapariśiṣṭa (of Udayana) 349-62
Nyāyaparísiṣṭaprakāśa (of Vardhamāna) 10, 314, 362-63
Nyāyaratna (of Maṇikaṇṭha Miśra) 344, 623
Nyāyaratnaprakāśa (of Vācaspati Miśra II) 11, 454-55
Nyāyasāra (of Bhāsarvajña) 8, 389, 615
Nyāyasāranyāmuktāvalī (of Aparārkadeva) 366
(*Nyāyasāra)Nyāyasaṃgraha* 366, 615
Nyāyasārapadapañcikā (of Vāsudeva Sūri) 11, 389-94
Nyāyasāratāparyadīpikā (of Jayasiṃhasūri) 10, 363-68
Nyāyasiddhāntadīpa (of Jayadeva Miśra) 12
Nyāyasiddhāntadīpa (of Śaśadhara) 394, 487, 593
Nyāyasiddhāntadīpaṭippaṇī (of Guṇaratna Sūri) 11, 394
Nyāyasiddhāntadīpaprabhā (of Śeṣāṇanta) 11, 472
Nyāyasiddhāntamāla (of Jayarāma Nyāyapañcānana) 618
Nyāyasiddhāntasāra (of Vāsudeva Miśra) 12, 492
(*Tattvacintāmaṇiprakāśa) Nyāyaśikhāmaṇi* (of Rāmakṛṣṇa) 622
Nyāyasūcīnibandha (of Vācaspati

Miśra I) 455
Nyāyasūtras (of Gautama) 6, 8, 88, 299, 318, 331, 336, 345, 349, 352, 354, 359-60, 362, 367, 390, 392, 425, 446, 450, 455, 466-67, 469, 496, 504, 523, 590, 615, 626
Nyāya(sūtra)bhāṣya (of Vātsyāyana) 336, 523
Nyāyasūtrānvīkṣikīnayatattvabodhinī (of Vardhamāna) 10, 314, 332
Nyāyatātparyaṭīkā (of Vācaspati Miśra I), see (Nyāya) Tātparyaṭīka
Nyāyasūtroddhāra (of Vācaspati Miśra II) 11, 455
Nyāyatattvāloka (of Vācaspati Miśra II) 11, 455, 459, 619
Nyāyavārttika (of Uddyotakara) 336, 436, 463, 523, 626
nyūna, see deficient formulation

obeisance, see salutation
object (*viṣaya*), intentional, see content
object
  external (*bāhyārtha*) 451
  of action (*karman*) 459
  of knowledge (*prameya*) 367, 372-73, 482
  sense 372
  supporting object (*ālambana*) 458, 523
oblation to fire 234
obligation 287, 289
obligatory rite, see rite, obligatory
observation, repeated (*bhūyodarśana*) 74, 178-83, 332, 476-77, 502, 623
obstacles, removal of 87, 316, 364, 424, 493
obstructing the occurrence of something (*pratibandhakatā*) 16
obstruction (*upādhi*) 72-73, 100, 102, 106, 121, 170, 173-74, 177-78, 180-83, 187-92, 222, 228, 327, 332, 344, 348, 370, 374, 384-86, 411, 418, 437, 443, 448, 453, 467, 476, 478-79, 503, 505, 527, 570, 579-84, 594-97, 606, 610, 631
  believed (*niścita*) 191
  doubted (*saṃdigdha*) 191, 343, 478-79
  fallacious (*ābhāsa*) 192, 416
obstruction-filled/-less (*(an)aupādhika*) 421, 436-37, 448, 463, 469
obstructor (*pratibandhaka*) 226-30, 264-65, 398, 554, 585-86, 611
occurrence (*vṛtti*) 413
  -exacting relation, see relation, occurrence-exacting
  unlimited occurrence (*apramitavṛtti*) 530
occurrent 53
oil, hot (*taila*) 34, 418
olfactory organ, i.e. the nose, see smell, the olfactory organ
omission, sin of (*pratyavāya*) 316, 457
omnilocated, see only-positive
omnipotence, see God's omnipotence
Omniscience 186-87, 217, 446
  Brahman's 404
  God's 225-26, 242
  limited 24
one (the number) (*ekatva*) 42, 319, 329, 372, 379, 444, 472, 564
only-negative agreement (*kevalavyatirekin*) 175, 195-97, 335, 346, 366, 383, 418-19, 438, 480, 616
only-negative definition 319-20
only-positive agreement (*kevalānvayin*) 171-72, 175, 190, 192, 195-96, 202, 347, 366, 383, 392, 419, 433, 438, 474, 503, 550-51, 571, 584
operation (*vyāpāra*) 44, 59, 87, 118, 238, 347, 442, 537, 541, 602
opponent's position (*pūrvapakṣa*) 36-37
organ, internal, see internal organ
organ, sense, see sense-organ
origin(ation) (*utpatti*) 322, 341, 578, 630
Orissa 489-90
overextension (*ativyāpti*) 167, 175, 267, 327-28, 383, 472-74, 482, 503, 515, 527-29, 532, 549-55, 563-64, 567-70, 588
overlapping, see cross-connection
overlooking a mistake (*paryanuyojyopekṣaṇa*) 361, 367, 409-10

overpervasion, see overextension
oviparous 321
ownership, see possessedness

p , see *pakṣa*
pada, see word
padārtha , see category
Padārthacandra (of Misaru Miśra) 491
Padārthacandrikā, see Saptapadārthīpadārthacandrikā (of Śeṣānanta)
Padārthadharmasaṃgraha (of Praśastapāda) 315, 317, 372
Padārtharatnamālā (of Jānakinātha Bhaṭṭācārya) 492
Padārthatattvanirṇaya (of Raghunātha Śiromaṇi) 6, 13, 35, 40, 47-48, 522, 529-35, 591
paddy 234
Padmanābha Miśra (1650) 374
Padmavatī queen of Pañcālabhūmi 454
pain, see frustration
  (e.g., in the foot) 148, 320, 326
Pākhaṇḍa 413-14
pakṣa (*p*) 36-37, 69-76, 110, 119, 127, 146, 170, 182, 189-220, 223, 241, 271, 331, 334-35, 344, 350-52, 355-58, 366, 378-79, 448, 453, 470, 474, 479, 481, 483, 485, 503-06, 550-52, 555, 560, 580-90, 594, 596, 606-07, 618
  being the *pakṣa* (*pakṣatā*) 193, 201, 344, 479, 485, 503, 584-87
  being other than the *pakṣa* (*pakṣetaratva*) 187, 191, 478-79
  pakṣadharmatā, see qualification of *p* by *h*
Pakṣadhara Upādhyāya, son of Vaṭeśvara 312-13
Pakṣadhara, the Vivekakāra (1450) 11, 313, 454, 470-71, 486-87, 620
Pakṣadhara Miśra, see Jayadeva Miśra
Paṇḍitavijaya (of Śaṃkara Miśra) 396
Pāṇini 369, 398, 539, 615, 626
paṅkaja, see lotus
Parabrahmotthāpanasthala (of Bhuvanasundarasūri) 472
paramāṇu, see atom
parāmarśa, see consideration
pāramārthika, see reality, *pāramārthika*
parārdha, see number, highest
parārthānumāna, see inference for others
pāratantrya, see bondage
paratva , see farness
paribhāṣā, pāribhāṣikī term, see term, technical
Parimala (of Divākara Upādhyāya), see *Nyāyakusumāñjaliparimala* (of Divākara Upādhyāya)
Parimala (of Jagadguru) , see *Nyāyakusumāñjaliparimala* (of Jagadguru)
parimāṇa, see size
pariṇāma, see transformation
pariśeṣānumāna, see inference, eliminative
Pariśuddhi (of Udayana) 318, 336
Pariśuddhinyāyanibandhaprakāśa (of Vardhamāna) 314, 336-37
parity (*samatva*) 349-58
parokṣatva, see mediacy
parrot 63-64, 243, 252, 254, 263, 341, 507, 517
parsimony, see simplicity
Pārśvanātha, temple of Śrī, at Harsha pura 471
part, see whole and part
  partless (*akhaṇḍa*) 38
Pārthasārathi Miśra (1075) 511
particle (*nipāta*) 315
  negative, see negation, negative particle
particular (*vyakti*) 416, 428, 431-32, 446, 514
  momentary particular (*svalakṣaṇa*) 55, 446
Pārvatī 396
paryanuyojyopekṣaṇa, see overlooking a mistake
paryāpti, see relation, numerical
paryudāsa, see absence, *paryudāsa*
passion (*kāma*) 368, 380, 393, 442
past
  life 93
  time, see time
Pāśupata 413
Paśupati, son of Vaṭeśvara 474
Patañjali, see *Yogasūtras*

Peddi Bhaṭṭa 380
penance (*tapas*) 237, 368, 393
perception (*pratyakṣa*) 22-23, 34, 55, 58-62, 66, 86-88, 91, 106, 109, 113-17, 127-28, 133-34, 144-45, 148-53, 156, 163, 165, 170, 210, 213, 218-19, 239-40, 254, 270, 325, 339, 343, 347, 364, 369, 378, 384-86, 405, 414-15, 418, 421, 433-34, 439, 443, 446-48, 474, 477, 496-500, 519, 530-34, 570-90, 594-95, 605, 608, 614-15
continuous (*dhārāvāhika*) 122
definition of 58, 116-22, 146
determinative (*vyavasāya*) 462
eternal (*nitya*) 58
God's, see God's perception
jñānalakṣaṇasannikarṣa perception 58, 61, 95, 420, 545, 574, 628
mental (*mānasa*) 95, 267, 365, 499
occurrent or ordinary (*janya*) 58, 118, 502
perceptibility 34-35, 531-32
sāmānyalakṣaṇasannikarṣa perception 58, 61-62, 81, 152-53, 157, 184-87, 213-15, 272, 303, 415, 420, 458, 462, 464, 573-80, 605, 628-30
simultaneous 149-50
yogic 58, 61, 118, 334, 365, 420, 442, 458, 462, 496-97
person (*puruṣa*) 211
pervasion (*vyāpti*) 5, 17, 69-81, 90, 110, 117, 162, 170-87, 194, 203-06, 217, 220, 223, 239, 249, 256, 260, 303, 332, 335, 344, 365-66, 381, 390, 411, 415-16, 431-32, 436-37, 450, 453, 462-64, 474, 476-79, 483-84, 501, 549-60, 563-64, 568-72, 581-84, 588, 604-05, 623, 627-28
awareness of 221, 345
comprehensiveness (*vyāptyanugama*) of 184
equi-/nonequi- ((*a*)*samaavyāpti*) 325, 332, 344, 398, 421, 437, 503
means of grasping pervasion (*vyāptigrahopāya*) 175-83, 502
negative pervasion (*vyatirekin*) 93, 589
-ness 182
Peterson, P. 592
phlegm, see humors
pitṛyajña, see rite, *pitṛyajña*
place, see space or spatial direction
plants 212, 216, 441
pleasure (*sukha*) (see also satisfaction) 424, 441, 450
poison (*kalañja*) 268, 272-76, 282, 305, 512, 544
Poona 455
positive entity (*bhāva*) 136, 190, 334, 570
(being) positive (*bhāvatva*) 532
postitive inference, see inference, positive
positive-negative agreement (*anvayavyatirekin*) 175, 192, 195-97, 347, 366, 419, 438
possessedness (*svatva*) 49, 533, 564
postfix, verbal (*dhātūttarapratyaya*) 538, 540
posterior absence, see absence, posterior
potency (*saṃskāratva*) 233
(*śakti*), see designative capacity
verbal potency, see designative capacity
pot (*ghaṭa, kalaśa*)
blue pot 534
potness 432
potency (as a category) 619
Potter, Karl H. 170, 178-83, 211-26, 423-50, 529-35, 541, 591, 632
pounding of grain 232-33
power, see causal efficacy
located power (*ādheya śakti*) 230-33
simultaneous (*sahaja-*) 230-32
to signify (*śabdaśakti*) 260
prabhā, see radiance
Prabhākara (700) 571, 627
Prābhākara Mīmāṃsā 8, 49, 55-66, 98-106, 109-10, 114, 117, 119-22, 126, 138-41, 151, 169-70, 178-82, 238, 252-57, 264-81, 284, 289, 292, 294-304, 335, 342, 372, 374, 396, 413-16, 419, 432, 446, 469, 495-96,

511, 513, 523, 541, 543-45, 592, 595-601, 610-15, 618-19
neo-Prābhākaras 108, 274
Prabhākaropadhyāya (1250) 314, 476, 478
practice (see also usage, practical), successful 92
Pragalbha Miśra (1470) 5, 11-12, 313, 473, 486, 491, 494, 554, 558, 621
pragmatic features (*prakaraṇa*) 255
Prajñākaragupta (910) 414, 618
prakaraṇasama, see neutralization
prakāśa, see illumination
Prakāśātman (975) 368
prakṛti 44, 336, 397
pralaya 509-10, 552
avāntarapralaya 412
mahāpralaya 412, 578
pramā, see knowledge
pramāṇa, see instrument of knowledge
Pramāṇamañjarī (of Sārvadeva) 616
Pramāṇapallava (of Jayadeva Miśra) 12, 487
Pramāṇa (or *Prameya-*) *tattvabodha* (of Vardhamāna) 507, 624
prāṇa, see breath
prāpti, see union
prarocana , see instigation
prasaṅga, see (1) result, unwanted, (2) question, continued
prasañjaka, see reasoning
prasaraṇa, see expansion
Praśastapāda or Praśastadeva (530?) 33, 35, 38-39, 42, 44, 317, 323, 325-26, 329, 331, 372-73, 387, 428, 526, 618
prasiddhārthakhyāti 364
praśna, see question
Pratāparāja 382
Pratāparudra 454
pratibandhakāra, see obstructor
pratibandhakatā, see obstructing the occurrence of something
pratibandhitva, see having its occurrence obstructed
pratidṛṣṭānta, see counterexample
pratigraha, see right
pratijñā, see thesis
pratijñāntara, see changing the thesis
pratijñānahāni, see violating the thesis
pratijñāsaṃnyāsa, see renouncing the thesis
pratijñāvirodha, see reason and thesis contradictory
pratirodha, see counterargument
pratiyogin, see (1) counterpositive, (2) referent
pratiyogitā, see counterpositiveness; being the counterpositive
pratyabhijñā, see recognition
Pratyakṣanirṇaya (of Vācaspati Miśra II) 11, 455
pratyavāya, see omission, sin of
pratyaya, see postfic
pratyayādhipati 523
pratyayavyāvṛtti, distinctness, revealed
pravartana, pravartaka, see inciter
pravṛtti, see activity
Prayāga (Allahabad) 424, 518
Prāyaścittaviveka 492
prayatna, see effort
prayojaka, see conducive
precedence, invariable, see *niyama*
precluder (*nivartaka*) 104
prefix (*upasarga*) 312, 316
prescription (*niyoga*) 511
presenceness (*bhāvatva*) 551
present, see time
preservation, instinct for (*jīvanadṛṣṭi*) 160
presumption (*arthāpatti*) (see also implication) 197, 229, 299, 303, 346, 392, 398, 415
parity through 354
prior absence, see absence, prior
priority, temporal (*pūrvatva*) 577-78
probability (*sambhāvanā*) 353, 371, 413-14, 421
produced (*janya*) 505
prohibition 304-05, 448, 460, 512-13, 543
prokṣaṇa, see ablution
prompting 274, 278, 510
property (*dharma*) 366, 389, 401, 413, 544
common or generic or consecutive (*anugata*) 97, 99, 179

composite/noncomposite (*sakhaṇḍa/akhaṇḍa*) 34-35, 40, 45
distributive (*vibhājaka*) 38
imposed, see imposed property
of pairs, etc (*vyāsajyavṛtti*) 17, 459, 566
-possessor (*dharmin*) 118, 324, 331, 338, 366-67, 387, 389, 413, 462, 465, 525, 544, 561, 575
specific (*asādhāraṇa*) 364
proposition, see sentence
assimilative (*atideśavākya*) 507
propositional
act, see awareness
attitude 29-30
proving what has already been admitted (*siddhasādhana*) 344-45, 465
proximity, see contiguity
pṛthaktva, see separateness
pṛthivī, see earth
psychology 71, 75, 607
putreṣṭi, see rite, *putreṣṭi*
pūjā, see worship
punarukta, see repetition
purāṇas 423
Puri 489
purification 394
acts of religious 237
purpose (*artha*) 235
purposive act, see act, purposive
puruṣa, see (1) person, (2) consciousness in Sāṃkhya
-*artha* 510
Puruṣasūkta 398
Puruṣottama, father of Vallabha 453
Puruṣottama Bhaṭṭācārya (1510) 12, 520, 524
pūrvapakṣa, see opponent's position
pūrvavat, see inference, *pūrvavat*
putreṣṭi, see sacrifice, *putreṣṭi*

qualificand, qualificandum (*viśeṣya*) 16, 25-33, 54, 90-97, 103, 106, 114-15, 125-26, 155, 158, 163-68, 225, 228, 242, 264, 286, 289, 291, 365, 494-95, 499-500, 539-42, 569, 575, 582, 584, 586, 597, 599-600, 610, 613
-ness (-*tā*) 16, 32, 330
qualification (*viśeṣaṇatā*) 25, 28-31, 89, 155, 337, 474
absential (*abhāvīya*-) 16
for a role (*adhikāra*) 408
of *p* by *h* (*pakṣadharmatā*) 170, 175, 194, 206-09, 220, 242, 249, 335, 347, 370, 386-87, 408, 411, 415, 504, 523, 616
-relation, see (being) qualified
spatial (*daiśika*) 16
temporal (*kālika*) 16
viśeṣaṇaviśeṣyabhāva 337
(being) qualified or qualifiedness or qualification-relation (*vaiśiṣṭya*) 50-51, 89, 127-28, 159, 161, 228, 346, 420, 453, 472, 490, 495, 500, 535, 575, 597-98, 602
qualifier (*viśeṣaṇa*) 16, 25-33, 59, 89, 92-97, 102-03, 114-15, 119-22, 125-27, 130-31, 155-58, 162-69, 186-87, 215-17, 225, 228, 241, 248, 267, 286, 289, 295, 329-30, 365, 373, 383, 451, 462, 478, 484, 489, 494-500, 539-42, 569, 573, 575, 579, 582-83, 594, 597, 599-600, 605, 610, 628
chief qualifier (*prakāra*) 26, 54, 92, 99-102, 106, 155-56, 164, 185, 194, 242-45, 264-65, 330-31, 400, 405, 415, 522, 545, 594, 610
qualifierness (*viśeṣaṇatā*) 16, 61, 66, 122, 130-33, 136, 156, 163, 331, 420, 497, 600, 628-29
qualifier-qualificand relation (*viśeṣaṇaviśeṣyasambandha*) 50-51
unknown (*aprasiddha*) 370
quality (*guṇa*) 15, 17, 38-45, 50, 122, 125, 127, 215, 323-32, 383-87, 413, 418, 427-29, 432, 444-46, 472, 510, 528-32, 550-51, 562, 567
locus-pervading/nonlocus-pervading 17, 39, 99, 129, 173, 328, 333, 420, 531, 49, 553-60, 569
manifest/unmanifest (*udbhūta/anudbhūta*) 40, 372
natural (*svābhāvika*) 434
produced specific quality (*vibhukārya*) 386

psychological 43
qualityness (*guṇatva*) 38, 188, 323-27, 384, 388, 418, 428-29, 432-33, 525, 527-28, 532
qualityness 525
specific (*viśeṣaguṇa*) 144, 147, 211, 321, 324-27, 388, 418, 424-25, 433, 439
quantification 7, 46
question (*praśna*) 407, 412, 417
awareness of, see understanding the question
-begging, see mutual dependence
continued (*prasaṅga*) 352
jñāpaka 352
kāraka 352
viparītaprasaktika 352
questioner 366
quibble (*chala*) 211, 361, 390, 411

R (e.g., NVR) = Rule
Rāḍhi class of Brahmins 473
radiance (*prabhā*) 144
rāga, see desire
Raghavan, V. 632
Raghunanda 4, 489
Raghunātha Śiromaṇi (1510) 3-6, 8-9, 12-13, 17-18, 23, 31, 33-50, 61-62, 70, 470, 487, 489-90, 492, 520-90, 624-31
Raghunātha Vidyālaṃkāra 520
Raghuvaṃśa 618, 620
Raja, K. Kunjunni 632
rajas guṇa 415
Rājaśekhara Sūri (1350) 10, 363
rājasūya, see sacrifice, *rājasūya*
Raktāmbara 414
Rāmabhadradeva 454-55
Rāmānuja (1120), followers of, see Viśiṣṭādvaita
Rāmānujācārya (1750) 55
Rāmeśvara (1420) 11, 368, 373, 380
Rārhī Brahmins 489
rasa, see taste
Rasārṇava (of Śaṃkara Miśra) 396
Ratnākarāvatārikapañjikā (of Rājaśekhara Sūri) 363
Ratnākara Vidyāvācaspati (1505) 12, 520
Ratnakīrti (1070) 618
Ratnakośa (of Taraṇi Miśra) 189, 337, 339, 344, 407-08, 411-12, 412, 463, 484, 511, 606, 623
Ratnaśekhara (1440) 471
Ravinātha 375
ray of light/fire 377-78
reality (*tattva*) 99, 317, 376, 392, 462
real entity (*vastu*) 405-06
knowledge of reality (*tattvajñāna*) 236, 318-19, 422, 450, 461, 469-70, 519, 524
neither real nor nonreal, see *anirvacanīya*
(*pāramārthika*) 403, 406-07
(*satya*) 399
reason (*hetu*) 405
and thesis contradictory (*pratijñā virodha*) 410, 464
changing one's reason (*hetvantara*) 359
reasoning (*prasañjaka, nyāya*) 198, 255, 258, 262
recension, extinct 342
recognition (*pratyabhijñā*) 44, 58-60, 113-14, 118-22, 145, 156-57, 170, 178, 333, 347, 374, 422, 438-39, 462, 465-66, 468, 495-97, 501, 509, 533, 595, 599
recollection, see memory
recurrence 121-22
reductio ad absurdum, see *tarka*
redundancy (*adhika*) 360, 366-67, 409-10
referend (*anuyogin*) 15-16, 365, 562, 632
referent (*pratiyogin*) 15, 122, 169, 365, 562, 632
reflection (*bhāvanā, vibhāvanā*) 380, 399
reflection (*manana*) 338, 400, 402, 406-07, 440-41, 497
reflection, subsumptive 504
regress, infinite, see infinite regress
regulator (*niyāmaka*) 127
reidentification (*anuvṛtti*) 431
rejecting the questions (*praśnaparāha*) 407
relatedness (*pratiyogitā*) 400
relatedness (*vaiśiṣṭya* or *sambandhaviśeṣaṇatā*) 107, 413

sādhyānutpattisama 353
-ness 7, 358, 556-57, 560, 562, 586
parity through 351-52
sādhyavikalatva 352
unknown *sādhya* 597
sages 441
Saha, Sukharanjan 65, 155-69, 292-300, 604
sahacarya, see collocation
Sahajasarvajña Viṣṇubhaṭṭopādhyāya 368
sahānavasthāna, see nonconcurrence
sahopalambhaniyama, see *niyama, sahopalambha*
Śaivism 374
sākāravāda 105, 115
sākṣāttva, see immediacy
śakti, see (1) causal efficacy, (2) designative capacity, weak (*vikala-*) 390
Śālikanātha Miśra (925) 372, 612, 620
salutation (*namaskāra*) 88, 315-16
sama, see parity
sāmagrī, see causation, collection of causal factors
samāhāra, see aggregate
samanādhikaraṇa, see collocation
sāmānya, see universal
sāmānyalakṣaṇāpratyāsatti, see perception, *sāmānyalakṣaṇā*
sāmānyatodṛṣṭa, see inference, *sāmānyatodṛṣṭa*
samartha, see efficiency/nonefficiency, causal
samāsa, see compound
samavāya, see inherence
samavāyikāraṇa, see cause, inherence
samavyāpti, see pervasion, equi-
sambandha, see relation
sambhava, see concurrence
sambhāvanā, see probability
saṃdhyā 394
sameness, see similarity
saṃghāta, see aggregate
(*Nyāya) Saṃgraha*, see *Nyāyasāra* (of Bhāsarvajña)
saṃkalpa, see (1) (awareness of) desire, (2) intention
Śaṃkarācārya (710) 407, 460
Śaṃkarakiṃkara, see (Bhaṭṭa) Vādīndra
Śaṃkara Miśra (1430) 5-6, 11, 33-35, 38, 40, 43-44, 46, 61, 70, 313, 363, 374-76, 395-454, 523, 617-19, 625
saṃketa, see signification
saṃkhyā, see number
Sāṃkhya 44, 336, 383, 397, 434, 439, 446
Sāṃkhyakārikās (of Īśvarakṛṣṇa) 336
saṃsāra, see bondage
saṃsargamaryādā 536, 540-41
saṃskāra, see trace
-*tva*, see potency
saṃvadana, see corroboration
saṃvara 414
samyaktva 55
saṃyoga, see contact
Sanātanī (950) 407
sandhyā, see sacrifice, *sandhyā*
Śāṇḍilya *gotra* 487
sannidhi, see contiguity
sannikarṣa, see relation
Santhal Parganas 376
sapakṣa (*sp*) 185-86, 192, 196, 200-03, 213-14, 220, 335, 352, 358, 370, 373, 433, 438, 481, 504, 581, 589, 594, 606, 618
sapravṛttinimitta 416
Saptapadārthī (of Śivāditya) 6, 616
Saptapadārthījñānavardhinī (of Jinavardhana Sūri) 10, 378-80, 616
Saptapadārthpadārthacandrikā (of Śeṣānanta) 11, 472-73
Saptapadārthīśiśubodhinī (of Bhairavendra) 12, 521
sarcasm 417
śarīra, see body
Sarisava 395
Sārvabhauma, see Vāsudeva Sārvabhauma
Sarvabhauma, S.C. 314, 519
Sarvadarśanasaṃgraha (of Mādhava/Vidyāraṇya) 313, 368
Sārvadeva 616, 618
Sarvajña, see Bhāsarvajña
Śaśadhara (1300) 36-37, 86, 394, 487, 593, 623
Śaśadharavyākhyā (of Pakṣadhara Miśra) 12, 487
śāstra, see (1) discourse, scientific, (2)

scripture
Sastri, Badrinath 322, 525
Sastri, Dundhiraja 197, 333, 338, 380-81, 452, 515, 587
Sastri Gaurinath 486, 490, 594, 621-22, 624
Sastri, Harihara 333, 452
Sastri, K. Sambasiva 389
Sastri, V. Subrahmanya 616, 623
Śatadūṣaṇī (of Vedānta Deśika) 618
satisfaction or pleasure (*sukha*) 43, 146-50, 153, 186, 214, 218, 225, 227, 268-70, 273-74, 280, 289, 305, 307, 325-26, 329, 393-94, 407, 412, 415-16, 426, 453, 478, 524, 529, 532, 579, 604
satkāryavāda 630
satpratipakṣa, see counterbalance
sattā, see existence
  svarūpasattā 457
satya, see reality, *satya*
Sautrāntika 382, 414
savikalpajñāna, see awareness, propositional
savyabhicāra, see deviation
Sāyaṇa 368
scepticism, see skepticism
science, Western philosophy of 70
script (*lipi*) 421
scripture (*śāstra, āgama*) (see also Veda) 235, 250, 333, 387, 401, 403-06, 423-26, 431, 440-43, 543
section of a work (*ullāsa*) 407
seed and sprout 114
self (*ātma*ʳ) 36-38, 43, 116, 118, 151, 211, 214-18, 225, 235-36, 321, 336, 340, 367, 372, 377-78, 386, 393, 399, 404, 406-07, 412-13, 419, 422-23, 427-28, 435, 438-42, 450, 468, 505, 518, 524-25, 529, 552, 600, 603-08
  self-caused (*svabhāvajanya*) 175
  self-dependence or -residence (*ātmāśraya*) 139-40, 383, 411, 438
  (*jīva*) in Jainism 414
  self-knowledge, see knowledge, self
  self-linking connector, see connector, self-linking
  multiplicity of selves 388
  perception of 122, 145
  self-occurrent (*svavṛtti*) 532
  self-revealing or -illuminating (*svaprakāśa*), see awareness, self-revealing
  supreme (*paramātman*) 529
Self (in Advaita) 406, 426, 452, 458, 461, 469, 626
Sen, Nani Lal 322-32, 382-88, 525-29
Sen, Prabhal Kumar 535-41
Sen, Pranab Kumar 604
sensation 55, 321, 466, 523
  beyond sensation (*atīndriya*) 326
sense-organ (*indriya*) 110, 113, 116-20, 122, 131-32, 134, 136, 138, 144, 146, 148, 151, 178, 184-85, 218, 250, 253, 296, 318, 331, 337, 364-65, 372, 378, 387, 391, 414, 419, 438-39, 453, 462, 466, 468, 476, 496, 498, 502, 525, 573-74, 582, 598-99, 602-03
sentence or utterance (*vākya*) 25, 197, 243-47, 251-52, 263-64, 298, 371, 451, 480, 541-42
  elliptical 285
  final letter of 436
  sentence-meaning, see meaning, sentence
  understanding of, see understanding, sentential
  Vedic, see Veda
separateness (*pṛthaktva*) 39, 413, 420, 444, 461, 530, 569
  of a single thing (*ekapṛthaktva*) 324
  of self from body 468
  of two things (*dvipṛthaktva*) 42, 329
Śeṣānanta (1450) 11, 382, 472-73
Śeṣa Śārṅgadhara (1420) 11, 33, 39, 47, 382-88, 472, 617
śeṣavat, see inference, *śeṣavat*
shape (*ākṛti, ākāra*) 43, 124, 166, 299-300, 580
Shaw, J.L. 592
shell 100-02, 109, 225
  conch 91, 97, 103
shoemaker, 376, 395-96
shuffling (*vikalpa*), parity through 351,

355, 362
Shukla, S.N. 398
siddhānta section of a discussion 36-37
Siddhāntamuktāvalī (of Viśvanātha) 626-27
siddhasādhana, see proving what has already been admitted
siddhi, see establishment
in yoga 447
sifting (*cālanīnyāya*) 557
signification (*saṃketa*) 308
silver (the metal) 100-15, 225, 244
siṃha, see lion definition
similarity (*sādṛśya, sājātya*) 119, 122, 124, 238-39, 300, 413, 416, 422, 495, 619
(*sādharmya*), parity through 349-50, 353, 355, 357
simplicity (*lāghava*)/complexity (*gau rava*) 31, 50, 102, 112-13, 116, 120, 123, 127, 130, 132, 147, 150, 152, 185, 223-24, 238, 247, 254, 257, 259, 265, 267, 273, 275, 280, 282, 285-86, 291-98, 303, 343, 348, 479-80, 484, 505, 519, 537, 539, 561, 563, 565-67, 572, 576, 579, 588-90, 598, 601
simultaneity 387
sin, see demerit
of omission 513
single, see one (the number)
Sinha, Nandalal, 423, 434
Śiva 282, 336, 347, 376, 395-96
Śivāditya Miśra (1150) 6, 167, 337, 378, 472, 616, 618
Śivapati (1420) 10, 313, 380, 374
size (*parimāṇa*) 35, 43, 141-44, 320, 325, 378, 418, 427, 441, 530-31, 561
God's, see God's size
large (*mahat*) 142-43, 190, 330, 348, 412, 523, 599
largest (*parimāṇamahat*) 388
of an atom, see atom, size of
small or atomic (*aṇu, pārimāṇḍalya*) 35, 43, 147-49, 319, 348, 372, 384, 499, 530, 600
ubiquitous (*vibhu*) 147-50, 326, 387, 414, 434, 439, 446, 497, 603
skandha 359, 414
skepticism 58, 75, 183, 572, 605
universal skepticism 93
sleep (*nidrā*) 393, 536
deep sleep 257, 419, 440
smell (*gandha*) 40, 123, 127, 335, 385-86, 414, 418, 427, 433-34, 441, 464, 472, 499, 531, 535, 603
-ness 123
nonfragrant (*asurabhi*) 328
the organ of 123, 388, 603
variegated 41
smoothness 321
smṛti literature 313, 396, 423, 491, 509-10
sneha, see viscidioty
Śodarpura family of Mithilā 395, 486, 492
ṣoḍaśin cup 543-44
Solomon, Esther A. 349-62
somasiddhānta 414
Somanathopadhyāya 211
Somasundarasūri (1404) 471
(Bhaṭṭa) Someśvara 51
Sondadopādhyāya (1310) 417, 475, 478
sophistry (*jalpa*) 366, 407, 409-10, 461
sound (*śabda*) 44-45, 124-26, 130, 149, 211, 216, 326-27, 331, 340, 373, 384, 386, 391-92, 413-16, 497, 508-09, 529, 622
-ness 125
noneternality (*anityatā*) of sound 263, 349-58
South India 380-81
sp, see *sapakṣa*
space or spatial direction (*diś*) 35, 37, 322, 378, 387, 394, 413, 415, 418-19, 435, 501, 529
(*ākāśa*), see *ākāśa*
spatial qualification, see qualification, spatial
sparśa, see touch
speaker's intention, see intention, speaker's
species, see particular
specific quality, see quality, specific
specifier, see determination

speed, see impetus
sphoṭa 436
śraddhā, see sacrific, *śraddhā*
Śrāvakapratikramaṇasūtraṭīkā (of Ratnaśekhara) 471
śravana, see hearing
Śrīdhara (990) 33, 43-44, 372, 374, 420, 444-45
Śrīharṣa (1140) 6, 53, 57-58, 81, 85, 343, 398, 407, 455-65, 477, 603, 619-20
Śrīkara (a Mīmāṃsaka) 514
Śrīkara Kubjaśaktivāda (1500) 12, 298, 492, 622
Śrīnātha Bhaṭṭācārya Cakravartin (1470) 12, 489, 553, 621
Śrotriya family of Mithilā 395
Staal, J. Frits 69, 593
Steinkellner, Ernst 314, 615
stem (*nāma*) 262
  verbal stem, see root
sthira, see continuant
sthitī, see maintenance
sthitīsthāpakatva, see elasticity
stimulator (*uttejaka*) 585-86
stotra, see hymn
stuti, see eulogizing
subdued (*abhibhūta*) 372
Śubhaṅkara, see Pragalbha Miśra
subject, see property-possessor
sublation (*bādha*) 91, 99, 105, 115, 190-92, 198, 208-11, 219, 248, 345, 402, 404, 411, 421, 438, 453, 456, 465, 481-85, 503-04, 517, 583
substance (*dravya*) 17, 33-38, 50, 122, 129, 143, 323, 328, 383-87, 413, 415, 418, 420, 428-30, 438, 444, 510, 525, 527-28, 530-32, 550, 558, 562
  all-pervading (*vibhu*) 377, 432
  -hood or -ness 74, 323-24, 418, 428, 432, 528, 551, 555, 567
  material substance (*mūrta*) 39, 327
  produced (*janya*) 384
substratum (*ādhāra*) 126
subtracting (*apakarṣa*), parity through 350-51
Sucarita Miśra (1120) 618
śūdra 337
suffering, see frustration
suffix, verbal (*ākhyāta*) 262, 311-12, 515, 535-41, 609, 626
  injunctive 302-03
  optative 277-82, 300, 305, 611-12
suicide 443
Śukadeva 236
sukha, see (1) satisfaction, (2) pleasure
Śūlapāṇi Miśra (1500) 12, 492, 622
sun 315, 385, 394
  's rays 34
superimposition (*āropa*) 181, 317, 333, 340, 364, 422, 441, 559, 560
superiority 394
superstratum (*ādheya*) 126, 627
supplementary passages (of the Veda) (*arthavāda*) 513
supportless (*aprayojaka*), a fallacy 102, 106, 126-27, 421
Sūryasūri (of Kashmir) 389, 617
suspicion 248
suvarṇa, see gold
SV, see awareness, propositional
svabhāva, see essence
svābhāvikasambandha, see relation, natural
svādhyāya 393
svagrāhasambandhaviśeṣaṇatā 130
svalakṣaṇa, see particular, momentary
Svapneśvara (1650) 489
svaprakāśa, see awareness, self-illuminating
svarga, see heaven
svārthānumāna, see inference for oneself
svarūpasambandha, see connector, self-linking
svātantrya, see liberation
svatva, see possessedness
Śvetāmbara 363, 414
Śvetāśvatara Upaniṣad 318, 372, 399
sweetness 123
Syādvādakalikā (of Rājaśekhara Sūri) 363
śyena, see sacrifice, *śyena*
Sylhet, see Assam
syllable 342
  final 436

tādātmya, see identity

taila see oil, hot
Taittirīya Upaniṣad 406, 415, 524
Tajjñānotpattisama 353
tamas, see darkness
tamas guṇa 315, 414
tāmasa beings 315
tangibility, see touch
tāpa, see affliction
Tāpagaccha 471
tapas, see penance
Taraṇi Miśra (1300) 206, 337, 339, 344, 410-12, 453, 511, 623
tarka 76-79, 179, 182-86, 224, 232, 343-46, 354, 364, 386, 399, 411, 462, 477-78, 502, 559, 572-73, 583-84, 605, 617, 623, 628, 631
  fallacies of 465
  supportive or favorable (*anukūla*) 190-91, 222, 344, 601
Tarkabhāṣā (of Keśava Miśra) 6
Tarkabhāṣā—Commentary (of Vardhamāna) 314
Tarkabhāṣā—Commentary (of Virūpakṣa Miśra) 12
Tarkabhāṣāprakāśa Commentary (of Rucidatta Miśra) 12, 492
Tarkabhāṣāprakāśikā (of Cinnam Bhaṭṭa) 10, 368-73
Tarkabhāṣāprakāśikāniruktivivṛti (of Viṣṇubhaṭṭa) 11, 380
Tarkacandrikā (of Śeṣa Śārṅgadhara) 11, 382
Tarkadarsanatirtha, Gurucarana 549-51, 553, 556, 566, 570
Tarkasaṃgraha (of Annambhaṭṭa) 382, 591
Tarkasaṃgrahakāra 382, 384-85, 387-88, 591
Tarkavagisa, Kamakhyanatha 239, 282, 294, 488
Tarkavagisa, Phanibhusana 453, 521
Tārkikarakṣāvyākhyā of *Saṃgrahavivaraṇa* (of Cinnam Bhaṭṭa and Rāmeśvara) 10-11, 358, 373-74
Tarkikarakṣāsārasaṃgrahaniṣkāntikā (of Mallinātha) 11, 465-70
taste (*rasa*) 40, 106, 327-28, 332, 378, 414, 427, 432-34, 499, 531, 604-05
  kṣara 328
  manifest 329
  -ness 123
  salty 328
  variegated 41, 320-21, 328, 333, 472, 499, 520
Tatachariar or Tatacarya, N.S. Ramanuja 86, 183-84, 193, 195-97, 492
taṭasthopalakṣaṇa (see also term, technical) 416
(*Nyāya*) *Tātparyaṭīkā* (of Vācaspati Miśra I) 463, 467, 523, 615, 626
tattva, see reality
  -*jñāna*, see knowledge of the truth
Tattvacintāmaṇi (of Gaṅgeśa) 3, 5-6, 10, 36, 46-47, 58, 61-62, 85-312, 314, 317, 374-75, 455, 470, 489, 492-93, 496, 580, 591, 593-615
Tattvacintāmaṇi—Commentary (by Narahari?) 473
Tattacintāmaṇyāloka (of Jayadeva Miśra) 4, 6, 8, 470, 473, 492
Tattvacintāmaṇi and -*Āloka*—Commentary (of Ratnākara Vidyāvācaspati) 12, 520
Tattvacintāmaṇi—Commentary (of Gaṅgāditya) 10
Tattvacintāmaṇi—Commentary (of Ghaṭeśa Upādhyāya) 10
Tattvacintāmaṇi—Commentary (of Śrīnātha Bhaṭṭācārya Cakravartin) 12, 489
Tattvacintāmaṇi—Commentary (of Tvantopādhyāya) 10, 374
Tattvacintāmaṇidīdhiti (of Raghunātha Śiromaṇi) 8-9, 13, 18, 43-44, 70, 470, 490, 520-22, 544-90
Tattvacintāmaṇidūṣaṇddhāra (of Narahari Upādhyāya) 12, 473, 491
Tattvacintāmaṇi (pratyakṣa) kṛṣṇa (of Kṛṣṇānanda Vidyāvinoda) 12
Tattvacintāmaṇimayūkha (of Śaṃkara Miśra) 11, 396, 421, 438, 446
Tattvacintāmaṇiprabhā (of Yajñapati Upādhyāya) 11, 380, 474-85, 621
Tattvacintāmaṇi—Commentary (of Mādhava Miśra) 491

Tattvacintāmaṇiprāgalbhī (of Pragalbha Miśra) 11, 486
Tattvacintāmaṇiprakāśa (of Janārdana) 12, 490
Tattvacintāmaṇivivecana (of Vidyānivāsa Bhaṭṭācārya) 375
Tattvacintāmaṇiprakāśa (of Rucidatta Miśra) 12, 183, 492-515
Tattvacintāmaṇiprakāśa (of Vācaspati Miśra II) 11, 455
Tattvacintāmaṇisārāvalī (of Vāsudeva Sārvabhauma) 12, 490
Tattvacintāmaṇiviveka (of Pakṣadhara) 11, 470-71
Tattvacintāmaṇyāloka (of Jayadeva Miśra) 12, 313, 374, 470, 487-89
Tattvacintāmaṇyālokaddyota (of Jāneśvara Vāhinīpati) 12, 520
Tattvāloka (of Vācaspati Miśra II), see *Nyāyatattvāloka*
Tattvaniraṇaya (of Pakṣadhara Upādhyāya) 313
Tauṭikas 446
teacher (*ācārya*) 422
tejas, see fire or light
Telang, M.R. 471
tense, perfect 315, 519
term
  complex 25
  general/individual 446
  technical (*pāribhāṣikī*) 98, 308-09, 418
(verbal) testimony (see also language) (*śabda*) 9, 23, 59, 62-66, 133, 156, 184, 198, 210-11, 226, 297, 341-42, 345-46, 364, 367, 371, 386, 389-92, 405, 415, 421, 442, 446, 448, 458, 467, 495, 507, 532, 534, 605, 614-16
Thakur, Anantalal 368
thesis (*pratijñā*) 356
  changing the thesis (*pratijñāntara*) 358
  contradictory reason and thesis 358-59
  renouncing the thesis (*pratijñasannyāsa*) 359
  violating the thesis (*pratijñāhāni*) 358, 409-11
thinking (*manana*), see reflection
thunder 125
tiger (*vyāghra*) definition 171, 550-51
time (*kāla*) 35, 37, 49, 214, 235, 271-72, 322, 387-88, 394, 413, 417-19, 434-35, 452, 457, 501, 529, 533, 551, 561-62, 576-78, 586, 627
  appropriate time (*avasara*) 323
  qualification, see qualification temporal
  rule of three times 359
Timmabhūpāla (1490) 12, 490-91
Trihut 490
tirobhāva, see envelopment
too-general (*sādhāraṇa*) 198, 200, 203, 464, 481-83
too-specific (*asādhāraṇa*) 198-203, 351, 433, 435, 464, 480-82, 504, 589
touch, the tactile organ (*sparśa*) 133, 143, 189, 320, 328, 334-35, 384-86, 414, 419, 427, 433-34, 437, 439, 531-32, 602
  hot/not hot (*uṣṇa/anuṣṇa*) 34, 325, 328, 377
  manifested/unmanifested 34-35, 143-45, 372, 378, 418, 453, 498-99, 506, 520, 530, 606
  variegated 520
trace, mental or impression (*saṃskāra, bhāvanā, vāsanā*) 19-21, 43-44, 103, 110, 113, 119, 122, 154, 156-57, 160-61, 178, 296, 325-27, 333, 335, 340-41, 347, 374, 380, 388, 407, 413, 415, 422-24, 427, 444, 450, 452, 462, 465, 477, 480, 497, 501, 516, 524, 533, 599
  exciter of, see exciter
  karmic (*apūrva*) 264, 270, 275-79, 300-08, 340, 343, 397, 401, 405, 442, 509-14, 519, 544, 609
  memory-trace, see memory
  unconscious trace 22
tradition (*sampradāya*) 478
  as instrument of knowledge 421
transformation (*pariṇāma*) 430
tree 33, 321, 441
Tridaṇḍimata, see Bhedābhedavāda of Bhāskara
Tripadavibhūtimahānārāyaṇa Upaniṣad 407

Tripuratāpinī Upaniṣad 399
tripuṭī 415
tripuṭīpratyakṣavāda, see Prābhākara
trustworthiness/untrustworthiness 250-51, 260, 448-49
truth or validity (*prāmāṇya, pramātva*) 22, 53-58, 64, 88-100, 102, 106, 108, 114-15, 209, 243, 245-46, 250-51, 257, 312, 341, 371, 403, 412, 451, 467, 484, 488-89, 494-95, 544-46, 562-63, 599
ascertainment of, extrinsic (*paratas*) or intrinsic (*svatas*) 54-57, 88-92, 95, 97-98, 391, 451, 494, 496, 516-17, 544
as distinct from validity 588
four noble truths 359
God's, see God's awareness
how grasped (*jñapti*) 88-97, 494
how it arises (*utpatti*) 97-98, 494, 592
of the Vedas 412, 451, 467, 484, 488-89, 494-95, 516
(*yāthārthya*) 126
truṭi, see minimum perceptibilium
tulya, see equipollence
Tvantopādhyāya (1400) 10, 374

ucyamānagrāhya, see (a fault) dedected even while the debater is speaking
Udayana (1075) 5-6, 33, 36-39, 42-45, 80, 85-86, 163, 168, 192, 225, 252, 281, 314-32, 338-39, 343, 345, 347, 349-62, 372, 381-88, 397-98, 410-11, 416, 420-22, 431, 437, 444-45, 450-52, 457, 460-67, 470, 491, 494, 503, 511, 513, 516-18, 523-25, 604, 617-18, 623-25
udbodhaka, see exciter
uddeśya, see (1) designated, (2) being the thing to be named
Uddyotakara (610) 17, 33, 66, 336, 349, 351-52, 355, 358-59, 364, 392, 411, 433, 436, 462
udvāpa, see discrimination
uktagrāhya, see detected after the argument has been stated
uncertainty (*varṇya*), parity through 351
uncertainty (*anadhyavasita*) 421
underextension (*avyāpti*) 167, 175, 327, 549-50, 552, 554, 567, 570
understanding
hearer's understanding 292
sentential understanding (*śābdabodha*) 284-87, 292-93
understanding the question (*praśnajñāna*) 407, 412-17
unestablished, see unproved
ungrammaticality (*apaśabda*) 367
unhappiness, see frustration
unintelligibility (*avijñātārtha*) 359-409
union (*prāpti*), parity through 352, 354
unity, see one (the number)
universal property (*jāti, sāmānya*) 16, 25-26, 38, 40, 42, 45-46, 49, 62-63, 66, 73-75, 98, 113, 117-19, 122-27, 137, 140, 143, 155, 164, 167, 179, 186, 214, 220, 222, 232, 271, 289, 292-300, 304, 309, 319-29, 337, 342, 379, 384-87, 390, 401, 405, 413-18, 427-32, 436, 443, 446-47, 459, 461, 469, 472, 478, 502, 514, 516, 519-20, 527, 532-34, 542, 545, 552, 555, 562-67, 573-80, 598-600, 615, 628
cross-connection of, see cross-connection
highest (*parā-*) 377
lower or specifying universal (*avāntarajāti*) 39, 316, 325, 385, 431
lowest (*aparā-*) 377
simple/complex (*akhaṇḍa/sakhaṇḍa*) 574
universal judgment 32
universal of a universal 578-79
universe (see also world) (*jagat, viśva*) 211, 322, 397
unlimited occurrence, see occurrence, unlimited
unmanifest quality, see quality, manifest/unmanifest
unproved or unestablished (*asiddha*) 101, 110, 146, 199, 207-09, 271, 331, 334, 344-45, 351-52,

356, 370, 386, 411, 421, 437, 481, 484, 503-04, 590, 616
ajñānasiddhi 481-82
āśrayāsiddhi (unestablishedness of *h* due to the unestablishment of *p*) 207-09, 345, 421, 438
pakṣāsiddhi 481-82
svarūpāsiddhi (unestablishedness of *h*'s belonging to *p*) 207-08, 356, 438, 465, 485
vyāpty- or *vyāpyatva asiddhi* (unestablishedness of *h*'s pervadability) 207, 360, 370, 421, 437-38, 453, 465, 590
upādāna, see materiality, *upādāna*
upādeya, see form, material
upādhi, see (1) imposed property, (2) obstruction
the word 370
vibhājaka, see condition, distinguishing
Upādhyāya, Padmaprasāda 338, 515
upakāra 413
upalabdhi, see awareness
upalakṣaṇa, see indicator
antarbhūtopalakṣaṇa 416
upamāna, see comparison
upanaya, see application
Upaniṣad (see also specific titles) 36-37, 399, 403, 407, 427, 452-53, 458, 515, 524, 625-26
upapatti, see equally tenable
upāsanā 277
upasarga, see prefix
upekṣā, see indifference
usage (*prayoga*) 239
usage, practical, speech-behavior (*vyavahāra*) 105-06, 114-15, 150-51, 154, 181, 263-64, 309, 436, 446, 477
utkarṣa, see augmentation
utkṣepaṇa, see lifting up
utpatti, see origination
utterance, see sentence
Vācaspati Miśra I (960) 224, 322, 355, 383, 411, 416, 418, 451, 453, 467, 534, 572, 576, 604, 615, 626
Vācaspati Miśra II (1440) 5, 11, 57-58, 61, 313, 375, 454-65, 619-20
vāda, see discussion
(Bhaṭṭa) Vādīndra (1225) 372-74, 385, 387, 394
Vādi Vāgīśvara (1050) 386, 388
Vādivinoda (of Śaṃkara Miśra) 11, 363, 375, 407-17, 421, 616
Vāgbhaṭālaṅkāraṭīkā (of Jinavardhana Sūri) 376
Vāhinīpati, see Janeśvara Vāhinīpati
Vaibhāṣika 414
Vaidyanātha, see Śiva
Vaidyanāthadhāma, see Devaghara
vairāgya, see detachment
*Vaiśeṣikasūtra*s (of Kaṇāda) 6, 318, 377, 427, 591
Vaiśeṣikasūtropaskāra (of Śaṃkara Miśra) 11, 35, 423-50
vaiśiṣṭya, see (being) qualified; relatedness
Vaiṣṇava 4, 489, 520
vaitaṇḍika 337
vājapeya, see sacrifice, *vājapeya*
vākya, see sentence
vaiyadhikaraṇya, see heterolocativity
validity, see truth
as distinct from truth 589
(Śrī) Vallabha (1140) 6, 8, 36, 42, 314, 334, 385-88, 396, 418, 452-53, 463, 507, 604, 618, 624
Varadacarya, K.S. 616
Varadachari, V. 38, 314-36, 338-48, 362-82, 397-422, 450-53, 455-70, 472-73, 492-520, 522-529
Varadarāja (1150) 370, 465, 468-69, 615, 617
Varanasi, see Banaras
Vardhamāna (the grammarian) 313
(Smārta) Vardhamāna 454
Vardhamāna (1345) 5, 10, 33, 35, 37-45, 85, 313-63, 374-75, 382, 396, 412, 464, 472, 507, 515, 518-19, 527-28, 615, 623
Vardhamāna Upādhyāya 396, 454
Varendra Brahmin 486
variegated, see color, touch, etc., variegated
varṇya, see uncertainty
vastu, see (actual) entity
Vāsudeva Miśra (1505) 12, 487, 492
Vāsudeva Sārvabhauma (1480) 4, 12, 48, 375, 473, 486, 489-90, 520-

21, 550, 553, 555, 558, 561-62, 621-22, 627
Vāsudeva Sūri (1420) 11, 389-94, 617
Vaṭeśvara (1340) 4, 10, 312-13, 375, 396, 461, 474, 491, 615
Vātsyāyana (410) 39, 44, 336, 349, 351-54, 358, 364, 411, 532, 604
Vattanky, John 36, 211, 591
vāyu, see air or wind
Veda(s) 63-64, 161, 211, 224-26, 231-32, 235, 263, 276, 278-79, 283, 287-88, 291, 305-06, 317-18, 321, 338, 342, 391, 399, 402, 414-15, 430, 440, 442, 451-52, 459-60, 493, 500, 507-10, 513
  eternality of 509
  God's authorship of, see God as author (e.g., of the Vedas)
  validity of 228, 339, 342, 391, 509
  Vedic injunctions, see injunctions, Vedic
  Vedic language or utterances 240, 244, 249, 251-53, 255-56, 258-59, 262, 379
  recensions of 509
  Vedic rites 234, 342, 371
Vedānta (see also Advaita) 357, 367, 510, 515, 620
Vedānta Deśika (1330) 375, 618
Vedāntakalpataru (of Amalānanda) 386
Vedantatirtha, N.C. 349, 362, 397, 519
vega, see impetus
vein (*nāḍī*) 218, 419
Venis, Arthur 465
verb (*kriyā*) 166, 262, 539-40
verbal awareness, see testimony
verbal form (*liṅ*) 415
verbal potency, see designative capacity
vibhāga, see disjunction
vibhājaka upādhi, see property, distributive
vibhakta, see manifest
vibhakti, see case-ending
vibhukārya, see quality, produced specific
vicious circle, see circle, vicious
vidhi, see injunction
Vidyabhusana, Satischandra 62, 86, 184, 196-97, 211, 238-39, 262-63, 282, 308-12, 363, 368, 396, 470, 593, 608, 617, 622, 632
Vidyanagara family 473
Vidyānivāsa Bhaṭṭācārya (1520) 374-75, 520
  Vidyāpati Ṭhakkura (1525) 453
  Vidyāraṇya (see also Mādhava) 368
Vidyasagara, Jivananda 563, 584
Vidyāviriñci, see Kṛṣṇānanda Vidyāvinoda
Vijayanagara 368, 616
vikalpa, see (mere) consideration, (2) construction, (3) shuffling
vikṣepa, see evasion
Vilāsakāra 469
Vindhya mountains 445
violence (*hiṃsā*) 276-77
vipakṣa (*vp*) 192, 195, 197, 200-03, 344, 370, 373, 433, 438, 481, 504, 551, 581, 588-89, 618
viparītakhyāti 364-65
viparyaya, see falsity
vipratipatti, see (1) alternative, (2) wrong understanding
virodhābhāsa 493
viruddha, see contradiction
virudhavyabhicāra, see counter-balance
Virūpekṣa Miśra (1494) 12, 491
visaṃvādinī, see deviant
viṣaya, see content
viṣayāloka relation, see relation of content and illumination
viṣayatathātva 56
viscidity or oiliness (*sneha*) 43, 321-22, 327, 434, 570
  natural (*svābhāvika*)/conditioned (*aupādhika*) 379, 433
viśeṣa, see individuator
viśeṣaṇa, see qualifier
viśeṣaṇatā, see qualifierness, qualification
viśeṣya, see qualificand
viśeṣyatā, see qualificandness
viśiṣṭa, see qualificand
viśiṣṭajñānatva, see awareness of relatedness
viśiṣṭatva, see qualificandness

Viśiṣṭādvaita 372, 616
Viṣṇubhaṭṭa (1420) 11, 368, 380
Viṣṇudāsa Vidyāvācaspati, see Ratnākara Vidyāvācaspati
Viṣṇupurāṇa 470
vitaṇḍā, see cavil
vītarāga, see free from passion
Vivādacandra (of Misaru Miśra) 491
(*Brahmasūtra*) *Vivaraṇa* (of Prakāśātman) 368
Vivaraṇa Advaita Vedānta 56
vivekākhyāti 364
viviparous 321
vivṛti, see description
voice (*vācya*) of a verb 537-41, 626
volition (*kṛti*) (see also effort) 186, 215, 221, 244-45, 282, 419, 461, 505, 511, 578, 610
  (*bhāvanā*) 264-68, 270, 274, 511, 609
  cause of volition 290
  eternal 407
  will to live 266-67
vp, see *vipakṣa*
vṛtti, see (1) indication, (2) occurrence
Vṛttikāra on the *Brahmasūtras* 424
Vṛttikāra of the *Vaiśeṣikasūtropaskāra* 432, 438, 443
vṛttiniyāmaka, see relation, occurrence-exacting
vyabhicāra, see deviation
vyadhikaraṇābhāva, see absence, locative
vyadhikaraṇāvacchinnābhāva, see absence limited by a property whose loci are different from its counterpositive
vyāghra, see tiger definition
vyākaraṇa, see grammar
vyakta, see manifested
vyakti, see particular
vyañjaka, see manifestor
vyāpāra, see operation
vyāpti, see pervasion
vyāpyavṛtti, see relation, locus-pervading
vyāsajyavṛtti, see properties of pairs, etc.
vyatirekin anumāna, see inference, negative
vyatirekin vyāpti, see pervation, negative
vyavahāra, see usage
vyāvahārika, see empirical level
vyāvarttaka, see differentiation
vyavasāyajñāna, see awareness, initial
Vyomaśiva (950) 33-35

waking state 403, 419
wandering, see deviation
warmth, see heat
water (*āp*) 33, 218, 320-22, 328, 379, 385, 413-14, 433, 441, 520, 535, 570
  -ness 130, 146, 433-34
  sipping (*ācamana*) 320
way of losing an argument (*nigrahasthāna*) 358-62, 366-67, 392, 409, 411-12, 482, 550
weight (*gurutva*) 43, 325-26, 334-35, 379, 418, 441, 472-73
  unmanifest weight 335
well-formedness 292
Western philosophy 21, 26, 29, 603
whole (*avayavin*) and part (*avayava*) 17, 24, 123-27, 217-18, 321, 333, 343, 420, 436, 526, 530-31, 600-01
whole, final (*antyāvayavin*) 386, 530
will, see volition
  God's, see God's will
wind, see (1) air, (2) humors
wine 414
withdrawal from activity (*nivṛtti*) 105, 107-08, 111-12, 427, 430, 511, 598
woman 337, 367
womb (*yoni*) 321, 453
word (*pada*) 240-41, 341, 371, 407, 416, 446
  words, knowledge of 616
  word-meaning, see meaning, word-
  -sequence 342
world (*loka*) 403, 405-06, 453, 460, 518
  Brahma-world 278
  creator of the world, see God
  (*prapañca*) 402-04
worship (*pūjā*) 316, 337-38, 368, 376, 393-94, 518
  God's, see God's worship
wrangling, see cavil

wrongly expressed (*asaduktika*) 349-50, 367
wrongly finding fault (*niranuyojyānu-yoga*) 361-62, 410
wrong understanding (*vipratipatti*) 367

Yajñapati Upādhyāya (1460) 4-5, 11, 48, 61, 313, 380, 454, 473-85, 487, 491, 521, 586, 621-22
yāma 393-94
Yamasama 487
yāthārthya 55
yatna, see effort
yoga, see etymology
yoga, *yogin* 217, 319, 337, 393, 413, 424, 442, 446, 519, 531
yogic power 422, 447
yogic practice 406
Yoga 60
Yogācāra 414, 451, 457
Yogasūtras (of Patañjali) 368, 393-94, 632
yogyānupalabdhi, see nonapprehension of what is perceptible
yogyatā, see fitness
yoni, see womb